THE SOUL ALWAYS THINKS

The Collected English Papers of Wolfgang Giegerich

The Collected English Papers of Wolfgang Giegerich makes the work of one of archetypal psychology's most brilliant theorists available in one place. A practicing Jungian analyst and a long-time contributor to the field, Giegerich is renowned for his dedication to the substance of Jungian thought and for his unparalleled ability to think it through with both rigor and speculative strength. The product of over three decades of critical reflection, Giegerich's English papers are collected in six volumes: *The Neurosis of Psychology* (Vol. I). *Technology and the Soul* (Vol. 2), *Soul-Violence* (Vol. 3), and *The Soul Always Thinks* (Vol. 4), *The Flight into the Unconscious* (Vol. 5), and *Dreaming the Myth Onwards* (Vol. 6).

For a full list of titles in this series, please visit *www.routledge.com/The-Collected- English-Papers-of-Wolfgang-Giegerich/book-series/CEPWG*

Titles in this series:
The Neurosis of Psychology: Primary Papers Towards a Critical Psychology (Volume 1)
Technology and the Soul: From the Nuclear Bomb to the World Wide Web (Volume 2)
Soul-Violence (Volume 3)
The Soul Always Thinks (Volume 4)
The Flight into the Unconscious: An Analysis of C. G. Jung's Psychology Project (Volume 5)
"Dreaming the Myth Onwards": C. G. Jung on Christianity and on Hegel (Volume 6)

THE SOUL ALWAYS THINKS

Collected English Papers
Volume Four

Wolfgang Giegerich

LONDON AND NEW YORK

First published 2010 by Spring Journal Books

Published 2020 by Routledge
2 Park Square, Milton Park, Abingdon, Oxon OX14 4RN
52 Vanderbilt Avenue, New York, NY 10017

Routledge is an imprint of the Taylor & Francis Group, an informa business

© 2020 Wolfgang Giegerich

The right of Wolfgang Giegerich to be identified as author of this work has been asserted by him in accordance with sections 77 and 78 of the Copyright, Designs and Patents Act 1988.

All rights reserved. No part of this book may be reprinted or reproduced or utilised in any form or by any electronic, mechanical, or other means, now known or hereafter invented, including photocopying and recording, or in any information storage or retrieval system, without permission in writing from the publishers.

Trademark notice: Product or corporate names may be trademarks or registered trademarks and are used only for identification and explanation without intent to infringe.

British Library Cataloguing-in-Publication Data
A catalogue record for this book is available from the British Library

Library of Congress Cataloging-in-Publication Data
A catalog record has been requested for this book

ISBN: 978-0-367-48523-8 (hbk)
ISBN: 978-0-367-48526-9 (pbk)
ISBN: 978-1-003-04145-0 (ebk)

Contents

Acknowledgments ix

Sources and Abbreviations xi

Introduction: "Thought": Some Signposts.................................. 1

CHAPTER ONE: The Lesson of the Christmas Tree 23

CHAPTER TWO: The Rescue of the World. Jung, Hegel,
and the Subjective Universe 53

CHAPTER THREE: Effort? Yes, Effort! 63

CHAPTER FOUR: Shalt thou build me an house for me to
dwell in? Or: Anima mundi and Time.
A response to Hillman's "Cosmology for Soul. From
Universe to Cosmos" 73

CHAPTER FIVE: The Dignity of Thought: In Defense of the
Phenomenon of Philosophical Thought 119

CHAPTER SIX: Is the Soul 'Deep?'—Entering and Following
the Logical Movement of Heraclitus' 'Fragment 45' 131

CHAPTER SEVEN: The Leap Into the Solid Stone 165

CHAPTER EIGHT: The Future of Psychology:
Its Going Under 173

CHAPTER NINE: The End of Meaning and the Birth of Man.
An essay about the state reached in the history of
consciousness and an analysis of C.G. Jung's
psychology project 189

    1. The self-contradiction inherent in the search for meaning .. 191

    2. In-ness as the reality of the pre-modern ages 193

    3. The end of in-ness 199

4. Two basic lines of reaction to "the end of in-ness" 203
5. Jung's idea of the death of symbols 205
6. Man the unborn 210
7. The birth of man 218
8. The fate of God(s) 224
9. Critique of the feeling of loss and need 230
10. The logic and genesis of C.G. Jung's psychology in the
 light of the question of meaning 239

The problem as it presented itself to Jung and its Solution or: SATURNIAN SWALLOWING – Sacrifice of the intellect and the exclusion of the problem of *form* – "The unconscious": Discovered fact or means to an end? – Downsizing and privatization – Privileging the raw – Permanent storeroom of images? No, "just in time" production! – Dissociation and the rescue of unbornness – Jung's semanticizing the problem of the "new form" – Token adulthood – Kronos swallows not only his children, not only childhood as such (the whole parent-child re lationship, the mode of upward looking), but also his children's *birth* – Archetypal psychology (James Hillman) or: ABSOLUTE SWALLOWING

CHAPTER TEN: The Soul as Axis of the World 285

CHAPTER ELEVEN: The Movement of the Soul 307

CHAPTER TWELVE: Psychology – The Study of the
 Soul's Logical Life 325

CHAPTER THIRTEEN: The Ego-Psychological Fallacy. A note
 on "the birth of the meaning out of a symbol" 351

CHAPTER FOURTEEN: Once More "The Stone Which is
 Not a Stone." Further Reflections on "Not" 363

CHAPTER FIFTEEN: "By Its Colorful Tunes the Lark Blissfully
 Climbs Up Into the Air." A Few Reflections on Soul-
 Making as the Making of Psychic Reality 379

CHAPTER SIXTEEN: Irrelevantification. Or: On the Death
 of Nature, the Construction of "the Archetype,"
 and the Birth of Man 387

CHAPTER SEVENTEEN: "The Unassimilable Remnant":
 What is at Stake? A Dispute with Stanton Marlan 443

CHAPTER EIGHTEEN: Imaginal Psychology Gone Overboard:
 Michael Vannoy Adams' 'Imaginology.' A Defense of the
 Image Against the Detraction by its Devotees 475

CHAPTER NINETEEN: *Psychologie Larmoyante*: Glen Slater, For Example. On Psychology's Failure to Face the Modern World 501

CHAPTER TWENTY: Jung's Idea of a Metamorphosis of the Gods and the History of the Soul 531

CHAPTER TWENTY-ONE: There Is Psychological Progress. Can There Be Progress of Psychology? 563

Index 591

Acknowledgments

Versions of the following chapters have previously been published elsewhere:

Chapter 1, "The Lesson of the Christmas Tree." A first very short German version of this paper was orally presented at the C.G. Jung Institut Stuttgart in 1984 and published in its *Institutsbrief*, No. 2 (1985), under the title, "Lichtsymbolik 1984." Largely expanded during the second half of the 1990s it became a chapter of an uncompleted book project in German on "The Meaning of Myth Today," and in this form was orally presented as one part of a lecture course at the C.G. Jung Institute Zürich during the winter semester of 2005-2006.

Chapter 2, "The Rescue of the World. Jung, Hegel, and the Subjective Universe" first appeared in *Spring 1987*, 1987, pp. 107–114.

Chapter 3, "Effort? Yes, Effort!" was first printed in *Spring 1988*, 1988, pp. 181–188.

Chapter 5, "The Dignity of Thought: In Defense of the Phenomenon of Philosophical Thought" first appeared in *Harvest. Journal for Jungian Studies*, vol. 43, no.1, 1997, pp. 45–54.

Chapter 6, "Is the Soul 'Deep?'—Entering and Following the Logical Movement of Heraclitus' 'Fragment 45'" was first printed in *Spring 64*, fall and winter 1998, pp. 1–32.

Chapter 8, "The Future of Psychology: Its Going Under," written in German and translated into Japanese by Toshio Kawai, was an invited contribution for a special millennium issue on "New Perspectives in Psychotherapy in the 21st Century" of *Seishin Ryoho* [Japanese Journal of Psychotherapy], vol. 26, no. 1, February 2000, pp. 33–40.

Chapter 9, "The End of Meaning and the Birth of Man. An essay about the state reached in the history of consciousness and an analysis of C.G. Jung's psychology project." A short oral version was presented before the Guild of Pastoral Psychology, London, in October 2003 and printed in the *Guild of Pastoral Psychology, Guild Lecture No. 284*, [London] 2004. The full version was first published on the Web in October 2003 (http://www.cgjungpage.org/articles/EndofMeaning.pdf) and printed in *The Journal of Jungian Theory and Practice*, vol. 6, no. 1, 2004, pp. 1–65, followed by extensive responses by Greg Mogenson, David L. Miller, John Beebe, and Terry L. Pulver and my response to the responses. I would like to express my sincere gratitude to the then editor, Stanton Marlan, for his uncommonly generous offer to devote an entire issue of this journal to the topic of this paper.

Chapter 12, "Psychology—The study of the soul's logical life" first appeared in Ann Casement (ed.), *Who Owns Jung?*, London (Karnac) 2007, pp. 247–263.

Chapter 13, "The Ego-Psychological Fallacy: A Note on 'the birth of the meaning out of a symbol,'" first appeared in *Journal of Jungian Theory and Practice*, vol. 7, no. 2, 2005, pp. 53–59.

Chapter 14, "Once More 'The Stone Which is Not a Stone': Further Reflections on 'Not,'" was printed in *Disturbances in the Field. Essays in Honor of David L. Miller*, ed. by Christine Downing, New Orleans (Spring Journal Books) 2006, pp. 127–141.

Chapter 17, "The Unassimilable Remnant'—What is at Stake? A Dispute with Stanton Marlan," appeared in *Archetypal Psychologies. Reflections in Honor of James Hillman*, New Orleans (Spring Journal Books) 2008, pp. 193–223.

As in the previous volumes of this collection of papers, I would again like to express my special gratitude to *Susan Giegerich* for checking through the manuscripts, to *Nancy Cater* and *Robert Gagliuso* for their production and typesetting work, and above all to *Greg Mogenson*, who not only as competent editor of these volumes, but also as colleague and friend accompanied the composition process of this volume and the writing process of many of the newer chapters with much sympathy, astute understanding, and valuable advice.

W.G.

Sources and Abbreviations

For frequently cited sources, the following abbreviations have been used:

CW: Jung, C. G. *Collected Works*. 20 vols. Ed. Herbert Read, Michael Fordham, Gerhard Adler, and William McGuire. Trans. R. F. C. Hull. Princeton: Princeton University Press, 1957-1979. Cited by volume and, unless otherwise noted, by paragraph number.

GW: Jung, C. G. *Gesammelte Werke*. Zürich and Stuttgart (Rascher) now Olten and Freiburg i:Br: Walter-Verlag, 1958 ff.

Letters: Jung, C. G. *Letters*. 2 vols. Ed. Gerhard Adler. Bollingen Series XCV: 2. Princeton: Princeton University Press, 1975.

MDR: Jung, C. G. *Memories, Dreams, Reflections*. Rev. ed. Ed. Aniela Jaffé. Trans. Richard and Clara Winston. New York: Vintage Books, 1965. Cited by page number.

INTRODUCTION

"Thought":
Some Signposts

Of course I am pleading the cause of the *thinking* man, and, inasmuch as most people do not think, of a small minority.

C.G. Jung[1]

The *sacrificium intellectus* is a sweet drug for man's all-embracing spiritual laziness and inertia.

C.G. Jung[2]

Moreover I seriously wonder whether it is not much more dangerous for the Christian symbols to be made inaccessible to conceptual thought and to be banished to a sphere of unreachable unintelligibility. ... man has the gift of thought that can apply itself to the highest things.

C.G. Jung[3]

One should probably not talk much *about* thinking, one should rather do it. But considering the title of this book, *The Soul Always Thinks* (a quotation from Bishop Berkeley[4]), and the fact that "thinking" or "thought" is surrounded by many popular

---

[1] *CW* 18 § 1616.
[2] *CW* 18 § 1643.
[3] *CW* 11 § 170, translation modified. "Conceptual thought": Jung's text has "*denkendes Begreifen.*"
[4] George Berkeley, *Principles of Human Knowledge*, § 98.

misconceptions and (often strongly emotional) prejudices, if it does not meet with downright rejection, it may not be altogether inappropriate here to summarily and sketchily compile a few notes on the topic of "thinking" and to introduce some distinctions.

1. Another statement by Berkeley tells us that, "Few men think, yet all will have opinions."[5] "Having opinions" is not thinking, but, we might add, people commonly believe they are thinking when in fact they merely have opinions (or shove opinions around in their minds). Thinking, so we learn from Berkeley (as also from Jung), is something rare, unusual. Nevertheless, because everyone has opinions, employs and applies opinions, and because of the confusion mentioned, everyone is convinced that without further ado he is able to think.

2. Our quotation contains two further insights. The first is that thought (in the strict sense) is to be understood as a verbal noun, i.e., as an act, movement, performance. Opinions can be "had," which shows that in them thought has become reified and frozen, and as frozen has become like merchandise. "Opinions" can be borrowed. They don't have to be our own. As a blatant example we just have to think of Jung's notion of what he called "animus-possessed" women (the same would of course apply to men) who are dominated by rigid opinions taken over from admired authority figures. This is not the case with thought. It is inherent in the form of thoughts, *if* they are truly thoughts, that they are always my own. They cannot be alienated. In order to *be* thought in the first place, thoughts need to be thought and in this way to come to life, much like music needs to be played. We cannot just avail ourselves of thoughts and pass this off as thinking. The utilization of thoughts, for example as arguments in support of one's position, is also nothing but an operating with opinions. "Operating with" of course also refers to an activity, but the critical difference to thinking is that such an operating has the thoughts (opinions) that it utilizes as a kind of ready-mades fundamentally outside of and vis-à-vis itself as operation; argumentation is operation *with* thoughts as static opinions. All life resides in what one does with the thoughts, while the thoughts themselves are frozen items. By contrast, thought proper is in itself life.

---

[5] George Berkeley, *Principles of Human Knowledge* and *Three Dialogues* (Oxford World Classics), Oxford University Press, 1999, p. 154. (From the Second Dialogue. Philonous is the speaker who makes this statement).

INTRODUCTION

3. This leads to the second insight to be gained from Berkeley's dictum. It involves the psychological difference, the difference between the human being (or the ego) and "the soul." Obviously, as "to have opinions" shows, opinions are a "possession" of the ego, and the utilization of opinions is a technical activity carried out by the ego. The subject or agent of thought proper, of true thinking, by contrast, is not the ego, not we people, but, mythologically speaking, "the soul." Thinking is a non-ego activity. It must not be confused with deliberate concoctions by the subjective mind. Ultimately, thoughts think themselves; all we do when we truly think is allow them to actualize and unfold themselves in ourselves. In *their* thinking, "the soul" displays *itself,* its own truths. *Cogitatio nostra non est cogitatio vulgi.*

4. When we speak in psychology of thinking, we should therefore by no means confuse it with Jung's "the thinking function," which refers to an ego operation. His whole typology of "orientation functions" is primarily seen from an ego perspective and from the point of view of the ego's practical, "survival" interests (its orientation in reality). The concept of these functions belongs to a technological fantasy, not to a "psychology *with* soul."[6] Especially problematic is the (in Jungian circles not infrequent) hypostatizing of the thinking function as if it were itself the agent that thinks ("my thinking function tells me..."). With such ideas one makes three mistakes: one starts out with a reductive unpsychological, technological notion of thinking; one dissociates oneself from the event of thought; and one commits a mystification, turning a mere function or habitual operation into a subject who allegedly performs this operation. Another terrible problem is that the concept of the typology of functions not only condones but also itself decrees and "institutionalizes" the popular absolute split between thinking and feeling, their mutually excluding each other. The soul, however, is a totality. We should not compartmentalize and dissociate it such that thinking becomes

---

[6] It should, however, not be overlooked that Jung himself, in the main body of his typology book (prior to Chapters IX and X ["General Description of the Types" and "Definitions"] and with his interest in the unconscious spontaneous workings of the inferior function in creative processes (philosophy, theology, poetry, etc.), goes far beyond the technical, personalistic sphere of ego interests and ego functionality into the dimension of truly psychological issues. Nevertheless, there is also a personalistic aspect of Jung's typological theory as a whole, and it is what more or less exclusively has dominated the typological interest of those who came after him.

4 THE SOUL ALWAYS THINKS

identified with abstract intellectualism. In reality, deep thinking and deep feeling go well together. In fact, deep thought presupposes feeling (see the section "Feeling as bridge to the soul" in Chapter 19 below).

5. The role of thinking in psychology can also not be to provide "a stronger philosophical frame" for psychology, as, for example, Glen Slater seems to think.[7] Psychology does not need and, if it is to *be* psychology, cannot be built on an *external, underlying* foundation. No need for an epistemological base, nor for a theory of science or a philosophy of psychology. It is the peculiarity of psychology that each time it works a particular matter it has to establish its own "philosophical" foundation anew and from scratch in and through this work. It has to acquire its ground as the *result* of its work, not as its external presupposition. It can only find, or rather not find but itself *produce*, its a priori as an a posteriori. Just in time production. And the only way it acquires this ground is by following the psychic phenomenon at hand into *its* (the phenomenon's) ground, and this is what we call psychological thinking. Intellectual rigor has to have its place in the very heart of psychology itself, not around it as its frame. The ousting of stringent thought from the precincts of psychology makes it possible for the mind to freely indulge in thoughtless feelings and unthought imaginings and thereby unwittingly to act out one's favorite prejudices (one's belief system).

6. Opinions are always opinions *about* something. The opinions themselves thus have that which they are about fundamentally outside themselves. As such, as alienated from their referents, they are abstract. Thoughts, on the other hand, because they think themselves, have no external referent. They simply unfold their own internal content. They have everything they need within themselves, which makes them concrete.

7. What also needs to be kept away from the psychological notion of thinking is "thinking" in the sense of formal logic. The latter type of thinking is concerned with the execution of formally correct technical operations upon propositions (= "opinions"), ultimately for the purpose of problem-solving. Formal logic is doubly abstract because it not only,

---

[7] Glen Slater, "Cyborgian Drift: Resistance is not Futile," in: *Spring 75, Psyche & Nature Part 1*, Fall 2006, pp. 171–195, here p. 190.

INTRODUCTION

as opinions do, holds the external referent of the statements outside of its own concern, but abstracts even from the material content of the statements themselves, only considering their general form, so that it can ultimately replace them by symbols.

8. In point 3 above I rejected the idea of the ego as the producing subject of thought and attributed a non-ego character to veritable thinking. It is the objective soul that thinks. (This statement could of course easily be misconstrued if one forgets that expressions like "the soul" or "the objective soul" must not be hypostatized. They are only a mythologizing [substantiating, "personifying"] *façon de parler*. It would be completely wrong to insist on rejecting the ego, or the thinking function, as the producer of thought only to thereafter posit the soul as its producer. I already hinted at the fact that, "Ultimately, thoughts think themselves." This is their non-ego character. The soul must not be naively imagined as the acting agent or already-existing producer, the mastermind, *behind* psychic phenomenology. Rather, the soul is autogenetic. The soul *makes* itself, which means that it first, and only, comes into being in and through its phenomenology, as the *result* of its productions, in our context as the inner depth and truth of the thoughts that think themselves.) But now comes a most important complication. The soul, this process of its self-production, must not be thought of as being something in terms of a formal-logical identity. Rather, the soul is *in itself* different. It is the unity of its own unity and its difference from itself, its bipolarity. Just as it unfolds its own *nature* as the psychic opposites of anima and animus and their dialectical interplay, so also it does its *thinking* at two different poles of itself, as objective and as subjective soul, i.e., in the actual deeds and the real development of culture (the *magnum opus*) "out there" on the one hand, and in the reflecting human mind on the other hand.[8] Thought, thus, is both (or can be either) the innermost nature of soul itself and (or) a mode of attending to soul. This is so because soul *is* essentially self-reflection. And just as anima and animus, despite

---

[8] Since I alluded to the *opus magnum* in connection with the development of culture, one might be inclined to parallelize the thinking of human mind with the *opus parvum*. But this would be a mistake, at least in our context. The *opus parvum* refers to the private psyche, which is a historically late historical acquisition, a peculiarity of modernity. Here, however, I am not concerned with the atomized individual's private thinking (which *psychologically*, from a soul point of view, is neither here nor there), but with the public thinking of the general human mind.

their opposition, always stay united within the soul as *syzygy*, so also do the two sides of the "always thinking" soul—soul itself and psychology—despite their opposition never lose their connection in the soul as the self-contradictory, dialectical *uroboros*.

9. For Heraclitus[9] who bestowed on all future thinking the philosophical term *logos*, this *logos* shows a similar bipolarity. As the *logos eôn*, the subsisting *logos*, it is the animating truth (*zoê*, life) in what is real, in the cosmos. "This world-order [*kosmos*], the same for all, none of the gods nor of the men has made, but it was always and is and shall be: an ever-living fire..."[10] It is the flash of lightning: "The thunderbolt steers all things" (Fr. 64 DK); it is the *aithêr* (Ether), the pure element of light of the fiery heaven. And this heavenly light is in itself *to sophon*, the primordial knowing or the pure element of all knowing. But the *logos* is at the same time also the corresponding small light in us humans, the light of the human mind (what later ages would call the natural light of reason), and in the last analysis the *logos* is this primordial self-division into these two poles of itself or their relation, their correspondence, the *harmonia* of opposites. Only like can know like. "If the eye were not sun-like, / How could we behold the light? / If God's own potency did not live in us, / How could what is divine delight us?" (Goethe. Cf. Plotinus, *Enneads* I, 6, 9: "What sees we have to make akin and alike to what is seen. Never would the eye have seen the sun if it were not itself sun-like..."). The condition of the possibility of truth is that our thinking and what our thinking is about have something in common. This insight, and the insight that *what* they have in common is the *logos*, was Heraclitus' discovery. The *logos* structures and permeates both the Real and the I. It too is uroboric.

10. However, the awareness of this undivided self-division is a historical achievement. And this awareness is the beginning of thought proper, of the ("always thinking") soul's now also having explicitly entered the *status* or *element* of thought, which had not existed before. Primordially, the soul's thinking had been completely submerged in deeds and facts, in ritual act. Ritual is unthought thought, the soul's

---

[9] For my understanding of Heraclitus I am indebted to diverse writings of Claus-Artur Scheier.

[10] Fragment 30 (Diels-Kranz), translation W.K.C. Guthrie, *A History of Greek Philosophy*, vol. I, Cambridge (Cambridge University Press: 1962), p. 454.

INTRODUCTION 7

thought sunken into acted-out deed. The *logos*, the heavenly light, was completely "imprisoned" (as the alchemists would later say about the Mercurius) in the concrete factualness of ritual performance. There was no need and no place for a thinking I, for a subjective soul that reflects. The sacramental deed contained, as it were, both the later "sun-like eye" *and* "the sun" within itself: it was logically self-sufficient, in itself illumined and self-reflecting all by itself. It needed no external subject for being reflected. It *was* the truth, it was the truth as existing fact or performance, which, however, means that truth itself was still occluded, not yet "born out of" its containment in the material reality of the ritual into the light of day. It had not come home to itself. The sacramental deed contained, and concealed, everything it needed within itself. No doubt, the human being was indispensable here too, but it was needed only as the doer of the deed, the executing celebrant of the ritual, but not in his own right as a light, a small subjective light that corresponds to the light in the real, and not as a knowing, comprehending, and speaking I vis-à-vis what *is*. On the contrary, man was absorbed into the ritual acts, sometimes even literally so by being sacrificially slaughtered. Heraclitus, by contrast, speaks on his own responsibility, however precisely in the name of the *logos* as the *xynon* ('the common,' the Relation),[11] and this shows that with him for one, the soul in addition to its "always thinking" has also entered its, the soul's, home territory, *the land* of thought, once and for all.

11. Myth does not have the same significance as ritual deed. It is, to be sure, an intermediate form between ritual and thought, but logically still belongs to the stage of ritual. It is, as it were, merely a secondary "commentary" on what is enacted in specific rituals, a description in narrative, imaginal form of what is logically going on in them. The truth that had been completely hidden in the materiality of the ritual deed becomes expressed in words. Nevertheless, this does not mean that truth would now, with myth's move from deed to word, have been truly "born out of" its imprisonment in factual performance. As "the true word" (W.F. Otto), myth is itself still an occluded form of truth. In the stories of myth it is not the human subject speaking about the world on his own responsibility. Rather, myth is the *telling*

---

[11] Heraclitus does not want us to listen to *him*, but to the *logos* that he is speaking about (fr. 50 DK).

of the truth of the man's being-in-the-world, a truth that had primordially expressed itself objectively in rituals. And just as man was only the executing performer of the rituals, so he is also only the hearing recipient of the myths as the true word. It is inherent in the form of myth that man is absorbed into it, rather than that he is the maker and inventor of myths. The *form* of submergence has not been overcome with the change from act to word (narrative).

12. So the acquisition of an awareness of the whole (so-to-speak horizontal) bipolarity of *logos* as the *logos eôn* and the *logos* in us is itself the one side of another (but now "vertical," i.e., historical) bipolarity, one side, that is to say, of the opposition or bipolarity between the stage of the ritualistic mode of being-in-the-world and the stage of *logos*, the thinking world-relation. This is an opposition which has frequently been articulated in the phrase "From mythos to logos" (a formulation which of course betrays ignorance about *logos's* true counterpart, namely ritual deed, mistaking its weak derivative, myth, for this counterpart). This move from the previous form to thought is not a gradual development (growth). Just like the soul itself, thought is autogenetic. The move to thought can only be brought about through thought itself, through its own revolutionary uprising of its own accord. Just as Athena at her birth jumped fully grown and fully armed into the world, so thought is suddenly there or not at all. But unlike Athena, thought can only *be* by having (logically) wiped away, canceled, everything particular that existed before. This is the reason why we have to speak of a violent uprising. We see this radical negation, Pseudo-Democritus' "nature conquers (or subdues) nature," in what we heard about Heraclitus. Where the world of myth is concerned with the inner logic of particular, concrete *intramundane* phenomena of life such as love, war, fertility, birth, illness and death, the gaining of prophetic insight, the quest for the soul's treasure, Heraclitus has risen to the pure ether of light as the universal medium in which whatever exists shows itself, or, in later terminology, as the abstract *principle* of knowing. Ultimately it is the move to the (as it were) empty *space* or the *vessel* for all knowing. In order to arrive at the awareness of this light, this space, this principle, the experienced world had first, in a radical abstraction, to have been totally emptied of any phenomenon, of its entire immediate sensory concreteness and particularity, of anything already known (with the one exception of

INTRODUCTION

the partly visible phenomenon of light itself[12]), so that only the empty "vessel" was left.

13. The word "abstract" in this context is equivocal. When it refers to the whole sphere of thought as such it characterizes the general nature of thought in contrast to the perception of the sensory world and to the mythic image or the imaginal at large as being based on their sublation *in toto* and as such being, in mythological parlance, underworldly, ghostly, as cold as the *psyche*. But when we speak of particular concepts or thoughts within this general sphere and say they are abstractions, the term points to an impoverished, deficient (although most frequent, commonplace) form of thought. Abstract intellectualism and abstract concepts in the sense of formal logic are characterized by their having their referents and reality outside themselves. But this abstract thinking is nevertheless the most commonplace. It is what for most people defines the terms thinking and concept. Modifying an alchemical phrase we might say, it is *cogitatio vulgi*. Which is strange since they all are familiar with and make daily use of the foremost example of a *concrete* concept, the concept "I" ("I" is a thought, nothing but a thought, that itself within itself *is*, or establishes, its own reality). But has not Heraclitus pointed out already that, "They divorce themselves from that with which most of all they are in continuous contact, the *logos*, and what they come across every day, that appears foreign to them" (Fr. 72 DK)?

14. At the other end of the bipolar *logos*, the I, we see a corresponding radical negation, which in the case of the I is a (likewise logical, not literal) self-negation. This move is reflected and becomes accessible to us in an episode within the innocent genre of a fairytale-like story in the Odyssey (probably written down around 720 B.C., several decades later than the Iliad, in other words, at the very beginning of the time of the awakening of the Greek mind). I refer to the remarkable scene where after he had escaped from the cave of Polyphemus Odysseus responded to the latter's question what his name was with: "Nobody." This his capacity to (logically) totally withdraw to "Nobody" reveals something absolutely extraordinary and new that

---

[12] For Heraclitus the light is, like the light of the sun, visible, empirical, but it goes far beyond this sensorily perceptible light to the pure ether of knowing which cannot be seen, but only thought. Although his thought partly *articulates* itself in images, these *are* not in themselves images, but veritable thoughts expressed in images.

would not have been possible on the level of mythic (ritualistic) being-in-the-world: the capacity to totally abstract from oneself. Only a human who has gained a distance to himself, who has logically departed from himself, disregarding *everything* he knows and feels about himself, in fact his entire immediate sense of identity with himself, can come up with the answer "Nobody." Through this self-negation the human being all of a sudden enters the drama of the human world-relation as an actor in his own right with his own judgement and of equal standing—as a subject—and thus becomes an I, when before he had only participated in the course of the world by executing (*enacting*), as a faithful child of the gods, certain rituals demanded by the gods.[13] And this his entering the drama, his himself becoming a full-fledged venue of the *logos*, is how the (uroboric) bipolarity between the subsisting *logos* (the logic of and in the real) and the subjective *logos* as human thinking is realized and it becomes explicit. Whereas before, the *essential* psychic relation[14] to or interaction with the world was the immediacy of the here and now of active ritual performance, the new essential soulful relation to the world is the in itself reflected one of *theoria*, contemplation. The negation of all the sensory phenomena freed the soul from its immediate involvement in and with the world as an immediate presence and opened the way to the possibility of universal *knowing* and, at a later time, even to *science*.

15. Whereas myth and ritual are relatively stable and persistent, remaining pretty much unchanged over centuries or even millennia, thought is in itself dynamic and progressive. It has its origin in an act of negation, of "pushing off from" what preceded it, and it exists only as this permanent self-origination or autopoiesis. This means that its uprising from out of the world of ritual was not a one-time act that once and for all created a new stage of being-in-the-world. Rather, by itself the state that was created becomes for it the new status quo from which it has to push off. Thought is inevitably self-reflective and applies itself to itself, to what it itself produced and what through this having

---

[13] Compared to the mind's judgment of reason, an enactment of a ritual seems to be active. But it is active only in a literal empirical sense, whereas the "passive" mental judgment is logically, psychologically active.

[14] In contrast to people's everyday practical and pragmatic interaction with the world.

INTRODUCTION   11

been *produced* gives the appearance of a new fixed and solid ground. Thought has *opus*-character. I use this alchemical term on purpose because the direction in which thought progresses is that of a deepening, a continued interiorization into itself, to the achieved status's as yet unseen inner ground, a refinement and distillation. A process of making explicit what was only implicit.

16. The same movement can also be described in nearly opposite terms, namely in terms of integration, if we describe it as the process of (thinking) *consciousness*. What appeared as simply given to, or as the *result* and semantic *content* of, consciousness, or as an object in front of consciousness, is slowly absorbed into the very form or syntax of consciousness itself, into its own *mode* of seeing and operating. It is turned into consciousness's own categories. Consciousness then has made what used to be the topic it was talking about its own standpoint. It has caught up with its own content or message, which in this way has psychologically been "born out of it."[15] What used to be, as it were, the "ceiling" above that it looked up to has become the "floor" it is standing on. For the resulting new consciousness the world naturally appears in a new light, and this newly perceived world is the new semantic content or object in front of consciousness that in time can again be integrated into the logical form of consciousness.

17. The relation between consciousness and the world corresponds to that between the subjective mind and the objective soul.[16] The process of thought proceeds via the tension between the two poles of the soul. Thinking consciousness becomes aware of the inner truth of the state of the world (the logical constitution of the actual mode of being-in-the-world). When through integrating this awareness a new status of consciousness arises, this not only leads to a new

---

[15] *Psychological* birth does precisely not mean the emergence of a new content the way biological birth means the appearance of a new separate being. Rather it means that the content in question becomes psychologized, distilled, evaporated, i.e., that *psychologically* it ceases to exist as a substantiated content in front of consciousness altogether and that instead it is integrated into the logical form of consciousness. (*Psychically*, however, the content of course remains in consciousness as a historical relic, as the corpse of its former animated self.)

[16] For Jung the objective soul was what he called "the unconscious," especially "the collective unconscious." But the really objective soul is the inner logical life in the process of culture. We must leave behind the fiction of "the unconscious," as if it were something psychologically real. It serves only as a kind of "screen memory" for the really objective soul.

perception of the world as pointed out in the previous paragraph. The new form of consciousness also slowly finds *objective* expression in the culture, in the way life is lived, how society is organized, in new modes of production and new cultural phenomena. The inner logic of the new awareness "materializes." And this means that the world experienced by consciousness (especially the consciousness of a new generation that takes the world into which it has been born for granted) has also objectively become a new one and now challenges consciousness to become again aware of the new logic animating it. The objective soul, the soul in the real, is always ahead of subjective consciousness—despite the fact that the objective soul is not a "metaphysical" entity, a wise agent, i.e., not objective in a naive literal sense, but nothing but the *result* of the objectification of the inner logical form acquired by the *former* subjective consciousness. The result is ahead of what produced it.

18. Once the soul has entered the stage of thought, there is no way back. This, however, does not mean that now ritual deed and mythic image have literally disappeared once and for all. Rather it means that they are now only sublated moments within a new, more comprehensive frame of consciousness. Whereas before, they had themselves been "state-of-the art," they now can survive only in four ways. In each they have to pay tribute to their sublatedness in a different way. (1) They can persist as long-lived isolated relics of the past within a wholly different cultural situation (and thus as foreign bodies in it). As such they can still be cultivated and retain their innocence, but are objectively out of touch with "where the real action is," reduced to a merely private, subjective validity. (2) They can survive *intellectually* and *aesthetically* as part of the cultural heritage for the educated part of society. (3) One can, against one's better knowledge, *pretend* that they are still valid. Here the reactionary, nostalgic ego-will for a revival (in contrast to the "survival" of [1]) is at work[17] and tries with lots of effort to cover up the images' as-if character, feigning their unquestionable authenticity. It is what we call *kitsch*. (4) In great literature and great art in general it is not the images as such but *the imaginal mode* as a mode of producing images for the purpose of

---

[17] An attempt at a revival indicates that the death or loss of what is to be revived has already been experienced.

INTRODUCTION

portraying the soul truth of the age that can still be valid. It can be authentic because here the very form of the images or imaginal narratives produced is no longer the innocent, naive form of image. It much rather *in itself* bears witness to its woundedness by reflection and thought, to its no longer being mythic image but image on the level of thought, and this is why, other than kitsch (which tries to simulate the obsolete naive form), it can give legitimate expression to the truth of its own age.[18]

19. Since for more than two and a half millennia the soul has been in the status of thought, even mythic images themselves must no longer be taken at face value, simply as images. They, too, must now be *thought*, reflected, interpreted. "But the mythological figures are themselves products of creative fantasy and still have to be translated into conceptual language" (*CW* 15 § 127). The wide-spread wish to keep rigorous thought out of psychology and to work with images just like that is the wish to *have licence* to freely fantasize, to merely entertain images as *immediately* relevant,[19] to have licence, too, to view even a thoroughly modern psychic phenomenon, across all the many historical gaps, in terms of some ancient mythic image or ancient god on the basis of no more than a merely *formal, abstract likeness.* Although this kind of association approach is not *totally* free, inasmuch as the imagination feels bound by the requirement that there be an abstract (merely semantic) similitude (but similitude nonetheless) between the items compared, it is nevertheless a variety of "free association," for two reasons. It is a desertion from the original phenomenon (which has everything within itself that it needs), a going off to *other* (similar) phenomena or images from other ages, *and* it abstracts from the rootedness of those phenomena or images each in its own concrete cultural-historical context with its own particular logic. It is an innocent Kore-like plucking of flowers into a colorful bunch (without, however, being followed by the ensuing appearance of a raping Hades). An "impressionistic" collage of spots of color for the sake of *impressing* consciousness, rather than a dwelling with the phenomenon to bring out its inner truth, its soul.

---

[18] 20th century art even seems to have made the woundedness of image its very message, whereas before in Western art, the imaginal was wounded, too, without, however, explicitly displaying its woundedness.

[19] Cf. also no. 5 above.

20. Thinking, by contrast, could be said to proceed in an alchemical style. The matter (phenomenon, image) at hand is first of all enclosed in a retort so that it is held tight, cannot escape, and, conversely, so that the *impression* it makes on us does not induce the imagination to wander off, on the surface level, to *other* "likenesses." The imagination must not be allowed to freely associate, to simply stroll along with the flow of associations of images taken from the mythologies of all times as they happen to come to mind in the psychologist. It has to stay put. This is also why Jung wanted us to write our dreams down as early as possible, because we need a fixed record of them, since memory and the imagination are unreliable. They do not simply record, but treat memories creatively; they *create* memories even while presenting them as mere recollections. Psychology needs "*documents* of the soul." Thought gives the phenomenon to be thought determinateness, turns it into a fixed starting point, our firm position for the time being. "This is it!" Thinking means to take the phenomenon itself seriously rather than as a trigger for our ruminations.

21. Now—this is the second step—it, the content of the vessel, has to show what it contains, implies, involves. The phenomenon is taken at its word. It is subjected to rigorous thought, that is, to a fermenting decomposition and distillation. Because it is taken at its word it has to prove what it is worth and where it leads. It has to *logon didonai*, account for what it says. What from outside at first appeared as "something," e.g., as an image, is, when one enters it and views it from within itself, revealed to be a complex process of its internal logical *life*. Thought is the move from an external impression, from a viewing *from* the outside, which shows the phenomenon as image or imaginal shape, to a seeing the image *from within*, as the logical process that constitutes it. The imaginal approach rests content with the image as the frozen result and external appearance (sort of the "skin") of this internal logical process, much like the looks of a person are the external appearance of all the physiological processes going on inside under his or her skin. Images *qua* images, i.e., as long as they are not thought, are necessarily abstractions, *contracted abbreviations*. It is true, Jung said "*image is soul*" (italics and the word "soul" [not "psyche"] by Jung in the original,

INTRODUCTION 15

GW 13 § 75), but this does not mean the reverse, that soul is image![20] In itself, in its innermost nature, soul is thought, is the marvel of mindedness, of (implicit and explicit) consciousness, the dialectical unity of self-production (self-presentation) and self-reflection. Image is merely one of the possible forms of manifestation of soul, one garb of soul as thought, and a shorthand form at that. Image needs to be thought in order to become written out in longhand.

22. Thought—thinking as a mode of attending to psychic phenomena, the mode of psychology—follows the process which internally constitutes the matter *all the way* to the utmost consequences lying in the matter.[21] It tries to exhaust the matter,[22] which is made to eat its own medicine ("self-application," letting its message come home to itself), and this is how it becomes slowly absolute-negatively interiorized into itself: *released* into its truth (which amounts, in alchemical language, to the freeing of the Mercurius imprisoned in the physicalness of the matter).[23] Thought reveals the hidden mercurial logic animating the matter, a logic which is not a static structure, but the whole complex process of its self-unfolding that psychological thought is called upon to go through once more step by step. We must neither identify the matter with its starting-point (the initial appearance of the image as image) nor with the result of the thinking

---

[20] This statement seems to be contradicted by Jung in *CW* 11 § 889, where we read that "Every psychic process is an image and an imagining..." But when we look at his own wording in *GW*, "Alles seelische Geschehen ist ein Bild und eine Ein-Bildung," we discover that Jung is not speaking of "an imagining" or a fantasy-activity at all. *Ein-Bildung* much rather means "giving (something) the form of image." Image (in Jung's sentence) is thus the result of a secondary formation of something that primarily is precisely not image. In the following clause, Jung also tells us *his view* of why (what for) this formation is necessary: in order for the soul processes to become phenomenal, accessible to consciousness. In other words, Jung is here not speaking of the innermost nature of the psychic or the soul.

[21] Thinking cannot rest content with and stop short at "paradoxes," "mysteries," "the unspeakable," etc. All these terms betray a standpoint that remains outside and perceives from outside. Instead of entering, it stargazes and marvels. Thought goes *into* the "paradox," which *ipso facto* reveals itself as a dialectical contradiction and unfolds its dialectic.

[22] "Only the exhaustive is truly interesting" (Thomas Mann).

[23] An example of thinking a matter in the sense of releasing it into its truth and interiorizing it into itself, in this case the "matter" of *metanoia, paenitentia* (repentance, lit. "a turning about"), might be the first of Luther's 95 theses: "When our Lord and master Jesus Christ said, 'Repent etc.' [Matth. 4:7] he wanted the believers' life as a whole to be a repentance." It is the move from the notion of repentance as a literal behavior with respect to a particular sinful action or thought (in other words, a notion held down in the "physicalness" of positivity) to a notion of repentance as a whole new mode of being-in-the-world.

16   *THE SOUL ALWAYS THINKS*

process. Both are abstractions.

23. Psychological thought in the spirit of alchemy is not our freehand designing of theories. It is not free-floating, like the imagination very often is. It is bound. Thinking means to think the *matter* at hand, the soul in the real. Thinking is essentially attached to, indeed, merely reflective of, something real, and as such it is a mode of attending to it. (This is also why in this book one will find several critical, if not polemical, responses to articles by other authors. In other chapters, I start out from and dwell on one tiny dictum or phenomenon. In either case, those articles, dicta, and phenomena, much like dream texts in analysis, provide a specific *documented* and well-circumscribed prime matter that can be more or less exhaustively thought through and mined for insight, so that thought has a concrete basis and support in the real. Penetrating analysis of mistaken views *ipso facto* reveals the more adequate views. And explicitly spelling out in detail what is wrong with a particular view guards us against unwittingly reverting to it.) In fact, thinking is not really *our* subjective thinking, but the thoughts' thinking themselves. It is the self-unfolding of the logical life, as which the matter itself exists—"the matter's cold march of necessity" (Hegel), the step-by-step self-unfolding of the implications and consequences inherent in the observation, idea, or thesis that one began with. It is one's following the thought's or "matter's" own internal dynamic, its will to come to its end. Thus it is "objective" thinking or the thinking of the objective psyche. *Our* thinking it is only to the extent that it is our "thinking-*again*" of *its* thinking, in much the same sense that Jung said, concerning one particular psychic phenomenon (dreams), "What the dream, which is not manufactured by us, says is *just so*. Say it again, as well as you can."[24] Thinking is the art to allow the matter that we are dealing with to speak for itself. Psychology is not concerned with what we, what people think, but with what "the soul" of/in the real thinks.[25] As such

---

[24] *Letters 2*, p. 591, to Read, 2 September 1960.

[25] The quotation marks around "the soul" indicate that I do not substantiate the soul as a separate producing agent *behind* the psychic phenomena, but know "what 'the soul' of/in the real thinks" to be a mythologizing (personifying) *façon de parler*. I also do not speak of "the unconscious," which is another mythological fantasy. "The soul" simply refers to the ongoing objective thought or logical life, *as which* psychic phenomena exist. Thoughts think themselves, and this their self-character is precisely the soul aspect of the inner logic of the real. "The real" in our psychological context refers to human (above all ritual) deeds and to what goes on in the process of culture.

INTRODUCTION 17

"thinking again" what the phenomena think, *our* thinking always comes after the fact. The owl of Minerva, Hegel had said, only begins its flight at dusk, when the day is over. Thinking thinks what has already happened and thus now *is*. However, our thinking, as our "thinking-again" what the phenomena think, is the way how *they* can be released into their truth, how their soul can become explicit, how they can come home to themselves, how their truth can be born out of them. The human subject as *artifex*, his thinking, is necessary. Schelling said that in man nature opens her eyes and beholds herself. It is not enough for the soul to *be* ongoing thought, existing logical life. It also, in addition, wants to be released into its truth, which, however, can only happen in and through human thinking ("thinking-again").

24. Here it becomes necessary to complement Berkeley's above statement about a first error concerning thought, namely the confusion of "having opinions" with "thinking," by another one about the opposite error: "People think that they are *not* thinking when in truth they are thinking," or rather: when something, "the soul," in them is thinking. Just as people think that thinking and feeling are mutually exclusive opposites (see no. 4 above), they also think that their emotions, their fantasies and images, and even more so their neurotic symptoms are *not* a thinking; they operate with a mindless abstract opposition. They think that psychologically there is something outside of thinking, in a similar way to how some think that one could be unpolitical. But, as Jung insisted, we are inescapably surrounded by soul on all sides. Everything psychological takes place on the stage of thought, even the fashionable rejection of thought as intellectualism in favor of "emotions" and "body." "The fact that consciousness does not perform acts of thinking does not, however, prove that they do not exist. They merely occur unconsciously and make themselves felt indirectly in dreams, visions, revelations, and 'instinctive' changes of consciousness, from whose nature one can see that ... they are the result of unconscious acts of judgment or unconscious conclusions" (*CW* 11 § 638, transl. modified). The question is therefore only *what* kind of thought it is: intelligent thought transparent to itself, or poor, occluded thought (unthought thought as "opinions," prejudices), or unborn, merely implicit thought (thought submerged in the form of emotion, revelation, symptom)? Truly outside of thought are only the dead

things and events of the world of positivity—but even their being outside occurs only *within* thought. People are usually incapable of understanding that, in themselves, symptoms, emotions, dreams, images are thoughts, although of course thoughts "imprisoned" in "the physicalness of the matter," thoughts sunk and frozen into positive-factual events and mental items. The same applies to cultural phenomena (cults, political constitutions, the phenomenon of technology-as-such, etc.). The soul *always* thinks, no matter how it displays itself and how deeply it sinks its thoughts into, and conceals them in, the "physical" of the matter. And we, too, think even when we have emotions, or entertain images, or have opinions. The only problem is that this is a poor thinking, reified thought, thought not come home to itself *as* thought and unconscious to and cut off from ourselves.

25. True thought, because it is not concerned with what *we* think, is ruthless, merciless (which is an effect of its cold, underworldly nature). Professional. What *we* feel and whether we welcome what it reveals and where it leads is of no significance. It is concerned with truth. Just like alchemy, thinking is not for sissies. One must not show too much of a soft spot for our personal feelings nor for the images in their innocent beauty nor for the things of the world in their natural appearance, nor cling too much to our desire for unbroken continuity, all of which point to a defense against the underworldly soul, to a wish to hold on to the day world. Alchemy ruthlessly pulverizes, flays, tortures, dissolves, putrefies its own prime matter, and thought proceeds via logical negations, the matter's self-negations. Explicit thought having *itself* brought itself into being through a radical negation and thus having lost the (logical) innocence or unwoundedness of the ritualistic mode of being-in-the-world[26] is not afraid of the discontinuities and ruptures that it may discover.

---

[26] The innocence of the ritualistic mode of being-in-the-world is *logical* or *psychological* innocence, not literal innocence. Having ritual slaughter as one of its foremost institutions it is of course anything but innocent in an everyday external (or psychic or semantic) sense. The same is affirmed by headhunting, scalping, by all sorts of initiation ordeals (circumcision, scarification, subincision, etc.) as well as by such motifs in mythology as dismemberment. What in initiation rituals is done to the body and the person and thus "acted out (upon an *other*: a human being)," in thought uroborically comes home to "the soul" (its thinking) itself and is thus released into its truth.

INTRODUCTION

26. Thought requires patience, and here we should also keep in mind that "patience" comes from *pati*, to suffer, to endure, to permit, and is related to "passive." Thought is not an ego activity, not a technique. Other than problem-solving, it is not out for immediate answers. Not we but the thought itself is the agent of its thinking. One has to be able, perhaps even for years, to go pregnant with the phenomena as *open questions*, pregnant precisely with what has *not* been understood. As Rilke once put it: "One must have patience towards the unresolved things in one's heart and try to *love the questions themselves*, like closed rooms and like books written in a foreign language. If one lives the questions, then one will perhaps slowly, without noticing it, one distant day live into the answer."[27] Our thinking is true thinking only if it is the question's own slowly growing in us and finally giving birth to the answer. The I is of course needed, in fact indispensable, but only as the place where the questions as seeds can do their own ripening. What we need to understand is that the questions have everything they need within themselves.[28] Answers that would need to be supplied to them from without may at times be technically helpful, but are psychologically irrelevant, indeed downright misleading: unpsychological.[29]

27. Abstract thought deals with universal, timeless structures or principles. Not so psychological thought, which, like alchemy, has a real, material base. It is always concerned with the real, with specific, concrete matters rooted in a determinate historical and cultural situation. When such a matter is hermetically enclosed in the retort, it is not this matter *in a narrow sense*, the pure matter abstracted from its historical and cultural context. No, when we enclose the matter in the vessel, we get its context, its historical locus, into the bargain, because the prime matter is only what it is if it is not severed from its

---

[27] Rainer Maria Rilke, *Briefe an einen jungen Dichter*, Leipzig (Insel: 1929), here: from the letter of 23 April 1904. My transl. and emphasis.

[28] Often readers would like to ask the author of a text to provide answers to their questions about it. But it is the text ("like books written in a foreign language") and not the author that needs to be asked. Similarly in dream interpretation, we have to ask the dream text about *its* associations or amplifications, rather than asking the patient, the dreamer, what *his* associations are (the dreamer *qua* dreamer should only provide objective, descriptive information about dream details or communicate factual knowledge he has about the persons or objects in the dream).

[29] This predicate ("unpsychological") applies to all causal-reductive thinking in personalistic psychology (explanations of psychic states from traumas or other bad conditions in early childhood).

context, much like a quotation is only this true quotation if it is not understood out of context. Of course, Jungian psychology is always in danger of substituting an ideal (universal, timeless) context ("the archetypes," "the imaginal") for the concrete real context in which the matter at hand is embedded. But true psychology proceeds from the methodological assumption that any prime matter has its own archetypal or soul depth within itself (and only within itself), rather than in an external ready-made archetypal frame of reference. And this its own archetypal depth it possesses in truth only if the prime matter is appreciated as this *concrete* prime matter *in its historical locus* rather than abstractly.

28. Because the concrete situation is part and parcel of the matter itself, psychological thought inevitably becomes aware of the fact that two semantically (content-wise) alike phenomena or images may nevertheless represent fundamentally different psychological realities because of their rootedness in the logic of different historical ages and cultures. Their different context (psychologically: the different status or logical constitution of consciousness, the different syntax) gives them an entirely different meaning and function. It alters their own logical form and thus makes them in fact in themselves different from each other despite their abstract, external likeness. While it is thought that opens our eyes to the syntax or logical form of phenomena, the awareness of the contrast between the syntactical and the semantic is in turn the soul's initiation into Time, history. And it is intrinsic to thought that for it, other than for myth, the semantics and the syntactical or logical form of one and the same phenomenon have fallen apart (just as for thought likewise the objective soul and the subjective soul fall apart): this radical difference is constitutive and reflects the fact that thought is not in the psychological state of innocence, since it had, after all, come into being by having broken with the primordial continuity and innocence characteristic of the ritualistic mode of being-in-the-world. Thought has been wounded by its knowing about Time. Because it has become conscious of Time, thought (we could also say: the soul in the *status* of thought, in contrast to the soul in the status of the basically static, "timeless" form of myth and the mythic imagination) is also in itself, and explicitly, historical in the sense of having a history and proceeding via successive stages (cf. no. 15 above). It carries within itself an acute sense of caesura and of the bygone.

INTRODUCTION

29. If psychology has become aware (1) of the logical life going on *inside* psychic phenomena and constituting them and (2) of the syntactical status *in which* they stand, it has arrived on the home territory of soul. Only with a sensitivity to the logical status of psychic phenomena can such psychological blunders be avoided as, to mention only one example, that of identifying "the ego" with archaic mythic images or notions: with Hercules, with the "solar hero."[30] And only with this sensitivity can psychology, conversely, hope to do justice to the soul where it is today, in our modern world. When turning to the history of the soul or to the spirit of an age, psychology must focus on the transformations of the general logical form of consciousness. It must not allow itself to be seduced to stay on the semantic level and cling to individual contents, symbols, dreams, images, ideas that come up in history. Unless an individual semantic phenomenon is seen in the light of the general syntax of consciousness of the historical period in question and shown to be representative of it, our focusing on it remains arbitrary and subjective. There are countless ideas, dreams, and images of all sorts at a given time. Only the awareness of the general logical form of consciousness prevailing at a specific historical locus and the logic of historical development gives to psychological investigation a certain objectivity, something to rely on.

30. By way of ending, a word on "therapy and thought." In the context of a psychology "with soul" therapy is not a project of *our* curing, correcting what is wrong, of efficiently getting results. The therapist is not a healer. Therapy does not *want* anything of its own accord. It does not have a program. All it wants is in each case to release whatever *is* into its depth, its truth. This is its *opus*. This is how it reaches soul, the soul in the real.

---

[30] "The ego" in the sense of Jungian psychology is a historical psychic product of Industrial Modernity, of the 19th century. There was no "ego" in archaic times, in antiquity, in the Middle Ages, and even the I in the thinking of Descartes must by no means be confused with "the ego" in the psychological sense. "The ego" presupposes the psychological end of classical metaphysics and religion; it presupposes the rule of positivism and the logic of "function" (Frege; instead of the metaphysical logic of the copula). One should not dress modern phenomena in the plumes borrowed from ancient myths.

CHAPTER ONE

The Lesson
of the Christmas Tree[1]

Christmas is associated for us with hopes for peace in the world (be they religious or secular), with giving and receiving presents, with cozy family reunions or merry festivities. But that the Christmas Tree could teach us something may be a surprising idea. However, as we will see, the Christmas Tree can indeed give us an important lesson, provided we look closely at how it shows itself and let this its *phainomenal* appearance speak, rather than taking it for granted.

If it is nowadays widely customary to set up at Christmas an illuminated tree, and if this custom that originated in German-speaking regions has spread over many parts of the world, even reaching Australia and Japan, then this is a case of the jutting of an ancient custom into our age. The question raised for us by this phenomenon is what is the situation in our time of authentic relicts of mythic experience from earlier times. In other words, is a symbol or ritual that *in itself* remains more or less the same as before immune to the changes in the character of the times in which it appears? This question raised by the Christmas tree can probably also throw a light

---

[1] The nuclear idea of this paper was first presented in a short speech at the C.G. Jung-Institut Stuttgart in 1984, printed in the *Institutsbrief no. 2* (1985), and expanded to the present length in 1997 as one chapter of an (unfinished) book-length manuscript on the meaning and role of myth today.

24   *THE SOUL ALWAYS THINKS*

upon the wider question how authentic, indeed how "archetypal" and "mythic" are archetypal experiences in dreams and visions today.

At our time Christmas has of course become commercialized and fallen prey to an "anything goes" attitude to such an extent that we can hardly dare to still consider a living myth to be at work in it. Through this process of commercialization and kitschification the symbol of the Christmas tree has itself suffered considerable modification. But as little as half a century ago this was not the case, and for this reason Jung was still able to counter the objection made to him that the custom of putting up Christmas trees had come up in relatively recent times (first documentation in 1660) and that this fact makes his interpretation of it as based in an archetype seem unlikely, with the comment, "On the contrary! The way the Christmas tree has caught on in various countries and rapidly took root, so that most people actually believe it is an age-old custom, is only further proof that its appeal is grounded in the depths of the soul, in the collective unconscious, and far exceeds that of the crib, the ox and the ass."[2] What we will have to focus on in the following is therefore the still intact Christmas tree of five or ten decades ago, which can still occasionally be found here or there, rather than the long devalued and kitschified tree that has been alienated from its own form and substance.

The custom of the Christmas tree allows us quite well to illustrate one essential feature of what is genuinely mythic in a wider sense (including myth, ritual, symbol), and Jung pointed repeatedly to this feature. It is the fact that ritual acts are "performed without thinking" (*gedankenlos vollzogen*)[3] and that one also usually simply does not have any clear ideas or thoughts about the myths and symbols that one uses. Apropos certain Christian mythological images (virgin birth, Christ's divinity, Trinity) Jung makes the following fundamentally significant statement: "It almost seems as if these images had just lived, and as if their living existence had simply been taken for granted without question and without reflection, much as everyone decorates Christmas trees or hides Easter eggs without ever knowing what these

---

[2] Georg Gerster, Interview "C.G. Jung und der Weihnachtsbaum" (in: *Die Weltwoche* [Zürich], Christmas 1957), reprinted in English translation "Jung and the Christmas Tree" in William McGuire and R.F.C. Hull (eds.), *C.G. Jung Speaking*, London (Picador ed., Pan Books) 1980, p. 333 (transl. modif.).

[3] *C.G. Jung Speaking* has "unthinking ritual act," p. 332.

THE LESSON OF THE CHRISTMAS TREE

customs mean. The fact is that archetypal images a priori carry their meaning within themselves so that people never think of asking what they might mean" (*CW* 9i § 22, transl. modified). In fact, mythic images were alive—this we have to conclude on the basis of our foregoing discussion—merely *because* one did not have any conscious ideas or knowledge about them. The original standpoint vis-à-vis them was thus "exoteric" in Jung's special sense: one cannot know what they mean, one cannot have conscious ideas about them, because all their meaning and everything that could be "thought" *about* them is still contained *within* the symbol or ritual act *itself* and has not yet been born out of it. As Jung had pointed out, they *are a priori* meaningful,[4] by themselves and in themselves, long prior to our turning our attention to them and they do not first become meaningful through *our* understanding or experiencing their meaning. Jung liked to illustrate this characteristic trait of cultic symbols with a custom of the African Elgonyi, with whom he had stayed for a certain length of time. He had asked them about traces of their religious ideas and ceremonies. However:

> They knew nothing of religious customs. But I did not give up, and finally, at the end of one of many fruitless palavers, an old man suddenly exclaimed: "In the morning, when the sun comes up, we go out of the huts, spit in our hands, and hold them up to the sun." I got them to perform the ceremony for me and describe it exactly. They hold their hands before their faces and spit or blow into them vigorously. Then they turn their hands round and hold the palms towards the sun. I asked them the meaning of what they did—why they blew or spat in their hands. My question was futile. "That is how it has always been done," they said. It was impossible to get an explanation, and it became clear to me that they knew only *that* they did it and not *what* they did. They see no meaning in their action. (*CW* 10 § 144)[5]

They not only did not know *what* the meaning of this action was, they also did at first not really appreciate it as a meaningful, let alone

---

[4] "A priori meaningful" = *pregnant* with meaning.
[5] Transl. modified. Italics added according to the almost identical description in *Erinnerungen, Träume, Gedanken*, p. 270. A similar report is given in *CW* 18 § 551, a somewhat shorter one in the cited Gerster interview about the Christmas tree, *op. cit.* p. 330f.

religious, ritual act, for when Jung asked them about their religious ceremonies for a long time they did not come up with the example of this custom. No exciting feeling of meaning, no sense of meaning. They simply did it. The ceremony was acted out completely without reflection, without great inner involvement, we might even say: routinely, as a mere fact ("*that* they do it") and for this reason it remained (certainly not unknown, but) completely without notice. "It is something that's always been done ..."[6] One did not entertain any thoughts about it.

> What they were doing was obvious to me but not to them. They just do it, they never reflect on what they are doing, and are consequently unable to explain themselves. They are evidently just repeating what they have "always" done at sunrise... It is most unlikely that these primitives ever, even in the remote past, knew any more about the meaning of their ceremony. On the contrary, their ancestors probably knew even less, because they were more profoundly unconscious and thought if possible even less about their doings. (*CW* 18 § 552)

This is an authentic, living ritual in which mythic meaning is active. We can here supplement Jung's report with an observation and reflection that Thomas Hardy gave us long before Jung. In *The Return of the Native* he wrote:

> A traditional pastime is to be distinguished from a mere revival in no more striking feature than in this, that while in the revival all is excitement and fervour, the survival is carried on with a stolidity and absence of stir which sets one wondering why a thing that is done so perfunctorily should be kept up at all. Like Balaam and other unwilling prophets, the agents seem moved by an inner compulsion to say and do their allotted parts whether they will or no. This unweeting manner of performance is the true ring by which, in this refurbishing age, a fossilized survival may be known from a spurious reproduction.[7]

Jung said that the Elgonyi performed the ceremony "certainly with a certain emotion and by no means merely mechanically" (*CW* 18 §

---

[6] Gerster interview, *op. cit.* p. 331.
[7] Thomas HARDY, *The Return of the Native*, Harmondsworth (Penguin Books) 1978, p. 178.

THE LESSON OF THE CHRISTMAS TREE

552). But this statement we've got to take with a pinch of salt. It would certainly be wrong to insinuate that rituals in early cultures were enacted "merely mechanically," for such a mechanical behavior is characteristic of very late ages; it is relative to the modern ego and its freely disposable will, relative also to the age of industrialization. The "purely mechanical" is the counterpart to our likewise modern wish to feel and experience. Both correspond to, indeed presuppose, each other, inasmuch as they are the two sides of one and the same *abstract* soul condition. Just as the persons enacting a ritual did not need to and were not able to have thoughts about it and to understand its meaning, they could also not have any deeply uplifting emotional experience through it. Both are "esoteric" in the special sense in which Jung uses this term: removed from the living symbol.[8]

To emotionally experience and understand the meaning of rituals is something that requires a conscious ego. But ritual, as long as it is still intact, is not celebrated *by* the ego. It is always the non-ego that enacts it and the latter is the addressee, if I may say so, of the mythic and symbolic. We may grant that the Elgonyi performed the ritual of greeting the sun "with a certain emotion," provided we put the emphasis on the word "certain" and mean by it no more than the general aura of "significance," dignity, maybe even "sacredness," but not a subjective emotion. It is decisive to see that feelings were precisely not important. "The only important thing is to do the ritual in the prescribed manner," said an expert of the world of ritual, Cesáreo Bandera.[9] He also points out that for example in the Spanish countryside professional female mourners are hired for a funeral, mourners of whom the person who hires them cannot assume that they personally and emotionally grieve. But this was from the outset not the point nor the reason why they were hired. The only thing that really counted was the meticulously accurate performance of the *objective* ritual act of mourning according to the ancient custom, I could even say: nothing else but *one's going through the motion* of mourning (provided this phrase is not meant in the usual derogatory sense).

---

[8] For Jung's term "esoteric" in connection with myth and symbol see CW 6 § 816, CW 18 § 632. Cf. MDR p. 332: "One does not even understand that a myth is dead if it no longer lives and is developed further" (transl. modified).

[9] In his contribution to the discussion, in: Robert G. Hammerton-Kelly (Hg.), *Violent Origins*, Stanford (Stanford Univ. Press) 1987, p. 187.

A minister, who during the 20s of this century [the 20th century] had his parish in a village in the Westerwald region of Germany, an area where time seemed to have been standing still, recounted the following. He had to perform a funeral. More or less all the people of the village were standing around the open grave, and the minister was ready to begin with the ceremony. He noticed two girls of maybe 17 years whose thoughts obviously were somewhere totally else and were vividly chatting about something very exciting for them. But suddenly it dawned on them that they were at a funeral, and in a flash they pulled out their handkerchiefs and burst into tears, because it was still the custom at that time in this village that all its female inhabitants had to cry during a funeral ceremony. This example demonstrates very nicely that what the custom demanded had nothing whatsoever to do with personal emotions. The custom did not demand subjectively felt grief, but objective mourning behavior.

Once more: Why is precisely the emotionless, *almost* mechanical enactment of the ritual a sign of authenticity? Because it shows that the mythic meaning is still completely contained and enveloped *within* the symbolic act *itself* and that man can only be blessed by it if he as an experiencing and feeling person takes second place to, gives absolute precedence to, the *self-sufficient* ritual, and, as it were, disappears in it by becoming no more than its marionette. Meaning is here not sucked out of the ritual for our benefit; the ritual is not used and consumed for the purposes of our experiencing and understanding meaning. The ritual is itself its own end. The ritual has life in itself. "The fact is that in former times men *lived* their symbols rather than reflected upon them [and, so we might add, rather than wanted to emotionally *experience* them]" (*CW* 18 § 551). They were no more and no less than *ta drômena*, "that which is enacted." And myths were *ta legomena*, "that which is told," what one says, not what one feels and believes. In much the same sense we find in Jung the statement: "Faust aptly says: 'Im Anfang war die Tat' (in the beginning was the deed). Deeds were not invented, they were done. ... Yet unreflected life existed long before man; it was not invented, but in it man found himself as an afterthought" (*ibid.* § 553). Man as afterthought! In this archaic situation man was made, if I may put it in this way, for the Sabbath and not the other way around. He has his life not within himself, in his own feeling and thinking, but his life is *inside* "that which is

THE LESSON OF THE CHRISTMAS TREE

enacted," inside the objective ritual, in his statue of god, in the sacred stone ("out there," as it were). It, the ritual, the symbol, the myth must increase, the I or the human subject must decrease.[10] This is the nature of ritualism and symbolism: what it is about is that (to express it merely by means of the example of ritual mourning by professional mourners) mourning has a real empirical presence in sensory form. All meaning, all psychic life is invested in this objectively existing sensory form. Meaning has not yet withdrawn from what is visibly enacted out there nor from the likewise objectively present image or statue into the inner of man's subjective faith and felt experience.

Despite the fact that our Christmas customs have on the one hand long been superimposed with commercialism, consumerism, and fashion trends, and on the other hand are exploited for our subjective felt experience (the Christmas mood and atmosphere), in other words, have become sentimentalized—nevertheless, only a few decades ago the Christmas custom with its candle-lit Christmas tree could still serve as an example of a living myth. For to the extent that for that time, too, it was true that, "You may ask many civilized people in vain for the reason and meaning of the Christmas tree or of the coloured eggs at Easter, because they have no idea about the meaning of these customs. The fact is, they do things without knowing why they do them" (*CW* 18 § 540), the people here in our latitudes were at that time in much the same situation as Jung's Elgonyi. Does this at least mean that it was *an authentic relict* of living myth? Let us mentally transport ourselves back into the time before the total commercialization of Christmas and allow ourselves to be told by the candle-lit Christmas tree itself, when it was still preserved intact, what has become of mythic meaning in the 20th century.

The original meaning of the Christmas tree had two distinct roots, a pagan and a Christian one. Part of the pagan symbolism are the evergreen world tree, the individual's tree of life, the mid-winter vegetation and solstice festival (which among Germanic peoples was celebrated with a burning Yule log), perhaps even the Levantine

---

[10] This wording is already inaccurate because it comes from within a post-ritualistic, post-mythological situation. For that type of man who lived in a world that was mythologically and ritualistically constituted, it needed no "must increase – must decrease." He found himself, as Jung put it, a priori as a mere "afterthought" in the ritual, which was that which was the actually real.

mythology of the dying god. If seen in its Christian context, too, the Christmas tree symbolizes the return of Light in the longest and darkest night of the year, in accordance with the promise: "The people that walked in darkness will see a great light" (Isa. 9:1). The illuminated tree leads directly to the Christian experience of the birth of light in the world: "O light born from light" (Martin Opitz). Christ is the "Morning shine of eternity / Light from the unexhausted light" (Christian Knorr von Rosenroth). Paul Gerhardt writes in his poem "Nun ruhen alle Wälder": "What happened to you, Sun? / The night has driven you away, / The night, day's enemy. / Begone. Another sun, / My Jesus, my delight / Shines very brightly in my heart." Pagan customs and Christian meaning are often superimposed; we could also say that the pagan customs were re-interpreted in a Christian sense. In the Bavarian Forest, Christmas was celebrated way into the 20th century with the burning of a log in which we easily recognize the Teutonic Yule log. Until the Gregorian Calendar was introduced 1582, St. Lucy's Day was considered the mid-winter day, the day with the longest night; now it falls on December 13. In Sweden it is still today an important holiday on which girls dress in white as "Lussibrud" (St. Lucy bride; Lucy or Lucia from Lat. *lux*, light) and, with a burning candle on their head, wake up their parents in the morning. The pagan mid-winter custom was rescued for the Christian age through being rededicated to a Christian Saint, Sancta Lucia. Both this Swedish holiday and Christmas celebrated with a candle-adorned Christmas tree are concerned with the birth of light from within the darkest darkness. No doubt, the burning Christmas tree, if *seen in isolation*, must be acknowledged as being a full-fledged symbol.

However, the question with which we will have to concern ourselves is precisely what happens to a symbol or ritual that *in itself* remained intact and unchanged when it is immersed into another epoch. Is myth, is ritual immune over against the character of that age *within which* it occurs? In other words: can myth be viewed *abstractly* all by itself, apart from the time in which it is embedded, or does this not ipso facto result in our having only an abstract view of it?

During the 17th century, when there is the first documentation of the Christmas tree (although the custom could well be much older), in an age, in other words, when people could only produce a miserable

THE LESSON OF THE CHRISTMAS TREE

light by means of a pine wood chip, tallow candle, or oil lamp and only if it was really necessary, and when for the most part it simply remained dark during the night, then a tree illuminated with numerous candles was truly able to provide an experience of the birth of light in the middle of the deepest night. Compared to the normally prevailing darkness or, at best, scanty lighting, the Christmas tree brought an otherwise unheard of bright light into the darkness of the night.

Peter Rosegger's story, "The First Christmas Tree in the Forest Home [*Waldheimat*]" may give us at least a vague idea of this experience (although only through the modern form of an already subjectivized sentimental recreation, which shows that, much like fairytales in our modern times, this example has to be seen as already having its essential place in the nursery).

The 19th century author recounts how as a student in a large city far away from his rural home he came back into the wretchedly poor forest farmhouse of his parents, when he had his first Christmas vacation. In the city he had heard for the first time of the custom of putting up a Christmas tree, which was still unknown in the remote forest region from which he came. All the evening lighting ever known in his parents' house was the feeble light of a pine wood chip on ordinary days and a candle—*one* candle—on holidays. The light that came from them was so meager, hardly worth calling light, that one could only recognize things after one's eyes had slowly become adjusted to it. As a student on Christmas home leave, in order to surprise his family, he secretly put up a candle-lit Christmas tree in the front room, and hidden behind the stove he looked at "the marvel of light the kind of which had never been seen in this room" and expectantly waited for the surprise of his unsuspecting parents, the farm hands, and above all his young brother, when they would enter the room. And he relates how when they had come his little brother "stared speechless. In his big round eyes the lights from the Christmas tree were reflected like stars."

Because in olden times a tree full of burning candles in fact brought a sensory illumination, it was also able to serve as a valid expression of the spiritual and cosmic enlightenment, that is, it could truly be a symbol. Expressed in psychological language: it brought about the psychically real and so to speak "automatic" transformation or transportation of psychic energy in the direction of the spiritual light. I say "automatic" because it was independent of whether one was willing or not, felt it and was consciously aware of it or not.

Today, by contrast, accustomed as we are to several-100 watt room and street illumination, we have to specifically turn off our electric lights in order to enjoy the dim light of a candle-lit Christmas tree. Candles today no longer provide, in the middle of the Christmas night, illumining light as the unquestionable ground of life. They quite conversely provide a cozy, moody semi-light through which we can recover from the otherwise prevailing basic brightness in which we live. We go literally and on purpose into a regression. Within *our* time we simulate once more the time prior to our brightly lit night. In this way, we play "night" once more, as it were, despite the fact that the night has long ceased to be night: a mythic power. In order to have it bright, we do not, like the Elgonyi, expectantly wait for the sun to rise in the morning, the sun that (temporarily!) triumphs over the darkness of the night. *We* live our lives, at least potentially, in eternal light, much like the Olympic gods, and, when we want to have it really dark, we need to artificially darken our rooms by means of shutters so that the city street lights and neon signs do not shine into them. And even a power failure, a black-out, as a *failure* of light, is precisely a confirmation of the fundamental rule of light.

When Paul Gerhardt, as we heard, was able to write in his poem: "What happened to you, Sun? / The night has driven you away, / The night, day's enemy. / Begone. Another sun, / my Jesus, my delight / Shines very brightly in my heart," then we see that he had his mental or soul place in an in-between stage between two conditions of the world. On the one hand, it was still possible for him to experience the night in a quasi mythic way, as a cosmic power: "The night has driven you away, / The night, day's enemy." It was possible for him because on the level of *immediate experience* the power of Night was still unbroken. There was not yet any electric light, no fundamental illumination of the night, that is, not yet the empirical-factual victory over the night, or expressed the other way around, not yet the fundamental dethronement of the mythic Night. For primordial experience the night was the never ageing producer of all things, daughter of Chaos, a powerful goddess, ruler of the All, for she quiets down everything, restrains all passions, and she is the cause of the origin of all things. She was what encompassed within herself the day and

THE LESSON OF THE CHRISTMAS TREE

the light. The Sun's light was day by day merely temporarily born out of the night, only to return ever anew in the evening into her as into its origin.

For Paul Gerhardt, however, the night is first of all no longer the all-encompassing great goddess and the native ground even of light, but "day's *enemy*." And secondly, the entire natural world, and inasmuch as the natural world is the condition of possibility of mythic experience, this mythic experience as such, are dismissed. "Begone," he says to the sun expelled by the night. The whole mythic world, night *and* sun or day, has been dismissed. *Another* experience ("Another sun...") takes its place, supersedes it. It is the inner, spiritual experience of the Christian truth which is completely independent of natural reality, of sensory experience. But of course, this experience that is independent of sensory reality and thus of mythic experience is here still a merely internal one, one of the heart. Factually, Gerhardt has to acknowledge the power of the night, and this is why he pronounces his "Begone," which defies it. The dismissal of mythic experience is only a subjective, psychological one, one in the interiority of the individual soul. It has not yet become the evident and absolutely true, objective reality. The "Another sun shines very brightly in my heart" is still dependent on whether a particular person believes in Jesus Christ and is truly fulfilled with this faith or that experience that corresponds to it.

Our present-day situation is totally different. The might of the night is objectively broken. She is not a goddess any more, indeed, it is quite impossible to ascribe to the night a power of being, substantiality, and personlike divinity. We do not have to say to the sun, defying the night, "Begone." For us the street lights go on automatically every night. The Christian overcoming of the night and, by extension, of myth as such has become an objective reality that is no longer dependent on one's subjective faith and on the heart's interiority. The victory over the night is a self-sufficient, self-confirming objective fact.

If we compare the symbol of the Christmas tree of 1660 with that of today (or rather 50 or 60 years ago), we see that even though there has not been a significant change in the external appearance of the symbol (as long as we look at it in isolation), this symbol has nevertheless experienced a complete *reversal* of its meaning because then and now it is immersed into two radically different world conditions or ages. Once upon a time it pointed forward, from darkness to light; today it regressively leads from the overbrightness of our modern, high-tech and highly rationalized world of consciousness into a relaxing dimness, psychologically speaking into a lowering of conscious awareness.[11] It is likely that this psychological recreational value of the Christmas holiday is one of the main aspects that has so far safeguarded its singular popularity above all the other major Church holidays (Good Friday, Easter, Ascension Day, Pentecost). Life today takes place in such a brightness of consciousness, is strenuous to such a degree, that a temporary, but *officially ennobled* and also by no means threatening (because totally controlled) sinking back into a twilight state is something enormously attractive.

A watershed seems to go right through the middle of the Christmas tree and to make the modern meaning of this symbol that points in the direction of the past run absolutely counter to the direction of the same symbol's original meaning pointing in the direction of progression. In order to establish this fact, no interpretation from us is needed. We do not have to meddle in with opinions of our own. Precisely when the symbol of the illuminated Christmas tree is still taken as a symbol, it reveals its truth by itself. We can tell what kind of "meaning" it has simply by having a good look at how it appears. For a symbol is only symbol by carrying its intellectual meaning *immediately within its sensory appearance* and possessing this meaning only by virtue of the latter. We cannot even say that lighting candles at Christmas amounts to one's "carrying coals to Newcastle," because this phrase suggests that the illuminated Christmas tree would simply bring additional light into a world that is already brightly lit to begin with. But in our case we are dealing with a subtraction. The light of the tree is not merely superfluous, it brings a loss of light.

---

[11] Here I will not go into that other important aspect of the Christmas tree, namely that today for public consciousness the needle tree, threatened by waldsterben, can hardly be an evident guarantor of eternally greening life. It is of course possible that consciousness subjectively still *entertains this idea*, but then, as a tree that is merely in one's opinion the guarantor of always greening life, it would only be a sign. A symbol, by contrast, has to be the true, best possible expression (not of one's subjective opinion or feeling, but) of something that cannot yet, or can never be, expressed otherwise. Obviously, an artificial Christmas tree of plastic, industrially manufactured, easily dismantled and re-usable every year, can hardly be an obvious symbol of ever again self-renewing life.

THE LESSON OF THE CHRISTMAS TREE

It does not amount to a promise of a future salvation. It is the hallowing of something like a "vacation from the ego world." Christmas is an oasis surrounded on all sides by technological modernity and thus a priori checkmated.

A true symbol is not, as we all know, an allegory in the sense of a pictorial representation of an already known concept. It is instead the best possible expression of something that is not yet capable of being conceptually grasped, but only intuited. The illuminated Christmas tree is today at best an allegory. As such it is only "esoteric" in Jung's sense and subject to consciousness's arbitrary disposal, a fact made perfectly evident in the artificial, dismantlable and re-usable tree. As a symbol, the Christmas tree is redundant, as jobless as a manual spinning wheel is in our present-day economy or a goose quill as a serious writing utensil. There is no work only it can perform. It can no longer really express a mystery, nor can it represent, for up-to-date consciousness, a still unconscious meaning that cannot otherwise be better expressed, because what it expresses has precisely already long been known.

A symbol stands or falls with its sensory form. If we today *truly* wanted to express the birth of light from within the deepest darkness in a symbolic, ritualistic way, we would probably have to detonate an atom bomb and expose ourselves to its shine, in order to have, at least from the sensory side, an experience of an "unexpressible" expressed "in *unsurpassable form.*"[12] Only against the foil of the explosion of light through an atom bomb could our present-day real brightness still, or again, be recognized, on the sensory level, as the benightedness of consciousness, as the darkness of the night which is the indispensable ground for the symbol of the birth of light. Anything beneath that level of light either confirms the brightness of consciousness prevailing anyway all around or serves one's pleasant restoration from it by way of an insular darkening amidst this brightness.

Consciousness therefore must artificially stultify itself and systematically scotomize the larger part of the reality known to it in order to be able to pretend before itself as though it would still perceive the candle-lit Christmas tree as a symbol of the birth of light "Amid the cold, cold winter, / And in the dark midnight." Today the

---

[12] CW 6 § 816, italics taken over from the German original.

Christmas tree only reaches the I or the ego personality, whereas an authentic symbol first of all addresses the soul or, as Jung would put it, the Self (which is not so much inside us but *in* which we have our place, being surrounded by it on all sides, from the front as well as the back, and from the side of the past as well as from that of the future).

Now we can also understand why the commercialization, the fashion trends, and the mechanization of the Christmas holiday as a whole and of the Christmas tree in particular (re-usable plastic trees, electric candles, trees in fashionable colors) could become possible in the first place. This was only possible because the symbol *is* a symbol no longer. It is non-committal. It is only a mock-up of itself, and as such it is, as a matter of course, perfectly legitimate for it to be manipulated at will. It is now in the process of losing even its allegorical character (through which it would still point to *something*) and becoming an empty form, a mere (by definition meaning-less) decoration, a self-sufficient display, in accordance with the major trend of our age toward, or deeper into, "medial" modernity.

What during our time in reality is (has been) happening to Christmas and to the Christmas tree must, however, be understood as the innocent self-representation of their true nature today. It is not an illegitimate abuse, not degeneration. What looks like abuse and degeneration is only a change, a change through which the external sensory form of that which once upon a time used to be a symbol is at long last brought into alignment with the altered situation (soul situation) in which it finds itself today. Precisely that Christmas tree which is subject to all sorts of fashions, and precisely that Christmas that is in openly kitschy form celebrated in a tourist beach hotel in the Caribbean confront us with our living present, because the way they are they *are* the real expression of *the pastness of what is past.*

It can be assumed that what we were able to see here does not only apply to the Christmas tree in particular. Rather, we can extrapolate what we found to the general fate of symbols and myth using the Christmas tree as a model. Today, in its obsolescence, it itself becomes a veritable symbol of the obsolescence of symbols in general. We merely have to allow ourselves to be taught by what it says: symbol and myth, both taken in that high sense in which Jung and the psychology that follows him take them, have been uncoupled from

THE LESSON OF THE CHRISTMAS TREE

the train of time and are now standing in the sidings, much like workers who in the course of modern rationalizations have become redundant, and, unhooked from working life, have been shoved to the sidings of State welfare.

As late as one and a half centuries ago Eduard Mörike in a poem ("*Um Mitternacht*," At midnight) was still able to evoke mythic Night one last time.[13] The fact that the illuminated Christmas tree lags hopelessly behind the state of technology or, the other way around, that technology fundamentally depotentiated that mythic Night is not something merely external and technical. Rather, it is the external, objectual mirror (or one single facet of a mirror consisting of innumerably many facets) of the state of our psychic reality reached today, the mirror of (as we might put it) solar consciousness. For the latter, however, the *logical form* of symbol and myth is something that only nostalgically, sentimentally leads back into oases of obsolete soul states. As such it can emotionally gratify ego-consciousness, but it no longer has any handle with which it could still reach and move the soul itself, the logical form of modern consciousness. The symbolic or mythological mode is relative to a (let us say) lunar consciousness, a consciousness for which Night was a real might and an all-comprehensive goddess, even if the sun god or the god of heaven were perhaps already in the foreground of conscious experience and religious practice. Solar consciousness is on a new storey. It is capable of still seeing through the glass floor which separates it from the hitherto sole, but now lower storey, down upon the myths and symbols that formerly used to express the soul's life and to set it in motion. It can recognize them exactly in their external form, but only as *historical* and in this sense as dead *forms* that remain on principle out of reach and depotentiated as far as it is concerned. Consciousness today is unhitched so that the "motor" of the symbols and myths runs idle. But the consciousness which is unhitched from them is not at a standstill. *It* is not what is checkmated. On the contrary, with tremendous power

---

[13] "Gelassen stieg die Nacht ans Land, / Lehnt träumend an der Berge Wand, / Ihr Auge sieht die goldne Waage nun / Der Zeit in gleichen Schalen stille ruhn; / Und kecker rauschen die Quellen hervor, / Sie singen der Mutter, der Nacht, ins Ohr / Vom Tage, / Vom heute gewesenen Tage. // ..." (Calmly Night ascended to the land. She leans dreamingly against the mountainside. Her eye now sees time's golden scales quietly balanced at rest. And pertly the springs rush forth, singing in the ear of their mother, the Night, of the day, the day that has just been. ...)

it is driven forward by a new, different, invisible engine towards an unknown future. To the extent that consciousness believes to search for its motor, as before, in symbols and myths, and for that matter in the *form* of the mythic at large, it remains unconscious about its own true motor that drives it ahead with an uncanny dynamics.

With these insights we have at least an initial answer to the other important question raised at the beginning, namely, whether an authentic archetypal experience in dream or vision today is an exception to the otherwise prevailing fact that in our days myth cannot succeed. If we take the illuminated Christmas tree as a model for the situation of symbol and myth as such today, we can say that our dreams may contain the (in themselves) most authentic and numinous symbols and mythic motifs and accordingly touch us deeply. Nevertheless, they have no chance. The character of the age pulls the floor out from under them. Or no, it is the other way around. The dynamic of the *soul's* life passes high over them, and they no longer rise into and reach the soul's life. They do not even touch it. They remain completely unrelated beneath the niveau at which the soul resides today.

The point is precisely that it is not the soul that is reached and addressed by the numinous symbols and myths today, but the ego personality. To feel and experience, to be deeply moved and touched, on the one hand, and to (esotercially) understand on the other hand are ego modes, not modes of the soul. The soul is interested, as we have already seen, quite unexcitedly in the *drômena* and *legomena*, in the *self-sufficient* TRUTH of what is true, its disclosedness. All it wants is that TRUTH finds an objective expression and presence. The mere fact that the experience of archetypal and mythic images is always viewed today from the perspective of one's own self-development, self-actualization, sometimes also self-stabilization, betrays the standpoint of the ego.

What we learn from our discussion is that we must not look at a symbol abstractly, in isolation from the particular world condition into which it is immersed. This is a great mistake so easily committed by us Jungians: one only sees the semantics and is blind for the syntax. One abstracts from the character of the age, from the truth of the age, and looks solely at the naked mythic motif itself, at the mere factual occurrence of mythic images, symbols, or behavioral patterns. One shows oneself quickly impressed by their undoubted "archetypal"

THE LESSON OF THE CHRISTMAS TREE

quality, by their obvious correspondence with impressive parallels from ancient mythologems, and believes that this alone shows that one is dealing with genuine myth. But it is only the *abstract* myth, the peeled-off mythic *form*. It is of course easy in our time to be blind to the abstractness of this so-called "mythic experience" because the abstract symbol serves as a stimulus for one's generating within oneself a (likewise abstract) sentiment, an archetypal feeling or atmosphere, just as in the case of the Christmas tree. When these two abstractions, the *formally* authentic symbol here and the *subjective* intensive feeling there, are joined together, they reinforce each other; the subjective emotion lends its power to the abstract form, the latter lends a reminiscence of meaning to the emotion, and the abstractness of both seems simply to drop away. Due to their vacuity the two opposite abstractnesses attract each other like powerful magnets and thereby seem to merge into an organic whole, a full-fledged both numinous and mythic experience, so that at the same time—seemingly—their abstractness is canceled out. Seemingly, because in truth what is passed off as a whole is and remains something artificially glued together from two dead things, abstract form here and abstract sentiment there.

The fact that today we are not allowed to look at a symbol or mythic motif abstractly in isolation and infer from it alone that we are still confronted with a real myth shows that the psychic situation of modern man has become more complex and that, as Jung put it (CW 9ii § 274), "far greater demands are made on present-day man than were ever made on people living in the apostolic era" (and of course, I add, by the same token in all truly premodern times). Formerly it was sufficient to look at one's dreams and visions, the symbolic statues, and the mythic tales. One did not have to become explicitly aware of one's era. It sufficed to pay "religious" (*religiose*) attention to the semantic contents of one's experience, the images. Why? Because the character of the time, that is, the logical constitution of man's being-in-the-world, fully corresponded with the mythic, archetypal character of the images. Inasmuch as both aspects did not fall apart, inasmuch as there was no difference between them, one was not (and could not be) in the least conscious of the second aspect, the question of the logical constitution of consciousness or of the condition of the world. One took into account only *what* was immersed into the character of the age and did not need to take note of more. That medium as well as

40   *THE SOUL ALWAYS THINKS*

the fact of the images' being immersed into a medium or soul condition could not be seen and reflected. In other words, one only saw the ontic entities, but not Being, only the semantic, not the syntax. The awareness of the Being *in* which an ontic entity has its place is, as always, only possible when the difference emerges for consciousness: when the inherent logical constitution of the objects and contents on the one hand and the logical constitution of the intellectual medium for whatever experienced content on the other hand have fallen apart.

As the previous quotation from Jung shows, he had become aware of the fact that, without calling it so, a *logical* difference separates us from the apostolic era, for example. After the quoted partial sentence the text continues,

> for them [the people living then] there was no difficulty at all in believing in the virgin birth of the hero and demigod, and Justin Martyr was still able to use this argument in his apology. Nor was the idea of a redeeming God-man anything unheard of, since practically all Asiatic potentates together with the Roman Emperor were of divine nature. We, by contrast, do not even have an insight into the divine right of kings any more! The miraculous tales in the gospels, which easily convinced people in those days, would be a *petra scandali* in any modern biography and would evoke the very reverse of belief. The weird and wonderful nature of the gods was a self-evident fact when myth was still alive ... "Hermes ter unus" was not an intellectual absurdity but a philosophical truth. On these foundations the dogma of the Trinity could be built up convincingly. For modern man this dogma is either an impenetrable mystery or an historical curiosity, preferably the latter. For the man of antiquity the virtue of the consecrated water or the transmutation of substances was in no sense an enormity... (transl. modified).

What Jung points to is the perfect agreement in antiquity between the semantic contents of myth (and symbols) and the general prevailing mindset or syntax of consciousness that entertained these contents and, by contrast, the rift between them in modernity. As far as its logical form is concerned consciousness in olden times was itself on one level with the miraculous stories told in myth. This is why they could not be a *petra scandali* for consciousness, but were easily embraced as self-

THE LESSON OF THE CHRISTMAS TREE

41

evident truths. Consciousness could seamlessly integrate them along with all its ordinary-life knowledge and every-day-type experiences. They were special, to be sure, but they were precisely not beyond all reason. They were "*philosophical* truths." They were *intellectually* acceptable as *arguments*, even more than acceptable: higher or highest truths. That for us these miracles are "scandalous," that the virgin birth and similar motifs present the greatest "difficulties" for us, that "Hermes ter unus" is an "intellectual absurdity"[14] for us, and that consciousness has to *force* itself with great effort against reason to believe in the Trinity (if it wants to do so at all), simply results from and displays the fact that we have logically left that level and now live high above it on a different level of consciousness. All these conceptions, although we still factually retain them as contents of our *historical* knowledge within consciousness (Jung said as "historical curiosities"), have nevertheless become fundamentally foreign to the structure or logical form of consciousness, veritable alien bodies within it, which consciousness *cannot* reconcile with itself without giving itself up.

The fact that those old ideas are "historical curiosities" for us is not something wrong, not a mistake. It is the innocent self-display of the fundamental difference, indeed incompatibility, between those older contents of consciousness and all other ordinary, intellectually acceptable contents of consciousness and thus the self-display of the fact that our consciousness contains two storeys within itself, the "lower" storey of the former level of consciousness represented by those obsolete contents or "historical curiosities" and the "upper" storey of modern consciousness. Our consciousness is "higher," not so much because it is above the old form of consciousness, but rather because it is a two-storey consciousness over against that one-storey consciousness of former days which could place the miraculous seamlessly side by side with the ordinary on one and the same level of consciousness.

---

[14] Or "an impenetrable mystery," which is really the same thing as an "intellectual absurdity." Both names express the fact that the content in question is absolutely indigestible, unintegrateable for consciousness, but in the one case this fact is given a benevolent interpretation, which is possible because the unacceptable nature of the content has been bracketed and safely encased in the (one could almost say: metalanguage) word "mystery," whereas the other interpretation is brutally honest because consciousness in this case exposes itself directly to the experience of this content. Much the same as about "mystery" could be said about another popular word for such contents: "paradox."

Jung of course substantiated and positivized the modern consciousness-*internal* difference between the "historical curiosities" on the one hand and all intellectually acceptable contents on the other hand as a radical external difference between "consciousness" and what he called "the unconscious" or "the collective unconscious." He hoped to thereby give to those historical curiosities a new quasi "ontological" dignity of their own, but had to pay for this maneuver the dear price of introducing an axiomatic split, a dissociation. Imaginal psychology, by contrast, tried to resolve the problem in another way, namely by, *on* the modern level of consciousness, simulating a new one-storey consciousness that can, just like that, feel at home with mythic images and effortlessly see present-day life events in terms of them. The price it had to pay for this harmonious view was threefold, first, a denial of the incontrovertible historical discrepancy, of the death of the gods and the obsolescence of the mythic contents, in logical terms, a denial of negation; secondly, an aestheticizing and poeticizing, a reduction of the mythic contents to metaphors, to rhetoric, to "the imaginal"; and, thirdly, a moralization, a split between a purified "anima-only" world of the images as something said to be soulful and the typically modern technical world as "the soulless." The imaginal has the abstract modern consciousness not so to speak vertically "above" itself, like Jung's "collective unconscious," but rather horizontally, although only as rejects, outside and vis-à-vis itself, on one and the same plane with the imaginal.

It is clear that with our two-storey situation of consciousness, as Jung had said, indeed "far greater demands are made on present-day man than were ever made on people living in the apostolic era." But it is also to be assumed that neither in Jung's way, with his dissociation between consciousness and the unconscious, nor in the way of imaginal psychology with its aestheticizing the "historical curiosities," have or can these far greater demands be really met. Both ways resort to tricks to get away from the problem without actually meeting those greater demands.

Be that as it may, we today are forced to take note of the historical discrepancy, and we all already have been and are doing this all along and inevitably, no matter whether we like it or know about it or not: namely in the form of a mute factual suffering from our time. It is a suffering from the loss of meaning, from a "metaphysical" homelessness

THE LESSON OF THE CHRISTMAS TREE

in the world, one's fundamental isolation as modern individual, the feeling of alienation. Very frequently we try to evade the necessity to consciously acknowledge this discrepancy, that is, to appreciate and reflect it. Factual suffering, as an emotionalizing of what is actually a truth, as the pushing of a truth off into the merely subjective sphere of sentiments and shelving it there, is, similar to acting-out, a compromise-formation and serves as a defense. It is only an implicit reflection: the reflection does take place, but it is still held down on the old stage and standpoint of a seemingly still unbroken consciousness, as no more than a disturbing painful factor within the latter, whereas it would be the real telos of reflection to overcome this *stage*. This reflection is not yet permitted to come fully home to consciousness, to be released into its truth, and thus to become explicit reflection. If this had happened, it would have become a new logical status, the new stage on which consciousness would then in fact stand and from which, as its real standpoint, it would experience what it experiences.

Nevertheless, regardless of whether the reflection is held down and pushed aside into a special feeling as a mere content (besides numerous other contents) within the old status of consciousness or whether it has become released into its own true nature and thus become the *total character* of a new stage for whatever content of experience, one thing is clear: the difference has been experienced once and for all and thus the rupture of time has happened; it is all over with myth. Because myth presupposes an unbroken relation between man and nature, between the constitution of man's being-in-the-world at the age in question and the logical constitution of the archetypal contents of experience, such that *within* what is a natural, sensory presence the nonsensory, intelligible infinite and archetypal is present. As people who have been reached by the psychic (soul) difference we have dropped out of that status of consciousness for which alone there could still be real myth and symbols (not merely sublated ones that have become abstract historical or aesthetic formations). What I just said is a description of the situation in terms of the loss we experience. The positive formulation would be: it is our task *in the status of reflection* (in it as a fundamental *stage* of consciousness and in the *form* appropriate to it) to determine our relationship to life and to the world in a completely new way and to learn to take our stand in that relationship.

The symbols and myths can no longer be a *present reality* for us, but only a *historical presence.*

The Christmas tree *as* symbol is obsolete because in the sensory medium a technical development has taken place which psychologically seen turns the sensory object of the Christmas tree inevitably into something historical, a kind of museum piece. In the Christmas tree just as well as in the lighting technology that prevails in everyday life we have clear documentation of the *sublatedness* of the sensory side of the symbol. When the sensory side of the symbol is either obsolete (the illuminated tree) or alienated (lighting technology) and in either case exists merely as a sublated symbol, then this not only renders the specific carrier for the symbolic expression (candle light) and the specific symbol (Christmas tree) obsolete, but also the symbol in general, the condition of the possibility of myth and symbol as such. This is why I said that the illuminated Christmas tree is the symbol of the obsolescence of "symbol" as such. The sensory can no longer be in itself an authentic, valid expression of intellectual, spiritual meaning. The form of image as such is what as far as mythic meaning is concerned has become absolutely jobless, functionless: precisely because the image, the sensory *form*, has become absolutely functionalized today. Image today is a means to an end, not an end in itself. This proves true even in psychology where images have the (of course unacknowledged) *technical function* of providing meaningful experience.

One might say that the functionalization of image is pathological. Maybe so. But this does not mean a lot. It does not alter the fact that the image can no longer be the medium of a manifestation of mythic meaning. In the total functionalization of the image—on the one hand in our being flooded with advertizing images for the purpose of marketing and on the other hand in our being flooded with television images for the purpose of infotainment—we constantly objectively present to ourselves the sublatedness of the sensory-imaginal, indeed, even the continued destruction of such a thing as *Sinn-Bild*, meaningful image, not to mention here the phenomenon of the digitalization of images and the entailing possibility of their manipulation. Advertizing and television are the visible demonstration of the *reductio ad absurdum* of image inasmuch as image *as* something sensory is supposed to at the same time have a *meaning.*

THE LESSON OF THE CHRISTMAS TREE 45

If at all, then a carrier of meaning could under these circumstances only be something like Paul Gerhardt's "another sun," in explicit opposition to the sensory sun, which as a natural phenomenon has been told to begone. However, the sun that Gerhardt had in mind is also no longer accessible to us, because it is superseded. His sun, his Jesus, still shone in the interiority of his heart. But we live in the age of *wahrgemacht*, realized Christianity, Christianity having become objective. Paul Gerhardt's *other* sun has long been shining for us objectively "out there," namely as electric light. And for this very reason it no longer *subjectively* provides meaning and has no longer the form of religion, let alone of myth—precisely because the Christian truth as well as its further expression, the light of European Enlightenment, have become *objective* in the electric light, so that Christian truth has come into a state where it is completely free of any need for personal faith and subjective fulfillment.

In the technical supersededness of the candlelight at the Christmas tree we can *pars pro toto* see the logical-psychological phenomenon that determines our entire soul situation: the fundamental technification and thus *sublation* of *nature in its sensory form.* One by one, all of nature as "naturally given" is logically being destroyed and given back to us only as either a *literally* technologically altered nature or as one that can only through technology be preserved or protected and is in this sense *logically* technified. Nature is in its very nature no longer natural. *It is already "other," already in itself reflection.* The point of technology is not only a pragmatic one of "technical progress" and alleviation of life. It also (and I would say: predominantly[15]) has a psychic (soul) meaning in the context of the alchemical *opus magnum* as which the history of the soul *is.* We are mostly blind to the soul side of this process. For this reason we usually think in all earnest that technology serves *our* practical purposes, that it exists for our sake and also ought to be there for our benefit. This is ego-psychological. Its true purpose, however, is a soul purpose. What we take to be the purpose of technology is only the piece of sugar with the help of which the trainer

---

[15] Possibly even exclusively. It is well possible that the enticement through the alleviation that technology brings is merely the sprat to catch the mackerel with, that is to say, that with which mankind is baited to go on a path of psychic development that takes place via technification. We think that we do it for our purposes and benefit, whereas in reality we are instrumentalized for the purposes of the soul, purposes that by no means are identical with our own ones.

trains his horse. Technology is the form in which an *objective* psychic transformation takes place, that is, a transformation of the objective soul. The psychological meaning of science and technology—the meaning of the soul *opus* that we refer to under these two names—is nothing else but the destruction of the naive apperception of the sensory and natural, through the objective transformation of the nature that is visible in pictorial shape into something that is always already reflected. Worded differently, the goal of the soul's *opus magnum* that we find ourselves today exposed to is the annulment of intuition (*Anschauung*) and imagination as organs of the experience of meaning. Provided that consciousness does not abstract from its real situation and stultify itself (which is of course always possible), there is one point where there can still be a true manifestation. But what still today can possibly be the object of such an experience (that is, what can be perceived as a symbol or a mythic reality) is no longer any individual sensory thing or event (such as the Christmas tree); the individual object is no longer by itself a *phainomenon* (something that manifests, displays, reveals itself). Rather, a phenomenon in the true sense that can still be intuited is now only *the whole*, only this one reality: the logical sublatedness of the sensory *per se*, of the entire natural world. He who has eyes to see can apperceive this *phainomenon pars pro toto* exemplified in the Christmas tree as well as in a thousand other individual "phenomena" of our age. (Of course it is the eyes of the mind that "see" here, i.e., *think*, not the literal eyes of the body.)

What one sees quite evidently in our example of the Christmas tree is that the symbol of the birth of light from out of the deepest darkness has been checkmated. It has long been infinitely surpassed, so that the illuminated Christmas tree now points into the reverse direction, into that of regression, into the benightedness of consciousness. Progression, the birth and intensification of light takes place somewhere else: in science and technology. Progression has, we can say by extension, emigrated from religion, from Christianity. Christianity has superseded itself as religion, it has progressed *beyond itself*, and thereby it left *itself as religion* behind (as something that has *the form of* religion, or insofar as it still tries to have the form of religion); along with all its religious symbols it left itself behind as museum-like antiquities of the soul.

THE LESSON OF THE CHRISTMAS TREE

Jung once said (CW 18 § 279), "My problem is to wrestle with the big monster of the historical past, the great snake of the centuries, the burden of the human mind, the problem of Christianity." If we take up for now only the one image of the snake from this quotation, we can say that the snake has shed its skin; it has left the form of its existence as religion behind itself as a lifeless skin and dead casing and, as a living snake, is now at work at some totally other place.

I said above in view of the insight into the technical supersededness of the candle-lit Christmas tree that, if anything, only the detonated atom bomb could be an appropriate expression of the birth of light from out of the night of the world. As much as this contrast can indeed help us to clearly perceive the obsolescence of the Christmas symbol, so impossible it is nevertheless for us now, after our extrapolation of what could be realized from the Christmas tree to the general situation of symbols, to still hold up this view. The point is precisely not that we have to choose between diverse sensory things or events, appropriate versus inappropriate ones, correct versus incorrect ones, obsolete ones versus those that "work." Especially the atom bomb makes perfectly clear that even the most extreme sensory medium or carrier could not have any mythic or symbolic potency any more. Fact is that the exploding atom bomb would only destroy physically, but not illumine spiritually and psychologically. No, the imaginal as such has become incapable of directly expressing meaning or truth. We have been expelled from the paradise of intuition and imagination and, in keeping with the insight that "far greater demands are made" on us, we find ourselves remitted to thought, to *the Concept*.

***

POSTSCRIPT 2008

From the very fact that the Christmas tree held this particular lesson for us we can even draw an additional lesson of general methodological importance for psychology. I will explain this by starting with a personal comment. Before I developed the ideas set down in this paper I was a strong admirer of Jung and thus rather uncritically accepted his teachings as simple truth. In other words, I had pretty much become identified with Jung's ideas and so also with his archetypal interpretations of symbols such as that of the Christmas tree. The first version of this paper 1984 marked the first instance of my emancipation from this unconscious identity with Jung's ideas. As long as the identity persisted, I would as a matter of course approach psychic phenomena with the methodological intent to see the archetype at work in them, or, with the intent of Hillman's archetypal psychology to view them "in terms of the Gods." The archetypal significance of symbols and, for that matter, of all psychic phenomena was taken for granted. In retrospect it becomes clear that this was a serious methodological handicap. Because only then, in 1984, when I let go of this fixation, was I all of a sudden free to see the Christmas Tree *against the backdrop of its own context* in modern reality. Before, this had been impossible. The theory of the archetypes or "the Gods" had occupied the place of the backdrop against which any individual phenomenon was to be seen. In other words, it had been inherent in the methodological approach that I would come to any phenomenon whatsoever bringing to it a ready-made stereotyped backdrop (the archetypal theory) which I impose on it, thereby displacing and replacing its own context.

Archetypal theory, used this way, was a prejudice, a prejudgment. It supplied once and for all a framework, one and the same framework ("the archetype is ageless and everpresent"), into which any phenomenon was a priori understood to fit. The phenomena were not allowed to come with their own backdrop, their own context. This was tantamount to seeing them only in isolation, forcing them to appear as free-floating ageless contents, cut off from their social, cultural, historical context (their *Sitz im Leben*): to be abstractions. Mind you, with the words prejudice and prejudgment I am here not criticizing the theory of archetypes as such. What I criticize is the *belief* in this theory, one's having become identical with it so that one routinely *envelops* in it any object of study as if in its self-evident backdrop. It is the use of the archetypal theory and the theory of the Gods as an *ideology*.

A "psychology in terms of the Gods" and of eternal archetypes is also a prejudgment in another methodological sense. Psychology should, strictly and exclusively, be a psychology in terms of the soul. "No man can serve two masters." A "psychology in terms of the Gods," that is to say, a psychology which wants to interpret psychic

THE LESSON OF THE CHRISTMAS TREE

phenomena (our symptoms, dreams, ideas, fantasies) in terms of the gods, is characterized by divided loyalties. It operates with and is committed to two separate explanatory principles or axioms, its own root-metaphor, "soul," on the one hand, and "Gods," on the other hand. The gods as timeless, invariant structures are logically set up as a given for the soul ("They are the lords of its realms of being," "The soul cannot be, except in one of their patterns. All psychic reality is governed by one or another archetypal fantasy, given sanction by a God"[16]), something logically external to its own sphere of jurisdiction. They are literally *pre*-sub-posed to the soul, and because of this their eviction from the notion of soul itself they are logically literalized and hypostatized (even if empirically they may be "imagined"). Since such a psychology operates with something ("gods") that it cannot account for in terms of its own root metaphor, soul, but that it simply has to take for granted, its "Gods" are irrational, indeed miraculous, factors[17] for it and have, within its theorizing, the status of mystifications. This is also what makes such a psychological position ideological.

By contrast, while by no means denying the essential importance of the gods for the soul, a psychology solely in terms of the soul would conceive of the gods as being themselves ("only") psychic *phenomena*, certainly foremost ones, but nevertheless on the same level with other psychic phenomena. They are products of the soul's fantasy activity or self-expression and as phenomena of its own making also its own property. As such, the gods are not exempt from but have their place *in* the soul's logical *life*. This is why gods have their own particular times in history and why they die from time to time, as Jung said (*CW* 9i § 22). It is a requisite for a true psychology to be able to account for the gods in terms of its root metaphor, the soul's making itself. And they can be accounted for because they are not supraphenomenal, not a *fundamentum inconcussum* for the soul *in terms of which* all the other psychic phenomena could be, and would have to be, interpreted.

By rejecting *belief* in the Gods and insisting on merely *imagining* them, archetypal psychology somehow admits their being soul phenomena and wants to see them as soul-internal. But by conceiving them as the governing lords of *all* psychic reality, it singles out and

---

[16] James Hillman, *Re-Visioning Psychology*, New York et al. (Harper & Row: 1975), p. 169 f.
[17] "Numinous borderline persons," *ibid.*, p. 169.

prioritizes as absolutely irreducible principles certain *particular* phenomena from the whole range of the soul's historical phenomenology, setting them up as timeless, universal, and absolute rulers over all psychic phenomena. Archetypal psychology is on the literal level certainly correct when it claims that its "concern is not with the revival of religion." But psychologically or logically it preserves the religious, believing stance and is its true, although unwitting concern the rescue of it. It has by no means overcome it, has not dethroned the gods, seen through them as historical products of the soul's own making, but has merely "swallowed" and thus "bracketed" the religious mode—encapsulated, camouflaged, suspended it, rendered it practically inconsequential—to in this way provide a safe *psychological* asylum for it during an age—modernity—that has psychologically outgrown religion and such a thing as gods. For *psychologically*, that is, for the soul, it makes no great difference if you ostensibly worship the gods (or the God) in the mode of religion or assure their survival in the well-camouflaged retreat of an openly untheological, rational theory that nevertheless within itself declares that "the Gods are never dead" and that the soul cannot be, except in one of their patterns. In either case the *religious* soul of old gets *psychologically* what it wants. Archetypal psychology's seeing through has to be applied to *itself.*

The meta-level lesson that the lesson of the Christmas tree itself holds for us is that each time we want to study a psychic phenomenon, instead of invariantly searching for a fitting myth, god, or archetype we have to look closely not only at this phenomenon itself, but also look for its own backdrop, that is to say, to allow this backdrop to be freshly *given* to us by the real phenomenon in question. A phenomenon is what it is not all by itself and out of context (*in abstracto*), just as a word means what it means only in and by virtue of the specific sentence (and life situation!) in which it occurs. The logical status of consciousness, the syntax of the specific mode of being-in-the-world at a given historical time, is thus intrinsically part of the essence of any psychic phenomenon or symbol itself.

The ideological use of the theories of the archetypes and of "the imaginal" are also unpsychological. Psychological phenomena are defined as having everything they need within themselves, even the backdrop against which they have to be seen. This is of course not an

THE LESSON OF THE CHRISTMAS TREE

ontological assertion, but a methodological maxim. With the a priori expectation to find an archetype or "God" in any given phenomenon this phenomenon is subsumed under an external premise, a program. Interestingly enough, in archaic times this was different. *Avant la lettre*, phenomena were indeed already "psychological" in the sense given, inasmuch as nobody approached them with a wish to see archetypes or Gods in them. Conversely, (certain) phenomena spontaneously showed themselves to be epiphanic.

CHAPTER TWO

The Rescue of the World
Jung, Hegel, and the Subjective Universe[1]

Barbara Eckman has to be commended for her important article on Jung and Hegel in *Spring 1986*,[2] since a decisive demonstration of "Jung's Hegelianism *malgré lui*" (p.96) has long been overdue. Her article gives independent support to a statement I had made only in passing in my Eranos lecture of the same year (1986): "... despite the rejection of him by Jung himself, Hegel nevertheless seems to be the only one who could provide to Jungian psychology the kind of logic with which alone it could truly comprehend and say what it has to say."[3] And I admire how she succeeds in elucidating such a difficult subject in a relatively short space

---

[1] I had originally entitled this article "Once More: Jung, Hegel, and the Subjective Universe." Shortly before its publication in *Spring 1987*, the editor (James Hillman) called me and suggested the present title, "The Rescue of the World. Jung, Hegel, and the Subjective Universe," because, he said, this article went far beyond a reply to Barbara Eckman's piece. I consented to this change, but ever after I regretted it because the notion of the rescue of the world, which comes from a Jung passage cited by me in this article, seems to get highlighted and endorsed when it is part of the title. But as a psychologist and psychotherapist I really have no stake in "rescuing," no matter what, let alone in the gigantic task of a rescue of the *world*. I consider it my job to try to see the soul in the real.

[2] Barbara Eckman, "Jung, Hegel, and the Subjective Universe," *Spring 1986*, pp. 88–99.

[3] Wolfgang Giegerich, "Das Bewußtsein, der zweite Schöpfer der Welt," *Eranos 55-1986*, Frankfurt (Insel) 1988, pp. 183–239, here p. 200.

54   *THE SOUL ALWAYS THINKS*

and in carrying her theme forward to what is truly the "heart of the matter," subjectivity and love.

Her conciseness due to the space available, however, may have had its price. Barbara Eckman may have arrived a little too quickly at the parallels between Hegel and Jung by not giving the "malgré lui" the necessary weight. So I want to complicate matters a bit.

Jung's rejection of Hegel is not a mere misunderstanding. Jung's determined, almost violent rejection must also be seen as the legitimate expression of a real and in a certain sense unbridgeable difference. To make this difference visible, I would like to start out with the thesis that, seen with Hegelian eyes, Jung's conception of psychoid archetypes *does not* overcome the Kantian bifurcation of subject and object, but is only *intended* to do so. Why is this? Because Jung contents himself with "results," whereas the Hegelian "Begriff" is the unity of the way leading to the result *and* the result. Jung thought he could make do with positing the psychoid archetypes, thereby claiming that there is something in which subject and object are one. What is posited and claimed to exist remains "out there," i.e. merely objective, even if it is the idea *of* something that is also working in and through us. It is only substance and not also subject in Hegel's sense. The theories of the psychoid archetypes as well as of synchronicity are theories of an ontic, "factual" reality (even if the factualness might be played down by calling the posited fact not a fact but a mere hypothesis), which shows that here we are only in the world of the *first* part of Hegel's *Science of Logic*, in the realm of being and of immediateness.

For Hegel, this is just the beginning from which we have to push off. "Being" has to be seen through to be mere "appearance" (which takes us to part two of Hegel's *Logic*), but later this "appearance" in turn proves to have been mere "appearance," which leads to the third and last part of the *Logic*, the realm of *Begriff* in the particular Hegelian sense. Jung, however, does not repel or negate the initial level, he purposefully settles there and cements his staying there by his empiricist, scientistic ideology.[4] And so he could gladly quote the *British Medical Journal* stating about himself, "He is an empiricist first and

---

[4] It should be noted that in reality the situation is much more complex. An accurate description of the logical locus of Jung's position would have to go beyond the simple linear succession of three parts of Hegel's logic and introduce internal differentiations, which however, for our purposes of a preliminary discussion, can be neglected. If such

THE RESCUE OF THE WORLD

last," without in the least realizing what a disservice he thereby was doing to his own work, quite apart from seeing where he was placing his psychology within the context of Hegel's *Logic*. Here we have a real blindness, but one that Jung passionately defended. Whenever he exercised conscious control over his theorizing and intended to be critical, he wanted to freeze his amazing psychological insights on the logically lowest level, the ontic level of "empirical findings," which held his insights imprisoned in the logical status of "substance" and prevented them from becoming "subjective" (i.e. psychological) in themselves (in contradistinction to merely being insights *about* something psychological). This alone is what made the essential move of Hillman's archetypal psychology necessary—with Jung against Jung. Archetypal psychology propelled itself from the initial level (which it called the literal) and thereby undertook some of the kind of work that Hegel termed "Anstrengung des Begriffs," by which he did not merely mean intellectual efforts, but more precisely the painful labor of going the way of the "Aufhebung" (sublation) of one logical level after the other. Jung did more than not undertake it. He rejected it with systematic intention.

This is where Kant comes in, or rather Jung's understanding of Kant. Jung was—and rightly so—afraid of falling back into the pre-Kantian metaphysical mode of thinking about the soul ("rational psychology"). Kant was concerned with the question: under which conditions could our thinking reach the world, if our thinking remained under the rules of formal logic; in other words, under which conditions could it be called 'knowledge'? And his answer was that we could know only under the one condition that our ideas did not claim to refer to the world in itself, but, loosely speaking, only to an essentially "artificial" world pre-fabricated or pre-processed by our own reason. This amounted to saying that we could know only if we used the designation 'knowing' for what was known to us to be not knowing in the proper sense of the word. If Jung had followed Kant he would have known that what he, Jung, envisioned as psychology (a psychology for which it would be essential to allow the "persons" in the

---

additional distinctions had been made, it would be possible to show that Jung's theoretical stance does not simply belong into the first part (being). Rather, it is to be located in the second part (that of *Wesen*), but there, within the second part, it represents a reversion to the first part...

"unconscious" to speak to us of their own accord, a psychology of real knowing—remember Jung's famous dictum about God: I do not believe, I know) is utterly untenable. For this was precisely what Kant had to deny categorically: that anything could enter our consciousness of its own accord, i.e. without being pre-organized by our mind. There could be no presences, only *our* representations.

Now, Jung of course could not conceive of psychology without an autonomous, and in the fullest sense of the word, real psyche initiating in us certain 'contents,' so that here we would have to speak of real knowledge in contradistinction to knowledge in the restricted Kantian sense. Jung would not have been Jung if he could have contented himself with the only kind of psychology permitted by Kant (the kind that studies behavior by means of truly empirical methods, tests, statistics, etc.). So there is this dilemma: Jung needed a psychology allowing for real input from the soul, which Kant had once and for all proven to be untenable (if the laws of formal logic remain in power). But Jung also had to steer clear from regressing to rational psychology, precisely because Kant had destroyed every legitimacy and credibility it once seemed to have had. Jung helped himself out of this dilemma by means of a compromise solution. He proceeded on the one hand with the kind of psychology demanded of him by his inner life. And on the other hand he believed that it would suffice to pay his toll to Kant simply by constantly assuring us that all his theoretical statements (about archetypes, synchronicity, the autonomous psyche, the psychoid, etc.) were not intended as metaphysical statements, but only as hypotheses, models or the like and that he was, e.g., not speaking about God himself, but only about the God image in the psyche.

It is obvious that this won't do. Jung himself knew better. He taught us to see through the illusion that by calling e.g. psychological powers "moods," "nervousness," "delusional ideas," in short, "symptoms" instead of "Gods" or "daimones," anything would be changed as to the reality of these powers. In a certain sense (this is Jung's insight), it does not matter to the God whether we serve him under the name of an "addiction" or under the name of "God." He demands and gets his due either way. *Within* psychology, Jung would think this way. However, outside psychology, when it was a question of the status of his psychological statements as such with respect to his theory of

THE RESCUE OF THE WORLD

knowledge, Jung would speak with another tongue. Here he would claim that *calling* a statement "merely psychological and not metaphysical" made all the difference. We, having learned Jung's lesson, see the illusion. Furnishing his theory with the label 'hypothetical,' assigning to it the value of a mere 'model,' does in no way detract from the reality of his psychological theories, i.e. from their logical (and psychological) status as 'metaphysical.' Jung paid Kant only a token toll, that of a change in how he *intended* his findings to be taken, without any change regarding the delimitation of which contents were to be accepted into empirical psychology and which not. But Kant's price is higher. Paying it would have meant for Jung to bar from his psychology as 'metaphysical' the greater part of the substance of what now makes up his psychology. It does not make any real difference whether we assert that we are speaking "only" about the God image in the soul or whether we believe to be speaking about God himself. In either way we speak about God. The difference is only cosmetic. The retreat to the "mere representation in the psyche" amounts to no more than a camouflage or a displacement in the psychoanalytic sense. If we think this retreat to be sufficient payment for the sacrifice Kant demands of us, we are like the primitive who took a meager chicken to the image of his God saying, "Behold, what a beautiful goat I sacrifice to you."

The problem is not that Jung was under the influence of Kant's philosophy. The problem is that he learned Kant's lesson only half-heartedly and took refuge in an easy way out of his dilemma. So it would be all wrong to free Jung from the supposedly negative Kantian influence. Quite to the contrary, it remains to us to apply relentlessly the razor of Kant's critique for the first time to Jung's psychology and to show him that while he *thought* he had based his psychology on Kant he had *in fact* unwittingly relapsed onto the pre-Kantian metaphysical level. The very mode by which he hoped to meet Kant's critique is what makes his ideas subject to this critique: Jung's asserting his findings to be of a strictly empirical and his theories to be of a merely hypothetical nature. Kant has shown beyond any doubt that precisely if such realities as the ones Jung discovered are considered part of the 'phenomenal' (positive-factual, we could also say 'literal') world, we have succumbed to metaphysics, to superstition, i.e. daimones and Gods as empirical literal realities, as (to use Jung's phrase) "archetypes in themselves." As long as Jung clings to his label 'empiricist first and last,' Kant would show him that he has no right to posit for example a psychoid archetypal level in which the subject-object dichotomy would be overcome.

What we have thought all along to be Jung's tribute to Kant, namely his empiricism and scientism, now proves to be his defense against Kant that was to shield the precious contents of his inner life against the full impact of Kant's insights. Jung's having avoided the unconditional surrender to "Kant" and, as a result, his needing to forestall the possible onslaught of Kant's implications by asserting that he already had heeded Kant's critique (inasmuch as he was strictly confining himself to the 'phenomenal'): this is what separates him from Hegel and may account for his *ressentiment*. Hegel, because he had paid the entire toll Kant demands, was free of Kant. He could overcome Kant by 'sublating' his critique through a critique of the critique. To Jung, who on the one hand had lost his metaphysical innocence through Kant so that he could not in good faith return to a naive metaphysical theory of the numinous depth of the soul, and who, on the other hand, had not sacrificed his naive relation to these depths, as would have been demanded by Kant's philosophy, Hegel had to appear at once as a temptation and a terrible threat. Jung, not having gone all the way through Kant, could not imagine that there might be land beyond Kant. And thus he necessarily had to see in Hegel the great danger of an inflation of consciousness by the unconscious, of taking as metaphysical, in the pre-Kantian way, such experiences as Jung was visited by.

In what Jung feared would have lain the real solution to his dilemma. To give up his defense against Kant would have meant to give up his insistence on being empiricist. Then he would have had to go through the same plunge into the depths *intellectually* that he had exposed himself to without reserve in his soul, in his *descensus ad inferos* during the time of World War I. And then he would have been open to Hegel. He could have acknowledged Hegel, not as a "psychologist in disguise" (*CW* 8, § 358), but as a brother in the spirit who had accomplished in the realm of philosophy proper, in the realm of *logic*, what he, Jung, had accomplished in the realm of psychology proper, the realm of living experience. Jung had found that his unconditional plunge into the inner depth had not meant the literal end of himself as natural man (death) and sane mind (psychosis). Rather, that kind of death was at the same time his rebirth as psychological man. Hegel could have shown him the equivalent on the intellectual plane: that the relentless living through the death of metaphysics as imposed by Kant did not mean absolute nihilism. Rather that kind of death of the precious contents of the old mythical, religious, and metaphysical tradition was at the same time their resurrection as "absolute knowledge" in Hegel's terms and as "psychology" in ours.

Of course, "absolute knowledge" sounds terribly like a relapse into otherwordly metaphysics. As such it has been misunderstood by generations of superficial and not so superficial readers of Hegel. What Hegel means, however, by "absolute" is anything but the "absolute" of traditional metaphysics. Hegel means that kind of knowledge that is "ab-solved" (freed) from the difference between the absolute and the empirical, the infinite and the finite. It means something very simple and "natural," something that might be compared to the logic or mode-of-being-in-the-world achieved by the Zen-Buddhist—or by him who can see the literal world with imaginal eyes.

This insight—that Jung denied Hegel the right to do in the realm of logic what Jung had done in the realm of the psyche—is the exposition of Jung's Hegelianism *malgré lui* as well as, we might add, of his anti-Hegelianism *malgré lui*. For it is not only that Jung is a "Hegelian" at heart (his personality No. 2) who consciously (his personality No. 1) rejects Hegel; he is also "anti-Hegelian" at heart. This because Jung defends the old ego and its logic, even where he consciously advocates a transformation process that requires the death of that ego and thus is analogous to what Hegel was striving for in philosophy. The "malgré" is emblematic of the dissociation that goes on *de facto* in Jung's psycho-logy. What Jung had personally experienced, himself performed, and professionally taught in regard to the psyche of psychology, he could not allow to its logic.

This dissociation accounts for the ultimate (not the preliminary) futility of therapy, even if it be Jungian therapy in the truest and deepest sense of the word. Jung said (*CW* 10, § 536) that the rescue of the world consists in the rescue of one's own soul. Put just like that, this statement is utterly and dangerously false, a fatal delusion haunting psychotherapy to the present day. *As regards* the rescue of the world, *nothing* is changed even if I (and thousands of other individuals as well) have undergone the most authentic individuation process bringing about a profound personal transformation. This process in my inner life occurs only in the psyche of psychology, leaving the old logic (which is what ultimately determines the status, or mode-of-being, of reality) intact. The individuation process is not enough. We cannot get away so cheaply, dear as it may be. We could learn from Hegel that Jung's statement could only become true if it were transformed into what Hegel termed the "speculative sentence" (i.e., the mirroring sentence): The rescue of the world consists only to that extent in the rescue of one's own soul that the rescue of one's own soul consists in the rescue of the world.

Therefore I would not want to present Hegel's idea of the World Spirit and Jung's idea of the psychoid archetype or of a subjective universe as if they were, just like that, the overcoming of the bifurcation of subject and object. They are not. It is not sufficient to propound the "right" ideas, to develop a world view in which the subject-object alienation is overcome. It is not sufficient to proclaim the *unus mundus*, the *anima mundi*, the oneness of physis and psyche at the psychoid or synchronistic level, etc. For these "right" ideas are placed into a world whose logic remains unchanged. Even worse, into these "right" ideas themselves is invested the old logic; "malgré" of *what* they say, they carry in their own implicit logical form or status the very alienation between subject and object that they are explicitly *intended* to overcome, and thus they unwittingly perpetuate it. Regardless of whether they are considered empirical findings, hypothetical scientific constructs, psychological images, a world view or ultimate truths, they have the logical form of ontic ideas: *our* ideas *about* existing factors or aspects. It is obvious that this logical form *is* the splitting of subject (we as the ones having the idea) and object (what our idea refers to). When we adopt the idea of the subjective universe, we by doing so fall into and enact the subject-object alienation that we intend to overcome. This shows that we are victims of and participants in a fraud. We have to see that we have no right to the idea of a world soul as long as our logic has not been transformed—so long as the logical form of our thoughts has not undergone *its* individuation process, to misappropriate Jung's term, or the "Anstrengung des Begriffs," to say the same thing with Hegel's expression. The mere ontic idea of the

THE RESCUE OF THE WORLD

"subjective universe" has to be subjected to the long and painful process of experiencing the destruction of the first part of Hegel's logic and of experiencing afterwards the destruction of the destruction. Then, and only then, would it have *acquired* the status of the Hegelian *Begriff* and then, and only then, would subjectivity (in the Hegelian sense of the transsubstantiation of substance into subject) not only be asserted, but actually prevail.

CHAPTER THREE

Effort? Yes, Effort![1]

If James Hillman imagines his way of speaking as a ball game, I would like to begin by saying that I am only too glad to catch the balls that he threw me (pretty hard ones, to be sure) and return them, perhaps with a little more momentum added and a twist given to them here and there. But first I have to take myself out of the position into which the title of his piece "Hegel, Giegerich and the U.S.A." put me, squeezed between a giant of thought and a superpower. I'm not going to return his balls up there in such lofty heights, but down here on an ordinary playfield, and am not going to answer as the voice of Europe replying to the voice of America, but as an individual listening and responding to another analyst and a friend.

The conflict between us as seen by Hillman should not be taken too literally. Hillman is not only jousting with me, but also jesting, posing as the typical American and playing the devil's advocate. Obviously, the man who devoted a book to the careful analysis of the *notion* of the anima, who reminded psychologists that neither Jung nor Freud had to cut their heads off; who adamantly argued for a non-agnostic psychology, and time and again insisted on discrimination,

[1] In *Spring 1987* I had published a paper, "The Rescue of the World. Jung, Hegel, and the Subjective Universe," having taking my cue from a previous article by Barbara Eckman in *Spring 1986* on "Jung, Hegel, and the Subjective Universe." James Hillman responded to my paper with his "Hegel, Giegerich and the U.S.A." in *Spring 1988*. The present paper is my reaction to Hillman's piece and was published together with the latter in *Spring 1988*.

is not exactly identical with the one who here tends to lightly dismiss, as secondary, thought, knowing, logic and who stylizes himself as a salesman, pushing his product "anima mundi" and advising us to sweet talk our way "and anything goes." Neither does the conflict between us fully coincide with that between Europe and the U.S.A. No doubt, his portrayal of America is a pointed description of powerful aspects of the U.S.A., but is this the only and full picture that the U.S.A. presents? Hillman is an American, but he is also a European himself, and not only by passport.

Conversely, one can certainly not say that Hegel's logic "so persuades the European mind that ...," because Hegel's logic has been terra incognita ever since Hegel's death in 1830. If it had persuaded the European mind, the history of the last two centuries would have been very different. And was it not precisely an American publication that printed both Barbara Eckman's and my plea for more Hegel, and now this discussion? I doubt whether such a paper would have been accepted by psychological journals over here and whether there are any colleagues in my country who would waste a thought on these questions. Also, I have no difficulties (nor would Hegel have any) with the idea of anima mundi, of "the essential poem at the centre of things," of visions, events as directly sensible, directly impinging as a self-display; and certainly the subject-object business is not *my* problem—I only alluded to it as one that was offered in the article which prompted me to write my piece and as a familiar example that needed no wordy explanations. And I wholeheartedly agree that the attempt to solve a problem may be a way to get stuck in it, indeed, to build it up.

So, to some extent the conflict between us is not simply there and not just the way it has been presented, but it is also artfully set up—perhaps to provide the playfield for our game. But in this game, I believe, some serious problems and maybe very real conflicts may surface.

One of these problems comes to light when Hillman says: "Speech before thought" or (interpreting my position) "Logic precedes existence" or "not ... in the terrain of thought but in the expression of things." Speech and thought, logic and existence, thought and things are set up as pairs of opposites within an either-or logic. Either logic or rhetoric is ontic. Either the one or the other comes first. Hillman

EFFORT? YES, EFFORT!

(here in this paper and contrary to his own convictions expressed elsewhere) draws a line and puts "how we know the world (epistemology) or order its thought (logic)" as less significant and less erotic on the one side of it and "how we enjoy, celebrate, complain, and argue the world" on the other. But what is being referred to by him under the label of logic is not the same "logic" as the one I talked about in my *Spring '87* piece. Neither is it in any way congruous with Hegel's understanding of logic. It is something else. My notion of logic is placed within another logic than that of either-or, and already here we get a first inkling of the inescapability of logic. Hillman has already made use of one brand of logic here, even while arguing against logic. And the brand of logic at work in his argument is not helpful: if you start out with an idea of logic that belongs to one side only, and that precedes speech or rhetoric or things or enjoyment (or, if you prefer, the other way around), and if you start out with one to which something can be "*reduced*," then of course the whole cause is already lost.

If we take the sentence about "how we know the world and order its thought" and "how we enjoy, celebrate, complain, and argue the world," my notion of logic is not found on one side of the line. Rather, logic is the investigation of the "how" on either side. There are many styles and levels of knowing, enjoying, complaining, and each has its logic. Nothing is to be "reduced" to logic, because the logic here in question is in things, in behavior, in speech. Things and thoughts don't have to be opposites; after all, our tradition has taught us that things are the thoughts of God. True, thought comes before speech, but only to the extent (and here I remind you of what I said about the speculative sentence in the other paper) that also speech comes before thought, for again our tradition tells us that in the beginning was the word (And God spoke...). There *is* a "before," but it must not be literalized and thereby be turned into something that can only be the exclusive property of either the one or the other.

Here I have to insert a short apology of Hegel. Hegel's *Logic* is at no point literal, and the category of opposition exits early from the scene in his book. It has rightly been termed a work that as a genuine philosophical one is in itself poetry. And what inspires it is Love. Hillman seems to imagine the *Anstrengung des Begriffs* in terms of a heroic effort to find a way out and to overcome a monster called the "split between subject and object," or whatever. Nothing of the sort obtains. Hegel does not seek a way out, but a way in, deeper and deeper. And it is not he who wants to overcome any problems, he is merely the spectator who watches the game of the logical categories, watches how they perish from their own inner contradictions, provided one does not freeze their game, not literalize them at any one point. Effort here refers to the patience to watch the entire "game" from start to finish, the patience of slow and very small steps. Hillman and archetypal psychology could find many of their own concerns in Hegel's logic in different guise, discussed at a very high level of reflection and thoroughly elaborated—but not to be had without some effort.

What I have argued so far could in the main be put down to misunderstandings and semantic problems (different notions connected with the word "logic"). But more is at stake. The real conflict has not been touched upon, or was so only when we found the literalist, oppositional thought pattern that split logic and speech apart, which is not in accordance with Hillman's own usual stance. Psyche must not be split off from her own logic, logic not from the soul: psychology must remain one word. And we must suffer the complication, if not contradiction, that psyche is subjected to an analysis of the logical status she is in, and logic moistened by psyche. Psyche alone, cut off from logos, will not do. The innocence of imagination by itself, of visions virginal just as they come, of rhetoric without logical awareness makes for poor psychology, poor *aisthesis*, poor poetry, and for a consumptive or maybe even phony anima mundi. We cannot afford the luxury of innocence any more—not just because doom abounds, but because we would fail and miss the very things we claim to be concerned about, psyche and world.

A cozy, romantic image: the one of the salesman pushing his product in the casual storefront and the black-suited Calvinist in the back room. That's how it may have been in the good old days. But haven't you noticed? Now we live in the age of supermarkets with self-service, store chains that do not belong to anybody, but to an anonymous and abstract concern. And all the commodities that you can buy there are the commodities of a throw-away society. So if you say that you push the anima mundi as your product, you should know what your thesis means and entails, and in order to know this you need to know the logic of advertisements, of pushing products, selling

EFFORT? YES, EFFORT!

something, of "everything is returnable," etc. The question is not simply whether it is the anima mundi you sell instead of cigarettes or soap or arms or Bibles, and not whether "I am comfortable with that" or "I'll buy it." If one thinks so, one has cut off the idea of the anima mundi from its context, indeed from the world (of which after all it was supposed to be an idea). An idea is not just what it is, pure and simple; it is itself *and* the context in which it appears and into which it is spoken.

Placing the idea of the anima mundi into the context of selling and marketing means reducing it to a throw-away commodity with no inherent worth. We cannot innocently and without further ado transplant into our age ideas that had their legitimate place in an earlier age, as if nothing had changed. Ideas, images are not just items side by side on the shelves in a supermarket of the imagination for us to pick out what we like and to return if I made the wrong choice. They also have their time.

It is too easy to call the Americans born-again Sophists, because the time of the splendid innocence of a first awakening from myth is once and for all gone. We live in an age that is the late result of a long process that was started by the Sophists, to be sure, but led through many stages of mediations. There is no way back from Ulysses' scar to Puer's wound (the scar, by the way, would be a good image for what Hegel means by *Aufhebung*: the scar as the *aufgehobene* wound). And it is one thing to say "sweet talk and anything goes" at the time around 500 B.C. and another to say it today, at a time when we have bombs and poisonous chemicals and gene manipulation. People today may be *playing* born-again Sophists or babes in the woods, but they are not, and they probably would do well to awaken to this insight. The babe cannot do much harm, it could only be hurt in the woods. But we have the real power to do a lot of harm.

It would make the Goddess Peitho turn around in her grave if she knew that she was placed, just as if she came off the shelf of an antiques store, into the context of modern "pushing products." Worlds separate her from the kind of persuasion going on in modern advertising and marketing. What once used to be a Goddess has been reduced to a mere instrument in the service of the only God of this age, Capital. (And here it would again be indiscriminate to liken Capital to ancient Mammon or to harmless premodern money.) The rhetoric and sweet

68   *THE SOUL ALWAYS THINKS*

talking at work in advertising has nothing to do with anima. On the contrary, it shows what once upon a time used to be anima enslaved in the service of almost its opposite. It is a rhetoric that does not truly enhance things, but fully renders them into disposable and exchangeable commodities whose only value lies in the question whether *I'll* buy, and like, and can use, them or not. I am not criticizing or arguing "against" this modern situation. I am arguing for discrimination, for knowing the discrepancy.

Neither can I put "Boreas" and "Jetstream" or "High Pressure System" into the same sentence as if they were only different names for the same thing. They are, psychologically and logically, very different realities, because they belong to different logical statuses. It may be true in poetry, *as in an asylum within* our world, that the trees are mended (Wallace Stevens). It is certainly not true in that *world*. And then again—if you closely listen to what the poet says, you will hear that he says the opposite of what he says. For if the trees are *mended*, they have not (as the sentence would suggest to a casual listener) returned to what they once were. Just like the scar is the sublated wound, so mendedness is the sublated tear. Heidegger (wrongly) ascribed to Hegel the statement, A torn stocking is better than a mended one.[2] Mended trees are what you find in nostalgic movies or novels. Where all seems well and whole, you can be certain to be in a place of mended things. Sure: they appear enhanced there, notable, valuable, of raised importance. But the appearance of this enhancement is deliberately produced by a very complex logic in the writer and reproduced by the same logic in the nostalgic audience, in such a way, however, that this logical production is kept subliminal, which makes the innocent consciousness believe to have had a direct *aisthesis*.

The icy wind that strikes my chest and disturbs the butts in an ashtray is by the same token *not simply* an "event directly sensible, directly impinging as a self-display." Our sensation is not all that innocent anymore. It has been affected by and gone through numerous stages of mediations and retains, as *aufgehoben*, within itself a long history of imagination, enlightenment, re-imagination, new enlightenment and all the tears and scars that go along with it, even if all this lies completely under the surface. The icy wind too is mended,

---

[2] Cf. Heidegger, *Vier Seminare*, Frankfurt 1977, p. 25 f.

EFFORT? YES, EFFORT!

if not rent (which, according to Heidegger's Hegel, would be the better state). We cannot sense the wind as the pre-Homeric Greeks did. We cannot undo the fact that ours are eyes that have looked through telescopes and microscopes and into television tubes and have been in museums and seen thousands of posters, art reproductions, statistical charts and scientific diagrams; and ears that have listened to motors, to the rumble of cannons, to string quartets and rock, to digitalized music. We cannot undo the fact that we know about sound and light waves. I claim that under these conditions the idea of the directly sensible icy wind—just like that, without further ado—is a cozy idea that misses what is to be seen or felt today, misses *today's* self-display and poetry in the things of nature: the wind, the tree, the bush, the doe are rent, scarred, even dead; they are the ghosts of what they once were. Such is the perception that would offer itself to an "aesthetic response" today (*if* we had the logical power to see such), just as to the (uncurtailed) perception of the Greeks, nature offered herself as Boreas, nymph, dryad, Pan, Artemis. For a full-fledged *aisthesis* is always the perception of the inner image in the phenomenon, i.e., of the thing *with* its aura, with the entire "world" (logical sphere) it represents, not of its positive-factual shape.

We need logic (in Hegel's sense), but not to indulge in academic desires for a theory of knowledge or to find out if such an idea as the anima mundi is "logically sound." We need logic for the benefit of a real aesthetic response to our world, for the benefit of the things in the world as it is today, so that they can be seen with soul. We need logic to educate and differentiate our senses to the degree of sophistication that would match the state of logical sophistication already real in the things of our world out there, which is a world of steel-and-glass architecture, asphalt streets, airplanes and spacecraft, electronics, computer tomography, shopping malls, etc. Tremendous changes have occurred since the days of mythological man: they are the assignment, we have to do our homework. Just as it will not do today to write poems like Goethe, or compose music like Palestrina or Bach, or paint like Leonardo or Monet, so it will not be enough that people "buy" the vision of the anima mundi just like that, as comfortable as they may be with it. I am very comfortable with Goethe or Bach, more than, e.g., with very modern compositions. But I know that they do not connect me with our world today. They keep me in the world of the good old days and my consciousness in the logical status that had been reached then.

Without raising into consciousness the subliminal logic inherent in our perceiving today; without the painful effort of, step by step, reconstructing in our frame of mind the history of logical transmutations that is condensed and collapsed into the things of our modern world and preserved in them, we are more or less like the followers of the Melanesian cargo cult. They did not see what their cult was to a large extent about: technical things like airplanes, watches, radios etc. What they saw were objects conceived within an "animistic" or "mythological" consciousness, by which objects they supplanted the products brought into their world from without. Their perception did not have the logical means[3] to *see* something as sophisticated as a plastic cup and all the other products of our industrial and high-technological society.

But neither does ours! We are blind to buses and butts in the ashtray, blind to the soul in all the things that come off the assembly line, and doubly blind if we believe to be seeing them. We may understand how to drive a bus, understand the mechanics of its motor and maybe even the physics behind it. But we lack the logical power to see it physiognomonically *for what it is*, i.e., in an equivalent way to how the early Greeks were able to see *their* world for what it was. Where we try to see a bus or an airplane physiognomonically, we restrict ourselves to that small and relatively unimportant part of its reality, i.e., to that harmless logical status, that it has in common with natural things (its bodily shape and face), as if the plane were perhaps a kind of bird, the parked bus in the sun something like a big shiny boulder, or what have you. We do not see it together with its sphere (the entire technological civilization with its abstractions, mass production, mass transportation, stress ...). A reductive physiognomonic perception. And a kind of *logical* "monotheism": one single logical plane or status for everything.

Logic as understood here robs psyche of the atemporal innocence with which she would cocoon herself within the Platonist kaleidoscope of her own eternal visions. Psyche alone, separate from the second half

---

[3] By this I in no way suggest a lower intelligence or any other inferiority. I am merely referring to something just as obvious as that they did not have the *technical* means to produce plastic cups or airplanes.

EFFORT? YES, EFFORT! 71

of 'psychology,' would draw the world, too, into this cocoon by flatly and effortlessly likening (leveling?) (archetypal) vision and (real) event, ancient and modern (*anamnesis*). Psyche alone would believe in the possibility of a Renaissance simply through the exchange of one's vision and by enwrapping oneself in belief, in an "as if." The logic element in "psychology" cuts through this cocoon and inflicts upon psyche a sense of a real world out there, subject to Irreversible Time, and thus a sense of irretrievable losses that are at the same time gains; a sense of a possible discrepancy between the logical status our attitude is in and the status reached by the objective world we produced for ourselves; a sense of many deaths to be died and resurrections to go through— which both together make up what Hegel's word *Aufhebung* manages to think as one.

"We shall overcome" may be a translation into American, but certainly not *of* aufgehoben. On the contrary, psychologically it is the slogan in which the preservation of the ego is made a maxim. It is the programmatic declaration of the refusal to suffer the death to be died by the present logical constitution of our consciousness. Sure, I heard this uncanny slogan often enough during the time of the Vietnam war. But I never heard that its second line would have been chanted by the crowds, the one that goes: "*et pereat mundus.*" Apparently nobody was aware that what they chanted had a second line, or better, a thorough bass. Indeed, they did overcome—but the bill for their overcoming was paid by millions of Cambodians and Vietnamese, who were murdered not as an unforeseeable misfortune, but as a result of the betrayal of the world inherent in the logic of "*WE* shall *overcome.*" Of course, it is also inherent in this logic that the will for self-preservation (for the self-preservation of our innocence) must be dumb to its own counterpoint. For if this will had become conscious of the fact that by saying, "We shall overcome," one is at the same time saying, "*et pereat mundus,*" this slogan would have lost its innocence and perished from its inner contradiction. And then the will for self-preservation, for whose sake alone this slogan had been invented, would have been—you guess what is coming: *aufgehoben*! *Aufgehoben* in what? Maybe in a love for this world that could allow us to open ourselves to its *reality*, even to its bitter, cold, and alien half, to make soul there too.

CHAPTER FOUR

Shalt thou build me an house for me to dwell in?
Or: Anima mundi and Time
A response to Hillman's "Cosmology for Soul, From Universe to Cosmos"[1]

When Hillman began to address the theme of anima mundi and thereby opened psychology from the narrow confines of the consulting room to the real world, I thought that this—in a way—radical move was not completely surprising, but rather a consistent development of the germinal ideas of archetypal psychology, which after all had begun with the idea of the *world* as the vale of soul-making. Inevitably, a psychology of and for the world will have to answer the cosmological question, a task Hillman turns to in the paper "Cosmology for Soul" first read in Japan in 1986.

This paper opens with the soul's "presenting complaint" about the neglect it suffers in the philosophical, scientific, and theological theories of the West. They are governed, Hillman shows, by a worldview that sees the world from the perspective of "universe," in contrast to the perspective of *kosmos*, toward which Hillman would like to reach.

---

[1] James Hillman, "Cosmology for the Soul. From Universe to Cosmos," in: *Sphinx* 2, London 1989, pp. 17-33. I had written the present paper shortly after this issue of *Sphinx* had appeared and sent it to Hillman as well as to Noel Cobb, the editor of that journal. But it remained unpublished.

74 THE SOUL ALWAYS THINKS

Whereas "universe" leads, monotheistically, to an all-encompassing, coherent theory of the world and to an experience of events in themselves insufficient and only meaningful as parts of the whole, so that abstract explanation is the proper response to them, "cosmos" leads to an altogether different stance. Its key notions are "sympathy of all things," "polytheistic," "sensuous" and "aesthetic," "an ever more profound appreciation of phenomena," and above all an "animalized cosmology." It would be inappropriate for me to summarize here what Hillman understands by "animalizing." This fascinating idea adds a whole other dimension to the description of psychology given in *Re-Visioning Psychology* by means of the four terms "personifying," "pathologizing," "psychologizing," and "dehumanizing." May it suffice to mention only a few major aspects implied by animalizing: the eachness of phenomena, immediate perception, and the self-display of interiority.

What emerges is a grand (and beautiful) vision. Hillman's proposal would open up the possibility of a completely different mode of experiencing, and responding to, the world, and one that would undoubtedly deserve the attribute "soulful." And yet, I believe that his answer in this paper does not really do what it is supposed to do. Precisely because the aim of returning soul to the world is so precious, I want to discuss (also by way of a new installment of our debate begun in *Spring 1988*) the problems I see with his approach, which in my opinion is counterproductive, contradicting its own purpose. It is all the more necessary to go into this because the problems I encountered seem to me to be dangers just as inherent in archetypal psychology as was the promise of an opening towards the world. Maybe archetypal psychology has come to a kind of watershed. It could go either way. It is vital to see what is at stake, in order to be able to make the moves that truly bring us closer to our common goal.

1. Self-contradiction One:
The plea for "cosmos" is out of touch with the actual world

What does it mean: to entertain Whitehead's idea of "nature alive" (p. 24), while at the same time the constant messages of the age are the destruction of the rain forests, *Waldsterben*, the extinction of many species, the pollution of the atmosphere and the oceans, the greenhouse

SHALT THOU BUILD ME A HOUSE? 75

effect, and the irrevocable destruction of the ozone layer, all of which together amount to an unmistakable message that (psycho-/onto-) logically the very notion of nature is doomed. Indeed, such an attempt would be a counterphobic defense. The idea of "nature alive" is a grotesque mockery in view of what is going on.

Can the "animal" serve as exemplary image for the cosmology of eachness, if inherent in the very idea of animal today is one of the following: 1) tourist attraction in zoo or reserve, 2) pet, 3) milk or meat producing machine within a highly industrialized farming enterprise, 4) biological organism and product of evolution, 5) guinea-pig for laboratory experiments, 6) artifact constructed by genetic engineering, 7) endangered species, 8) extinct? The animal which could be once spoken of as "each according to its kind" (p. 32) doesn't have any reality anymore. It is spurious. An image without footing in the actual world.

What does it mean to propose the idea of the immediate perception (p. 27) of the animal and of an aesthetic, sensuous response to events ("an ever more profound and differentiated appreciation" p. 23), when, at the same time, millions of people go about with walkmen dulling their senses, dulling themselves into an obliviousness to the world around them; when millions see the world not only *in* television alone, but also, while not watching TV, *through* television as their spectacles; when we have left the earth and look down at it and at ourselves from outer space?

Ours is the age of prefabricated houses, pre-processed convenience foods, plastics, flowers that are programmed to bloom on demand, mass-produced commodities, disposable items, the devaluation of everything (throwaway watches and 20 million dollars Picassos), printed books and posters, every value and every thought dictated and packaged by the mills of advertising, buildings and statues poured out of concrete, mass transportation, rock festivals, statistics, reproductions and photocopies, sound-engineered music on discs or tapes. We buy our houses, cars, TV's and furniture on credit (the banks mediating between ourselves and what we "own"); we travel by car and airplane at high speed ruthlessly past or over phenomena, openly demonstrating our (not personal, but logical) contempt for them (no sense of eachness and no appreciation). And we communicate via satellites. If this is not enough to convince us that the mere mention of immediacy (p. 31) is tactless: the objective psyche expressly imagines our time as the age of the mass media (mass vs. eachness; media vs. immediacy). This imagination is no mere fancy, it is incarnated, institutionalized. And the media are not just one of the many phenomena *in* our world, they are the *medium* in which we all live and experience the world, being surrounded by them on all sides (which is reminiscent of Jung's definition of psyche!).

Where are we when we speak at such a time of immediacy and animalizing? In proposing a return to "animal faith," "nature alive," and a cosmology of eachness, Hillman seems to me (here, not elsewhere) to be out of touch with our time and actuality. I am almost reminded of Honecker, celebrating now, in October 1989, the glory of 40 years of "socialism" in the German Democratic Republic as its people are demonstrating on the streets against this very system or simply turn their back on it and depart. Or of Everyman's advice for someone in a deep depression ("stop brooding, think positive, go out to parties, that will take your mind off things and cheer you up"). Not listening to what is really going on, to the truth of today. Not going into and along with the pathology (in the sense of "like cures like"). Instead, a condemnation of the present view and an allopathic attempt at healing: *from* "universe" *to* "cosmos," disease and health being located in two separate, alternative archetypal structures.

To whom does Hillman speak? For prehistoric hunters his message might have been appropriate since it would have been their truth— except that by *lecturing* about *this* truth, the latter is already lost and destroyed. That's the problem with immediacy. Even for the first agriculturalists, immediacy and the "animal" were already things of the past. They were already on the way to the idea of "universe." When they planted the seed, they weren't saving the phenomenon, weren't answering the shine of its display with an ever more profound appreciation: they deserted (buried) it, and together with it the immediate present (presence), in favor of an almost "eschatological" hope for a rich harvest, overarching a long time span. And their fruits were *planted* ("posited"), not presenting themselves of their own. No immediacy any longer as it indeed existed for the hunter, who had to face the animal, here and now, if he wanted to eat: a face to face immediate encounter, authenticated by the simultaneous presence of life and death. *Kairós*. This animal was an "each," whereas the seed is

SHALT THOU BUILD ME A HOUSE?

an anonymous, interchangeable mass product. Until the age of Goethe and Mozart, one could still believe to be living in a logically agricultural world. Today, however, we know that we are at least as far removed from the agriculturalists as they were from the big-game hunters. Modern man has become a physicist instead.[2]

Hillman uses the word "return" in the neoplatonic sense of *epistrophé*. But from the present discussion we see that what it means has in actuality the character of a return in Rousseau's sense. His is a nostalgic, romantic position. What he says is a piece of "archaeology," a reconstruction of how we think today it may once (in prehistoric times) have been. But his paper does not expressly present it as a reconstruction, does not admit that this is merely of archaeological significance, merely museum stuff. It presents the "cosmos" view as a possibility for the present and future. The legitimate value of an acknowledged reconstruction would be that it could help us discern more clearly our own situation against the foil of this archaeological fantasy. It could provide more differentiated categories for understanding our place in history. It could show us *what* it is that we have irretrievably lost, so that we might be able to consciously and without reserve take leave of it. And I believe that this is what Hillman's paper, *malgré lui*, really does and where its importance is.

The very notion of nature doomed; the "animal" spurious; "immediate perception" obsolete; the idea of "cosmos" an atavism: this is what needs to enter consciousness; it does not need to be counteracted or remedied.

2. SELF-CONTRADICTION TWO:
The proposed view is based on an overall metaphysical position to fight which is its declared purpose

The only way to justify the return to cosmos, animal, eachness, immediacy in view of today's actuality and to give these otherwise utopian ideas weight and substance would be by means of some theory of decadence or decline (from true to false) or some other non-temporal dualistic scheme (e.g. the struggle between two principles like good and evil). Then one could argue, "yes, indeed, today we have no

---

[2] This statement is of course not in reference to a literal profession. It refers to the general logical status of modern man.

immediacy, the animals are endangered, we live with anonymous, mass-produced things. But this is precisely the problem, a disease, a wrong to be cured. Today's reality has to be dismissed as soulless, as a deviation (Fall) from the cosmos in which the soul could feel at home and which therefore is a higher state of the world: a higher truth." This seems to be the position that Hillman adopts in this paper. On the one hand: "Lift repression and the cosmos appears as it is, ... in its actual truth, beauty and goodness" (p. 29). And on the other hand, (universe is a fantasy) "that *wrongs* the soul by posing the *wrong* inspiration for its formulation" (p. 30, my emphases).

Hillman might not agree. He could say that he is not concerned with a higher truth, but only with the soul's well-being (which is the psychologist's legitimate calling). After all, he presented us with the soul's presenting complaint from the outset. It is not a question of Hillman's higher truth, but of the soul's suffering from the universe view and needing another view of the world to become well again. But if he argued like this, he would not see that the distinction between a healthy and a sick state of soul (especially when the sick state is actual and the healthy one only wished for) is just another variety of the metaphysical / moral distinction between right and wrong, higher truth and deviation from it. The "cosmos as it is in its actual truth" (as opposed to as it is when repressed) *is* that very kind of metaphysical higher truth that he normally would not want to have anything to do with.

If that is the case, Hillman has deserted here his earlier insight that pathologizing is a legitimate way of soul-making and the soul's *own* self-expression. At least he has deserted it as far as the perspective informing this entire essay is concerned; for as a content this insight is explicitly recalled in this very paper (p. 19). Now he is operating (consciously or unconsciously) within a dualistic metaphysics of two contradictory principles (soul versus soullessness; actual truth, beauty and goodness versus historical perversion through human wrong-doing: non-acknowledgment and repression; these formulations show that in this view the dualistic position leads to the implication that man is to be blamed, much as in theology and ego-psychology).

Such a metaphysical position contradicts the immediacy and eachness aimed for. It would be an overall, "universal" theory (to overcome which is the very purpose of this paper). But it is also obvious

SHALT THOU BUILD ME A HOUSE? 79

that the allopathic approach in this paper needs this metaphysical position or is one expression of it, because, with a logic of abstract identity, it distributes health and disease unequivocally, the one to one side (cosmos), the other to the other side (universe). The front between good and bad is clearly defined. The dialectical logic underlying the idea of pathologizing as soul-making has disappeared.

If, on the one hand, only by means of a theory of decadence can the wished-for return to the cosmos view be reconciled with the actual character of present day reality and thus avoid the stigma of being utopian, and if, on the other hand, such a theory runs counter to and thus defeats the message of this paper, we get into a twofold deadlock: (1) Ideas of "animal" and "eachness" (once they have no relation to actuality anymore) cannot be formulated without their becoming utopian; as utopian, they would undermine the paper's purpose of providing us with a keener sense of immediate actuality. (2) One cannot aim at animalizing and cosmos without rejecting the present situation (universe view) as fundamentally wrong, soulless. By rejecting it, the very "universe" logic (overall metaphysical principle) is used that the paper wants to overcome, thus again running into contradictions.

3. SELF-CONTRADICTION THREE:
The irreality of the form of discourse defeats the content of its message.

Hillman's message is the certainty of the animal and "an animal display." But what his piece itself does or is, as a form or style of discourse, is the very opposite: instead of an animal self-display, a lecture *about* self-display and a plea for it—in other words a sermon preaching this message, promising us a better alternative to the universe idea. The animal that the paper has in mind could not talk *about* its ways, and it would not have any alternatives. If it did, it would have left the very mode of existence that it were talking about. But Hillman presents us with two options to choose from, and the favored option, cosmos, does not present *itself*. In fact, it is presented as a fantasy about a mode of being whose actuality is lacking. We hear only what *would* happen if we followed the "cosmos / animal" perspective instead of the universe one. The paper abounds with subjunctives: "Were animals

80   *THE SOUL ALWAYS THINKS*

to define consciousness..." (p. 26), we "would not depart from the palpable: we would have no hidden God, ..." (p. 25), "And the animal ... would not vote for the Christian ... cosmologies" (p. 24), "the ego ... would melt into air," "The West would not have to turn East" (p. 27), "we would not greet the stranger..., inquiry itself would be..." (p. 29), "we would realize..." (p. 30), "would" several times on p. 31. Obviously we are not dealing with *Dinge an sich* (p. 31) here, not with "Facts: hard, real, naked, true" (ibid.). We are dealing with possibilities, with ifs and whens and woulds. Idle, unreal, irreal. "Let us suppose..." (p. 32): *We* are doing the supposing (sub-ponere) and talking, *we* present a possibility, *we* have to *give* first place to animals (p. 28)—and show thereby that what we present does not and cannot display itself.

The subjunctives could of course be edited away. But that would be cosmetic surgery and not get any closer to "cosmos" and self-display. The woulds are appropriate. They are the legitimate expression, or reflection in language, of the actual nature of the prevailing logic (one of allopathy, of alternatives). One could say that they are the self-display of the irreality (obsoleteness: only archaeological significance) of the idea presented or the sign indicating that Hillman unwittingly *knows* the cosmos / animal idea to be irreal.

Christian preaching is consistent in message and style. Its message is the overcoming of the [natural] world and the promise of a better beyond, authenticated by a transcendent God. And its mode of discourse is preaching, claiming, promising, believing, admonishing, a mode that likewise establishes a beyond (the split between the subjective act of talking or believing and the object referred to). Mode and message are one. Hillman's "sermon," by contrast, tries to achieve the impossible: it proclaims and wants to bring about the overcoming *of the overcoming* of the world and it believes that such action would amount to a return from the transcendent beyond to the immediate, to eachness, to innocence.[3] This is a self-contradiction. Putting up the immediate as a goal already sets it up as a beyond, and one that is beyond any immediate self-display.

---

[3] Innocence here is logical innocence. In its content it may be very sophisticated and complex, e.g. by encompassing the pathological and allowing for imperfection, the incomplete and "unwholesome" (p. 29).

SHALT THOU BUILD ME A HOUSE?

So is there really no "wholly other (Otto)" (p. 29) in the view Hillman proposes? Yes, it is true, the cosmos view does not have need nor room for a "wholly other" "that breaks through ... into the interior castle of the 'unrelated' individual...." But is not this no-wholly-other view supposed to be itself wholly other with respect to the universe view? Not just other, not just "an altered theory of the universe, a newly modelled home" (p. 30), but truly *wholly* other, having "torn down the very idea of home and the hope that would build one"? The wholly other has not disappeared: it only changed from intentional object or doctrinal content to a mode of being, or quality, of the view itself. It has merely been "integrated," the projection (hypostasis) having been withdrawn. The return to the animalized cosmos does not free us from Otherness by allegedly placing us into the world just as it is.

4. SELF-CONTRADICTION FOUR:
The conflict between the "animalized cosmos" and "cosmos as perspective"

Hillman speaks of cosmos and universe as two "perspectives" and wishes to shift from the latter to the former. This tells us something about the logic of perspectives and the relationship between a perspective and what is seen from it. It appears as if we had on the one side the actual, literal world (the things, events as such) and on the other side, completely separately, perspectives as a kind of dressing for this world, as if it were up to us to dress the naked world with the perspective of our choosing. We would be like a mother standing in front of a closet pondering which clothes to select today to dress her child in. We appear to be completely free to pick the one or the other perspective and then apply it to the actual world, a world as equally ready to be cloaked in "cosmos" as in "universe" (even though, from another paramount perspective, namely Hillman's own, the one cloak may appear to be more becoming to it than the other). In this fantasy, I am not bound by a certain archetypal perspective, a certain God that I have to serve whether I like it or not, simply because I am His child and claimed by Him; and the world does not come with a certain real perspective that determines how we have to see it and that we are more or less "stuck" with, as children of our time and by way of a tribute to be paid to the spirit of the age.

The very point of perspectives as used here is that they have no reality-value, no binding force of their own. If they did, we could not shift perspectives. Perspectives have to be free-floating possibilities without roots in a given real situation. Then one can indeed "shift the universe," and without heroic labor at that. Because now one is in a realm of freedom, in a kind of Hessean glass-bead game where one can effortlessly move from perspective to perspective. It is as easy as the surgeon's shift from syringe to scalpel or scissors, or the carpenter's from hammer to pliers. But one has paid for this effortlessness by the loss of the unrelenting realness of the world, to reach which one has originally set out. Now one can at best *claim* (preach) that the subject-object relation falls into the abyss it created itself (p. 29), but the approach via perspectives contradicts this claim and perpetuates the subject-object split, because views (perspectives) have the actual object that they view (Kant's *Ding an sich*) outside of and vis-à-vis themselves, forever out of reach. That is how a perspective is defined.

But if "cosmos" is the perspective to which the notion of self-display belongs, it cannot be a perspective to which we can shift at will. The cosmos "perspective" would have to be something inherent in the world itself and its natural self-display: the native skin of the world so to speak rather than one of many coats. The animal described in this paper has its very nature in its "absolute knowledge" (p. 27), i.e. in that it does not (cannot) have views or perspectives (just as it does not have clothes that it could put on or take off). It *is* what it "thinks" and it "thinks" what it is and does. The animal's logic is in its organism and life. It exists as its logic. But we, merely by putting on a fur coat (the "perspective" of immediacy), will never reach the immediacy and certainty with which the animal wore the same coat as its own skin.

The idea that the perspective of cosmos has to be, as it were, like the animal's own skin seems to be a thought in Hillman's mind, too. For he imagines the shift from universe to cosmos as the lifting of a repression, as a result of which lifting the cosmos will appear again in its original "truth, beauty and goodness" (p. 29). In other words, the world seen from the universe perspective is to be compared to a dog or monkey dressed up artificially in clothes; we just have to take off the distorting outfit, and we will see the animal again "as it is." The universe perspective is then an artificial costume, and the cosmos

SHALT THOU BUILD ME A HOUSE?

perspective is not really a perspective (*our* perspective) at all, inasmuch as it is the natural self-display of the things in the world.

So on the one hand, "cosmos" and "universe" have to be freely exchangeable perspectives, for how else could we shift the universe? We must move in the realm of possible (not-real) views in order to effortlessly move from one to the other. My real view, one that clings to me as my skin does, I cannot change like clothes. On the other hand, "cosmos" and "universe" have to relate to each other as thing-in-itself and artificial perspective or as natural self-display and perversion, primordial truth and repression of truth.

5. Self-contradiction Five:
The return to "cosmos" is the move into "universe"

It seems that by viewing universe as a perspective and cosmos as truth, the derealization of the animalized cosmos is avoided and that a return to it (qua lifting of the repression inherent in the universe perspective) becomes a real option again. But by lifting a repression we do not return to the primordial truth having supposedly prevailed prior to the repression. We move on to an entirely new situation. The innocence of the animalized cosmos lost due to the alleged repression cannot be regained. The shift from universe to cosmos, even if it were possible, would not be able to undo the artificiality and arbitrariness inherent in the act of shifting by which the cosmos perspective would have been reinstated. The fantasy of the world "as it is" in its virginal freshness has to be seen through. It is self-contradictory. The return to the world in its original "truth, beauty and goodness" or to *Dinge an sich* "real, naked, true" is the opposite of what it purports to be. Rather than a return, it is the move into a new future, and rather than the return to cosmos, it is the move ever deeper into "universe." Why?

By striving for a return to immediacy we are moving further away from it, inasmuch as immediacy is the unreflected state that the soul in fact happens to be in initially, whatever state it may be, in our case the "universe" condition. By advocating a shift of perspectives, Hillman makes us self-conscious of the prevailing perspective and robs us of whatever remainder is left of unreflected animal certainty that our (universe) vision of the world was equipped with initially. He robs the universe experience of its unquestionable self-evidence. He confronts us with a choice, and thus, rather than letting the subject-object relation fall into oblivion, he adds to this split inherent in the universe constitution of the world an additional split, that between cosmos and universe, so that now we are twice removed from animal certainty.

The opposition of "true but repressed" and "false but real" is the means by which we can free ourselves from the immediacy of the "animal" (or the immediacy projected onto it). By declaring the present situation to be wronging the soul and by positing some original truth that we have deviated from, the soul can sever itself from its embeddedness in actuality, in its actually prevailing experience of the world (which today seems to be the world as universe). It gives the soul a position vis-à-vis and outside itself (outside its view). It enables the soul to turn against herself (her actual condition). This oppositional fantasy is the knife that allows her to pull the skin off the anima(l)'s, i.e. her own, body in order to render this skin into a fur coat that it can put on or take off at will. The soul has to invent for itself some "other" original state from which we have fallen, it has to create in itself the fiction of a need for a redemption, it has to put up for itself the idea of a primordial nature to "return" to: in order to alienate itself from its own life as it is and to venture upon a path of—an entirely new, artificial, technological future.

Hillman's return to immediacy via the cosmos perspective is in itself a *technological* project, the artificial project of a kind of face lifting or rather skin (or heart?) transplantation for the world (shifting the universe). But one that in order to appear convincing and authorized has to disguise itself as the "return" to a primordial truth (the old face's return to the original skin of youth—a ghostly fake) and as the "lifting" of a repression, just as *our* "Unbehagen in der Kultur" (Freud) that the soul created for itself in order to propel itself away from the real condition of immediacy onto a trajectory of scientific and technological development is taken literally as the soul's own complaint and as a condition that wrongs and represses the soul.

Now we are in a position to better understand that by (within the universe stage of consciousness) entertaining the ideas of cosmos and animal and of a Fall from them, and by trying to return to them, we do not really leave the universe stage of consciousness; we only reaffirm and self-display the inherent character of this stage of consciousness as one alienated and dissociated *from itself.* This stage

SHALT THOU BUILD ME A HOUSE? 85

of consciousness *comes* as a self-division, as the imagination of itself as a perversion. Both, the "universe" *and* the "cosmos" perspectives, that is the entire opposition between them, belong into the "universe" stance towards the world. The idea that it is a Fall from some original truth does not describe its genealogy, but is the content or message that it wants to bring; it is its telos. The Fall, thus, is not a historical event, it did not happen to consciousness from "outside," but it is consciousness' own, innate state, its core, a way it imagines itself. And this imagination is what defines this consciousness. So the longing for a return from the Fall *is* the very way in which the Fall, i.e. that consciousness that is divided against itself, actualizes.

If we do not want to fall for the fiction of cosmos as the primordial truth and yet honor it as the soul's own fiction, we can comprehend cosmos and universe as the names for two stages of consciousness imagined by the universe fantasy and irrevocably separated from each other by "historical time." If we truly listen to the soul's fantasy of "cosmos," then cosmos can never be thought of as an origin to return to. "Cosmos" comes as a thing of the past, truly obsolete, dead, forever gone. There is no wrong condition to be righted. The very message of the fantasy of a Fall is that we cannot look back. The door to paradise has been locked. The Fall if understood propels us ahead. And thus (again: if seen through) it can only be a historical imagination serving as a foil to help us more clearly see, and more soulfully inhabit, our own inalienable situation, that of "universe."

6. SEEING THROUGH "PERSPECTIVES"

We have already seen that the perspectives gained by means of reflection and by abstracting them from real experience are mere possibilities and as such irrealities. Real they are only while completely fused with the things seen in their light, so that the thing *is* the way it is seen. But we have also seen that perspectives can be treated as if they were real entities. How is this possible? The idea of the world "as it is" in contradistinction to the universe perspective is the product of an artificial operation. It owes its existence to the splitting of the "phainomenon" into two halves, the thing as it really is and the perspective in which it is seen. The two moments of the phainomenon that appear only to a subsequent reflection are literalized and hypostasized. The world is spoken about as if it existed independently of the respective perspective in which it is seen, and perspectives are now treated as if they were things separate from the phainomena of which they were an inherent and inseparable moment.

Just like the skin can be turned into fur coats by killing the animal and pulling its skin off and by further preserving it by means of tanning and moth balls, so archetypal perspectives can be abstracted from real historical situations (stances) of man's interaction with the world after "killing" (rendering obsolete) the actual stances in question; and then they can be preserved by means of some kind of imaginal freeze-drying and be elevated to the status of atemporal essences. Just as fur coats refer back to some real animal now dead and forgotten, so perspectives refer back to real, but forgotten situations of our human past. And much like furs are stocked and offered for sale in our stores so that anyone (with enough money,[4] that is) can buy and wear them, regardless of his or her actual standing, so we keep a stock of possible perspectives to choose from according to our momentary likings. Once we have a supply of diverse cloaks, we can choose which one to wear or to dress "the animal" in at will, according to how we wish the animal to appear. In other words, perspectives are tools by means of which we can change the world according to our interests. Perspectivism is part of a technological approach to the world.

It is the same as with the Platonic Forms. They are, as Bruno Liebrucks has so convincingly shown,[5] abstractions, catapulted into heaven and there brought into an orbit at the exact speed necessary to give them, with respect to any point on the revolving earth, the appearance of standing still, of fixed stars: eternal truths. Thus their historicity and temporality can be obliterated, or rather obscured. And they can serve as firm points of reference for manipulating reality. They are so many Archimedean points from which to unhinge the world from its "natural" (mythologically experienced) constitution and to transform it into a revolutionized technical reality.

Just as prehistoric man manufactured knives and hammers from stone, wood or bone, so Plato manufactured logical tools called eternal

---

[4] For perspectives, the necessary "money" would be education and intelligence, as well as the freedom and luxury of a bourgeois existence.

[5] See especially Bruno Liebrucks, *Sprache und Bewußtsein*, 7 vols., Frankfurt/Main (Akademische Verlagsanstalt, later Peter Lang) 1964–79.

Ideas out of phenomenal experience. The Ideas or perspectives are the first satellites mankind sent up into space. By redirecting our experience of life on earth in a controlled way via these satellites orbiting up there as eternal truths (possibilities)—much as today our communication is literally redirected via communication satellites—we have become able to free ourselves from immediate experience and to subject the world to those possibilities of our choosing. The Platonic Forms are the logical preparation and prerequisite for the technical and industrial revolutions. We need reliable (eternal) Ideas or perspectives to technically change the world. They are not a way to knowing and truth, but instruments to alter reality by.

The tool character of the "archetypal perspectives" and Platonic Forms remained and remains a secret. What is a mere instrument for establishing or maintaining, vis-à-vis the real complexities and contradictions of experience, a logic of identity to transform the world and life technologically is treated as if it were of *theoretical* significance. Perspectives are believed in. But the fact that the tool character of Forms or perspectives remained a secret is not a mere fault. Their instrumental character *must* not be seen through, if they are to do their job. One *has to* believe in them as in unshakeable truths if the world is to be completely remodelled.

7. THE FEAR OF PHILOSOPHY AND THE FORSAKING OF THE EARTH

One's operating on the level of possible perspectives is the indication that one has left the earth, left actuality and its self-display; one has gone up into a beyond (a realm of "atemporal" ideas, general essences, free-floating views). The cosmos / animal perspective may be fascinating. But because it is no more than a perspective (an option, an "as if") there is no way to *really* get to what it is the option of (especially in this case, where what you want to get to is the opposite of an option: animal certainty). If the idea of an animalized cosmology is out of touch with the actual world, it turns out to be a worldless idea. It is not at all a fantasy inspired by the anima *mundi*. Rather in this theory we witness how the anima *alba*, enclosed within and untouched by world, believes to be outside and in touch with the world merely by presenting its own inner fantasy of the world without, its fantasy of an anima mundi.

It is the problem of Moses and the promised land, where the problem, however, is not with Moses, but with the "promise." For the logic of promise is that it places that which it promises out of reach. You can only talk and dream about it, hope and long for it, or, of course, you can also *pretend* to be there, in the Honecker style, or like fathers playing with their children: consciously going beneath their consciousness.

So far my critique of the idea of shifting the universe and of the shift of perspectives has been a critique of Hillman's allopathic stance and of his move into a platonistic beyond in his paper. Now, by collecting a few images and formulations that reveal the attitude at work here, I want to turn to another aspect of this shifting: shiftiness, evasiveness, as opposed to holding one's ground, trying to solve a problem with effort and courage, working something out exhaustively.

Very early in his paper, Hillman introduces us to three great dangers: three insuperable monsters guarding the gates (to a cosmology for soul) (p. 18). What does he do vis-à-vis this threat? He does not meet the demons; he wants "to *side-slip* these dangers" (my emphasis, as in the following citations too).

The three monsters have to do with a) an exhaustive study disproving all other approaches in the spirit of the redemptive hero, b) using and literally believing in big, metaphysical words and abstract concepts, c) the desire to give an all-embracing answer. By contrast, Hillman's way of side-slipping is by means of telling a *tale*. Similarly, the shifting of the universe is done by *imagining afresh*. No work, no labor, no big concepts.

"But we are not as tired as Atlas who carried the universe on human [?] shoulders. We have long ago put down that heroic fantasy" (p. 28).

"The idea of cosmos *spares* philosophy so much of its efforts" (p. 29).

But sparing philosophy its efforts is not all. "The return (epistrophé) of cosmology to *kosmos* also leads to an *emptying out* of all first causes, single equations, ontological grounds. ... Being *evaporates*..." (p. 23). In other words, philosophy as such is deprived of its essential content and concerns, drained of its life force and thus will simply dissolve (one must assume), just like we heard that the ego "would melt into air, leave not a rack behind" (p. 27).

So far my collection of passages and images. I believe that these admittedly few bits and pieces reveal an underlying attitude of

SHALT THOU BUILD ME A HOUSE? 89

fundamental importance not only for this paper of his, but also for much of archetypal psychology in general.

What is it that they reveal? A tremendous pull away from matter, and toward an emancipation from actuality. A desubstantialization. A refusal to accept and meet a problem with its own weight and solidity, as given to us by our history and in our actual situation. In this paper, Hillman does not begin with the pathology, the real, the "facts" (e.g. with walkmen, drugs, the irrevocable encirclement of modern consciousness by the media on all sides, the Bomb, dying forests and endangered species) as his prima materia to be cooked, or worked on in some other alchemical way, but he begins with an alternative to all this, with a longing, a remedy. And to give this longing or wish the semblance of actuality, he forsakes actuality in favor of the (platonist) realm of Ideas by talking about archetypal perspectives, and as if these modes of viewing the world were independently existing entities. Hillman does not just perform an alchemical operation of vaporization, even though the word 'evaporate' is used. Such alchemical operations would be performed for the purpose of obtaining a (vaporized) product, but here, there is no product. Whatever there was is emptied out and disappears into air without, as is expressly stated, even leaving a rack behind. Voided, annihilated—not by an action, but by the omission of any action, in other words because the philosophical problems are nothing to begin with. Just Maya.

You therefore *have* to side-slip. To take the big problems of philosophy seriously would be to walk into a trap, would mean to give credit to what is, in actuality, a mere illusion, delusion. "Being" (capitalized) as just a big inflated balloon. Trying to face philosophical questions would be nothing but blowing more air into this balloon, feeding the inflation. Just leave such questions alone, evade them, refuse to tackle them—and they will fall to nothing. This is at bottom the position.

8. SELF-CONTRADICTION SIX:
The polytheistic multiplicity of perspectives as logical monotheism

It is one thing if reflection uncovers the perspective actually prevailing in a given experience of the world and another thing if perspectives as free-floating possibilities are employed with a view to changing and correcting what is thought to be a wrong experience of the world. What I said about perspectives above is not to deny nor to belittle their value as a critical instrument of self-reflectively and after the fact becoming aware of our modes of seeing (our actual ones, the ones we are really in) and of the Gods inherent in them (seeing through). As such, the discovery of perspectives (and the re-interpretation of the archetypes as perspectives, whereas the late Jung still tried to hypostatize them as "archetypes-in-themselves") was undoubtedly a major psychological breakthrough, in fact, one of the constitutive discoveries of psychology proper. Through it psychologizing became possible, the creation of that inner space between ourselves and our beliefs, emotions, behavior that can be called psychological awareness. It is of tremendous therapeutic importance in dissolving neurotic or other fixations, allowing us to gain a certain distance to what we have gotten stuck in. But of course, this kind of critical self-reflection also moves us away from animal certainty.

By the same token, side-slipping can be a very important therapeutic tool. Many patients walk into the trap of a problem, not realizing that trying to solve the problem (trying to free themselves, e.g., from a mother complex) is the very way to feed this complex, to tighten the bind. A complex does indeed not care, if I may use this personifying language, if one serves it positively, by affirming what it wants, or negatively, by organizing a personal crusade against it. Either way it gets what it wants: blind attention. The only way to stop this vicious circle is by letting the complex *be*, by refusing to fight it. And sure enough, this is how many a complex vanishes into air (though maybe not without leaving a rack behind). Or rather: how we move out of its blinding and compelling spell to a level where we can *see* its logic.

But perspectives and the idea of a polytheistic psychology can also be in the service of defending us from the weight of earth and the bond of Time (history) by presenting us with so many options to choose from. The ideas of perspectives and polytheism seem to have the function of supporting this general attitude. The way archetypal psychology makes use of these ideas and terms gives them an unclarified ambiguity or equivocation which comes in handy.

SHALT THOU BUILD ME A HOUSE?

In order to look at this it is best to go to the discussion of perspective in *Re-Visioning Psychology*, in particular to the "Excursion on Perspective in Painting...." There we read on p. 212 that the Renaissance achievement of spatial perspective reflects, among others, the theme of Hillman's book: "the simultaneous apperception of the soul's multiplicity, its several points of view coalescing as perspective." This sentence is not easy to understand. But if my reading is not all wrong, I assume that it wants to claim the Renaissance invention of perspective for (psychological) polytheism; perspective in painting as one place where the Renaissance appreciation of the soul's multiple points of view supposedly becomes evident.

This is one of the few assessments in *Re-visioning* that I could not follow, already when I first read the book. Is it really possible to connect perspective in painting with multiplicity and polytheism? I think that the very contrary is true. Perspective was the final victory of monotheism. Everything in a painting had now to be subservient to one single eyepoint that is the overall ordering principle, forcing everything in the painting into a systematic totality, while not itself part of the painting. It remains outside. It is the unnoticed "unmoved mover" (Aristotle). The mover, because the invention of perspective is not a sign of an increased awareness of the natural self-display of things, but the invention of a highly artificial construction, by which the unmoved mover subjugates the world to his own design. Now nature does not present itself anymore, we present it. A complete revolution: from man being subject to the self-presentation of phenomena, to man as the modern subject, subjecting nature to his own scheme, to his viewing in an active, aggressive sense.[6] This phenomenon (that there is now this invisible eyepoint) is a "visible" self-display of what Jung had in mind with his theoretical construct of the ego (defined as the unnoticed, invisible, but all-controlling center of consciousness, whereby consciousness in turn is defined as the sphere of those contents that are connected with this center. The kind of connection prevailing here is not a concrete one [like ropes], but might be imagined in terms of the vanishing lines of perspective.). And the invention of perspective during the Renaissance is the self-display of the historical

---

[6] It is the revolution that I described at length as that from "Angeblicktwerden" to "Selber-Blicken" in my *Die Atombombe als seelische Wirklichkeit*, Zürich (Schweizer Spiegel Verlag, Raben-Reihe) 1988, esp. part I, chapter. 3.

emergence of the ego in the sense of a monistic organizing principle of consciousness.

Fig. 4.1: Albrecht Dürer, woodcut from "Unterweysung der Messung," Nürnberg 1525. Note the sharp point of the instrument fixing the painter's gaze so that a single unshifting eyepoint results as well as the subjugation of nature/anima to an artificial grid.

Dürer's woodcut is both a drawing of applied perspective and one *about* perspective. As such it shows the hidden logic inherent in perspective. The sharp point of the instrument fixes the painter's gaze into one single, unshifting (unmoved) eyepoint (as if obeying Mt. 6:22, "if therefore thy eye be single, thy whole body shall be full of light") and subjugates nature / anima to an imposed artificial grid. This picture demonstrates to us what actually happens in perspective: everything in the world is "uni-versum" (directed to one point, organized or constructed from one focus). Perspective *is* the self-display of the universe conception of the world.

Each time we look at a painting with spatial perspective, we are forced into a stance where the world is contained in a single homogenous geometrical space (= ego-consciousness) and we are ritually trained to *become* the single eyepoint from which everything seen will obey the all-encompassing law of this unmoved mover. Each painting is a celebration of the singleness of the modern subject's eyepoint. Each one reaffirms the modern ego's need for a systematic totality and its claim to exclusive sovereignty. In earlier medieval paintings (as well as in the non-perspective painting of other ages and civilizations) each thing presented itself from its own angle, each according to the needs of its most essential characteristics. In the same painting, one thing might be seen from the front, another from the

SHALT THOU BUILD ME A HOUSE?

93

side or from on top, one from a distance, one from up close—many eyepoints at once. Even different parts of one and the same thing might be presented from different points of view. There was no unified, monocentric ego, no monotheism of consciousness. The "perspective" was, so to speak, each thing's own perspective, and its "vanishing lines" didn't lead outside the painting, they didn't vanish in the infinitely distant nowhere of a single focal point functioning as a projection of the viewing ego. The things had their focal point in themselves. The Renaissance invention of perspective, however, expropriated the focal points from the things themselves and made them into the ego's property.

But how could Hillman connect perspective with multiplicity in the first place? This is where the ambiguity comes in. It is the unclarified difference-and-identity between the single eyepoint and the many standpoints. The one and the many. Hillman knows that this is not the formula to comprehend the difference between monotheism and polytheism. A common view would be to equate monotheism with the one and polytheism with the many. But the entire problem of the one and the many belongs to the side of monotheism, whereas polytheism is to be sought on this side of the opposition of one and many. The key term here is eachness, or to be more precise *Jeweiligkeit*, each at its own moment (when its Time has come) and according to its kind. An individual painting with perspective shows only the One (the single focus). The many appear in the multiplicity of paintings, each being painted from a different standpoint. But the ontically many paintings and the many standpoints are all psychologically or logically monotheistic, because all affirm one and the same homogenous space and the fundamental singleness of focus. Monotheism does not mean, "there must be only one single painting." There is room for many paintings, just as there is for the pluralism of scientific models, philosophical paradigms, or, in a modern democratic society, for the pluralism of world-views, religions, political opinions. This pluralism is that of and within monotheism, made possible by the constitution of the world as "universe." Absolute monotheism: the One being so unshakable that it can be absolutely indifferent to the many. It does not matter what you believe or from what point of view you look, because all standpoints confirm the single eyepoint anyway.

94   *THE SOUL ALWAYS THINKS*

The fact that archetypal psychology's polytheism tends to be empirical (ontic) multiplicity within a logical monotheism is borne out by imaginal constructions such as Guilio Camillo's Memory Theatre, often cited as an exemplary model backing archetypal psychology's polytheism. It is a depiction of the "universe" view: one single room (scheme) for all the many images. A kind of pictorial encyclopedia[7] or the framework for one. And secondly, does this Memory Theatre not bear witness to the status of archetypal perspectives, namely as logically obsolete and antiquarian: the "Gods" mere museum stuff, mummies in show-cases, uprooted from their embeddedness in real life and historical situations? Each one neatly and safely in his own box. Jung seems to have seen what their status is; his assessment was that the "Gods" have become diseases and that Zeus no longer governs the Olympus, but the plexus solaris. Can one not smell the stuffiness of this theatre? And thirdly, Camillo's Theatre displays the technical character of the images / perspectives. It is Camillo's tool chest so to speak.

By the same token I wonder whether perspective in painting can be interpreted as particularly indicative of the "depth dimension of the soul" (ibid.). Isn't it rather that the notion of depth fundamentally changed: from imaginal to imaginary, illusionistic depth, from soul depth to literal, geometric (i.e. external, superficial) depth? Isn't perspective much closer to Galileo after all than to Plato or Plotinus? Or do we even have to realize that Plato is closer to Galileo than we liked to think? (Of course, art would not be art if it couldn't give expression to the depth of the soul even in the medium of the "flat," naturalistic depth created by perspective.)

Spatial perspective makes depth *vanish* in the beyond. Along with depth, the inherent worth of all visible things in the world *vanishes* in literal infinity. The vanishing lines suck out the metaphysical dignity of all individual things portrayed in the painting. What is visible in the painting is fundamentally devalued (secularized), in favor of the one transcendent eyepoint (outside the painting, in the viewer) who, being the sole owner of worth,[8] is the source of

---

[7] The word "encyclopedia" is by the way also a 15th cent. Renaissance coinage, bearing witness to the uni-versal interests of that age.

[8] This worth manifests itself as the aesthetic feeling experience of the art enthusiast who, by consuming the work of art, edifies himself.

SHALT THOU BUILD ME A HOUSE?

any secondary worth that the things emanating from his vision may still have (eyepoint = ego = Christian God; the latter being as much above his creation [transcendent] and all-controlling as the eyepoint is with respect to the painting).

I said that the ambiguity in the words perspective and polytheism may come in handy. It is the ambiguity between each and many, between truly polytheistic Jeweiligkeit and pluralistic indifference, the distinction left unclarified. And it is the ambiguity of the word (and the movement of the) Renaissance, which concealed its essentially Christian-modernist essence under a colorful Greek coat. With the word "perspective" one could at one and the same time refer to the Gods and their archetypal backing of our actual human views *and* move in the realm of that monotheistic indifference that alone provides the freedom to shift perspectives without much effort (the realm of Nietzsche's perspectivism, of Vaihinger's "as if," of Hesse's glass-bead game; cf. also Wittgenstein's language games). The term Jeweiligkeit implies each (each God, archetypal phenomenon etc.) if and when its Time has come (actually come!), when it actually displayed itself. In other words, Jeweiligkeit has the reference to Time, actuality, history within itself. It is grounded. *Within itself* it reaches out to the concrete real situation. You cannot ask here: which perspective is better for soul? What is good, what is bad? No game-playing here. You have to ask: Whose Time is it now? What does this situation and the God constellated in it demand in the way of service? Believing in shifting perspectives, in side-slipping, in simple re-imagining, shifting visions and re-framing, by contrast, is moving within a utopia. It doesn't really "matter" anymore (because the relation to matter, to material, historical concreteness has been severed). Instead, the only limitation on one's choice of perspective in this realm of pluralistic indifference can be the extraneous and idealistic concern for what would be better for soul (*ideally*, i.e. according to our opinion). Decisionism.

Here we are at the watershed I mentioned in the beginning. It was hidden in the ambiguity of the ideas of perspectives and polytheism. Archetypal psychology can move either towards the licence of many free-floating possibilities or towards actuality binding us with the bond of Ananke; towards the atemporal or towards the eachness provided by historical time.

9. The Christian character of Renaissance
paganism and naturalism

Contrary to appearance and to popular opinion, paintings with perspective are the first instance of "abstract" art. The naturalism of Renaissance painting is abstract. It does not depict the actual natural world, but an artificial construction, one, however, that is now claimed to be *the* true image of nature as such. This is exactly parallel to what happened in the modern sciences. They claimed their artificial constructs to be a simple discovery of the true laws of nature ("Naturwissenschaft"). This is just as much a delusion as was the belief of the Renaissance that perspective was the rediscovery of how the ancients saw, whereas it is the first occurrence of a thoroughly Christian, monotheistic vision in painting.[9] Renaissance painting is the first truly Christian painting. Earlier Christian art depicted Christian themes, to be sure, but it did so in a still mythic, pagan way. Now, with the Renaissance invention of perspective, one did not even have to portray Christian contents anymore to create Christian art, because every painting, even with secular themes, was the depiction and reenactment of the Christian vision. Christianism had been "integrated" and was now the objective *style* of seeing. We could also say it had changed from a particular theme of our culture into the logic of our culture or into the unconscious horizon within which any theme was seen.

Twentieth century "abstract" art is merely the manifestation of a dawning consciousness of what the previous naturalism had actually been all along. The Renaissance delusion has now objectively (not necessarily subjectively) been seen through. It can now be openly admitted that its naturalism in all its beauty is abstract; this admission now displays itself visibly in painting. Similarly, Kant means that place in philosophy where man begins to become conscious of the fact that the sciences do not enable us to *know* the world, but provide only access to an abstract construct of the world (what he termed "Erscheinung"), one, however, that allows us to manipulate the world.

---

[9] I am not in a position to pass judgment on the question to what extent the Renaissance in general may or may not have been deluded about its being a rebirth of the views and values of the ancients and of pagan (polytheistic) modes of thinking, concealing the decidedly Christian direction of its achievements.

SHALT THOU BUILD ME A HOUSE?

The Renaissance painters still believed to be painting natural scenes. They believed in a Renaissance, in a rebirth of how the ancients saw (= how things really are). They did not understand the fact discussed above that the fiction of a rebirth is the way into a new and different future (away from what it is to be a rebirth of). They could not know yet that what they actually depicted were neither natural things nor the "cosmos," but the *sublated* (or superceded, "aufgehoben") cosmos, cosmos or nature *as* the platonic Idea of itself, i.e., the "universe" that turns the portrayed things logically into the shadows of mere shadows. What they painted were those shadows, but they did not paint the portrayed things expressly *as* the shadows of shadows. Unsuspectingly, they saw them only empirically, still from the point of view of the "natural mind," where they appeared as aesthetically beautiful and ideal. They did not see them logically, just as Plato, unaware of the logical status of his (platonic, atemporal) "Ideas," could still innocently believe in their total beauty and goodness, whereas we today, who are now physically surrounded by them, live with them and use them on a daily basis (all the commodities of our technological civilization) are much more apt to shrink from them, often in some kind of horror.

This is because we begin to see the soullessness of those beautiful platonic essences, their ghostly abstractness, and to see through to their logical status, their utterly technical, instrumental character (Bruno Liebrucks). (Technology seems to *display* the *logic* of the realm of Ideas.) Plato could not see the dialectical identity of the shadows of shadows in the cave, on the one hand, and the sun or the Idea of the Good, on the other. He could not see that what *empirically* was the way to his brightest light *was logically* the way into the cave and to those shadows that he thought he was leaving. But by leaving, *within* his fantasy, the shadows he didn't really leave anything, he stayed in the same fantasy. He merely established it as the new way to see the whole world: the world as needing to be left behind since it is a world of shadows of shadows. Plato only *blinded* himself to the *truth* of his own sun, turning against one entire half of his vision, the one that presented the unknown *logical status* of his conscious, explicit goal. *For the truth of his sun is the cave.* And this truth takes hold of man to the same degree *that he blindly believes in the converse: in the sun as revealing the truth about the cave.* Plato's sun is merely the instrument that allows the real things of this world to be turned into shadows of shadows (= technical objects). What Plato really left behind (the mythic situation and the world as it was experienced from within it) is totally outside his parable. This corresponds to what I tried to show above: that Hillman does not seem to realize that by moving towards the fascinatingly beautiful idea of an animalized cosmos he is logically moving towards a dead and ghostly past[10] that in actuality only confirms what he is trying to get away from: the universe.

It remained a task for our century's painters[11] to paint the "natural" things of the platonist-Christian universe (that formerly had appeared to be only of ideal beauty) in their abstractness and to thereby slowly open our logical eyes. It is psychologically vital not to split the abstract paintings of this century off from the beautiful depictions of Renaissance painting, as if they were two separate realities, but to hold the connection and see that the former merely reveal the logical status of or truth about what the latter used to present empirically, from outside. This is similar to the way in which formerly, as long as a merely empirical approach prevailed, technology was only seen in idealistic terms (progress), whereas now, when the pollution and waste problems confront us with the *logic* at work in technology, everyone is shocked. It is pretty much as if we had gone out to a restaurant for a fancy dinner and, having just been thinking of the enjoyment, would be terribly shocked when at the end the waiter presents us with the bill. As if we had not been able to know about the cost from the outset.

10. THE INSUFFICIENCY OF (PURE) PSYCHOLOGY.

At the surface, there is no self-contradiction in the move away from heroic effort, from the big terms of philosophy and from addressing certain problems like Being, first causes, truth etc. *as philosophical* ones.[12] Hillman's is in this respect a legitimate position. And more

---

[10] "Past" here is the word for the logical status of being obsolete and abstract. It does not suggest that the animalized cosmos was an actual reality in some literal past. I have no way of knowing about that. Sure is that today it is an archetypal fantasy.

[11] Remember, this was written in 1989.

[12] It would be contradictory only if it were supposed to be a move towards the world. But this contradiction has already been discussed in the first section above. Here we are looking into the question of the validity of moving on the level of possible perspectives as such. That they too have their own, but very subtle, internal contradiction (namely between their conscious empirical aspect and the unconscious logic of the matter) should have become apparent from what I said about Plato and the Renaissance.

SHALT THOU BUILD ME A HOUSE? 99

than that: it is the position that makes psychology possible. It is that stance that provides the real emancipation of psychology from philosophy, from the spiritual, mind orientation (just as it provides the emancipation from the stance of the natural sciences). So what is my objection?

First, let me stress that I do not want to fall behind the achievement of this stance back to the pre-psychological position of philosophy. The psychological awareness gained through the idea of perspectives and seeing through shall not be forsaken. My objection is rather that this move is not enough. It is still contained within the innocence of the personal, human, merely subjective—despite the emphasis on archetypes, collective unconscious, and dehumanizing. It is, to use the language of Hillman's 1989 Paris lecture on yellowing, still "white psychology," what I termed "pure, or mere, psychology."[13] It has forsaken the relation to the earth, to actuality. This dehumanization is still a brand of humanism, and this anima mundi is still in a bubble, not reaching out into the actual world.

Psychologizing does not exempt us from philosophizing.

Concerning the argument against philosophy, we have to make a few distinctions. First, the distinction between literalism (taking a problem literally and getting stuck in this literalism) and taking a problem, our real problem, seriously in the sense of trying to give an honest answer to it (not *the* answer, but our answer, as best we can). Both are not the same. The one is a predicament or fallacy, the other a necessity. We have to address our actual problem, but our attention to it does not have to be the blind one of fighting it or adoring (indulging in) it. Our attempt at a solution can also be that respectful devotion that would no more than *know* (comprehend) it in depth, in the sense of that kind of comprehending that would at once imply our being comprehended by it.

Second, we have to distinguish between the labor due to an identification with the hero and the effort of modestly, diligently, patiently doing our job, the job that is waiting to be done, provided for us by our actual present-day societal situation. This job is nothing else but the slow opus in the alchemical laboratory-and-oratory. And

---

[13] W.G., "Die Syzygie. Über die Wirklichkeit der Welt oder die Not der Psychologie," *Eranos 57-1988*, Frankfurt (Insel) 1990, pp. 235-305.

conversely, we have to distinguish between seeing through (which is a critical instrument of utmost importance) and getting out, escaping. A crucial distinction. Seeing through frees us of our unconsciousness, literalism and psychological unawareness, but it does not have to, indeed it must not, imply an attempt to get out of our concrete situation (not even if the latter happens to be a terrible predicament) into the realm of free-floating as ifs. If psychologizing means to free us from our literalisms by opening up a middle space of psyche between physics and philosophy, and if philosophizing means to give a committed answer to whatever questions are actually raised for us by our situation, then the question is not "philosophy or not?," but "how philosophy?" (prior to psychology, i.e. literally, or after it, with psychological awareness).

Even the fear of the hero has to be reviewed. It is intolerable that archetypal psychology pronounces a lump-sum verdict against particular archetypes, like the hero or Apollo. With what justification? Each archetype has its traps and dangers, but each potentially also provides its own access to the depth of soul. It is not worse to be inflated by the hero or identified with Atlas than to be identified with, say, the anima or Hermes. The problem is not the hero, but the inflation, which can occur in the domain of any archetype.

This is not a plea for a heroic attitude. In this anti-hero and unheroic time the dangers of the hero archetype are not particularly great anyway. Generally, we are far too lazy, easy-going and unpompous, also too full of feelings of inferiority to be likely victims of a hero identification. Of course I agree that any such hero identification has to be seen through and possibly dissolved. But I cannot consent to that global discrimination (hardly reconcilable with a polytheistic stance) against the hero and against Apollo that is used mainly either as an excuse or as a club with which to kill in the bud any attempt at a committed and exhaustive answer to a given problem—for the (probably unconscious) purpose of keeping psychology "white," unburdened by the actual predicaments of our age.

Third, by the same token, we have to distinguish between evading our actual situation and a mercurial, evasive style *of approaching* it. Alchemy teaches us that the committed effort at working on the opus can go along with a hermetic style of consciousness.

SHALT THOU BUILD ME A HOUSE?

My question is: Can re-imagining, can (pure) psychology provide the answer to our problem? Side-slipping, shifting perspectives may do the trick. But will doing the trick do? Do we not need more than a trick, more than freedom from literalism? Namely an authentic access to our real age and world with its weight and substantiality? Becoming aware of the perspectives one sees from is only an instrument for one particular situation (that of a too literal consciousness, one stuck in a fixation). It is not a panacea, just as in alchemy calcination and the bath in water are operations applied only for certain conditions, a too moist or too dry soul, respectively. But above all, it is only an answer to a condition of the soul *in* us (narcissistically), not to that of the world and to our being-in-the-world (our world relation). With shifting perspectives something shifts, but not what is supposed to shift: the condition our world is in. There is another view, but the actual world stays the way it was.

For how could shifting our perspectives change the condition of the present-day world, if that condition (i.e., its logic) is *not* just a view in our mind, as white psychology imagines, but an actual condition that is only to that extent "in here" that it is also "out there," incarnate, inherent in things and institutions (TV's, satellites, advertising, credit cards)? Would changing our perspectives make the credit card system, speculation on the stock exchange, dependence on satellites and television, mass-transportation and telephones, our whole industrial civilization melt into air? This would be the illusory hope (and hubris) of white psychology: just change the individual, his perspectives and attitudes, and this will change the world. But the problem—the logic of our actual situation—is taken out of our hands (namely: out of our subjective mind: our viewing). It is invested in the material culture and has its own momentum, its own demands and consequences. Sure, we can change our minds, but so what? It would be a change only in a sphere that does not *matter* anyway, the limited sphere of our personal freedom, the realm of indifference, what I call *Frei-Zeit* (religious, political beliefs, world-views, feelings, tastes, preferences, etc.).[14]

The only chance to reach the actual situation would be for psychology, within itself, to open itself up to "philosophy" (if this is

---

[14] See my *Drachenkampf oder Initiation ins Nuklearzeitalter*, Zürich (Schweizer Spiegel Verlag, Raben-Reihe) 1989, esp. Part II.

the name for taking our problems as actual [not only psychological] problems). This would mean to be again concerned with truth (whatever that means), a true answer to our situation, a serious, committed response as best we can. The detailed and in depth elaboration of the logic, the Notion, *Begriff* (Hegel, Science of Logic, part III), of our situation. No need to avoid big words and so-called abstract concepts anymore. Because we now realize that as modern men we think in those big words anyway (even if we take refuge in images), so that it is much better to try to do a good job of it than to hope to evade them. And so: No tales and images anymore. That is, tales and images only for didactic or rhetorical purposes, not as a substitute for addressing the problem on the level it shows itself today: a logical one.[15]

If psychology first shuts its doors to philosophy *and then* becomes aware of its own narcissism, where can it turn? The door to the consulting room and to the interiority of the individual is locked for it. There is only one opening for it: it will inevitably be driven to seeing activism as the only avenue to the real world remaining available. This activism of the former psychologist will probably be of a softer and more subtle nature than the usual one; it will still be intellectual and imaginal, not literal, an activism of words and thoughts and demonstrations, since it carries those traits within itself from its past as former psychology. But activism nonetheless: in the sense of a direct response to the world. This may be a way to the world as reality (*Realität*, the world inasmuch as it can be manipulated), but certainly not to the world as actuality (*Wirklichkeit* in Hegel's sense) and as anima mundi. Along with philosophy, psychology would have forsaken the theoretical terrain in favor of the truly terrible naiveté of an imaginal variety of *Action directe* and fallen into the same trap that Marx walked into by opting for practice instead of theory. Marx was no longer able to hold his ground in the insight that theory[16] *is* the place "where the action is." Underlying this crudeness is a false split between the two, theory appearing as merely academic (ivory tower), practice

---

[15] Here I have to add that on the other side of logic (once we have thoroughly gone through it) there may well be a return to myth and images, but on a new level.

[16] Not to be confused with mere *Frei-Zeit* theorizing, which emerges only as a result of the very split between theory and practice that Marx advocated.

SHALT THOU BUILD ME A HOUSE? 103

supposedly being concerned with the real.[17] Aristotle knew that theory is the highest form of practice. (As Hillman knew in his other writings too.) I would say it is the depth or soul dimension of the world, the dimension where our problems are rooted, where they can be seen for what they actually are, whereas all practice opposed to theory is muddling in the realm of the merely symptomatic. The alchemical "practice" took place in the laboratory, not on the street, and it was embedded and grounded in the oratory's thinking work.[18]

We are not really free to choose the perspective of cosmos / animal and reject the universe perspective, just because we like the cosmos idea better and it seems to be healthier. It is wishful to think that the universe perspective is just a perspective and as such disposable at will. The "universe"-Gestalt of the world is the very fact (hard, real, naked, true) that Hillman believes can only be had in a beyond, in the wholly other cosmos / animal perspective. The "universe" is a fact because that is how we actually live and think—and not only we subjectively, but how the world truly and "objectively" affords itself to us, how it is logically constituted today. It would be naive to suppose we could, just like we change a coat, shift the universe towards cosmos or whatever, just as naive as to believe one could, effortlessly, walk out of a severe neurosis. Perspectives, as mere possibilities, do not have a connection to actuality within themselves.

For those living in an ice-age, it would not do any good to shift perspective to "interglacial period," instead of waiting for the climate to get warmer. In fact they would do well to tune into the idea of "ice," so as not to be neurotically split off from their situation. The universe view is of course not an "outside" climate to the same degree as is the ice-age. That is why there is more for us to do in response to it. But it nevertheless has the same degree of relentless realness, giving way only

---

[17] This split is to bring about our emancipation from actuality (the bond of necessity) and our ability to confront actuality with the wish to impose a different (supposedly better) condition / system / perspective upon it. The split creates the very type of (carefree, Frei-Zeit) theory that it polemicizes against under the label of ivory tower, as well as the emptied out world of positive facts that it tries to change by brute force (action).

[18] We don't have to identify the modern alchemical "laboratory" with the consulting room of personal therapy and confuse my rejection of "the street" (acting out) with an attempt to lock psychology up again in the consulting room. Laboratory and oratory having been seen through as imaginal topoi; they seem to me to have merged into one. Today the labor is thought, to be done in those remote, icy recesses in the psyche that I call logic and truth. This laboratory-and-oratory is no ivory tower. On the contrary, it is the only place where actuality, the world can be truly reached.

104 *THE SOUL ALWAYS THINKS*

to an actual, not a wished for (proposed) change of psychological climate (perspective).

To really think in terms of the animal and of things as they are means to return such qualities as "cosmos" or "universe" to the real things themselves (here: to the world) as their "factual" property,[19] whereas here they are abstracted from actuality and thought of platonistically as *our* free-floating perspectives to be exchanged at will.

We are not "fully there" in the animal sense (p. 31), i.e. not in the actual world, as long as we think in terms of perspectives. We are there when (or to the extent that) we recognize what once was held to be a perspective to be the actual, present, hard-fact-like Gestalt o r truth of the phenomenon itself. This Gestalt, today the "universe," is the unity of the world's actual being *and* our seeing, in short: it is our actual *Weltbegegnung*.

Is the place we get to by side-slipping the three monsters really the same place we wanted to reach originally (namely through that very gate that they guard)? Are *they* fooled, or rather *we* ourselves? Take note: it is the monsters that are posted in front of the gate to the promised land by *our own* fantasy, our own way of experiencing the problem. Do the demons, if and when they actually appear to us, not demand payment in hard cash? "Denn Opfer verlangt der Himmlischen jedes. Wo aber eines versäumt ward, Nie hat es Gutes gebracht" ("For each of the gods demands sacrifices, But if one sacrifice was neglected, Never was it of advantage" Hölderlin). I have no choice as to which archetypes I serve. I have to attend to the situation as it actually is (affords, self-displays, itself).

We have to give an exhaustive answer. For only those problems that have been exhausted (which is the opposite of Hillman's "[Being or whatever] evaporates") will loosen their hold on us and can disappear, freeing the way for something new. Of course, the work on an exhaustive answer is dangerous. Hillman is right, the monsters are there. But a possible failure is no excuse. We have to try. The demons have to be met.

Does the idea of cosmos still "spare philosophy so much of its efforts," once it has become apparent that this idea, as beautiful a truth

---

[19] There is no conflict between this return and the one in the sense of epistrophé, because they are answers to different questions. The latter is concerned with the archetypal depth of a phenomenon; this return, by contrast, has to do with a very different question, that of "the human (timeless) mode of seeing" vs. "the actual world at a concrete moment."

as it may be, is nevertheless not the truth of our age? What good is a truth that is not ours? Does it become ours by our admiring or preaching it? If there is to be a shift, the full weight of history will have to be shifted. A real path has to be traveled. And that takes effort and time.

And: Is this side-slipping concordant with the "evermore profound and differentiated appreciation" of the phenomenon (that which presents itself)? The wish to avoid the monsters seems to me to be the very non-acknowledgment, obscuring and repression that on p. 29 is imputed to the sciences. But then, is there really a repression going on in the sciences, or do they not much rather very faithfully, law-abidingly, and animal-like trod along their path according to their kind? Their kind, however, happens to be one that in contrast to the cosmos idea leads to the step-by-step, ever more profound destruction of the natural world. They are not merely carnivorous, but naturavorous. Their eating away the naturalness of the world can easily be mistaken for a repression. But destruction or killing is not repression. It has a different purpose (telos): the psyche's killing of its own (and our) logical innocence (an innocence that Hillman, like Rousseau, et al., would here defend or rather *restore*, for in reality he has already lost it long ago).

11. CONCLUSION:
Hic Rhodos, hic salta

I said that a real path has to be traveled. This is a path not from here to there, "from universe to cosmos," but one further and further down into the here—to its ground, its end.

To return to the image of skin or fur. As humans we have the freedom to change our coats without dying. The animal that loses its fur is dead. But the level of our fur coats that we can change freely, effortlessly and without danger (the level of our "fashions," of *Frei-Zeit*) is not the one on which our real problem (the problem taken up by Hillman in this paper) is. The problem of the anima mundi involves our actual skin, the organ that is the meeting point of man and world, the symbol of our *Weltbegegnung* and *Weltumgang* (encounter and interaction with the world).

Why do we have to stick to the image? Is this only for methodological reasons, to be good phenomenologists? It is primarily because only those images or perspectives are worth talking about that are actual, actually ours, i.e., that, long before *we* stick to them, we *are* stuck with and stuck in as in our (psycho-)logical skin. And the remedy is not a change or shift or alternative ("allo"-pathy). It is at best like the snake's shedding of its skin—slow, itchy, maybe even painful, and in any case requiring lots of effort so as to (possibly) give room to a new skin from *underneath*, in the same old place.

The real pathology (the "universe") would have been the place to look for the cure, especially when the topic that the therapy is concerned about is the anima mundi, rather than merely some subjective attitude.

When King David had the idea of building a temple for the Lord, he sought the opinion of the theological expert, Nathan, to make sure this novel idea was all right. "Nathan said to the king, Go, do all that is in thine heart; for the Lord is with you." This is the *immediate* judgment of theological or religious common sense: as a matter of course, so the ordinary religious mind thinks, it must be pleasing to God to get a temple built for himself. Nathan supported what is obviously a pious project.—"But at night the word of the Lord came unto Nathan, saying, Go and tell my servant David, Thus saith the Lord, Shalt thou build me an house to dwell in? ... when thy days be fulfilled, ..., I will set up thy seed after thee, ..., He shall build an house for my name..." (2 Samuel 7). It turns out that the Lord was, after all, *not* with King David and with what was in his (and in Nathan's) heart. The undoubtedly well-meaning and pious wish is revealed to have merely been an ego wish, as we would put it today, and Nathan's first, immediate judgment ("the Lord is with you") as only his "day" opinion and as a subjective, human-all-too-human interpretation of what God wants. It was terribly naïve to think that the pious character alone of a project is already sufficient proof that it indeed comes from God, rather than from strictly human intentions. Jung was not so naïve. He was well aware of the possibility of a discrepancy between our pious intentions and the will of God ("They use the Word to protect themselves against the will of God" *CW* 18 § 1637. The church "serves as a fortress to protect us against God and his Spirit" *CW* 18 § 1534). However, Nathan was not totally sold on this his own "day" view (the assessment by the subjective mind), but opened himself also to the

SHALT THOU BUILD ME A HOUSE?

"night" view, the actual word of the Lord himself—in Jungian terms: to the view of the non-ego or the objective psyche. The fact that Nathan had *second* thoughts and overcame his *immediate* view about what is pious—shows that he *was* a theological expert, after all.

The psychological greatness of this story lies in the fact that within itself it establishes the psychological difference, the difference between the subjective and the objective psyche, and that it shows that the latter only comes about through the explicit negation of the former. The story first makes Nathan give his subjective opinion, and then forces him to go back to the king in order to revoke his former expertise. Nathan, and through him this story, pushes off from an initial ego assessment to the soul standpoint.

Much like Nathan, Hillman gives us the (psychologist's) expert opinion as to what kind of house, what kind of cosmology, the soul surely must want, and in what kind of house it surely must feel neglected, "utterly contingent" (p. 20) and repressed. It seems perfectly obvious to our human, well-meaning psychological view that the soul, as a matter of course, wants ensoulment and abhors the abstract and soulless "universe" of modern science and technology. This is *immediately* plausible. Who would disagree? But the point is that this is the subjective popular or "day" view about the soul's need. The wish to move "from universe to cosmos" stems from psychological common sense, from ordinary conventional ideas about the soul, from an ego prejudice about what the soul wants. *People's* opinion. It therefore is an instance of the very "humanism" (in Hillman's sense) that he rejected in *Re-Visioning Psychology* ("Archetypal Psychology Is Not a Humanism," p. 171). Just as apropos the Nathan story, we can say here, too, even if *mutatis mutandis*, that it is naïve to think that the soulful character of a project is by itself already sufficient proof that it comes from the objective psyche. The *anima semantics* of Hillman's program, the fact that this program has the *anima mundi* as its content and aim, does not guarantee that it is also animated by a truly psychological syntax. Indeed, does not the very fact alone that Hillman has a program (his own agenda)— rather than simply presenting a *theoria* in the old sense (his view of how things *are*)—reveal his piece as on the syntactical level being an ego project? *Du merkest Absicht, und du bist verstimmt* ("You sense the agenda and you become disgruntled" Goethe).

What is missing in Hillman's text is an equivalent to the second part of our Biblical story, "But at night the word of the Lord came unto Nathan, saying ..." From beginning to end Hillman remains sold on his immediate "day" view of the matter. Expressed in alchemical terms it is the view from the standpoint of the *unio naturalis*, of innocence (unwoundedness), immediacy. There is no internal critique, no second view, no retraction/revision of the "humanistic" day view and thus no pushing off from it to the soul standpoint, from the viewpoint of the *unio naturalis* to a *contra-naturam* one. But for psychology, this two-stage logic is indispensable. To be sure, the negation does not have to occur, as in our exemplary text, in the form of literally two consecutive positions. It is also possible, and even more refined, if there is only one position whose logical character, however, consists in its having in itself its having-pushed-off from the corresponding initial position and in its *existing* as the latter's negation—in other words, if the two-stage logic is no longer merely semantic but has become syntactical, the logical form of what is stated. Without (logical) woundedness—without incision into the immediacy of one's immediate views, without its negation—no psychology.

In personal psychology, one main aim of "individuation," according to Jung, is our liberation or emancipation from the suggestive power (*Suggestivgewalt*) of unconscious images (*CW* 7 § 269). Similarly, psychology itself, as a discipline, needs to liberate itself from the suggestive or seductive power that the whole "ensoulment" rhetoric has for the *unio naturalis* consciousness. It is *natural* or naïve (from Lat. *nativus*) consciousness that (mis)takes the (semantic) talk about soul and feeling and instinct, about myth and meaning and *anima mundi*, about symbol and image and the imaginal for *ipso facto* psychological discourse.

No doubt, the notions of "sensate particulars" and "palpable things" (ibid.), of "the sympathy of all things" (p. 23 and 30), "animal faith" (p. 24), "the soul's delight in tales" (p. 33), or generally the lofty talk of eros, *aisthesis*, mythic certainty, as well as the conception of *kosmos* as implying "sweet song" (p. 21) are beautiful ideas and tempting indeed. But psychology must not succumb to their sirenian allurement. It cannot afford to adopt these notions as its own aims and values. It must not turn particular *phenomena* into its own *categories*

SHALT THOU BUILD ME A HOUSE? 109

by which it judges the whole range of psychic phenomenology. If it did, it would be *dogmatic* and judgmental, having given absolute priority to certain elements from the phenomenology of the soul. Psychology would have turned into ideology and serve the *weltanschauliche* longings of the modern ego that is discontent with how the world is developing, and *we* would have become inflated. No, no. Jung was right to warn us against succumbing to the suggestive power of unconscious images or ideas, and "cosmos" and "animal faith," "aesthetics" and "ensoulment" are such unconscious ideas. Not that there would be anything wrong with all the beautiful notions mentioned. They all deserve attention. But they are merely particular contents or motifs to be studied by psychology in those cases where they actually occur in, and apply to, the life of the soul (the same as, for example, the motifs of the virgin birth, the solar hero, the great mother, the forbidden chamber, the puer, the anima). The fact that the motif of the virgin birth is a topic of psychology does not mean that psychology *believes* in virgin births. Likewise, that *kosmos* is a topic of psychology cannot mean for psychology to believe in it, just as psychology cannot conversely be sold on the idea of the universe either. *All* these ideas should never be raised from the phenomenal level to the status of psychology's own categories or guiding principles. As I said, that would be dogmatic, even a kind of idolization. Not even the anima (Lat. for "soul") can be psychology's guiding principle, because it, too, is only one particular form of manifestation of the soul at large, one of its moments.

It is not merely that dogmatism is in itself incompatible with psychology; it also has the inevitable consequence that it becomes partial. But psychology must not take sides. It must not put restraints on how the soul is allowed to show itself. No a priori fixing of what is included and what is excluded from the definition of soul. No binary opposition such as "pro cosmos, contra universe." For a real psychology, "cosmos" is as good as "universe," the classical anima as good as modern technology and science, Orpheus as good as Hercules, just as for a natural scientist, say a biologist, a weed is as good as a rose, a rhinoceros as a gazelle. What alone counts for the psychologist in this regard is (a) whether an idea is psychically *real* in general, (b) to what degree it is indeed real in a given *actual situation*, and (c) *what particular* soul aspect (soul logos), soul status, soul truth, or soul potential is expressed in it.

Isn't it that we have to listen to the actual phenomenology of the soul itself—the soul in the real—as the only authority, rather than to the personal opinions of psychologists? Do we not merely have to perceive, in the sense of "scrupulous observation" (p. 26), *which* kind of house the soul *has actually* built for itself today and what is psychologically right or wrong today? Isn't the Real the locus from which "the word of the Soul comes to us"—*provided*, of course, that we are willing to leave the day standpoint behind and listen to the Real truly "at night," that is, seeing through its "day" appearance to its "night" aspect, "night" truth? The true "expert opinion" is already there (perfect tense): in our actual relation to the world, but of course only *for* the "nocturnal"[20]—psychological— standpoint. And true psychology is always *theoretical* in the sense of "looking backwards" to what already has manifested. It is merely reflecting, not designing projects and programs. No plans, no wishing and wanting.

And therefore: Is it we who have to build a house for soul? Are we to be its architects? Or isn't it that the soul builds its own house in and through us, and that this building, otherwise called soul-making (the soul's own making of itself), is going on all the time, even at the time of "universe" and in the manner of soulless science, technology, and advanced capitalism? *So that we can never fall out of soul?*

Of course, Hillman expressly stated that he has "torn down the very idea of home and the hope that would build one" (p. 30). But this tearing down occurs in the service of *his* search for a cosmology for soul. A non-home is as much a variety of home as the anti-hero is one type of hero. Tearing down the very idea of home is the mode of building this non-home for soul called "cosmos." But then the soul could ask, "Shalt thou build me a (non-)house to dwell in? Shalt thou tear down the idea of home to build me a cosmology supposedly better for me?" After all, the Lord in the David-Nathan story didn't insist on staying in tent and tabernacle. He did want a firm home. Why couldn't the soul too have wanted to move out of its previous dwelling place, the tent of eachness and immediacy, into a solid home, an overall theory, the "universe"?

---

[20] We could also say "underworldly," or "contra-naturam," "Mercurial," "absolute-negative."

SHALT THOU BUILD ME A HOUSE? 111

Once this has come home to us, we will see ourselves forced to admit that what is wrong, soulless, pathological does not present a principle wholly other, outside and contrary to soul. The "universe" view *with* its (admitted) soullessness is an event within soul, an instance of soul-making. It is not due to a repression that must be lifted, but is the objective psyche's legitimate self-expression, her own active imagination—one, however, in which the soul chose to wrong and hurt the soul, just as Pseudo-Demokritos said, "Nature delights in nature; nature subdues nature; nature rules over nature." The contra-naturam move is itself an inner necessity of what the alchemists called nature. Soul or nature in this sense is all-comprehensive.

We are surrounded by psyche on *all* sides, said Jung. If this is so, how could our reality ever be truly not soul? Soul is inescapable. Sophocles in his *Trachinian Women* (last line) said something similar in the terms of his time and with respect to the general divine lawful order of the world: "and [there is] nothing of all this that is not Zeus." Hegel expressed the same idea again in a different language when he said, "... was wirklich ist, das ist vernünftig" (Preface to *Grundlinien der Philosophie des Rechts*). Jung's dictum means that out of everything we see, soul is looking at us. Not: "only in this eachness does soul exist" (p. 30). Who are we to say? Who are we to put restraints on the soul's liberty to show itself as it pleases, who to limit the scope and depth of its logos (Heraclitus)? Can we pin down soul to one definition of itself? Even the soulless universe of the modern philosophers, scientists and theologians is not outside soul, but a manifestation of it. It is the home that the soul, and no one else, laboriously built for herself during the last few millennia.

No dualism anymore, no Fall from truth to perversion, but a historical change ("Gestaltwandel," metamorphosis) *of* the soul's truth from one of its manifestations to another, from tent to solid temple, from cosmos to universe. And instead of that Fall, *archetypal psychology's* fall from the platonistic realm of atemporal archetypal ideas (in the sense of that "polytheism" that is imagined like a kind of lofty supermarket for 'Gods' and perspectives, all neatly lined up on the shelves, from which to choose the one that is most to one's liking) down to earth and into temporality. Archetypal perspectives *have their Time.* They are bound to (are the property of) a concrete historical situation. Now "cosmos" and "universe" are recognized to be in a diachronic relationship, separated by a historical rupture between distinct stages of consciousness (actual modes of being in and relating to the world): Very different archetypal "perspectives" prevail in the age of man as physicist than in the age of man as big-game hunter or of man as agriculturalist.

Psychological polytheism of perspectives, by placing cosmos and universe and all the other principles side by side as so many options, accounts for and takes care of the conflicts between our different needs as well as between those needs and our present-day reality. It organizes all differences as synchronic, parallel possibilities under the same roof (cf. Camillo's Memory Theater) and thus harmonizes them, protecting us from the pain of feeling the longing for something that we have lost and are separated from by a gulf, the gulf of diachronic change and of our particular place in history. This polytheism is thus a way to stabilize consciousness in its present stage by immunizing us from the contradictions inherent in our real situation. Since polytheism paradoxically allows us to retain the (monotheistic) belief in the single roof, the idea of "house" (= stage of consciousness) does not have to fall apart into "many houses," many fundamentally different Memory Theaters, most of which are decidedly not ours and inaccessible (and thus also irrelevant) to us, because they are the houses, or stages of consciousness, of other ages and other peoples. By presenting us with limitless possibilities and in the paper I am responding to especially with "cosmos" as options for us, it offers ways to at least seemingly, namely nostalgically, satisfy soul needs that otherwise would remain unfulfilled. They would have to be unmitigatingly suffered as both *indispensable* for the soul and yet *incompatible* with the actual stage of consciousness we are in. This contradiction would tend to tear consciousness apart and thus explode it, forcing it onto a radically new level—if, through the palliative of free-floating options, the conflict between the indispensibility and the incompatibility were not superficially reconciled and if the soul needs were not defused of their "metaphysical" claim to *actuality*. Psychological polytheism a compromise formation?

We may ask why nature would want to conquer nature, why soul would want to turn against herself, even violate herself. If she actually does want to do this, the reason would have to be, I suppose, that, as implied by Demokritos, there is an inherent need in the soul to kill

SHALT THOU BUILD ME A HOUSE?

her own innocence, to break her own pleroma, to stop her "sweet song" (p. 21), to intercept her direct self-display, and, imposing continence on herself, to abstain from her "passionate participation" (p. 29).[21] No more immediacy, no more direct presence, no more eachness. Quoth the raven: "Nevermore." Now psyche "displays" itself as its own Other and confronts itself from outside itself (today even literally: from satellites in outer space)—without, however, truly leaving itself.

It follows that the presenting complaint with which Hillman begins his paper is not the soul's own complaint, as he would have it, or it is only the complaint of one soul person in us, the nostalgic, antiquarian (*ewiggestrige*) soul, not of the soul that is so to speak "state of the art,"[22] at the forefront of life. The latter engages in science, technology and industry, in advertising, the media, artificial materials (plastics, e.g.), in short: in an abstract and utterly mediated relation to the world (via all kinds of devices: telescopes, microscopes, computers, radar...), it enjoys leaving the earth for outer space, enjoys overcoming nature. To conquer herself, this is what the soul wants today. We (i.e., the person in us that stays bound to what once was) may not like it (just as Honecker, a true *Ewiggestriger* ['die-hard old reactionary'], doesn't like it that his people don't want his kind of socialism), but that is not the question. The question is: what do the people, what does the soul actually want (in contrast to: what *should* they / it want[23])?

The Hillman who lets the soul pronounce this kind of presenting complaint and is informed by a dualistic vision of universe versus cosmos is not the same as the one who, to mention just one example, once said, "Technology is cursed by our mechanical idea of it. ... Technical things are neither silent, obedient slaves, nor mere manufactured products of other machines... They are concrete images of animation, locations of the hylic anima..."[24] The latter Hillman wouldn't have had to reject the "universe" as soulless (therefore no need

---

[21] In my Eranos 1988 paper (see footnote 13 above) I presented this inherent tension within the soul as that between the *soul as anima* [= innocence, pleroma; first phrase in Demokritos' dictum] and the *soul as animus* violating the anima [second phrase in Demokritos' dictum]. This tension is, however, not just a self-laceration on the part of the soul, but occurs within and for the sake of the *soul as syzygy* of anima and animus [alluded to in the third part of Demokritos' dictum].

[22] Art here = the *ars* of the alchemical opus.

[23] "Should" points to the program *we* assign to the soul, our agenda.

[24] J. Hillman, "The Imagination of Air and the Collapse of Alchemy", *Eranos 50-*

114   *THE SOUL ALWAYS THINKS*

for the soul to voice its presenting complaint[25]), but he could have appreciated it as a manifestation of the anima.[26] With my critique I mobilize Hillman against Hillman.

But if we can never fall out of soul and have to accept what she built for herself, what about therapy? For of course, the soul does want therapy. It is not enough that things simply are and continue the way they are. But therapy does not have to be correction, *our* setting right (moving from a wrong archetypal perspective to the right one). It can be the alchemical work with the prima materia as it is actually given. In our context therapy can mean no more and no less than, first, the scrupulous observation of what kind of house the psyche actually built for itself in our concrete situation, second, the wholehearted acknowledgment of this house *as the soul's own house*, and, third, the ever more profound and differentiated appreciation of this house as such, i.e., the full comprehension of its logic with all its inherent contradictions. This, too, would require a "shift" of perspective. But here it wouldn't be we who shift from one to the other perspective, and perspectives wouldn't be modes of seeing or tools that we choose according to our purposes. It would be a "shift" that befalls us and that we would have to suffer through as the collapse of our entire "world" (stage of consciousness). With this in mind, I believe we can safely say the following:

What is psychologically wrong with "universe" is not that it "allows the soul only a minuscule and utterly contingent place" (p. 20). Rather, "universe" is cursed by our soulless interpretation of it: by our refusal to uncompromisingly acknowledge and appreciate the *soulless* "universe" as the modern *soul's* authentic home.

1981, p. 327. Similarly he wrote another time: "Science is not soulless at all. ... For science, also, is a field of soul-making provided we do not take it literally on its own terms." (*Re-Visioning Psychology*, p. 169). To take science or the universe "literally on its own terms" would be what I called above the day perspective, the conventional common sense view of it.

[25] It also needs to be noted that Hillman does not show in any way that it is really the soul who is complaining. Rather than really "allowing soul a voice" (p. 17), he is the one who is speaking. He merely puts his own discontents (as well as those of many contemporaries) concerning modern civilization and science into the mouth of the soul. He uses (not the soul, but) the fantasy of "the soul" as his front.

[26] Of course I would not use the term anima here. Technology has moved out of the sphere of the (soul as) anima, let alone a "hylic anima," but not out of the soul (as syzygy) altogether, which is the main point here. See my Syzygy paper referred to above.

SHALT THOU BUILD ME A HOUSE?

In sticking to "universe," we do not have to undialectically and altogether dismiss Hillman's vision of an animalized cosmology for soul. To the contrary, what I had to say here proceeded from the admission that the universe idea wrongs the soul; I have made use of the animal perspective throughout this paper, firmly basing my argument on it. And only because I did so, did I have to reject Hillman's view, for, as I showed, by staying with the cosmos / animal perspective one cannot be true to it. It contradicts and undermines itself. To be really true to it means to give it up, to leave it behind as a thing of the "past." We do justice to the message of the animal *only* if we stick to the "shine in the display" of what *displays* itself today: the "universe"—even if this is the display of an anti-animal (universal, totally mediated) situation; and it is precisely a betrayal of animalizing to want to realize it directly, naively. It is no longer as simple as that. The world, and with it the animal, have become fundamentally different. What I termed the change *of* truth from one of its manifestations to another could also be described as a metamorphosis *of* the "animal" *from* 'immediacy' and 'eachness' *to* 'mediation' and 'universality': from natural[27] animal to contra naturam animal.

Why the refusal to acknowledge the (semantically) soulless "universe" as (syntactically) the modern soul's authentic home? Do we fear to suffer the Contradiction? The loss of the ego's sanity of mind? The violation of our logical innocence, our *unio naturalis* status? The abyss of a dialectical logic? The death of the white soul, i.e., of our pure, "nice" conception of it?

Cosmology for Soul? It is already there. It is our actual cosmology, provided that we own it *as* the soul's.

POSTSCRIPT 2008
What is psychologically at stake with the category of 'Time'?

Jungian psychology is, among other things, characterized by the notion of the objective psyche, i.e., the not-subjective psyche. It is not enough for psychology to talk about the objective psychic, to have

---

[27] "Natural" here is of course not the equivalent of "biological" (nature in the abstract sense of modern science or "the physical in the matter" in the sense of alchemy). Rather it refers to the mode of experiencing the animal and the world that came "naturally" to man, a mode in which the imaginal or mythical dimension of the world were included.

and entertain this notion as a semantic content of its teachings. The inner form of that consciousness that entertains this content must correspond to what the content is about and, to put it the other way around, the essence of the content in question must have come home to the very constitution of consciousness. Only if the notion of the objective psyche is also reflected in the very structure or logical form of psychology itself has this notion become a truly psychological one. This is where historical Time comes in. The awareness in psychology of Time as something essential to reckon with is, as it were, the placeholder or representation within the theoretical framework of psychology (or within the logical form of psychological consciousness) of the *idea* of the objective psyche. It is the sense of Time that grants the objective psyche its objectivity. If Time is given a place in the way psychological thought is set up then the semantic notion of the objective psyche has also become syntactical. The form of consciousness then backs up what it is talking about, preventing the latter from being merely maybe beautiful, but empty words. If Time as an essential category or factor to pay tribute to in psychology is scorned in psychology, then this psychology does not really within itself allow for the objectivity of the objective psyche that it may nevertheless proclaim. But this is putting it too mildly. We must rather say, then the form or syntax of consciousness contradicts the objectivity of the objective psyche even while this consciousness may semantically insist on the idea of the objective psyche: the structure of hypocrisy.

"The imaginal," no matter how disturbing or painful particular images may semantically be for the subject, syntactically is always subject-syntonic. Any image that comes to us is automatically *our* image, and we as subject are immediately absorbed into the sphere of this image. Such is the might of the "suggestive power" of images and of the logical character of the imaginal. The imagination, if it is conceived as timeless, creates a syntactically harmonious, concordant, uniform space with no real otherness, a space of innocence (logical unwoundedness); expressed in negative terms, the imaginal enwraps us in a bubble. Time, by contrast, forces an awareness of what is outside and independent of this bubble. A true non-ego. It is Time alone that provides for us Hillman's "Facts: hard, real, naked, true" in a psychological sense or Jung's "the psychic in its objectivity, hard as

SHALT THOU BUILD ME A HOUSE? 117

granite and heavy as lead" (*CW* 17 § 303, transl. modified). Time implies that there can be images or truths that are *not* ours, that truly belong to *other* ages and peoples and that for that reason can possibly also become *syntactically* disturbing, because they relativize ourselves and our truths, our form of consciousness.

A second aspect of what Time brings to psychology is Necessity, Ananke, as discussed above. The soul as objective psyche has its own time or rather times in the plural. So I am not free to imagine what I like. I cannot simply chose images that belong to other ages or cultures. Not all images—although I can certainly *abstractly* entertain them in my mind—are *psychologically* available to me. My time gives me, prescribes to me, those images and that truth that are mine, that I have to live in. I am not the subject and producing agent of the imagination; *we* do not imagine (imagine in the sense of the *imaginatio vera*), the objective soul does it for us, and *historical time is nothing else but the process or opus of the objective soul's ongoing imagining.* "... without history there can be no psychology, and certainly no psychology of the unconscious" (*MDR* pp. 205f.). Therefore the imaginal, provided it is understood as *imaginatio vera*, does not liberate us from Time in the sense of that "anything goes" that Hillman comes up with[28] when he feels cornered by my insistence on history, or in the sense of that "[e]scape from temporal determinism" that he hails in his open letter to a Brazilian group of seminar participants.[29] I have to look and see, and allow myself to be taught, *what* the objective psyche's real fantasies and truth are into which I have been placed. No choice. No simple "shift in vision" that "makes for a whole new ball game."[30] Only—if anything constructive at all—a better, clearer, more deepened awareness and understanding of what my time's objective vision is and how and why it evolved from what preceded it.

---

[28] See James Hillman, "Hegel, Giegerich and the U.S.A.," in: *Spring 1988*, pp. 177–180, here p. 180.
[29] James Hillman, "Divergences. *A propos* of a Brazilian Seminar on Giegerich/ Hillman – Organized by Marcus Quintaes," 2008.
[30] "Hegel, Giegerich and the U.S.A.," *op. cit.*, p. 179.

CHAPTER FIVE

The Dignity of Thought
In Defence of the Phenomenon of Philosophical Thought

Tougas' paper in the last issue of *Harvest* on "Taking Women Philosophers Seriously"[1] is not at all written in a polemical style nor does it appear to be an attack on anything. Its character and purpose is rather to *plead* for something, such as for the personal presence of the philosopher in his thought, for instilling thought with love and a sense of forgiveness, and her well-meaning motivation is "to teach these guys" [i.e., male philosophers as well as psychologists who call themselves "post-Jungian archetypal"]. She asks, "If we love them, how can we help them?" It will be the task of the present paper to show that what she wrote nevertheless amounts to a perhaps unwitting attack on thought. My own motivation is neither as altruistic nor as missionary as hers in that I would want to help and teach *her*. My concern is to restore a sense of respect for the dignity of thought proper.

THE ABSTRACT CONCEPTION OF THOUGHT

"What I and women philosophers I know ... give is not 'better abstraction' or 'a more correct metaphysical system,' but rather erotic

---

[1] Cecile T. Tougas, "Taking Women Philosophers Seriously", in: *Harvest. Journal for Jungian Studies*, vol. 42, no. 2, 1996, pp. 35–42.

relation, a feeling sense that demands that abstract concepts be connected to the fullness of the experience founding them. We women know that we must always feel what we say as we are saying them" (p. 40f.). There is a fatal flaw in these sentences. This flaw is not the idea that there has to be an erotic relation and that thought needs to be connected to the fullness of the experience in which it is rooted. That can be accepted. The flaw is that she does not say what *specific* kind of erotic relation has to be present for thought to be thought and what the nature of the specific experience of a thinker is (and has to be) if it is to qualify as thought proper. To her, psychologists of the archetypal school "are playing with images or concepts as a substitute for engaging in personal erotic relation with real people" (p. 40). So the erotic relation that she and women philosophers add to philosophy is personal relation with real people. Correspondingly, the fullness of the experience she has in mind has to do with one's personal suffering in life, such as from a divorce; "the ideal must be intimate, closely felt, and *mixed with the ordinary necessities of life*" (p. 41, my emphasis).

Oscar Wilde once said, "Only superficial people insist on looking beneath the surface." In a similar way we could formulate, "Only people who do not know the experience of real thought imagine (not *think!*) thought as something that *needs* to be connected to the fullness of experience, *needs* to be supplemented by feelings and by erotic relation to real people." Why are people who insist on looking beneath the surface superficial? Because they cannot see the depth that is right there in the surface itself inasmuch as *their* seeing (not the surface) lacks the necessary depth. By the same token, the idea that thought is wanting, that it needs something else which must be "given" or supplied to it, is testimony to the fact that one is operating with an abstract, impoverished idea of thought. Thought is reduced to "abstract thought," it is "nothing but" thought. It is only because one starts out with a deficient idea of thought, that one feels (correctly) that it is insufficient and thus needs to be connected to real life, which has to be sought outside of thought (in the necessities of ordinary life, in one's personal feelings, in relations with real people). It cannot be within this kind of thought, which, by definition, is dead.

Thus this impoverishment of thought is not thought's fault, but the fault of one's own abstract conception and one's ignorance about what thought is. It amounts to a defamation to charge the

THE DIGNITY OF THOUGHT

archetypalists among the Jungians with "playing with images or concepts as a substitute for engaging in personal erotic relation with real people." I am not thinking here of a defamation of the character of those persons (even though it may entail that, too), but of a defamation of thought itself. Thought is implied to be nothing but a substitute for something else that is the real thing. What a defamation, too, of the thought of philosophers, if this thought is claimed not to be connected to the fullness of the experience founding it and to be lacking in feeling and erotic relation! Thought (and of course I am talking only about real thought, the thought of true thinkers, not of what colloquially might also go under the name of thought), *thought has everything it needs within itself.* It needs nothing that would have to be supplied to it from outside to make it complete or to give it life. All it needs to come to life (and to *also* unfold the wealth of feeling and eros invested in it), is a thinking reader, someone who has access to the level of thought.

Tougas is of course right in demanding that thought be connected to the fullness of the experience founding it. But the fatal flaw in her argumentation is that she does not realize that the experience in question here has to be a very specific one in order for what results from it to be thought in the first place: Needless to say, it has to be a *philosophical* experience from the outset, the experience *of thought,* a *thinker's* experience, not just any other, ordinary life experience, like that of a divorce or how one's "2-year-old son used to wake up in the night, crying and gnashing his teeth" (p. 42), experiences that anybody (a carpenter, a businessman, a politician, a journalist) might have, too. Such experiences do not qualify as ones that could found thought in the first place. They are extraneous to it and are thus only disturbing. Thought, just like poetry, painting, music, is complete in itself. It has its own dignity because it is founded in itself, in the thought experience. And Tougas' views amount to an attack on thought because they attempt to destroy the dignity of thought as a figure of life in its own right, and because she tries to replace it with a reductive conception of thought as heteronomously founded in experiences alien to it.

Similarly, the eros needed for thought must be *philosophical* eros from the outset, an "erotic relation" to the matter of thought, *if* the phenomenon of thought is to exist at all. No question, an erotic relation to real people is a fine thing. Who would want to miss it? But it is neither sufficient to create thought, nor relevant to thought. It is a different figure of life (one which has a dignity of its own). By mixing the two figures, both lose. Thought appears as abstract and in need of supplementing, and the erotic relation to a friend can probably also not be allowed to be just what it is. Just like thought itself, a love relation, *as* that which it is, could be one mode to experience the absolute; the idea behind connecting it with philosophical thought, however, might imply, according to the thinking prevailing in Tougas' article, that it needs to be "philosophically" ennobled, which to my mind would be a way of putting it down. It is not in need of any such ennoblement, being complete and perfect in itself. It also (just like thought) has everything it needs within itself, its own spirituality, too (which is even true for a purely *sexual* relation).

What Tougas misses in thought is all there from the beginning (provided we are really talking about thought proper). Thought has its own inherent passion. But of course, this passion is a passion precisely *for* the internal *logical* life of concepts, for "the cold march of necessity of [or: inherent in] the subject matter itself" (Hegel), not an ordinary life passion for other things or for people. How could it be thought if it were otherwise? Whoever is incapable of feeling the passion and sensing the intense life inherent in the seemingly cold and abstract thought of Aristotle, Descartes, Kant, to mention only a few truly rigorous thinkers, has simply never entered the land of philosophy. He has no inkling of what thought is (maybe reducing it formalistically to "making logical distinctions" or having opinions and being able to support them by arguments[2]). He has not been reached and touched by the reality called thought. He is, as it were, colour-blind or like someone who can appreciate works of art only as capital investment, or if they are "true copies" of nature. He imagines thought from outside of thought.

Tougas' thinking is dissociated, or dissociating, thinking. She operates within a split: abstract concepts on the one side, feelings and eros on the other side. The great mission, and feat, of what she calls "women philosophers" is supposed to be to glue the two together

---

[2] Logical distinctions, opinions and argumentation are not the *differentia specifica* of thought (in the sense of philosophical thought). They are also indispensable in all sciences and even in everyday practical life. We could not even survive on a very basic level without making logical distinctions.

THE DIGNITY OF THOUGHT 123

"again" and thereby rescue the poor male philosophers who are helplessly lost in abstractions. But this idea that there are two separate halves that need to be conjoined is what splits them up in the first place. This idea *is* the attack on thought, its (unwitting) destruction, inasmuch as it *violates thought's intactness*. It deprives it of its integrity, its innate wholeness. This view condemns thought to death: to be lifeless, abstract, a corpse, and sets up woman as the creator God, secondarily blowing life into the primarily dead body of thought. But life does not come from outside. You can blow as much as you want. Life comes from within, through the self-organization of "dead matter," as even biology begins to realize. All you do when bringing in to thought your own subjectivity, personal feelings, and erotic relations, is to pour a soup of sentiments over the still lifeless concepts, thereby for the unthinking public maybe disguising their lifelessness, but for anyone who *thinks*, making all the more painfully and embarrassingly aware of it. It is like someone who believes that lyrical poems need to be illustrated by drawings or photographs as a crutch in order for their images to come alive for us, and who ipso facto denies the inherent life and self-sufficiency of the poetic image.

The phrase "the abstractness of thought" has two very different meanings that need to be kept apart. Thought as such is abstract in a first sense in that it is constituted by the abstraction or divorce from ordinary life, personal feelings, "natural" conceptions of the common sense mentality. This is what makes all thought, as it were, ghostly by comparison with the experience of ordinary life (a fact which, psychologically speaking, is due to the animus, who first of all is a killer[3]). That is its distinction. Thinking, reflection owe their existence to a negation. Alchemically speaking, they are an *opus contra naturam*. They presuppose a "death": the dissolution of the *unio naturalis*, and take place on the radically new level of the *unio mentalis*.

Now I come to the second sense of "abstract thought." If a particular instance of thought is abstract in this sense, this is a *flaw* or *shortcoming*, and no longer the distinction constitutive for *all* thought. The best example for abstract thought is mathematical thought or the thoughts of formal logic. Scientific thought is also essentially abstract, inasmuch as it has the reality of what it is *about* outside of itself. All theorizing

---

[3] W. Giegerich, *Animus-Psychologie*, Frankfurt a.M. et al. (Peter Lang) 1994.

about ... is abstract. Especially so are all "ego concoctions." Thought proper, by contrast, such as the thought of great philosophers, is always concrete and not abstract in the second sense, even though, of course, it is abstract in the first sense. Thought is concrete because it contains the fullness of life and comprises reality within itself. It is the *comprehension* of the Real, the bringing to light of the inner logic of the Real. The second sense abstractness (that *some* thought has) can, in addition to the aforementioned examples, also come about when one splits thought apart, cutting it off from its rootedness in the *Concept* of the Real and from its *own internal* logical life, thereby alienating it from itself and consequently trying to found it instead in the experience of one's personal ordinary life in order to compensate for its self-created abstractness. This is the subjugation of thought under the personal. It has been imperialistically deprived of its autonomy and sovereignty. We can say, the problem of thought is thus not *that* it is abstract in sense one, but *if* it is abstract, in sense two.

"Metaphysics cannot create what is already there" (p. 41). This is either a triviality expressing the experience of the common sense personality, in which case it is not a philosophical statement, or it is a highly problematic assertion put down dogmatically and thus thoughtlessly, in which case it is also not philosophical. It is not even an abstract thought, but just an opinion. I merely mention the idea of the "social construction of reality" or Hölderlin's idea, so important for Heidegger, "*Was bleibet aber stiften die Dichter*" (What is lasting is founded by the poets), or Jung's idea of consciousness as the second *creator of the world* in order to point to the kind of questions that come up once the level of common sense experience has been left and the level of thought has been reached.

Thought is not everybody's cup of tea, nor does it have to be either. Not everybody must be truly touched by the experience and reality of thought. Conversely, there is nothing wrong with being predominantly interested in one's subjectivity, in personal erotic relations with real people and, e.g., in looking at life "from mother's point of view" (p. 40). All this is an interest or project in its own right. But such a project is not the project of "thought" or "philosophy." To confound these two distinct and incompatible projects is unacceptable.

Recently I read a newspaper article about a school in Oakland, California, where the predominantly black students were consistently

THE DIGNITY OF THOUGHT

extremely poor in English because they are used to speaking what is now sometimes called "ebonics" (from "ebony" and "phonics"), the street language of black neighbourhoods. The school board tried to solve the problem by simply making ebonics the accepted standard. If they had succeeded, all students would suddenly have good grades in English. This reminds me of Tougas' project. She wants to retain a connection to ordinary life feelings, and yet wants this (in itself legitimate) interest to be taken seriously as a *philosophical* interest. In trying to convert her male philosopher friend to her views and to "teach" all the other thinkers her good news, she even goes beyond what that school board did. She tries, as it were, to make every student in every school nationwide speak ebonics in their English courses, and thus to redefine the notion of English in terms of ebonics.

Again, I am not trying to put down ordinary life experience and also not ebonics. As a living language, ebonics has its own dignity. But it is different from proper English.

For the Oakland students, there are two distinct spheres, the street (or home) and school. Each sphere has its own separate language. They have to know *when and where* to speak the one, and when and where to speak the other. It seems to me that Tougas' scheme does not allow for a similar distinction. It does not provide thought, on the one hand, and personal erotic relations or subjective feelings on the other hand, each with its own when and where. She offers only one single sphere in which both concerns have to find their place as immediately connected. It all has to happen at once. She fights discontinuity and insists on undisturbed unity. This takes us to our next section.

MODERN SUBJECTIVISM

This is a more psychological issue. "Who" is the subject of thought proper? When our author writes to her male philosopher friend that "Not having your personal presence in your paper disturbs me greatly"(p. 41), she not only insists on an unbroken continuity from the personal to thought and on a monism of space or place, as we indicated in the last paragraph, she also, I would think, identifies all subjectivity with what we call the ego. It is the ordinary ego personality speaking when she says, "We women know that we must always feel what we say as we are saying it" (p. 41). The ego pushes to the foreground. "We, we." But is thinking in the sense of philosophical

126   THE SOUL ALWAYS THINKS

thought an ego activity? Or is not the subject of thought a non-ego, a non-I? Is real thought not much greater and bigger than the person of the thinker? Does real thought not *happen* to the thinker (often fatefully so) so that when expressed it could well be that it cannot be immediately felt and adequately understood by him or her? Does thought not have its own inherent subjectivity, its inner necessity and dynamics, as attested to by Hegel's formulation quoted above concerning the "cold march of necessity of the subject matter itself"?

All this seems to be anathema to our author. She wants both to be taken seriously as a philosopher and yet hold on to the unbroken continuity of her conventional personal ego. Her piece as a whole is one extended attempt at a preservation or rescue of the sense of "ordinary personal identity" *as* the exclusive identity, which is threatened, it seems, by any philosophical thought, because real thought indeed does not support this sense of ego-identity. Thought is based on the experience of a discontinuity. But here, there is no room for alterity, for what Jung termed the collision with the non-I or the "objective psyche" (to which true thought, as a product of the soul, belongs). Our author wants to hold thought down in the familiar sphere of the ego-personality and its commonplace, human, all-too-human experience. This is why she reproaches archetypalist thinkers saying, "They all forget that in the beginning they were infants, born of women..." (p. 40) But is the real thinker of the thought born of woman? Does he, *inasmuch* as he is thinker and not a private individual, have his *beginning* (his *arché*) in the infancy of the human person that he of course also is? Jung at least was able to entertain the idea that we humans are not only autochthonous, earthborn (and this includes mother-born) *animalia*, but as twice-born are rooted in the Godhead, in spirit, just as one of his prime therapeutic concerns was that one learn to *detach* oneself from one's ideas and images, de-identify oneself from them, so as to be able to take a stand *objectively vis-à-vis* them. No immediacy. *Distance* from oneself. Awareness of the non-I and of the *autonomous* subjectivity of the mind's products.[4] This is what Jung had in mind, whom Tougas, after all, seems to accept as an authority.

---

[4] In the same issue of *Harvest* immediately preceding Tougas' article Greg Mogenson reminded us, in his intelligent "Re-constructing Jung," of the importance of discontinuity and the "objectification of impersonal images" for Jung ("not signs of human relationship, but autonomous symbols of an unknowable, unconscious power," p. 32).

THE DIGNITY OF THOUGHT

Tougas assentingly quotes Victor Hugo, "The ideal must be breathable, drinkable, and eatable by the human spirit" (p. 41). Hugo has "*à l'esprit humain.*" Tougas ignores completely that this very quotation that she uses as an authority contains a non-I: *esprit.* Is she as ego personality identical with the *esprit humain*? She uses Hugo's statement as if it had only read "the ideal must be breathable, drinkable, and eatable," period. What this other subjectivity is *to whom* the ideal is supposed to be breathable and eatable and how it relates to the conventional ego-personality is of absolutely no interest to her.

Is a medieval altar-piece in any way wanting as a work of art if in it we do not feel the personal presence of the painter and his private life situation at the time of painting it? We cannot tell from the painting whether he was happily married or had just had a terrible marriage crisis, whether he had a 2-year-old son waking up at night or whether he was in grief on account of a death in the family. Do we have to be greatly disturbed by our not being able to sense his personal presence? We may not even know his name, and yet his work may be perfect. It does not need the personal presence of the painter. Should not the same apply to a work of thought?

A thinker has a job to do. His virtue is his capacity to abandon himself to the inner necessities of his thought, indeed, to disappear as much as possible in it, so that the living truth and depth of the thought itself as an "objective," autonomous reality may shine forth. Even a thinker who in fact put his own person as an "I" into the foreground, Nietzsche with his *Ecce homo*, did not *immediately* and *spontaneously* talk about his *private* life and feelings. The "I" in chapters like "Why I am so wise" is an already mediated, reflected I, an I that has, having gone through a negation, been incorporated into the abstract realm of philosophical thought.

This self-abandoning dedication to the matter of thought and this voluntary submission of the person to serving the subject matter itself is an expression of the philosophical eros. Is the insistence on one's personal presence in thought not a sign of self-centeredness? Of course not so much a personal self-centeredness (as a character trait), but rather the general *ideological program* of self-centeredness as such, the counter-program to philosophical love, the love of and for thought in its abstractness?

128   THE SOUL ALWAYS THINKS

In *The Return of the Native*, Thomas Hardy wrote, "A traditional pastime is to be distinguished from a mere revival in no more striking feature than in this, that while in the revival all is excitement and fervour, the survival is carried on with a stolidity and absence of stir which sets one wondering why a thing that is done so perfunctorily should be kept up at all. Like Balaam and other unwilling prophets, the agents seem moved by an inner compulsion to say and do their allotted parts whether they will or no. This unweeting manner of performance is the true ring by which, in this refurbishing age, a fossilized survival may be known from a spurious reproduction."[5] *Mutatis mutandis* this is also the true ring by which authentic thought may be known from displays of modern subjectivism with its excited emotionalism and spontaneity cult. What Hardy said does not, as he seems to imply, only characterize "fossilized survivals." It is the character of all genuine ritual, which never had been emotional, but had been sober and matter-of-fact from the outset. Those who perform a ritual are in service to something that requires to be done. They don't "express *themselves, their* own feelings." As persons, they are not important. They often even disappear behind a mask, allowing some other person, a god, a spirit, to take over. They are important only to the extent that they have a job to do: to perform the ritual, to make it possible for *its* inherent truth to appear. The inner compulsion that seems to move them does not come from their own interior or subjective drives, it is the inner ("objective") necessity of the ritual itself binding them. Rituals, as long as they are intact and have not been reassigned to serve either one's desire for personal self-gratification or as emotional, spiritual entertainment of tourists, do not have to be subjectively understood and felt. They have to be *performed*, and correctly so. Thought follows the same laws.

In concluding I want to return to the question of *when and where* what belongs. "But thou, when thou prayest, enter into thy closet, and when thou hast shut thy door, pray to the Father which is in secret" (Matt. 6:6). There is a legitimate place for the expression of one's "*feelings* of sorrow and grief" (p. 42) as well as for all other personal feelings and private affairs. This place, I feel, is the privacy of "one's

---

[5] Thomas Hardy, *The Return of the Native*, Harmondsworth (Penguin Books) 1978, p. 178.

THE DIGNITY OF THOUGHT 129

closet" *or* the privacy of one's relation to intimate friends, loved ones, family, analyst, priest.[6] Maybe I am very old-fashioned; in this day and age the very idea of privacy is of course being destroyed in the media and through the avid support of the public (intrusive yellow journalism, reality TV, public confessions on TV about intimate aspects of a person's life and so on). Nevertheless, it offends my sense of propriety and of style if, in a *work* of thought (which as thought by its very nature belongs to the public domain, to *l'esprit humain*) or in a *presentation* (or publication) before a general audience (an audience consisting largely of strangers), the author enters with his or her personal feelings about his or her private affairs, where such confession is not necessitated by the inner logic of the subject matter at hand. I would call this indecent exposure.

---

[6] A public place where intimate personal feelings may be expressed is art, lyric poetry. But this is something different. By having been transported into the "objective" medium of art, the merely personal has been detached from the privacy of the person and has thus received a public status.

CHAPTER SIX

Is the Soul 'Deep'?
Entering and Following the Logical Movement of
HERACLITUS' Fragment 45 (DIELS)

"Is the soul 'deep'?"—this question does not seem to make sense within depth psychology, inasmuch as the soul's depth is one of the presuppositions given with the very definition of the field as such. The well-known fragment 45 (Diels) of Heraclitus'

> You would not find out the boundaries of soul, even by travelling along every path: so deep a measure does it have.[1]

has often been taken as the probably earliest explicit formulation of the insight into the depth of the soul, and Heraclitus for this reason has been considered one of the ancestors of depth psychology.

But does this dictum really advance the thesis of the depth of the soul? And if it should turn out that his statement is about the depth of the soul, what then is the precise meaning of "depth" or "deep" here? These are questions that can reasonably be posed.

Focusing on an ancient text with such questions in mind does not make the following discussion a philological or historical study. Its interest is in the soul, but since the soul cannot be approached immediately, the particular style of psychological investigation has to take the form of *commentary* on given "documents of the soul." The

---

[1] G.S. Kirk and J.E. Raven, *The PreSocratic Philosophers*, Cambridge (Cambridge University Press) 1977, p. 205.

psychological question is not, cannot be, what and how the soul *is*, but how the soul is *reflected* in its manifestations. We are not as naive as to want to take on the soul directly. We have understood that psychology is the study of the *reflection* in some mirror and not the study of *what* the mirror image is the reflection *of*. This turn to the already reflected is not a trick to get at the otherwise invisible soul after all, and not a second-best substitute for "the real thing." On the contrary, we know that the already reflected *is* psychology's "real thing."

Apart from the question of the range of meanings of the Greek word used here for "deep" (*bathýs*) three features of our quotation demand attention.

1. If one approaches our fragment with the expectation that it is the *locus classicus* about the soul's depth, one is surprised to find upon closer look that Heraclitus does not say that the soul is deep. He uses the word "deep" with respect to the soul's *lógos* (which in the above English version has been rendered as "measure"). The *lógos* is deep. Whether this also makes the soul deep is an open question.

2. We tend to connect "depth" primarily with verticality. Thus Hillman, after quoting our fragment, stated, "Ever since Heraclitus brought soul and depth together in one formulation, the dimension of soul is depth (not breadth or height) and the dimension of our soul travel is downward."[2] And in a footnote to the quotation, he adds, "Soul is not in the surface of things, the superficialities, but reaches down into hidden depths, a region which also refers to Hades and death."[3] Now, is it not strange that the fantasy which Heraclitus presents to us in the longer part of this fragment is one of horizontality, a movement on the surface of the earth? When Thomas Mann opens his novel *Joseph and His Brothers* with the sentence "Deep is the fountain of the past," we know immediately that the perspective is downwards. Here, however, there is no image of a fountain, no suggestion of "abyss," "ground," "underworld," "bottom" or "bottomlessness." There can be no doubt that Heraclitus is primarily thinking in terms of breadth. He speaks of "every road (or path)," of traveling, of borders, limits. Roads always follow the surface of the earth. They may go up

---

[2] James Hillman, *Re-Visioning Psychology*, New York et. al. (Harper & Row) 1975, p. XI.

[3] Ibid., p. 231, note 6.

IS THE SOUL 'DEEP'?

a hill and down into a valley, but they never leave the surface and they serve the purpose of taking you horizontally from here to there. (The journey to the underworld does not proceed on *roads*.) Furthermore, the word translated as "to travel," *epiporeúesthai*, with its prefix *epi-* explicitly suggests horizontal movement. It is typically used for the *marching* of an army and for any *traversing* of an area, an aspect which is reinforced in our quote by the idea of the boundary or border, which you encounter after having completely traversed a region or country. There is also an additional word in the text, *iôn* (present participle of *iénai*, to go, to walk), which in modern translations is frequently left untranslated because its meaning is felt to be contained in that of "traveling," but which is apt to strengthen the fantasy of horizontal movement. And conversely, there is nothing in the text to suggest a climbing or descending. One might, of course, think that Heraclitus' argument could have been: The horizontal movement is inadequate to the soul, therefore we have to come to the conclusion that the proper dimension of soul is the altogether different one of depth and downwardness and *not* horizontal extension, *not* breadth. But as the word *houtô [bathýn]* (*so [deep]*) shows, there is no contrast established between the first and the second parts of the fragment, the horizontal fantasy precisely leading up to and supporting the final statement.

3. How very strange that Heraclitus would, when thinking about the dimension of the soul (*psychê*), come up with the image of traveling along roads at all. Nobody today whose purpose it is to search for the limits of soul would start out from the idea or image of a search in the outside world, because it is understood that the soul's limits are not to be found there in the first place. Isn't the soul something invisible, immaterial, nonspatial and, above all, something *in us* to begin with, so that any movement along *roads* in external reality (regardless of whether meant literally or metaphorically) is on principle simply missing the point? Unless, of course, Heraclitus' *psychê* is not defined to be "inner" (inside humans) versus "outer," but extends out into the world. Then this would logically be where it is primarily to be sought; whatever the Greek or the Heraclitean notion of soul might be, the choice of image makes it clear that *psychê* must be such that to search for its boundaries out there by traveling along every road *has some plausibility*, even if perhaps only a preliminary one. It cannot be part of the psyche's a priori definition to have its locus *in* ourselves

134   *THE SOUL ALWAYS THINKS*

and to consist of what is going on in us, *our* emotions, thoughts, images, desires, etc.

The last part of our text about the depth of the soul's measure or *lógos* is not the important part of our fragment. It presents only the result or conclusion of a thought process, a result that is hardly more than a brief, abstract *name* for the insight to be transmitted. The insight itself, what it amounts to and the way it is acquired, can be learned only from the first sentence about the search for the psyche's boundaries. It will not do to jump on two single words ("deep" and "soul") in the text and, regardless of the context and thought process in which they occur, attribute to them whatever meaning *we* ordinarily associate with them, in order to exploit them for our own purposes. Also, we must not stand in awe in front of the alleged mystique that "the soul is deep" and mindlessly repeat this slogan as a static article of faith. Fragment 45 expressly speaks of traveling. But even if it did not, we would still have to honor Heraclitus as a thinker and our fragment as an instance of living thought, in other words as *movement*. It would be an insult to Heraclitus to intimate that all he wanted to do with this fragment was to lay down a kind of "golden word of wisdom" about the soul's depth. Not wisdom, not a gnome, not a static and ready-made truth, but a thought! We have to enter into the precise and intricate thought process that Heraclitus condensed into this fragment and *think* it, reconstruct it, that is to say, follow its internal movement; we have to unfold what he presents in the nutshell of one sentence. In order to do this, we must leave behind all the baggage that we bring along, all our preconceived ideas about the nature of the soul, even about its "depth," and in fact submit to the very journey upon which our text sends us, in order to find out for ourselves where this movement leads and what its results are.

Heraclitus sends us out to search for the soul's boundaries. In order to do this, we are supposed to go forward and travel along not one road, but along every (possible) road, in all possible directions, and we are to travel each of these roads, as it were, all the way (as the sense of "traversing" contained in *epiporeúesthai* implies). The philosopher subjects us to a mental experiment; it is obvious that empirically we could not travel every road to its end (especially during an age when traveling a road meant to walk by

IS THE SOUL 'DEEP'?

foot or to ride on horseback). Life is too short, our physical strength too slight. No, we do not have to physically leave home. We have to set out on an expedition in the mind. Suppose, Heraclitus tells us, there were no limitations at all as to time and strength, no human shortcomings, no finite nature of human existence, and we had the capability to actually travel every single road all the way (one could even extend his idea by including our modern technical means of transportation: motor-ships, aircraft, spacecraft, and transform Heraclitus' statement into the following: suppose we were factually capable of searching every spot in the entire universe)—we would nevertheless find out that we *cannot* find out the boundaries of the soul.

The idea is by no means the human impossibility of ever getting to the limits of the soul. The problem is not a practical one. Heraclitus is not trying to tell us that this task is too immense or difficult *for us*. Rather than about us and our insufficiencies the fragment is speaking about the nature of the soul, as the last sentence concerning "the depth of its logos" makes clear. The point is that on principle the soul's boundaries cannot be found; they could not even be found by a superhuman. That is to say: there *is* no boundary, the soul is limitless, infinite. This is a difficult thought. What does it mean?

One might think it means that one's travel could go on and on, endlessly. But such a sense of infinity is not supported by our fragment. This would be what philosophically is called the "infinite progress" and what has been shown by Hegel to be the "bad infinity" of "bad metaphysics." The insight that Heraclitus has gained and pronounced would not have been taken to heart, or we would not abide by it, because we would still be hoping for some boundaries, even though it has been understood that we will never arrive. Heraclitus' insight is definitive, that is, it puts an end to any search for the boundaries of the soul. His insight a priori renders any attempt to find out the limits of the soul absurd. This entire project is frustrated, negated; it is *shown* to be not only futile, but also unreasonable from the outset. We do not end up with the indeterminateness of a "depth" in the sense of an endless extension into the distance (regardless of whether it be horizontal or vertical). No, the whole orientation towards a bottomless depth, the infinitely self-perpetuating expectation of an end to one's search in some unreachable future has been ruthlessly cut off. No "not yet" in a forever deferred future, but the conclusive "no" that here and now terminates any flirting with the idea of a limit of the soul out there.

The result that we end up with is paradoxical: the insight is that the soul has "no limits," but this insight turns out to be in itself a terminating thought and as such a new limit. The final outcome of Heraclitus' reflection is not a total limitlessness at all. The closure that cannot be found *in fact* or *in re* (as *the soul's* closure) turns up anew *in the mind*, inside *our* thinking as *its* closure, as a limiting thought that terminates our endless expectations and our search for a boundary. Heraclitus' reflection, rather than altogether depriving us of a sense of boundary, brings about a transportation of "boundary" from the sphere of the real into that of the mental or notional, from the "object" (the soul, psychological reality) into the "subject," from the ontological to the logical. The boundary is interiorized.

Another paradox is that we had to actually and committedly undergo the search for the boundaries by traveling every road in order to find out that this search is unreasonable.

The soul has no limits. This is a contradictory idea. "Border" means two things: a) limitation, end, constriction, enclosure and b) a *bordering on* some other, something new, foreign, and in this sense an opening to new regions or countries. If the soul has no boundaries, this results in a *reversal* with respect to the two aspects of "border." Where "border" means limitation, the soul is unlimited, infinite; where "border" means opening to an outside, we have to realize that the soul has *nothing that* it borders *on* and that 'soul' thus implies absolute confinement.[4] Conversely, this reversal of the natural order of things shows that with his "no limit" insight Heraclitus is not merely *using* the word "soul," but is touching the reality we mean by 'soul,' for the soul is an "inverted [or upside down, inside out] world" (Hegel), it is *contra naturam*.

We are hopelessly enclosed by the soul. There is nothing outside the psyche, no other, nothing new. The notion or logic of the soul precludes a beyond, an "abroad." We cannot get out. There is never any point where there would be a demarcation line separating what is inside the soul from what is out there. We are hopelessly stuck *in* the

---

[4] This is not physical or imaginal, but logical confinement. There is no narrow prison cell outside of which freedom would begin. In this prison you are free to go as far and wherever you want. It is imprisonment in the *infinity* of the soul.

IS THE SOUL 'DEEP'?

soul, that is to say, in its absolute interiority. No exit[5], no escape. I want to elucidate this notion of absolute interiority in the sense of an inescapable enclosure by turning to another text from another civilization in which *mutatis mutandis* "the same" idea is presented in much more detail and plasticity, although with respect to the presence of God rather than to the *psychê*. It is a text from the Old Testament, Psalm 139, lines 1-16.

> O Lord, thou hast searched me, and known me. Thou knowest my downsitting and mine uprising, thou understandest my thought afar off. Thou compassest my path and my lying down, and art acquainted with all my ways. For there is not a word in my tongue, but, lo, O Lord, thou knowest it altogether. Thou hast beset me behind and before, and laid thine hand upon me. Such knowledge is too wonderful for me; it is high, I cannot attain unto it.

> Wither shall I go from thy spirit? or whither shall I flee from thy presence? If I ascend up into heaven, thou art there: if I make my bed in hell, behold, thou art there. If I take the wings of the morning, and dwell in the uttermost parts of the sea; Even there shall thy hand lead me, and thy right hand shall hold me. If I say, Surely the darkness shall cover me; even the night shall be light about me. Yea, the darkness hideth not from thee; but the night shineth as the day: the darkness and the light are both alike to thee. ...

> My substance was not hid from thee, when I was made in secret, and curiously wrought in the lowest parts of the earth. Thine eyes did see my substance, yet being unperfect; and in thy book all my members were written, which in continuance were fashioned, when as yet there was none of them.

What Heraclitus presented summarily in one sentence and in the one thought of traveling "every" road, the psalmist spells out, as it were. In his mental experiment the psalmist really travels every possible road in all directions. Whether he were to go to the end of the world in the east where the sun rises or in the utmost west where it sets in

---

[5] Heidegger translates *peírata* (boundaries) on the basis of his understanding of the Greek sense of *psychê* as "Ausgänge (der Seele)" (exits, openings or outlets of the soul), see his *Heraklit*, Gesamtausgabe vol. 55, Frankfurt am Main (Klostermann) 1979, pp. 282, 297, 303f.

the ocean, whether he were to go up to heaven or down into the underworld, he is forced to realize that he would nevertheless be enclosed in God's presence. Whether he be in motion or at rest, he cannot escape. Even the seeming privacy of his thoughts and the darkness of night (or the darkness, we might add, of the "unconscious"), indeed, even the prenatal past are not areas that would provide at least some theoretical outside. What the psalmist expresses is the insight into his being inescapably surrounded on *all* sides, in time, empirical and cosmic space as well as in the inner realm of one's thoughts and feelings. Everything, his whole existence, is absolutely contained in an absolute ("autonomous," "objective" and a priori) knowledge, a *being known* that is experienced as an imprisonment.

If there is no escape and no outside, then there is only interiority: *absolute* interiority. Absolute, because this interiority is not the counterpart of an exteriority; it is "absolved" from the opposition of inner and outer. This interiority is unchallenged: infinite. Our habitual notion *of* interiority or the "inner" is abstract or *external*, because according to it the inner has its other, the external, *outside* of itself, on the other side of the border between them, and it, the inner, is just as external to the outer world. Our psalm drives home the realization that every conceivable "outside" is already (a priori) *inside* this all-encompassing knowledge. We are thus forced to advance to a sense of an "inner" interiority that has interiorized even the very notion of an "outer" into itself. On the level of consciousness reached by the psalmist and by Heraclitus, a "real" outside has become inconceivable. We are absolutely locked, be it into the interiority of a being known by God (Psalm 139) or into the interiority of the *psychê* (Heraclitus, fragment 45).

Driven by the wish to get out, the psalmist tested every imaginable kind of "outside" in his mental experiment and experienced how the hypothesis that there could be a way out was falsified. In this way he painfully acquired for himself a new status of consciousness determined by the notion of an inescapable interiority. Even though Heraclitus gives us only the briefest condensation of his mental experiment, we can assume from what he said that his thought process was "the same" and we see that it led to the same result. The first aspect of this result is the imprisonment character of our containment in the soul. But

IS THE SOUL 'DEEP'?

there is also the other aspect of the "no boundary" insight: that of the *infinity* of the soul. It is unlimited. We already know that this infinity cannot mean an unending extension into the distance, neither spatially nor in time (past or future). The *knowledge* that there *is no* boundary works as a new unsurmountable boundary at which, as if by a brick wall, our striving to get to a limit in the endless distance is repulsed. *It is thrown back upon, and reflected into, itself.* The new boundary is the *absolute* "prison" wall that is absolute because it does not separate freedom outside from imprisonment in here. Inasmuch as the soul's infinity is itself absolutely enclosed in the soul's absolute interiority, it cannot escape further and further into extendedness. It is turned back inside, forced within: interiorized into itself.

But when the relentless orientation towards spatial extension into an endless distance is forced back and has to return within, whither can it go? It inevitably has to explode the literal, natural, namely *spatial*, notion of the "inner" and thus to open up an entirely new *dimension*, that of "intension." But no, "explosion" is already wrong; it is still tied to the extensional orientation. We have to speak of an implosion. But again, this is not the adequate expression, implying too violent a process. The infinite interiority or interiorized infinity comes about through the alchemical, logically negative process of an internal putrefaction, corruption, fermentation, sublimation of "whatever is there" ever deeper into itself.

This conquest of the dimension of an intensional or "inner" infinity amounts, however, to nothing less than a breakthrough through spatial thinking altogether. And this in turn is the breakthrough through the mode of imagination and into that of reflection, of thought proper. Heraclitus is driven beyond the imagination. Similarly, the psalmist is driven beyond the imaginal, beyond myth. Not only all empirical places on the surface of the earth and the whole world of nature, but also the strictly imaginal or archetypal *topoi* heaven and underworld are once and for all sublated in favor of the new dimension of an all-encompassing, all-pervasive *knowing*. The importance of the mental sphere is emphasized by the inclusion of one's hidden thoughts (plans) and as-yet unspoken utterances in this aforecoming being known. There is a radical, revolutionary shift as to the locus of human existence. Now human existence has its *primary* place within an inescapable "being *known*" and no longer, as in the times of polytheistic myth, in naive, simple *being*, in the cosmos, in nature. What we witness in this psalm is the origin of a first awareness of "consciousness," in other words, of a *real* consciousness *of* consciousness and thus the beginning of a sense of the psychological. Latin *con-scientia* as well as Greek *syn-eidêsis* make use of a prefix meaning "with" to express the notion of consciousness, because consciousness is more than a simple knowing; it is comprehended as that knowing that the being who is conscious shares with an *ideal observer* (who is, in the case of the Biblical author, God, but could just as well be, for example, a Kantian transcendental consciousness, a universal consciousness-in-itself). The (innocent, natural[6]) *being*-in-the-world (and thus ontology) is superseded by a being in the notional sphere of reflection, consciousness, logos as "broken" (reflected) or sublated being. From *mythos* to *logos*.

Because this psalm is a text from the Bible and on the surface speaks about and to God, we tend to read it theologically, in terms of piety. But a theological reading cannot do it justice. It would belittle its importance and neutralize its revolutionizing impact by enveloping it regressively in a conventional faith. Our text is above all an essential document in the history of the soul, bearing testimony to the rise of a new status of consciousness. We must not be blinded by the word God and our "natural" reaction to it. This text is not *about God*, as if God were first of all a given positivity whose nature would here be described. Many mythical gods had the attribute of being all-knowing. But in the world of myth the god was the "substance" and his knowing was one of his "attributes" or qualities. Here, it is the other way around. The text is about an inescapable *knowledge*. The psalmist wants to flee (not from *Him*, who happens to be all-knowing, but) from (His) *knowing*, (His) spirit, (His) presence. The psalmist rose to the insight of an inescapable containment in a nonspatial realm of reflection or of an "objective" (not subjective, not his personal) self-knowledge ("con-scientia"), and, as was to be expected, he gave this absolute containment the name "God."

But whether "God" or "psyche," the actual experience in the psalm and in the Heraclitus fragment is analogous, the only difference being

---

[6] I use "natural" in a psychological, alchemical sense, not in an abstract naturalistic or positivistic sense (as in biology or physics). The natural in terms of *human* existence is an animated, spiritual natural to begin with: the imaginal perception of the world. Myth and ritual are what is natural to the soul.

IS THE SOUL 'DEEP'?

that in each case different moments of the same experience are being stressed. The Biblical text, by personifying this sphere of reflection, emphasizes its wholly-otherness, its objectivity and autonomy vis-à-vis the I, whereas the aspect that the newly discovered "being known" is a *self*-knowledge is kept in a subliminal condition; the psalmist feels the need to distinguish and distance himself from this self-knowledge. This is why the motif of escaping is in the foreground. It is terrifying to find oneself expelled from the innocence of one's native embeddedness in myth and to awaken to an awareness of the reflectedness of existence as such. The psalmist's fleeing is driven by his wish to return into the innocent, unreflected state of *being*-in-the-world (that state of being characterized by myth and ritual)—a forerunner of the romantic longing "Retour à la nature." But the first emergence of this longing to be relieved of the burden of consciousness (in the sense of *Selbstbewußtsein*, a consciousness *of* consciousness) and the attempts to escape the broken, reflected state of being already come with the insight into their futility. No indulging in a nostalgic illusion. In fact, it is probably only *through* the feeling of the loss of oneness, the loss of an embeddedness in myth and ritual, and *through* the insight into the impossibility of a return to the innocence of being that the new sense of "in-ness" in a self-knowledge is acquired. The attempt to get out of his containment in God's knowledge is, dialectically, the mode in which the psalmist *really* acquires the idea of this containment for himself and more and more settles in it, definitively removing human existence from its surroundedness by myth and instead grounding it in reflectedness; precisely by trying to escape he brings the insight of his inescapable containment in God's knowledge home to himself.

Heraclitus, by contrast, is not especially interested in getting *out*. He would want to positively *reach* the boundaries by traversing the whole space of his containment in *psychê* from here to there. From the outset, his view stays much more within. And his notion of *psychê* is accordingly one that stresses the connection of this "objective" reflection to the human being, to ourselves, as *our* psychological existence. From his version of the insight it is not too difficult to get to our modern notion of the psyche as self-relation, self-reflection. But of course, in the idea of self-relation the otherness that was highlighted in the Biblical text is not totally lost either; it is inherent in it as a

142   *THE SOUL ALWAYS THINKS*

sublated moment, inasmuch as the self that does the reflecting and the self that is being reflected are both identical *and different.*

The different realms and things in the imaginal have boundaries. For example, heaven, earth and the underworld are clearly demarcated spheres. Sea and land, valley and mountain border on each other. If the soul has no boundaries, it cannot be of an imaginal nature. The insight gained by Heraclitus that the soul has no boundaries puts an end to any thinking about it within the realm of the imagination and, all the more so, within the space of sensory intuition. When in the logical status of consciousness reached by Heraclitus it comes to the soul, thinking in spatial terms as such is reduced to absurdity. The soul is not *res extensa*, it cannot be conceived in terms of extension, regardless of whether literal or imaginal extension. The soul is *res cogitans* and the appropriate approach to it is thus in and by thought. If we accept the message of Heraclitus' fragment, we have to realize that the realm of psychology begins where the imagination has been superseded.

There are two obstacles to this understanding.

(1) With the terms *res extensa* and *res cogitans* we enter the territory of Descartes. Now, in many quarters and also in archetypal psychology, Descartes meets with contempt. He is treated like an (intellectual or psychological) criminal responsible for the fundamental split expressed by the opposition of the aforementioned terms. This is not only unfair, but also unpsychological. Descartes did not *do* anything; he is not responsible for, not guilty of, a splitting. He merely expressed the split that was constitutive for the modern soul condition, and thus a modern truth. If anyone is "guilty" here, it is the soul. Descartes conscientiously did her bidding, no more. And in a way we can see this distinction or opposition of his already prefigured in Heraclitus' dictum. Blaming Descartes is a defense (in the psychoanalytic sense of the word) against having to acknowledge the fundamental psychological revolution that has long taken place and that brought about an irrevocable rupture, experienced as the loss of myth and the estrangement from "nature." Expressed in positive terms, it was the acquisition of a broken, reflected and reflecting consciousness. We do not have to fight or undo "Descartes." We have to take him further, "think him onwards" (to play on Jung's oft-cited formulation, "to dream the myth onwards"). This is why when I say

IS THE SOUL 'DEEP'?

that the soul is not *res extensa*, the latter expression is not exactly identical with the meaning and function it has in *his* thought.

(2) There is the idea that by resorting to the imagination this split could be healed again. The imaginal is imagined (not *thought!*) to be neither a Cartesian *res extensa* nor a *res cogitans*. It is supposed to be exempt from this distinction. It is said to be an intermediary third. But things are not as simple as that. To be sure, the way Descartes' oppositional pair is set up, the imaginal does not fit in, just like that. But this does not mean that it would not be covered by his scheme. On the contrary, it *is* nothing but the compromise formation between his opposites. If it does not belong on either side and is not a totally different third either, what else can it be? It exists as the *whole opposition* collapsed into one, but in such a way that within this One the opposites are internally immunized against one another and their dangerous conflict is thus defused and suspended: stalemated. As such, the imaginal in modern psychology is the disguised internalization of the very Cartesian split as a whole that it openly scorns and for which it is said to be the solution. How come?

Image is shape and shape is spatial. On this count, the imaginal is undoubtedly *res extensa*. But it is extended matter only as far as the *content* of the image is concerned. Its logical *form* (as image in the imagination or as idea in the mind) is, of course, not extended. Through its form it partakes of the nature of Descartes' *res cogitans*. By holding content and logical form of the image strictly apart, each to one side, the idea of the imaginal *is* the trick that allows having it both ways. It is the trick of trying to do justice to *res extensa* and *res cogitans* at once, however *while* preventing the self-contradictory nature of this undertaking from becoming apparent and effective, which would lead to its self-destruction. The trick is to camouflage the simultaneous obedience to both and to systematically distribute the opposites neatly each on one side. The sanity of the mind is thus rescued. One's falling into the contradiction and into the ensuing dialectic is avoided. Imaginal psychology can indignantly reject the diagnosis of its being firmly rooted in Cartesian ground: when the character of the extendedness of the content of its images is pointed out, it quickly insists on its non-extended ideational *form*; and when conversely the ideational character of the form or status as images is stressed, it disowns having any part in the *res cogitans* and produces as counter-proof its connection, by way of metaphor, with the sensory, physical world.

The standpoint of the imaginal is the (hypostatized, reified) act of skillfully and instantaneously switching between the Cartesian opposites, so that it never has to show its true colors. As the movie projector's speedy sequence of separate images creates the impression of one continuous moving image, so here the speed and the subliminal nature of the switching back and forth makes its act character and the inherent contradiction between the two sides disappear in the impression of a resting, static, in-itself reconciled image. The idea of the imaginal is not really a third, not really something new and other beyond the Cartesian opposites. It is the artfully produced illusion of something other, a splendid show.

Here it may be time to return to the final sentence of Heraclitus' fragment: *houtô bathyn lógon échei*, "so deep a measure does it have," "so deep is its meaning," "such is the depth of its meaning"—to cite only three of a multitude of renderings. It has already become obvious that Heraclitus' fragment is not concerned with depth in the sense of verticality and a downwards movement, but also not with extension in a wider sense. This is why the translation "so deep a measure" is ruled out for us, also for linguistic reasons; for Guthrie's argument against Kirk's thinking in terms of "vast extent" is conclusive: "but βαθὺν λόγον ἔχει would seem a rather recherché phrase to express simply 'so extensive is it.'"[7] The Greek word *bathýs* like Latin *altus* means both deep and high (cf. "altitude"), in other words vertical extension, but it can also have quite different meanings. It (and the noun *báthos*, depth) can be used in a decidedly horizontal sense to indicate width (such as that of a shore, the wide extension of a courtyard or the depth of a battle-line). Indeed, Plato uses the plural of the noun to refer to all three dimensions of a solid (length, height and depth). It can also have nonspatial meanings and designate the density of a forest or of a fog, the thickness and length of hair, the intensity of a color, the strength of a storm, the high degree of wealth or of a debt, the craftiness of a person, the profundity of an argument.

---

[7] W.K.C. Guthrie, *The earlier Presocratics and the Pythagoreans*, vol. I of his *A History of Greek Philosophy*, Cambridge (Cambridge Univ. Press) 1962, p. 477, note 1.

IS THE SOUL 'DEEP'? 145

So we might think that we are better off with the other translations given above that speak of the depth of *meaning*. For now depth is used no longer literally, but metaphorically, imaginally. Apart from the fact that this would be a rather banal, trite wisdom for the discovery and formulation of which one would hardly need a philosopher of the rank of Heraclitus, does the metaphorical depth get us any further? By no means. In fact, the move to the metaphorical merely *obscures* that nothing has changed as to one's dominant orientation. If the soul has "so deep a meaning," I am still, and remain, standing at the place where I have always been and from there merely look into an assumed distance. Whether I am doing this literally in external space (in the area of physical vision) or metaphorically in the realm of the imagination, or in "the depth of feeling" (e.g., through the puer's nostalgic longing, *póthos*, for faraway and fundamentally unreachable places) makes no difference. Whether depth of measure or depth of meaning, in both cases it is the same *refusal* to get going to the boundaries and to get Heraclitus' message about the pointlessness of any orientation into the distance (a message which I cannot really get unless I have relentlessly tried to get there and actually experienced a failure).

Heraclitus does not, as we with our talk about the depth of the soul's meaning, end up with the vagueness of an undecided question, and the boundary does not fade away in an endless distance, that is to say, in the fuzziness of a mysterious and mystifying idea of depth. Heraclitus has come to a determinate and definitive conclusion. He did travel all the way to the boundary, for how else could he have found out the truth about it? The question about the boundaries is decided. And it has consequences. There is a closure. We have to see through the intellectual idea of the depth of the soul's meaning and the analogous feeling attitude of *póthos* and recognize it as the (however glorified) neglect or hesitation to actually try to get to the end. By holding on to the idea of "depth," one pretends that there might still be some boundary and a beyond after all, only so far away that our arrival there is forever postponed, deferred. One simply ignores that the "no boundary" insight has long been acquired, and that thereby any longing into the distance and any imagining in terms of vast extent has once and for all been cut off.

146   *THE SOUL ALWAYS THINKS*

This small example concerning the idea of the depth of the soul brings to light the structural deficiency of the imagination *if* it is supposed to be the predominant function for approaching the soul and for understanding its nature, in other words, its deficiency for doing psychology. "The soul's depth" is the formula describing in a nutshell the nature of the imaginal approach: with this stance one is just *daydreaming* of something that is by definition not supposed to ever be actually attained. One is just "tele-visioning": envisioning, peeping, viewing, romantically expecting (*ex-spectare*, to look out) from a distance into the endless distance. The imaginally understood image is nothing but the visualized or reified "depth" (endless distance) itself. It can be adored from afar, but cannot be known. The imaginal stance allows one to stall, to hold back, to reserve oneself, inasmuch as belief in the soul's depth arrests midway, or prevents altogether, the internal movement ("traveling") that the Heraclitean statement speaks about. The imaginal stance speaks with a split tongue. It says "no boundary," but it continues to be on the lookout for one. The insight of the "no boundary" does not come home. The recoil is avoided. The old orientation out and away into (literal or metaphorical) space is rescued and the reflection into itself, this essential result of Heraclitus' motion, does not happen.

In this way, the *real* depth aimed at by Heraclitus is avoided; that depth which is the "depth" of the soul's *logos*: logical "depth," the "depth" of thought, in contrast to sensory, or imagined, or felt depth. If you follow Heraclitus' movement, you start out from thought and end up with thought. This has to be shown.

I said that Heraclitus did travel all the way. But his traveling was neither literal movement nor imagined movement. He did not picture his journey and where he would arrive. Nor did he stay at home. What he did was to travel without leaving home, and to stay home by way of the most extensive traveling, that is to say, he traveled in thought: *he thought through* the idea of traveling every road to the boundaries all the way, with all its consequences, just as the author of Psalm 139 did. Their traveling was negated, sublated, alchemically decomposed traveling from the outset (which already comes out linguistically in what is in translation the subjunctive: "would not find," "if I were to ascend to heaven"). It is only in thought that you really arrive at the soul's boundary, which however is that sublated boundary consisting

IS THE SOUL 'DEEP'?

in the very insight that there is no boundary. It is only in thought that you arrive in soul country. For the imagination there cannot be the insight that there is no boundary, because it resorts to the idea of depth, a premature idea of depth, which is the noun for the act of deferring the boundary forever and thus for avoiding closure. It keeps the boundary question in the dark. Heraclitus' thinking-through all the way to the very end the idea of a (literal or imaginal) search for the boundaries of the soul, and his in fact *arriving* at the inescapable insight that there is no boundary out there in the realm of extension, amount to a *closure of the mode of imagining* (which is always space-bound). He conquers the non-space of thought for the soul, thereby removing the soul from its exile in myth or mythically imagined nature and returns it into its native country. He fetches the boundary that was not to be found out there back home as the "determinate nought" (Hegel) of "outside boundary," as *sublated* border and as the inalienable property of the mind: as truly inner or internal boundary.

The imagination inevitably has to imagine the border out there, in the distance, at the margins. But Heraclitus (logically, not physically!) *draws the border or margins inside, into the center, thereby establishing interiority* (a revolution that the perceiving and imagining mind cannot survive; it is at once sublated and becomes *thinking* consciousness). For the real "inner" is not something *located* inside of something else. It is not a location at all; as a location it would still be an abstract or *external* notion *of* interiority. No, the real "inner" is what has nothing outside of, or external to, itself, no boundaries that would be out there, at its margins. The true inner is defined as that whose interiority has, in a revolutionary reversal, surrounded the very notion of "outside," "margin," or "border" and internalized it into itself. The inner is thus what has the outer truly within and not outside of itself. Only this self-contradictory, "crazy" relation is what constitutes interiority. But something that has the outside (its own outside) truly *inside itself* can, of course, not be imagined any more. It can only be thought. And because the "land" of soul is constituted by interiority, it is verily accessible only to thought. It is in itself an Inverted World and as such unimaginable.

What becomes of the boundary when it has truly been interiorized? It now can be seen to be the contradictory nature or dialectic of the soul's logical life. As such, it is the liquefied, vaporized, sublimated border, border no longer as a static line, but as a living *complexio oppositorum.*

Now we are in a better position to understand what the last sentence of our fragment (*so deep a logos does it have*) means. Far from suggesting a mysterious depth of the soul, an endless extension of its measure or its meaning, it tells us how *bathýs* (unfathomable, complex, intricate, subtle, counternatural, "twisted," "crazy") its *lógos* is. Why *logos*? Why not, e.g., "how *bathýs* the *nature* of the psyche is"? The answer is that the status of consciousness reached here does not allow Heraclitus any longer to naively speak of a "nature" of the soul. He says the soul's *logos* is "deep" because soul is not an existing entity, not ontic; it is *sublated* nature, *sublated* myth, or it is logical; it is nothing else but the *relation* of a dialectical reversal, an inversion. It is absolutely misleading to say that the soul is deep. When we say this, we inevitably imagine it as a "something" that extends out into an imaginal distance. But the soul is not a "something," it is "reflection into itself." It is a logical relation, a relation that exists only in and for the mind; it is the status of absolute interiority, which, as we have seen, is that unimaginable, because self-contradictory, relation of outer and inner where the outer is inside the inner and the inner thus encloses all, even its own outside. The external is now only a *sublated moment* within the internal.

This is why Heraclitus' "so deep a logos does it have" is somehow analogous to the psalmist's "Such knowledge is too wonderful for me; it is [too] high, I cannot attain unto it." In both cases it is a question of logic, of conceptual comprehension (which is experienced as "deep" or as "too wonderful"). In fragment 45 as well as in Psalm 139 we witness the first emergence of the conscious awareness of this unheard of new dimension of absolute interiority or internal infinity. The psalmist calls it "such knowledge" (the all-encircling knowledge of God), Heraclitus calls it the psyche whose boundaries cannot be found out there (because the psyche as internal infinity *is itself* the all-encompassing boundary).

The idea of an all-encircling and inescapable knowledge is too wonderful, too high, in short, incomprehensible for the psalmist, because his is only the first dawning of the insight of the inescapability of consciousness. He is, as it were, getting a glimpse of something that

IS THE SOUL 'DEEP'?

explodes the stance of mythologizing or imagining consciousness, but he is getting this glimpse from "beneath," while he is still viewing from within this old stance of consciousness. Therefore he necessarily experiences it as an incomprehensible wonder, because within it he naturally does not have the logical means to comprehend it. But this does of course not mean that what he caught sight of would indeed be incomprehensible, absolutely irrational. On the contrary. It is that new form of consciousness that in all *essential* regards orients itself in life by means of the abstractness of rigorous thought and conceptual comprehension, because it has sublated the modes of sensory intuition and imagination. It cannot be imagined any more. So the problem with it is not at all that it is truly incomprehensible (as the psalmist suggests), but that it is *unimaginable.* Having *within* the horizon of a perceiving and imagining consciousness caught sight of what is utterly beyond this horizon and implies the very destruction of the imagining mode as consciousness' dominant mode amounts to a summoning to be initiated into the new logical level of consciousness through a logical revolution. You cannot have an inkling of the inescapability of reflection without having fallen under an obligation: to allow the new "content" to alchemically decompose your old frame of mind and the old logical constitution of your world. What at first appears as a content *of* consciousness is in truth the seed of what wants to become a radically new *form* of consciousness at large.

This is where the idea of the soul's depth comes in. It, too, expresses the dawning awareness of something that explodes the horizon of the imagination, but it also defuses this "content," which threatens to decompose the whole status of consciousness, by re-integrating it into the old status of consciousness. It holds what wants to be the promise of a new *form* of consciousness down in the status of a mere *content* of the old, imagining consciousness, freezing its internal dynamic, its corrupting, fermenting power. How can it do this? By depriving it of its logical, notional, intellectual claims and challenge and instead translating it into the harmlessness and fuzziness of a mere romantic *feeling.* Emotions, feelings, are an excellent packaging for safely storing the logical or "metaphysical" dynamite of contents away. If you construe a conflict as an emotion or feeling, you have successfully removed it from the battlefield of truth and reduced it to the banal level of personal, subjective, or interpersonal problems. Emotions, if

150   *THE SOUL ALWAYS THINKS*

taken *per se*, are in the life of the soul what the *ad hominem* argument is in a discussion. The intellectual substance of "depth" in "the soul's depth" is near zero. It is a vague feeling. And it is a black hole that swallows within it all precise thinking. It is the name for the *unthoughtness* of Heraclitus' message to us, and for the refusal to allow it to work on our consciousness.

I expressed the view that what Heraclitus and the psalmist discovered explodes the whole sphere of mythological imagination. But we now have to realize that the idea of absolute interiority, of an internal infinity, of an all-surrounding logical life and an unreachable boundary is not new. In fact, it is a constitutive idea of mythology itself. There is the Greek myth of Okeanos, the "origin of the Gods," "the generation of all"; there is the corresponding Egyptian myth of the primal Ocean Nun, the "World Encircler" and "Father of the Gods"; there is the Germanic uroboric Midgard Serpent, to mention only three examples from three different cultural spheres. I will concentrate on the Greek myth. Okeanos[8] (the name is said to be of Semitic origin and to mean "circling") is the mythic image of the soul's logical life as stream (continuous streaming, fluidity), as unending circulation (returning into itself), as unreachable outermost border of the world separating Being from Non-Being, and thus as all-encircling as well as all-permeating circumference of Being. If the world-encompassing Okeanos separates Being from Non-Being, what is outside of its limits is nothing, in other words, the world has no outside, no beyond. Okeanos is not a border *between* two realms, like borders in ordinary reality, from which proceed, as it were, two vectors, one out and one in. Being the outermost end of the world, he is exclusively pointing inwards: all rivers, springs, wells, the entire sea, they all continuously originate from him and flow into the world; he is the generation and circumference of all that exists. You could not reach this boundary, because however far you might go and whatever distant and unheard-of place you would reach would ipso facto be encircled by all-encircling Okeanos. Okeanos is in this sense much like what

---

[8] See my paper "Deliverance from the Stream of Events: Okeanos and the Circulation of the Blood," in: *Sulfur 21* (Winter 1988), pp. 118-140. Now Chapter Twelve in my *The Neurosis of Psychology. Primary Papers towards a Clinical Psychology*, Collected English Papers, vol. 1, New Orleans, LA (Spring Journal Books: 2005), pp. 233–255.

IS THE SOUL 'DEEP'? 151

we call the horizon, which one cannot reach either, because it moves along with one wherever one goes.

In the image of Okeanos the mythological imagination imagined *its own* engendering origin: the constituting principle of mythologizing itself. Okeanos is the image of the world's absolute containment, the world's inescapably being locked in, *thrown back upon itself.* He is the image of the *internal boundary* of everything in the world. By grace of this boundary everything is "inner"; there is, for mythic experience, no "*outside* world," nothing "external," no natural world in the modern sense of a *res extensa.* The world is not positive fact, not "whatever is the case," not mindless matter, not mere *Vorhandensein.* As long as there is an Okeanos, it is a priori a world *in itself reflected,* which is what makes it imaginal. Okeanos guarantees the absolute interiority and *inner* infinity of the whole world, and thus also of everything that exists in this world. By inescapably locking everything within, Okeanos is what enables and forces (potentially) everything to be experienced as "inner," as animated, spirited from within by an ultimately divine image as its soul. This is why Okeanos is the Father of all the Gods, the father, we might say, of all images. He prevents things or events from being seen in terms of extension and exteriority by forcing all thinking and all vision into that interiority of each thing or event that is the divine image, word or meaning it contains.

But if mythology already contains the idea of absolute interiority and is even conscious of the fact that this is what it is constituted by— what is new with Heraclitus' and the psalmist's insight? Not the content or substance. The content is ancient mythological stock. New is only the *logical form* in which this substance is now conceived. Already myth *is* logos, *is* reflection, *is* thought, *is* absolute interiority. But it is logos cloaked in natural imagery; it presents absolute interiority projected into its other, the "*extended* matter" of the imagination, in other words, in a mode opposite to what it is about. This is why myths are paradoxical: Okeanos, who represents the idea of absolute interiority, is imagined as a river *out there* at the very margins of Being. This image thus necessarily turns our orientation towards the outermost distance and holds it thus in a spatial fantasy, while at the same time *telling* us that all rivers flow from out there inwards, in other words, that the essential movement goes in the opposite direction. By contrast, the psalmist does not *imagine* a world-encircling *river* any

152   *THE SOUL ALWAYS THINKS*

more. He *thinks* of an inescapable *knowledge*. He and Heraclitus reduce the idea of the literal or imaginal move into the distance to absurdity and thus overcome the imaginal mode once and for all, thereby sublating the ancient idea of an absolute containment, by both overcoming the mythical idea of an Okeanos and regaining it in the *mode* of reflection and on the *level* of conceptual thought.

It is with this revolutionary change of the mode or *form* of consciousness that psychology becomes possible as well as necessary. As long as the form of consciousness was truly imaginal (mythic), there was no place for psychology, because then the soul, as it were, spilled out into and all over nature. It "extended" itself. Psychology, however, is the soul returned to its home ground, reflected into itself, not into its other, nature. As long as consciousness was informed by myth, humans could still feel that they lived *in the world*, *in* nature, *in* the cosmos. This is impossible for us. We *know* that we live *in soul*, in consciousness, in God's knowledge, and that the world is irrevocably outside.

I n order to understand Heraclitus' fragment and to put it into perspective, we have also looked at Psalm 139 as well as at the myth of Okeanos. It now remains for us to clarify how the Heraclitean conception relates to Jung's psychology and vice versa. In *CW* 8 § 680 we read,

> We are in truth so wrapped about by psychic images that we cannot penetrate at all to the essence of things external to ourselves.

Does this not sound like an (unintended) rewording of Heraclitus' "You would not find out the boundaries of soul, even by traveling along every path"? No exit out of psychic reality. We are totally surrounded by soul. Clearly, this is the idea of the psyche's absolute interiority in itself.

But then we also have to note that in the same sentence Jung posits an essence of things *external* to the psyche, which is incompatible with the "no exit" idea. Jung simultaneously holds two mutually exclusive views. It is not that with the second view the soul's absolute interiority is relativized. Rather, *as* absolute interiority it is in toto suspended in the opposite conception, in a linear orientation of extension and exteriority. Even if it is practically inaccessible, *theoretically* there

IS THE SOUL 'DEEP'?

nevertheless does exist for this stance an exit out of the psyche; the soul does have an "outside" of itself. Jung operates with the idea of a beyond on the other side of "a barrier across the mental world" (*CW* 18 § 1734), in other words with the very idea of an outer boundary that Heraclitus as well as the psalmist had reduced to absurdity. This second stance is thus diametrically opposed to the insight Heraclitus had gained. Jung leaves the boundary "out there," and unreachable, while Heraclitus had interiorized it into the soul.

Jung is thus speaking with a split tongue; he has two separate truths that he holds apart by means of a systematic complementary distribution. When *doing* psychology (when speaking *within* the field of psychology), he totally subscribes to the "inescapable interiority" idea, sometimes even giving psychology the rank of a super-science, a "science" *of* the sciences (inasmuch as all sciences are expressions of the psyche, too). But when he reflects *about* psychology and presents his overall theory of knowing, he ultimately invalidates psychology by embedding it in an overriding stance for which precisely the *essence* of things is located beyond that unsurmountable boundary, in the "things external to ourselves." What from within psychology is personally felt, and explicitly declared, to be of utmost importance, to *be* the *essential* (our processes of transformation and individuation with all the precious images of ultimately divine matters they involve us in) has only ("nothing but"!) the logical status of a kind of personal entertainment in a bubble that has both the real essence and the essence of real life outside of itself. Psychology is fenced in, encapsulated in a reserve or asylum, one could also say in a playhouse. Within this playhouse it is free, infinite, or, putting it the other way around as Jung did, it does not have "the advantage of a 'delimited field of work'" (*CW* 9/I § 112), but psychology as a whole *is* defined as a "delimited field." You have to play dumb and suppress your knowledge about the real state of affairs (namely, that the essence is out there) in order to be able to take psychology fully seriously. In other words, you have to act *as if* you were taking it seriously.

That the essence of things outside of ourselves is said to be totally out of reach, and the barrier to be unsurmountable even for "the boldest leap of speculation"[9] has the result that for all practical intents

[9] *CW* 18 § 1734, translation modified.

154   *THE SOUL ALWAYS THINKS*

and purposes the exit out of the psyche can be neglected. Within psychology it does not take effect. But this does not alter the fact that the (practically ineffective) idea of something external to the psyche *psychologically* is very powerful: it is what *really* determines *the theoretical validity and logical status* of things psychological. Psychology is under the spell of the orientation towards an "outside."

The ruling power of this orientation is not even destroyed for Jung by the fact that his view involves him and us in a (faulty, undialectical) contradiction. For if it is true that we are so wrapped about by psychic images that we cannot penetrate at all to the essence of things external to ourselves, we cannot know in the first place that there are things external to ourselves, because this idea would necessarily also be no more than a psychic image. It would be a fantasy on the part of the soul, a soul content that the soul *within* itself *projects outside of itself.* Within psychology Jung, of course, insisted that projections have to be withdrawn. But when it comes to the soul's projected imagination of its own other, he instantly dropped the psychological approach like a hot potato, insisting on taking this (soul-internal!) projection of something external as bare fact. Whereas within psychology the soul was all-surrounding, psychology itself was set up as bordering on, and totally encircled by, an external other: "real" reality.

Why would Jung resort to such a split-in-itself, dissociated conception? This question strikes at the heart of his psychology project and touches on its basic fault. An answer would involve a thorough analysis of the whole of his psychology including a fundamental critique of his notions of "the unconscious," "the inner," "psychological reality," "personality" and thus also "Self" as well as of his psycho-biography. This is beyond the scope of the present paper. Some aspects of an answer I tried to provide in my article, "Jung's Betrayal of His Truth: The Adoption of a Kant-Based Empiricism and the rejection of Hegel's Speculative Thought."[10] Here I want to point out merely one benefit of this dissociation.

By fundamentally "doing psychology in," i.e., defining it as having to do with an "inner" in an abstract, *external* sense, so that he would have *two* mutually exclusive ultimate commitments, and by correspondingly inventing himself as two *alternating* subjectivities

---

[10] In: *Harvest* 44, No. 1, 1998, pp. 46–64.

IS THE SOUL 'DEEP'?

(personality No. 1 and personality No. 2), Jung could continue operating on the level of the *contents* of consciousness without having to become conscious of, and take responsibility for, the problem of the logical *form* of consciousness. I have stressed that Heraclitus, by fetching the notion of boundary from out there onto the home territory of the soul as the self-contradictory, inverted notion of its *inner* or internal boundary, had decomposed or corrupted once and for all that form of consciousness that orients itself primarily by means of sensory intuition and imagination. Instead he advanced to a thinking, reflecting form of consciousness as the only adequate mode in which to think about the soul. Two and a half thousand years after Heraclitus, Jung hoped to get away, in his conception of the new field of "the psychology of the unconscious," with staying at the old level of consciousness and feeling exempt from having to *think* the prime matters of soul. The split to which he resorted enabled him to provide, on the one hand, a playground for all the mythical images and ideas of the soul, a playground unhindered by any metaphysical claims that they would inevitably involve a modern consciousness in, and, on the other hand, to pay tribute to the reality that the times of myth (of a oneness of soul and nature, of a truly imaginal *form* of consciousness) were irrevocably bygone and that we had long arrived on the level of a broken, reflecting consciousness. He satisfied two opposite needs, not, however, by logically reconciling them, but by switching back and forth. In other words, he acted the rupture out instead of remembering, interiorizing it.

I used the image of the playhouse for psychology and said that psychology is free and unlimited within this playhouse, whereas the playhouse itself is defined as a "delimited field." It is, of course, *the personality* that is the reality reflected in this image. The structural setup of psychology with the duplicity of a total surroundedness by psychic images *and* of an unreachable reality external to ourselves is perfectly mirrored in the idea of the unconscious *in* the personality (the abstract "inner") *and* the real world all around it (the abstract "outer"), which in turn is mirrored in the distinction between the subject- and the object-levels of dream interpretation. Here, too, we see how Jung acted out. He internalized the psyche *into the person* instead of reflecting (inwardizing) it *into itself*! This is the result of

156 *THE SOUL ALWAYS THINKS*

his clinging to the mode of sensory intuition and imagination, which forced him to absolutely hold on to something positive and empirical-factual, the human personality. It prevented him from "*remembering*" the soul's need for an internalization, which, if "remembered," would have been an *absolute-negative* interiorization.

His acting out on the theoretical level is what most distinguishes his conception from both that of Heraclitus and that of the Okeanos myth. The latter two did not act out, nor were they split. They were both "whole." The unshakeable foundation of Jung's whole setup was the abstract, external, unpsychological border (his "barrier through the mental world") that separated "inner" and "outer" as mutually exclusive opposites standing, as it were, back to back, much as the two half-circles in Jakob Böhme's "broken" mandala (◗◀).[11] This dissociation was the tribute he had to pay to modernity, and it was what drove his "striving toward wholeness." Because Jung externalized the abstract boundary (i.e., left it "out there"), he did not penetrate to a psychological (interiorized) notion of the inner. As his internalizing the inner *into something external*, namely into the "positive fact" called human being shows, his psychology as a whole remained *ultimately* subject to positivity and external thinking, as much as he tried to acquire a real sense of soul.

The Okeanos myth is totally different. It started out from a non-abstract idea of boundary, from absolute interiority, but *it externalized this only secondarily* by imagining it. This secondarily *externalized* true interiority resulted in man's real being *in* the world, being *in* nature, which in turn meant that man was able to experience nature from within: as animated, divine, full of meaning. With Heraclitus the situation is again wholly different. Like Jung he started out with the external, abstract idea of boundary. This shows that from the outset he was in "reflection" and no longer in "myth." Embeddedness in nature was once and for all bygone. But then he drew the external boundary within, thereby opening up the dimension of absolute interiority *on* the level of reflecting consciousness and paving the way for a true psychology.

Another small example may illustrate the fact that Jung tried to achieve on the level of contents (observable, empirical, i.e, *external,*

---

[11]See Jung, *CW* 9/I Fig. 1, p. 297.

IS THE SOUL 'DEEP'?

"facts") what he had theoretically excluded and vehemently prohibited on the level of logical form (his own thought, the theoretical setup of psychology). I am talking of his theory of synchronicity. In his well-considered thought, the "inner" was, on the one hand, separated from the "outer" (the object external to ourselves) by an unsurmountable barrier, as we have seen. But, on the other hand, Jung showed them to be united in certain empirical (so-called synchronistic) *events*, a union which seemed to promise no less than an ultimate overcoming of the gulf between physics and psychology. Through the observation of "facts" he tried to get in through the backdoor what he had thrown out through the official, dedicated entrance. How can a psychologist put the burden of proof or authority on the empirical, on the observation of external facts? How can he want to get *himself* out of the firing-line, posing as an innocent, neutral observer? The implications of the theory of synchronicity absolutely threaten, indeed shatter, our accustomed world-view. But Jung did not take responsibility for his theory. *He* was not to blame; he had nothing to do with it; he had not on his own come up with a "metaphysical" claim of an ultimate oneness; he had only *discovered* certain "empirical facts" about the deepest, psychoid nature of the collective unconscious. Shameful.

The subject, you yourself, your *own* thinking, have to take full responsibility for whatever is stated in psychology, because the *only* entrance to psychology is through *my* (each person's) own subjectivity, which in turn is only accessible *speculatively* by reflecting myself in some other (in a given manifestation or document of the soul) and through absolute-negative interiorization. It is not accessible empirically through introspection (which is merely a literal, positive return home, inasmuch as it looks at the subject only as its new *object* of study, never reaching psychological interiority).

We see: Jung was still trying, as it were, to "travel every road out there" in search of the boundaries of soul. Declaring himself to be an empiricist means he believed, so to speak, to have to find the truth about the soul "on the street." But 2,500 years after Heraclitus and more than 100 years after Hegel, he could have and should have known that psychology begins with the return home. Not a literal return in space, but a logical one through the logical reversal of the ordinary relation of inner and outer. By cementing his empiricism, Jung in contrast to Heraclitus *protected this empiricism from its having to suffer its own natural fate*: its sublation through the inevitable experience of *not* finding out the boundaries out there. Jung arrested the search midway by resorting to ideologizing: he claimed that the road *is* the goal. This claim is ideological because it cloaks a subjective *refusal* (the refusal to expose his empiricism to its fate) in an allegedly objective truth. But what this claim says *is not* simply the truth. What it amounts to is the freezing of the search, not in the physical or imaginal sense of immobilizing it (halting it in its movement), but on the contrary, in the logical sense of freezing its movement *as movement*, so that it can go on and on and on. It can never arrive anywhere. The search cannot find its natural end. It is endless in the sense of "bad infinity." In other words, his claim is the ideological equivalent to the sentiment expressed in the idea of the soul's depth. Despite his many revolutionary moves in many areas of psychology, Jung was, in the very heart of psychology itself, namely where it is a question of its logical constitution, what in politics is called a reactionary: by staying on Heraclitus' "roads" he protracted the modes of sensory intuition and imagination and defended against the necessity of entering thought, which would have transported him to the outermost boundary of the "no" instantaneously. Thus he successfully prevented the experience of the recoil of his outwards movement (his empiricism), of its being thrown back upon itself and the ensuing reversal of his logic. Not the road is the goal. The goal is the actual, committed arrival at, and ever deeper penetration into or submission to, the "no" of the "no boundary" insight, in other words, the absolute-negative interiorization. The "road as the goal" is the *positive* negation of the goal. But psychology requires the *negative* negation.

It is not enough to *teach* the *unus mundus* and the *complexio oppositorum* and not enough to *have* and *experience* dream or visionary images thereof. That's not psychology at all, because it's still projected into positive "fact" or natural "event." What good are images from the unconscious *of* the self and wholeness and *of* an *unus mundus*, if the very systems of the unconscious and consciousness and of man and world are divided against each other by an unsurmountable barrier? Has wholeness become *real* if I dream an image of wholeness? Is a divorce or an estrangement between husband and wife healed by seeing a movie about a perfect marriage? What good is the experience of

IS THE SOUL 'DEEP'?

synchronistic events if the union of physis and psyche occurs only in the "object" out there, the event, but *excludes its own inner* from this union: namely me, my subjectivity, my conscious mind? That it does exclude my mind is obvious from the fact that I have to experience synchronistic occurrences as miraculous (as "too wonderful, too high, I cannot attain unto them"). Jung's answers to the problem of the great split in the Western soul and of the psychic opposites are mock solutions because they sidestep the actual problem. They *must* sidestep the actual problem because they are systematically set up to occur on the one side only—that of the images or experiences—when the actual problem is the division between the two sides—the images there and our subjectivity or thought here. This is why any approach concentrating on facts, felt experiences, images, the imaginal jumps too short. It stays on the one side of the split that it wants to overcome.

There is only one answer to the problem of the split and the opposites. *I* have to slowly and painfully learn to become able to *truly* think, to *conceptually comprehend*, the union of opposites—where true thinking does not mean that I push ideas around in my head, but that I *exist as* this living comprehension, i.e., as the existing Concept (Hegel). This comprehension has to have become the explicit and *real* logic of my conscious awareness of my being-in-the-world.

The neurotic split in the Western psyche is not actually pathological. What makes it pathological is that it is not *understood*—not understood as a "symptom" (manifestation) of the fact that in the history of the soul consciousness has advanced to an awareness of *itself* as a determining factor and as one half of the whole, an awareness that simply *requires* thought and dialectical logic. It requires the alchemical corruption of the empirical stance into a speculative one. The painfully experienced split is no more than an invitation to consciousness to allow itself to be initiated into thought and to become *thinking* consciousness *sensu strictiori*. It is only because this invitation is refused, consciousness stubbornly cocooning itself in the innocence of its outdated imagining mode, that the split becomes truly neurotic, pathological. The "neurotic" split is an artifact. It *is* our letting the "barrier through the mental world" remain out there as a positive barrier, in other words, it is our neglect to (like Heraclitus) interiorize it, to reflect it into *itself* (not into ourselves, our "inner"!). Jung by and large tried to locate, and cure, the split *out there, in the psyche of the person*. But this is not where it is. The soul is not split, it is not in need of wholeness, because *it* is always whole. The split is in Jung's (and our) frame of mind; it is produced by his obstinate empiricism, image-fixation and speculation phobia, that turns the soul's *inner* boundary (its internal contradiction, or the dialectic, of its logical life) inside *out*, translating it from the negativity of the soul into the positivity of imagined realities, so that the inner boundary all of a sudden appears as a hard "barrier" or positive rupture between two separate, unambiguously distinct, ontologized realms, the positivized inner (or psychic, "the unconscious") and the likewise positivized outer (or the "objective" world): exactly like the two back-to-back half-circles of Böhme's split mandala. But, of course, you need the split out there if you want to be the innocent neutral observer and psychology to be a natural science.

Why do we have neuroses? Apart from the external (not yet psychological) aspect of the contingent conditions lying in one's personal biography, there are two psychological reasons. The first is that the soul's internal boundary (= its dialectical life) is turned inside out, resulting in (1) a factually existing split or rupture and (2) a positivizing frame of mind. The second reason is that, due to this compulsion to positivize, the personality is identified, i.e., *becomes identical*, with the (now abstract, external) boundary and thus has to personally *exist as* the embodied barrier that holds two sides apart—dissociates them.

Returning from the individual neuroses to the cultural neurosis in the singular, we can say that the personality has become the existing boundary by having been interposed, like a wedge, right into the whole of experience so as to be the partition wall dividing this integral whole into two opposite classes of experiences, those that "seem() to us" to be "derived from a 'material' environment to which our bodies belong" (= the outer), versus "others, which are in no way less real," but "seem to come from a 'spiritual' source" (cf. *CW* 8 § 681), such as our dreams, fantasies, thoughts. We call this intercepting, interposed personality the "ego personality." Existing as the embodied border that splits the world into two, "the physical world" here and "the spiritual world" (ibid.) there, it is fundamentally Janus-faced. It has two

IS THE SOUL 'DEEP'?

separate truths, two antipodal "source(s) of psychic contents that crowd into my field of consciousness" (ibid.), two opposite orientations. It switches between looking out (extraversion) and turning in (introspection, introversion): it *is* the neurosis. That the ego personality *is* The Neurosis does of course not mean that in all cases it would also have to *have* a personal neurosis in the clinical sense. On the contrary. The more it *is* the neurosis, the more it is likely to be free from neurotic disorders; the more it is plagued by an individual neurosis, the more it probably refuses to *exist as* the neurotic split. And Jung's typological doctrine (about extraversion versus introversion and about the incompatibility of thinking and feeling) is the celebration and justification of the neurotic split by raising it to the rank of a general theory.

The insight into the "ego personality" as Head of Janus supports our view expressed above that "inner" and "outer" are both equally external. They are like looking left and turning around to look right, or like looking north and turning around to look south. *Dream images as such are not "inner" in a* PSYCHOLOGICAL *sense.* They are "inner" only for the mindless understanding of everyday consciousness that takes the mere name "inner" for the real thing, clinging to an *external* sense of the inner-outer opposition. Dream images are just as much outer (empirical) facts as the stones, trees, animals, people I experience in the physical world, and they have *their* real inner, namely me ("my field of consciousness"), likewise outside of themselves. That we arbitrarily call a class of *objects* vis-à-vis ourselves (thoughts, feelings, dream and fantasy images) *inner* is only a sign of the ruling abstract sense of boundary and of the internalization of this external boundary into, or its identification with, the positivized human personality. And it is the sign of a defense against the soul and its absolute-negative interiorization, its reflection-into-itself; it is the sign of a wish to do psychology, but nevertheless to keep the I out so that it can be the self-identical empirical scientist; and it is a sign of the avoidance of thought, logic. If a certain class of phenomena are supposed to be the "inner" as opposed to others as "outer," and if there is a hypostatized object called "the Self," I myself as subjectivity am exempted; I do not have to become aware of myself. It's *all* out there. Psychology, however, begins where *any* phenomenon (whether physical or mental, "real" or fantasy image) is interiorized absolute-negatively into itself and I find myself *in* its internal infinity. This is what it takes, psychology cannot be had for less.

Interestingly enough, I can "get out" and feel exempted only by *getting in* right in the center of experience as such, so as to *be* the dividing barrier. This contradiction results from the dialectical nature of existence. The ordinary ego personality and the consciousness of the scientist are the barrier in that they hold the archetypal, religious, metaphysical aspects of experience behind their back as so-called superstitions or at least "merely subjective," in order to have only positivized facts in front of themselves. Jung, the psychologist of the collective unconscious, invented a second way of getting out by getting in even deeper. How did he preserve his neutrality? He did not simply turn around so that he would look at the psychic images, while having the positive facts of reality behind him. Rather, he *widened* our ordinary vision or our ordinary sense of the real so that it would include the ordinarily ignored archetypal aspects. We already know that extraversion and introspection are equally external. How then did he *exist as* the barrier and what did *he* keep behind his back? Jung kept the religious, metaphysical dynamite contained in the soul's archetypal fantasies and ideas behind his back. He could look at the mysteries of Gnosticism, Christian dogma, metaphysical conceptions, even at the weirdest delusional ideas and superstitions without any threat to his common sense, because he had interposed himself right in the middle of these ideas or images, dividing their *archetypal content* as legitimate psychological interest ("psychological reality") from their inherent *claim to truth*, which had to be excluded by penalty of one's sanity of mind.

In other words, Jung repeated the same division with which positivistic science rid itself of any religious or metaphysical implications, only now on a deeper, more refined level: He applied it precisely to what the other sciences had systematically excluded. The cleaver with which he was able to interpose the scientific ego personality into what science had hitherto *had* to keep behind its back was his invention of a second, special kind of reality or truth, the aforementioned *psychological reality*. This ingenious invention permitted him to subject even the archetypal ideas or the imaginal to the same positivizing that formerly had cleared "nature" from any archetypal "projections." "When psychology speaks, for instance, of the motif of the virgin birth, it is only concerned with the fact that there is such an idea, but it is not concerned with the question whether such an idea is true or false in any other sense. The idea is psychologically true inasmuch as it exists" (*CW* 11 § 4). Here we see not Occam's but Jung's razor at work. The archetypal substance is cut apart, castrated, deprived of its claim to truth, reduced to the mere factual "occurrence" (*ibid.*) or existence of its abstract content. This is—*horribile dictu*—archetypal positivism, positivism applied to the imaginal itself! *Psychological* truth is here defined precisely as what excludes real truth, real truth which *has* to be kept behind the psychologist's back. So Jung rescued the imaginal contents for the scientific approach by paying for it with their soul: their claim to truth; nevertheless he sold the resulting leftover as *the* definition of psychology! All this, in order to avoid falling into dialectical logic and speculation.

But now we have to realize, too, that the personality as Head of Janus already *is* the dialectic, the existing Concept, only turned inside out and thus in its frozen, hardened shape as literal border or dissociation. This is also why it needs, and has, the sentimental idea that "the soul is deep" to console it for, and to disguise, its own *logical* petrification. In the romantic sentiment it has the split-off other side inherent in the dialectic (other than its contradictory nature), namely the dialectic's interiority and fluidity as the soul of *all* reality and as logical *life* (an interiority that is now, in the guise of this romantic sentiment, *also* abstract, externalized, reified). If Heraclitus can be considered the Father of psychology, psychology has to learn from his fragment (1) that the notion of soul hinges on actually getting to its *boundaries* and thus on a sense of opposition or contradiction (inner–outer), (2) that getting there is only possible through and in thought, and that it is *negative* arrival, or arrival at a "no," being permeated by this "no," (3) that such an arrival leads to an absolute-negative interiorization of "boundary," resulting in an interiority through which (4) the boundary is decomposed as the positive barrier that it used to be for the imagining mind and is vaporized into the fluidity of living *dialectics*. Such is the depth of the soul's *logos*.

CHAPTER SEVEN

The Leap Into The Solid Stone or The Breakthrough Into Interiority

In the El Capitan Canyon Seminar I discussed in detail the psychology or dialectical logic of the glass mountain fairy tale.[1] It was about an *upwards* movement into transcendence, to the absolute embodied by the princess sitting on the mountain top, and the dialectic of this movement up the slippery mountain was that the goal could precisely only be reached via the absolute failure of the people attempting to reach it. Similarly, in the previous chapter ("Is the Soul Deep?") I discussed the movement to the *outermost* boundary of being. Now I want to discuss a very different topic, the movement *into* the true inner, true interiority. And yet, as we will see, the logic of the three movements is much the same.

I will begin with a legend of the Crow Indians who belong to the Sioux.

> *A boy had fallen with his face into the fire in the cabin. Because he did not want to be seen with his marred face in the camp, he ran away and remained missing. Much later, two women, a mother with her daughter, had been abducted by another tribe and tried to get back to their own people. This was very difficult. They had to*

---

[1] Wolfgang Giegerich, David L. Miller, Greg Mogenson, *Dialectics & Analytical Psychology. The El Capitan Canyon Seminar*, New Orleans (Spring Journal, Inc.) 2005, here pp. 9–24.

166   *THE SOUL ALWAYS THINKS*

> *stay for some time in a mountain area with a deep canyon. They are helped by that missing boy who had meanwhile grown into a man. He provides hides for a tent, etc., for them. The mother suggests to her daughter that she should become the wife of this man. However, he did not live out in the open, in a hut or tent, but in the solid, impenetrable rock into which he was wont to enter through the smooth wall of the canyon. The daughter knew that she could not enter. She had to see whether there might be an opportunity where she might get in. Therefore she waited until the man came out. When he went back in, she followed him and lay down inside by the entrance. But he sent her away. The same happened three times, and the fourth time he saw how brave she was and took her as his wife.*[2]

The point here, of course, is that the Crow man did not live in a niche or some other kind of hollow place in the rock or between rocks. He lived in the very rock itself, in the impenetrable rock. And he did not enter it through a crack or opening. He miraculously went into the solid wall.

It might perhaps be helpful, considering how strange this idea is, to supply a bit of support from other stories with a similar motif.

> *In central-European mountains there are many rock walls that open themselves for him who comes at the right moment or has a miracle key.*

> *In a local legend from Alsace, the father of Saint Odilia wanted to force her to marry a certain man. She ran away, kneeled in front of a wall of rock in order to pray. The rock opened, enclosed her and let her out only after the father had given up his plan to marry her to that man.* Again we have here a dense rock that nevertheless under certain circumstances or for certain persons becomes a place to be in.

> *In a local legend from Carinthia a poor farm worker who because of his poverty cannot marry his bride runs with his forehead against a grey stone half the size of a man. Now he notices a small door in the wall of the rock, goes into a gallery and comes into a large hall shiny with gold and silver. A beautiful woman fills his pockets with rocks, leads him to an armchair out of silver where he falls asleep. When he awakens, he is outside, and there is no door in the rock any more.*

---

[2] According to Heino Gehrts, "Vom Wesen der Steine," in: *GORGO 11* (1986), pp. 3–27, here p. 20.

THE LEAP INTO THE SOLID STONE   167

> *Now he believes to have dreamed. But when he comes home, he finds out that he has been away for seven years and that the stones that the woman had put into his pockets are nuggets of gold, so that he now can marry his girl.*
>
> *In his* Heimskringla Snorri Sturluson *describes how a Swedish king by the name* Sveigðir *in the evening of a holy day entered into a solid rock that was as large as a house and did not return. His whole life long he had desired to encounter the god Odin. For that purpose he had undertaken a five year journey east. Now back at home again, a dwarf, standing beneath the door to the stone beckons him and tells him: there, in that stone he was going to meet Odin. The king leaped into the stone, and the stone closed itself behind him.*[3]

The soul, it seems, when it wants to imagine the idea of its own interiority, presents us with the image of a solid rock or a stone wall. From our everyday point of view this is absurd. But this absurdity is the purpose, or I should rather not speak of absurdity, but of the total *self-contradiction* that we find in these stories. The impenetrable rock, in and with its very impenetrability, is nevertheless open and clear. The stone half the size of a man contains a gallery in which a full-grown man can walk upright and even a large hall. We have here images of the impossible.

Normally, if on your way forward you run into a wall out of rock this wall is experienced as an obstacle blocking your way, an impasse, a dead end. And normally the image of an impasse arouses the desire to turn around and to seek one's fortune somewhere else. But *this* dead end *is* the goal for the Swedish king, *is* the rescue for Saint Odilia, *is* the solution for the poor farm worker. The wall *is* the opening, the rock the clearance. The obstacle *is* the entrance.

What occurs here is rather something like one's breaking through the "soundbarrier," into a completely new, other dimension. This is why one has to take the image of the dead end very literally. At its end there is a real ending, a closure. An absolute stop. No continuation. One has reached the end of the world, i.e., the end of the ordinary, empirical, positively existing world, the end of the old dimension, and with the breakthrough through the wall one has not merely overcome

---

[3] All examples from Gehrts, op. cit. p. 18. The last one in *Snorris Königsbuch* vol. 1, in *Thule vol. 14*, Jena 1922, p. 38.

an obstacle so that one can continue one's way beyond it, whereby what is beyond it is the continuation of the ordinary empirical world. No, one has altogether left this world and been catapulted into a wholly other one, the realm of the soul. The ordinary world has disappeared and been replaced by a totally different one.

It is a sudden inversion from impasse to opening. We know from Gestalt psychology how the line-drawing of a cube (a so-called Necker cube) can "flip-flop" (it looks like a cube shown from above and then suddenly it appears as a cube shown from below), or how with the "figure and ground" illusion one's perception of one and the same picture of a vase may fluctuate between seeing a white vase on black background or seeing two black profiles of faces with white space as background. These are empirical phenomena within the psychology of Gestalt perception, and which way you see the figures does not make a fundamental difference. Both ways of seeing in each case remain on the same ontological or logical level, while in our topic, that of the rock that opens, we are dealing with a breakthrough from one dimension into a new one. Nevertheless, this trivial empirical phenomenon of a "flip-flop" can serve as an imaginal bridge to the understanding of the kind of inversion that takes place here on a more fundamental level. It is one and the same rock that is both at once, impenetrable obstacle and opening, clearance, and thus it is self-contradictory, although it is, just as with those perceptional illusions, always only either the one or the other version that is real for you at a time. For the Crow woman the canyon wall was an absolute obstacle while she was sitting in front of it alone. But when the rock dweller had appeared, she could follow him inside without difficulty. The poor farm worker ran with his head against a solid stone that was of course impenetrable for him. And at the end of the story, it is impenetrable again: no door was to be seen, and so what had passed in between appeared to him as a mere dream. But in between he had indeed been inside the stone, but this had meant that while there he had left the ordinary world.

The "flip-flop" like inversion may even have been made possible by the blow against his head when he ran with his forehead into this stone. The blow is the physically real, undeniable confrontation with the obstacle as obstacle, with its hardness and absolute impenetrability. The real experience of the impasse, of the futility of any attempt to

THE LEAP INTO THE SOLID STONE 169

move forward is, it seems, the precondition of the breakthrough into the other dimension. In the case of king Sveigðir the five year long journey east in search of his god had proved to him the absolute futility of a literal, positive search for god. This insight was *his* sound barrier and as such it was the impenetrable rock into which he could leap. In the case of Saint Odilia, it was the utter hopelessness of her attempt to run away from her powerful father and her bridegroom that opened the rock wall for her and turned the very obstacle into her protection. It was the absolute impasse that opened a way out for her; it was precisely the very hopelessness of her plight that by totally enveloping her with no escape provided her protection. The fact that in this legend she arrives at a wall of rock indicates symbolically that she has realized the total futility of her attempt to run away. She has arrived at a dead end. But this dead end *is* her rescue. Here one is reminded of Hölderlin's all-too-often-quoted lines, *Wo aber Gefahr ist, wächst das Rettende auch*, "But where there is danger, there rescue is close." However, what we are concerned with here, goes far beyond this dictum. In the latter, danger and rescue seem to be two different things (which is emphasized by the word *auch*, "also"), but here we do not have a duality of plight and hope. Rather, the absolute impossibility is in itself the rescue. There is only one thing, one reality, the rock, which is the image of impenetrability *and* opening at once. This self-contradictory nature is the very point of the rock image.

So we can say that the impenetrability is needed, indeed, required, if there is to be a breakthrough into the other dimension. The absolute obstacle is in itself the entrance to initiation. Without the obstacle, no initiation.

What is that which rescues? How can the relentless experience of the absolute hopelessness of her situation *in itself* become the shield and refuge for Saint Odilia? And why would her father all of a sudden change his mind? A still other way to ask the same question is: what is this other dimension that opens up within the impenetrable rock, the hopeless plight, the futility of the attempt on the part of the Swedish king to find the god Odin? This dimension is that of the soul's interiority.

But with this term we have only explained *ignotum per ignotius*, the unknown through the even more unknown. And rather than inserting our conventional, ready-made concept of the inner into the above sentence, we have to conversely allow ourselves to be taught for the first time from the Swedish king's leap into a stone, or from Odilia's flight into the rock of her hopelessness, what psychological interiority is.

It is precisely Odilia's relentless realization and unreserved, active acceptance of the absolute futility of her attempt to run away from the threat posed by her father which opens up the psychic space of interiority and protects her from the threat. As long as she was hoping to be successful in her flight, she would remain threatened by the possibility of being reached by her persecutors. Why should they not be able to follow her wherever she went and capture her? As long as she relied on an escape in the realm of positivity, through literally running away or by hiding behind a literal bulwark, she could be reached, because she would then stay on the same level with her pursuers. But the moment she left this level and entered another dimension she was safe, not literally so, but logically or psychologically so, because now she was logically out of reach for her enemies.

This leap or breakthrough is possible only through the self-application of the notion of flight. By firmly bedding herself in the hopelessness of her situation she escaped from the notion of escape. She turned the running away against itself, thereby negating it, but not merely in the sense of simple negation, which would have amounted to a resigned giving in to her father's wish. No, even with this negation of her flight she stayed faithful to her purpose of fleeing. Hers was a negation *of* the negation *of* her impulse to escape. She applied the notion of the flight to the notion of flight itself and thereby interiorized the flight into itself even as she interiorized herself into the notion of the absolute hopelessness of her situation; we could also say she escaped into the futility of escape, so that her escape was *sublated* escape.

But this was the real escape, the escape from the *level* of positivity into logical negativity. Here she was absolutely out of reach, because (1) having escaped from the notion of escape she had become immune to her pursuers; and on top of it (2) the latter could not possibly follow her into the sphere of logical negativity or interiority. Why not? Because her pursuers were not fleeing and were not in an absolutely hopeless situation, so that they of course could not negate the flight from the absolute hopelessness, let alone negate this negation. As pursuers they were condemned to stay in the realm of positivity. And so precisely by having escaped from her need to escape them was Odilia absolutely

THE LEAP INTO THE SOLID STONE

171

safe from them. There was not a literal rock that miraculously enveloped her. It was the other way around. The fact that she willfully settled in the total futility of an attempt to escape and ipso facto had become aloof to all the terrible things that could possibly be done to her *was* in itself the impenetrable rock that protected her. If we viewed her personalistically as a real human being and not a figure in a legend, we could perhaps say that she had acquired and withdrawn into what might be called a new, previously unheard-of firmness of character, a firmness as impenetrable as a rock. She had made herself *independent* of external events, of course not physically independent, but logically so. She had conquered the space of interiority.

It is probably because she had escaped into the logical independence from all external threats that her father changed his mind. Unreachable in the space of interiority and negativity as she was, he had lost her, lost his power over her. So he gave up.

From what was just shown, we can see once more quite clearly the strict identity of open clearance and impenetrable rock. Before I had tried to approach our motif by alluding to perceptional "flip-flop" experiences. But there is not an inversion. There is the simultaneity, the contradictory identity of the opposites. Before I had said that the hard rock is the entrance. But it is not only that. By passing through an entrance you leave it behind. But here the hard rock *is* the opening, and the open space of interiority *is* the enclosing and protecting rock.

Now we understand why there must be a dead end and why the open clearance does not lie beyond the wall of stone, but in the impenetrable stone of the wall itself. If the wall were no more than an obstacle to be overcome, then consciousness, even if it had overcome the obstacle, would remain in the same dimension that it had set out to overcome. After the overcoming of the obstacle one would be back to business as usual. The positive overcoming of the obstacle would tie one to the positivity of the obstacle, just as Odilia's pursuers stay stuck in the world of positivity. It is the impasse alone that negates the positivity of "mere obstacle" and ipso facto produces the breakthrough through the "sound barrier" into the completely other sphere of logical negativity and interiority, which consists in the sublation of the sphere of our conventional existence.

When the soul is interested in portraying its own true interiority, it uses the image of a stone or a wall of rock. This image helps us to distinguish true interiority from the false one that comes today mainly in two versions.

The one is the psychologistic inner, the interiority of introspection and self-growth, the whole interest in oneself and what goes on within oneself, the focus on those abstractions that we call our emotions, affects, wishes, fantasies—the emotions and fantasies of the cut-off, worldless, private individual.

The other is the interiority of esoteric spirituality, such as the *mundus imaginalis* or the idea of "higher worlds."

The rock saves us from both. True interiority is not in us and is not anything esoteric. It is in the rock. And the rock is out there in reality; it is, for example, the real plight of Odilia. It is very concrete, the experience of "no exit," of absolute futility. Whereas the glass mountain tale presented the sphere of negativity as transcendence, the rock teaches us that *this transcendence* is immanent or is *this-worldly* transcendence. Whereas the Kena Upanishad had taught that "not what the eyes can see, but what opens the eyes is the Brahma," the impenetrable rock now teaches us that that which opens the eyes is not something spiritual in the lofty sense of esotericism, mysticism, or spiritual exercises above and separate from normal reality. Just as the spirit Mercurius is in the matter, so is true interiority in real life out there. What opens the eyes is precisely the hard encounter with that certainly visible and tangible solid "rock" in our worldly reality that consists in the irreducible insight that our striving has run into an impasse.

It opens our eyes to the large hall out of silver and gold or to the sphere of Odin, but it does so only provided that instead of, in view of the obstacle, simply turning around again in resignation or despair we hold our place in the absolute contradiction of dead end and continued faithfulness to our purpose. Because then the experienced stone wall interiorizes our progressive movement into itself so that it becomes an in itself recursive progression.

CHAPTER EIGHT

The Future of Psychology: its Going Under[1]

If now at the end of this century, which in the field of psychology had such a promising beginning with the pioneer achievements of Freud, Adler and Jung, we look at the present state of (therapeutic) psychology, it presents itself in a deplorable state.

First of all it shows a picture of confusion: several hundred different psychological schools, theoretical conceptions, and practical approaches exist side by side without inner connection—a state of affairs that is rather intolerable for anyone with a sense of scientific responsibility.

Secondly, at least in the West the credibility of depth psychology as a whole has been disputed during the last few years; more and more the experts in psychiatry and psychology tend to lean toward a *biological* (genetic and biochemical) view and method of treatment. The more the prestige of biological psychiatry increases, the more Freud, for one, is charged with having been the inventor of possibly exciting fictions which belong much more in the domain of the arts and belles-lettres than in that of a scientific psychology.

---

[1] This was written in German in 1999 as an invited contribution to the "New Perspectives in Psychotherapy in the 21st Century" special millennia issue of *SEISHIN RYOHO* ("Japanese Journal of Psychotherapy") and published there in a Japanese translation by Prof. Toshio Kawai in vol. 26, no. 1, February 2000, pp. 33–40. I am indebted to Prof. Yasuhiro Yamanaka for his asking me to contribute to this journal.

The third problem that exists for depth psychology, especially for the Jungian direction, is popularization with its ensuing watering-down effect. What makes this so dangerous is that ultimately, in the long run, it has a diluting effect also on professional psychotherapy and psychological theory. Along with this popularization (*pop psychology*), the clear difference tends to become dissolved between psychology on the one hand and, on the other hand, superstition, esoteric beliefs, or, in the mildest case, the irrational abuse of psychology for the gratification of one's personal *emotional-ideological* needs during these times of radical change and a widespread feeling of unease.

A fourth threat to depth psychology comes from the State. In times when the supply of money runs short, the State tries to save on social expenditure. But at the same time it also has to see to it that sufficient psychotherapeutic care is available for the population. A third factor is that there is an increasing tendency to establish laws governing the profession of psychotherapy, to introduce State regulation and supervision for its execution, whereas previously it had been possible for psychotherapy to be performed in a more or less law-less, unregulated realm, in a freedom that is so necessary if therapy with its to some extent subversive, if not anarchic character is to be what it is meant to be. These political necessities plus the worries on the part of psychotherapists about how to make a living puts the issue of *money* emotionally and factually in the center. Content issues ultimately have to take second place. The different schools of psychotherapy struggle with each other for the best access to available State or health plan funds. All this in turn not only has the consequence that psychotherapy becomes bureaucratized (which is incompatible with what it is about); it also has the consequence that the therapeutic schools are exposed to an inappropriate external pressure to justify their existence by proving their efficacy in terms of purely technical thinking by means of statistical investigations and external (non-psychological) definitions of what "success" is. Naturally, this has a detrimental effect on the mental attitude of all those working in the field of psychotherapy because they come under an ever greater influence of the tendency to give psychotherapy a scientific cast and to make it more technical. Such a tendency completely contradicts the actual task of psychology and

THE FUTURE OF PSYCHOLOGY   175

psychotherapy, which is precisely in an age of the absolute rule of technology and capitalism to serve a wholly other reality, the soul.[2]

Truly dismal prospects. All this could be reason enough to look ahead with desperation to "the psychotherapy in the 21st century" and to predict its end. When in 1927 with respect to religion Freud felt the need to speak of the *Future of an Illusion*, he was perhaps in truth, but unwittingly, talking about the future of psychoanalysis and psychotherapy themselves. It is not impossible that the whole undertaking of depth-psychological, therapeutic psychology will prove to have been a fiction of the 20th century. But prophecies are not my business. There can always be surprising turns. Let us leave what will really happen with psychology open.

Although I do not want to risk in the following any predictions of my own about the future, I nevertheless do want to look *ahead*. However not ahead in time on the literal, factual level, but—by *psychologizing* the concept of "future" itself—ahead towards the *inner telos*, the *essential determination* of psychology. A telos is the future that is no longer understood in an external-temporal, but in an essential or logical sense. Undeterred by the present real situation of psychology in the world, undeterred also by the unlikelihood of such a line of thought as the one I want to follow, I would like to trace out the path on which to my mind therapeutic psychology would have to move in the future. In other words, I would like to determine the future *task* that its own inner nature, from within itself, assigns to psychology and to which it would have to apply itself. Whether it will in fact take this course, whether it will indeed tackle this task, is not our topic.

Where does that path lead? What is the telos, the task, of therapeutic psychology that it would have to take upon itself during the 21st century? I pointed out that the present condition in which

---

[2] With this comment I do not want to affirm the popular view of an absolute incompatibility of technology and soul. With respect to any "acting out" and promoting literal technology (the work of our technicians, engineers, and scientists) and any technological or scientistic as well as utilitarian thinking the soul is, to be sure, "wholly other." But this does not mean that this great phenomenon of technology itself would be soulless. As I insist in my *Technology and the Soul* (2007, vol. 2 of the present collection of my English papers), it is precisely psychology's task to discover the soul, the Mercurial spirit, at work in or behind the amazing development of technology. Technology has to be seen through, precisely because of the otherness of the soul. In the age of technology it is psychology's task not to be misled to think that technology were itself a technical phenomenon. It is a soul phenomenon.

psychotherapy finds itself could be a reason to predict its end during the coming century. Now I propose the thesis that it is precisely the *task* of psychology *to go the way into its going under*. It is clear that *this* "going under" is a different one from the aforementioned "end." What had before been stated with this term was that therapeutic psychology would be totally finished. The present thesis claims the exact opposite, that in its going-under psychology would have its true *future*. It will be the task of the following discussion to elucidate what this going under is in which psychology would find its fulfillment and reach its telos.

Before I can devote myself to this topic I must first explain what the standpoint and starting-point is from which I approach it. Today's generally prevailing view about research is that it ought to be interdisciplinary. Just as in the practice of science and business team work is preferred, so all important questions are supposed to be tackled across diverse disciplines. Our time is on principle decisively against closed systems and stands up for diversity, plurality and fundamentally *open* theories. Any belief in a center is disapproved of. "Dissemination" and "difference" are today's mottos.

In view of all the many schools of depth psychology, let alone psychology at large, it might in this sense suggest itself to take into account as many theoretical orientations and practical approaches as possible in order to assemble from each what shows itself to be useful and convincing and in this way to correct the onesidednesses of any single orientation. Indeed, whereas only a few decades ago a wish to demarcate, if not hostility, and competition, determined the relation between the diverse psychological schools, it seems to become much more common today to make attempts at communication across the dividing lines between the schools.

As humanly commendable as such an open communication-oriented attitude is, I cannot follow this syncretistic endeavor in the case of depth psychology. My instinct and my theoretical convictions say no. Rather, with full determination I stand up for onesidedness. Without regard to what is said and done to the left and to the right of me, I want to go more and more into the depths at the *one* point at which I stand, that is, I want to go all the way through with that theory or school to which I belong. Not a glance across the fence to others, not an expansion into alien regions, not a comparison and mediation

THE FUTURE OF PSYCHOLOGY

of one's own discourse with the many other ones all around oneself can qualify as the essential direction in which depth psychology has to move. Psychology is the discipline of interiority. The movement of psychological thought can only be that of a continuous absolute-negative interiorization into itself (deeper into the position that is one's starting point). The contradictions inherent both in one's own position itself and between it and its full realization are here, so to speak, the rungs of the ladder that leads into the depths.

The ground on which I stand and from which (and the horizon within which) I approach the topic that is up for discussion here is that of Jungian psychology. It is my *Hic Rhodus, hic salta*. I will therefore argue completely internally.

With this description of the direction of movement of a true depth psychology I have unexpectedly already presented a first, rough, but nevertheless the decisive determination of that *going under* that is the telos of psychology. It is that absolute-negative interiorization, psychology's going under into its own *internal* ground, its concept, its essence. It is precisely this pull into its own inner ground or *Abgrund* (abysmal depth) that is the distinguishing mark of psychology, that which turns (at least could turn) psychology into psychology in the first place and what naturally also fundamentally sets it off (would set it off) from the world of the sciences. The latter are always oriented outward, away from themselves towards objects ("ob-jects"), towards some other. In addition, this its distinguishing mark also sets it off from people's so-called everyday life-world. And in this regard my decision without looking left or right unreservedly to allow myself to fall into that psychology that I belong to is in itself already a kind of going under on my part, or the first step of such a going under.

Without going under psychology could not be more than behaviorism. For where and how else would there be interiority, where and how else "soul"? We have gone beyond that status of consciousness where we could still believe in "the soul" as an existing entity, in "*the* unconscious" as a mysterious reality behind the scene, or in the "inner" which is supposed to be literally inside a person (somewhere in his head? In his body enclosed by his skin?). No, the inner, the depths, or the soul exists only in and through the going under on the part of psychology itself into its actual inner ground, in other words, only as (logical) *movement*, not as an existing place or entity. Soul is the inner of every real, however 'the inner' in the sense of "what is seen *from within.*" But psychology is only able to see *from within* if it has gone under into its own inner ground and has thus arrived "within": has made interiority its *principle.* Interiority can exclusively be reached *negatively,* only through a going under or fall into one's own inner ground. Everything into which I move from outside in a positive sense of literal movement (or into which I try to get via introspection or empathizing) remains external.

A true fall into the inner ground stands at the beginning of C.G. Jung's psychology. Jung's entire psychological orientation is grounded in those experiences that he had following his going under. After his separation from Freud he went into a phase of disorientation and was afflicted with an enormous inner pressure and a stream of fantasies. Jung's condition has been interpreted as "a creative illness" (Ellenberger), but also as a "longer psychotic reaction." His going under is related in *Memories, Dreams, Reflections.*

> In order to grasp the fantasies which were stirring in me "underground," I knew I had to let myself plummet down into them, as it were. I felt not only violent resistance to this, but a distinct fear. For I was afraid of losing command of myself and becoming prey to the unconscious—and as a psychiatrist I realized only too well what that meant. After a prolonged hesitation, however, I saw that there was no other way out. ...
>
> It was during Advent of the year 1913—December 12, to be exact—that I resolved upon the decisive step. I was sitting at my desk once more, thinking over my fears. Then I let myself drop. Suddenly it was as though the ground literally gave way beneath my feet, and I plunged down into dark depths. I could not fend off a feeling of panic. ... (pp. 178 f., transl. modif.)

Jung's plummeting into the depths did, however, not lead to the literal annihilation that he had feared. "But then, abruptly, at not too great a depth, I landed on my feet in a soft, sticky mass. I felt a great relief." A vision set in. Later, many other visions followed, and in the course of these visions Jung encountered in a certain figure emerging in them, in Philemon, something like his "guru," his teacher or mentor who initiated him into psychology inasmuch as he taught Jung the notion of the *reality* of the images, the notion of psychic reality.

THE FUTURE OF PSYCHOLOGY

Jung's going under was not a one-time event. Rather, Jung fell frequently back on the idea of a going under as a methodical aid for entering the inner depths:

> In order to seize hold of the fantasies, I frequently imagined a steep descent. I even made several attempts to get to the very bottom. The first time I reached, as it were, a depth of about a thousand feet; the next time I already found myself at the edge of a cosmic abyss. It was like a voyage to the moon, or a descent into empty space. First came the image of a crater, and I had the feeling that I was in the land of the dead. (p. 181)

His going under proves to have been a *descensus ad inferos*.

Now we must nevertheless raise the question: is what Jung experienced really that going under which I said amounted to the future of psychology? Certainly not. Psychologically it shows serious flaws which, however, are merely different aspects of a single *proton pseudos*.

Jung took the necessity of a plunge *literally* and *personally*. He identified himself with this task. This had the effect that his going under and what succeeded it was pushed off onto a sideline, namely into his private felt experience, and that, conversely, what was actually sought, namely the true, the *logical* going under, the going under of psychology into *its* ground, was avoided. Jung *acted out* the going under on the literal level of subjective, felt experience. He absorbed it into himself, appropriated it (cf. his phrase "to seize hold of the fantasies"). He performed it in the imagination (within a vision) as a *literal* emotional event within himself, and in this way he unwittingly protected *psychology* from *its* having to suffer its going under. His going under only belongs to his personal biography. It is only important for him alone. But for psychology and for us his having gone under is only an interesting report, it is what is nowadays called a piece of "information." The demand later put forward time and again by Jung in other contexts, namely that we ought to *distinguish* ourselves from the archetypal ideas (in this case: from the idea of a *descensus ad inferos*), was here not heeded by Jung himself. To distinguish myself from the soul means to realize that the psychic process is not about *me*, is not *my* personal process, that *I* am not its aim and focus, and it is not intended for *my* benefit. The soul is an end in itself. When Jung in retrospect states, "I needed, however, to take the risk of trying to *gain*

180   THE SOUL ALWAYS THINKS

power over them [the emotions and fantasies]" (p. 178, transl. modif., my emphasis) and that he was afraid to "*becom[e] prey to* the unconscious" (p. 178, modif., my emphasis), we see how for him the unconscious is set up as a monster to be fought. This brings the fact out into the open that he as the empirical person that he was was identified with a Herculean stance towards the underworld.

It is true, with a certain justification one could call these deep experiences during this period a "creative illness" in analogy to a "shaman's illness." But with this view we already touch upon what is problematic here. If it is really a case of such an "illness," then Jung performed before himself, just as in archaic times, the dramatic play of a personal going through a kind of initiation ritual (Jung himself speaks of his "experiment with the unconscious" (p. 181). But such a thing as an initiation to be personally experienced had only its legitimate place in that psychic status in which "the person" was still *symbolical to itself,* in which it was logically, to the highest degree, *released* into the course of events and did not preserve itself vis-à-vis the events, in other words, in which it was so to speak a pure *bearer* of masks,[3] the mere place of apparitions. The moment, however, when man became an ego personality to himself and claims for himself a solid, permanent identity of his own *vis-à-vis* whatever happens, when he takes himself as person literally, then a niveau of consciousness has been reached that makes it psychologically illegitimate to think that oneself could still be the subject which would have to live through an "initiation" (quite analogously to how it is no longer psychologically appropriate, as it still was in pagan times, to see and adore in the sun, the sea, or in other natural objects veritable gods and spirits). To still want to personally and in earnest experience an initiation is now *regressive* (unless it is merely a simulation serving one's spiritual entertainment).

The place and the subject of what in former days was the initiation process is now the *logos*: what is necessary is *psychology's* (and thus consciousness's) going under into *its* internal ground, into its *Concept*. It is not Jung's, not the psychologist's nor the patient's (the analysand's) going under into *his* or *her* personal unconscious. It is psychology that is the true subject of this going under. This is the first point.

---

[3] Cf. my paper, "The Lesson of the Mask," in: W. G., *The Neurosis of Psychology. Primary Papers towards a Critical Psychology,* Collected English Papers vol. 1, New Orleans (Spring Journal Books) 2005, pp. 257–262.

THE FUTURE OF PSYCHOLOGY

The second point refers to the logical form: the going under, instead of being something literal, a special act, event, or experience in time, must have become the logical "structure" of psychology, the logical form of consciousness and that means it must have become *syntactical*. As long as it is still an emotional experience, as long as it is imagined as a process of images, as it is acted out as an internal adventure, it still remains semantic, a content, objectified—and thus it is externalized, unpsychological.

The third point concerns the whereto of the going under: Jung still plunges down into an external, namely *spatial* depths ("it was like a voyage to the moon"). That is to say he does not really drop into an interiority, but precisely falls outside of himself, and so he also lands in his first vision on a ground that is an other, something alien for him, something *upon* which he then literally stands (with his feet) as upon his external, sensibly-given foundation. We see that the going under has not yet become psychological, internal to itself. It is still imagined. The *psychological* ground, by contrast, would not be a literal foundation, a basis or floor for the feet, but *sublated* ground: the Concept, the inner essence, the mind (mindedness) that fills, animates, guides me, and that only in this sense also "carries" or "supports" me.

It is worthwhile—beyond the internal logic of the plunge itself— to also think about the reasons that necessitated this form of the *descensus ad inferos*. From his own point of view Jung's situation at that time appeared as follows: He was threatened and attacked by unconscious emotions and, in order to seize hold of the fantasy content hidden in them and to escape a psychosis through this grasping them, he had to undertake the venture of his going under. But I think we must not sight unseen take over this interpretation of his situation. For it is begotten by the atmosphere of the crisis itself and, as a simple self-articulation of this atmosphere, justifies it. However, we must not, as Jung himself knew, "fall for" the "conjecture"[4] (today we would perhaps call it "ideology") generated by a psychic crisis itself, but must rather see through it. In our case it is reasonable to precisely reverse the causal relation: the fact that Jung was stuck in his personalistic prejudice and for this reason found *himself as person* identified with "the true subject" of the psychological process was the reason why the

---

[4] Cf. *CW* 10 §§ 356, 365.

danger of psychosis existed in the first place. Only on account of the identification of the ego personality with the true subject of the soul's process did he, if I may express myself this way, come under fire of the emotions and images. And by undertaking to risk his going under in order to get the upper hand over the images, he merely legitimized the personalistic prejudice and proceeded, syntonically with it, further on its ground. It was not "the unconscious" that compelled him, as if it were a beast of prey ready to devour him, to face it at highest personal risk. Rather, it was the unreflected prior dogma of the personality as the true subject and as the framework that is supposed to contain the soul's concerns within itself, in other words, the psychologistic squeezing of the soul's life into the cramped vessel of the modern personality, that conversely forced the psychic contents into the shape of "the unconscious," an unconscious, which *ipso facto* threatened to explode the personality. The modern personality is one which takes itself literally.

From Jung's perspective (just as from that clinical perspective mentioned above that diagnosed a "longer psychotic reaction"), the crisis appears as a natural event, something that is simply given as a fact, a fateful happening, and the sole question in this situation is whether and how the person befallen by it can get through the crisis. By contrast, it is my opinion that we must not take the surging tide of emotions and images, i.e., the incidence of the crisis, simply for granted as a given fact. Much rather, the critical situation itself must already be viewed psychologically: not as fate, an "objective necessity," but so to speak as "artificially" posited and staged by the soul solely on the basis of *its* own necessities. Viewed in this way, namely as a purposive arrangement, a literally "functional" disorder brought on for a very particular purpose, Jung's crisis during those years was a truly *psychological* crisis, by no means caused by nonpsychological empirical conditions originating in his personality or biography (e.g., constitutional factors, vicissitudes in early childhood, his having been conditioned by a certain adverse family constellation), but brought about solely by or rather *for* soul purposes, logical purposes. It was so to speak Jung's "*hystérie grande*" (Charcot), not as private person, but as a psychological theorist.

What was all this about, what did it happen for? In the course of his mythological studies Jung had arrived at insights that take effect

THE FUTURE OF PSYCHOLOGY

above all in the chapter "The Sacrifice" of his work *Wandlungen und Symbole der Libido* (1912) and which he knew would cost him his friendship with Freud. Through the break with Freud Jung was not only mentally isolated, totally thrown back upon himself. For him (for whom according to his own profession "making 'theory'" was a "form of existence" "as necessary for me as eating and drinking" *MDR* p. 327, transl. modif.), the fact that those insights had also thrown him into a fundamental *theoretical* conflict carried much more weight than the personal rift with Freud. Jung had realized—this is how we can describe his insight today—that the psychic, the soul,[5] was in itself (a) noetic, a world of meanings, (b) historical, (c) "theo-logical" ("saying the god"), and (d) (logically) infinite. This discovery was devastating for the natural-scientific conception of psychology. But as much as Jung was willing for the sake of his new insight to sacrifice his friendship *on the personal level*, it was absolutely out of the question for him to forego *on the theoretical level* the natural-scientific credo that he shared with Freud and his age. This *theoretical* sacrifice he did not want to make; nor was he able to sacrifice his convictions about the nature of the psychic.

Consequently, the only option that in principle remained was the sacrifice *of the* theoretical, that is, the *sacrificium intellectus*, the renunciation of consciousness—the sinking of the psychic into unconsciousness: *the* (so-called) unconscious.

The intellectual dilemma was—for a person for whom making theory was "a form of existence as necessary as eating and drinking"— so terrible that it could not even become conscious and explicit. *This* is the reason, I think, for Jung's "disorientation" during that time. The actual conflict had to be resolved beneath the threshold of consciousness, without the participation of his waking intelligence or a sense of intellectual responsibility, or rather precisely not *resolved*, truly settled, but altogether eliminated, rendered harmless. But how?

Through nothing else but that very crisis, "the creative illness," "the longer psychotic reaction." This crisis has to be comprehended

---

[5] The word "the psychic" in English creates problems of equivocation. It can refer to the psyche (then it is *das Psychische*) just as well as to the soul (then it is *das Seelische*). It therefore can mean either one of the opposites contained in "the psychological difference," which is the difference between psyche (as part of human biology) and soul, or between the psychic in the narrower sense (*das Psychische*) and the psychological (the logos of the soul). In this paper it generally means *das Seelische*.

as the performance of a *ritual* or as an *arrangement* in Alfred Adler's sense. Rituals are methods for the *real, objective* logical transformation (not a technical-practical transformation) of reality beneath the threshold of conscious thought, namely in the medium of the sensible and visible. The particular ritual that is our topic here had the task of transporting the nature of the psychic discovered by Jung (which as something noetic and "theological" was essentially infinite, unfathomable, incapable of being positivized, i.e. something logically negative) into the personality—into the so-called "inner"—, to imprison it there in the form of the so-called unconscious of this personality and thereby to *logically* tranquillize it.

Freud's "unconscious" had been biological from the outset, or at least rooted in biology. As a matter of course *his* "unconscious" therefore had its place a priori inside the individual human organism. Jung, by contrast, had experienced the psychic as a mental "world" of "cosmic" dimensions, a world of meanings, universal objective symbols. This was *his* truth. For him *this* a priori *not*-biological psychic had to be logically subjugated to the "person" for the first time and imprisoned in the latter. For this purpose "the psychotic reaction" was required. While *objectively* it drew like a funnel the emotions and images with their full impact upon and into him as their literal target, it made him *subjectively* be their overwhelmed victim (cf. "becoming prey to the unconscious"). This Jung's, on the *empirical experiential* level, being personally endangered to the highest degree by a psychosis served the purpose of the *real logical* defusion and translation of the infinite, quasi metaphysical psychic into "the inner," where it became "the unconscious": what once would have been absolute truths was reduced to merely "psychological truths," subjective experiences.

By exposing himself to the danger of an explosion of his personality, Jung was able to furnish absolutely convincing practical-factual evidence—as much for himself as for others—that the psychic is logically contained in the personality, encircled by it, and that it threatens the personality *only from within*. Speaking in terms of the psychological difference we can say that the psychological was reduced to the psychic (here "the psychic" in the narrower [biological or anthropological] sense).

This meant that Jung's dilemma had now been eliminated. "The unconscious" had now been construed as a natural force. And as a piece

THE FUTURE OF PSYCHOLOGY

of nature working from within man, it was just an empirical object, a fact in the positivistic sense, purely "objective" (Jung: "the *autonomous* unconscious," "the *objective* psyche"). As empirical object and force of nature, the unconscious could, to be sure, still empirically threaten the consciousness of the *private individual* (with inflation or psychosis), but it could not logically threaten the *general* natural-scientific *logic* of psychology, let alone the public mind, the form of its binding knowledge as such. Psychology itself was logically immune to and fundamentally vis-à-vis "*the* unconscious." This was the one side, the side of "syntax" or "logical form." "Semantically" (on the content level)—that is, *after* its *logical* domestication and containment within the boundaries of the "inner" of the personality—this unconscious was, however, at the same time allowed and able to be again that spiritual world of infinite extent and full of divine meaning (the "collective unconscious"). By the same token, on the empirical experiential or behavioral level, especially in analysis, the logically immune consciousness (this is what we call "the ego") could, and was allowed to (indeed was to some degree supposed to), be deeply taken hold of, shaken, and transformed by this content side of the unconscious—as private person.

The way the dilemma was removed was thus by its being introjected or incorporated into psychological theory as a logical split within it, which is a solution analogous to the defense mechanism of "identification with the aggressor." What used to be a dilemma for the *psychologist* had now become an internal part of the very structure of psychology itself, in the form of a dissociation between psychology itself as natural science *and* what it is about, soul (mind[edness], meaning, archetypes, God); between consciousness *and* the unconscious; between "logical" *and* "empirical"; syntax (form) *and* semantics (content).

In order for the two split-off sides not to fall totally apart, a containing third, and a strict focus on it, was needed. But as this third that was supposed to perform the actually *logical* function of *copula* or *vinculum* something positive-factual was chosen: the idea of the personality, because the personality is indeed *utriusque capax* and therefore in principle (although not always in reality) holds the two dissociated sides together. Psychology had to be personalistic. But this type of a third only holds the dissociated sides together in a literal

186   *THE SOUL ALWAYS THINKS*

(external) personal union ("physically," as it were, just as a building encompasses different rooms or storeys within itself). It does not unite them "alchemically" or logically: through an intrinsic *coniunctio oppositorum*.

Now it becomes clear why Jung had to draw the necessity of a going under absolutely personally upon himself: because it was of highest importance for his project to establish the personality as *the* arena and solid framework of the psychic (the soul's life).[6] It needed Jung's *personal* crisis in order to transplant the psychic from the vastness of the world of the mind into a tightly enclosed personality, and from the status of public validity and objective truth to that of merely private subjective experience. Through Jung's having come close to a psychosis and his letting himself personally in for a going under into his inner visions, the glance of the subject doing psychology *had been* turned away from the wide world of the mind inwards, and the psychic, the noetic, had been established as the inner, the unconscious.[7]

Therefore not a creative illness. No individuation process of the person C.G. Jung. All this had nothing to do with him personally, at least not directly. It was much rather—precisely through his personal entanglement—the inaugural ritual of *psychology* as the "psychology of the unconscious" (a term that Jung frequently uses as a name for the psychology he established). A very revealing title. For it is clear

---

[6] What was actually his own fabrication of the unconscious was later projected out by him into cosmic space and mythologized or mystified as a grand natural event: "spirit ... has descended from its fiery heights. But when spirit becomes heavy it turns to water..." (CW 9i § 32) "Since the stars have fallen from heaven and our highest symbols have paled, a secret life holds sway in the unconscious. ... Our unconscious ... holds living water, spirit that has become nature [naturhaft, physical]..." (§ 50, transl. modif.). A "fall of the stars" and not a fabrication! But we also see that the ritual that he lived through did not have the character of an *initiation into* be it "the unconscious" or be it the mysteries of the "metaphysical" world of the stars, the spirits, and gods, but was precisely the process of the fabrication of "*the* unconscious" through the transplantation of the "metaphysical" mysteries that used to be in the whole wide world all around us into the narrow confines of the "inner" of the positive-factually existing individual.

[7] In Jungian psychology after Jung, i.e., in archetypal psychology (James Hillman), the unconscious was liberated from its personalistic imprisonment and turned into "the imaginal." But it is essential to realize that psychology did by no means thereby return to the status *quo ante*, as some might perhaps want to imagine, but that "the imaginal" much rather is a derivative of the positivized unconscious: its airy, free-floating variety. It is semantically freed, but does not *logically* leave the precincts established by "the unconscious" and the personalistic move. Nor does it overcome the aloofness of its position over against its contents. Whereas in Jung this aloofness had a scientist cast, it now is, very different and yet the same, that of an aestheticism.

THE FUTURE OF PSYCHOLOGY 187

that the name "psychology of the unconscious" *actually* (even though unintentionally) pronounces psychology's (or consciousness's) having become unconscious and being systematically kept unconscious. After all, "the unconscious" is not something that existed from time immemorial and that happened to be *discovered* only during the 19th /20th century (much like America had existed all the time, but became known to the Europeans only through Columbus). No, the so-called "discovery" of the unconscious is the reflex or symptom of the exclusion of myth, ritual, religion, and metaphysics from man's public and binding knowledge, an exclusion which occurred during the 19th century. "The unconscious" is sunken cultural assets, a religious-metaphysical "final disposal site." It is thus without future.

As "psychology of the unconscious" Jung's psychology is and remains final-disposal-site psychology because in itself it is designed to take what it, with its one hand (empirically and semantically), raises into consciousness and, with its other hand (logically, syntactically), to hand it over at the same time to the unconscious (which simply means: to keep our binding knowledge—consciousness—free of it). For this was absolutely essential to Jung: despite all one's making conscious and digging up unconscious contents, never to infringe on the logical innocence and untouchability of our knowing itself. Only the personality (as that which experiences, views, interprets) was allowed to and was supposed to be touched by the unconscious, but not the binding knowledge of our time itself, not psychology, because then psychology would have committed the grave crime of having transgressed the borders to metaphysics. "*The* unconscious" is a theoretical artifact, the result of a psychology which is pinned down to being a natural science and *ipso facto* needs to hold off the psychic (the soul's life) at a distance. According to this scheme, psychology must never become internal to itself, never become psychological. It needs to stay alienated from itself. The contents of the unconscious had to retain at all cost the form of objectivity and externality. "Internality" can here only mean literal in-ness in a person. Even after having been made conscious, the contents had to stay purely *contents* of consciousness, but were not allowed to dare to transgress the limits set for them and to unhygienically enter into the *logical form* of knowledge itself. Because if that would have happened, psychological theory would have lost its natural-scientific insulation vis-à-vis its object and would have turned into *speculative knowledge*.[8] Psychology would have become infected by its object, by the latter's mind or spirit nature, its historicity and infinity, by the dimension of meaning and religious experience that its object entails. Or, which is the same thing, psychology as knowing or theory would have gone under into the object of its knowing—and precisely thereby it would for the first time have become autonomous and inward, for the first time truly *psychological*.

Jung's going under shows itself to have precisely been a mode of avoiding the true going under, to have been a substitute for it. The true going under is thus still wanting. It is the task of the future and at the same time it is also that in which consists the future of psychology. It is not sufficient for psychology to dedicate itself time and again merely to the therapeutic Sisyphean work upon the unconscious of the *persons* who come into therapy, which is a Sisyphean task because the very structure of psychology, its systemic unconsciousness,[9] and *its* refusal to go under into its speculative inner essence, *logically* themselves generate ever anew and keep alive "*the* unconscious" (and along with it the neurotic dissociation of consciousness), that very unconscious that by its *empirical* therapeutic and research endeavors[10] it attempts to connect with consciousness. Also in the interest of its therapeutic work with patients, psychology's going under is indispensable.

---

[8] It is interesting that it was precisely his sticking to the modern logical form of knowledge (natural science) that allowed Jung to give his psychology on the *content* level the obsolete form of a *mythology*, the mythology of the unconscious.

[9] I mean that unconsciousness that psychology systematically firmly establishes in the theory of "the unconscious."

[10] They amount to an acting out.

CHAPTER NINE

The End of Meaning and the Birth of Man

An essay about the state reached in the history of consciousness and an analysis of C.G. Jung's psychology project

> But who longs for life to such a boundless extent? Precisely that person who does not possess it and wanders off the beaten track: the solitary individual.
>
> Siegfried Kracauer (1913)

One of the most persuasive voices that during the last century raised the question of the "meaning of life" or, as we might also say, the question of "mythic," "religious," or "metaphysical"[1] meaning, was that of C.G. Jung. His thoughts about this topic moved between two poles. On the one hand there is his relentless *diagnosis* that "No, evidently we no longer have any myth."[2] "Our myth has become mute, and gives no answers."[3] Today "we stand

---

[1] I use "metaphysical" in two different senses, in a loose sense, where it is more or less synonymous with words like "transcendental," "supernatural," or "higher," and in a strict sense, where it refers to the Western tradition of metaphysics as a First Philosophy, a tradition that began, say, with Heraclitus and ended with Hegel. The context should make clear which meaning the word has in each case.

[2] *MDR* p. 171.

[3] *MDR* p. 332.

empty-handed, bewildered, and perplexed [...]"[4] "There are no longer any gods whom we could invoke [...]"[5] Jung even went as far as to state that "it would be far better stoutly to avow our spiritual poverty, our symbol-lessness, instead of feigning a legacy to which we are not the legitimate heirs at all."[6] Jung was very much aware that modern man dwells with himself alone, "where, in the cold light of consciousness, the blank barrenness of the world reaches to the very stars."[7]

The other pole of his thinking about meaning comes to the fore when to the quoted diagnosis of his ("No, evidently we no longer have any myth") he immediately reacts with the surprising question, "But then what is your myth? The myth in which you do live?" Jung did not take "no" for an answer. He was of the opinion that meaning is indispensable and that the loss of meaning in modern times is the ultimate reason for neurosis. Neurosis is due to the "senselessness and aimlessness" of the lives of those who suffer from it.[8] "Everything is banal, everything is 'nothing but'; and that is the reason why people are neurotic."[9] "You see, man is in need of a symbolic life—badly in need."[10]

Both the diagnosis of the loss of meaning and the idea of the dire need of meaning (which come nicely together in Jung's statement, we "cannot even get it into our heads that no myth will come to our aid although we have such urgent need of one"[11]) are nothing new. They had already been experienced and struggled with in different ways for at least one hundred years prior to Jung. The 19th century had not only discovered what was to become known under the catch-word "nihilism," defined by Nietzsche as the lack of a goal, the lack of an answer to the "What for?"; it had also desperately tried, in ever new utopian schemes, to provide a new, ultimate goal of life. To mention only three examples, Kierkegaard had proposed a leap into faith, Marx

---

[4] *Ibid.*
[5] *CW* 18 § 598.
[6] *CW* 9i § 28.
[7] *CW* 9i § 29. (The *CW* have "to dwell with itself alone," where "itself" refers to "spiritual poverty." It is, however, also possible (and, I feel, more likely) to understand Jung's phrase, *"um bei sich einzukehren,"* in his text as meaning "in order to dwell with *oneself* (alone)" or even better: "in order to hold communion with oneself" or "in order to search one's soul.")
[8] Cf. *CW* 16 § 83. Also *CW* 11 §§ 509, 514, 516.
[9] *CW* 18 § 627.
[10] *Ibid.* § 625.
[11] *MDR* p. 332f.

THE END OF MEANING AND THE BIRTH OF MAN

had promised the communist society, and Nietzsche had put all his hope onto the longed for advent of what he imaged under the symbolic name "Dionysus," who would come to and inspire "Ariadne," the deserted soul ready to receive Dionysus, thereby ending the sterility reached in the 19th century.[12]

1. THE SELF-CONTRADICTION INHERENT IN THE SEARCH FOR MEANING

One might think that the diagnosed loss of meaning is the cause, the search for meaning the result; further, that the loss of meaning is the "illness" while the sought-for meaning would be the cure. But "loss of meaning" and "search for meaning" have to be seen as rather the two sides of the same coin. Just as it is the sense of loss of meaning that creates a craving for meaning, so it is the idea of the dire need of a higher meaning that makes real life appear as intolerably banal and "nothing but," merely "*maya* compared with that one thing, that your life is meaningful."[13] The more you long for meaning, the more banal life gets; the more banal you feel life to be, the more you will say with Jung: "My whole being was seeking for something still unknown which might confer meaning upon the banality of life."[14] There are not two phenomena here but only one. The search for meaning is the opposite of itself. It is what turns reality into that very senselessness that it intends to overcome; it is itself that symptom or illness the cure of which it claims to be. The longing for meaning is deluded about itself.

What is the delusion? The search for meaning seeks something that cannot be sought because any seeking for it destroys what is to be gained. Meaning is not an entity that could be had, not a creed, a doctrine, a world view, also not something like the fairytale treasure hard to attain. It is not semantic, not a content. Meaning, where it indeed exists, is first of all an implicit *fact* of existence, its *a priori*. It can never be the answer to a question; it is conversely an unquestioned and unquestionable certainty that predates any possible questioning. It is the groundedness of existence, a sense of embeddedness in life, of

---

[12] See Claus-Artur Scheier, *Nietzsches Labyrinth. Das ursprüngliche Denken und die Seele*, Freiburg, München (Alber) 1985.

[13] *CW* 18 § 630.

[14] *MDR* p. 165.

192 *THE SOUL ALWAYS THINKS*

containment in the world—perhaps we could even say of in-ness as the logic of existence *as such*. Meaning exists if the meaning of life is as self-evident as the in-ness in water is for fish.

Myth, religion, metaphysics—they were never *answers* to an explicit and pressing question about the meaning of existence, such as when, e.g., William James in 1897 raised the question, "Is Life Worth Living?" No, they were merely the concrete *articulation* or *formulation*, in imaginal form, and, in the case of metaphysics, the *explication*, in the mode of thought, of the form of the *factually existing* in-ness in, or groundedness of, existence at each historical locus respectively. The tales of myth, the religious practices, doctrines or dogmas, the elaborate systems of metaphysics, spelled out in different modes the logic that factually governed a people's lived life. They were the self-expression in consciousness of the meaning that was. This is why myths, rituals, and metaphysics simply told—and celebrated—the truth. That was their job. Just as fish could never seriously question the meaningfulness of being in water, so from the age of myth through the end of the age of metaphysics, i.e., through the time of Hegel and Schelling, man could not possibly have in all earnest raised the question, "Is Life Worth Living?" *as a real, more than merely rhetorical, question.*

If in the 19th century the question of the meaning and worth of life all of a sudden—or by and by—became possible, indeed serious and pressing, a radical change in man's being-in-the-world must have had taken place. Man must have had stepped out of his previous absolute containment in life, so that he now was both enabled and forced to view life as if from outside, because only in this way could *the whole of* life become thematic in the first place. Now, with the question about its meaning and worth, existence as such had become a vis-à-vis, as it were, which is the opposite of in-ness. Man now for the first time had a *position to* the world per se.[15] The question of

---

[15] "Aber das Neue dieses Vorgangs liegt keinesfalls darin, daß jetzt die Stellung des Menschen inmitten des Seienden lediglich eine andere ist gegenüber dem mittelalterlichen und antiken Menschen. Entscheidend ist, daß der Mensch diese Stellung eigens als die von ihm ausgemachte selbst bezieht [...] Jetzt erst gibt es überhaupt so etwas wie eine Stellung des Menschen." Martin Heidegger, "Die Zeit des Weltbildes," in: *Holzwege*, Frankfurt a.M. (Klostermann) 1972, p. 84. (The problem of this passage is only that Heidegger retrojects a modern [post-metaphysical, 19th century or later] situation already into the last epoch of the age of metaphysics, the time from Descartes to Hegel. On this retrojection see Claus-Artur Scheier, "Die Sprache spricht. Heideggers Tautologien," in: *Zeitschrift für philosophische Forschung*, vol. 47, 1993, no. 1, pp. 60–74, here p. 69.)

THE END OF MEANING AND THE BIRTH OF MAN

meaning is the mark of the modern period after the conclusion of the age of metaphysics at the beginning of the 19th century.

Now we understand why the modern search for meaning is necessarily self-contradictory. The search for meaning is in truth, but secretly, the longing for a state of in-ness, but since the question about the worth and meaning of life has existence as a whole in its field of vision, it inevitably positions us outside and vis-à-vis life. The search for meaning unwittingly has to construe that which it desires to be the logic or *syntax* of life as a *semantic content*, as a kind of doctrine of wisdom or a creed or ideology, ultimately as a commodity. This is why today meaning exists in the plural of numerous competing meanings put up for sale on a large "meaning market" by a whole "meaning industry," and why we are in the position of customers who have to make their decisions and choices about these "meanings."[16] Even if we "buy" a certain meaning and immure ourselves in it, nothing can undo the fact that it is a secondary acquisition and that our in-ness in it, if it comes to exist at all, is like that in a house that we ourselves built or rented, not that kind of a priori and irrevocable in-ness that was actually sought.

In addition to the intellectual contradictoriness inherent in the question of meaning there is also an emotional contradiction: we could not even seriously *wish* to find in fact realized what our search for meaning is in truth seeking. The kind of in-ness that is longed for, if it were indeed realized, would be intolerable for the modern subject. It would collide with our inalienable insistence on emancipated individuality and rationality. It would necessarily be felt as imprisonment, as a nightmare, of which the 20th century experience in totalitarian states and with fundamentalist sects has given us a taste.

A few exemplary facts may serve as suggestive illustrations to evoke at least some sense of the unquestionable containment that once was, since I cannot give the elaborate exposition here that this topic would deserve.

2. IN-NESS AS THE REALITY OF THE PRE-MODERN AGES

We must distinguish between ancient conceptions and tales, on the one hand, in which the absolute in-ness has become expressly

---

[16] Cf. the "selling God" concept of American social scientists.

articulated, a content of conscious awareness, and, on the other hand, factual phenomena of the way life was lived that betray that man's containment in nature was the prevailing actual reality.

Examples of the articulation of the sense of metaphysical in-ness are certain geographical and cosmological views of the mythological age. The earth was imagined as a circular disc surrounded by a stream (the Greek Okeanos, the Egyptian Nun) or a serpent (the Germanic Midgard Serpent) or a solid girdle or band comparable to the tire of a wagon wheel (the Altai mountain range). This "World Encircler" or "Bitter River" (as the Egyptians or Babylonians, respectively, called it) was the border between Being and Non-Being and created an inner space into which human existence was absolutely locked. No exit. Whereas the name Bitter River suggests the bond of necessity (Ἀνάγκη) that unrelentingly encloses human existence, the idea of the circle implies that existence is existence at a center.

Through this center went the World Tree that both held apart and connected the three levels of the cosmos: the underworld below, the earth in the middle (appropriately called "Midgard" in Germanic mythology) and heaven above. Midgard as the locus of human existence sandwiched between underworld and heaven is already suggestive enough of the sense of in-ness. But the widespread myth of the separation of the world parents, Mother Earth and Father Heaven, adds an even stronger and more dynamic note. The world parents were originally lying in eternal embrace upon one another. Their children had to live between their bellies in eternal darkness and without space and air to breathe, until one day an especially strong son brutally disrupted the *gamos* of the World Parents and lifted Father Heaven up into the heights so that that openness that we call the *world* of man, in contrast to the mere physical environment, was created. The interesting point here is that with respect to the question of containment the situation after this feat of the culture hero is exactly the same as before; his opening up of the world did not provide a release from the enclosure. The children of Heaven and Earth remain surrounded by their parents regardless of whether they are pressed between their united bodies or whether there is an open space or "clearance" between Heaven and Earth in which they can walk erect, breathe freely and orient themselves in their world. Both images represent a situation of absolute in-ness. It is therefore not surprising

THE END OF MEANING AND THE BIRTH OF MAN 195

that the Orphics thought of the cosmos as a cave and of human existence as an existence in this cave, a conception that might be linked to the widespread ideas of heaven as a vault or tent. In such figures as that of the Greek Atlas whose task it was to constantly hold the vault of heaven up so that it would not crash back down upon the earth, the experienced inescapable in-ness of human existence has found its explicit expression.

Having the fiery heaven, the realm of the gods, above him, man was *essentially* upward looking. The ancient Greeks even derived the very etymology of the word for Man, *anthrôpos*, from *anô athrôn* (he who looks upwards, to the sky/heaven). Worship, devotion[17] was his nature. There was a fixed border above, the moon, which separated the sublunar sphere from the empyrean. This fixed limit gave a hold to the upward looking, made it determinate and concrete and prevented one's glance from simply disappearing in the indifference of an infinite void.

The sense of embeddedness is also reflected in man's ancient self-understanding. We have already heard that man conceived of himself as the child of Mother Earth or Mother Nature and Father Heaven, and his relation to all the gods was that of a child looking up to parents. The Greeks spoke directly of Father Okeanos and Father Zeus, Christianity of Our Father in Heaven. And the Catholic Church still perceives itself fundamentally as the Mother of all believers, thereby confirming the metaphysical child status of man and thus the stance of upward looking, the native stance of the child towards father and mother.

This ancient sense of containment is best expressed in the description with which Jung summarized what he learned from the master of ceremonies of a tribe of Pueblo Indians about their stance in the world. "They get up in the morning with the feeling of their great and divine responsibility: they are the sons of the Sun, the Father,

---

[17] The etymological sense of "devotion" from Lat. *de-votio, de-vovere* seems to be in opposition to "upward looking." In the ritual of *devotio* a warrior was consecrated (or consecrated himself) to the underworld, to death (see "Blood Brotherhood, Blood Revenge, and *Devotio*: Glimpses of the Archaic Psyche," in: my *Soul-Violence*, Collected English Papers vol. III, New Orleans, LA [Spring Journal Books] 2008, pp. 267–315). But the literal direction is not essential here. There was an "upward looking" even in the devotion to the gods of the underworld (regardless of whether it was a case of literal *devotio* or of devotion in the generalized sense of worship). Without this upward looking, there would be neither gods above nor below.

and their daily duty is to help the Father over the horizon—not for themselves alone, but for the whole world. You should see these fellows: they have a natural fulfilled dignity."[18] They are "fulfilling [their] role, [their] role as [...] actors in the divine drama of life."[19] We have here not only the sense of containment and fundamental upward looking on account of their status as children or sons of a divine Father, but more fundamentally that of metaphysically being enveloped in a divine drama. Living life means to fulfil one's role as an actor in this drama. We are *in* this greater drama and do not each have to live life merely on our own account.

The nature of the particular role to be fulfilled by these Pueblo Indians strikingly reveals their sense of being fundamentally enveloped in nature. They have to help the sun to wander across the sky. In other words, they have to ritually accompany or soulfully tune into a pre-given movement that is precisely absolutely independent of and unswayed by any human doings and attitudes, utterly beyond human reach, following as it does the relentless laws of physics, of natural necessity. The point of their ceremonies was obviously not a real help in the sense of practical effectiveness, but merely the humble, obedient synchronizing of the movement of the human soul with the unshakeable laws of nature. This corresponds to the fundamental sense of not empirical-practical, but metaphysical powerlessness that we find at this stage of cultural development. Man experienced himself primarily as a thread in the fabric of nature, without any arbitrary volition of his own (Heino Gehrts). Even where man interfered with nature, such as when tilling the soil, erecting a house, or, above all, in his sacrificial killings, these human interventions were, in a sense, decidedly not his own doings, doings, metaphysically speaking, on his own responsibility, but rather re-enactments of exemplary acts originally performed by gods. And even these re-enactments were ultimately not the work of the human actors, but rather of the gods who acted through them.

---

[18] *CW* 18 § 630. We should here, however, keep in mind that the necessity to help the Sun to continue to go across the sky and thus to prevent a general darkening (doom) of the world has a rather sinister side to it. With another people, the Meso-American Aztecs, this helping the Sun to be able to continue its daily course took the form of the sacrificial killing of people in huge numbers, whose hearts had to be cut out and offered to the gods.

[19] *Ibid.* § 628.

THE END OF MEANING AND THE BIRTH OF MAN 197

All the examples given so far mainly belonged to the archaic stage of consciousness and culture characterized by myth and ritual. But the sense of embeddedness *mutatis mutandis* prevailed also after the transition from the mythological or ritualistic age to the time of religion and classical metaphysics. We have already heard of the Christian Father in Heaven and the Roman Catholic's existence in the fold of Mother Church. We can also refer by way of one single example to Romans 8:38f. in which the certainty is expressed "that neither death, nor life, nor angels, nor principalities, nor powers, nor things present, nor things to come, Nor height, nor depth, nor any other creature, shall be able to separate us from the love of God, which is in Christ Jesus our Lord." Christian man's containment in the love of God is absolute. As to metaphysics (in the sense of First Philosophy) I will here only point to the logic of the judgment (*Urteil*), in which the copula is the abstract-logical analogue to the mythological-imaginal figure of Atlas who at the same time is keeping apart and uniting the opposites. The copula guarantees the real union of subject and predicate, the universal and the particular, implying the Ground, or Being, that encompasses and produces both extremes and is in turn ultimately grounded in God. The thought of classical metaphysics possesses a fulfilled center.[20]

The views in which the sense of in-ness articulated itself are one thing. As views, ideas, they could possibly be mistaken, superstitious, fictitious. But it can be shown that the articulated *sense* of in-ness in turn articulates the in-ness in fact inherent in the actual conditions of the practical reality of life at those times. Again I can merely mention a few points by way of suggestion.

First, the ethical and intellectual life of each present generation was embedded in the age-old tradition of the fathers. Each present derived its truths from what Eliade called *illud tempus* or from the ancients. All thinking and experience were enwrapped in the inherited views.

---

[20] The logic of the judgment in the context of the metaphysical tradition and in contrast to the modern logic of the proposition (Frege) has been analyzed and discussed in many writings by Claus-Artur Scheier. See e.g. his "Die Grenze der Metaphysik und die Herkunft des gegenwärtigen Denkens," in: *Abhandlungen der Braunschweigischen Wissenschaftlichen Gesellschaft*, vol. XLVI, 1995, Göttingen (Verlag Erich Goltze) 1996, pp. 189–196, as well as "Russels Antinomie und der Heraklitische Anfang der Logik," in: Rainer Enskat (ed.), *Erfahrung und Urteilskraft*, Würzburg (Königshausen & Neumann), pp. 43–54.

Second, the individual had his reality and substance not in himself but in something larger, logically speaking in a universal, be it the family, the clan, the tribe, or a corporation, which was the only true real and of which the individual was no more than sort of a fall-out, an emanation.[21] He likewise had his Self and his soul not in himself, but in the king, the tribe's medicine man, the Pharaoh.

Third, there was the inescapable dependence on nature. The talk of Mother Nature was not so much a metaphor as a factual reality. Man was at the mercy of nature when it sent earthquakes, droughts, floods, and he relied on nature for his subsistence. To be sure, man was also a producer, but even in his own production he showed himself to be the child of nature, because his producing was only an alteration of things previously produced by nature, logs, rocks, sheep and cows, grain, etc. And the mode of human production was the imitation, *mimesis,* of nature's way of producing, which is even reflected in much of the Western pre-modern theory of art. Man's productivity was not yet conceived as creativity.

Fourth, the factual in-ness also showed in the unquestionable resigned submission of people to fate, to the vicissitudes and rigors of nature, to the whims of the rulers, to God's inscrutable ways.

Fifth and finally, if, as Jung claimed, the primitive Australians, e.g., sacrificed two-thirds of their conscious lifetime to what he called the "symbolic life"[22] and if the public and private life of people in all other former cultures had similarly its center in their cults, we see that upward looking was more than an inconsequential subjective attitude, it was a practical reality. From a strictly financial point of view it is absolutely amazing how much, for example, the Egyptians invested in their pyramids and tombs that did not serve any immediate practical purpose for the living. It expressed their metaphysical devotedness to something larger in which human existence as a whole was contained.

---

[21] By way of one example I mention only the common phenomenon described in Acts 16:33: "[...] and was baptized, he and all his [...]" The head of the household is converted to Christianity and his whole family and dependents have to follow suit. Another example is the power that genealogy had over people's self-understanding and the use of patronymics (logically one had one's identity in being son or daughter of ...).

[22] *CW* 18 § 649.

THE END OF MEANING AND THE BIRTH OF MAN

3. THE END OF IN-NESS

All that was described concerning man's metaphysical containment in nature during the ages of myth and metaphysics is no more. In the modern age that began with the 19th century, Atlas lost his job; there is no above and below in a universe in which the earth is no longer in the center, no longer Midgard. The ideas of the center, of above and below, have cosmologically become simply meaningless. Without Atlas constantly holding Heaven and Earth apart, the world parents have collapsed upon each other, into positivity, so that the metaphysical difference between Heaven and Earth, as well as the difference between the earth, the moon, the sun, the planets and stars has disappeared. The essential duality of this earthly world, on the one hand, and a transcendent one, on the other, is simply gone, a state which is reflected in the search for a *uniform* world formula. There is now positivistically only one metaphysically homogenous stuff out of which the "universe" (no longer *kósmos*!) as a whole is made up. The place of planet Earth in what was the *kósmos* has become absolutely indifferent and insignificant. Long before man's flight to the moon and the launching of unmanned rockets to other planets, the unsurmountable limit between the sublunar sphere and the fiery heaven as the realm of the gods had been abolished. Even with the aid of the largest telescope men will, Jung once said, discover behind the farthest nebulae no fiery empyrean, "and we know that our eyes will wander despairingly through the emptiness of interstellar space."[23] No world encircling Okeanos relentlessly encloses us with the bond of necessity in the here and now. We even have managed to look down upon the Earth from outside, from outer space.[24] The stance of a metaphysical upward looking has become impossible. The soul has left the Earth as its inescapable locus and thus lost the former sense of in-ness.

The opposite change seems to have taken place with man. The individual, the singular has established itself as the center and as the ultimate real. Corporations and society have lost their metaphysical substantiality and realness, having become reduced to "col-lectives,"

---

[23] *CW* 9i § 31.

[24] Cf. our orientation on the earth via GPS, our remote sensing with earth observation satellites. Cf. also the proliferation of science fiction books and movies about star wars, etc.

aggregations of atomic individuals on the basis of the idea of social contracts. Genealogy has lost the power it used to have in one's self-understanding; the modern individual no longer comprehends himself primarily as "son of ...," but as his own center and center of his world. To be "I" means to have established oneself as all by oneself being the *origin* of one's coordinates. Likewise, ideas and concepts have lost their former status of ultimate realness as "universals" in the neoplatonic sense, a realness superior to that of the particular and the concrete individual who had formerly only possessed reality to the extent that he *participated* in and was subsumed under the universal. The most easily accessible illustration is sexual liberation. Formerly there was a clear idea of what "a man" and "a woman," their true nature and accordingly their roles in society, were. The *concept* was *physei*, it immediatedly expressed, nay, *was* the nature and true reality of things and people. The particular individual had his or her truth and reality only in and through the concept, and this is why deviant feelings and inclinations, such as homosexual ones, were utterly "untrue," "not real," perverse, *despite* their occurring in fact. Today, what actually occurs in individuals in all their diversity *is* the only real, and ideas, concepts, roles are seen as no more than human constructs. The singular has emancipated itself from the universal concept, which is now in fact reduced to a *flatus vocis* or experienced as a mere human instrument of oppression.

In a similar way man has psychologically, even if not completely factually, emancipated himself from the vicissitudes of fate, from the rigors of nature and from the arbitrariness of rulers. Formerly these forces were experienced as self-evident aspects of the *nature* of the world that one had to helplessly let be: "The Lord gave, and the Lord hath taken away; blessed be the name of the Lord" (Job 1:21). Today there are strong ideas that logically, even if not always factually, man can insure himself against the blows of fate and that pain and illness, to some extent even aging and death, are unacceptable wrongs to be corrected by human technology. There is even the feeling that I have a *right* to a pain-free and happy life. Although empirically and practically our technical means are still ridiculously limited compared with the effects of weather, earthquakes, volcanos, floods, tornados, illnesses, etc., psychologically or logically, that is, as far as man's *real* self-understanding and self-definition is concerned, there are no limits

THE END OF MEANING AND THE BIRTH OF MAN

to what can on principle be done by man. Man, nobody else, is now the one who is in charge and holds the responsibility for the existence or non-existence of the world, the continuity of life on earth, the protection of the environment.

The cult of the ancestors has been replaced by the idolization of childhood and youth; instead of the orientation towards the knowledge of the dead ancestors, the ancients and wise old men or women, and instead of the cultivation of and respect for tradition, modernity is characterized by the need for individual originality and constant innovation as well as the delight in irreverence and provocation (modern art!).

As to human productivity,[25] man has begun with the technical appropriation of the production processes that once were the unfathomable secrets of nature. This is most apparent in the area of genetic engineering and reproduction. Formerly the only way to improve or change animals and plants according to our human needs was by means of breeding. Today biotechnology has advanced to the possibility of creating new types of organisms by directly *designing* them. Similarly in the human realm it is now possible to have sex without children and children without sex. Before, reproduction could only be brought about by allowing *nature* to do *its* work of reproduction through, so to speak, one's ritually re-enacting the marriage of Father Heaven and Mother Earth. Today it is more and more becoming possible to directly, technically, control the reproduction process. With the possibility of artificial in vitro insemination and even the feasibility of artificial uteri, the meaning of "blood relationship" ("blood is thicker than water") has logically disappeared; the bond between family members will logically no longer be nature-based, but only social, psychological, contingent: it seems likely that one day not too far away babies will be designed, laboratory-produced from the best, healthiest but anonymous "raw materials," so that a father will no longer be father because he fathered his child, but only because he held the office of "father," and the sense that one continues in and through one's children will have no basis in fact anymore; the very idea of "mother" and "father," indeed of the

---

[25] On the revolution of the form of human production and its philosophical implications see C.A. Scheier, *Ästhetik der Simulation*, Hamburg (Meiner) 2000.

mother and father archetypes, will have lost their integrity. Even if this mode of reproduction should prove practically too difficult, *logically* the fundamental rupture with the natural way of reproduction and the loss of innocence *has* already taken place.

But these are only the most blatant examples for a change that has been inherent in the Industrial Revolution from the outset. With the beginning of modern chemistry with Lavoisier at the time of the French Revolution, human production is no longer restricted to the mere alteration of the products of nature (*natura naturata*), but itself behaves like the *natura naturans* by, e.g., producing artificial substances that do not occur in nature. We have "designed matter" and even "intelligent materials." Nature has abdicated as "Mother" and unfathomable origin; it is now a mere raw material for human production and partially itself already a human product, the borders between "natural" and "artificial" being fundamentally blurred, which corresponds to the other fact already mentioned that it is now man who has to protect nature as his "problem child."

Where formerly man was entirely dependent on the sources of energy provided by nature, on horse power, wind and water, he now has technically appropriated the power to produce energy for himself when and where he pleases, earlier by means of steam engines, now also by means of various types of motors, batteries and atomic energy. It is a part of this change that *Nyx*, the Night, once a venerable, potent, substantial reality in her own right and a goddess, is now reduced to no more than an absence of daylight that can be compensated for, and fundamentally depotentiated, by electric light. The pun "the world is getting light" refers to the fact that whereas the earlier heavy industry had to rely on coal and steel machine tools, a process has now started where coal will slowly be replaced by hydrogen, the lightest element, as an energy carrier, and machine tools more and more by lasers, which are light.

Clearly, man's embeddedness in nature is over. But since the meaning of "meaning" is nothing else but in-ness, it is obvious why the last two centuries had to experience a loss of meaning,[26] a sense of alienation and nihilism. As Jung stated, the "soul has become lonely;

---

[26] To avoid misunderstandings I want to point out that "meaninglessness" or "loss or end of meaning" refers only to meaning in the material sense ("meaning" as in: the

THE END OF MEANING AND THE BIRTH OF MAN 203

it is *extra ecclesiam* and in a state of no salvation."[27] The soul is likewise *extra naturam*. With this insight we have returned in our discussion to, and provided an underpinning for, Jung's initial diagnosis, "No, evidently we no longer have any myth."

4. Two basic lines of reaction to "the end of in-ness"

In view of this fundamental change, two opposite stances are possible. One can *either* try to hold on to and defend the truth of the past *against* the real situation produced by historical developments *or* own up to the new situation into which history has placed us and allow oneself to be taught by it about how to think. Both reactions involve us in a dialectic.

By allowing itself to be placed into the real situation the second option lets go of the *former* definition of in-ness, namely, the child status of upward looking and the sense of containment in nature, while in fact continuing the real in-ness, which however now happens to be the in-ness precisely in the situation of "meaninglessness." According to this stance history is, as it were, the soul's alchemical retort, and we collectively are the prime matter in this hermetically sealed retort and are transported through one phase of history's alchemical opus after the other, each time finding ourselves in an entirely new world situation.

By longing for "meaning," the first option defends, to be sure, the old sense of in-ness, i.e., the in-ness in the former situation, but therefore has to renounce what it actually most desires, in-ness as an actual reality, which, however, today would be the in-ness in the utterly new psychological situation of being *extra ecclesiam et naturam* and not the in-ness of old. Either way, a loss is unavoidable.

Inasmuch as the first option tries to dictate *what* the kind of in-ness that it wants has to be, it must be comprehended as the egoic revolt against the soul's alchemical process, the attempt to remain exempt from having to undergo the transformations of the soul's logical life from stage to stage. It insists on having meaning, i.e., the status of

---

meaning [*Sinn*] and worth of life, mythic or metaphysical meaning). "Meaning" in the formal sense ("the meaning [*Bedeutung*] of such and such a word, sentence, text," etc.) remains of course unaffected.

[27] *CW* 18 § 632.

in-ness, while itself *imaginally* placing and holding itself outside the containment in the alchemical vessel of history. From outside the vessel, it can prescribe and demand the status that it thinks should be and criticize and condemn what it thinks is intolerable about the situation that is. It is in this sense that, e.g., Jung, as we already heard, declared mythic meaning to be indispensable and meaninglessness to be the unbearable cause of psychic illness. When you are *extra ecclesiam*, so he stated as a veritable scaremonger, "then things really become terrible, [...] you are confronted with all the demons of hell"[28]; before you "there yawns the void [*das Nichts*]," and you "turn[-] away from it in horror."[29]

Threatening with the horrors of the void is one strategy of those who insist on meaning. Another favorite strategy for the same purpose is interpreting the change that occurred in terms of a psychology of blame. The change is viewed as a decline, decadence, a mistake, as sick; it is due to our fault, our hubris, our neglect and forgetfulness. It is all our guilt. The West has *squandered* its spiritual heritage, Jung stated.[30] We have been too rationalistic, too patriarchal, too one-sided. So now, this conception claims, we have to humble ourselves and turn again to the ignored unconscious as the true source of meaning.

This strategy operates with a structurally neurotic split between the soul and the ego, the soul and the rational intellect. It follows the thought figure "*omne bonum a deo, omne malum ab homine.*"[31] Even if Jung occasionally was ready to state that "I am convinced that the growing impoverishment of symbols has a meaning [...],"[32] which would imply that it is a necessary development in the history or alchemy of the soul and thus the soul's, not our, doing, his dominant position was the one about our fault.

The problem with this view is that it represents the very arrogance of the ego that it decries. The humble submission to the unconscious is only an *empirical* behavior, an acted-out attitude that conceals the inner *logical* pompousness of one's insisting on being something grander than what one happens to be. It is the insistence on being an

---

[28] *Ibid.*
[29] *CW* 9i § 28.
[30] *Ibid.*
[31] Criticized by Jung *CW* 11 § 739.
[32] *CW* 9i § 28.

THE END OF MEANING AND THE BIRTH OF MAN

actor in the divine drama, the sons of the Sun, the Father, like the Pueblo Indians, or "the 'age-old son of the mother'", "the 'old man,' the 'ancient' [...] who has always been and always will be,"[33] like Jung. It is the insistence on a metaphysical or mythical garment that gives us a higher status.

The first option, a negative interpretation of the fundamental change from myth and metaphysics to modernity, does not work. So much has become clear. We have to turn to the second option, that is to say, to let ourselves be placed by the soul's process into the situation that is. It must teach us how to interpret our situation.

5. JUNG'S IDEA OF THE DEATH OF SYMBOLS

As a model for the general line of such an interpretation we can lean on a conception by Jung, a very different one that, however, seems to be rather isolated in his work and inconsequential for his further thought. It is his view of the symbol to be found in the section "Definitions" of his *Psychological Types* (§ 816).[34] Jung writes:

> So long as a symbol is a living thing, it is an expression for something that cannot be characterized in any other or better way. The symbol is alive only so long as it is pregnant with meaning. But once its meaning has been born out of it, once that expression is found which formulates the thing sought, expected, or divined even better than the hitherto accepted symbol, then the symbol is *dead*, i.e., it possesses only an historical significance. We may still go on speaking of it as a symbol, on the tacit assumption that we are speaking of it as it was before the better expression was born out of it. [...] For every esoteric interpretation the symbol is dead, because esotericism has already given it (at least ostensibly) a better expression, whereupon it becomes merely a conventional sign for associations that are more completely and better known elsewhere. Only from the exoteric standpoint is the symbol a living thing.

Here, concerning the *meaning* of a symbol, Jung operates with the images of pregnancy and birth, and concerning the *interpretation* of a

---

[33] *MDR* p. 225.
[34] Cf. for a similar view *CW* 18 § 632. Cf. also: People "do not realize that a myth is dead if it no longer lives and grows." *MDR* p. 332.

symbol, with the ideas of exoteric and esoteric standpoints. The symbol is only the unfinished embryonic form of a given meaning. As long as the symbol is alive its meaning is still unborn, has not fully seen the light of day. The birth of the meaning at once means the death of its former embryonic form, i.e., the death of the form of symbol, and it means that this meaning has received a *better* expression. The death of a symbol, inasmuch as it amounts to the birth of the better formulation of what it is about, is thus by no means to be viewed as an intolerable catastrophe. It is a transformation that, to be sure, goes along with a loss, but ultimately is a gain, a progress, just as in the case of the transition from biological pregnancy to birth. It thus is precisely the meaning's *destination* to die *as symbol* and thereby to be born out of its initial enveloped form of mere pregnancy (implicitness, *Ansichsein*).

The *interpreting mind's* movement is the converse to the movement of the meaning. As long as the meaning is still hidden in the belly of the symbol, the mind views or divines it from outside; this is what Jung calls the mind's exoteric standpoint. The birth of the meaning out of the symbol goes hand in hand with the mind's initiation into the meaning so that it understands the meaning from within itself and is fully conscious of it; the meaning then has become explicit, *conceptually* comprehended (= the esoteric standpoint), which, however, is naturally tantamount to the loss of its mystique. It has become demythologized and desacralized and now is merely an ordinary content of consciousness (Jung says "conventional sign").

So we have to understand that "in-ness in meaning" (= the living symbol still merely pregnant with *its* meaning) and "exoteric standpoint" are descriptions of the same situation from opposite sides.

This passage by Jung about the symbol is one of the rare moments where he rises up to a truly dialectical thinking in terms of a Hegelian sublation.

Jung spoke here only of the history or fate of the meaning of individual symbols. In the case of the death of one individual symbol through consciousness' transition from an exoteric to an esoteric standpoint toward it, it may well be that this loss is compensated for by the emergence of a new symbol pregnant with a different meaning so that there is a new fascination. This is what had in fact happened

THE END OF MEANING AND THE BIRTH OF MAN 207

in history many times; there have been numerous periods of cultural crisis when the old gods or symbols had lost their conviction and new ones had not fully taken hold of people, but were slowly emerging. Just think of the major transition from polytheism to monotheism. These times of transition were times of *empirical* and temporal suffering from the loss of meaning, while the fundamental, logical in-ness continued even across the period of its empirical absence. This type of change and predicament could be compared to the unrest during a removal, when one is no longer in one's old home and has not yet moved into one's new home.

But now, when we transfer what Jung said about the individual symbol to our topic, the question of the meaning of human existence as a whole, we are confronted with a historical rupture of an entirely different character and order of magnitude; this change is no longer comparable to a removal, which, being no more than a change of location or environment, does not immediately and essentially affect the identity of the person moving. It is more like the transformation in puberty, e.g., when there is a substantial change in the identity and redefinition of the person himself or herself from child to man or woman, respectively. The house may stay precisely the same. What is here, as it were, reconstituted is the person himself in that house. He all of a sudden wakes up still in the same unaltered house, but *as* another.

The notion of "change" has become "sublimated," reflected (interiorized) into itself: change here no longer means locomotion of an intact substance or subject, but rather internal ("alchemical") transformation of this substance or subject itself. The notion, one might say, is no longer acted out (nota bene: acted out on the conceptual level!), but "*erinnert.*" The movement has fully come home to that which formerly was merely moved around.

For the "symbol" that we are talking about now is meaning *as such*, Meaning with a capital M; it is myth, the symbolic life, the imaginal, religion, the grand narratives—not *this* myth or religion or grand narrative nor *this* meaning, but myth or religion pure and simple, Meaning altogether. And the "meaning" (lowercase) that has been born out of *this* "symbol" (i.e., out of Meaning capitalized) is Man himself or consciousness as such, human existence at large. Because consciousness has been born out of them, myth as such, religion altogether, higher meaning at large now possess only historical significance; they still exist, but in the plural, and shrunk into the reduced status of commodities—*dead* meanings. If they are nevertheless still used today to hold consciousness in their sway and thus to create a new secondary mystique or aura, a new sense of in-ness, then they can function this way because they now have the status of (spiritual) drugs used to benumb consciousness or to give it its highs.

Myth, religion, the grand narratives as a constituting *form* of consciousness *have* to be dead: the birth of *their* "meaning," Man, out of them is tantamount to the fact that man's *interpretation* of this "meaning," that is, his interpretation of himself, has now become esoteric in Jung's sense. Man now understands and views himself *from within* his consciousness and thus *as* consciousness, *as* linguistic, *as* the process of interpretation and symbol-formation. To the extent that the interpretation has left the outside, exoteric, standpoint, the *contents* of consciousness (the former symbols, mythic images, religious conceptions) can no longer be naively taken at face value and believed in as objects per se, as primordial epiphanic phainomena. They can and must now be seen as products of the human mind, as "conventional signs," not symbols in the lofty Jungian sense; indeed as signifiers, ultimately as letters, as writing, *écriture*, to be read and interpreted, not to be believed in and to be given over to or enwrapped by.

Under the present conditions, when "symbolic life" or Mythic Meaning as such (rather than only this or that symbol) has become questionable, there could only be a new "symbol" pregnant with new meaning, a new "myth" or religion, a new in-ness of human existence, if we were willing to follow Nietzsche in his dream of the coming overman. If man, as Nietzsche claimed, is something that must be (and can be) overcome, if man is indeed a rope tied between animal and overman, then and only then can the old in-ness that has come to an end with the death of God and myth be superseded by a new in-ness, a new state of pregnancy with meaning. For the transition from man to overman is neither like a locomotion (a removal from one house to another) nor like a transformation as in puberty, in which there is a kind of redefinition or reconstitution of one and the same subject. It is rather a new *creation* of a new man and as such the *substitution* or

THE END OF MEANING AND THE BIRTH OF MAN

replacement of the present logical substrate of consciousness, man as he has been known, by a different substrate, a radically new, other definition of man with a new, other mind; not a natural continuation of the evolution and history of consciousness, but a truly new start. The overman being an unknown future would be a new symbol whose "meaning" has not been born out of it yet for present man's understanding. With respect to it the mind of present man which has become esoteric to itself would again be exoteric to this new definition of man.

Once consciousness has become conscious of, and esoteric in, itself, the condition of the possibility of a new in-ness would be a fundamental rupture, a discontinuity of the interpreting mind. But now we have to understand that the idea of a *discontinuity* in the definition of man given with the duality of man and overman and the succession from the one to the other is paradoxically a desperate attempt to rescue the *continuity* of the sense of in-ness in meaning as a constituent, and thus indispensable, part of the definition of human existence. Just as previously the succession of ever new symbols in the history of man had in fact guaranteed that man had never *fundamentally* (logically) fallen out of his sense of in-ness, despite the many periods of cultural crisis in which he was forced to suffer through the empirical loss of his *particular* in-ness in the respective old symbols.

However, since Nietzsche's idea of the overman has become apparent to have been a utopia, even a phantom, we know we cannot hope for a possible successor to man. The inevitable continuity of man means that he will have to hold his place in the loss of in-ness in meaning and that this loss will fall upon him as a fundamental, irrevocable, *logical* one; no new double will relieve him of his having once and for all been born out of meaning and protect him from being initiated into this change by this change itself, when it comes home to him and works upon him alchemically (in the sense of a fermenting decomposition and reconstitution). *This* loss is not an interlude. It makes a *real* difference. But rather than inflating man into an overman, it forces man in his concept of himself to come down from his former lofty height and to live *without* being dressed in any splendid religious or mythical garments.

210   *THE SOUL ALWAYS THINKS*

6. Man the unborn

According to a popular idea, man is the naked ape.[35] This idea had already been popular in antiquity. In Protagoras's myth, related by Plato,[36] man is represented as by nature "naked, without shoes, without cover, without weapon." By comparison with animals, nature has been a stepmother for man (the topos of the *natura noverca* existed at least from the 5th century B.C. onwards). Many philosophers and anthropologists have pointed out that man is a *Mängelwesen* (Herder), a biologically deficient being. Human culture has consequently been interpreted as man's compensation for his biological deficiencies. Without refuting the biological legitimacy of such views and the underlying observations, I propose a different thesis. Harking back to Nietzsche's idea of the overman, I call man, i.e., precisely man as he has been known, the "overanimal" and insist that it is in turn the animal, the ape, that is naked by comparison with man. Just as Nietzsche's overman—if he had come into existence—would logically have been a new creation, while physically remaining man, so man has in fact logically been, and is, a new creation, while biologically remaining an animal.

The animal, as Plato already pointed out,[37] wears its blanket or bedding as its natural fur undetachably upon itself. Physically it is dressed in a protective cover. But logically or metaphysically, it is naked. It is directly thrust into and exposed to the environment and has to live all for itself, on its own account, for better or for worse. There is nothing in between it and external reality. It is in itself complete, autonomous, self-sufficient inasmuch as it has everything it needs for adapting to reality within itself. It has been equipped by nature with its own laws, its instincts. Exclusively with what it has in itself and what it is, it takes life or the environment in its stride. The animal knows no fooling. No illusions, no hopes, no utopias, but also no meaning and no upward looking. This is its nakedness. The animal is very realistic, rational, and sober; as Jung

---

[35] Cf. Desmond John Morris, *The Naked Ape*, New York (McGraw-Hill Book Company) 1967.

[36] Plato, *Protagoras* 321e.

[37] Plato, *Protagoras* 321 c 6.

THE END OF MEANING AND THE BIRTH OF MAN   211

stated, it is a well-behaved, law-abiding citizen in nature.[38] It is an absolutely mature adult, *and*: mature by nature, thus inalienably so. Its way of living life is downright professional.

So we can say that the animal is fully born into the world. Birth means the transition from the containment in a protective womb to the naked exposure to a cold, dangerous environment. Birth also means the transition from being automatically and constantly provided for to the experience of need, and to having to take care of one's needs all by oneself. Already the newborn baby all of a sudden has to do its own breathing and sucking; newborn animals already have to compete with each other for the most food, and often run for their lives, all the more so the grown up animals.

Literal birth is just the beginning of birth in a wider sense. To be *fully* born, and this will have to be kept in mind for the following discussion, is paradoxically synonymous with being fully adult, fully mature: neither dependent on parents, but all on one's own, nor shielded from the environment by any intermediary, but nakedly exposed to it. When this state is reached, then and only then has birth been concluded.

Turning here from animal to man, we immediately see that man prior to modernity is the opposite on both counts. He was fundamentally in a child status, upward looking to the gods, his world parents, or to God, his Father, and contained in the fold of Mother Nature, Mother Church, or some other uterine vessel. What was the cult of the ancestors other than the celebration of the "child's" respect for timeless spiritual parents? Metaphysically, man was not "man for himself"[39] and living on his own responsibility. Rather than carrying his laws as his natural instincts within himself, they had to come to him "written on tablets" from above and outside. The ultimate responsibility for his own doing, too, rested with the gods. Even as the mature adult that he certainly was *psychically*, even with that "natural fulfilled dignity" that Jung had observed in his Pueblo Indians, *psychologically* (logically or metaphysically) man was decidedly a child; indeed, that empirical dignity and maturity was precisely the result

---

[38] C. G. Jung, *Visions Seminar* I (9 Dec. 1930), Notes of Mary Foote, p. 282, quoted in J. Hillman, "The Animal Kingdom in the Human Dream," in: *Eranos 51-1982*, p. 313.

[39] Cf. Erich Fromm, *Man for himself* (1947).

of the Pueblo Indians' logically being and staying the sons of the Sun, their Father; they derived their strength and authority from their "religious" relation to him. By the same token, the initiation rites at puberty, to be found in traditional societies in most parts of the world, had, to be sure, the task of transporting a person from childhood into social adulthood. But they fulfilled this task precisely by logically initiating the initiate into *metaphysical childhood*. And as late as the 20th century, the realization of the deep, inner child-status of man ("the *filiatio*—the sonship of God"[40]) was an idea very dear to C.G. Jung's heart, a central psychological goal.

Man (I am here not speaking about the empirical individual, but, on the logical level, about Man at large, his "humanity": the *concept* of man as and in which we all live) is not born directly into the environment, not "thrust into existence," as the 20th century existentialists thought. He is born first of all into and contained in myths, meanings, ideas, images, words, creeds, theories, traditions. They stand irrevocably between him and external reality, so that he is not naked, and it not either. Everything in the world is hopelessly enwrapped in mythical garments; nothing is just what it pragmatically is. Tools, weapons, things and events in nature, regardless of whether big or small, the activities of daily life: everything has its story about its primordial divine origin and cosmic significance, and this its mythical or metaphysical reality is its primary reality. Naked reality is fundamentally out of reach. When man came into this world, he *ipso facto* had entered into One ongoing, continuous, and all-comprehensive Dream, a dream from which there was no awakening since this dream was his real world and life, his "reality principle." What we call consciousness is just as much part of *this* Dream as are the many particular literal dreams (which normally are thought to belong to "the unconscious").

Or we could say he entered into One Sandplay, with the difference to ordinary sandplays in the context of sandplay therapy that it was not an event or intended performance *in* the course of life, but that life itself and as a whole (and not only one's own life, but the life of people collectively, as it extended over millennia) was this Sandplay, the real world (nature, the cosmos) being its sandtray and the real

---

[40] Cf., for example, (*MDR* p. 333).

THE END OF MEANING AND THE BIRTH OF MAN

people, animals, plants, things, events its toy figures. *While* a sandplay is played, *while* a dream is dreamed, they are absolutely real, the one and only reality. The reality of the waking mind simply does not exist for the dreamer and his dream. The dream has no other world outside of itself. In the same way, the One Dream or Sandplay as which life was lived did not have the problem of truth as *adaequatio intellectus et rei*. Truth was "absolute"; it *was*, existed: physically, cosmically. Things and events *were* the mythical, imaginal apperception of them, and myths *were* the real nature of reality. One might even claim: *Anima naturaliter realista* ("the soul is by nature a realist," realist here in the sense of the medieval universals controversy).

Man is fundamentally unborn. Despite his literal biological birth, he has logically never left the in-ness in a womb. In being biologically born, he only *exchanged* the biological womb for another, a metaphysical womb, the womb of Meaning. Personalistically expressed, man managed to *in fact* take the logical sting away from birth (birth where is thy sting?[41]), the logical (not emotional, not empirical) trauma of the radical and irrevocable rupture that birth meant for the animal in that birth ruthlessly expelled it from in-ness in a uterus into naked exposure to the environment. Man managed to logically defeat birth in its literal biological dimension and use it for a purpose not intended, *contra naturam*. With respect to its intended purpose (naked exposure to the world, expulsion into adulthood) birth was forced to miscarry. It was forced to simply lead into another state of unbornness, another childhood.

How did this work? Through a fundamental inversion. Man gave up the instincts that belonged to him qua animal and *logically* extrajected the instinctual knowledge from within himself out into the environment, the whole universe—similarly to how we today *empirically-technically* launch satellites into outer orbits. He thereby gave up the fixedness, certainty and empirical realness of his natural knowledge as each individual's private property for the openness, uncertainty and virtuality of mental conceptions belonging to the community of humanity at large. In this way a virtual uterus was formed, one encompassing even the external physical environment as a whole, into which *biological* birth would still thrust man just as

---

[41] Cf. 1 Cor. 15:55.

before. With this inversion the in-ness in a womb could be retained even across the event of factual birth, and the birth into mature adulthood, as it is obtained by animals, could be forever postponed. On the other hand man could become physically naked, unprotected, deficiently equipped with instincts, because metaphysically he never left the protectedness of the embryonic stage.

If in this way natural birth was, as it were, cheated out of its reward and used for another purpose, what then was the reward of this re-designation? It was the genesis of mind, soul, *logos*. By man's foregoing that his biological birth had the result of, and exhausted itself in, *his* full-fledged birth into the naked existence in the environment, i.e., into the maturity and adulthood of self-sufficient animal existence, his biological birth was freed to give birth to something else, something incredible and unheard of before: the invisible and intangible metaphysical dimension of meanings, the realm of consciousness. It is a virtual reality, and because it is virtual, it does not do away with the biological altogether. What is born here, is also the *difference* between biological and metaphysical birth, or in more general terms, the difference between the empirical ("literal," positive-factual) and the logical, between the psychic and the psychological.

So when man is born in the literal sense, he is not really born at all. He merely exchanges the biological womb of the mother for a second womb, the spiritual womb, the amniotic sac of the mind, images and meanings. Man is not born directly into the environment. He is "born" into his *being mind and soul.* Much like astronauts do not really venture into outer space, but stay in their spaceships or space-suits that protect them from outer space, so man, even when literally, biologically, born into the environment, is logically not directly exposed to the environment like an animal, but enters the environment only safely encapsulated in the space-suit, or should we say environment-suit, of his images, ideas, concepts, words.

When I just said that man was born into his *being* mind and soul, this was a bit premature. The space-suit image is more correct. It makes apparent that the person in the space-suit and that space-suit itself are in principle separable as two distinct "substances." Pre-modern man as individual was *in* mind and soul. He lived fundamentally cocooned in his images and conceptions. Mind and soul were outside, around him, in the *world.* As we have seen, ideas and concepts were

THE END OF MEANING AND THE BIRTH OF MAN   215

immediately real, hypostases in the Neoplatonic sense. *They* were the true nature of things. On the other hand, there is a shortcoming in the image of the space-suit. It suggests something too rigid. So let us shift to another image and say that man was floating in mind and soul as in his secondary amniotic fluid.

The animal is driven from within itself by its instincts, as if from behind. Thus it is *fundamentally* unconscious; it has its laws contained in its bodily-rooted innate release mechanisms always in its back. Man, by contrast, has the equivalent of instincts, the laws or the logic of his human nature and of his life, no longer in himself in the form of release mechanisms, but outside, as the *horizon* of his *world* (in the cosmos, in the stars, in the things and events of nature) and he has them in the *form* of divine figures and messages. And the knowledge about the logic of his nature comes to him fundamentally a posteriori, partly as spontaneous visions, revelations or apparitions, partly as something to be read in the world, partly and mostly through the age-old traditional store of images and conceptions of his people that have to be taken over and filled with new life by each new generation. This is why man is fundamentally conscious, by nature and inalienably so: the "laws" of his nature are *before* his mind, they have the *form* of *knowledge* for him; he sees them out there in the (mythically or imaginally perceived) natural world as his mirror. He is "overanimal," man, human, *because* he *gave up the unconscious inside* (his instincts) *for* having his "laws" out there in the form of an enveloping horizon and because he gave up the mechanical nature of natural laws rooted in the individual body for the mental, notional, cultural and communal form of *knowing* his "laws." The ancient symbol of trees having their roots in the sky and growing down to earth might reflect the inversion discussed here.

The difference between the unconscious of the animal and human consciousness is *only* that the animal carries its laws and logic within itself as bodily-rooted innate release mechanisms, while man has his laws and logic conversely out there all around himself as an horizon and thus as knowledge; but there is, at the outset, no difference as to the certainty of "knowing." From the beginning man was, like the animal, adapted to the world and at home in it. Despite the logical a-posteriority of his essential knowledge (the knowledge concerning the logic of his own nature), human existence began with answers, not questions. No real questions, no puzzling riddles. Man was born into, and it thus began with, the answers; man was embedded in them on all sides. Puzzling questions are only the late result of a long cultural development. This is why human existence *logically* always had its place in paradise, while only *empirically-practically* being life "after the Fall." Paradise and life outside the garden of Eden were only narratively, not logically, divided by a "before" and "after." Logically they were simultaneous, as the two sides of the same coin. The real division is between "logically" (or "metaphysically") and "empirically" (or "positive-factually"); or between "in the depth of soul" and "in external reality": Paradise or the Golden Age had been the *logical* truth *of* man's *empirical* existence in the fallen world or the Iron Age, the Indian Kali Yuga.

The animal does not *know* what it is doing. It simply does what it has to do, without *con-scientia, syn-eidesis*. This is the difference to the situation of man. Since he *is* (exists as) consciousness, he knows what he is doing, or has done, or has to do. However, to begin with man does not know about his knowing, he is not conscious of this consciousness of his; he views the contents of his consciousness—his truths—as if they were things, natural objects, external facts, rather than being aware of the fact that what he sees in nature as divine figures are the *mirror images* of the internal logic of his existence. This not-knowing came home to Jung when he was with an East-African tribe and asked about a ritual performed by them: "'It has always been done,' they said. It was impossible to obtain any explanation, and I realized that they actually knew only *that* they did it, not *what* they were doing. They themselves saw no meaning in this action."[42] We could say that early man only knows the answers without knowing the corresponding questions and without knowing that they are *answers to* questions. "I am inclined to believe that things were generally done first and that only a long time afterwards somebody asked a question about them, and then eventually discovered why they were done."[43] In other words, early man is not able to view the answers as logical (events of and within the mind, logos), but apperceives them only ontologically. Returning

---

[42] *MDR* p. 266, translation and emphases adjusted by me according to the German original.
[43] *CW* 18 § 540.

THE END OF MEANING AND THE BIRTH OF MAN 217

to our earlier image we could say that the space-suit despite being in principle separable, was not seen as separate. It was like one's skin. There was no distance to it, much like the embryo is distancelessly at one with its amniotic fluid.

In the beginning there were the answers. But in contrast to animal instincts, the answers that man was living with were not absolutely fixed. They did not have the form of abstract universals, principles. They were concrete universals, reflecting the specific culture of each people, because although they were experienced like "stars" (as strictly objective entities, truths of nature, even as personified figures), they actually, though secretly, were "satellites": having passed through the mind and having been launched by it up into the sky and out into the natural world. Since the form of the answers was mental, cultural and communal, there was room, within a certain range, for variety and development, from individual to individual, from one people or tribe to another, from eon to eon. And because human knowing came essentially from outside, rather than from inside the physical body, the condition of the possibility of a later development toward a distance to and a critical questioning of the images and ideas was inherent in this essential knowing from the outset.

The price, however, for the soul's and consciousness' birth into the world, for their becoming real, embodied, was that man stayed fundamentally unborn. And yet, this re-designation of biological birth was not without radical consequences also for him. It catapulted him into a new form of existence. Although his physical birth did not really bring about his *birth* in the full sense of the word, it nevertheless brought about the *begettal, conception* and thus the *embryonic* existence of man *as "overanimal":* as *human*, as a being living primarily neither in his animal body, nor in the physical environment, but in images and ideas, in myths and metaphysics, in creeds and ideologies, as his *contra naturam* womb. Man's body and the whole physical environment are *inside* his mind.[44] They have been interiorized, integrated, *er-innert* so that *as external factual reality* they are nevertheless only sublated moments in consciousness.

---

[44] Not inside his brain, his head: the mind is the horizon of the world!

7. The birth of man

Modernity is characterized by the fact that man has emerged from his in-ness in a horizon, from his containment in a womb; all the facts discussed in the chapter "The end of in-ness" above are evidence to this development. Of course I am here not speaking about empirical individuals. When I say "man" here, I am speaking about the general form of the logical constitution of being human, the concept or logic as the medium of the existence of a concrete empirical individual. Man has emerged from the ocean of meaning. He raised his head above the surface of the ocean and now has it out in the open. He has awakened from the One Dream or Sandplay that existence in the world had been and now is fundamentally and irrevocably *extra ecclesiam*, as Jung had pointed out, as well as *extra naturam*. He has lost his myths, his symbols. He now looks back down upon consciousness at large from outside. The flight to the moon and beyond to other planets, the observation of planet Earth from satellites, the looking back down upon the Earth from outer space: all this is the *technical* objectification of the *psychological* fact that consciousness has now taken a position outside itself and has become aware of *itself* and of man *as consciousness*. He has hatched from the Orphic world egg. The tell-tale sign for this in the history of thought is the "linguistic turn," the awareness that everything we are dealing with is first and foremost linguistic, semiotic, information, that man himself is language.

For the in-ness in the pre-modern situation had also been containment *in* language. When one has one's logical place *within* language, the words as positivities (phonetic sound clusters), as factual means of expression, are completely unobtrusive. They do their job, but do not push themselves into the foreground. Man is here completely given over to the *meaning* of the utterances; he dwells solely with the ideas or the things and events referred to, using the words and their sounds merely as something to push off from into the realm of meaning.[45] Consciousness floats in meanings. The words and grammar, i.e., language as such, are taken for granted, much as fish take water as the element of their life for granted. Although the words, syllables, sounds of language do of course not do their job as *silent*

---

[45] Here meaning is obviously used in the formal (logical and linguistic) sense.

THE END OF MEANING AND THE BIRTH OF MAN

servants, they nevertheless become audible for the sole purpose of immediately dying away again, because only *as* having faded away do they release their meaning. The death or sublation of the words as sounds *is* the meaning of the sentence. This and the fact that consciousness more or less exclusively dwelled with their meaning is why the word, the sentence, the poetic image are here immediately the true and the real.[46] They are *die Sachen selbst.* The call to be heard in the 20th century from Husserl, "To the things themselves," would not have made any sense here. Language here is in itself symbolic (in the weighty sense that was also Jung's), if not epiphanic (of course epiphanic on the mental or logical level, not experientially, religiously). This symbolic nature of *language* survived even the mind's explicit emancipation in philosophical *thought* during the course of the Middle Ages from the Realism of universals and the emergence of Nominalism.

The modern situation, by contrast, is characterized by the fact that man has logically (not always experientially) fallen out of his containment in language, with the result that now language is first of all comprehended as an *instrument* for communication. As such it is an object vis-à-vis, it has become explicit. Man has been born out of it, too, and now views it from outside.[47] This division is paralleled by another one, that between the mind and the world, the "things themselves": now consciousness has become fundamentally *intentional* ("being-directed-toward"). And a third split is brought by man's having fallen out of language, namely, that the word itself falls apart into "signifier" and "signified." The sign as such, the sound, the letter begin to be obtrusive, forcing themselves into the foreground, insisting on being something in their own right ("L'instance de la lettre").[48] The sign that does no longer exist for the only purpose of having to die away drives a wedge between the mind and (linguistic) meaning. The understanding of language shifts from a symbolic to a semiotic one, and thought in general from the contents *in* the media to the

---

[46] As I pointed out: *anima naturaliter realista.*

[47] The statement by Theodore Savory in 1967, "There can be no doubt that science is in many ways the natural enemy of languages," sheds a light on the extent of this alienation.

[48] That this is not merely a fundamental shift in the deep constitution of the soul, but has obvious effects in practical reality can be seen from the incredible increase today of puns, of toying with words and signs ("4" for "for," "I ♥ NY") as well as the proliferation of acronyms instead of *words.*

awareness of and concentration upon the media themselves as well as from semantics to syntax, to logical form.

The (spatial) image of outer space from which man is looking back down upon consciousness (and nature and language) is tricky, possibly misleading. For this looking back down upon consciousness occurs only *within* consciousness. There has not been a literal move out of consciousness. The move into the outer space beyond consciousness in order to see it from outside is dialectically the interiorization (*Er-innerung*) of the whole of the former consciousness into itself. It is similar to an involution. Consciousness only gets out of itself by pulling itself into itself. Reflection. Above I said that mind and soul, that images and concepts, were a kind of space-suit with which man ventured into the physical environment and that this pointed to an in principle existing separability of the space-suit and the person in it. Now, what has happened with modernity is that this separation has taken place. Man has become capable of seeing this "space-suit" from outside as a vis-à-vis, as a system of *signs* used by him. However, man did not learn to see his space-suit from outside by stepping out of it and leaving it behind, but conversely, by now interiorizing, integrating mind and soul, his former amniotic sac, into himself via a fermenting corruption of its hard substantiality. He absorbed the sublimated or vaporized result of this disintegration process into the very definition or concept of himself, just as originally the entire environment had been interiorized into mind and soul as their sublated moments. Man has occupied, "cathected," his space-suit or "uterus," so that the "external" *substance* (the neoplatonic real universal, objective truths, as ontological) has transformed into the status of "subject" and man can now finally be said to really *be* mind and soul, to exist as mind and soul. He has now *in fact* comprehended himself as a sign-using, the linguistic being, and (which is the same thing) that which formerly had been ontic (the *nature* of things as such) he has comprehended as *his* signs. Thus he also can be said to know not only *that*, but also *what*, he is doing.

This is the birth of man as the overanimal, his having come of age and become adult in his humanness. He has left "father" and "mother" to stand on his own feet; he has come out of the protective shell of the world egg, out of the in-ness in between Heaven and Earth, and, himself now *being* consciousness and comprising the former Heaven

THE END OF MEANING AND THE BIRTH OF MAN 221

and Earth as sublated moments within himself, is for the first time ruthlessly exposed to life or reality *in metaphysical nakedness*. What nature brought about in the animal right from the start with the animal's biological birth had been the fact that the born animal lost any protective womb and was exposed naked to the environment, all for itself, for better or worse. Modernity finally achieved the same situation in man *as human*, who had hitherto been on all sides enveloped in meaning. Now he has to exist all for himself, in what Jung once called the "illimitable loneliness of man."[49] It is, figuratively speaking, the inevitable metaphysical loneliness of Aquarius, the water-bearer, the sovereign Lord of the media, who has left the former containment in the waters. It is, literally and figuratively speaking, man as fundamentally existing "*extra ecclesiam*," in the fresh cold air out there in the open and in the soberness that this condition entails.

Of course "God is dead," as Nietzsche has said, and of course "There are no longer any gods whom we could invoke to help us," as Jung had said. How could there be gods, how an upward looking if there is no above and below in the metaphysical sense, no Atlas holding Heaven and Earth apart anymore, and if man *essentially* looks down upon planet Earth and himself from outer space? Gods can *be* only for the fish swimming in the water, for a consciousness still contained in the amniotic sac of its images and ideas perceived as *substances*, Neoplatonic hypostases, the truth of nature itself, things-in-themselves. Gods can only be for the man who still is in between Heaven and Earth and as such has to be fundamentally, that is, logically, an upward looking being. They could only exist as long as *nature* was the ultimate horizon and absolute limit of human production. The fundamental unsurpassability, immutability and transcendence of nature was their *sine qua non*, because such a nature was the condition both for the metaphysical child status of man and for the extrajection of the internal logic of human existence, first into the cosmos (myth), later into the status of objective hypostases (philosophy), and thus for the stance of upward looking. Once man has learned to interfere with nature itself, thus sublating it, taking charge of it, once the fish has emerged from the waters and transmuted into Aquarius, the whole logic or mode of upward looking as such is over. And *ipso facto* the very notion of "god"

---

[49] *Letters 2*, p. 586, to Berann, 27 August 1960.

THE SOUL ALWAYS THINKS

has become impossible, inasmuch as the gods *are* nothing else but the imaginal, personified figures into which the various distinct forms of upward looking or worship have congealed and become objective for consciousness. Aquarius looks back down upon the waters from which he emerged and also down upon the fish in it as discarded, outgrown elements of his former *history*. The condition of the possibility of the sacred, the numinous, of mysteries, of the symbolic life, of myth and religion—each taken according to its *highest determination*—has disappeared.

Why are the religious symbols and ideas obsolete, rituals at best commodities, the religious practice no more than a (lofty, spiritual) hobby? Because they are fundamentally sublated; they have no logical task anymore for consciousness. The task that religion once had had has been fulfilled. The "meaning" that it once was pregnant with has been born out of it, the "better expression" has been found: consciousness has caught up with the message that it had projected out as its contents, as symbols in Jung's sense. Religion had been the objective representation, in imaginal or in conceptual form, of the inner logic of human existence. But now consciousness has integrated its former contents into itself as the form of its logical constitution. Whereas before consciousness had had its truth or logic, its self and highest essence, out there as its objective contents and *ipso facto* had had to be upward looking, this truth has meanwhile come home to consciousness itself; much like a sugar cube dissolves in coffee, so has what had formerly been seen as solid substance dissolved into the form of consciousness itself. Thus it seemingly vanished, but it is still there: it only disappeared as a concrete visible (or imaginable) object, while it is present as a quality: the sweetness of the coffee, the logical form of consciousness, its categories. Consciousness has recognized *itself*, its own structure, in its formerly projected or extrajected contents. It has comprehended them as the mind's self-portrait.

The entire third epoch of Western metaphysics (from, say, Nicholas of Cusa via Descartes, Spinoza, etc. to Hegel) experienced, i.e., *thought*, the world-subject no longer as the Father (Zeus) as in Antiquity, nor as the Son (Christ) as in the Middle Ages, but as Spirit (in Christian terminology: the third person of the Godhead) and therefore as Subjectivity. And the *opus magnum* of this epoch was the completion of the logical integration and realization of the notion of

THE END OF MEANING AND THE BIRTH OF MAN 223

spirit. As Spirit, God is no longer a substantial Being (Father or Son). He has, as it were, dissolved into spirit. He has been alchemically distilled, evaporated.

Therefore, to still preach religion in all earnest—instead of seeing, appreciating, and studying it strictly historically—means to carry coals to Newscastle. It is like making a present of a primer to a high-school graduate or, if we consider the oppressive and stultifying character of such endeavors, like squeezing an adult into a crib.

Just as on a personal level one cannot go back behind puberty (except—partially and seemingly—for the price of neurosis), so there is on the cultural level of consciousness no way back to the gods. Once the sugar cube has been dissolved in the coffee, it cannot be made undissolved. As Jung said (without, however, fully taking his own medicine), "We cannot turn the wheel backwards; we cannot go back to a symbolism that is gone. [...] I cannot go back to the Catholic Church; I cannot experience the miracle of the Mass; I know too much about it."[50] This knowing too much about it is the sign that the meaning has been born out of the symbol that had formerly only been pregnant with it. It is the sign that Jung's consciousness looks back down upon the miracle of the Mass as if from outer space, the sign also that Jung no longer knows only *that*, but also *what*. But the Catholic Church with the Mass is here of course only one example. Not only the semantics of one particular religion, not even all religions, but the syntax of religiousness as such has dissolved, because it has been integrated into the *form* of consciousness. Once Jung wrote about the Gnostic at the beginning of the Christian era, "Longingly he looked back to the world of the Father, but it was lost forever, because an irreversible increase in man's consciousness had taken place in the meantime and made it independent."[51] The same applies to our modern situation, but with even more validity.

It has been said about Pythagoras, who believed in the transmigration of souls, that when he erected himself and craned his neck with all his mental powers he was effortlessly able to view every detail in his ten or even twenty former lives.[52] This is exactly the situation of modern consciousness, only that *it* does no longer have to

---

[50] *CW* 18 § 632.
[51] *CW* 11 § 203.
[52] Empedokles, fragment 129.

act out this craning one's neck subjectively, through particular acts, in the spirit and context of a mystery religion of personal salvation. As *inevitably* historical, modern consciousness is logically once and for all in the *status* of the "craned neck." This status is objectified and institutionalized in the field of historical research, which has the task of extending and differentiating, quite soberly and far from any mystifying religious hope for salvation, our historical awareness so that we might be able to see before us, with ever higher degrees of sophistication, more and more different and ever earlier formations (*Gestalten*) of the human mind's former lives. Even the biological theory of evolution is testimony to the fact that consciousness has fundamentally come out of the in-ness in the waters and is once and for all a historically backward looking one instead.

The gods have not become diseases, as Jung and Hillman wanted us to believe, they have become *memories*, memories of former modes of man's being-in-the-world. I have been speaking of "former lives" and of "discarded, outgrown elements." I could also speak of obsolescence. However, this needs some qualifications. What has been discarded is not the elements and contents themselves, but their, or our, claim to their being in the status of a present reality, of numinosity, of sacred mysteries. This status they had for the fish. For Aquarius, they are all still there, and to be sure even as a source of inspiration, but only in Mnemosyne. They are *historical* presences.

8. The fate of God(s)

What is left of religion once its substance has been integrated into the logical form of consciousness is only the "conventional sign," the conventional forms without living substance: the dead snake skin after the living snake has moved out of it into new fields. One can, however, inflate even a dead snake skin and replace the life that it does not have of its own account with one's own breath. Even if the sugar cube cannot be got back from out of the coffee in which it has been dissolved, there is nevertheless still its paper wrapping that can be refolded so as to simulate the former sugar cube in its wrapping. Thus fundamentalism uses the old dogmas and fills them with the subjective zeal stemming from the feeling of lack and thereby gives a secondary rigid stability and seeming life to them. Or one can use the snake skin like an amulet;

THE END OF MEANING AND THE BIRTH OF MAN

conventional forms of religion can serve as a kind of spiritual pacifier for want of a living truth; the fossil pointing to a former real life can be used as a *token* satisfaction of one's need for a symbolic or metaphysical life; the appearance can be taken for the real thing, with the same kind of silent conspiracy that is found in the tale of the emperor's new clothes. Or, a third possibility, one can use the old forms as a mere stimulant for an attempt to work oneself up into strictly subjective heightened emotional states that have very little to do with the experienced truths that the old forms in themselves were about, the religious origin of the stimulant sufficing to gloss over the merely subjective emotions, so that the impression is created that the religious or metaphysical needs are taken care of.

There is one, and only one, way how religion can today still be a *present reality* and not just a commodity and hobby. Under the conditions of modernity, the price for giving religion the status of present reality is, however, that it has to be reduced to the *zero grade* of itself, religion without any dignity, any substantial content and any conscious awareness. Where does religion as present reality show today? Only in the momentary acts of certain irrational, meaningless crimes: in the *action directe* of the bombings and shootings, e.g., of the Una bomber and the Columbine and Erfurt high school shootings, in certain cases of sexual abuse and murder of children, etc. Here, the numinous is an immediate reality, as a *tremendum* breaking through the indifference and "banality" of everyday life, and as an overwhelming power "religiously observed" by the individuals committing these crimes, who usually give up for their passion any hope for a future happiness. But the numinous is here a reality for only one short moment, without substantial dignified content, totally abstract and absolutely blind, bringing not the least spiritual reward (blessing, illumination, experience of meaning) for anybody. It is just the empty shell of religion, the abstract naked form of the sacred, and as such the legitimate form of religion as a living reality *today*.

Two possible mistaken conclusions need to be discussed here. First, with respect to Nietzsche's statement "God is dead" Jung pointed to the psychological fact that a psychological, especially archetypal, content does not simply get lost; if you declare an archetypal content, e.g. God, to be dead, you yourself become identical with that content

226 THE SOUL ALWAYS THINKS

that you declared dead; you become inflated by the God-idea and possibly psychotic.[53] However, this is only true under two conditions: first, that the doing away with God is only *semantic*, the elimination of one particular element in a system of thought that leaves the old syntax or the system itself, the logical constitution of consciousness, intact. It is a totally different situation if what is negated or rendered obsolete is the entire previous *syntax* or *logical form* of consciousness; if e.g., as in modernity, human consciousness has emerged from its containment in nature and is now looking back down upon it as if from outer space. Secondly, the elimination of God would have to be one's personal doing (both personal, as by the ego, and active doing). The danger of inflation does not exist if, as during the 19th century, the "God is dead" dictum was the late, painful realization of a situation that had come over consciousness as an accomplished fact brought about by history, by "the soul" itself—"because an irreversible increase in man's consciousness had taken place in the meantime and made it independent."[54]

Another mistake is that frequently the ideas of the death of God and of the loss of meaning are not carried to their logical conclusion. There is, e.g., a Death of God theology, in other words, a theology that wants to heed the death of God and integrate it into theology, but nevertheless continue to exist as theology. This is a self-contradiction, one, however, that is already inherent in the statement about the death of God itself. This statement, while *semantically* declaring the death of God, *syntactically* posits God and preserves him beyond what is happening to him in this sentence. It could only be true as a transitional statement and for the short time of the transition. If one really gets the message that the statement wants to transmit, then the end of the sentence (the predicate) destroys and does away with the beginning (the subject) altogether: it is dead and gone. This means that once we have understood the meaning of this sentence, the *notion* of God no longer exists for us: the former numinosity implied by this word is simply gone and has no chance anymore, because the

---

[53] "The tragedy of *Zarathustra* is that, because Nietzsche's God died, he himself became a god [....] He to whom 'God dies,' will become the victim of 'inflation.'" *CW* 11 § 142 (modified according to *GW*). Cf. *CW* 10 § 437 and *Letters 2*, p. 168, to Victor White, 10 April 1954 ("Through the negation of God one becomes deified, [...]")

[54] *CW* 11 § 203, where Jung, however, uses these words not with respect to the modern situation, but to that of the Gnostics.

THE END OF MEANING AND THE BIRTH OF MAN

whole mode of upward looking, of which the experience of numinosity was the expression, is over. The notion of God has become demystified, maybe in the spirit that expresses itself in Lichtenberg's witty remark: "Just as one paints a zero above the heads of saints."[55] We then cannot even speak of the death of God anymore because such speaking would precisely evoke the notion of God once more, even while semantically declaring Him—him merely as sort of incumbent in the position of God—dead. The position, office, or throne of God would remain even after having become vacant. Psychologically, that is, for the soul, it never makes any difference whether you call something dead or alive, whether you love or hate it, support or combat it. The only thing that counts psychologically is whether its *concept* or *position* is important to you one way or another. But "God is dead" means that the *position* of "God" has disappeared. God can now, much like Ether or phlogiston, only be a content of historical knowledge.

Therefore the fear that through the death of God man becomes inflated is ungrounded, as is the fear that man has become "godlike" or "equal to God" on account of the fact that with the enormous advances in nuclear physics and genetic biology together with the corresponding technologies, incredible powers to destroy and create are now lying in human hands. We find this fear expressed in Jung: "[...] never before was the power of absolute destruction given into the hand of man himself. It is a 'godlike' power that has fallen into human hands. The *dignitas humani generis* has swollen into truly diabolical grandeur."[56] This fear in addition to being ungrounded also contradicts itself; it implies that the overcoming of upward looking as such, which is the specific message of the "death of God" statement, has not been allowed to happen at all; that instead a mere transferral is imagined: man is conceived as still upward looking, only now upward looking to himself instead of to God, and likewise as now assigning numinosity and an aura to himself. Not the *dignitas humani generis* has swollen into truly diabolical grandeur, but Jung uses blown up *categories* with which he interprets the historical change, one that

---

[55] Georg Christoph Lichtenberg, *Sudelbücher* I, Heft F, No. 167. In: *Idem, Schriften und Briefe*, vol. 1, ed. by Wolfgang Promies, München (Hanser) 1968, p. 485. My translation.

[56] C.G. Jung, *Letters 2*, p. 225, to Pater Lucas Menz, 22 February 1955. Cf. also "[...] that the cosmic power of self-destruction is given into the hands of man and that man inherits the dual nature of the Father." *Letters 2*, p. 167, to Victor White, 10 April 1954.

228   *THE SOUL ALWAYS THINKS*

he observes correctly. It is the consciousness which uses terms like "godlike" and "diabolical" for this technical advance and for the advance of consciousness that is inflated, a mystifying one. The acquisition of the destructive and creative power that is now in the hand of man is only quantitatively different from the conquest of fire and the invention of bow and arrow by early man, not qualitatively. It is not that the prehistoric advance was harmless whereas today's is diabolical.

The fear of man's inflation on account of the enormous increase in technical power is the opposite of what the insight into the death of God means and of what actual effect the fact of the increase in technical power has. Psychologically, this fact *objectively* makes more humble, makes "so disappointingly simple"[57] (quite apart from what people's subjective attitudes may be). The fact that "God is dead" merely means that man has become psychologically of age; it allows him to become more humane. It has its own logic. The increase in power puts in fact the heavy burden of an unheard-of responsibility upon man's shoulders, a burden that *inevitably weighs him down* in his soul, rather than leading to a sense of grandiosity or to hybris. It even produces quite a bit of depressiveness. Man is more and more reduced to a functionary in the organization of society and an operator of machines, he *bedient* them (as their servant). Much of his own intelligence he has abdicated in favor of his computers, robots, artificial intelligence. He sits for hours in front of television, often watching downright stupid, utterly banal quiz and reality TV shows, etc. He wears the most casual clothes. When he has his picture taken, he prefers decidedly informal poses or spontaneous snapshots. All pompousness and sense of dignity (Jung's *dignitas humani generis*) is gone. The higher consciousness *objectively* goes along with a lower, more modest self-assessment. No need for moral exhortations in this regard. Moral exhortations do not reach the objective, logical level of man's constitution anyway.

Much the same as what has been said about the death of God idea applies to the idea of the loss of meaning. If we really listened to what it says, we would understand from it that meaning is simply no topic anymore. As a topic or notion it is dead and gone. We cannot even speak of its loss, because then we would secretly resurrect and hold

---

[57] Jung used this formulation for his own "empirical standpoint." *Letters 2*, p. 573, to Robert C. Smith, 29 June 1960.

THE END OF MEANING AND THE BIRTH OF MAN

on to it as a logical *category* that merely today happens to be empirically empty.

This vacuum would then necessarily create a craving, an obsession with the search for meaning. But the vacuum is only the result of the fact of the loss's having been reductively held down in the status of a semantic event and thus something particular. The vacuum, and with it the addiction, immediately disappear if the "loss," initially experienced as semantic, is allowed to infect and permeate the syntax of consciousness as such. The experienced "loss" wants to come home to consciousness, be integrated into it; it wants to "initiate" consciousness into the "loss" as its new truth, which initiation would mean the transformation of consciousness as a whole through a decomposition and reconstitution of it. But very often people prefer great and endless semantic/empirical suffering over logical transformation, over an initiation occurring once and for all.

So far I criticized the inconsistency in the two statements concerning the sentence *subject*, "God" or "meaning," respectively. But a corresponding inconsistency applies to the predicate, too, to the ideas of "loss" and "death." Both words suggest that what they name should actually not be and thus nourish our contrary expectations: death and loss should not have been. And therefore both statements try to make us aware of a new situation while viewing and evaluating it from the standpoint of the old situation. So the statements themselves implicitly *resist* that very transformation from old to new that they explicitly want to bring to awareness. The statements let themselves in for the new only as far as the (semantic) contents are concerned, but retain the old unaltered expectations and values, the old logic or level of consciousness. They give the information without letting themselves be informed by it. They present us with a disappointment, disillusionment, without leading to the necessary radical *dis*-illusionment: the destruction of the former illusionary expectation; they invite us to a resignation, but do not advance to the re-*signation*. Resignation is the defense of the unaltered old hope together with the admission of its zero fulfillment (= the vacuum). Consciousness holds on to the *logic* of hoping while holding the experienced and admitted non-fulfillment down in the status of a semantic content, a mere piece of information about an empirical lack. Because the experience is sealed in this status of a particular, the syntax of consciousness is immunized against being infected by its own content. The re-signation, by contrast, replaces the old hope or thesis by a new one (places life under a new sign) on the basis of what has been learned from experience. If the above statements about the end of God and meaning were allowed to go all the way, then they would decompose the very ideas of "loss" and "death" (in this connection) altogether.

So at this point I have to criticize my own use above of the phrase "end" or "loss" of meaning as a mere concession to the prevailing, but inappropriate interpretation of what is actually the phenomenon of a "birth" *from* the standpoint prior to the birth.

9. Critique of the feeling of loss and need

Apart from this destruction of the *notion* of loss itself, is the loss of meaning really a *loss* in the first place (simply on the phenomenological level)? Is it a *loss* that I have moved out of my parents' house, the house of my childhood, and learned to stand on my own feet? Is it not a gain (a gain at least just as much as it may at first have been *felt* as a loss)? One does not have to go quite as far as St. Augustin who wrote, "But who would not recoil and, confronted with the alternative of either having to die or to become a child once more, would not rather choose death?"[58] in order to be fully convinced that the move from childhood to adulthood is a boon, that it "has a meaning" and "is a development that has an inner consistency" (to say it with the words with which Jung greeted the "the growing impoverishment of symbols"[59]).

This insight presses the following questions upon us. Is it really so terrible to live without a higher meaning? Is it really the void that yawns before us when we are without it? After all, Homer, Dante, Shakespeare, Goethe, Praxiteles, the Chartres cathedral, Leonardo da Vinci, Mozart, Plato, Thomas Aquinas, Hegel, etc. etc. remain— incredible, inexhaustible riches. Are they not enough, more than enough? What about the smile of the person who passed me this morning on the street; the rays of sunlight falling through the leaves of a forest; the happy events of a true meeting of minds, the friendship of a friend, the love of one's spouse—are they all void, banal, "all *maya*

---

[58] St. Augustin, *De civitate dei*, Book 21, chapter 14.
[59] *CW* 9i § 28.

THE END OF MEANING AND THE BIRTH OF MAN   231

compared with that one thing, that your life is meaningful," as Jung wants us to believe?[60]

Here we can return to the discussion of the correct understanding of "loss" and warn against mistaking the expressions "metaphysically naked" and "poverty." "Poverty" does not refer to a state like that of the poor in Third World slums; "nakedness" not to the condition of the beggar who was clothed by St. Martin. The idea of "loss," rightly understood, refers exclusively to the loss of an excess, of a grandiose self-stylization, of giving oneself airs, not to the loss of substance. This is why I cannot agree with Jung when he states that we are not the legitimate heirs of the Christian symbolism, because we have "squandered"[61] it. Of course we are the legitimate heirs of our Christian heritage and of our whole Western cultural tradition. The loss that occurred is not the loss of the substance of Christianity and metaphysics, but only of its "validity" (to use Jung's word, see below page 241 with note 86), its numinous aura, that is to say of it *as a present reality* and *immediacy*. We have not outgrown our heritage, but the *immediacy* of its "possession," our feeling *immediately* identical with it. We have lost the possibility to strut around in it as our true garment: to think that *it* is we or we it. We have only lost this pompousness. Everything else is still there. We have only become conscious of it, no longer only knowing *that*, but also *what*.

Similarly, the "illimitable loneliness of man" is only the (metaphysical) analogue of the (empirical) loneliness of the individual who has left his parents' home to stand on his own feet. As such, it is the precondition for human fellowship, friendship and love.

There is no need for "meaning," for the state of in-ness, for myth or religion as a present reality. On the contrary, we can, now that the gods have become memories, devote ourselves to all the riches of Mnemosyne freely, without having to hold our breath in awe. Let me mention just one example as an illustration. As long as the Bible has the status of a sacred book, one cannot read it freely on one's own account. It makes on us an absolute metaphysical claim for submission and worship. One must hold one's breath while approaching it. There is always the atmosphere of an "ought" enveloping us on all sides. Thus

---

[60] The idea of "that one thing" follows the paradigm of Matthew 13:46 ("Who, when he had found one pearl of great price, went and sold all that he had, and bought it.")

[61] *CW* 9i § 28.

it is logically (not necessarily empirically) intimidating, and suppresses any natural curiosity in it arising spontaneously from within us as the real empirical persons that we are. What a relief when the Bible is discovered to be a historical book, a document in the history of the human mind or soul. Now it can be fascinating reading and stimulate an interest in its serious study, but only because it has been desacralized, demystified. Only what is on principle allowed to be liked or disliked, found interesting or boring, wise or stupid, is open to our genuine personal interest (in contrast to an imposed obligation to venerate). This is the gift of the sense of history.

By contrast, if today the Bible is still offered as Holy Writ or, in general, if religion is preached as a present reality and myths and symbols are presented as numinous presences, then they have necessarily become commodities, because they now are supposed to provide *particular* felt experiences or ideological views that, although they occur *within* the general state of a modern consciousness that has emerged from in-ness, nevertheless are supposed to simulate the former sense of in-ness that has precisely been outgrown.

One can, to be sure, agree with Jung when he states that, "Meaninglessness inhibits the fullness of life and therefore is equivalent to illness,"[62] *provided* one understands this sentence appropriately, reading it against the grain, i.e., against Jung's probable intention. The feeling that there should be a higher meaning of life and that it is missing *is* the illness.[63] But this is not how the sentence is meant. Rather it interprets absence as an unbearable loss and the *need* for meaning as an anthropological constant and thus as self-evident and inescapable (whereas it is a "reaction formation" in response to the modern situation). But as the example of most people living in the modern world shows, one can live quite well without meaning, just as the normal adult can live quite well without parents. It is not *necessary* to process *neurotically* one's leaving one's parents behind oneself.

---

[62] *MDR* p. 340.

[63] A completely different phenomenon, the feeling of loss of meaning as part of serious (not-neurotic) depressions or grave personality disorders is of course also pathological, but it has nothing to do with our topic here, mythic or metaphysical meaning. It is a psychic (quasi biological) illness, a disturbance of one's vitality, not a psycho*logical* illness, an illness of the soul or mind.

THE END OF MEANING AND THE BIRTH OF MAN 233

Furthermore: does the lack of "that one thing," meaning, really make you neurotic? I claim there has not been one case where the meaninglessness of life was the cause of illness. Using a Nietzschean figure of thought I say, it is "a lack of philology: one constantly confuses the explanation with the text." The suffering from the "senselessness and aimlessness" is "a formulation, not a cause,"[64] of neurosis. It is the expression of a neurotic pretentiousness, a claim to metaphysical grandiosity. It is the delusion that life is only life if there is, like in dog races, that never-to-be-reached one thing, the sausage, to race after. Therefore, a person who seeks that one precious thing, meaning, "Is like a beast, on barren ground led around in circles by an evil spirit, while all around there are beautiful verdant pastures," as Goethe put it.

Jung refused to see this. To be sure, he saw the danger of a pointless seeking. He once tells us that "On my many travels I have found people who were on their third trip round the world—uninterruptedly. Just travelling, travelling; seeking, seeking." One such woman he asked, "'What for? [...] What are you trying to do that for?' And I was amazed when I looked into her eyes—the eyes of a hunted, a cornered animal [...] She is nearly possessed [...]" But then he continues, "And why is she possessed? Because she does not live the life that makes sense. Hers is a life utterly, grotesquely banal, utterly poor, meaningless, with no point in it at all. If she is killed today, nothing has happened, nothing has vanished—because she is nothing. But if she could say, 'I am the daughter of the Moon. Every night I must help the Moon, my Mother, over the horizon'—ah, that is something else! Then she lives, then her life makes sense, and makes sense in all continuity, and for the whole of humanity."[65] And, we might add, then she would be cured.

What Jung does not realize is that his proposed cure is just a repetition of that illness that he himself diagnosed correctly, and not a cure at all. By mimicking the Pueblo-Indian model, he only prescribes more of the same: "Daughter of the Moon"—this is absolutely out of reach for a modern woman; it is precisely an idea that could *only* be sought in an endless, futile search. Thus Jung conjures up the very transcendence the longing for which is the cause

---

[64] Friedrich Nietzsche, *Die Unschuld des Werdens. Der Nachlaß*, ed. Alfred Baeumler, vol. 1, Stuttgart (Kröner) 1956, pp. 306f. (#953).
[65] *CW* 18 § 630.

of such seeking. Jung's suggestion feeds her neurotic craving, her "addiction." For what is she chasing after if not after some such mythical garment to dress herself in as in her "mummeries"[66]? It is her very problem that while as a modern woman she *cannot* possibly say anything like what Jung suggested, she *nevertheless* thinks she ought to be able to; it is her problem that *on principle* there are no mythological garments that would fit her, but that she nevertheless is unconsciously convinced that it is indispensable to have one. This is the neurotic trap that turns her into the pointless seeker, the hunted, cornered animal which Jung saw in her eyes.

A real cure would have to move into the opposite direction. It would have to make her fully aware that unconsciously she obviously thinks she ought to be the daughter of the Moon or some such thing and that this is why she is desperately traveling, constantly seeking; in other words, that she—as does Jung here—tries to solve her problem on the semantic level while trying to keep the syntactic level intact. A real therapeutic move would have to make her aware that her problem is a syntactic or logical one and to confront her with the exaltedness, inflatedness of these unconscious demands and expectations, which—much like Kitsch—are the result of a semantics that is not backed up and authenticated by the scope, form and sophistication of the syntax. Why should she not be able, like everybody else, to find satisfaction,[67] *contentedness*, in ordinary life? Perhaps by cultivating her garden, doing her daily duties, enjoying some good books and exhibitions, giving her neighbors a hand— perhaps also, and above all, by devoting herself to some useful task that would allow her to discover and employ *her* specific potential for being productive. Everybody surely can find some area where, some way how, to be productive. Why must she make such a fuss, unwittingly give herself airs as if she were perhaps a secret Queen in search of her missing crown insignia and the recognition due but denied to her? Why can't she be her ordinary self and find the way into the simplicity of life and of being human? Why can't she understand that there is nothing to be sought, nothing that would be somewhere else, be it in the future or in transcendence? Why can't she see that "this is it!"? It is this real life of hers that contains everything it needs within itself.

---

[66] Cf. *CW* 9i § 27.
[67] Lat. *satis* = enough.

THE END OF MEANING AND THE BIRTH OF MAN

This life of hers here and now that has already been going on *is* the source and circumference of all happiness, productivity and fulfillment possible for her. Nothing needs to be sought at all. On the contrary, her seeking is her running away from her fulfillment.

Jung does not really listen to what the Pueblo Indian, whose model he was following, had told him and what he himself wholeheartedly had agreed with: "There is nothing to be looked for!"[68] There really isn't. It's all there. This message of the Pueblo Indian would have seamlessly fitted to Jung's own advice when he opted for spiritual poverty: "*um bei sich einzukehren,*" which *we* might render now as: in order to unreservedly enter one's own life "as it really is," (although Jung, as we have seen, had something else in mind in that passage: introversion, turning to one's unconscious, one's dreams, etc.)

Why is there nothing to be looked for? Because rather than their being the distant object of a quest, fulfillment and bliss depend on the *degree of one's own wholehearted dedication* to what *is* (whatever it may be) with one's specific productive powers (however great or small and of what nature they may be).

Jung once wrote, "The greatest limitation for man is the 'self'; it is manifested in the experience: 'I am *only* that!'"[69] *Is this not ENOUGH?* Do I really have to be *more* than I am, do I really need the higher orders of a "symbolic existence in which I am *something else*, in which I am fulfilling my role, my role as one of the actors in the divine drama of life"[70]?

What a presumption! And conversely, what a disparagement of ordinary human life, which is cast away as "grotesquely banal, utterly poor." In 1959, two years before his death, Jung wrote about himself, "The journey from cloud-cuckoo-land back to reality lasted a long time. In my case Pilgrim's Progress consisted in my having to climb down a thousand ladders until I could reach out my hand to the little clod of earth that I am."[71] A charming statement. And yet, as long as one insists on being "something else" and playing one's "role as one of the actors in the divine drama of life" one is psychologically (logically) still up in cloud-cuckoo-land, still living with grandiose

---

[68] *CW* 18 § 630.

[69] *MDR* p. 325. It must be noted, however, that Jung's next sentence shows him moving back into transcendence again.

[70] *CW* 18 § 628. My emphasis.

[71] *Letters I*, to Freud, 11.II.10, note 8, p. 19. From letter by Jung of 9.IV.59.

ideas. And the very formulation that Jung uses shows that he has not really come down. Because if one is really down, one cannot reach out one's hand to the little clod of earth that one is, inasmuch as being down means having *comprehended* that one *is*, and has always been, *just* oneself. As long as I want to reach out my hand to myself, I as the one who reaches his hand out still believe to be something else from, and above, the "clod of earth" whom I graciously befriend. The idea that I would have to come down and humble myself *is* already presumption, arrogance. The noble attitude of humility is the way in which the simple recognition that in truth I am and have always been down here is kept at bay. There *is* nothing and nobody to whom I could lower myself, because the so-called clod of earth is myself.

On the other hand, the expression "clod of earth" puts me down far too much, in a similar way to how the formulation "grotesquely banal, utterly poor" disparages our ordinary earthly existence. I am not a clod of earth, but a human being with a mind. The implicit viewpoint from which Jung speaks in this statement is one high up from where he looks down upon himself, which contradicts his explicit message that he has come down.

In the "Retrospect" of *Memories, Dreams, Reflections* Jung assentingly recounts the "fine old story about a student who came to a rabbi and said, 'In the olden days there were men who saw the face of God. Why don't they any more?' The rabbi replied, 'Because nowadays no one can stoop so low.'"[72] With this idea, Jung achieves two advantages, a "theoretical" and an "ethical" one. As to the "theoretical" advantage: by resorting to a trick, the trick of "stooping to conquer," Jung can act as if in objective reality nothing had changed. The loss of God is only our fault, it is merely subjective. If only we stooped low enough, everything would be fine: God would still be visible, we could have his unmediated epiphany after all ("*Urerfahrung*"!). As regards the ethical stance, Jung sells indulgences: if only we concentrate all our efforts on the *subjective and positive behavior* of stooping and of in this way personally *acting out* a literal, external humility (this is the price for the indulgence), he dispenses us from the real, the *psychological* humility: the humility of objectively, logically—namely in our *knowing*—bowing to our truth; the truth

---

[72] *MDR* p. 355.

THE END OF MEANING AND THE BIRTH OF MAN

that metaphysically we *are* already at the bottom, i.e., there where we know (not God, but) the very notion of God to have become untenable, let alone the possibility to see "Him" face to face. Thus Jung allows us to take refuge in happy unconsciousness; he lulls himself and us into a theological-metaphysical slumber. He does not realize that his holding on to the idea of the necessity of such a stooping *is* the very arrogance, *hubris*, that he blames modern man for. Just like a person's putting himself on stilts does not make him or her great, so conversely the subjective (psychic, empirical, literal) act of stooping does not undo the objective (logical, psychological) presumption, but only conceals and thus affirms it.

When I am "*only* that," I am without higher orders, even without the mythical garment of an endowment (be it by Nature or by the Creator) with the "dignity of man" or "inalienable human rights," these inflated modern ideas. I cannot bask in the shine of an eternal truth, an absolute ideal, or higher values that would be in my possession. No such thing has revealed itself to me and claimed me. And yet, this does by no means mean that "anything goes." I am not without truth, norms, values. But they conversely receive their authority and reality only from *my* being-so and *my* standing up for them. In this sense, they are fundamentally contingent, subjective: human, all-too-human; there is no essential difference to my liking this food or art or music and disliking that. What gives them their objectivity is the objective fact of my being-so. In the "Prologue" to *Memories, Dreams, Reflections* Jung wrote, "Whether or not the stories [that he was going to tell] are 'true' is not the problem. The only problem is whether what I tell is *my* fable, *my* truth."[73] This is said in the spirit of truly being "*only* that."

Certain things, views, possible behaviors, etc. happen to be incompatible with who and how I am. *This* is the only "proof" I have to offer for my truths. Here I stand, I cannot do otherwise. But here I *do* stand, and really *stand*.

In a way, I have, in metaphysical regards, returned to the status of hunters and gatherers. Metaphysically, I live from hand to mouth. In some 19th century popular novel by Karl May, the narrator—all alone in the emptiness of the prairie in the Wild West—comes across another lone horseman. When this other person is told that the

---

[73] *MDR* p. 3.

238 THE SOUL ALWAYS THINKS

narrator is an author who writes novels about his travels for other people to read, he finds this very comical because, as he says, he for one would not dream of shooting game for other people, but only for his own sustenance. This is not an overly intelligent scene. Nevertheless, the point is well taken. I have to live *my* life on *my* own account, even with respect to my truths and values.

The reference to hunters and gatherers and to living from hand to mouth should not suggest that I find my values on the street like ready-made things or on the market-place "out there," like commodities, nor that just any momentary impulse could be declared to be my truth. In order to find *my* truth and my *truth*, I have to perceive, alchemically speaking, as the *homo totus* and observe, while focusing on the *logos* as the soul of my world, my wholehearted responses.[74]

There is a point in Goethe's *Faust* where old Faust assessing his life says, "So far I have still not fought myself out into the open. / Could I remove magic from my path, / Altogether unlearn the magic charms, / Were I standing, Nature, in front of you one man alone, / Then it would be worth the trouble to be a human."[75] Our situation is different. *We* do not have to fight ourselves out into the open. *We* do not have to remove magic from our path. Magic, that is, the sympathetic world-relation, the mode of in-ness, metaphysics, is something *we* only know from hearsay. *We* have each long been standing vis-à-vis an "alienated," sublated nature, and each of us one person alone and metaphysically naked. Should it not be true for us, too, that—precisely for that reason, precisely because the birth of man has been achieved— it is worth the trouble to be a human?

---

[74] On the relation of hunt and truth see my *The Soul's Logical Life*, Frankfurt am Main etc. (Peter Lang) 4th ed. 2008 (1st ed. 1999), ch. 6 "Actaion and Artemis," pp. 203–275.

[75] Joh. W. v. Goethe, *Faust. Eine Tragödie*, 5th Act, Mitternacht, lines 11403ff., my translation. ("Noch hab' ich mich ins Freie nicht gekämpft. / Könnt' ich Magie von meinem Pfad entfernen, / Die Zaubersprüche ganz und gar verlernen, / Stünd' ich, Natur, vor dir ein Mann allein, / Da wär's der Mühe wert, ein Mensch zu sein.")

THE END OF MEANING AND THE BIRTH OF MAN 239

10. The logic and genesis of C.G. Jung's psychology
in the light of the question of meaning

The problem as it presented itself to Jung and its solution or: Saturnian swallowing

Jung's root experience was that modern man is, both in the literal and in the wider figurative sense, *extra ecclesiam*: "no more protected," "no more in the *consensus gentium*," "no more in the lap of the All-compassionate Mother. You are alone [...]"[76] We have no myth anymore. An irreversible increase in man's consciousness has made consciousness independent.[77] It has been born out of the containment in meaning.

This experience was his particular version of the experience shared by all the great thinkers of the 19th century, who had described the same historical rupture in other terms: as alienation, nihilism, loss of faith, etc.

Jung was well aware that this state of affairs, the loss of meaning, was the historically singular character of the modern world. "This is a new problem. All ages before us have believed in gods in some form or other." The "impoverishment of symbolism" is "unparalleled."[78] "[...] we have reached a significant turning point of the ages [...]"[79]

Like the other thinkers of the 19th century before him who had experienced this loss or rupture, Jung too found it intolerable and wanted to overcome it. In his eyes, life after the end of meaning and the birth of man at bottom "is a life utterly, grotesquely banal, utterly poor, meaningless, with no point in it at all."[80] So the life task set for him was to restore meaning, "the symbolic life." His project had to be—here I use part of a formulation Jung used when quoting Freud's description of his, Freud's, concern—to erect "an unshakable bulwark against the black tide of"[81] mythlessness. And so it makes sense that late in life he could declare that, "The main interest of my work is not

---

[76] *CW* 18 § 632.
[77] Cf. *CW* 11 § 203, where Jung, however, used this formulation for the psychological situation at the time of Gnosticism.
[78] *CW* 9i § 50.
[79] *MDR* p. 334.
[80] *CW* 18§ 630, where Jung is, however, speaking by way of example about the life of one particular person only. But the implication of this example is universal.
[81] *MDR* p. 150.

concerned with the treatment of neurosis but rather with the approach to the numinous."[82]

But how could you restore something that had been lost? Jung's predecessors, the thinkers of the 19th century, Feuerbach, Kierkegaard, Marx, Nietzsche, had offered various *utopian* promises or hopes. None of these had had enough power of conviction to lastingly bind the collective mind, and especially after Nietzsche's collapse due to his realization that his expectation would and could not come true, the lesson of the 19th century about the untenableness of utopias had been learned. They were too airy, too exalted, too speculative (in the derogatory sense). The 20th century's thinkers were no longer utopian. Utopian thinking had meanwhile sunk to the level of political ideology and hard-core power politics. For Jung, too, the utopian solution was not workable. Coming after Nietzsche and his exalted, high-falutin style, Jung, in typical early 20th century fashion, now wanted a solution based on solid and sober science, empirically verifiable. The decidedly anti-utopian attitude of Jung's comes out most definitely in his programmatic profession, "Some seek gratification of desire and some others fulfilment of power and yet others want to see the world as it is and leave things in peace. We do not want to change anything. The world is good as it is."[83]

Nor could Jung simply revive the past. "We cannot turn the wheel backwards; we cannot go back to a symbolism that is gone."[84] "[...] the wheel of history cannot be turned back. Even the Emperor Augustus with all his power could not push through his attempts at repristination."[85]

The present was unacceptable; to expect a salvation from the future untenable; a repristination impossible. The fourth possibility, a broken, reflected, historical relation to the spiritual treasures of the past, was absolutely insufficient for Jung: "In the end we dig up the wisdom of all ages and peoples, only to find that everything most dear and most precious to us has already been said in the most superb language. Like greedy children we stretch out our hands and think that, if only we

---

[82] *Letters 1*, p. 377, to Martin, 20.VIII.45. (*Briefe I*, p. 465, gives the date of this letter as 28.VIII.45. Which is right?)

[83] *CW* 18 § 278.

[84] *CW* 18 § 632.

[85] *Letters 2*, p. 226, to Pater Lucas Menz, 22 February 1955.

THE END OF MEANING AND THE BIRTH OF MAN

could grasp it, we would possess it too. But what we possess is no longer valid [...]"[86] Jung was "greedy," he wanted to possess like children possess, with "validity," that is, with the sense of immediate, unbroken oneness with and in-ness in what one possesses. "My psychological condition wants something else. I must have a situation in which that thing becomes true once more."[87] Jung insisted on meaning as a *present, immediate reality*, as a numinous "*Urerfahrung*" or "*Urerlebnis*" (primordial or originary experience, directly from the source, not mediated by tradition or historical knowledge nor distorted by conscious reflection and elaboration), "*Urerfahrung*" here and now! Not only the meanings of former times contemplated in Mnemosyne.

How can consciousness, once it has been born out of the in-ness in meaning and its *irreversible* bornness has been fully realized, become unborn again? How can the essential thing become true once more if you neither have the option of the forward movement into utopian hopes nor of a backwards movement to the past, and on top of it are unrelentingly committed to empirical evidence? There is only one solution: to go within, to work with the distinction or split between outside and inside. Inside and outside are not opposites like left and right, lying next to each other. The one is within the containing other. Already on an abstract-formal level, the inner provides in-ness.

Therefore, in order to establish the division between inside and outside, consciousness had to be taught to be its own Kronos-Saturn. In personal union, consciousness had to be both Kronos (enveloping outside) and the child newly born to him by Rhea and swallowed by him (contained inside). Consciousness had to dissociate itself into the modern, adult consciousness, on the one hand, that realized and accepted its irrevocable bornness and, on the other hand, into itself as the just-born child, the innocent babe prior to its becoming aware of its bornness and being sicklied over with the reflectedness of modernity.

This is a second division, the split between substantial content and logical form, more specifically the dissociation into the *abstract form* of consciousness (its capacity of rational reflection, the scientific mind, the empirical observer, alchemically speaking the *vas*, the retort)

---

[86] *CW* 9i § 31.

[87] *CW* 18 § 632. "That thing": immediately before, Jung had spoken of the miracle of the Mass and of his not being able to go back to the Catholic Church.

242   *THE SOUL ALWAYS THINKS*

on the one hand and into the likewise abstracted, cut-off traditional (mythical, imaginal, metaphysical) contents of consciousness on the other. As the fully born abstract-formal consciousness it was Kronos who swallowed itself (its contents) as the newborn. These contents were *newborn* because they were no longer the original contents firmly embedded in, and the property of, a living religious or metaphysical tradition. They were the contents already released from Mother Church or from the Western tradition of metaphysics, which is why Jung called them "autonomous," "spontaneous," and facts of *nature*: they were free-floating, contingent. The break with tradition had happened. The images and ideas ("the archetypal images" or what archetypal psychology would term "the imaginal") were already the modern, abstract, uprooted version of the traditional contents ("*Urerfahrung*" and "arche-types": sort of coming directly from heaven), much like the altarpieces in museums are the abstracted modern versions of the same altarpieces in the original churches and embedded in a living cult.

This act is the invention and manufacturing of "the inner" and "the unconscious." Consciousness exists now twice, once as "the ego" or consciousness in the narrower sense (the modern rationalistic mind as mere form or vessel or function) and once as "the unconscious" (as a treasury of substantial images). By virtue of its having been swallowed and thus deprived of the possibility to participate in the practice of the job of consciousness (reflection, rational examination, which is *essentially* public), the swallowed consciousness is ipso facto *un*conscious, while the swallowing mind is, to be sure, consciousness in the narrower sense, but only an empty form, totally divorced from the contents it might entertain and on principle released from any intellectual responsibility for the unconscious images. The conscious mind is *only* the passive recipient of images from the unconscious. "We have simply got to listen to what the psyche spontaneously says to us. [...] Say it again as well as you can. [...] What is the great Dream? It consists of the many small dreams and the many acts of humility and submission to their hints."[88]

The inner is not utopian, because, e.g. in the form of dreams, it is "now," immediate, and accessible to empirical observation. But being

---

[88] *Letters 2*, p. 591, to Sir Herbert Read, 2 Sept. 1960.

THE END OF MEANING AND THE BIRTH OF MAN 243

"now," it is also not identical with the *real* modern present, the public world of today, because it has been set up in contradistinction to that present. It is ready to be the re-collection of the past *as* a (simulated) present reality—a present reality, however, which in turn, as *simulated* and by definition *unconscious*, secretly is in the logical status of "past." Jung may in some dim way even have been aware of the simulatedness of modern unconscious images. At any rate, in the 1925 seminar on *Analytical Psychology* he stated concerning his own fantasy of Elijah and Salome: "I had read much mythology before this fantasy came to me, and all of this reading entered into the condensation of these figures,"[89] an admission in greatest contrast to his usual thinking in terms of the origin of fantasies directly from the collective unconscious as well as to his view that the unconscious is pure nature.

I compared the swallowed contents to items in a museum. But of course, the unconscious must not be conceived as a museum. The museum is, as it were, the institutionalized and objectified Mnemosyne. It is the expression of the *historical* relation to the riches and the wisdom of all ages and peoples. We cannot stretch our hands out and hope to grasp and possess the objects on display: the glass of the showcases or in front of the paintings makes us quite literally aware of our unsurmountable logical distance to them. *Only* by swallowing, interiorizing, the contents of the former tradition into "ourselves" as our unconscious could "that thing become true once more" without our either having to escape into a utopian future or having to try to turn the wheel back. Only by swallowing could one get meaning (in-ness) as a *present reality* (a so-called "*Urerfahrung*") under the conditions of irretrievably having lost one's in-ness. Only by swallowing could the impression be created that the images emerging from inside are absolutely spontaneous and pure, pristine nature, and our experience of them experience directly from the source.[90] For the Saturnian swallowing is nothing else but the creation of a state of secondary

---

[89] C. G. Jung, *Analytical Psychology*. Notes of the Seminar Given in 1925, ed. by William McGuire, Princeton (Princeton University Press) 1989, p. 92. Greg Mogenson kindly pointed out this passage to me.
[90] "The richest yield of all is naturally to be found in the primary material [*Urmaterie*] itself, that is to say in the dreams, which are not thought up or "spun" like a yarn [*ersponnen*: hatched, contrived, devised]. They are involuntary products of nature, spontaneously expressing the psychic processes without interference of the conscious will." *CW* 18 § 1282.

244   THE SOUL ALWAYS THINKS

unbornness for Saturn's children after the fact of their having been born and a freezing them in an embryonic state, in order to prevent their ever becoming part of public intellectual life. Similarly the imaginal contents have already been released from religion and metaphysics; but by confining them in the unconscious, they are once and for all prevented from "growing up": getting out and taking part in public intellectual life and being in turn affected by its transformations. Instead, the intellect has to take them as indisputable facts of nature, not as its own property and productions, on the one hand, nor as something it is fully accountable for, on the other hand.

Kronos as *father* creates a secondary, unnatural womb for his already-born children. The invention of the unconscious is likewise the device by which *modern* consciousness *as abstract form* can be used for the purpose of serving as a protective womb for traditional knowledge and imitating a sense of in-ness.

Jung could of course himself not be fully conscious of the fact that the logical origin of his "collective unconscious" was a strategic act of logical splitting and swallowing. After all, if he had been conscious of it, he could not have believed in the collective unconscious. Nevertheless it did not escape him that the unconscious is a result, the result of a downgrading and downsizing as well as an internalizing, privatizing of the contents of the former public traditional knowledge, of myth, religion and metaphysics. This comes out, at least indirectly, in such quotes as the following. "Since the stars have fallen from heaven and our highest symbols have paled, a secret life holds sway in the unconscious. This is why we have a psychology today, and why we speak of the unconscious."[91] "When our natural inheritance has been dissipated, then the spirit too, as Heraclitus says, has descended from its fiery heights. But when the spirit becomes heavy, it turns to water [...]" We are "children of an age in which the spirit is no longer up above but down below, no longer fire, but water."[92] "The rift in the metaphysical world has slowly risen into consciousness as a split in the human psyche, and the struggle between light and darkness moves

---

[91] *CW* 9i § 50.
[92] *CW* 9i § 32. I changed "was" in "the spirit was no longer [...]" into "is," because there is no apparent reason why Jung's present tense "ist" in German should be rendered with a past tense.

THE END OF MEANING AND THE BIRTH OF MAN   245

to the battleground within."[93] The work of the psychotherapist "is accomplished in a sphere in which the numen settled [or immigrated] only recently and into which the whole weight of mankind's problems [*Menschheitsproblematik*] has moved."[94]

Indeed, even the very idea of swallowing occurs in Jung's own thinking, although he speaks of it only from a critical distance:

> Well, after all we managed—for first time since the dawn of history—to swallow the whole primordial animatedness of nature into ourselves; not only did the gods descend (or rather were they dragged down) from their planetary spheres and transformed into chthonic demons, but ... even this host of demons, which at the time of Paracelsus still frolicked happily in mountains and woods, in rivers and human dwelling-places, was reduced to a miserable remnant and finally vanished altogether.[95]

Sacrifice of the intellect and the exclusion of the problem of *form*

The image of the fallen stars is most revealing. Once visible for everybody and objects of public veneration and of a conscious upward looking that the intellect did not need to be ashamed of, they are, now that they have been sunk and logically entombed in the unconscious, inside and *fundamentally* unconscious, not admissible to public thought and not under the obligation of being the subject of a *lógon didónai* (rational accounting for). The intellect must not touch them. "You must not allow your reason to play with" them,[96] says Jung with a formulation that betrays the total immunization of these contents from the point of view of the other, the intellect's, side, because the intellect is devalued as "our playful intellect"[97] and thus as per definitionem incompetent in matters of higher meaning: "Our intellect is absolutely incapable of understanding these things."[98] No

---

[93] *CW* 13 § 293. *GW*: "der Kampf des Lichtes gegen die Finsternis verlegt seinen Schauplatz ins Innere derselben," viz., "der menschlichen Seele." The interior of man is turned into the new, previously not existing battleground.

[94] *CW* 16 § 449, translation modified. *Menschheitsproblematik*: not particular problems that might come up, but something like the problem of human existence as such.

[95] *CW* 10 § 431 (transl. modified).

[96] *CW* 18 § 617.

[97] *Ibid.*

[98] *Ibid.*

doubt, there is a type of intellect that is incapable of doing justice to such things, a positivistic, rationalistic, utilitaristic thinking. But why does Jung restrict himself to this narrow-minded sense of "intellect"? This would by no means be necessary. It is his choice. Therefore, despite the form in which his statement is presented, one must not mistake it for an innocent statement of fact, a mere observation. It is rather a refusal or prohibition: "do not touch symbols with the intellect! The intellect shall be excluded on principle!" Since the unconscious in Jung's sense is the realm of symbols and archetypal images and has been declared off limits for the intellect, the notion of the unconscious *is* in itself a *sacrificium intellectus*, for it has the reverse that the intellect has to stay fundamentally blind with respect to them, as much as it may or is supposed to take note of them as *facts*. It is precisely their fact character that ensures the intellect's essential blindness, impotence and immunity with respect to them. The intellect must not enter them thinkingly. This means that ultimately consciousness has to be in itself unconscious: both sides of the pair of opposites, consciousness and the unconscious, are *together* the unconscious.

The last quoted sentence about the absolute impotence of the intellect concerning rituals and symbols appears embedded in the following context. "The sad truth is that we do not understand it [the secret of virginity and the virginal conception] any more. But, you know, in former centuries man did not need that kind of intellectual understanding. We are proud of it; but it is nothing to be proud of. Our intellect is absolutely incapable of understanding these things. We are not far enough advanced psychologically to understand the truth, the extraordinary truth, of ritual and dogma." What does this statement tell us? First Jung says we do not understand such secrets any more, which implies that in former times they were understood. But then he realizes that formerly, when ritual and dogma were still alive, there had not been a need for an understanding at all. We heard already from Jung that in primitive societies, people only knew *that*, but not *what* they do. "They see no meaning in their (ritual) actions." "[...] things were generally done first and [...] only a long time afterwards somebody asked a question about them [...]" An understanding was simply not necessary at the ritualistic stage of consciousness. The need for an intellectual understanding arose only

THE END OF MEANING AND THE BIRTH OF MAN   247

much later, but particularly in modern times. It arose due to the emergence of consciousness from its previous in-ness and at the same time it is a symptom of this change. It was a firm conviction of Jung's that modern man needs to understand.[99] After all, Jung knew this need from his own youth. While in confirmation class, the catechism bored him terribly, except for the paragraph about the holy trinity. He reports how he waited impatiently for the moment when this topic would be explained and how terribly disappointed he was when his father, the minister, said that they were going to skip this section because he did not *comprehend* anything about it himself.[100]

Inasmuch as Jung felt that we "are not far enough advanced psychologically to understand the truth [...] of ritual and dogma," one would have expected that Jung would have had the wish to advance our intellect so that it might slowly become able to understand. Instead he systematically excluded the intellect. As excluded, it, too, was immunized. It did not have to fear to be affected, *in its own logical form*, by the unconscious contents it became conscious of. We have here a structurally neurotic split: intellect and contents are set up in such a way that they do not affect or infect each other.

Thus the notion "the unconscious" does not really mean a realm, region or agency in the psyche. It primarily is a label that declares the contents to which it is applied as *fundamentally* taboo, untouchable: inaccessible to conscious knowing and intellectual penetration. This label puts them into a particular *logical status*, the status of irrevocable un-consciousness. It erects an unsurmountable, namely logical, barrier. To be sure, consciousness is permitted to look at the "contents of the unconscious" through the glass pane of the logical isolation ward that they are now confined in, it is even permitted to use the method of "amplification" and morphological comparison upon them, in other words, it is allowed to know *that* (the facts, the phenomenology), but it is absolutely forbidden to know *what*. The barrier is only not noticed because our subjective feeling experience, our being emotionally impressed by their numinosity, feigns an immediate proximity, much

---

[99] A general and for Jung unusually radical plea for "thoughtful understanding" (the German has *denkendem Begreifen*, which is closer to "intellectual comprehension" or comprehension in stringent thought) is to be found in *CW* 11 § 170.

[100] *CW* 9i § 30. *MDR* p. 52f.

like our empathy and compassion with a sick person behind the glass pane of an isolation ward seem to penetrate through the glass—without however being able to do away with it.

This split, in order to be possible, required a deeper unspoken split: the split between the semantic and syntax, between content and logical form. What Jung really excluded was the level of form. He semanticized both the unconscious contents and consciousness (the intellect[101]). Only because the question of logical form was systematically excluded could the two sides of Jung's opposition, the conscious intellect and the unconscious images, be successfully immunized against each other (i.e., could the swallowing of the one by the other happen in the first place). An infection (be it one-directional or mutual) could only have occurred on the level of form. *It* is where (and how) the two could touch. The problem of form or syntax having been eliminated once and for all, both sides were safe (where "safe" also means fundamentally unconscious). Due to this semanticizing, consciousness is systematically restricted to the knowing of the "that" and blinded to the "what," for the "what" would be nothing else but the logic of the phenomenon. Ultimately, *the exclusion of the level of form* is at the bottom of the Jungian notion of the unconscious, and it is what renders his *entire* "psychology of the unconscious" (as Jung liked to name his psychology) itself unconscious. The phrase "[...] of the unconscious" is here, *malgré lui*, a *genetivus objectivus* AND *subjectivus*.

In the passage in which Jung said that he cannot go back to the Catholic Church and cannot experience the miracle of the Mass because he knows too much about it, he continued: "I know it is the truth, but it is the truth *in a form* in which I cannot accept it any more. I cannot say 'This is the sacrifice of Christ,' and see him any more. I cannot. It is no more true to me; it does not express my psychological condition. My psychological condition wants something else. I must have a situation in which that thing becomes true once more. I need *a new form*."[102] Here Jung ran into the problem of the logical form, of syntax versus semantics. Semantically (as far as the

---

[101] The semanticized intellect is the intellect viewed as an abstract instrument and the semanticized consciousness is consciousness interpreted as *abstract* "form": empty vessel.

[102] *CW* 18 § 632 (my italics).

abstract "that" is concerned), the miracle of the Mass was still the truth for him; but history had catapulted him into a new situation so that the resulting "psychological condition" of his demanded a corresponding new form for the traditional metaphysical contents, too. And here we see that the *new* form was for him—the *psychologized*, interiorized, privatized version of the former mythical and metaphysical knowledge. Only as psychologized (i.e., turned into something *psychic* and precisely not left as something psychological), only in this "new form," could the past become true once more; the locus of "where the true action is" had to be transferred to the inner in positivized man.

"The unconscious": Discovered fact or means to an end?

The statement, "Since the stars have fallen from heaven and our highest symbols have paled, a secret life holds sway in the unconscious. This is why we have a psychology today, and why we speak of the unconscious," tells us more about the origin of Jung's psychology and the necessities of Jung's intellectual development in particular than about the history of the soul at large. It lets us see that Jung did not *discover* the unconscious simply by in his work as psychologist having stumbled across certain facts that necessitated this concept. *He was not first a psychologist, who then also happened to discover the collective unconscious.* He was not destined, sort of by birth, to become a psychologist. He could have chosen and been great in all sorts of other professions. No, it is the other way around. *He had to become a psychologist because "the unconscious"* (in his sense), to be more precise: the invention and establishment of the idea of the unconscious, *was the only avenue open to him* for successfully tackling his project. He needed the unconscious, because (a) he had the one supreme goal of restoring, under the conditions of modernity, mythic meaning as a present reality—without either resorting to utopia or to a repristination, (b) because it so happened that this goal could only be achieved through the Kronos-like interiorization *into* the individual human being (= through the psychologizing) *of* "the stars" (= the contents of the former myths, religion and metaphysics): "All the gods and demons, whose physical nothingness is so easily passed off as the 'opium of the people,' return to their place of origin, Man [...]"[103]

---

[103] *CW* 18 § 1366.

250   *THE SOUL ALWAYS THINKS*

Psychologism[104] itself—that is, the translation of all great religious and metaphysical ideas and issues from *world* or *cosmic* problems, and *public* problems, and problems of the *thought* of "the whole man," into psychological, merely internal ones, ones *in* man (where man is conceived as a *positivity*)—was the solution to his problem. But only a *Notlösung* (an expedient, a stopgap, a subterfuge). It of course had to be a *Notlösung* because what was really sought (a new form of in-ness, a secondary unbornness) was a *contradictio in se*.

Thus it was the fact that "psychology" provided the only way remaining for Jung's goal to become possibly reached that determined the profession he chose.

Downsizing and privatization

One major disadvantage of this psychologizing from *our* point of view is that it has to be psychologistic. Jung could not really comprehend the soul as logical life. He could not move from the level of semantics to that of syntax. He could not see that the "subject" of psychology is not the individual person and his or her inner feeling experiences, but "man at large," the notion of man, consciousness at large: the logic of our concrete being-in-the-world in a given historical situation. Jung had to downgrade and downsize the *opus magnum* to the *opus parvum*. Thus he was quite one-sidedly of the firm opinion that, "If the individual is not really changed, nothing is changed."[105] The reverse of this, namely, that nothing is changed if *only* the individual is changed and *not also* and even predominantly the logic of being-in-the-world at large, he was not able to see.[106] Jung wrote: "[...] does the individual know that *he* is the makeweight that tips the

---

[104] Jung defended himself in anticipation against the charge of psychologism in *CW* 11 § 751 and footnote. But the concept of psychologism he addresses himself to is very different from the charge raised against him here. I agree with Jung that he is not an adherent of psychologism in the sense that he has in mind.

[105] *Letters 2*, p. 462, to James Gibb, 1 Oct. 1958.

[106] Jung's early insight (1912) that "the apparently individual conflict of the patient is revealed as a universal conflict of his environment and epoch. Neurosis is thus nothing less than an individual attempt, however unsuccessful, to solve a universal problem [...]" (*CW* 7 § 438; cf. *CW* 7 § 18: "Neurosis is intimately bound up with the problem of our time [*dem Problem der Zeit*] and really represents an unsuccessful attempt on the part of the individual to solve the general problem in his own person.") was not revoked by him, but did not have any further consequences. At least here Jung moved away, in the general form of his thinking, from a personalistic view. Here for once he stresses (a) in contrast to the inner or the unconscious in man the environment, the real world in

THE END OF MEANING AND THE BIRTH OF MAN 251

scales?"[107] "Essential is, in the last analysis, only the life of the individual. This alone makes history, here alone do the great transformations first take place [...]"[108] "[...] that *he* [the individual] is the one important factor and that the salvation of the world consists in the salvation of the individual soul."[109] But how can the individual really change, if the logic has not changed—the logic, which is the heart and soul, and as such also the all-pervasive medium, of reality, of real human existence?

Part of the following statement has already been quoted above. The psychotherapist "is not just working for this particular patient, who may be quite insignificant, but for himself as well as his own soul, and in so doing he is perhaps laying an infinitesimal grain in the scales of humanity's soul. Small and invisible as this contribution may be, it is yet an *opus magnum*, for it is accomplished in a sphere in which the numen settled [or: immigrated] but lately and into which the whole weight of mankind's problems [*Menschheitsproblematik*] has moved. The ultimate questions of psychotherapy are not a private matter—they represent a supreme responsibility."[110] This cannot stand uncontradicted. We see here how Jung inflates the significance of, and mystifies, the therapist's work in the consulting room, while downsizing the *opus magnum*. Not unlike the primitive who went to the altar of his god with a chicken under his arm saying to the god, "Behold, here I am sacrificing a beautiful goat to you," Jung wants to pass off the private matter as a publicly significant one, the opus parvum as the opus magnum. He believed the psychology of the unconscious to be the *fundamental* science (the science of the ground of all sciences[111]) and by attending to the unconscious to have arrived

---

which we live, and (b) in contrast to an abstract (archetypal) universal the conflict of the epoch, the historical moment. However, the particular content of his thesis is debatable. I doubt that *neurosis* is indeed an attempt to solve a universal problem of *the epoch* and thus an addressing of the true problem of the age. I tend to think that in neurosis a battle is fought that has long been decided by history. The problem of neurosis would then not merely be that its attempt happens to be unsuccessful, but that the attempt is a priori not all that important as Jung wants to believe.

[107] *CW* 10 § 586. According to § 523, "the individual human being" has to be "in the centre as the measure of all things."

[108] *GW* and *CW* 10 § 315, the first sentence is my translation.

[109] *CW* 10 § 536.

[110] *CW* 16 § 449, translation modified.

[111] "Every science has so to speak an outside; not so psychology, whose object is the subject of all science [the subject that produces and as such is behind all science]." *CW* 8 § 429, translation modified, the text within the square brackets is my elucidation.

directly at the place where the real action is: "[...] the real problem will be from now on until a dim future a psychological one."[112] The psyche, the unconscious within, is thought to be the true "battleground"[113] where the ultimate decisions are made. To be sure, the work of psychotherapy has its own significance and represents a responsibility. But there is no fundamental difference to the significance of other significant occupations, like those of the teacher, the judge, the garbage man, the merchant, the factory worker, the doctor, the secretary, etc. Of course, if it is a question of no more than an *infinitesimal* grain that is put in the scales of humanity's soul, then Jung is right in asserting that psychotherapy may make such a contribution—because any action, omission, thought might be such an infinitesimal grain; psychotherapy is here not privileged. But as far as the *Menschheitsproblematik* is concerned, psychotherapy *is* insignificant. It is fundamentally a private matter, fundamentally *sublated, disengaged*, belonging at best, as it were, into what Husserl called the "life-world," but more appropriately expressed into the sphere of spare-time entertainment, into a playground (that playground that often is in psychotherapy, with an ennobling word, called *temenos*). The *opus magnum* is somewhere else: in those works that articulate and change the *logic* of our being-in-the-world.

But Jung wanted to rely on semantic events: experiences from the unconscious, personal dreams and the like. As we already heard: "What is the great Dream? It consists of the many small dreams [...]"[114] What a letdown! A few sentences earlier Jung had—correctly, I think—still said, "It is the great dream which has always spoken through the artist as a mouthpiece." The "great dream" as conceived in this statement is precisely not the sum of the private "small dreams," but a totally other phenomenon: the work of *great* art, which is a priori public, belonging to the whole nation, if not humanity,[115] and the product of the whole man (*homo totus*), including his wakeful consciousness and all his

---

[112] *Letters 2*, p. 498, to Werner Bruecher, 12 April 1959.

[113] *CW* 13 § 293. *GW*: "der Kampf des Lichtes gegen die Finsternis verlegt seinen Schauplatz ins Innere derselben," viz., "der menschlichen Seele." The interior of man is turned into the new, previously not existing battleground.

[114] *Letters 2*, p. 591, to Sir Herbert Read, 2 Sept. 1960.

[115] Once Jung expressed as much: in the sphere or at the stage of artistic creation it is "no longer the individual who experiences but the whole people [...]" *GW* 15 § 162 (my translation; this phrase is missing in *CW*).

THE END OF MEANING AND THE BIRTH OF MAN

intellectual power. Great art and, by the same token, great thinking, do not come out of "the unconscious" conceived naturalistically and positivistically as a mysterious anthropological constant and a reservoir of timeless archetypes, not out of the personality of the individual (his interior). They come out of *the real, concrete historical situation* of each respective time, out of the fundamental truths, the open questions and deep conflicts of the age that press both for an articulate representation and an answer. *They* (the truths, questions and conflicts of the age) are the source, the *prima materia* and the real subject of production ("creativity"). And they are neither individual nor "collective" but— logical (which takes us into a wholly other dimension), and as such (only as such) they are "as above, so below," as inside, so outside. In them and in the great works produced by them, not in himself, not in his "unconscious," man has his *soul* and this is why the locus of "the whole weight of mankind's problems" is those great works. In them and their succession we find the *opus magnum.*[116]

The great artist, the great thinker is consequently he or she who (not as person with his or her interior, his or her unconscious, but *as homo totus*) is reached by them or, the other way around, in whom, because he is reached and claimed by them, the great questions of the age ferment and can work themselves out. The great artist or thinker is no more than an alchemical vessel in which the great problems of the time are the prime matter undergoing their fermenting corruption, distillation, sublimation and of course articulation. And the real artifex of the work is ultimately the mercurial spirit stirring from within the *problems* of the age themselves. The great thinker and artist is thus he or she who can allow the Mercurius in the great questions of the age to do its stirring within himself or herself.

For Jung, however, all this is different in three regards. (1) The battleground is within, *Man* as individual person being for him, in true psychologistic manner, the "place of origin"[117] and the locus where the numen and where the expression of the present state of the great questions of human existence are to be found today; (2) the prime

---

[116] One single time Jung saw it the same way: The work of art "rises far above the personal and speaks both *from* the mind and heart, and *to* the mind and heart, of mankind." *GW* 15 § 156, my translation. "[...] the poet expresses the truth of all people," ibid., § 159, my translation.
[117] *CW* 18 § 1366.

254   *THE SOUL ALWAYS THINKS*

matter or mankind's problems are decidedly atemporal (timeless archetypal patterns); and (3) he refused to accept as fundamental the difference between the great and the minor, the exceptional and the commonplace,[118] the *opus magnum* and the *opus parvum*. He refused to see that archetypal images do not per se indicate and guarantee greatness[119] and that the small dreams of the ordinary individual are only of private, personal significance. He assigned to dreams as well as to the work in the consulting room a completely exaggerated, almost religious significance far beyond the *limited personal* importance that they do indeed have. *They* are the new locus of the numen for him. Almost anybody can have dreams. Thus it was Jung himself who prepared the way for the condition of today's Jungianism: for the prevailing subjective,[120] *fundamentally* amateurish and popular character of the typical Jungian publication, on the one hand, and for the inflated, phony spirit in which use is made of symbols and myths as well as of words like "the sacred" and "the numinous," on the other. Which is the one side of a coin whose other side shows in the fact that Jung's work did not attract and inspire great minds, thinkers, writers, artists, in obvious contrast to Freud's work, and academically stayed a non-entity.

A part of and precondition for this was the substitution of truth by *Erleben* (the felt experience). The abstract felt experience, regardless of what it was the experience of, was what ultimately counted, as long as it was an experience from the unconscious and as such "pristine nature." The content could be anything, inasmuch as for anything an archetypal or mythical paradigm can be found. Here Jung's scientistic empiricism and his subjectivism (personalistic, anthropological stance) join forces.

What is the problem with the felt experience (*Erleben, Urerfahrung*)? It is that it systematically excludes and abstracts from the logic of the situation: from the implicit, unspoken logical (or ontological) premises inherent in the constitution of consciousness as

---

[118] Edgar Wind, *Pagan Mysteries of the Renaissance*, revised and enlarged edition, New York (The Norton Library) 1968, p. 238.

[119] Archetypes occur also in the popular and trivial and in banal works as well as in Kitsch. The archetypal character of something is no criterion of greatness and psychological importance. Anything can be archetypal.

[120] Psychological thought as each person's free associating, free fantasizing from out of his or her own "psyche."

THE END OF MEANING AND THE BIRTH OF MAN 255

well as in the historical locus one happens to be in. What really counts, the psychological ground of our existence at the given historical moment, is a priori kept out. It is not put at stake, does not enter the process. The felt experience thus precisely excludes the soul of the situation, trying to pacify us instead with abstracted semantic contents (images), on the one hand, and, as their counterpart, with likewise abstracted subjective emotional reactions, as a bait. Emotional events such as "primordial experiences from the unconscious," as impressive and moving ("numinous") as they may be, are essentially *idiosyncratic*.[121] Psychically[122] they may be important, psychologically they are irrelevant.

In what Jung said about the immigration of the numen and the relocation of the *Menschheitsproblematik* shows again very clearly his mode of reacting to, and disposing of, his own awareness that human consciousness has emerged from its former containment in meaning. Three aspects can be distinguished.

First, instead of letting this fundamental change really come home to "the numen" itself as *its* decomposition, sublation, fermenting corruption, *its* "death," he lets it merely suffer a locomotion that allows to hold the numen as such intact despite this radical change of place. He responds to the emergence of consciousness with a submersion of the (unaltered, unaffected) numen: "It is one of the self-delusions of our time to think that the spirits do not ride again [...] We are removed only from the place of such happenings, carried away by our madness [*Wir sind nur von dem Ort solchen Geschehens entrückt oder verrückt*]. Those of us who are still there, or have found their way back again, will be smitten by the same experience, now as before."[123] Nothing really happened: "[...] nothing changes but its name, [...] Our consciousness only imagines that it has lost its gods, in reality they are still there [...]"[124] The phrase, "Those of us who are still there" points of course to the (secondary restitution of) unbornness, the attempted denial of the emergence of consciousness *after* the fact of the insight into the emergence.

---

[121] The term "collective unconscious" must not blind us!

[122] The psychic life in man is part of human biology, ethology ("the behavior of the organism"). The soul, by contrast, is fundamentally *contra naturam*. It is logical life.

[123] *Letters 2*, p. 612, to Olga von Koenig-Fachsenfeld, 30 November 1960.

[124] *Letters 2*, p. 594, to Miguel Serrano, 14 September 1960.

Second, by opening up a new battleground for the numen or the whole weight of the *Menschheitsproblematik* inside man, Jung deprives the public sphere of its status as the real and only battleground, the place of the soul's *opus magnum*. What happens out there is now devalued as "nothing but." The real place where the action is, where the soul is, is supposed to be the unconscious. All psychological attention is diverted away from what is going on in art, philosophy, technology, economics, etc. and channeled to the unconscious of the individual and its private products, above all dreams.

When Jung said that "this particular patient" "may be quite insignificant," he caught a glimpse of something important. But we have to generalize his comment. Not this particular patient is insignificant, while certain other ones might not be. To the extent that we *all*, qua individual persons, are patients (literally or deep down or at least potentially), we *and what goes on in us* are indeed quite insignificant. Jung also saw that what ultimately counts is what is in the "scales of *humanity's* soul." He even entertained the idea of an "individuation of *humanity*," as A. Jaffé stressed. Here he was very close to true psychology, to the logical dimension that is the soul's home. But all this he nevertheless stuffed into the individual, thereby miniaturizing it. All significance was projected into what Jung *in nuce* had already seen through as "quite insignificant." He did not free his view from its personalistic, anthropological fetters. Even the individuation of humanity was ultimately seen as occurring only in the personal individuation process, that in turn was pretty much conceived as a process of personal salvation.[125] The latter was what Jung put all his hopes upon. To be sure, he conceived of a *transpersonal* and *objective* psyche, but what kind of transpersonality and objectivity was this? The notion of transpersonality was locked into the *semantic* sphere: the archetypal images occurring in the *personal* psyche were said to be of a transpersonal nature and part of the objective psyche. *Syntactically* Jung did not allow his term "transpersonal" to break out into the open, to a transpersonality that was *in itself* transpersonal, impersonal, objective (instead of subjective-personal): mercurial, the inner logic of the historical situation that we are in.

---

[125] Cf. for example the already quoted statement, "[...] that the salvation of the world consists in the salvation of the individual soul." *CW* 10 § 536. (The German word that Jung used was not *Erlösung*, but *Rettung*, rescue.)

THE END OF MEANING AND THE BIRTH OF MAN

The question arises: If he was so close to the insight that not the individual but the objective, transpersonal Mercurius or the *logos* is the actual subject of psychological life (and therefore, by the way, also the subject-matter of psychological research[126]), why could he not free himself from the personalistic and miniaturized? Why could he not break out into the open, into the realm where the invisible soul's real battlefield is: the realm of thought, culture, art, science, economics, etc.? Why could he not look for the stirrings of the hidden Mercurius there? The answer is: Because then it would necessarily have become obvious (and he would have had to let himself in for the insight) that meaning, in-ness, myth are once and for all over. He would have had to enter modernity without reserve and allow man to be *born*, to have escaped from any uterine vessel and mythical garb, as well as allow the spirit to have escaped from the bottle. But of course, the very purpose of his psychology project was to seal the spirit again in the bottle after its escape[127] and to swallow the already born children—in order to simulate the *salus* that exists only inside the *ecclesia*. Furthermore, he would have had to entrust himself to the truly (even syntactically) *objective* (impersonal, suprapersonal) logic of the soul's life and give up the longing for a subjective, personal individuation and salvation process with personal experiences of "meaning." He wanted to *have* meaning, immediately possess it. After all, his was a counter-factual rescue project. So on both counts his psychologistic move was consistent and indispensable.

Third, the new duplicity of battlegrounds goes along with a structurally "neurotic" dissociation: The public arena with all the philosophical, art and other cultural, social, economic, political developments is the place where *in fact* the action is—*but* it counts as "nothing but," mere "ego"-stuff, in the last analysis as a place of delusion and madness (cf. the phrase "carried away by our madness"); the private arena of the processes in the unconscious is the place where supposedly the numen has settled and the ultimate human questions are decided, the *opus magnum* is accomplished—*but* it is irrelevant in the real world, nobody cares about, or notices anything of, it (except maybe for a few enthralled Jungians and their analysands).

---

[126] In contrast to the study of people's psyche as part of human biology in the widest sense ("behavior of the organism").

[127] Cf. *CW* 13 § 250f.

258 *THE SOUL ALWAYS THINKS*

Privileging the raw

Another aspect of the tendency away from great art or thought was that Jung usually privileged the productions of "subculture"-type movements (like alchemy)—the raw (i.e., rather inferior texts by mediocre authors) over the refined (i.e., products of the greatest minds and artists).[128] Similarly, he privileged the unconscious, the spontaneous (dreams, visions, paintings from the unconscious). The rawness of dreams or alchemical writings was of course so important because Jung, after all a contemporary of Surrealists like André Breton and André Masson with their automatic writing technique, believed to be allowed to see in spontaneous and unconscious production the hallmark of immediacy: the direct, unfiltered *revelation* of "*the* unconscious" as pristine nature and ultimate origin (this is why he spoke of *Urerfahrung, Urerlebnis, Uranschauung*). Jung was guided by the naive belief that the raw or immediate were truer than the great, than the refined and developed, the exceptional in Edgar Wind's sense. "Why have we not long since discovered the unconscious and raised up its treasure-house of eternal images? Simply because we had a religious formula for everything psychic—and one that is far more beautiful and comprehensive than immediate experience."[129] The idea that the far more beautiful and comprehensive religious formulas, the late result of a long cultural development and the product of the thinking of generations, *is* the true origin (the "archetypal" in the strict sense), whereas immediate experience is only a deficient and preliminary mode of it, did not occur to Jung. He (as psychologist, not private citizen) precisely preferred in art only "the purest and most naive form," "the simplicity and naïveté of presentation, which is entirely devoid of any 'psychological' intent"[130] as well as, we might add, entirely devoid of any cultural refinement and mental processing. As far as I can see there is only one place where Jung came close to admitting that the cooked—the distilled, refined, sublimated—is primary and the raw secondary. This was in a passage about the artist and the work of art. There he said, "That which in the last analysis is the subject that wills in him [the artist] is not the man as person, but

---

[128] Cf. Graham Hough, "Anima and Poetry," *Spring 1973*, pp. 85–96, esp. p. 87, and David L. Miller, "Fairy Tale or Myth?," *Spring 1976*, pp. 157–164.

[129] *CW* 9i § 11.

[130] *CW* 18 § 1280.

THE END OF MEANING AND THE BIRTH OF MAN

the work of art."[131] The work of art, the final product, as the first cause of the production.

Alchemy could have taught him: *Quod natura relinquit imperfectum, ars perficit*, a statement frequently cited by him, but not properly understood and heeded. What does this statement tell us? Not the *prima materia*, not *Urerfahrung*, not the "small dreams" (as spontaneous "nature products"[132]) are the true essence, but the accomplished *result* of the *Work*, the result of the prolonged[133] human effort at *processing* the prime matter: the *lapis*, the *quinta essentia*... It is precisely not enough "to say again as best one can" what the "small dream," which Everyman can have, says. Only through artful processing and refining can the small dream obtain the depth and importance that it can possibly have (for the individual) and only through the *greatness* of the mind (*artifex*) that performs such processing can perhaps the quintessence, the Mercurius, be reached.

The "anima"-only definition of the soul makes our modern real world and our intellectual products appear as the opposite of, or external to, soul. Jung was generally not willing to consider the possibility that the move *away from* myth and into modernity occurs *within* the soul and *as* her work,[134] so that precisely *other* phenomena than those of the "symbolic life" and dreams and visions might express the need of *today's* soul, and so that the notion of soul would have to be expanded to include the anima's other, the animus.

Permanent storeroom of images? No, "just in time" production!

On the other hand, as far as dreams and visions are concerned, Jung was not ready to consider the possibility that they are the very way in which the Saturnian swallowing takes place. The way Jung imagined dreams, one would have to think of the unconscious as a kind of sack full of archetypal forms and of dreams as what leaked out of this sack into consciousness. But there is no such sack. There is no unconscious as a stationary container, nor as a place, a layer (realm) or

---

[131] *GW* 15 § 157, my translation. The wording in the English *CW* is too unspecific.

[132] I ignore here the fact that in reality dreams are not as innocent ("pure nature") as Jung would have it. Their phenomenologically obvious spontaneity is the result of the obliterations of the mediation and human reflection that brought them forth. Theirs is a secondary, produced immediacy.

[133] *Ars longa, vita brevis est.*

[134] Except in a few isolated comments, such as those quoted below, see footnote 154.

agency. The unconscious is the *temporal (momentary) process* of a redefinition, reconstitution of specific contents: the act of Kronos' swallowing. The unconscious is not ontological, not an entity, but *performative*. It is *only in* the production and the products (the dreams, etc.) and their *interpretation* as contents of the unconscious, and it is produced in each such interpretation anew. There is not a substantiated unconscious as their producer *behind* the dreams. Again, Jung did not listen to his Pueblo Indian who had shown the way by saying, with respect to the visible, phenomenal Sun, "This *is* the Father; there is no Father behind it. [...]"[135]

The act of Saturnian swallowing, as which the unconscious exists, must not be imagined as a literal translocation from outside to inside and the storing there of the translocated contents. No, it is merely the *transformation* of the respective contents out of one *logical status* into another. It is the act of assigning to contents the logical status of being absolutely unknowable to the intellect. It (and thus the unconscious) is the momentary act itself of dreaming, of *pro-ducing* dreams (visions, etc.) and viewing them *as* expressions of "the unconscious." In and through this productive and interpretative act alone the modern soul "swallows" the contents of our cultural, spiritual heritage, contents of public thought and engagement, and translates them into the form of its own pristine property, as pristine as if they had directly fallen from heaven. It reproduces them (a) in the form of unique *events*, as *my private, subjective experiences*, and (b) as contents of *the* unconscious (as absolutely spontaneous nature products and as fundamentally inaccessible to the public mind, the intellect). The process as which the unconscious exists is dialectical: it is only the *production* (bringing forth) and *expression* or *emergence* of the images (from inside out) that is their *interiorization* (from outside, from the public mind, in). Their "rebirth" as consciously remembered dreams from "out of the unconscious" *is* the way in which they receive their status as contents of the unconscious and thus as secondarily unborn. Both movements occur "at once." They are only one self-contradictory movement.

---

[135] *CW* 18 § 688.

THE END OF MEANING AND THE BIRTH OF MAN

Dissociation and the rescue of unbornness

The metaphor of the stars having fallen from heaven allows us to add an essential qualification of our image of the swallowing Kronos. This image, coming from the pre-modern, even the mythological age, still operated with a simple binary division, putting the father on the one and the children on the other side. But now, in the modern situation, it is no longer as simple as that the father swallows his children. What is swallowed now is the *whole concept* of *childhood* as such, i.e., the whole "human child – divine parent" *relationship*, the stance of upward looking per se, the entire relation of above and below. That which used to be the whole former *kósmos*, the whole mode of being-in-the-world, has been *sublated*, reduced to an internal moment within a new, larger mode (or constitution of consciousness). Man has interiorized his entire former in-ness into himself. He as modern consciousness is the new "Kronos" who swallowed the entire old "Father Kronos – his children" relationship, thereby establishing his "unconscious." But we could also turn it around and say: by reducing what used to be its whole world-relation to a sublated moment within itself, consciousness pushed off from this world-relation and catapulted itself to a formerly unheard-of new level. The fish swallowed the "water – fish" relation and thereby turned into Aquarius, who has emerged from the waters.

The image of the stars having fallen from heaven makes us aware of the *pivotal nature* of the unconscious. The stars—the goal of man's upward looking—are no longer above, but down below in the unconscious, a toy version of stars and heaven. So we have to look down upon the stars now, down from the height of modern consciousness. We speak of "introspection," which is the looking from outside (in)to inside, from ego (in)to self, from consciousness (in)to the unconscious inside ourselves. This is the one perspective. But the stars contained in the unconscious are still *stars*. So there is a new starry heaven, a new above and below, a new God-image. From the point of view of "the unconscious," we have to and are able to look up to them again. There is thus also a new in-ness, a new stance of upward looking to a new transcendence (although one that as a whole is internalized, sublated).[136] The unconscious is in this sense the former (relation to the) mythic or metaphysical heaven, *only in little and in image*, and no longer cosmic (the real natural world), all around us and part of official public knowledge and reflection. It is the swallowed, miniaturized, but also check-mated, truth of former ages. Thus, what had admittedly been lost in full size and in real could be recovered in little and in image by means of "the unconscious."

Instead of a full-fledged sublation (reduction to a sublated moment) we get a dissociation: two simultaneous, but mutually exclusive truths between which we can switch. The negation that had historically happened could not be totally denied—it was too obvious—, but Jung refused to go wholeheartedly through with it. He insisted, as we heard, on having "a situation in which that thing becomes true once more" in "a new form."[137] With the introspective direction, consciousness as fully born looks down upon the former stars from outer space; as the swallowed consciousness on its night-sea-journey, conversely, it has a (Disneyland kind of, simulated) heaven and God-image above itself and is in the mode of upward looking. Empirically, for the dreaming ego, there are still the stars, still the numinous and luminous god-image(s)—but interned into the *unconscious*: the very light of the stars and gods has in itself become fundamentally, namely logically, occluded, obsfucated.

The notion of the collective unconscious, which has modern consciousness ("the ego," "ego-consciousness") outside itself, is thus *in itself* witness to the fact that the birth *has* happened. As the swallowed *notion* of childhood, it is the positivized negative (in the photographic sense) of accomplished adulthood. It is a compromise formation between the acknowledged existence *extra ecclesiam*, after the emergence from in-ness, on the one hand, and the refusal to be unreservedly informed by this existence because of the insistence on achieving a new in-ness, Saturnian style.

This pivotal sense of the unconscious is best illustrated by the way it was literally acted out by Jung in the organization of his life. I am referring to the two places between which Jung divided his life, his

---

[136] That it was a new *upward looking* and *in-ness* shows that it was precisely the *old* form. However, that it was a *new* (internalized, psychologized) upward looking suggested a "*new* form" to Jung.

[137] *CW* 18 § 632.

THE END OF MEANING AND THE BIRTH OF MAN 263

ordinary house in Küsnacht and his "tower" in Bollingen. Although they are literal places, I also consider them concretized metaphors for psychological *topoi*. Küsnacht was the place of truly modern consciousness that had "emerged from the waters." Here Jung while working at his desk had to stare into the face of Voltaire, whose bust was on his desk. Here Jung was the scientist who dug up facts, nothing but facts, about the soul. Here Jung abhorred any speculation transgressing beyond the Kantian "barrier across the mental world,"[138] especially any hypostatizing, sternly insisting that he only presented hypotheses (or, even more modestly, that he only named and described phenomena).

By contrast, "At Bollingen I am in the midst of my true life [*in meinem eigentlichsten Wesen*, lit. "in my truest nature (or essence)"], I am most deeply myself. Here I am, as it were, the 'age-old son of the mother.' That is how alchemy puts it, very wisely, for the 'old man,' the 'ancient,' whom I had already experienced as a child, is personality No. 2, who has always been and always will be. He exists outside time and is the son of the maternal unconscious. [...]"[139] "At times I feel as if I am spread out over the landscape and inside things, and am myself living in every tree, in the plashing of the waves, in the clouds and the animals that come and go, in the procession of the seasons. [...] here is space for the spaceless kingdom of the world's and the psyche's hinterland."[140] These feelings, where they occur, may be authentic and beautiful experiences. But whereas for the truly modern consciousness they would, *as* these authentic experiences, be not more than particular subjective events in one's personal psychology, contingent and metaphysically indifferent, Jung gives them an ontological status as expressive of his "*eigentlichste Wesen*" and of "the spaceless kingdom of the world's and the psyche's hinterland." Clearly, at Bollingen, Jung is still unborn. "Bollingen" is the place (*topos*) that has the function of allowing Jung, although he is on the literal level already born, nevertheless on the logical level to return into a state of unbornness.

The superlative form (*in meinem eigentlichsten Wesen*, in my truest nature) is revealing here. The relation of Küsnacht and Bollingen, outside and inside, is not that of false and true, but of true and more

---

[138] *CW* 18 § 1734.
[139] *MDR* p. 225.
[140] *MDR* p. 225f.

264   *THE SOUL ALWAYS THINKS*

true (or truest), *eigentlich* and *eigentlichst*. One would expect that "eigentliches Wesen", "true nature," would be enough. But Jung uses the superlative, which has the unintended effect of weakening the meaning and at the same time suggests that the Bollingen experience is not the innocent self-display of his truth, but a secondary stylization. "Bollingen" is only a small oasis in the middle of the modern world, a tiny private psycho-Disneyland. "Küsnacht," by contrast, is everywhere. And Bollingen is not an authentic, original remains of the former world amidst the modern world. It is—obviously—an artificial construction *by the Küsnacht Jung*. So it has its secondariness written on its face.

While in Küsnacht Jung is consciousness at the Aquarius level, at Bollingen he is the fish swimming in the waters. It is noteworthy in this context that Beckett recounts having heard Jung make the following comment, after a lecture about the case of a young girl, "In the most fundamental way, she had never been really born. I, too, have always had the sense of never having been born."[141] His psychology, which he often termed the "psychology of the unconscious," is the worked out *theory* and program of unbornness.

Jung comes to us in the scientist's clothing, but inwardly he is dressed in the glory of the mythical garment of the "age-old son of the mother." Officially he is the (psychologically) fully adult modern man, but privately he is the archetypal mother's grandiose child. Officially he shows himself in his metaphysical nakedness, but within himself he harbors the majesty of an "actor in the divine drama of life." Is he not himself the very "beggar who wraps himself in kingly raiment, (the) king who disguises himself as a beggar,"[142] that he warned against?

Jung's semanticizing the problem of the "new form"

Above I pointed out that Jung had run into and become aware of the problem of form ("I need a new form"). But after what we have worked out we see that he did not at all take up the challenge of the

---

[141] Quoted from the dissertation (Pacifica Graduate Institute, 2003) on *The Absence of Myth* by Sophia Heller, who cites James Olney, *Memory and Narrative*, Chicago (Chicago Univ. Press) 1998, p. 325, who in turn quotes Beckett directly from Charles Juliet, "Rencontre avec Beckett," see Charles Juliet, "Meeting Beckett," tr. Suzanne Chamier, in *TriQuarterly*, 77 (winter 1989/90) p. 14.

[142] *CW* 9i § 27.

THE END OF MEANING AND THE BIRTH OF MAN

problem of (a new) form. As I showed, he even radically eliminated the level of form from his psychology. The new "form" that he did discover or gave to things (psychologization) was only a downgrading and downsizing (and a change of location: "no longer above, but below"), that is to say it remained external. The *internal logical form* of the contents themselves was precisely not touched. But of course, the whole project of Jung's psychology served the purpose of evading the real problem of the internal or logical form: the new form *had* already been provided by the real historical situation and was what Jung rejected, obviously had to reject, in favor of his "flight into the unconscious."[143] What was this really existing new form? That all the contents that he was interested in were in the status of historical presence and no longer in that of a present reality ("no longer valid"). Jung, not being able to go the way of a repristination nor to content himself with having mythic meaning only in Mnemosyne, needed to *smuggle* the traditional metaphysical contents *in their traditional logical form* into the new situation and to palm them (in their old form) off on himself—himself in what he called "my psychological condition," which was the condition of modern consciousness that could not return, e.g., to the miracle of the Mass because it "knew too much." In order to achieve this he had to surreptitiously replace the idea of "new *form*" by the idea of a "new *vessel*, container, wrapping." A vessel is an external form. If form is taken as a vessel, then form itself has been semanticized, turned into its very opposite: a thing, substance. The new vessel that Jung invented for the mythical images was "the interior in man," "*the* unconscious." *It* is the so-called new "form" in which modern consciousness ("my psychological condition") can receive the old contents (*in* their old form!) into itself without either having to give up its own modern form or having to criticize these contents for their old form, be it by simply rejecting them altogether as superstition and obsolete or be it by taking them merely historically or deconstructing them. Here we see one root of the amazing fact that Jung denied himself any access to the level of logic, syntax and logical form, logical status, although only in them can be found what can be called the *soul* of real life.

---

[143] W. Giegerich, "The Flight into the Unconscious: A Psychological Analysis of C.G. Jung's Psychology Project." Psychology at the Threshold. UCSB, Santa Barbara, CA. September 2000 (audiotape, Sounds True Recording, Louisville, CO, 2000).

266   *THE SOUL ALWAYS THINKS*

What at Bollingen are revelations from the unconscious is, for the intellect of the Küsnacht Jung, simply provable observed facts, facts sealed in "unconsciousness," that is, in mindless factuality, in the prohibition to *think* them: the prohibition to allow the mind to be "infected" by them and to turn object (or content) into subject. The sugar cube is sealed in plastic foil so as not to dissolve in the coffee. The unconscious contents are deposited in the unconscious as in a CASTOR® container that, under penalty of either psychosis or of disqualification because of metaphysical transgression, is forbidden to be opened. They must not be released into the unfathomableness of their truth. The unconscious is indeed a "casket for storage and transport of radioactive waste," as it were, but not because archetypes and Gods are allegedly still alive and thus as dangerous as radioactive materials, but only because *if* we, *as* the modern consciousness that we are, would nevertheless still believe in them and take them *as* present realities, we would then, and only then, be threatened by inflation or psychosis. Their "radioactivity" is nothing else but the discrepancy between *their old logical form* and the logical form *of modern consciousness*. This form discrepancy alone is what makes the old contents threatening in the sense of inflation or psychosis for a consciousness inevitably informed by the new logical form. For a pre-modern consciousness, whose logical form had been that of in-ness and upward looking *anyway*, they had not represented a fundamental problem. The situation is totally different for a consciousness that is in "outer space" vis-à-vis itself, in other words, for whom the level of logical form or syntax has become indispensable.

What in Küsnacht—outside the CASTOR container—are merely "statements of the psyche," e.g. merely God-*images* in the soul,[144] at Bollingen—inside the container—are transcendent realities (a *vox Dei*[145]) that require our service ("to serve a god is full of meaning and promise because it is an act of submission to a higher, invisible and spiritual being"[146]). This fundamental duplicity, also expressed as the split between personality No. 1 and personality No. 2, has two

---

[144] "When I say 'God' I mean an anthropomorphic (archetypal) God-image and do not imagine I have said anything about God. I have neither denied nor affirmed him [...]" *Letters 2*, p. 54, to Haberlandt, 23 April 1952.

[145] Cf. *CW* 18 §§ 603 and 601.

[146] *CW* 13 § 55.

THE END OF MEANING AND THE BIRTH OF MAN 267

advantages for Jung. Since as the scientist, Jung does not have to take *intellectual* responsibility for his inner existence as the age-old son of the mother, the danger of becoming *personally* inflated or psychotic from his entertaining such a self-definition is warded off. And yet, since at Bollingen he is in his *truest* nature and the scientist has psychologically just the status of his façade, being ultimately just *maya*, "a good exterior 'dans ce meilleur des mondes possibles,'"[147] he can psychologically reap the benefit of the grandiosity and metaphysical meaning that it entails.

The subject that is at Bollingen (No. 2) cannot be infected by the "radioactive" (inflation-causing) material inside the container because it left its modern mind and its intellectual responsibility back in Küsnacht, with No. 1. As long as one is logically only *dreaming* "at Bollingen" (dreaming the myth onwards), one is safe. "Dreaming" here means: experiencing with a fundamental mental reservation, with the knowledge that it is *only* a "dream," an "*Urerlebnis*," only a *statement* by or *image* from the unconscious, and that the "dream" has outside of itself the "outer space" of modern consciousness and "real life" as the unquestioned real reality and reliable ground of our existence. "Dreaming" means to be at least implicitly aware of the fact that what is seen and felt in this state has its place only in a kind of segregated psycho-Disneyland. The real, even though unspoken, logical premises of our modern existence have been put between brackets so that they do not enter into the "*Urerfahrung*." But the moment one's neurotic dissociation is not airtight and one happens inadvertently to be present with one's whole waking mind that takes intellectually *seriously* what it experiences, the moment one unreservedly stakes even one's sense of reality and of one's real existence—ultimately one's real ontology and logic—: then one is in danger of being exposed to the contents' radioactivity.

As far as Jung's deepest need and supreme interest, the restoration of meaning, is concerned, psychology is an emergency stopgap. It is not an advance to a new level of consciousness, not an opening up of a fundamentally deeper mode of comprehension of the problem at hand. It moves thought to a sidetrack and a fenced-in private

---

[147] *Letters 1*, p. 171, to Hermann Hesse, 18 Sept. 1934. The original formulation is: "eine gute Exoterik."

playground rather than continuing, and contributing to, the historical evolution of the mind: because it did not provide an answer to the question of logical form *on the level of logical form*. Jung *saw* the problem of form, but answered it on the semantic level.

We should, however—this is essential—not make the mistake of interpreting this duplicity personalistically as Jung's idiosyncracy. Rather we have to comprehend that it *had to be this way* if Jung wanted to solve the task he was confronted with: the problem of meaning as it was set for him at this particular historical moment. And thus we have to comprehend that it is merely an illustration of the concept of man underlying Jung's psychology of the unconscious. The split and the pivotal character are part of the program. Jungian psychology wants to teach us to comprehend ourselves in the same way and to live our lives accordingly.

If one wonders why Jung had to have this project of establishing "a situation in which that thing becomes true once more" in "a new form," despite of its having obviously been rendered obsolete by the history of the soul and what the historical purpose of such a futile project might have been, my answer is that the factual obsolescence was probably not enough. The attempt to re-establish or rather to simulate the former situation had to be made for the sole purpose of *objectively* carrying it to absurdity. Consciousness had to learn in practice, by experience, the hard way, that it does not work. Only in this way is the wish to hold on or return *really* (and not only *in mente*) worked off and has consciousness unreservedly arrived in the modern world.

Token adulthood

It fits to the attempt to rescue unbornness that Jung could conceive of "(psychologically) fully growing up" (on the personal level) only as an *exchange* of the (childish) dependence on literal parents for the (mature) dependence on higher, divine parents. Above I mentioned that puberty rites in traditional cultures initiated into empirical adulthood precisely by logically initiating into metaphysical childhood. It is as if Jung's thinking about the transition from childhood to adulthood went along the same lines. Neurotics, he says critiquing Freudian psychoanalysis, "can only regain their health when they climb out of the mud of the commonplace. [...] How are they

THE END OF MEANING AND THE BIRTH OF MAN 269

ever to emerge if analysis does not make them aware of something different and better, when even theory holds them fast in it and offers them nothing more than the rational and 'reasonable' injunction to abandon such childishness? That is precisely what they cannot do, and how should they be able to if they do not discover something to stand on? One form of life cannot simply be abandoned unless it is exchanged for another."[148] And this "something to stand on," this other form of life to be exchanged for the neurotic or childish one, is—according to Jung—the awareness and attitude of being the child of divine parents. "[...] The fantasy of sacrifice means the giving up of infantile wishes. [...] But man cannot leave his previous personality and his previous objects of interest simply as they are, [...] Here religion is a great help because, by the bridge of the symbol, it leads his libido away from the infantile objects (parents) towards the symbolic representatives of the past, i.e., the gods, thus facilitating the transition from the infantile world to the adult world."[149] The move from literal parents to their symbolic representatives is most distinctly expressed in Jung's statement already quoted above about the ever-seeking traveling woman, "But if she could say, 'I am the daughter of the Moon. Every night I must help the Moon, my Mother, over the horizon'—ah, that is something else! Then she lives [...]"[150] A real birth of man, such as the birth of the symbol's meaning out of the symbol, is unthinkable for Jung. Childhood cannot really be left behind. It can only be transformed (or transported) from a literal to a logical or symbolic level. A successful transportation *of* the *childhood* status to the symbolic level is then—oddly enough—called maturity: "transition to the adult world."

Despite his insight into the "illimitable loneliness" of man, Jung was not ready to comprehend logical adulthood as the self-contradictory task of *oneself* having to *be*, to *exist as*, the very ground and the only ground one is standing on (just as personal adulthood means that I myself have to be my own mother and father for myself). No other ground, no uterine vessel. To be sure, he raised the rhetorical question, "Or is there something in ourselves that commands us to go in for no mummeries, but perhaps even *to sew our garment*

---

[148] *MDR* p. 166.
[149] *CW* 4 § 350.
[150] *CW* 18 § 630.

ourselves?"[151] But what he did and wanted us to do was the opposite: to slip into some ready-made archetypal garment to be discovered in the unconscious, in our private dreams. If there was anything that Jung did *not* want us to do then it was to really sew our garment ourselves. He was not even ready to uncompromisingly comprehend adulthood as metaphysical nakedness, which would be the prerequisite for really wanting to sew one's own garment, a garment that as self-made would be an ordinary outfit, not a majestic archetypal one. He thought that you simply cannot do without divine parents; you need to find some other, transcendent ground to stand on (although now of course, in the 20th century, this transcendent ground was *internally* "transcendent" for him: psychologized).

In this way the *logic* of the child-status stays the same, whereas the revolutionary fact that we have reached the age of personal-biological as well as cultural-historical majority is theoretically taken care (and disposed) of by a mere substitution of the *incumbents* in the office of parents, in the personal case, and, in the cultural case, by a mere substitution of one place and dimension of the parents (the public world of thought about, first cosmic, later metaphysical realities) for another (the interior of private images and feeling experiences). And "sewing one's garment oneself" was secretly reversed to mean the *personal* introspective search for a garment in *one's own* inner second-hand shop, the unconscious. Tailoring was out of the question.

Jung declared his readiness stoutly to avow our spiritual poverty, our symbol-lessness; he even spoke of a vow of spiritual poverty in analogy to the monks' vow of worldly poverty.[152] This shows once more his whole ambivalence or duplicity. The exalted language ("vow," with the associations of the life of monks, which is a metaphysically rich life *ad majorem dei gloriam*, and of heavenly reward for earthly poverty) contradicts the semantic message ("spiritual poverty"). The consciousness that is speaking is still up in the clouds; it is still firmly informed by the logic of religion and metaphysics, but *what* it is saying is that it wants to avow its metaphysical nakedness and renounce all riches. The point that needs to be made is that there is nothing to be

---

[151] *CW* 9i § 27, my italics.
[152] *CW* 9i §§ 28 and 29.

THE END OF MEANING AND THE BIRTH OF MAN 271

renounced. Nothing needs to be done. We do not have to come down from cloud-cuckoo-land, we do not have to stoop low (as Jung had suggested): because we in fact *are* already down on the earth, we *are* metaphysically naked, *really* naked; we do not have any symbols or myths that we could still give up. Jung's (to be sure casual) fantasy of a vow is another small indication that he remains stuck in personalistic and egoic thinking, here a thinking in terms of our efforts for the right way, ultimately for personal salvation. He does not advance to the truly *psychological* level: to the understanding that all that is needed, but also required and indispensable, is the conscious *recognition* of the logic that is and the accompaniment by us, with our *wholehearted feeling* and *intellectual comprehension*, of this logic in its self-movement.[153] Earlier I pointed out that Jung sells indulgences. Egoically he demands a psychic attitude or behavior (i.e., an acting out) in return for which he dispenses himself and us from having to respond psychologically, which here would mean our simply suffering the *truth* of the situation to come home to, permeate, and transform consciousness.

In one of the rather rare instances where Jung does not blame us, the ego, or the conscious intellect, for the historical development, but appreciates it as stemming from the soul,[154] he himself says that "the darkness of our soul" "hollows out and hacks up the shapes of our culture and its historical dominants. We have no dominants any more, [...] Our values are shifting, everything loses its certainty, even *sanctissima causalitas* has descended from the throne of the axiomata and has become a mere field of probabilities."[155] We simply *have* nothing. How could the really poor take a vow of poverty and renounce

---

[153] What I here charge Jung with is very similar to what he himself once charged "modern man, disguised in the figure of Faust" with: "Instead of comprehending [*erkennen*, to know, see through] the drama, he has become one of the figures in the drama" (Jung refers to the Paris-Helena scene of Goethe's *Faust*, *CW* 12 § 558, transl. modified).

[154] As also in the statement from *CW* 11 § 203 already quoted above and in a letter: "Man is compelled by divine forces to go forward to increasing consciousness and cognition, developing further and further away from his religious background because he does not understand it any more." *Letters 2*, p. 436, to Kelsey, 3 May 1958.

[155] *Letters 2*, p. 590, to Sir Herbert Read, 2 September 1960. Much the same had already been observed by Karl Marx a century earlier: "All that is solid melts into air, all that is holy is profaned, and man is at last compelled to face with sober senses his real conditions of life and his relations with his kind," Karl Marx and Friedrich Engels, *Manifesto of the Communist Party*, in: Marx & Engels, *Basic Writings on Politics and Philosophy*, ed. by Lewis S. Feuer, Anchor Books edition, 1959, p. 10.

(be it worldly or spiritual) riches? All we have to do is to refrain from secondarily pretending something else: from giving an inflated and thus phony significance to our personal dreams, to symbols and myths; from using the words "gods," "archetypes," "numinous," etc. lightly, for commonplace motifs and experiences. The fantasy of a vow shows that Jung's is only a token admission of the poverty that is. And indeed, just as the monk exchanged his worldly riches for spiritual and heavenly riches, so Jung's psychology exchanges the conscious riches of our cultural, religious and philosophical heritage, the riches present only in Mnemosyne, for the riches of or in the unconscious. This heritage he had, as we have seen, precisely systematically cast away (as having been "squandered" by us), for the very reason and the only reason that it was present *only* in Mnemosyne and thus "no longer valid"[156]: not a present reality.

Kronos swallows not only his children, not only childhood as such (the whole parent-child relationship, the mode of upward looking), but also his children's *birth*

"Bollingen" as well as "the unconscious" are secondary and insular. The modern world is all around them. Birth has already happened. But part of the logic of "the psychology of the unconscious" is that the secondary is declared to be primary (the second-hand shop *as* the place of *Urerfahrung*) and the late historical result is declared to be the secret origin. "Probably it [viz., the unconscious or the hinterland of man's mind] was always there, in every culture. [...] But no culture before ours felt the need to take this psychic background as such seriously."[157] Today "All the gods and demons, whose physical nothingness is so easily passed off as the 'opium of the people,' return to their place of origin, Man [...]"[158] The thesis is that the 20th century idea of the collective unconscious is actually the (formerly unknown) origin of all.

To represent this idea of primordial origin is also the function of Jung's ahistorical "archetypes" (as anthropological, if not cosmic, constants: synchronicity!). At a time when de Saussure (1906) had

---

[156] *CW* 9i § 31.
[157] *CW* 10 § 161. I altered the translation of the second sentence according to *GW* 10.
[158] *CW* 18 § 1366.

THE END OF MEANING AND THE BIRTH OF MAN

273

demonstrated that in the system of language the function of signs is not determined by substrates of meaning, but by differences, Jung resurrected, with his concept of archetypes, the idea of subsisting units of meaning: meaning as natural facts, not product of the activity of the mind (and thus not the mind's own property); meaning ontologized and hypostatized, timeless constants. The mind is conversely imagined to be the product of, and passively informed by, the archetypes.

The statement about all the gods and demons returning to their place of origin, Man, could have been the insight into what I described under the title of the birth of man, into man's having come of age, his having outgrown his metaphysical parents—*if* the inserted clause polemicizing against the "opium of the people" idea did not betray that it is used in the opposite direction, for rescuing the divine parents by psychologistically stuffing them into the unconscious that is inside Man. So this one sentence shows the Kronos strategy in action, the bornness *and* the swallowing of the born, the re-mystification of what has already been seen through as the mind's own production.

The secondary is assigned the status of the true origin. This is the first inversion. Similarly, the fundamental privacy and idiosyncracy of the unconscious is hidden and compensated for by declaring it to be in itself *collective*. But the Jungian term "collective" is not the public, not the official, not the communal, not "the soul's" *logical* life! It is the a priori *swallowed, done-in* public. The real public remains unaffected outside, taking its own course.

This leads us to a third inversion. Although the unconscious is insular in the world of consciousness, we as conscious personalities are said to be surrounded on all sides by the unconscious. The fantasy of being surrounded by the unconscious on all sides had only become possible because Jung had *systematically excluded* major conscious and public areas of modern reality (and cultural history at large) from being considered as relevant parts of the *phenomenology of the soul*: Philosophical thought was put down as merely intellectual speculation; the art of his time (e.g., the Cubists) was simply ignored by Jung; "Marx" and the whole economic reality remained outside, as did the advancement of technology, industry and the changes in the structure and organization of society; other modern phenomena were dismissed as mere mass phenomena (which they of course often were; but even *as* mass phenomena they are an indirect expression of the modern soul, too). By contrast, dreams, visions, myths, symbols were privileged as the true documents of the soul, soul thereby reductively limited to its "anima" aspect.[159] "Only the symbolic life can express the need of the soul."[160] Only the raw shows the soul in its unfiltered truth, as we saw above. For this reason probably, Jung could conversely *mystify* other modern banal mass movements and appropriate them for his archetypal theory, if only they seemed to be loaded with enough primitive emotion. Thus he misinterpreted the Nazi movement as expressive of an archetype, even a god (Wotan), and thereby attributed a psychological depth to it that it surely did not have.

Likewise, while the contents of the unconscious are actually the abstracted historical past, a task for the future is nevertheless attributed to the unconscious. "That is modern psychology, and that is the future,"[161] Jung said at the end of his talk about "The Symbolic Life." And somewhere else, as we already heard: "[...] the real problem will be from now on until a dim future a psychological one."[162] Jung's "myth of consciousness" needs to be mentioned here in particular. According to this myth God wants to incarnate, and become conscious, in man. Now, what goal for the future is this? It is a goal that history already reached with the conclusion of the age of metaphysics and the entrance into modernity at the beginning of the 19th century. That very consciousness that previously had been extrajected to the horizon and objectified in the idea of God in heaven has already been integrated into the form of consciousness. Why else would modern consciousness have experienced the death of God? "God" could only die if the meaning of this symbol had been born out of it, only if what consciousness previously had still needed to *have* in the form of a semantic content or substance ("projection") had meanwhile come home to consciousness itself, that is, had entered its own syntax or logical constitution, its own *being*. The "death of God" experience is precisely the indication (the symptom) of the fact that God's incarnation in man has happened.

Today, this new consciousness has existed as an objective societal or cultural reality (even if not so much subjectively) for about two

---

[159] See my *Animus-Psychologie*, Frankfurt am Main et al. (Peter Lang) 1994.
[160] *CW* 18 § 627.
[161] *CW* 18 § 639.
[162] *Letters 2*, p. 498, to Werner Bruecher, 12 April 1959.

THE END OF MEANING AND THE BIRTH OF MAN

centuries. But it is declared to be the future goal. However, the future goal only in little and in private: only as the goal of the inner process of the unconscious, cut off from the real development of consciousness in public cultural life.[163] Jung wanted an onwards movement, but one where we dream the myth onwards[164]: (a) *dream*, (b) the *myth*. It is the fish or unborn consciousness that "dreams," that in fact *does* not only dream (as a specific activity or event), but whose whole existence *is* one Dream. Aquarius or born consciousness has awakened from this Dream and no longer dreams (which does not preclude its still having literal dreams); because it has integrated the content of the former Dream into its form of consciousness, it *is* itself, and has to *be*, what the Dream used to be about.[165]

This move was a necessity for the project of Jung's "psychology of the unconscious." Since the point of this project was to have in-ness come true once more in a "new form," the really existing state of bornness in the sense of Aquarius consciousness had to be put down as utterly banal (or, of course, as unbearable or dangerous). But it could not simply be rejected and left outside. The idea of the "higher," born consciousness, of awakening from the dream, of Aquarius consciousness had to be appropriated by the unconscious as its own property so that the really existing Aquarius consciousness would through this privation be in fact depotentiated and could no longer threaten the position of the unconscious with the claim that it, public consciousness, was the "higher" consciousness and the unconscious, as it were, "old hat."

By the same token, the unconscious had to bring the idea of future development under its control. It could not leave the promise of the future resting with the official (public) intellectual and social history. The potential of "future" and of "advancing to a new, higher consciousness" had to be taken prisoner for[166] the unconscious as the

---

[163] One has to see this also in connection with Jung's idea of a "secret history," sort of a hidden undercurrent under that history that is accessible to the public mind.

[164] *CW* 9i § 271: "The most we can do is to *dream the myth onwards* [...]" But this is not exactly the same as the German original: *GW* 9/I § 271 ("Man *träumt* bestenfalls den Mythus weiter [...]").

[165] Once awakened, consciousness can reflect about ("interpret") the dream that it had had (= our spiritual heritage) in all its details, and treasure it in Mnemosyne.

[166] I take this phrase "to take prisoner for [...]," which goes back to Gregory of Nazianzus ("we take prisoner every thought for Christ," in: "In Praise of Basil" [*Pat. Gr.* 36, 508]) from James Hillman's "Psychology: Monotheistic or Polytheistic," in: *Spring 1971*, pp. 193–208, here p. 202 with note 15.

exclusive locus of the course of what for Jung was the *real, essential, deep, hidden* history. Declaring the stage of consciousness that has already been reached in the present to be the distant goal of the future is how Kronos swallowed not only this or that newborn child, but *bornness as such*; how in-ness "pocketed" its own opposite, "being born out of it." The birth of higher consciousness is now defined as an event *in* the unconscious. Only with this fundamental swallowing has "the unconscious," and thus the sense of in-ness, become absolute.

The future, in this way logically entombed in the unconscious, is an a priori defused future, a literally *past* future, a future that from the outset has already been overtaken by real developments. Just as the Jungian unconscious is the metaphysical past *as* a seeming new present, but a present that has the real present ("Küsnacht") outside of itself, so *this* future is actually our really existing present. But since it is our present only as image, as reconstructed within the enclosure of the miniaturized inner world that simulates the former state of in-ness (to have overcome which and pushed off from which is the very character of our *real* present), it must necessarily appear *as* the great future goal for mankind to strive for and the goal of human history at large.

For Jung the *real* (already existing) Aquarius consciousness is in psychological outer space. This becomes apparent from his interpretation of two of his late dreams, the one about the UFOs with the magic lantern pointing straight at Jung and the other one about the meditating yogin who had Jung's face. As to the first, Jung comments, "Still half in the dream, the thought passed through my head: 'We always think that the UFOs are projections of ours. Now it turns out that we are their projections. I am projected by the magic lantern as C.G. Jung. But who manipulates the apparatus?'"[167] Jung takes the dream image of the UFOs literally, on the "object-level." By hypostatizing them, he gives them a "metaphysical" interpretation, which as the natural scientist in "Küsnacht" he would have to abhor. He even toys with the idea of a mysterious mastermind behind the scene that is not suggested by the dream at all. He never considers the possibility that the UFOs in the dream represent his own Aquarius consciousness from which he dissociated himself, extrajecting it into

---

[167] *MDR* p. 323.

THE END OF MEANING AND THE BIRTH OF MAN 277

psychological "outer space" and reducing it to a mere technical apparatus (cf. his view of the intellect as an arbitrary, more or less irresponsible function of thinking things up, or as mechanical function in the sense of formal logic), and that it might be the purpose of this dream to re-establish a connection, to heal the dissociation: to allow Jung to comprehend himself as thinking self-relation.

Much the same can be seen in his reaction to the second dream. "I started in profound fright, and awoke with the thought: 'Aha, so he is the one who is meditating me. He has a dream, and I am it.' I knew that when he awakened, I would no longer be."[168] Again he takes the dream naively literally, metaphysically, as a dream about the question of his life or death. He sees a transcendent being in the yogin whom he identifies with his self, his "prenatal wholeness," that "meditates my earthly form," which in turn would have no more than the status of Maya, in keeping with Eastern philosophy.[169] A *psychological* interpretation, by contrast, would have to see the dream as expressing the idea of the soul's self-relation. We might say that the dream tries to make him aware of the fact that the yogin is his own, but disowned and exoticized (yogin!), modern consciousness. A modern consciousness, however, that is dreaming and not awake, as it would be befitting for the Aquarius stage of consciousness. The "yogin's" dream invents or stylizes him, Jung, as the author of the "psychology of the unconscious," as, say, the "Bollingen" person,[170] as the "unborn." And *this* person and along with it "the unconscious" would naturally disappear when this self-definition or self-stylization is given up. The ultimate telos of the dream, this Jung's own reflection shows, is the waking up out of the state of dreaming with the result that "I would no longer be." This death of the Bollingen person would be the final birth of man, the emergence from the waters. But again this thought came to Jung only as an unconscious one, in the form of a dream and as a possibility of, and projection into, the future, a post-

---

[168] *Ibid.*

[169] *Ibid.* p. 323f.

[170] Or, to be more exact, as the Küsnacht person who, after all, is defined as being no more than the "exoteric" shell around the Bollingen person as the true self. The problem of the Küsnacht person is that, because he always has Bollingen and his unbornness as his ultimate truth in the back of his mind, he does not à corps perdu give himself over to modern (Aquarius) consciousness, which for that very reason can imaginally only appear as the figure of a kind of alien belonging to outer space.

278   *THE SOUL ALWAYS THINKS*

mortal potentiality[171] (that Jung could not even envision as solution, redemption, but only as the literal death of himself as human being).

Archetypal psychology (James Hillman) or: Absolute swallowing

From here I want to have a quick look at the only important further development of Jung's psychology, archetypal psychology, in order to describe its logical genesis. Its origin had been Jung's standpoint. Rather than deserting this standpoint in favor of a personalistic developmental, clinical orientation, but also rather than being faithful to the letter of the Jungian *doctrine*, like orthodox Jungianism, archetypal psychology was faithful to the *dynamic and telos of the movement* performed by Jung: it radicalized Jung's move to a situation in which the past (mythic meaning) becomes true once more, figuratively speaking: the move to "Bollingen"; this move now became a one-way journey. Jung's psychology had been elliptic, it had had two focal points, "Bollingen" and "Küsnacht." Hillman abolished, as it were, the "Küsnacht" position altogether: he abolished from his theory Jung's scientific claim, the theory of compensation, the "archetypes in themselves," the interpretation of images as "symbols," Jung's "theology," even the Jungian interest in "meaning" (the big question of the meaning of life). Now "Bollingen" has no counterpart, no opposite any more. It is limitless, absolute, total, while with Jung it had still been insular and only one "half" of the whole truth. For archetypal psychology "Bollingen" is everywhere, now infinitely extended to comprise even its former opposite, "Küsnacht." This is why archetypal psychology was able to make the move "from mirror to window,"[172] the move from introspection and the consulting room into the real world at large, the city. But of course, thus subsumed under its opposite, *this* Küsnacht *ipso facto* is "Küsnacht" no more. It is the bollingenized city, the city absorbed into "Bollingen," the city seen romantically—mythically, imaginally, aesthetically, poetically, in terms of beauty and sensual

---

[171] Jung was very "impressed by the fact that the conclusion of *Faust* contains no conclusion[.]" (*MDR* p. 318). "[...] Faust's final rejuvenation takes place only in the post-mortal state, i.e., is projected into the future." *CW* 12 § 558. "It is an unconscious reality which in Faust's case was felt as being beyond his reach at the time, and for this reason it is separated from his real existence by death." *Letters 1*, p. 265 (to Anonymous, 22 March 1939).

[172] James Hillman, "From Mirror to Window. Curing Psychoanalysis of Its Narcissism," in: *Spring 49*, 1989, pp. 62–75.

THE END OF MEANING AND THE BIRTH OF MAN 279

certainty. It is no longer that city (the modern world *as* modern, *as* abstract and alienated, *as* devoid of Gods) in hard contradistinction to which Jung had erected his fantasy world out of stone at Bollingen as the bulwark against the banality and meaninglessness of "Küsnacht."

It is as if the naive puer who had been swallowed by Kronos (the position of Jung) now in turn decomposed the swallowing Kronos from within and absorbed him, so that only the swallowed puer remains. But this disintegration of Kronos is paradoxically the final victory of Kronos, who in this context is nothing else but the wish to retroactively prevent the birth that has already happened and to forever keep the puer in his naivety and secondary unbornness. If the swallowed children disintegrate and absorb that which swallowed them, then the swallowing has, to be sure, not been undone (this would have had to be their being disgorged again) but become invisible, obliterated and thereby immunized; it is no longer a special act, nor does it require a separated-off place ("inside"); furthermore, due to the incorporation, it has become the swallowed children's own attitude (similarly to how hostages of terrorists often take over their abductors' views in the sense of an "identification with the aggressor"). Kronos no longer needs to have a separate existence, he and his swallowing now fulfill themselves through his counterpart, his first victim: the swallowed puer, himself. Kronos' swallowing has been carried to its ultimate conclusion, has now become complete: absolute and eternalized. The swallowing has swallowed *itself*.[173]

Thus, by sublimating, evaporating the Jungian "Bollingen" (as a special literal place and a special intellectual *topos* in contradistinction to "Küsnacht"), archetypal psychology has turned the swallowing/unbornness into the logical character of the whole, into a "perspective," a "style" that, e.g., allows the modern "universe" in the sense of science to be seen *as* (as if it were) the "kósmos" of old,[174] the modern world at large *as* the world in little and in image, the real present *as* the once-more-come-true past, the world full of Gods. Archetypal psychology does not need to take the Gods ontologically and theologically as

---

[173] The swallowing completes itself via four stages (or moments), the swallowing (1) of the children, (2) of the child-parent relationship as a whole, (3) of (the children's) *birth* as such, (4) of the swallowing itself. The swallowing obliterates itself, becomes invisible. Thus a new seeming innocence (sensual directness) is artfully produced.

[174] James Hillman, "Cosmology for Soul. From Universe to Cosmos," in: *Sphinx 2*, 1989, pp. 17–33. For a detailed discussion of Hillman's paper see Chapter Four above.

Jung did; it takes them "psychologically," "metaphorically," "imaginally." The upward looking is correspondingly no longer a literal and subjective act and attitude; archetypal psychology itself *is* now the *sublated, distilled* upward looking, an upward looking which has receded from the level of behavior or psychic phenomenology into psychology's objective logical *form*. It is now, as it were, "institutionalized."

Although archetypal psychology moved from introspection and the consulting room out into the real world of the city, it did not truly get out into the open. What appears as a move out into real life, in truth is conversely a pulling in of all of reality. The world seen as image (image in this sense) is inside Kronos' stomach, secondarily unborn. It has all been taken prisoner for Kronos. Archetypal psychology is the logical *completion*, not a revision or reform / revolution, of the Jungian undertaking.

Archetypal psychology abolished Jung's distinction between the archetype in itself and the concrete archetypal image without getting rid of the archetypal altogether, just as it kept on talking about the Gods without wanting the Gods to be taken theologically. For this reason, the "image" in archetypal psychology is—as far as its self-interpretation is concerned—not like the image in *medial* modernity. The medial image has no archetypal depth to it, no Gods in it. It is plain show. The logical origin of the notion of image in archetypal psychology, by contrast, is (a) the reflection (interiorization) of Jung's "archetype in itself" into Jung's "archetypal image," so that the difference between them is canceled, and (b) the explosion of the "archetypal image" from its status of literal image as psychic event or phenomenon (image in the narrower sense or *symbol*, e.g., dream symbol), so that it now would be enabled to "swallow," and thus encompass, all the real phenomena and events out there. But of course, if seen through, archetypal psychology's "image," its "imaginal," its "metaphors" *are*, while seeming to be its opposite, in themselves the very "*impoverishment* of symbols" that Jung spoke about, the *celebration* of this impoverishment, and as such nevertheless an expression of medial modernity. What in the world of industry and economy and consumerism is the fetish of *Ware*, commodity (Marx), in archetypal psychology is "image."

THE END OF MEANING AND THE BIRTH OF MAN 281

Everything in the world has its archetypal depth and its God within itself. It is in itself image in this new sense: contained in "the imaginal." In-ness or unbornness now does not only have nothing outside itself, it has also incorporated the very idea of "external reality 'outside the window'" into itself and has thus brought it logically under its own control: in-ness has become absolute. This is what is reflected in archetypal psychology's notion of *beauty* (which is not literal beauty in opposition to the ugly, but the phenomena's absolutely unchallenged containment in the imaginal). "Beauty" here takes the place that "meaning" used to have for Jung. It is the successor concept of "meaning," its further determination, its sublimated, distilled, evaporated: *sublated* form.

Thus Hillman followed, just like Jung did in his own somewhat different way, the old neoplatonic impulse that attributed the higher (or even exclusive) reality to the universal idea and allowed the singular to be considered real only in a secondary sense, namely inasmuch as it participates in the truly real. In themselves the phenomena are *maya* (for Jung) or caught in literalism and part of the "fallen world" (for Hillman); they need to be compensated for by special experiences (dreams, archetypal *Urerfahrung*) in the one case and "returned to the Gods" (*epistrophê*) in the other.

Since in archetypal psychology the singular as such has its archetypal depth or its God within itself, no longer outside and above itself, the pressure upon the individual to conform to an external norm so characteristic of former (pre-modern) times is simply gone. As shown above by way of one example, homosexuality was formerly seen as perverse, as a violation of the *idea (concept)* and thus the *true reality* or *nature* of "man (male)" or "woman." People *had* to quite practically "return" their individual lives to this universal idea. In archetypal psychology, by contrast, each individual inclination or behavior, even if it is distorted, pathological or perverse, is in itself an archetypal image with its own beauty,[175] and to "return" it "to the Gods" means now to find the gods in whose mythology such pathological or perverse behavior occurs and who for that reason authorize it archetypally.

Here it is easy to see that two fundamental tenets of archetypal psychology follow directly from its basic move beyond Jung, from its

---

[175] For Hillman, beauty is, as I pointed out, not to be literalized!

exclusively settling in the "Bollingen" position and reflecting the archetypal into the now "aesthetic" image. These tenets are the polytheistic stance, which goes along with an emphasis on "eachness," and the idea that pathologizing *is* soul-making. Each individual *feature*, as distorted and pathological as it may be, is a phenomenon or image in its own right and with its own archetypal depth. As great as the difference of the empirical-practical consequences of this type of theory is to those that the former type of neoplatonic attitude had, the fundamental logic is structurally the same in both. It has only been a bit more sublimated, distilled.

Jung had needed to put his fantasy, because it was a counter-world to the real "utterly banal" world of his time, literally into stone[176] in order to give it solidity and conviction for himself as the immediate "present reality" that it was supposed to be. Having distilled and sublated the Jungian position, archetypal psychology no longer has this need. A "stone character" (here called "sensual certainty") comes for it from the real world "outside the window" (which as a whole has been absorbed into "the imaginal") as well as from the indisputable realness of each phenomenon, while the poetic or imaginal character of this world comes from the bollingenizing vision in which archetypal psychology cocoons what it takes note of or with which it coats it. Both aspects come together in archetypal psychology's particular theory of the "aesthetic."

* * *

There have been those who try to make Jungian and archetypal psychology appear as "post-modern." They don't see that both psychologies are, in slightly different ways, attempts to avoid modernity, to avoid having to unreservedly experience *transformation*, *initiation* into the modern form of consciousness.[177] To be more precise, both psychologies semantically indeed take note of modernity, while

---

[176] His tower and stone monuments at Bollingen. "Word and paper, however, did not seem real enough to me; something more was needed. I had to achieve a kind of representation in stone of my innermost thoughts [...]" *MDR* p. 223.

[177] And yet this is so obvious. Jung's unrelenting concern for the quest for meaning, his belief in archetypes as subsisting units of meaning, his theology, his idea of the individuation process with its confirmation of the subject, his commitment to "center," "self," mandalas, to "the circumambulation of the center," his insistence on direct experience (*Urerfahrung*) and thus immediate presence should dispel any doubts.

THE END OF MEANING AND THE BIRTH OF MAN

283

syntactically or logically they try to hold onto (or to secondarily recreate, i.e., simulate) a decidedly pre-modern level of consciousness. The dialectic of this split between the semantic and the syntactical, between the imaginal and the logical form, is that precisely with the very wish to rescue or simulate the old level of consciousness they syntactically are themselves very much subject to and exponents of modernity, whereas their semantics is the semantics and (sublated, semanticized) syntax of the past (their "myths," "gods," their Gnostic, alchemical, Renaissance models, their sense of meaning or, more distilled, of the "aesthetic").

CHAPTER TEN

The Soul as the Axis of the World[1]

I look upon the topic that I have been asked to discuss today as a *thesis*, a radical, revolutionary thesis. For millennia, the axis of the world had been conceived, e.g., as a tree, the World Tree at the center of the earth, rooted in the underworld and extending into heaven. Or, during the last two thousand years in the Western world, it had been known to be Christ, the Son of God, the Redeemer of mankind, and the alpha and omega. And now all of a sudden it is "the soul" that is declared to be the axis of the world. Truly, the thesis which substitutes the soul for the World Tree or for Christ amounts to a radical shift, in fact a revolutionary deed! It will be the task of the following reflections to explore and examine this shocking thesis. Is it legitimate, does it ring true? What made this shift possible and necessary? How is this idea to be understood, that is to say, what is the precise meaning of "the soul as the axis of the world," or better: what does the meaning of this phrase have to be if it is to make sense?

Before we can turn to this task, it will, however, be necessary to make ourselves consciously aware of the dangers given with this idea, so as to be better able to avoid them. We have to contemplate what

---

[1] Invited opening lecture at the XIII Simpósio International da Associação Junguiana do Brasil, Canela, Rio Grande do Sul, Brasil, November 2005 on the general theme of "A psyche é o eixo do mundo."

the effects of such an idea might be on the consciousness that entertains it. What can it do to us? I see above all three dangers. First, there is the danger of inflation. Especially if we keep in mind that the idea of the soul as *axis mundi* comes in some way as the modern successor notion to Christ as the *axis mundi*, we can realize how easy it could be that this idea goes to the heads of us psychologists, such as when Jung declares the psyche to be "the world's pivot" (*CW* 8 § 423). The soul could appear as the most important reality, as the Absolute, and inasmuch as we might view ourselves as the experts, attendants, and servants of the soul, we and our field, psychology, might get a blown-up sense of importance, too. In view of this danger it is helpful to remember that psychology (and by psychology I always mean "psychology *with* soul") is a *quantité negligeable* and has only a niche existence in our world. It is no more than a peripheral phenomenon and by no means the heart and center of real life. It is of personal importance only to a tiny proportion of the world population and has no real significance for what is really going on in the world—in politics, in economic life, in the entertainment sector. It has the character of a private luxury in an affluent society rather than a necessary staple. During the 20th century, which in some way was *the* century of psychology, it was still easy to place great utopian hopes on psychology, such as the epistemological hope that psychology could be a super-science, a science of all the sciences, and the therapeutic hope that it could be the rescue of the world or at least bring about the healing of the modern predicament. But now that we have gone through a period of "Freud bashing" and of the decay of Jungian psychology to pop psychology and a New Age ideology, now that we have left the phase of industrial modernity behind and entered the phase of "medial" modernity (the age of TV, mobile phones, game-boys, information and communication), we know that the "century of psychology" is over and are thus in a better position to see through the inflation and delusion that prevailed in those utopian hopes.

The second, related danger is that of a psychological totalitarianism. The idea of the *axis mundi* is by definition the idea of a center, and inasmuch as the center rules over the entire sphere of which it is the center, we might be seduced into believing that psychology could indeed claim the whole of the world, the All, for itself. What the first danger was in a subjective emotional sense (all-

THE SOUL AS THE AXIS OF THE WORLD

importance), this second danger is in a formal, quantitative sense (all-comprehensive scope of jurisdiction).

Let me note here in passing that paradoxically both the sense of all-importance and of all-comprehensiveness are legitimate, even indispensable, attributes of "the soul." What turns them into the dangers described is only that, and if, they are taken personally and are thus proudly experienced externally, positively, or literalistically as properties of *our* field, psychology. By contrast, as qualities of "the soul" they are what they are only as logically negative, "sublated" (*aufgehoben* in Hegel's sense) qualities, qualities that have been interiorized absolute-negatively into the soul. In the imaginal language of alchemy, they are qualities existing only *in Mercurio*, not in empirical-factual reality.

These two dangers are apt to remind us of the necessity for psychological consciousness to come down to earth from what Jung called cloud-cuckoo-land and to conceive of psychology as having quite modest goals, concrete, earthly, pragmatic goals. All that psychology can do and is supposed to do is to accompany in feeling and thought the actual movement of "the soul" or the mercurial spirit in the course of events and to try to make sense of it, thereby freeing the soul or spirit from its imprisonment in the opaqueness or occludedness of the factual.

The third danger is of a rather different nature. By harking back to an ancient mythological and thus imaginal idea and by inevitably evoking the notion of "the world out there," the idea of the soul as the *axis mundi* might invite us to fall for the temptation to indulge in a kind of metaphysical world view. But as psychologists, we have to be wary of not catering to our own or the public's ideological needs, in other words, ego needs. This is all the more important because a "world view," *Weltanschauung*, as the picture of the "world out there," inevitably involves us in externality, in the world as an object given to a subject, and thereby makes us lose the very soul that according to our present thesis is supposed to be the axis of the world. Psychology is the discipline of interiority. It cannot afford the luxury of thinking about its subject-matters in terms of external objects. Whatever is supposed to be a topic of psychology has to have been placed, so to speak, into an alchemical retort and hermetically sealed within it, the hermetic seal indicating the absolute exclusion of externality. The hermetic vessel is (the image for) interiority pure and simple, i.e., interiority *without* the idea of anything around and outside of it.[2]

What we therefore have to be wary of here is ulterior motives and strategic interests that might creep in by possibly being that which unwittingly "fires" our interest in the idea of "the soul as the axis of the world." Psychology is only possible as *inhibited* desire, *negated*, *sublated* interest. Even such a beautiful desire as that for an ensouled world is, I am sorry to say, unpsychological, because *as* desire it ties us to and confirms our naturalness and the natural (i.e., naturalistically perceived) world, and *ipso facto* prevents psychology as the *opus contra naturam*. From the outset, psychology has to take place in the negativity of the soul, or in what mythology imagined as "the underworld," in which, as you know, the blood-soul, the *thymós*, and thus the affects, emotions, passions, the libidinal desires had no place. The question, therefore, is not whether *what* is desired is soulful or soulless; no, the naturalness which is the nature of desiring as such is the problem.

After these cautions we are ready to begin with our examination of the idea of the soul as the axis of the world. The first thing we have to realize is that we have inherited the idea of the world axis from very ancient mythological thought and transferred it to our modern concept of psyche or soul. It is not an idea that originated on the ground of modern psychology itself. In order to understand *what* it is that we now attribute to the soul (rather than using this idea mindlessly as a cliché), it will be necessary to explore what the ancient mythological idea of the *axis mundi* psychologically entails and involves.

The mythological axis

The axis of the world is an idea known to virtually all cultures on earth and had many different imaginal forms. The most important and obvious, explicit form was that of a tree, the World Tree, in Germanic mythology an ash tree named Yggdrasil, in Slavic cultures often an oak tree. Sometimes it is also simply a column. Another form was that of a giant or culture hero who forever had to carry the vault of heaven on his shoulders, the most familiar example for us being the

---

[2] On this type of interiority see especially my "Closure and Setting Free or: The Bottled Spirit of Alchemy and Psychology," in: *Spring Journal 74* (Alchemy), Spring 2006, pp. 31–62.

THE SOUL AS THE AXIS OF THE WORLD

Greek Atlas. But the axis could also be imagined as a ladder or rope connecting heaven and earth, or even as only a *virtual* axis that went through particular places that marked the center of the earth, such as through the *omphalos* (navel) of the earth at Delphi. Common is also the idea that a particular sacred mountain rises from the earth to heaven and in this way represents the axis of the world. Examples are Mount Meru in Hindu mythology, Mount Kailash in Tibet, and Mount Olympus in ancient Greece.

One significant difference between these various conceptions is that the World Tree, or the ladder connecting heaven and the earth, or the giant holding up the vault of heaven exist only in the imagination, while, e.g., Mount Kailash or Mount Olympus are visible places in geographic reality. This takes me to a third way the *axis mundi* can appear, namely diverse man-made objects representing the world axis; I mention only the stupa of Hinduism reflecting Mount Meru, or the three-step temple mountains and pyramids, the staff or scepter to be found in many cultures, the totem poles among Native Americans, and the maypoles in Europe. In all these latter cases, we have attempts at a tangible representation and symbolization of the actually irrepresentable axis of the world. It is this irrepresentable imagination of an axis that we have to direct our attention to because it is the underlying idea that provides the basis and matrix for all the other forms.

VERTICALITY

The first feature of the mythological idea of an *axis mundi* is that it introduces a sense of verticality. What is most important here for us to understand is that this verticality is not plain, empirical verticality, but psychological verticality. *Verticalitas nostra non est verticalitas vulgi*, we might say, adapting an adage of the alchemists. It is to be assumed that many smaller land animals like mice or rabbits that live in fear of birds of prey above them have a clear sense of verticality, just as a dog has who experiences how an animal that he chased escaped up a tree that the dog cannot climb. But the horizontal orientation and this ordinary sense of verticality, too, remain *both* within the whole sphere of *psychological horizontality*, that is to say, within the sphere of the earthly instinctual drives and interests in self-preservation and well-being, the sphere of positivity.

By contrast, the notion of the axis of the world does not refer to an empirical fact. It is logically negative. To mimic the form of a statement by Heraclitus: Even by traveling along every path on earth you could never find the World Tree. It does not exist in the realm of positivity, but is fictional, that is to say, something that exists exclusively in the imagination, in the soul. But this fictional axis of the world is the center pole on which the world as such rests and on which it stands or falls!

Precisely because it is not positively real, the notion of the axis of the world bears witness to the fact that through a logical revolution man had *contra naturam* burst open his being enclosed in this realm of horizontality and established the positively nonexistent, logically negative dimension of verticality, and that he "then" had psychologically once and for all taken his home in this nonexistent sphere. It is precisely by basing human existence on and establishing it in something that does *not* positively exist that it was possible to break psychologically or logically out of the merely-empirical, factual world to which man as animal belonged and as organism continues to belong. Through this opening up of a totally new dimension of existence and settling therein, the animal named *homo sapiens* became a human being. What happened here is as revolutionary, incredible, indeed impossible as would be the breakthrough of a two-dimensional being through the two-dimensionality of the plane into the third dimension of verticality. *From the point of view* of the logic of the myth of the World Tree, animals are, as it were, "two-dimensional" beings and all animal and plant life takes place on the "two-dimensional plane" of positive-factual existence, for which, conversely, that verticality about which the myth of the World Tree speaks is simply nonexistent.

The World Tree image, despite the fact that, as an image of a living organism which grows and ages with time, it includes some sort of movement, is nevertheless a basically static, stationary image, as is also the image of Atlas who carries the vault of heaven, or even more so that of a world axis in the shape of a column. But as such they all are nothing else but the congealed or frozen image of what is actually a revolutionary deed, a logical act or movement. Mythology makes this deed or act character explicit, too, however in a separate mythologem, that of the separation of the World Parents Heaven and Earth by one of their sons. The brutal separation of the copulating World Parents

THE SOUL AS THE AXIS OF THE WORLD

through the castration of Father Heaven and his being stemmed up into the heights amounts to the creation of an open space, a clearance (*Lichtung* in the sense of Heidegger). As such it is the creation of the dimension of what a later postmythological (philosophical) age would comprehend as mind or soul or consciousness, while mythology qua mythology precisely had to imagine it out there in spatial terms as a natural "nothingness" in the cosmos. This stemming up is also the image for man's psychological rousing and erecting himself to an upright carriage. In retrospect we can see that myth in general is the articulation of the inner logic of human existence *as an existence in consciousness*, however an articulation in alienated form, "projected" out in physical images. At the time when the notion of the mind or, even later, the notion of consciousness could be conceived, that which myth had to imagine out there in nature had come home to human thought a little more.

Just as the images of the World Tree, World Column, and Atlas *are* in themselves the (more or less) immobilized, stationary images of a highly dynamic act of separation, so the mythologem of the violent disruption of the eternal *gamos* (marriage) of the World Parents and the lifting up of Father Heaven *is* that version of the static World Tree image that displays its inner nature of dynamic act. The two versions are representations of the same mythic idea or truth, but from different angles. It is not that they are two separate myths, the one telling about a one-time *event* or *deed* that once, way back in the primordial beginning of time, had happened, whereas the other one describes a permanent cosmological condition of the present cosmos as the result of that former event. No, what seen from outside is the static distance of Heaven and Earth is in itself a revolutionary act and activity. The cosmo*logical* state is in itself cosmo*gonic*.

Conversely, the violent disruption of the embrace of Heaven and Earth is not really a literal positive-factual *event* at all. Like all mythic "events" it never happened, but always *is* (Salustios), in other words, it is the permanently ongoing inner logical truth of the image of the World Tree. Because both the eternal *gamos* of the World Parents and the violent disruption of this *gamos* are mythic stories, we must not conceive of them as we would of events or conditions in empirical reality. In terms of empirical reality, the violent tearing apart of the copulating Heaven and Earth and the castration of Father Heaven

292 THE SOUL ALWAYS THINKS

would mean that the *gamos* is once and for all ended. This deed would have been the cause of a lasting effect, of a radical change. But mythic events do not happen in time, and so there is no change. Rather, both the separation through castration and the eternal embrace are, as Salustios said, *always*, which means that they are simultaneously true, which is of course contradictory. There is really an unrelenting disruption of the *gamos*—and yet this *gamos* also continues undisturbed. No sequence, no before and after: not first a condition of total union of Heaven and Earth, then the ruthless deed of the culture hero with his sickle, with the result of the new condition of an open space separating once and for all the bodies of the World Parents. There was never a time before the separation and thus also no time after it, because, as we said, this deed itself never happened, but always *is*.

To reconcile the notion of a sudden violent deed with the notion that it is permanently ongoing we have to comprehend it as an action that never took place but "always already" *has* happened. This event had at no time been a present. Rather, at all times it has its place in the perfect tense. At all times it is already over. As such the story of the disruption of the *gamos* does not tell us how, through what event consciousness, the mind and soul, was caused and came about, but what consciousness *is*, what internally constitutes it. It spells out the logic of consciousness, albeit in imaginal form. Consciousness is that present that is what it is in that it within itself posits this deed as already having happened. And by firmly basing itself on this position it establishes itself as consciousness. Consciousness *exists as* the "impertinent" assertion of "always already having the conquest of verticality behind itself." The cosmogonic displays the *logical* or *negative* or *actuose* nature of the cosmological state of the world—the structure (better: logic) of consciousness.

Mind, soul, consciousness are thus not natural facts but essentially *performative* or, to say it with the already employed medieval philosophical term, *actuose*.[3] They exist *as* one's actively holding oneself in that counter-natural condition of having the logical act of the

---

[3] On the basis of the Biblical designation of God as "the living God," the medieval theologians comprehended the true nature of God as *vita* (life) and this *vita* as *actuositas*. God is not (statically) an entity who is alive, but he *is* life. Whatever cannot be thought in terms of a thing-like substrate, but needs to be thought as ongoing performance or enactment is "actuose."

THE SOUL AS THE AXIS OF THE WORLD

separation of the World Parents behind oneself; as one's relentlessly basing oneself on the presupposition of this deed as an accomplished fact, as a truth, although one knows full well that it never happened in a positive-factual sense. Consciousness exists as the "crazy" venture (a logical, not behavioral venture) of unconditionally using as one's *foundation* something that does not positively exist, but is built in the air. It of course has to be this way, for how else if not by, as it were, clutching at thin air could something as unlikely as consciousness come about? How else could it be, so to speak, the two-dimensional being's real breakthrough through the two-dimensional plane? As long as any solid positive fact would be taken as the true basis of human existence, the human being would stay the animal that he is, too, and would be confined to the "two-dimensionality" of the natural and physical.

The performative nature or actuosity of consciousness, too, is displayed in a special image, namely in the figure of Atlas who has to ceaselessly hold up the vault of heaven. The moment he would tire and stop, mind, soul and consciousness would cease to exist, too, reverting to the material or physical world, the world of positivity, which would take over again, much like the moment when ancient Maya cities were deserted, then the primal forest took over again.

In the myth of the separation of the World Parents as well as of the World Tree, mythological man unwittingly articulated, confirmed, and celebrated the fact that he existed, not in the biological body and in the positivity of the physical world of things, but in the negativity of mind and soul. And in the image of Atlas mythological man clearly represented to himself his implicit knowledge that consciousness is not a natural or ontological state, but a constant effort and achievement *contra naturam*, though of course an effort not on the level of empirical-practical behavior, but in the psychological background, that is to say on the level of the logic of the soul. As this effort or performance, consciousness is a bit like fire which exists only as the process of burning and for as long as it burns. Mythological man had physical reality, including his own physical body, *in* the mind or soul, namely as his own conceptions, images, and notions of things natural. The mythic images mentioned served the purpose of time and again assuring him of his wholly other place of existence and of his counter-natural nature as a fundamentally upward-looking being—upward-looking of course

294 *THE SOUL ALWAYS THINKS*

in the sense of psychological or logical verticality, not of literal, *spatial* verticality: as a being with a heaven. Here it is interesting to note that there was no word for "world" or "universe" in early Greek. The word *kósmos* for the All came up only during the 5th century B.C. Before that the early thinkers used the word *ouranós* (sky, heaven) instead. In a similar way we still use the Latin expression "*toto coelo* different," different by a whole sky or heaven, i.e., by a world, by a whole universe.

I discussed the simultaneity of the two contradictory ideas of the eternal embrace of Heaven and Earth and of their being separated by the World Tree or World Pole or by a figure like Atlas holding up the vault of heaven. But now we have to gain the additional insight that the idea of the world axis embodied in the aforementioned images in itself expresses both aspects, union and separation, oneness and distance. The world axis at once holds Heaven and Earth apart *and* connects them. As axis it is of course also a *ligamentum, vinculum, copula*. So the world axis has to be comprehended as the *imaginal* form of the notion of the unity of union and separation. It is in itself dialectical. In Goethe's *Faust* Faust in the very beginning has a vision of the macrocosm, where he sees enthusiastically how celestial forces rise and descend and pass on to each other golden buckets, and pervade the All from heaven to earth. This poetic description adds a sense of movement to the static image of the axis. As the self-contradictory unity of unity and distance the axis is the frozen image of what seen from within is the simultaneity, the pulsating life, indeed the identity, of two opposite movements up and down, joining and dissevering.

CENTER

After my discussion of the first feature of the *axis mundi*, the sense of verticality, I turn to the second feature, the axis as the idea of a center. During the years between 1951 and 1967, when Hungary was still under a communist regime, Hungarian ethnographers did ethnographic field research in a Hungarian peasant village by the name of Átányi, which is only 120 km from the capital of Hungary. The researchers were told by inhabitants that as schoolboys they often loitered around the village, "went to the church and talked as follows: We know that Hungary is in the center of the world. Átányi is in the center of Hungary, the church is standing in the very center of the

THE SOUL AS THE AXIS OF THE WORLD

village. Thus we stand in the center of the world. They observed that the sky is highest above the Átányi church, sloping in a circle all around: this must in fact be the center of the world!"[4] For the boys, the church steeple pointing to the sky visibly marked the *axis mundi*. But it was not only the schoolboys who thought that way. The idea of the church of Átányi being the center of the world was prevalent throughout the community. There even was a local song celebrating this idea. The amazing thing for us is that here we find an archaic mythic idea as a living fossil during the second half of the 20th century in a European village that had not only been subject to communist indoctrination, but whose inhabitants read books and newspapers and had severally as soldiers been in foreign countries during two World Wars.

But what is more important for us is the fact that the villagers knew full well that the neighboring villages each held the same idea about their own church and village, that this was, however, merely jokingly noted and did not have the power to change their deeper conviction. Empirical observation would certainly also have shown them that the sky seems highest *wherever* they stand. The same was true in antiquity. The Greeks had their center or navel of the earth in Delphi, but in each major temple there was also the center of the earth and it contained, as a sign thereof, a stone navel. In other words, *the* center of the world was simultaneously in many places, and whereas for us the plural of centers would either destroy the very idea of there being a center or destroy the unity of the world, for the mythologically experiencing mind the empirical fact that *the* center of the earth occurred in the plural left the idea of center intact. It is similar to how other mythological ideas had simultaneously mutually excluding answers, e.g., that the underworld was located far away in the outermost West as well as underneath one's feet.

We can conclude from this that for the mythological mind the axis of the world was not an empirical reality, not a positive fact. No villager of Átány, no ancient Greek would have believed that the same empirical object, say one's hammer or plough, could simultaneously be in several places. But what was true for the things in the sphere of positivity was not true for something like the *axis mundi*. The latter

---

[4] Edit Fél and Tamás Hofer, *Proper Peasants. Traditional Life in a Hungarian Village,* Chicago (Aldine Publishing Company) 1969, p. 17.

belonged to a different order of reality. It was a priori immune to the laws prevailing in the ordinary everyday reality of things. If we restrict Lévy-Bruhl's much disputed intuition about a prelogical mentality of the primitives to the sphere of mythological objects and topics rather than understanding it anthropologically as a lack of the intellectual capacity on the part of those *peoples* to think logically, in other words, if we comprehend it as a thesis about an *objective quality* of the contents of myth themselves and not about a subjective deficiency, we see that there is a lot to be said for this intuition.

At any rate, if the fact that the inhabitants of the neighboring villages can with the same right as the inhabitants of Átányi claim that their church steeple is the center of the world and that this observation does not invalidate, indeed, *not even compete with* the latter's notion, we see that the *axis mundi* concept must be part of a reality *sui generis* over against the things of the empirical world. This is what makes it independent of rational objections and conflicts with observed empirical data. Because it does not have its place in the ordinary phenomenal world, it does not compete for being true with observations in the everyday world and with common-sense reasoning, and therefore it is not affected by them either. Thus we must conclude that it receives its authority, its conviction, its truth from some other source than experience in external reality. The question is from where? We might be quick to say, from the soul or from the unconscious. But this information would amount to no more than two words that tell us nothing; they merely cover over and hypostatize the void of our not knowing. We have to find a different approach.

INTERIORITY

What we found so far as centers of the earth was always at a fixed location: this village church, the sanctuary of Delphi, various temples. But now we have to add a different whole set of centers to our list, namely *essentially* temporary centers. In the mythological world, whenever a ritual was performed, the place where it was performed *ipso facto* turned into a center, into *the* center of the world. A ritual could only *be* a ritual and be effective if it was performed from out of the true center of being, both in the spatial sense (the place of the *axis mundi*) and in a temporal sense (the origin of the world). Now

THE SOUL AS THE AXIS OF THE WORLD

the interesting point is that in order to perform a ritual you did not necessarily have to go to a given place already known and marked by tradition to be the center of the world. The performance of a ritual did not have to rely on an already existing center. In many cases it was the other way around: the performance of the ritual that you performed originally *established* the center *ad hoc*. The spot where the ritual was performed turned, for the duration of the ritual and by virtue of its power, into the spot where the *axis mundi* both penetrated the ground below and rose to heaven.

So the mythological and ritualistic idea of the center of the world was not one of a literal center in the geographical sense, a priori not a center in terms of external reality. To use a post-mythological expression: this center was a "metaphysical" reality. It was originally produced in and as the depth and interiority of the here and now of the ritual that was in fact performed. It both was the result of the interiorizing movement constitutive of rituals and stayed confined within this *ad hoc* movement as the latter's property. We might of course be tempted to say that the factor that brings forth the idea of the axis of the world and performs rituals in the first place is the soul. But rather than in this way hypostatizing the soul as a factor behind the scene, I suggest the reverse: the ritual act that through itself establishes a center, i.e., the movement into the depth and interiority of a here and now, is in itself what we mean by "soul." The soul is not a something, a substance or entity[5] or a subject that would perform such movements. *This interiorizing movement itself with nothing behind it*, this type of logical life, *is all there is*; it is the only reality, but where it in fact occurs, there, we can say, "soul" is happening. "Soul" is merely a name we give to this real movement and event.

We have to go a little deeper with the idea that a ritual creates the center of the world. In the literature by scholars of religion one can often read that the performance of a ritual is a reenactment and repetition of a primordial deed performed *in illo tempore* by a god or mythic culture hero. While it is not wrong to say this, the understanding that we are apt to give to the notion of reenactment and repetition is in my estimation wrong; it does not do justice to the

---

[5] I disagree with Jung when he stated: "I firmly believe however that psyche is an οὐσία." *Letters 1*, p. 540, to Victor White, 31 December 1949.

logic of myth and ritual. When we think in terms of reenactment and repetition, we tacitly operate with our own world relation and our own post-mythological sense of time. But what we have to realize is that during the ages of myth the logic of time and world was an entirely different one. The primordial origin was not really in the past, in our historical sense of past. The world of myth and ritual is a world that does not yet have, nor operate with, a notion of the past. The origin is only in the present, as its own *depth*. This is why we have to turn the sequence around. The origin of the world comes into being only through, and *during the occurrence* of, the celebration of a ritual. The primordial deed exists exclusively in and by virtue of each present ritual. The ritual itself, *each time it is performed*, creates "for the first time" that which it is said to "repeat." There has never been that primordial deed performed by a god or culture hero in the literal past that could be literally repeated by the priests performing the present ritual.

The logical constitution of that consciousness that was informed by myth and ritual did not, like we do, *presuppose* the world as a finished positive fact and a fixed given. The world was not a decidedly external reality opposite to an epistemological subject, a reality that therefore would have needed to be *explained* and adapted to. The ritualistic mind qua ritualistic, rather than having the world vis-à-vis itself, is still truly within the world and thus logically at a place where the world is originally or primordially in the status of becoming or being created, or conversely, the world has not yet been released from its containment within the interiority of human experience into an *objective* factual existence prior to and independent of whether it is experienced or not. It has not been *released* from "the soul" into positivity.

So the logic of ritual is that it *within itself* creates that which it imitates and reenacts. It creates within itself that very center of the world as the metaphysical locus for its occurrence that it needs in order to *be* a true ritual in the first place. In other words, it creates within itself the very condition of its own possibility! It within itself creates the primordial origin as its own internal standard and measure for how it is presently to be performed. That which is said to be a primordial act *in illo tempore* has its own origin and *illud tempus* in the inner depth of the present of a performed ritual that is nothing else but the

THE SOUL AS THE AXIS OF THE WORLD

repetition of this primordial act first created by this repetition. Such is the dialectic of true rituals. If it were otherwise, if they simply repeated an event really *external* to themselves, rituals would indeed be no more than as what Jung felt the first Communion he had experienced to be, namely nothing but "a wretched *memorial* service with [...] flat bread and [...] sour wine" (*MDR* p. 55, my italics). "I [...] had expected something—I knew not what—to happen, and nothing at all had happened" (p. 54). "It had proved hollow; more than that, it had proved to be a total loss" (p. 55). It did not have that effect that alone would have proven that it had been a ritual in the first place. Obviously, it had degenerated into a merely formalistic reenactment, which in turn shows that it had not taken place at the center and origin of the world at all, but was a behavior that originated and stayed in external, positive-factual reality.

The dialectic of a reenactment (in the true ritualistic sense of the word) is that you have to have interiorized into the present ritual act the god's primordial deed of which this ritual is supposed to be a reenactment and you have to have logically interiorized the god himself into yourself. The ritual has everything it needs within itself, even its own primordial origin, even the god who performed the ritual deed "for the first time." A ritual has self nature. It stands or falls with its capacity to establish a fulfilled present. And a fulfilled present is one that has the center and origin[6] of the world within itself. There cannot be a fulfilled present, and thus also no ritual, for a psychological condition for which the origin and center is outside, in the historically perceived past, in empirical reality out there or in a beyond.

After this lengthy discussion we understand what the source of the authority and truth of the mythic idea of the center of the world is and that it can in no way be dependent on experience in external reality and on rational reasoning. The source of authority is the self nature of the center of the world. It is the logic of interiority. It is the fact that the mythic center of the world is within. Within what? Personalistic psychology would answer here: within the psyche, within us, within our inner. But this would be a naive positivization and reification of the "within." The mythic center of the world is within *itself.* Only as such can it *be* center of the world in the first place. The

---

[6] And of course the *finis* or *télos* of the world, too.

true center cannot have the spot at which it is located outside itself, because then this place would itself be ec-centric. The center must also be the center for its own location and not the other way around. It is this logic of self or interiority that makes the mythic idea of the center unassailable for any empirical objections.

THE MODERN AXIS

Having familiarized ourselves with what the mythic idea of the *axis mundi* as the sense of verticality and center involves, we have to note that we moderns are totally removed from it. It has become impossible for us to seriously believe in a World Tree or Atlas and a center of the world. The more spiritualized successor notion of the world axis, Christ as Mediator between Heaven and Earth, and more specifically the vertical bar of the Cross, have lost their conviction for modernity at large, notwithstanding the fact that individuals in their private subjectivity may still be believers. What is even more significant is that

(1) the idea of heaven and the distinction between a sublunar and a superlunar sphere have completely disappeared. We are convinced of the basic uniformity of the universe. Human identity as a logically upward-looking being has been replaced by the positivistic exploration of outer space. The sense of verticality is absolutely gone; modern thinking is decidedly horizontal and a *serial* thinking (whereas formerly thought knew itself to be based on a Ground). The neurosciences even try to reduce the mind and consciousness itself to nothing but chemistry and brain events.

(2) We live irrevocably in an *external* reality defined as positive fact. We have the world as object vis-à-vis ourselves as subjects. The world for us is literally our "environment." For us there is fundamentally a historical past that precedes the present and thus is essentially outside of it. We do not understand ourselves as selves, but know to have our origin millions of years back in biological evolution.

(3) Both modern thought and social reality have done away with the idea of center altogether. Any word ending in "-centrism" has become a dirty word. What is celebrated today is dissemination, difference, différance, dispersion, multitasking, multiplicity, (so-called) polytheism, multiculturalism. Modern logic, both as the special

THE SOUL AS THE AXIS OF THE WORLD

philosophical discipline and as the actual *spiritus rector* of modern thought, has even gotten rid of the copula, a world-shaking change.

We would be fooling ourselves if we pretended that all these ideas are merely subjective opinions or scientific theories, hypotheses that psychologically could be simply brushed aside. No, regardless of what we subjectively feel and think, the things I pointed to are symptoms that show our psychological *reality*, show where we objectively stand today psychologically. There is no way back.

In this situation we are faced with the thesis expressed by the topic of this symposium: "the soul as the axis of the world." Now that we collectively do no longer believe, and cannot possibly believe, in the World Tree, in Atlas, in Christ, should it be possible to simply raise the psyche to the vacant throne of the *axis mundi*? Under what conditions and in which way would this make sense, could it ring true—rather than being an empty ego assertion, a case of wishful thinking, an escape into ideology? These are the enormous questions that we are faced with here. We cannot simply follow Jung's externalizing (undialectical) conception of a hypostatized, reified psyche as "the world's pivot" (*CW* 8 § 423) *opposite* to the world ("a disturber of the natural-laws-governed cosmos," ibid. § 422, transl. modified), as much as I concede that "the soul" is *contra naturam.*

We also have to realize that there are two much more likely candidates for the idea of the present-day axis of the world: money + the media. We witness today the gigantic translation of everything in the world into the terms of money. We are only at the beginning of this revolutionary process. Money has of course always been an important power. That "money makes the world go round" or *Geld regiert die Welt* is proverbial. But in the past, it exerted its power only innocently via people's subjective love of it, their *natural* greed as well as need for it. In this case the real axis was not money at all, but human desire, human nature. Today, however, money has become emancipated from nature, from human wishes and decisions and is on the way to becoming absolute. In the present stage of advanced, unrestrained capitalism it has acquired an inner necessity and dynamic all of its own and has become self-serving, self-contained, an end in itself. Formerly only people wanted more money. But today it is money itself that demands to become more, and ever more, for its own sake, for no other purpose than multiplying *itself.* It is true, people, too, are still personally craving for money and in need of money; they sometimes even let themselves be bribed or sell themselves, or commit crimes, as in olden times, too. But this is trivial, part of human frailty, I might almost want to say, kid's stuff. In its most advanced form, money ruthlessly dictates what has to happen, without the least concern for what it means for people, for what people think and wish. It is not persons (the evil capitalists, the global players at the stock exchanges, the directors of hedge funds, the CEOs) who are to be blamed. It is the other way around: they are, as the last term spells out, no more than the chief *executive officers*, the officiating servants who have to do Money's bidding. Even the subjective wish of and pressure exerted by the shareholders that the value of their stock increases is in the service of Money and not the other way around.

In Philippians 2:9ff. Paul writes, "Wherefore God also hath highly exalted [Jesus Christ], and given him a name which is above every name: / [So] That at the name of Jesus every knee should bow [...]; / And that every tongue should confess that Jesus Christ is Lord [...]." Are we today not witnessing a process where this statement could *mutatis mutandis* be made about Money? No matter whether we subjectively understand and accept it or no—private individuals, whole companies, the work force in companies, and even whole nations are *objectively* forced to bow their knees at the name of Money. Even things, animals, the trees of the rain forest, values, ideals have to experience their sublation as substances in their own right and with a dignity of their own and find themselves reduced to their naked worth in money—money not in the substantial, thing-like sense of gold, not even of paper money, but as totally abstract, impersonal, imageless, irrepresentable value per se, as a mere number, quantity per se, i.e., money as the pure concept of itself, money distilled, sublimated, having *in fact* become the logic of itself, money fully interiorized into its notion. Money has finally come home to itself, after two and a half millennia of having been in the alienated, ec-centric, reduced status of a mere *means* to subjective human ends. Now, money has become its own center. Now the proverbial "money makes the world go round" has finally come true.

Similarly, The Media (including the whole modern sphere of communication and entertainment) today have emancipated themselves from their former status of means to the end of transporting

THE SOUL AS THE AXIS OF THE WORLD

contents and have become "self-important," self-centered, an end in themselves, all contents having been reduced to mere occasions for The Media to come into action. *They* determine politics, our perception of reality, the topics of discussion, our desires. "The Media" have become the message (to adapt a dictum by Marshall McLuhan). Both the modern form of Money and that of The Media amount to the real end of the metaphysics of substance and the translation of anything substantial, semantic, natural into the near-absoluteness of logical form, syntax, logical movement, "spirit." Both are the Same, although not alike.

SOUL

And yet I think that even in view of the sheer overwhelming power of [Money-and-The Media] as the new true Lord and Mediator of the world, the true new *axis mundi* that makes the world go round, a case can be made for the soul as the axis of the world. This requires two steps. First we have to experience what happens when "the soul" is inserted into the statement about the *axis mundi*. All three concepts (axis, soul, world) must be exposed to each other and allowed to affect, transmute, indeed revolutionize each other. Secondly, we have to draw the consequences of both our insights about [Money-and-The Media] and the results of the first step. I begin with the first step.

The axis, having become the soul, suffers itself a psychization or spiritualization. It can no longer be imagined in ontological, substantial, and spatial terms as a literal axis, as a tree, pole, ladder, or giant. The substantiality and material nature of those imagined axes has become alchemically dissolved and evaporated, so that the new "axis" takes on the meaning of the inner *spiritus rector* of what is, the meaning of what the alchemists would have called the mercurial spirit in all reality, and what we today in our language have to call the logic or syntax of the world.

The soul, assigned to the world, ceases to be the soul in the sense of personalistic psychology that concentrates on the *opus parvum*, on the development of the individual, on one's self, one's individuation (in Jung's sense). It bursts open its imprisonment inside the human being, where it would be seen as the sum-total of our private feelings, ideas, affects, desires, dreams and visions, and instead becomes public, objective, itself taking on a *world* character. Its true home and "place of operation," if I may say so, is now understood to be the world at large and not just the consulting room. As the *axis mundi* it is no longer reduced to Erich Neumann's ego-self axis. It now can be recognized as the *opus magnum*, as the soul of what is really going on in reality all around us, in the major processes of the economy, technology, science, the arts, etc.

And the world itself? The concept of it, too, becomes psychized, distilled, that is to say, the world loses the hard-core positive-factualness attributed to it in our naive imagination, where it is *hypostatized* as natural (physical) existence, as an absolute given, as the universe that independent of our mind and our thinking *is* the way it is. Now, by contrast, the world itself can be seen through as "world pictures," as models of the mind, as *text* to be read and interpreted.

We see how by placing the notions of soul, axis, and world into one sentence something starts to move, the concepts come to life and interact with each other, the fixed meanings that each of them may have seemed to have are brought into a fluid state.

Now I come to my second step. Whereas Jung in 1934 felt the need to warn against "the allurements of the exotic fragrance" of the East and instead urged that we "dwell with our own situation, where, in the cold light of consciousness, the blank barrenness of the world reaches to the very stars" (*CW* 9i § 29, transl. modif.), it may be much more necessary in Jungian psychology today to warn against the allurements of nostalgic, nebulous ideas about a romanticized *anima mundi*. If the soul is the axis of the world, we are bound to look for it in what is really going on in the world and refuse to entertain an idea of a "nicer" free-floating soul cut off from and in opposition to the real world, which then in turn is easily seen as the Fallen World. But there is only one world, and it is in itself the unity and tension of its perfection and its "fallenness." We must not, in Manichean style, dissociate into two what is a single dialectic and play the one moment against the other. The spirit Mercurius is *in* the matter—even precisely in the "stinking matter," and thus that soul which is conceived as the *axis mundi* can also only be sought in today's concrete reality the way it happens to be. We cannot start out with a preconceived ego idea of what "soul" in *our* eyes should be, but have to let reality show us what and how soul in fact is. And we must not with teenager innocence

THE SOUL AS THE AXIS OF THE WORLD 305

give soul a semantic definition as if it were one "sweet" part of, one "romantic" entity in the whole world over against other "tough" parts of reality (anima in contrast to animus; soul in contrast to ego world or body or spirit; that which is "soulful" in contrast to what is rational, cold, technical). For if it is the *axis mundi* (which, as we have seen, is not itself an entity in the world, but the notion of its center), it can only be defined logically, syntactically, formally—as that which is its own center: as interiority as such. *Anima nostra non est anima vulgi.*

For this reason we must not construe a mutually exclusive opposition between [Money-and-The Media] as the axis of the world and the soul as the axis of the world. On the contrary, we have to realize that the new reality of Money-and-The Media, which, as we have seen, have become their own centers and make the world go round, *are* the first immediacy of the soul as *axis mundi*—to be sure, only its first immediacy, not yet its full realization. For while it is true that Money-and-The Media have finally come home to themselves and that they have been interiorized into their own concept, we must now note that this concept itself has not yet fully come home to itself. The concept's home-coming, its interiorization into itself—and this alone would be the soul—has not yet happened. Inherent in both phenomena there is still a difference, a dissociation into two, which is also mirrored in the very fact that there are these *two* manifestations of one and the same concept. Despite the fact that money in its present unrestrained form is highly spiritualized—billions of dollars, while we are sitting here, electronically constantly coursing above our heads with the speed of light—there is, precisely by virtue of this technical form, still a remainder of positive-factualness, physicalness, and sensualness that has not yet been distilled and evaporated. The modern form of money is the empirical, objective reality of sheer fluidity, of movement for movement's sake, and as such the objective reality of the concept of the soul's logical life, but it is this fluidity, movement, and life still only as the *concretistic* (literalistic, positivized) form of fluidity. The concept still has that which it is the concept of outside of itself. Thus it is still in the state of self-alienation and externality. The same applies *mutatis mutandis* to The Media, where the internal dissociatedness shows in its dependence on something external for being able to be what they are, on semantic contents, however contents that are essentially inauthentic for it, merely fuel to be consumed. The media need scandals, tsunamis, catchwords, celebrities—not to celebrate *them* as important truths, but only to burn them up in order to keep *themselves*, their own movement, going. Similarly we have in the world of Money the phenomenon of hostile takeovers of companies—not in order to acquire them as valuable, treasured assets, but to dismantle them and sell their parts for a profit. The consumptive nature of The Media-and-Money shows them to be positive realizations of logical negativity.

But whereas for our personal, subjective psychology the alchemical adage may be true that "in our patience we have our soul," we can know that only in this alienated, concretistic form can we today have the *real* (not just imaginal), *objective* soul as the axis of the world. In this form it is today's stage of the prime matter of the *opus magnum*, awaiting its further *real* distillation during the next few centuries.

CHAPTER ELEVEN

The Movement of the Soul[1]

Very often myths have been understood as a kind of early prescientific attempt at explaining the world. But myth, at least genuine myth, is neither an attempted *explanation* nor about the *world*. Myth is always the self-expression, self-representation, self-depiction of "the soul," its nature, its logic, its life, each particular myth being a depiction of the whole soul in one finite perspective (or one moment of its logical life) and, of course, in the medium of images of the natural world, the cosmos. All the different myths are so many "definitions" of one and the same, "the soul," definitions, however, not in conceptual language, but in pictorial garb. The myth of the axis of the world, e.g., shows, as we have seen yesterday, "the soul" as internal distance, as clearance and openness, as verticality and centeredness. Such a wholly different myth as that of Okeanos, the river at the outermost edge of the earth, indeed at the border between being and nonbeing, is just as much an image depicting the logical nature of "the soul," only this time focusing on very different properties of it. Okeanos is a river whose waters flow forward and return again into themselves. So this mythic image depicts the character of the soul

---

[1] Invited lecture at the XIII Simpósio International da Associação Junguiana do Brasil, Canela, Rio Grande do Sul, Brasil, November 2005 on the general theme of "A psyche é o eixo do mundo."

308 *THE SOUL ALWAYS THINKS*

(a) as ultimate horizon of any thought, imagination, any content or experience,

(b) as constant flowing, pure streaming, sheer fluidity, as *being* movement rather than being an entity that also moves,

(c) as movement that streams back into itself and thus is circular, uroboric, *self-reflective* and *self-referential*, it *is* self, *is* inner infinity, and

(d) as self-contradictory, for in returning into itself, it is its own source. It does not originate in a spring, which in turn would be dependent on some other, on rain. But its source is at the same time its mouth. It does not flow into some other body of water. Its beginning is its end and vice versa.

I said that the Okeanos myth was a wholly different myth from the one of the world axis. But if the axis marks the center and Okeanos the horizon or periphery of the world, we see that they are complements of each other. *Together* they are the mythic representation of the one concept of the soul as circle.

I will not continue to list all sorts of other myths to show what diverse aspects of the logical nature of soul *they* represent, nor will I complete my description of what the image of Okeanos shows (the four features mentioned by no means being all that can be said about Okeanos). The reason is that with the mythic image of Okeanos I have already arrived at my theme for this lecture, the movement of the soul. Okeanos is the image for the first of five kinds of soul movement as which soul *per se* exists.

I.

This is not the kind of movement with which "the soul" would manifest itself in empirical life and as which it could be experienced. For the image of Okeanos is, just as is that of the *axis mundi*, not taken from natural reality. Okeanos is not the sea or an empirical river as real phenomena. No, it is imagined both as a nonphenomenal fantasy river and one fantasized as being at the outermost edge of being; as such it is beyond experience. It is the image of a border concept, of the concept of that which makes any experience and imagination possible in the first place, which is why Okeanos was also appropriately called "the generation of all." Okeanos is thus the mythic or imaginal

THE MOVEMENT OF THE SOUL

309

form of the *thought* that during a later philosophical age would be termed "the *a priori*" or, more specifically, "the *a priori* condition of the possibility" of experience, just as the *axis mundi* is the imaginal form of the copula of metaphysical logic.

The mythological idea expressed in the Okeanos myth is in a way also corroborated by much later philosophical and psychological thought. Plato defined the soul as τὸ αὐτὸ κινοῦν , that which moves itself (or by itself), the self-moved cause of all movement (*Phaidros* 245c, similarly *Nomoi* X, 896a), that whose nature it is *to be* movement. This idea is echoed more than two millennia later when James Hillman refers to the autonomous psyche as "the self-moving, self-forming activity of the soul."[2] Plato's conception has its specific ground in and function for Plato's whole psychology, indeed for his cosmology, which we will not need to go into here. We content ourselves with finding in philosophical thought another support for the notion of a *psychê* that is itself the cause of its own movement. As such it is its own motor, and a motor that does not need fuel (which, by the way, would exclude the idea that the soul could *be* moved by something external, and this in turn would exclude the concept of emotion in its literal sense from the theory of "the soul": *e-motio*, 'being moved out, expelled from, one's own natural state'). But if "the soul" is its own motor, the question arises what is this its motor and how does it function?

Here I go back to the observation that in the case of Okeanos its source is at the same time its mouth. This makes Okeanos similar to what the image of the uroboros, the "taileater," the snake that bites its tail, tries to depict. But this latter depiction has the disadvantage that qua depiction it prioritizes as the mouth and the tail two distinct points in the entire circle formed by the body of the snake. But in Okeanos every point of its entire course is at once source and mouth. While the uroboros as a natural, sensual image retains and affirms the difference between a beginning and an end as two distinct positive-factual and thus visible parts of the whole, beginning and end in the case of Okeanos have completely disappeared in each other so that no specific point at all, and at the same time any and all points of it, are its beginning and its end. Source and mouth have become totally

---

[2] James Hillman & Paul Kugler, "The Autonomous Psyche: A Communication to Goodheart from the Bi-Personal Field of Paul Kugler and James Hillman," in: *Spring 1985*, p. 146.

negativized, sublated, reflected into each other. They are no longer empirical features. They have receded from the imaginal figure into the mind as its concepts or logical categories. Just as Okeanos as a whole is not an empirical experience, nothing natural, not even fully imaginal, so also its source and mouth or beginning and end can only be thought, no longer imagined. Even if Okeanos is given by *name* the sensual shape of a river, it is actually the abstract concept of a circle that has only secondarily been given a pictorial naturalistic form.

If each point of the "river" Okeanos is "source" and yet at the same time also "mouth," this would require that the water coming from the source has, as it were, already *instantaneously* rushed all around the whole circle to be able to flow back into the source. If there were the tiniest delay, the identity of source and mouth, the fact that one and the same point is simultaneously both, would be destroyed.

Now we can answer our question of what the motor of the self-movement of the soul, as depicted in the image of Okeanos, is. It is the *logical* motor of dialectical contradiction, the internal contradiction of the strict identity of identity and difference, of source and mouth, or beginning and end. The beginning, when it begins and in order to be able to begin, must always already *have* completed the whole "future" movement to the end. Only then is there the strict identity of source and mouth; only in this way can the beginning have its own end behind itself as what "fuels" it and propels it forward. The source, under the conditions of circularity with no input from outside, can only be gushing source if it is *a priori* itself fed by what is gushing forth from it. Another way to describe the contradiction is to say that each point and all points in the periphery of a circle are the beginning of the circle, so that no point has the beginning outside and behind itself, no point is secondary, only product. Or we could say that each *point* on the periphery of a circle is in itself the whole circle, inasmuch as it must already have completed the circle (since each is the beginning and as beginning simultaneously also the end).

A movement that has already completed what it nevertheless is supposed to still bring about, can, of course, not be imagined. It can only be thought; it has its "existence" only in the ideal realm of thought. But the circle, both as an idea in the mind and as a graphic figure, is the visible or imaginable sign into which the thought, as which the circle *is*, has been collapsed. The circle is the abbreviation

THE MOVEMENT OF THE SOUL

that stands for a living thought that as that which it is in its own terms has disappeared in the abbreviation. The motion can no longer be seen in the figure of a circle, because a circle is (mental) *image* or visible picture and thus partakes of positivity inherent in the spatial nature of the imagination. The circle seems to be at rest, static, motionless. Nevertheless, it *is* motion. The fact that it thus is the contradictory unity of motion and rest tells us that the motion we are concerned with is not empirical, natural movement in time. It is the movement of thought itself: thought's own movement, absolute-negative motion. In Okeanos the mythological imagination *represented* pictorially (but thus, because of the pictorial form, also necessarily *concealed*) the *thought* of "the soul's" logical life as self-moving thought.

The first type of the soul's movement that we have been discussing so far is absolutely self-enclosed. It describes what the soul is in the remoteness and inaccessibility of its own truth, in its almost "autistic" reality, the soul *in abstracto*, in its absolute ideality.

II.

In a powerful distich the poet Friedrich Schiller stated that the soul cannot express itself, because if the soul *speaks*, it is no longer the *soul* that is speaking.[3] In other words, the soul is truly "autistic" for Schiller. It cannot really come out and open itself. However, he does not deny that the soul also displays itself and becomes visible. What he nevertheless claims is that there is a fundamental gap between the manifestation and that whose manifestation it is supposed to be, a logical rupture in the identity between the two. I reject this conception. "The soul's" logical life is more complex.

I therefore begin the discussion of the second type of soul movement by stating that it is the soul's own need to break its own self-containment within its circular movement and to open itself, to release itself from the ideal sphere into otherness and to enter the real world, the world of nature. The pure thought of "the soul" *per se* wants to immerse itself in the muddy waters of the sensory world. This is why Father Okeanos is explicitly described by Homer as "the

---

[3] Fr. Schiller, Xenien und Votivtafeln.   "Sprache.
Warum kann der lebendige Geist dem Geist nicht erscheinen?
Spricht die Seele, so spricht ach! schon die *Seele* nicht mehr."

generation of all," as "the origin of the gods." Despite his forever streaming back into himself, he is also absolutely productive-creative. All rivers, springs, wells, and the sea originate from him. Okeanos is the unity and difference of two kinds of movement, of the self-contained uroboric movement of "the soul" *per se*, and its procreative movement, i.e., its self-expression, self-representation, self-display. It is the unity of the ultimate periphery or horizon of the world as such *and* of all that appears within this horizon as the phenomena of the natural world. However, those phenomena not in the sense of positive facts, but as the living, soulful appearance of the phenomena—the natural world cloaked in mythical garments. Father Okeanos is responsible for what Jung would call "God's world" or what we could also call "anima world," the imaginal world or the land of the soul. The imaginal world is the pure movement of Okeanos *released* into the muddiness of sensuality and spatiality. The second type of movement is what in psychology is called projection, though of course not projection as people's doing, but as projections by Okeanos, the all surrounding soul, itself. It is the dressing up of nature as a "cosmos," an ordered world of beauty and divine dignity.

But as we know, this movement does not *appear* as projection and a dressing up of something that "before" had been naked positive fact. No, it *appears* as the opposite of a projection, as the *spontaneous, natural* self-manifestation and self-revelation of nature itself, as *phainomena*, as epiphanies of their own accord happening to people and showing the deeper truth of the world. And this is perfectly in tune with the mythic Father Okeanos. For all those waters that originate from him flow inwards, not outwards. His opening up and expressing himself stays exclusively within the horizon established by him; his circle is not burst open; everything produced by Okeanos remains within the self-containedness of his streaming. So Okeanos is the mythic image of *interiority as such*, of *inner infinity*, and thus of soulfulness. His procreation is not material-factual production. It is interiorization, inwardization of what is already there. This is why myth tells us that what Okeanos generates is flowing water, i.e., animating moisture and fluidity as such, as well as all the gods, i.e., the divine imaginal depth of what is, rather than all the objects in the world. But the character of *his* interiorization, the interiorization in the context of the second type of soul movement, is paradoxically a *pro-jective* enwrapping of

THE MOVEMENT OF THE SOUL

reality in mythic or fantasy image. The land of the soul thus appears as an *outer* world, the world *around* us, *in which* we live, the world constituted by a center and a vertical *axis mundi*; what is in fact the self-depiction of the inner nature and logic of "the soul" appears *as* (as if it indeed were) the real outer world itself, nature, the cosmos— the veil of Maya according to Brahmanism.

Because Okeanos, within himself, immersed his waters into the muddiness of the sensory world, we can understand why the imaginal world has to be intrinsically polytheistic, a manifold of diverse figures, relations, stories. The difference, on the one hand, between Okeanos as the stream that returns into itself (i.e., as the oneness of the circle) and, on the other hand, the experience of the imaginal world created by him as a dispersed multitude of separate, even autonomous archetypal forces, is similar to that between a ray of light before and the same ray after it has gone through a prism. The polytheistic form of the mythic world must not be literalized and positivized, as if there were indeed separate departments presided over by the different gods. All the many gods are so many "definitions" of the whole, each from another finite perspective.

If we stay with the mythological imagination we see why Schiller's fear is ungrounded. Because "the soul's" self-expression remains *within* itself, within the uroboric circle, the identity of the expression with the expressing soul is guaranteed. The soul's speaking does not at all leave the circle of the soul's interiority and inner infinity, and thus also does not lose its intrinsic continuity with it.

We even have to go a radical step further and reverse the order of 'first' and 'second' soul movement. The myth of Okeanos (as described in section I) is itself part of the soul's *self-articulation* (discussed in section II). If the soul had not already been *speaking* we would not have the image of Okeanos in the first place. What we described as the first type of soul movement needs now to be seen through as itself being one of those many projections that belong to the second type. The myth of Okeanos is just one myth (a story told) among the whole range of myths. That which is said to be the creative origin of all mythic images is itself a produced product. So our move from the first type to the second type is not a linear movement. It is itself circular, and inescapably so. To the extent that Okeanos is the origin of all mythic imaginings, mythic imagination is conversely the origin of the idea of

314   *THE SOUL ALWAYS THINKS*

Okeanos as origin. The horizon of all images is itself an image, is itself contained in what it contains. We cannot go behind the production to an abstractly pure origin of it. The origin is itself interior to itself. It is as if the prismatic spectrum of light produced as one of its moments the idea of the light prior to its dispersion through the prism. The relation is dialectical, contradictory: self-reflective. The soul shows itself to be *absolute* interiority.

III.

In section II, I warded off the misconception of projection in the context of Okeanos as people's doing. Now, with the third type of soul movement, the notion of an active involvement of people needs, however, to be introduced. There are incisive, invasive acts performed by man with which he cuts in to, and imparts himself on, the natural course of events. The prototype of this act may be Kronos's outrageous disruption of the eternal *gamos* of the World Parents, by castrating Father Heaven with his sickle and stemming him high up, a deed which is, as we heard yesterday, tantamount to the establishment of the axis of the world or to the erection of man to his upright carriage in the psychological sense. This is not a happening, but a deed. Especially all sacrificial slaughterings, as diverse as their particular character and meanings may be, contain as one of their aspects that they reenact this violent deed. Indeed all rituals as such are incisive acts intruding into what simply *is* and happens.

While in section II, I showed that Okeanos is the irreducible generation of all, I now claim that the human invasive act as it is exemplified above all in sacrificial killings is the condition of the *a priori* possibility of "Okeanos" and all that he produced, i.e., of the whole mythic imagination and the mythically experienced cosmos. The self-contained circle of "the soul" (section I) and of the mythic world as a whole (section II) owes its existence to a *counter-natural* act, the daring impertinence on the part of man not to let things just happen, but to rise up and violently impose himself on that which simply *is* and happens. The emergence of soul presupposes man's self-risk through coming forward, *facing* nature, willfully de-ciding (from Latin *caedere*, to kill) and thus also exposing himself.

THE MOVEMENT OF THE SOUL

However, this self-risk and exertion of the will is not something that occurs on the level of empirical behavior. It, too, is essentially a *logical* background act that precedes all factual sacrifices and rituals, which in turn merely reenact this primary logical act that never happened in empirical time, but only becomes present and real in each ritual through such reenactment. In addition, my mentioning the will should not mislead us to assume a willfulness in the modern sense, as the will of a person as subject, as an ego will. Here this willful act is, paradoxically, itself still a natural occurrence. It is nature's or "the soul's" own rising up in man and its own cutting into itself (in accordance with the "axiom of nature" by Pseudo-Democritus). This is also why the human sacrificer is not really himself the one who performs the killing. It is ultimately the god—the soul—who does the killing through him. So rituals are the manifestation of a human I, however of a still only *implicit* I, an *implicit* deciding will, an I and a will that have not yet been realized as man's personal I and will, but both happen to him as natural events.

IV.

While rituals are acts performed by humans, but not by the human ego-personality, the human as person in his own right comes into play in the fourth type of soul movement. This is the movement of initiation. "Initiation" comes from Latin *inire*, to enter, to go into. Again it is "the soul" that now forces man to interiorize *himself* into the truths of the soul, which are the soul truths of the tribe having come down through tradition. It is a process of personal experience through which the person not only exposes himself to the truths, but also acquires them as personal treasures. This appropriation for the individual person in turn also supplies fresh lifeblood to the inherited contents, which otherwise might be in danger of becoming rigid and sterile formalities. The self-inwardization into the soul's truths (in the particular form of one's own tribal tradition) is indispensable for that movement that was discussed in the previous section to be possible in the first place. You cannot, just like that, commit a sacrificial killing. In order to be a sacrificer you have to have undergone an initiation. A ritual has to be performed from within its own truth, a truth personally

316   *THE SOUL ALWAYS THINKS*

acquired as one's living possession through one's initiation. Otherwise it would not be a ritual, but merely empirical behavior.

So this self-interiorization is the ultimate origin of all the soul's movements discussed before in sections I–III, however, it is an internal origin. On man's relentless counter-natural self-abandonment in initiation depends the possibility of the incisive act, on which the possibility of the world as soul world or mythological world depends. And the mythic imagination in turn produces, as the self-reflection of its own condition of possibility, the idea of a mythic Okeanos as the procreative horizon of all myths and all soulful experience. But conversely, the condition of the possibility of initiations is, of course, that there is an Okeanos as a uroboric stream as the outermost limit of being (because initiations have to take place within absolute interiority, within their own truth, or else what you get is not initiations, but ordinary ego experiences). So the circularity expressed in the image of Okeanos reoccurs as the second self-contained circularity of the unfolding of the four forms of soul movement.

V.

The four types of movement constitute the inner life of the world of myth and ritual, the anima world. It is a world which, because its logic is self-contained and circular, could in principle continue forever, *if* there were not in addition a totally other soul movement! By way of introducing it I will adduce a few ideas and statements by Jung. He speaks for example of a "... view of the world that had sprung from the decay of Olympus and the transformation of the gods into philosophical and theological ideas."[4] At another time: "Many of the earlier gods developed from 'persons' into personified ideas, and finally into abstract ideas" (i.e., concepts) (*CW* 13 § 49). This is Jung's theory of the "metamorphosis of the gods," which formula he took over from a book title (1920) by the cultural philosopher Leopold Ziegler.[5] About the apparition of the so-called "Radiant Boy," which was felt as an evil omen, Jung writes, "It almost looks as though we were dealing with the figure of a *puer aeternus* who had become inauspicious through 'metamorphosis,' or in other words had shared the fate of the classical

---

[4] *Letters 2*, p. 337, to Père Bruno de Jésus-Marie, 20 Nov 1956.
[5] For a detailed discussion of this idea see Chapter 20 below.

THE MOVEMENT OF THE SOUL   317

and the Germanic gods, who have all become bugbears" (*CW* 9i § 268; cf. *CW* 13 § 246). A last quote: "The iconoclasm of the Reformation, however, quite literally made a breach in the protective wall of sacred images, and since then one image after another has crumbled away. They became dubious, for they conflicted with awakening reason. ... That gods die from time to time is due to man's sudden discovery that they do not mean anything, that they are made by human hands, useless idols of wood and stone" (*CW* 9i § 22). To this we might add Jung's ideas about the "death of symbols," which I discussed elsewhere.[6]

We see immediately that what is here referred to as the metamorphosis of the gods is something totally different from what metamorphosis means in mythology and, e.g., in Ovid. There it had always meant a merely semantic change that logically or syntactically remains within the sphere of myth. But in what Jung hints at we see processes at work that amount to an attack on mythic imagination as such. It is not only that many or all images crumbled away. No, it is much more radical: the *form* of image itself crumbled away. Divine image turned ultimately into abstract concept. Metamorphosis thus means here, rather than a transformation from one imaginal shape into another, the transition from imaginal shape to the shapelessness of intellectual or logical form and thus the revolutionary break with myth altogether. It is a breakthrough through the world constituted by its being absolutely enclosed by Okeanos, a breaking out of the interiority of the world into a logically exterior world or rather into the world *as a now logically exterior one, i.e., an only positive-factual world.*[7] The imaginal and the anima world, or Jung's "God's world," appear as a soap bubble that has burst or has to be burst.

The movement that we see here at work is a soul movement, too. But it is totally different from the system of the four types of movement described above. It is a movement that can be described as an *opus* in the sense of alchemy. The alchemical *opus* is fundamentally different from ritual, which is not *opus*, but deed. *The world of alchemy and the*

---

[6] W. Giegerich, "The End of Meaning and the Birth of Man: An Essay about the State Reached in the History of Consciousness and an Analysis of C.G. Jung's Psychology Project," in: *The Journal of Jungian Theory and Practice*, Vol. 6, No. 1, 2004, pp. 1–65. Now Chapter 9 above. In Italian: *Idem, La Fine del Senso e la Nascita dell'Uomo*, Milano (La biblioteca di Vivarium) 2005.

[7] This breakthrough has "birth" character.

318 THE SOUL ALWAYS THINKS

world of myth-and-ritual are psychologically incommensurable. Myth, ritual, initiation serve the soul purpose of *celebrating* the soul's logical life, of sensually and imaginally displaying its truths (contents), giving them an objective presence in empirical reality, and thereby at the same time of ensouling the world. This is the soul's *natural* drive.[8] It corresponds to the first part of Pseudo-Democritus's axiom, "nature enjoys nature."

But alchemy is an *opus contra naturam*, "the soul's" attack on "the soul's" own *natural* desire, a dissolution of and break with the *unio naturalis*. It's work follows the soul's other drive expressed in the second part of Democritus's axiom, "nature conquers nature": the drive to bring closure to that very world as a whole that is enclosed in itself, closure to the self-contained circular movement, thereby applying Okeanos's closure to itself. By the same token it brings an end to interiority and infinity. What we call *opus*, no longer drifts, as it were, from content to content within the polytheistic manifold of the imagination. It sticks to one content (its prime matter) and works it, works it usually cruelly,[9] in order to push off from its initial natural form and to reach higher, more distilled forms of the same. It is nothing like an initiation, like one's self-exposure to the interiority of a situation, to the divine image as its inner truth. No, it is destructive, negating, sublating work imposed upon the matter as if from outside the uroboric-okeanic containment, with a view to *change* the form of truth itself, to bring about a fundamentally new level of truth.

The world of myth-and-ritual was the world around the *axis mundi*. In it the soul displayed itself in spatial terms, in the cosmos, in sensory imagery. But along with the breakthrough through the formerly absolute horizon provided by Okeanos, which is tantamount to its total abolishment (inasmuch as Okeanos *is* only if it is the absolute horizon), the vertical axis of the world has disappeared, too. It changed into the time axis, into the sense of history as linear directionality. The world of myth was a world of eternal present without

---

[8] To avoid confusion I must point out that since this natural drive is a drive of *"the soul"* and the soul is in itself counter-natural, this the soul's *natural* drive is nevertheless in itself counter-natural (see above the counter-naturalness of Okeanos's identity of beginning and end, of ritual as counter-natural deed, of initiation a counter-natural self-abandonment. All this is part of the soul's *natural* longings)!

[9] It is the work of negation. Alchemy speaks of *mortificatio, putrefactio, divisio*, of pulverization, flaying, decomposition, *solutio*, etc.

THE MOVEMENT OF THE SOUL

history and future. In it, the counterpart to the present was, with Jean Gebser's term, the (atemporal) Origin, in Jung's term the archetypal realm, in other words, the "metaphysical" depth dimension of the present itself, its inner infinity. But now there is along with history also a real past external to and the cause of the "present," and there is now just as much an open future, so that the former sense of present is destroyed, the new form of "present" being so to speak the zero point squeezed in between past and future. This new type of movement is a process that is propelled forward to ever new stages of itself, ever new statuses of consciousness.

While the aim of the sphere of myth and ritual was, as I said, the ensoulment of the natural, sensually given and spatially experienced world, its ensoulment through the self-display of the logic of the soul projected upon the screen of nature, the alchemy of history is no longer aimed at and interested in the natural world. Its prime matter is consciousness itself, consciousness's distillation and further development.

This helps us to see what the soul purpose of this movement is. The soul wants to come home to itself. This implies that to begin with it had not been at home. We have to realize: myth, this beautiful, rich anima world, this view which makes us humans truly feel at home in the world because it is a world of pure interiority in the soul, *is* nevertheless the form of *"the soul's"* self-estrangement. It is the form in which the soul gives itself the form of "otherness," the form of *contents* of consciousness imagined in the externality of (outer or inner) space. The work of the alchemy of history, by contrast, has the totally counter-natural goal of fetching "the soul" home from its self-alienation in the cosmos by dissolving the *unio naturalis* (together with our *participation mystique* with nature) and by integrating what it had invested out there in the form of semantic contents into the very form (or logical constitution) of consciousness itself. The soul wants to become explicitly apparent and be objectively known *as* what it is—absolute negativity and interiority. The interiority that formerly, in myth, had been displayed and acted out as the soulful character of the world out there is now itself to be interiorized into itself. This is why alchemy's mercurial prime matter had to be consciousness.

320   *THE SOUL ALWAYS THINKS*

The opus of the alchemy of history began, say, two and a half millennia ago and has many phases. In an extremely large-scale overview we can distinguish three major phases.

(1) In a first phase the soul was extracted from the natural world, in which it had objectively been invested, and gathered into One; in ancient Israel and in the sphere of religion into the notion of an Absolute, the monotheistic God above and outside the world who was ultimately, in Christian times, realized to be mind, *logos*. Thus the soul as mind or logos received independent, extraterrestrial reality, apart from nature and the cosmos. Similarly, in ancient Greece and in the sphere of philosophical thought the whole mythically perceived natural world was sublated and contracted into the notion of Being as distinct from, and as the object of, thinking, so that here, too, the mind or *logos* established its independence over against what is. And here, too, thinking was first of all the work of the divine *nous*, which made it possible for the religious and the philosophical traditions to merge.

(2) In a second phase, the otherworldly mind came into the world again, down to earth, and settled in man. It came home to man that what had been sought up in heaven had already been here in himself as the *mens humana*. Through this influx of spirit, man discovered himself as existing *as* consciousness, *as* subjectivity, and thus turned into a personality with individual dignity. This phase was by and large concluded by around 1800.

"The soul," by having shown itself to be consciousness rather than a content of consciousness, i.e., an object in the world, had come home *from* externality. But this still does not mean that it had come home *to* itself. What had so far been achieved was only the full realization of the interiorized *general form* of consciousness, of what the alchemists called the *unio mentalis*. As such it was still something like a promise of a future that needed to be fulfilled, a projection that needed to be caught up with. To this end the work had to be repeated once more: now on the material, semantic, pragmatic level, the level of the contents of consciousness. So during the first half of the 19th century, this level began to force itself to the foreground as the new prime matter, in the form of the new phenomena of Positivism, Materialism, Industrialism, Imperialism, of socio-political utopias and the literalism of personalistic psychology. With the latter, interiority as such was now

THE MOVEMENT OF THE SOUL

itself positivized: the soul was being interiorized into man, but not yet into *itself*, because man let himself be seduced into seeing *himself* as *the* locus and container of "the soul," a delusion acted out, among other things, in the form of psychoanalysis in the widest sense and personal self-search. Man identified himself with the subject, for whom the world was this subject's object out there.

(3) The task of the third phase, in which we still live, therefore is to radically decompose and evaporate *substantiality as such*, first, the substantiality of the contents of consciousness, i.e., in the subject's external world, as well as all his ideologies, ideals and values, and later the substantiality of the notion of "conscious subject" itself including its newly acquired inflated sense of importance as "an individual" and "a personality." This work was mainly performed, first, by the Industrial Revolution and, since the last few decades, in a much more subtle way by [Money-and-The Media]. Money and The Media are huge psychological machines for the execution of this aspect of the *opus contra naturam.* Each in its own specific ways consumes the independent dignity of whatever it gets hold of. Their character is decidedly vampirical and voracious. They suck out the lifeblood of whatever content or reality and leave the latter behind as a soulless corpse. Is there anything holy or beautiful left once The Media, especially television and advertising, have gotten their hands on it? Is there anything left whose substantial dignity would still have remained intact once it has been apperceived in terms of today's advanced, unrestrained form of capitalism?

Man is thus objectively taught to *release* all semantic contents of consciousness (in fact, the whole natural world, which Jung had stubbornly still wanted to experience once more as "God's world") into the state of positive-factualness and thus to *abandon* it to utter meaninglessness, soullessness, i.e., indifference.

The immediate result for us of the *opus contra naturam* is therefore that the world lies before consciousness as a dead object, mere raw material for human production and disposal. This is that situation where, as Jung put it already 70 years ago, "in the cold light of consciousness, the blank barrenness of the world reaches to the very stars" (*CW* 9i § 29). The soul's homecoming from *its* alienation reciprocally leaves us humans alienated from the natural world. What else could "dissolution of the *unio naturalis*" mean, what else could an *opus contra naturam* bring about but the total irrelevance, for the soul, of nature and of an imagination that feeds on nature?

But the dissolution of the substantiality of the "objective world" is concomitant with the dissolution of the substantiality of the subject itself. Man as individual is nowadays forced to experience his "redundancy" and unimportance, his irrelevance; in his logical status as subject he is now more and more being logically dissolved and disintegrated into "anonymous," subject-less processes, webs of relations, and movement *per se*, for which the keywords globalization, networking, World Wide Web, communication, information society, international money transactions serve as indications.

These phenomena have already objectively the character of selves and of self-sufficient, self-organizing fluidity that is also the character of "the soul." And yet there is obviously still a rest of positivity and externality left in them, so that in them the soul has not really come home yet. This rest of positivity and externality, just like the logical statuses of substantiality and subject before, would also need to be absolute-negatively interiorized into itself if the soul is supposed to become apparent as itself, as pure interiority. But this would require an additional phase. About this phase I cannot speak anymore today, not only because my time is up, but also because this phase has not become a reality as yet. It is still a matter of the unknown future. All I can already say is two things, first, that it would probably require our own wholehearted self-exposure to this process so that it could come home to, i.e., transform the logical form of, consciousness. This would be the return of the self-risk, inherent in the outrageous incisive *act* of the sacrificer, in mirror image, as just as outrageous *"passive"* self-risk.

Secondly, if the process of the negative interiorization into itself would have been completed, "the soul" would probably have become apparent as being Love (with a capital L). Love would be nothing else but Okeanos from which we started out, but Okeanos finally fully interiorized into itself and thus come home to itself after its former exile in the imagination's sensory world. [Money-and-The Media] are, as I said yesterday, only the first immediacy of the soul; but they are, as such, stages on the way to Love. Love, of course, not in the abstract humanistic and egoic sense of *our* love of all mankind, not in the silly sense of "make love, not war," not as a personal emotion, desire, passion,

THE MOVEMENT OF THE SOUL

attraction, preference, all of which would still be positivities and subjective. No, *infinite* Love as *objectively* existing Concept (the self-comprehension of the mind), Love as absolute logical negativity, fluidity, interiority, Love as "self," inner infinity and absolute horizon, and in this sense as the *liquefied* axis of the world, the axis absolutely interiorized into itself.[10]

But for the time being these are only empty words whose being filled with concrete, experiential meaning and historical reality is still very much up in the air.[11]

---

[10] The first form of the axis had been spatial and cosmic, the second form temporal (evolution). Space and time are the form of the soul's externality.

[11] What I did not go into in this paper, in connection with the last type of the soul's movement (section V), is the specifics of the dialectic of (a) the soul's pushing off from a given status of consciousness and reaching out for something that is still in the future, still an unreal projection through which the soul is ahead of itself, and (b) the consequent necessity to catch up with the projection, to make it real, back it up through integrating the projected idea into the form of consciousness and (c) the additional materialization, objectification, institutionalization in society and practical life of the acquired new status of consciousness. The last aspect is a kind of sedimentation. It is the basis from which the pushing-off movement can begin again. Very important here is the role of the generation difference. For the new, young generation, which is born into the situation of the institutionalized new status of consciousness, this status is starting-point and not (as for the old generation) result. (See on this last point Chapter 21 below.)

CHAPTER TWELVE

Psychology—The Study of the Soul's Logical Life

In 1956 Jung lamented that "my later and more important work (as it seems to me) is still left untouched in its primordial obscurity."[1] This is probably still true today to a large extent. What Jung suggests in this statement is that there is a considerable difference between his earlier and his later work. His later work is not just a further elaboration in more detail and expansion of his beginnings, nor merely a partial modification. It is something in its own right and, as he felt, more important.

From Jung's assessment we could conclude that now, more than four decades after his death, it is our task to finally do justice to his late work. But I think that this would not be enough. Or, to do justice to his late work would have to mean more than simply trying to understand it and basing our own work on it. Rather, we have to go *with* Jung *beyond* Jung.

It is not enough to listen to and be faithful to the letter of the explicit Jungian teachings. As Nietzsche once pointed out, it would be a poor way of repaying one's teacher to stay his *disciple* forever. We have to further develop the impulses lying in his work, impulses that Jung himself did not fully develop and base his work on. Our loyalty has to be to the living spirit stirring from within Jung's work, to the

---

[1] *Letters 2*, p. 309, to Benjamin Nelson, 17 June 1956.

unresolved problems that have come up through his work, to its internal necessities. Orthodoxy is not the best way to be true to Jung. This attitude, by the way, corresponds to Jung's own attitude toward Freud. In the same letter as that in which he quoted the just mentioned view of Nietzsche, Jung wrote: "The problem nearest to Freud's heart was unquestionably the psychology of the unconscious, but none of his immediate followers has done anything about it. I happen to be the only one of his heirs that has carried out some further research along the lines he intuitively foresaw."[2] What Jung here implies is that he was the only true heir to Freud's project precisely by having deserted the literal Freudian school, and instead having taken over as his personal responsibility the deeper concern that was the driving force behind Freud's research.[3]

In order to give some idea of the direction that this further development needs to take, I will at first compare and contrast two titles of works by Jung. By drawing an imaginary line between the standpoint implicit in the wording of the first title at the one end and the standpoint implicitly expressed in the second title at the other end we get a kind of vector that we will have to follow in our own attempts. Inherent in the development of Jung's psychological thought there is a certain hidden teleology, and our thinking has to be committed to the *telos* or *finis* (finality) rather than to the historical origin that lies behind it, in keeping with Jung's own view (which he expressed with respect to the psychology of neurosis) that "any historical deviation is a detour, if not actually a wrong turning" (*CW* 10 § 363, transl. modif.).

An early work that dates back to the year 1916 appeared in a revised version 1928 under the title:

The Relations Between the Ego and the Unconscious.

Jung's main work of his later period is

Mysterium Coniunctionis
An Inquiry Into the Separation and Synthesis of Psychic Opposites in Alchemy

---

[2] *Ibid.*
[3] Cf. my "Jungian Psychology: A Baseless Enterprise. Reflections on Our Identity as Jungians," in: Wolfgang Giegerich, *The Neurosis of Psychology* (Collected English Papers, vol. 1), New Orleans, LA (Spring Journal Books) 2005, pp. 153–170.

THE STUDY OF THE SOUL'S LOGICAL LIFE

In the earlier title we have the idea of two entities who will be in a changing relation with each other. It is similar to two people, let's say a man and a woman, who may fall in love with each other, marry, have terrible fights, start to hate each other and finally may get a divorce or may also reconcile themselves with each other again. Logically speaking there are first these two persons and secondly they enter, in addition to their individual existence, into a relationship with all its possible vicissitudes. The essential point for our present discussion is that there is a separation and independence of, if not split between, the existence of the persons on the one hand and how they behave or what happens to them, on the other; philosophically it is the difference between substance and accidental property. The same two people might also not fall in love with each other and yet keep existing. The same can be said about the Ego and the Unconscious. There first of all exist, according to the fantasy of the title of this work, an ego as well as an Unconscious in the psyche, and secondly those existing psychic entities relate to each other in varying ways; their relation may be a constructive-creative one or, conversely, have the form of a dissociation. But no matter how they may specifically relate to each other, it is only the vicissitudes of life which the two existing psychic entities are subject to. A substantiating or reifying thinking is at work here. We could also call it "ontological" inasmuch as it starts out with the idea of subsisting entities.

The thinking underlying and expressed in the wording of the second title is totally different, despite the fact that both seem to speak about the same subject-matter. At first glance we might think that the psychic opposites could precisely be compared to a married couple, and the synthesis or *coniunctio* on the one hand and the separation on the other hand could correspond to the marriage and the divorce of the couple, in other words, to the harmonious and productive relation versus the dissociation between the ego and the unconscious. But the point is that in this new thinking there are no subsisting entities any more. Jung does not speak of the ego and the unconscious, not of man and woman or male and female, not of mind and body, spirit and matter, heaven and earth, or what have you. He is no longer concerned with any substance, any entity. Instead of referring in terms of an ontological or substantiating thinking to the psychic opposites as subsisting entities he simply expresses the abstract notion of the oppositional *structure* or *form* of the psychic. It is the internal nature of the psyche that it is oppositional, we could also say self-contradictory. That is all. *What* the opposites are is here not said, and it cannot, should not be said in the context of this late work, because this would be a relapse into the substantiating style of thought that this title has long left behind.

Instead of having two subsisting entities that are then said to be in opposition, we have here the notion of an in-itself oppositional structure as the primary (irreducible, *unhintergehbare*) fact so that all specific opposites that may appear on the phenomenological level are merely secondary *illustrations* or *exemplifications* or *costumes* of the fundamental (and actually *irrepresentable*) oppositional structure. And the terms separation and synthesis (or union) indicate the nature of this oppositional structure, namely that it is not really a "structure" at all (which would, after all, imply something ontic, subsisting, and static or rigid), but rather a movement, a living tension, the fluid interplay of separation and synthesis, of difference and identity. The psyche is here envisioned as pulsating life. We are with this thinking on the level of this life *itself* (life, movement *as such*) and no longer on the level of beings, items, or entities *that* live or move or relate. In other words, the separation of psychic entities from what secondarily happens with or to them does no longer exist here. The form of 'entity' has itself been "alchemically" dissolved into what formerly would have been seen as their relation to each other, so that only this *relation* in its fluidity is left.

Jung also developed, in his mythologizing way, the view that there are two forces in the psyche, which he called anima and animus, and that they form a couple or syzygy. Both anima and animus mean soul or mind, in Latin often synonymously without distinction.[4] It is Jung who makes use of the gender difference of the two words to give their sameness, expressed in their common word stem (*anim-*), consistently different definitions. If we take this view seriously, it follows that there can be three fundamentally different conceptions of psychology. Psychology can be construed from the standpoint of soul as anima,

---

[4] Cicero translates both Greek *psychê* and *nous* by *animus*. In Augustinus, both *anima* and *animus* can without distinction apply to the human soul. For Lucretius *animus* is soul (as located in one's chest), whereas *anima* means life (as a quality of the whole body). Ficino sometimes uses both terms interchangeably in one and the same paragraph.

THE STUDY OF THE SOUL'S LOGICAL LIFE 329

but it can also be construed from the standpoint of soul as animus, and finally also from the standpoint of soul as the syzygy itself. Because Jung uses mythological imagery, the idea of the syzygy of anima and animus can thus itself be seen through as being the perception of the relation of anima-animus from the first point of view, that of the anima. The anima *imagines* this syzygial relation in the naturalistic imagery of a marriage, just as it imagines also itself as well as its other, the animus and everything else, in naturalistic images (for example, itself as a nixie, a nymph, an age-old, but ever-young mysterious woman, as a mist above a bog, etc.). The same could also be seen in terms of the animus-position, where everything would no longer appear in the guise of personified figures and natural images, but as concepts, for example, of forces, tendencies, parts of the personality. In both cases the syzygy would be envisioned from the worm's-eye view, from the standpoint of the separate figures or concepts that are brought into a union by the syzygy *above* them, like a roof or umbrella.

But psychology can also rise to the level of the syzygy itself. However, if it does so, if it takes the standpoint of the "umbrella" itself, the syzygy will no longer be that umbrella above and encompassing anima and animus, and the latter two will *ipso facto* have disappeared as something in their own right and been reduced to internal *sublated* moments of the syzygy. There will then no longer be a yoke (syzygy lit. = yoke) that would connect two separate entities together. The only thing left will be the syzygy itself as an in-itself dialectical movement, as the unity of the unity and the difference of itself. From here we could say that the second of our two Jungian book titles speaks from the standpoint of the syzygy itself. Psychology has here in fact caught up with and integrated an idea that it had before only entertained as a vaguely intuited content of consciousness, so that now it is finally itself informed by this idea in its very style of thinking. The idea is no longer a content that it entertains and teaches; it has come home to psychology and revolutionized it. And what it had imagined as an umbrella or roof above to be looked up to has become the ground on which psychology stands, the perspective that informs it.

So with respect to the earlier title, we can note a fundamental paradigm shift. A shift from a "semantic" to a "syntactical" level of psychology, from "ontological" to "logical" thinking, from "imaginable substance" to "abstract form or constitution." The former title implied a psychologistic, personalistic psychology because it presupposed the human person as the foundation or container or subsisting substrate of the life of the soul. The pulsating life that the later title is about is no longer tied to the human person as substrate. It is self-sufficient, so that here psychology has finally come home to itself and is no longer alienated from itself. This pulsating life is logical life, not empirical process; it is the dialectical, self-contradictory movement of union *and* disunion. Separation and synthesis obviously represent logical relations or operations, however, *as* logical operations, not operations performed by us, by the subjective mind, but by "the soul" itself, or rather not even performed by the soul, but operations *as which* "soul" exists.

These brief comments may already have given us a clearer idea of why Jung was right to have said that his "later and more important work [...] is still left untouched in its primordial obscurity." Psychological thinking is usually still stuck in personalistic modes.

Now it is also true that the text that follows after this magnificent title of Jung's late book is not always up to the high level of psychological thinking achieved in the wording of the title. It is for this reason that we today have the task of going with Jung beyond Jung, the task of proceeding to the standpoint of the fluidity of the logical life as which the soul *is*.

The following expositions serve the purpose of trying to get us a little closer to that standpoint or level on which we can understand what is meant by the conception of the soul's logical life, which is dialectical life.

But first I will have to address the possible incredulity that the notion of "the soul's *logical* life" may give rise to in some readers. Has the depth-psychology of the past century not taught us that the soul is instinct, desire, emotion, affect, feeling, "the unconscious," irrationality, pathologizing, numinous (and fundamentally incomprehensible) image, etc.—at any rate anything else but "logical"? In response to this objection I have to point out two things.

The first concerns a merely *semantic* problem that causes a misconception. "Logical" in the incriminated phrase does not amount to the assertion that psychological life always behaves in accordance with the rules of formal logic, that it is "correct thinking," rationalistic, calculated, plausibly argued. "Logic" can be understood in two

THE STUDY OF THE SOUL'S LOGICAL LIFE

different senses. The first one is that of a special discipline in the department of philosophy; logic is here essentially conceived as an *instrument* for correct thinking, for becoming more easily able to distinguish false from true forms of reasoning. This is what one could call, with Kantian terms, the *Schulbegriff* (the school or academic concept) of logic, in contrast to its *Weltbegriff* (world concept, cf. *Critique of Pure Reason*, B 866). In terms of the latter, the *conceptus cosmicus*, logic means something totally different. The philosopher who introduced the notion of *logos* into Western thinking, Heraclitus, spoke of the *logos eôn*, the subsisting logos. We also speak, for example, of the logic of revolutions or the logic of capitalism. Karl R. Popper wrote a book entitled *The Logic of Scientific Discovery*. Pascal spoke of the logic of the heart. Closer to home we have the following sentence by Jung: "By [x, y, z] I mean the tendencies or determinants that produce culture in man with the same logic as in the bird they produce the artfully woven nest, and antlers in the stag" (*CW* 4 § 665).

Jung did of course not want to suggest that stags or birds took courses in Formal Logic and when they want to grow antlers or build their nests, they reason them out, applying the laws of formal logic. What is meant in all these statements is the fact that inherent in the diverse phenomena talked about there is a certain *logos eôn*, a consistent pattern and momentum, we could also say that in their development they follow certain internal rules, an inner necessity. One stage brings about a *determinate* other stage which in turn is consistently followed by a third one, etc., where the sequence is not brought about by an external cause-effect mechanism, but an internal position, response-to-the-position relation (which is why it belongs to the sphere of logos). The stages develop a particular dynamic of their own, independent of or maybe even absolutely contrary to the intentions of the human agents through whom the phenomena come about (the latter possibility being especially blatant in "the logic of revolutions"). Similarly, the notion of the soul's logical life suggests—in a first regard—no more than that the life of the soul, both its life as a whole and that of its individual moments (or truths),[5] is the self-unfolding of its own internal logic.

---

[5] With Jung we could speak here of "archetypal" moments or truths, such as the moments of love, of strife, of birth, of the puer, of virginity, of illumination, etc.

332   *THE SOUL ALWAYS THINKS*

The second point to be made in response to the objection mentioned concerns the conventional (*modern*) ideas of soul as instinct, desire, emotion, affect, feeling, imagination, etc. The work of the later Jung presented us with alchemy as a theoretical model for psychology. Alchemy conceives of its *opus* as an *opus contra naturam*, and one of the main first objectives of the Work is the dissolution of the *unio naturalis*. If the soul is conceived as essentially and primarily being affect, emotion, instinct, desire, etc., it is clear that the standpoint of such a view is precisely that of the undissolved *unio naturalis*. It is a naturalistic stance that clings to such notions by way of its definition of psyche or at least by way of what for it are the innermost core and basis of things psychological. And the psychologist who entertains such views is overly impressed by the physical aspects of experience. Desires, affects, emotions are always partly physical, rooted in the body.

But can psychology afford to demand that in an analytical process the natural union be dissolved while itself holding on to that very union? What psychology wants to achieve on the experiential level of dream work and the therapeutic process it must itself have achieved as a matter of course in its self-constitution. Psychology must not constantly defer into the future, load onto the shoulders of its analysands as *their* task, and carry before itself as its preached message what is first and foremost its own job. Its work can only truly be *contra naturam*, if the radical cut that separates it from "nature" lies behind it and it firmly stands on the ground of the irrevocably *dissolved unio naturalis*. Otherwise it will inevitably be condemned to stay ego psychology, personalistic psychology. Even mythological thinking supports this thesis, inasmuch as *psychê* had originally its place in the underworld and was the name of the bloodless shades there who could only whisper. The word itself refers to the coldness of the breath of wind that is felt as coming from ghosts, the dead.

"Logical" in the phrase "the soul's logical life" thus also has the second meaning of cold, abstract, formal, irrepresentable—if you wish to express it in mythological terms you could also say ghostly. The term "logical" comes as a narcissistic insult to the ego, the ego that naturally clings to the natural and wants to shift the burden of the *separatio* (if it becomes aware of it at all) away from *itself* to the experiential level and to the level of its contents of consciousness (its

THE STUDY OF THE SOUL'S LOGICAL LIFE

333

teachings) in order for the *logical structure* of consciousness to be able to remain in its virginal innocence as "natural" consciousness. But psychological consciousness has to take its own medicine, nay, it *is* only psychological consciousness in the first place if its having taken its own medicine lies behind itself.

Because of the described ruthless dissolution of the *unio naturalis* the soul's logical life is abstract. However, as the *logos eôn* it is the soul in the Real and for this reason it is always *concrete* in the sense that it is the logical life in real phenomena, existing logic. By contrast, formal logic or mathematics are abstract in the sense that they have the Real that they may be applied to logically outside of themselves. Inasmuch as formal logic is conceived as a mental instrument for correct thinking about the Real, it is clear that it is divorced from the Real. The usual way in which the term "concepts" is comprehended and used, they are abstract concepts in the sense of tools for comprehending something. All ideas, theories *about* reality, all explanations of reality are abstract in this sense. But there is also the concrete Concept, the existing Concept that we are concerned with in psychology. So we see that we get two very different senses of "abstract" or "Abstractness." It is crucial to clearly keep them apart. The logic of the soul is cold, abstract, underworldly by comparison with any naturalistic thought and feeling, but nevertheless very much concrete by comparison with the abstract concepts in the sense of formal logic.

While in my original list of those notions that seem to contradict the conception of the soul as logical life I had also included the numinous *image*, in my discussion so far I omitted the whole question of image and the imaginal. But now we have to take a look at it. Ultimately, the presence of the imaginal style of thinking is evidence of the undissolved *unio naturalis*, too. A superficial glance at alchemy is enough to show us that it is past the imaginal style, that it not only preaches dissolution, but actively practices it. When, for example, it uses formulas like *lithos ou lithos*, the stone which is not a stone, and when it gives the alchemical stone a thousand other, often contradictory names, it makes it impossible for consciousness to stay with the *image* of "stone." The imagination, which is always naturalistic, is upset. The very image character, the pictorial apperception of the idea of stone is destroyed. The same is true of the operations performed by alchemy.

334   THE SOUL ALWAYS THINKS

Putrefaction, fermenting corruption, pulverization, distillation, etc.
are all aimed at violently decomposing the imaginal shape of the matter
worked with. Alchemy is not tender-minded with respect to "image."

Bishop Berkeley, in accordance with the entire tradition, explicitly
stated that "the soul always thinks." One should not understand this
sentence abstractly and exclusively, as if the soul never desired,
imagined, felt, got emotional, etc. No, what is meant is that even when
the soul is not thinking in the narrower, rigorous sense of the word,
but when it is imagining things or feeling passionate emotions, it
nevertheless thinks, only in an obscured, beclouded way, implicitly
and of course unwittingly. From Jung we hear that, "The fact that
consciousness does not perform acts of thinking does not, however,
prove that they do not exist. They merely occur unconsciously and
make themselves felt indirectly in dreams, visions, revelations, and
'instinctive' changes of consciousness, from whose nature one can see
that ... they are the result of unconscious acts of judgment or
unconscious conclusions" (*CW* 11 § 638, transl. modified). Even
psychogenic body symptoms and affects are at bottom thoughts, but,
as it were, "materialized" thoughts, thoughts submerged, sunk into
the natural, physical medium of body or emotion. Image is thought
submerged in the murky natural(istic) element of space and time and
material form. Conversely, thinking is sublated imagining (sublated
pictorial representation). And a psychology informed by alchemy
would have the task of freeing "the spirit Mercurius," i.e., the thought
that is imprisoned in "the matter" (in the image, the emotion, the
body symptom), imprisoned in the Real. In general, we could establish
the following series: body symptom is submerged emotion, emotion
is submerged image, image is submerged thought, and conversely,
thought is sublated image, image is sublated emotion, emotion is
sublated body reaction or behavior.

In view of these ideas James Hillman once confronted me with the
critical question of whether there could indeed be an imageless thinking
and pointed to the dictum by Aristotle (*De anima* 431 a 16), "The soul
never thinks without an image." I have two answers to this question.

First, one has to read the cited statement by Aristotle in
conjunction with his discussion in *De memoria* 449 b 31 ff.: The image
(*phantasma*) of something quantitative leads to the knowing (the
thought) of something non-quantitative. Inasmuch as the soul *thinks*,

THE STUDY OF THE SOUL'S LOGICAL LIFE

it does *not* think the image *the way* it is imaged. Thinking works against the particularity of images. It "contradicts the imagination" (*De insomn.* 460 b 16-20). What thought concentrates on is precisely something else than what is imaged, something that the imagination can never represent. The thinking soul that Aristotle is speaking about is the *human* faculty of thinking (which apparently initially leans on the imagination, but only in order to transcend it and get to the soul's home territory of thought). Aristotle's "prime mover," however, is *noêsis noêseôs*, pure, imageless thinking, thinking that thinks *itself* and not some other. And even the human *nous* is the organ of principles (*archai*), which as such cannot be imagined. (More or less the same is true for Plotinus.)

Secondly, we do not have to accept in the first place the initial statement that the soul never thinks without an image. To be sure, as we have just heard from Hillman (but also relativized), according to the long Aristotelian tradition we think in images. In some way, this tradition was still at the root of early-modern representationalism. And even later, Kant discovered the "hidden art in the depths of the human soul," the art of the a priori productive and unconscious imagination (*Einbildungskraft*), and Fichte as well as Schelling, building on Kant's discovery, incorporated their own different versions of it into their own different schemes.[6] However: Hegel, after his early beginnings, in his mature philosophy, dethroned the productive imagination as the ultimate ground of object consciousness. The inner movement of his theoretical "Psychology" goes beyond the imagination and shows that not it, but *reproductive memory* makes the transition to thought. Hegel insisted that we think in names,[7] in the *words* of language (which interestingly enough reminds us of the thousand names that alchemy gave to the *lapis* or to the prime matter, etc.). "In the name, *Reproductive* memory has and recognises the thing, and with the thing it has the

---

[6] See the excellent study by Reinhard Loock, *Schwebende Einbildungskraft. Konzeptionen theoretischer Freiheit in der Philosophie Kants, Fichtes und Schellings*, Würzburg (Königshausen & Neumann) 2007.

[7] G. W. F. Hegel, *Jenaer Systementwürfe III*, in: *Gesammelte Werke*, Hamburg 1968 ff., vol. 8, ed. R.P. Horstmann and J.H. Trede, pp. 185 ff. Idem, *Enzyklopädie der philosophischen Wissenschaften III*, §§ 458–64. See also Alfredo Ferrarin, *Hegel and Aristotle*, Cambridge (Cambridge Univ. Pr.) 2001, pp. 287–308, and *idem*, "Logic, Thinking and Language," in: Rüdiger Bubner and Gunnar Hindrichs, *Von der Logik zur Sprache. Stuttgarter Hegel-Kongress 2005*, Stuttgart (Klett) 2007. Jens Rometsch, *Hegels Theorie des erkennenden Subjekts*, Würzburg (Königshausen & Neumann) 2007, pp. 204–217.

name, apart from intuition and image." "Given the name lion, we need neither the actual vision of the animal, nor its image even: the name alone, if we *understand* it, is the unimaged simple representation. We *think* in names."[8] I can speak about my father (and full well know what I am talking about) without having to produce the image of my father. I understand the word monster in a sentence even if no concrete image of one emerges in my mind. We probably could not successfully communicate at all about more complex matters if we had to produce the corresponding image for each and every word used in our sentences.

Whereas the image retains the tie with the natural looks of whatever its content is, the name of things ("table," "house," etc.) refers indirectly and arbitrarily to it, the signifier (the sequence of phonemes in oral, of letters in written language) has here no relation to the sensible appearance of the content. This is why the same object has totally different-sounding and unrelated names in different languages ("table," "Tisch," "mesa," "zhuōzi"). In language, spirit has arbitrarily assigned certain sounds of its *own* production to the respective content and thus, even while possibly referring to things, nevertheless stays with what is its own property, rather than maintaining, with a narcissistic tenderness toward itself, the inner continuum with the given (the *participation mystique* in Jung's sense). This is precisely the problem with the imaginal and even with symbols: they reaffirm the continuum with the natural likeness despite all subjective effort not to read them literalistically. The real, objective (logical) cut is avoided. Names (of things) or words are signs, not symbols. "When the Intelligence has designated something, it has finished with the content of the Intuition and has given to the sensory substrate [i.e., to the word-sign, the sound cluster, W.G.] as its soul a meaning *alien* to it."[9]

For Hegel, images belong to a still dreaming spirit; spirit (mindedness) awakens only in the realm of names, which, to put it in our alchemical terminology, are the existing evidence that the break with the *unio naturalis* has already occurred and accompanies language as an always already *accomplished* break. Now I would go a step further and say that pictorial thinking in images, while empirically and

---

[8] G. W. F. Hegel, *Enzyklopädie* § 462 and note.
[9] *Ibid.* § 457, *Zusatz*.

THE STUDY OF THE SOUL'S LOGICAL LIFE

experientially maybe coming first, is *logically* secondary because it presupposes language, thinking in words (names). Without language no metaphors and no images, either.

We also know that already small children are in fact capable of imageless thought, namely when they learn to say "I." "I" is pure thought. It is not image, not a representation (*Vorstellung*). "I" has no specific qualities or characteristics, because every human being (despite their great differences in looks, size, skin color, sex, age, character traits, gifts and weaknesses) can say "I." However, "I" is a thought as *existing* concept, *as a real.* If it were a representation, it would precisely not be "I" (but rather a specific "something") and could not perform what the concept I in fact achieves.

The last-mentioned point about the I can serve as an access to another essential aspect of the idea of the soul's logical life. It is clear that the I is not thought up (concocted) by the child, just as the antlers are not thought up by the stag. Paradoxically, the thought of I is not *made* by us, not an ego-thought. Thought here does not refer to the Jungian orientation *function*, to an explicit act of thinking. It is not a subjective achievement. It is a thought that happens to and in the person. The person is just the place where this objective thought occurs, just as the nest-building and the growth of antlers occur as objectively ongoing thoughts, thoughts not "subjectively" thought by the bird or stag, respectively. The idea of the soul's logical life thus operates with the idea of the objective psyche, with non-ego processes. Adapting an alchemical adage we could say: *Psychologia nostra non est psychologia vulgi.* Psychology is the study of the self-thinking, self-unfolding, and self-realizing logic of real life (or individual phenomena of real life); it is the study, e.g., of what the Roman Catholic Mass, what the Philosophical Tree, what the Trinity, what the Flying Saucers "think" (to allude to some subjects treated by Jung). It is not the study of what *people* think, imagine, feel, e.g., *about* the Mass or the Trinity, not what they intend, wish, all of which would belong to a personalistic or ego or naturalistic psychology. "*Our* psychology" has left the anthropological fallacy behind.

Only in this way does it also become possible to distinguish, concerning the great transformation processes in our time (keywords: globalization, advanced capitalism, computerization, internet, television, advertizing, information society, etc.), the subjective preferences and personally culpable behavior of the agents operating in those spheres from those changes in which it is nothing else but the action imperatives of the objective logic of the economy, of technology, etc. that are responsible for the developments, even though they, too, are empirically of course brought about through human agents. And only in this way can we acknowledge and appreciate this objective logic as the soul's opus or, alchemically (and thus imaginally) speaking, as that of the spirit Mercurius and must not, in terms of ego-psychology (which only knows of the opinions and motivations and behavior of *people*), disparage it as the evil, sinister work of those human agents who in reality happen to be the (sometimes, but of course not always, even unwilling) instruments of its realization.

Along with this break with personalistic psychology we have also broken with the romanticized idea of soul that wants it to be something nice and harmless, a supporter of our ego wishes for "meaning," self-importance (called "individuation") and a "return to nature." Psychology is a serious business and not in the service of our wishful thinking. We have also left the consulting room behind, of course not totally, but as the *main* place of the *opus*. The consulting room is only the place where we systematically focus on the *opus parvum*, the "small work" of only private significance. The main place of the soul, however, the true laboratory or retort of the *opus magnum* is history, the real historical process. Psychology thus does not have, as already Jung stated, a delimited field (*CW* 9i § 112); it is not one specialty side by side with all the other sciences and humanities. Rather, as depth-psychology it studies the internal objective logic—the mercurial spirit, "the soul"— in all real life processes and phenomena *inasmuch* as they already have been subject to the mind's attention, reflection, and interpretation. This inner logic cannot be known a priori. It needs to be found out *ex post facto* and is again always a matter of interpretation.

When saying "The soul always thinks" we must of course (see our initial critique above of any substantiating thinking) not imagine that there is a soul (as a substance or entity, an author or agent) which also, in addition to its being there, spends its time with the activity of thinking. The use of "the soul" in this statement is only a mythologizing manner of speaking, not a hypostasis. There are not two things: the soul plus its thinking. There is only one thing, the

THE STUDY OF THE SOUL'S LOGICAL LIFE 339

actually occurring logical or thinking life itself, with nothing (no literal, substantiated soul) behind it; but this ongoing objective thinking is itself what receives, in our rhetorically still mythologizing mode of expression, the traditional name of "soul."

In order to bring out another important advantage of the logical over against the imaginal perspective I will by way of example have a brief look at the interpretation of sexuality in psychology.

In the early days of Freudian psychoanalysis the life of the soul was predominantly seen in the realm of sexuality. Sexual needs, desires, behaviors, perversions, secrets of a person were interpreted as what the soul is basically and ultimately about. The soul = sexual libido. Jung did not agree. For him, too, sexuality was of greatest psychological importance, but not the sexual as such, rather it as that which sexual phenomena expressed. Jung took the sexual ideas and behaviors *as symbols*.

What does this mean? Jung saw *the psychological difference* at work in sexual phenomenology. A given sexual symptom, behavior, or fantasy was for him in itself different, in itself divided; it was the unity of two "realities": (a) the *phenomenal* aspect, the obvious, manifest sexual content, the empirical behavior or clinical symptom, and (b) what the phenomenal aspect symbolically represented and expressed and what was precisely *not* manifest, not phenomenal. It was fundamentally hidden, invisible, even downright *unanschaulich* (irrepresentable), completely abstract, non-objectual (*ungegenständlich*). It could be represented only indirectly, namely symbolically. But the symbol just as much *concealed* as it *revealed* the soul. It concealed what it represented because the symbolic expression was a garb or garment in which the irrepresentable soul manifested itself.

This has several consequences or implications. 1. The sexual phenomenon could not be taken at face value, not literally. Inasmuch as it was a garment for something else, its true meaning was not identical with what this garment was about. Sexuality, viewed psychologically, was not about sexuality, but about the soul as something in its own right. Although the particular symbolic garment that the soul chooses to cloak itself in is by no means totally indifferent and arbitrary, but has its own significance, nevertheless different garments, different symbols could in principle have been used instead. There are many ways in which the soul can express its ideas. 2. Being a symbol, the

340   *THE SOUL ALWAYS THINKS*

sexual phenomenon (or any psychological phenomenon) within itself negates its own phenomenal, manifest, empirical aspect and points to what it is not, to the soul meaning expressed by it. There is a logical activity going on in the symbol. We could almost speak of a logical drama:

1ˢᵗ act: the invisible "soul" or logic expresses itself in symbolic garb, it manifests itself phenomenally, e.g., in a sexual phenomenon, i.e., it makes itself visible. The irrepresentable represents itself in this symbol.

2ⁿᵈ act: the phenomenal or obvious aspect of the symbol negates itself, sort of saying: "*I (the way I look)* am *not* what I am about. Don't take me at face value. I am not really about sexuality at all."

3ʳᵈ act: The phenomenal aspect of the symbol pushes itself off from itself and points to some other, something hidden, invisible as to that which it is actually about. It says: "I am about this not-phenomenal other," namely, we could add, about "the soul," its logical life.

4ᵗʰ act: The symbol says: "But only through me (this my garb) can you get an access to this other. The latter is not wholly other, not anything outside of me, the way a speaker exists outside and independently of his sentences. That other to which I point, as that which I am actually about, exists exclusively within me myself; there is nothing behind me. I *am* its valid and true representation, its best possible representation. And more than that: that other represented by me exists only through me, is produced by me, posited by and within myself, precisely through my negation of myself." In other words, what was described as the 1ˢᵗ act, namely that invisible logic that creates the symbol, can now be realized to be created by and within the symbol itself.

5ᵗʰ act: The symbol says: "Because my meaning is absolutely negative, I really mean *nothing*, but of course not simply nothing, nothing in the sense of total emptiness, but nothing in the sense that I mean exactly what *I* phenomenally *show* and represent."

The symbol *is* this internal drama, all five acts or moves of this drama simultaneously, not successively. What from outside appears as a symbol, one unitary phenomenon, *is*, seen from within, this dramatic movement. It is a *logical* drama, i.e., not one played out in time and empirical reality, but behind the "face" of the symbol, and the logic of the symbol is a circular, uroboric logic. The end result of this logical drama returns to where we were at the very beginning.

THE STUDY OF THE SOUL'S LOGICAL LIFE 341

But this does not imply that we could simply eliminate and forget about the intermediate acts of this drama. No, the end contains all the stages that the movement passed through within itself, so that the end is not at all identical with the beginning. It is immensely enriched.

The foregoing, though in itself not a highly significant example, has been chosen here because, being relatively simple, it allows me to give a brief illustration of how the "logical" approach is capable of viewing the inner workings of a phenomenon *from within*. Neither the empirical nor even the imaginal approach are capable (or willing) to do this. They tend to describe phenomena the way one looks at things, from outside. While it is clear that the empirical approach observes and theorizes from the standpoint of the subject opposite to the phenomena as object, its viewing remaining external, it is not quite so obvious that the imaginal approach also views from outside and from a vis-à-vis position. Inasmuch as for it the image is *poetic* image, there is no doubt for it a certain inwardness in the image. And yet, the imaginal approach persists in beholding, envisioning, perceiving the image, that is to say, in always keeping it logically before consciousness, even if empirically the image may be kept in the back of one's mind for the purpose of seeing life phenomena through or by means of it. The interiorization into the phenomenon perceived as image remains incomplete, which is of course concomitant with the fact that this approach shrank away from the break with the *unio naturalis*. It is in love with the image and wants to keep it intact as a whole; it aims at *Facing the Gods* and the phenomena. It negates any literalism of the image, but is careful not to hurt the image itself (in contrast, e.g., to alchemy's blunt "the stone that is not a stone" and its destruction of the gestalt of the matter). Seeing through phenomena to the god is, to be sure, a deepening of one's viewing. But it nevertheless merely continues the direction of one's glance from outside. In addition, the god discovered is discovered through an external method, that of establishing likenesses (a given phenomenon and a mythic divinity given by tradition as a kind of ready-made). Seeing through is precisely not the phenomenon's self-revelation, its own speaking, its showing what its hidden inner essence, its soul, is.

Seeing phenomena *from* within is what we call thinking. Psychology has to *think* the phenomena, in contrast to merely "watching" them from outside and connecting them to appropriate

342   THE SOUL ALWAYS THINKS

myths. The "logical" approach destroys this intactness of the image, disrupts the tie with the natural likeness, by entering, penetrating the phenomenon so as to understand it on the basis of the workings of its inner logic. The difference between the imaginal and the logical approach is perhaps comparable (and here I of course make use of a naturalistic and as such external comparison) to that between the aesthetic appreciation of an animal as a shape (a "face," a natural appearance) and anatomy's dissecting-and-reconstructing work upon it, or better yet: physiology.[10]

The point I am making here I can illustrate by going back to the above-discussed topic of image versus words of language and to an objection to my view raised by Hillman from his image-devoted view.

> In his reply to Marlan (in the essay generously contributed to the book [p. 204] Marlan edited in my honor), Giegerich writes that we think in words of language and not in images. I'd say just the contrary. Words are themselves images. The history of language as supposed by Barfield and Vico suggests that polysemous metaphors and poetic analogies give birth to denotative concepts and singleness of meaning. Language can never free us from its primordial mother, the sensory, the natural, the physical, the implication of an *anima mundi*— a soul in and of a natural world, even if that natural world is always "unnatural." ...[11]

Before I come to the point that I want to make, I first have to make a few comments on Hillman's thesis. No doubt, there are contexts in which "words are themselves images." But the fact that words are themselves images is true only for words on a meta-level of speaking, words used in special moments or contexts of *eminent speaking*, such as in poetry, religious dogmas, myths. It is not true in ordinary-life speaking, in scientific language, in intellectual discourse. As I pointed

---

[10] Jung of course abhorred physiology. He explains his aversion with the cruelty of vivisection, which we can easily sympathize with. But it may in addition be indicative of a deeper unconscious reason, his tender-mindedness with respect to the intactness of image. Rather than thinking the images in the sense of an intrusive reconstruction of them from within their own internal logical life he preferred to merely reflect them against the backdrop of some external given (or imagined as given) other, namely myths and archetypes.

[11] James Hillman, "Divergences. *A propos* of a Brazilian Seminar on Giegerich/ Hillman – Organized by Marcus Quintaes," open letter 2008. My reply to Marlan referred to by Hillman is reprinted in the present volume as Chapter 17.

THE STUDY OF THE SOUL'S LOGICAL LIFE

343

out above, even in ordinary speech, when talking about a lion or one's father, people do not necessarily produce images, but understand what is meant. The point is here that it is the particular use made of, or reading given to, words that turns them into images, whereas in themselves they are by no means images. Only in such cases it may be true that far from "freeing us from" natural imagery, language precisely cocoons us in images and metaphors.

But even in poetry and religious language this must not always be true. Is the word rose, even in a poem, necessarily a true image or not perhaps much rather a name that we understand without image? Is the word "God" an image or not an unimaged *concept* that at times is only secondarily concretely imagined?

Above all, does the metaphoric use of words rely on the word as image or not precisely on it as mere name? Are metaphors not fundamentally based on a conceptual understanding? "He was a lion in battle": does this metaphor mean that we should imagine the fighter as having a mane, claws, and a tail and using his teeth in fighting valiantly? Does it not precisely forget about the concrete image, "the sensory, the natural, and physical" aspect of "lion," and solely concentrate on the *concept* of "fierce fortitude"? We even have to say categorically that *unless* "the sensory and the physical" are left behind, a *metaphorá*—a transference from one sphere to another—cannot take place. If the visual image stayed intact, the word to be used metaphorically would keep stickily clinging to the literal meaning. The unimaged name is the *sine qua non* of any metaphor. Metaphor and imaginal image are very different things. The fact that the metaphoric use of words seems to be inherent in human language from the outset only underlines, rather than refutes, my thesis that we think in words (as names) and that the condition of possibility of language is, as Hegel convincingly argued, its having radically left behind image as such and all sensory, natural basis in order to *give* itself "from scratch" its own fresh beginning.

Of course, Hillman contrasts "polysemous metaphors and poetic analogies" with "denotative concepts and singleness of meaning." This reduces the problem that we are here concerned with to the abstract opposition of polysemy versus singleness of meaning. This is an altogether different topic from that of word as unimaged name without sensory, natural base versus word as "natural" image. If used as what distinguishes the one from the other, polysemy versus monosemy are false categories. The singleness of meaning applies only to *abstract* concepts. But not all concepts are abstract. There are also concrete concepts, which are just as polysemous and infinite as Hillman's metaphors (e.g., "I," or "God"); conversely, many metaphors are characterized by the same singleness of meaning as abstract concepts (for instance, our example of "lion" as fierce fighter). But the real issue here is the very different one from the polysemy/monosemy one, namely whether there is, to put it in Hillman's terms, a given "primordial mother" nature *behind* language or whether language is the *free* production of the soul's logical life.

After these corrections, I can come to the point I wanted to make about the difference between the imaginal and the logical approach or that between the aesthetic appreciation of an animal as a natural appearance and anatomy's dissecting-and-reconstructing work upon it, or better yet: physiology. When we deal with dreams, with myths, with poems, with the imaginal, we are a priori immersed in a world of images as already existing, as ready-mades, so to speak, as already *produced* images. When we speak and when we imagine, we often simply make use of the meanings provided by our respective language and "act out" their potential for polysemous metaphors and poetic analogies, without wasting a thought on how these meanings come about, how they are produced, on the invisible, unconscious production process itself.

But surfing on the waves of language, taking its meanings for granted, "acting out" its potential is not enough in psychology. We also have to "remember"—to remember how the soul or mind *makes, generates* those meanings, namely by using and basing itself on absolutely meaningless and arbitrary acoustic signs (linguistic sounds or sound clusters) freely articulated (voiced) by the mind or soul itself. First of all, these sounds are not sounds of purely natural origin at all like the sounds of animals, but, as phonemes, parts of a *system of distinctions*, elements in *complementary distribution*, and as such a priori products and property of the mind. And secondly, in speaking these sound signs or phonemes are by no means held on to. Rather, the soul pushes off from those signs, which, as sounds, are fundamentally

THE STUDY OF THE SOUL'S LOGICAL LIFE 345

temporal and immediately die away. They must die away in order for the *meanings* of the words and sentences to be produced. The sounds of the words by themselves have no meaning. Their meaning is not inherent in them, not their permanent possession. Only in the dying away of the sounds the meanings come into being. No, there is no "primordial mother" behind language, nothing that would exist as a substance; on the contrary, the notion and feeling of an *anima mundi*, of the natural, or of a primordial mother exist only because they are secondarily *produced* by means of a certain use of language. To assume anything substantial like a primordial mother, like the sensory and the natural *behind* or *outside* of language, amounts to an illicit metaphysical hypostasis (even if it is meant only metaphorically), a mythologizing "projection" or "extrajection."

Inasmuch as the sounds of language are acoustic signs, we could of course call them something sensory and physical, the only sensory and physical substrate that language relies on. But the point is that in using those sounds to create words that can then be images, the mind precisely strips them of their naturalness, removing them from their natural context and appropriating them for its own mental sphere. It takes away their seeming substrate character, by letting the sounds die away and by pushing off from the sounds to meaning. This sensory is no more than a catalyst, a fleeting aid, that is completely left behind and thus does not enter the final product.

To be sure, Hillman qualifies his statement by adding, "even if that natural world is always 'unnatural,'" which is (or would be) the very point, but he appends this only as an inconsequential afterthought because he does not take the medicine contained in this insight. If he took it, he would see that there is, as far as anything "primordial" is concerned, only the absolute negativity of the mind's own work, its own free production process, and that his (Hillman's) "the sensory, the natural, the physical" are themselves only *concepts* already *created* by and within the mind through its naming and its availing itself of in-themselves meaningless and, in addition, negated sound signs. They are, if I my say so, home-made, the mind's own property. They are produced results, not given, found, perceived. Quite conversely, what in a human context we call perception is only made possible by the mind's production of meanings and images. What we do not have a concept or at least some vague idea of we cannot even perceive. We perceive in images and concepts made possible through the unimaged words of language.

As psychologists, we must not "fall for" the images secondarily created in language. We must not take them literally. We have to see through them, see through "the anima mundi," through "the sensory, the natural, the physical," through "the imaginal"—and not see through to "*the gods*" who are themselves *produced* images to be seen through. No, we have to see through to "the soul," to the soul-*making* that goes on in the words and images by means of meaningless and arbitrary acoustic signs. Otherwise we make an ideology out of the *anima mundi* and the imaginal.

In addition to the contrast of animal as existing entity and visible shape versus the anatomical and physiological study of animals I now want to mention two further (although remote) analogies to the point I have been making here. The first one is the distinction made in philosophy between *natura naturata* (nature as it appears to us, nature taken for granted as a given fact) and *natura naturans* (nature as it produces itself). The former notion is formally on the same level as "Words are themselves images" (which applies only to the words as results of language), whereas the latter betrays an interest in the production process that generates that which we know as nature in the *natura naturata* sense and is thus formally equivalent to an interest in how the mind produces its words and images.

My second analogy comes from psychotherapy. Jung warned psychologists, when they try to understand neuroses, against taking the neurotic conjectures (fantasies, the whole impression created by a neurosis) literally at face value and falling for the neurotic complications, thereby riding the same hobby-horse as the neurotic patients. Jung realized that the point of neurosis is to produce certain effects, to give itself this or that appearance, to create a certain impression, to seduce consciousness (both the consciousness of the neurotic himself and that of the people around him or her, including the therapists) into believing in the impression created. Jung wanted us to understand that neuroses are productions, *arrangements* (Alfred Adler), staged dramas and how and why they were staged. He wanted us to "remember" (rather than to contribute to the "acting out," on the theoretical level, of the neurosis). And to "remember" here means

THE STUDY OF THE SOUL'S LOGICAL LIFE

to reconstruct its internal logical genesis, its genesis from the soul.[12] So in this area, Jung moved his focus from the product to the production that resulted in the product.

By the same token, when Jung states that "The psyche creates reality every day" (*CW* 6 § 78) or conceives of consciousness as "the second creator of the world"[13] it is for psychology not sufficient to rest content with the result of this creation, with the fantasy images and the imagined world taken at face value and to explain them in terms of myths, archetypes, or gods as givens. If we want to be serious about the creative nature of the psyche, then we (a) must not hypostatize the soul as a substance or agent behind the scene that produces images through a particular faculty that it has called fantasy or imagination, and (b) we have to learn to reconstruct the images and psychic phenomena from within themselves, from out of their inner logical life *as their soul*. This means we have to give up the idea of anything primordial altogether, be it the sensory, the natural, the physical or be it archetypes as a priori given irreducible origins. All we have is produced results, whose production process is hidden.

Reconstruction means that the logical approach does not really "view" (watch, observe) the psychic phenomena's inner workings from within, as I once said above, but much rather itself goes through, and actively performs *as its own acts*, the individual steps of the internal self-movement as which a given image or psychic phenomenon *is*. In this way it does not merely look at the image as this logical drama's finished result vis-à-vis itself. In the case of such viewing this drama itself disappears behind the face that the finished result shows (or rather: always already has disappeared, has been obliterated). Because such a reconstruction performs the steps of the internal logical life constituting the psychic phenomena, the opposition of subject and object no longer exists. The phenomenon has come home to consciousness and consciousness has inwardized itself into the phenomenon. This unity or inwardness is only possible in one's *thinking* the phenomenon.

---

[12] This has to be sharply distinguished from the conventional depth-psychological attempt to conceive neurosis in terms of a biographical genesis in infancy or childhood and in terms of causality (external conditions, traumatizations, etc.).

[13] For example *Letters 2*, p. 487, to Tanner, 12 February 1959.

348   *THE SOUL ALWAYS THINKS*

Whereas ancient myths, symbols, local legends, cults might easily seduce us into using an imaginal approach and this means simply view them "in terms of the gods" since they themselves innocently present their truths in imaginal garb, it would, in the case of fundamentally *modern* phenomena, be a serious mistake to try to face them in order "to see through to the divine image." We would simply miss them if we tried to see modern phenomena like neurosis (in the realm of the *opus parvum*) and the enormous changes in the areas of the economy, technology, social organization, etc. (as part of the soul's *opus magnum*) in terms of the gods or archetypal images. Truly modern phenomena are in themselves far too "cunning" as that one could hope to do justice to them beneath the level of their logic. In earlier times "the soul" was content with simply *producing* and *displaying* its inner truth in imaginal shape, that is, in the result of its self-display. The essence of the events of life and of the known aspects of reality could adequately be captured in and condensed into the images of specific gods. This is no longer the case in modernity. Our life is far more complex, indeed complicated. In our time "the soul" has advanced to an awareness of its own production process and brings this out into the open. This is what its emphasis is on, and this is why modern phenomena in themselves have the nature of processes, complex logical relations, transactions rather than thing-like appearances. Just think of money. It is today not gold coins, but what happens in the global money-markets, investment banking, etc.

After having given some idea of what "logical" in the phrase "the soul's logical life" means and why the logical approach is indispensable for psychology, I want in conclusion to provide a few hints about the "life" that I have in mind here from a larger historical perspective. Before I was more concerned with the internal logical life constituting individual phenomena.

Historically, above all two distinct aims of movements need to be distinguished. First, there is the aim to form a soulful tradition and constantly renew it. Here the soul is interested in displaying its inner truths, in other words, in producing "products" (psychic phenomena) as results. This aim is realized in the dialectical interplay of the two movements of what in conventional depth-psychology has been called "projection" and "integration into consciousness." Projection here is to be understood in the widest sense: the need of "the soul" to give its

THE STUDY OF THE SOUL'S LOGICAL LIFE 349

own inner, totally irrepresentable logical life an objective representation or expression by sinking itself into the medium of the natural, in the form of cults, customs, images, myths, works of arts, culture at large (see above what was said about the "1ˢᵗ act" in the inner drama of a symbol). An opposite movement, which however belongs to the same sphere, comes from the need of the soul for the "initiation" of individual consciousness into the inner spirit of those objective representations, so that what at first was externalized may come home to consciousness and through this homecoming be filled with fresh lifeblood.

The second aim of the soul's logical life is to overcome itself, to emancipate itself from itself. This is the "alchemical" work of history, which is a history of the development of consciousness. Development here means consciousness's pushing off from its initial stage, negating and sublating the latter and *ipso facto* reaching a new stage, from which the same process can begin again. In Jung this theme of progression through sublations occurs especially in his ideas about the death of symbols and the "metamorphosis of the gods"[14] (one single example: a "... view of the world that had sprung from the decay of Olympus and the transformation of the gods into philosophical and theological ideas,"[15]). In each of the new stages reached the soul realizes and fulfills one potential of itself and brings out into the open one more aspect of its own nature.

The *whole* life of the soul is comprised in the one axiom of Pseudo-Democritus with its three stages, "Nature delights in nature [this corresponds to the first aim: the cultivation of traditional culture through projection (or objective representation) and initiation-integration], nature subdues nature [this corresponds to the step-by-step emancipation of consciousness, the alchemy of history as *opus contra naturam*], nature enjoys its mastery over nature [which we should not imagine as the utopia of a final stage, but as the soul's enjoyment of the specific fulfillment reached at any stage]."

---

[14] On the metamorphosis of the gods see Chapter 20 below.
[15] *Letters 2*, p. 337, to Père Bruno de Jésus-Marie, 20 Nov. 1956

CHAPTER THIRTEEN

The Ego-Psychological Fallacy
A note on "the birth of the meaning out of a symbol"

In his "The Mystical Symbol: Some Comments on Ankori, Giegerich, Scholem, and Jung" in the *Journal of Jungian Theory and Practice* (vol. 7, no. 1, 2005, pp. 25–29), Sanford Drob argues—seconded by Micha Ankori in his "Rejoinder ..." in the same issue (p. 31)—that "Both Scholem's understanding of the symbol and the kabbalists' notion of infinite interpretability pose significant challenges to Giegerich's declaration of 'the end of meaning.'" This is in no way the case. He can only think so because he does not see *my* argument; what he sees and criticizes is a view that he unwittingly substitutes for my view. The thesis in my "End of Meaning" article is by no means threatened by the ideas that "the symbol is *sui generis*" and that it is open to "an indefinite, if not infinite array of interpretations." I have no problem with these ideas.[1] Jung also becomes a victim of the same misconstrual. It makes Drob see an opposition or conflict between certain statements of Jung's where in fact there is no conflict, because the statements referred to are fully compatible. Thus after quoting Jung's idea from *Psychological Types* about the symbol that "once its meaning has been born out of it ... it

---

[1] I would, however, have a problem with Scholem's view, cited by Drob, that "the mystical symbol is a window into 'a hidden and inexpressible reality.'" This is obviously a metaphysical or ideological assertion. But as such it cannot pose a challenge for a psychological theory either.

is *dead*, i.e., it possesses only an historical significance," Drob states, "Jung, however, was not consistent in this view. For example, he later stated that 'no intellectual formulation comes anywhere near the richness and expressiveness of mythical imagery.'" Jung's two statements are compatible because they are answers to two different questions and for this reason cannot get into each other's hair. Drob seems to confound these two distinct issues.

What are the two questions? As to the first I start out with Drob's sentence, "While it is true that some symbols, for whatever reason, cease to stimulate interpretive possibilities, and thus 'die' ..." and note that Drob does not totally dispute the idea of the death of symbols, but that he has no explanation to offer for why and how the death of symbols is possible and, further, that he does not find this question worthy of consideration. How can it be that a symbol that enthralled people for centuries all of a sudden loses its power over their psyche? It is precisely this question that Jung answers with his theory, in *Psychological Types*, of the *birth* of the symbol's meaning out of it, in contrast to the symbol still *pregnant* with meaning. This is a question that has to do with the history and phenomenology of the soul's life in empirical reality.

When Jung, by contrast, says that "no intellectual formulation comes anywhere near the richness and expressiveness of mythical imagery," he is concerned with a totally different question, namely that of what a symbol *is* (when and as long as it is alive), a question about its particular dignity, its special nature and essence, in contrast above all to "sign" and "allegory." This is a logical question, a question of definition. Anyone can see that this view of the (it is safe to add: *infinite*[2]) richness and expressiveness of mythic imagery can with ease be inserted into the other statement, where it would then elucidate the "symbol still pregnant with meaning." The theory of the death and merely historical significance of a symbol precisely presupposes this (allegedly late and "not consistent") view of the symbol's richness. The symbol can only lose its richness and expressiveness if it possessed it before.

---

[2] Jung was well familiar with Goethe's, Creuzer's, Bachofen's theories of the symbol and concurred with them from early on. The infinite and thus ultimately indescribable richness of the meaning of a symbol was by no means a new acquisition by the older Jung in contrast to the Jung of the *Psychological Types*.

THE EGO-PSYCHOLOGICAL FALLACY

353

I said anyone can see it. But why then did Drob not see it? The reason, it seems to me, is his surreptitious replacement of Jung's (and my) view of the birth of the meaning out of the symbol by another, absolutely incompatible view, which comes out most clearly in his phrase, "the possibility or even the *necessity* of providing them [the symbols] with rational translations and interpretations." Drob asserts that "for Giegerich, with the birth of meaning out of the symbol, the symbol is finally understood," which is in a way backed up by formulations in my essay (in which I tried to *interpret Jung's* comments rather than speaking on my own), but is nevertheless a fundamental misrepresentation of my argument, since "understood" for him refers to *our* understanding, our interpretations, whereas in the context of the pregnancy-birth idea it means that it is the meaning itself that revealed its secret, that *it* has opened up like a blossom. Not, however, 'out there' as something to be watched, but by unwittingly having imparted itself to consciousness, by objectively having come home to and having revolutionized the logical form of consciousness. Therefore the symbol is not finally understood (by us, in the personalistic sense), but its meaning has been born out of it! A significant difference that deserves a few comments.

I worked with Jung's metaphor of *pregnancy* and *birth*. Drob instead works with the concepts of *interpretation* and *translation*. The difference between these two stances is crucial. What is the difference, indeed, opposition between them? We have to discern several aspects.

(1) The pregnancy-birth opposition is a metaphor from natural conditions or events. The ideas of "interpretation" or "translation," by contrast, are taken in their literal sense and can be taken in this way because from the outset they already refer to *mental* events. They involve the subject-object hiatus. The symbol is the object; the interpretation given is an event in the subject, in the mind of the ego-personality. This split plays no role in the pregnancy-birth imagery. The metaphoric birth of the meaning that the symbol was pregnant with is the (in a certain sense of the word) natural, spontaneous self-movement of the meaning (above I used the image of a bud opening up into a blossom). The event that happens here takes place solely on the side of the "object," the psychic phenomenon. The subject with his ideas and sentences does not enter in. We do have to stick to the image. A born baby is of course nothing like a human

354   THE SOUL ALWAYS THINKS

"interpretation" of what one surmises was hidden in the mother's belly. No, it is itself the hidden embryo that now, however, has come forth from out of its hiddenness.

(2) With pregnancy and birth we are talking about a status or condition change of one and the same entity, substance, or matter. "Birth" is the metaphoric description of a transition that can be observed, much like an alchemist observed the change of the matter in his retort, e.g., from blackness to whiteness. The ideas of a translation and interpretation, by contrast, operate with a duality, with two separate entities. Whereas the embryo is gone ("death" of the symbol) once the baby has been born, precisely because it turned into and lives on in the born baby, a translation is a new, additional product that leaves intact behind it the original that it is the translation of. Similarly, an interpretation is a new reality in addition to that which has been interpreted. Now we have two things, the original "text" and its interpretation/translation, both divided by an ontological gap.

(3) The unborn-born pair of concepts distinguishes between *statuses* or *conditions* of one matter. In the case of the interpretation-thesis, this distinction is replaced by another one, the "*real*" (text as fact) vs. "*ideal*" (interpretation as view, opinion) opposition, in other words, an opposition between two ontological realms. Because the difference is ontological, there cannot be a transition from the one to the other. They stand vis-à-vis, divided by a fundamental hiatus.

(4) Drob speaks of *providing* symbols with rational translations and interpretations. This wording is, I admit, completely appropriate for his "interpretation" thesis. *We* provide the already existing symbol with something; the interpretation has its origin in us, in the subjective mind; it is produced by us (on our own responsibility). It is a kind of thesis, hypothesis that we supply to or 'put under' (*hypo-*) the symbol. This shows that with his "interpretation" thesis about the "birth of meaning" Drob clearly views this idea from an ego standpoint. "Meaning" (in this context), since it is viewed in this way, immediately evokes the conception of our assigning our explanations, opinions to the symbol. It is all our activity, our thinking. *We* try to makes sense of a symbol, *we* try to figure it out.

The *birth* of meaning idea, understood in its own terms, is completely different. Here we are talking of an event that is the previously unborn meaning's own doing, its further development, its

THE EGO-PSYCHOLOGICAL FALLACY

coming to light. "Meaning" now has absolutely nothing to do with interpretations provided by the subjective mind. The birth image indicates that this theory is from the standpoint of "objective psychology." What *we* think or feel about a symbol, what interpretations or translations we *provide* for it, all this ego-stuff is irrelevant for an objective psychology. "Meaning" here is a *reality* in its own right. It is something (I might even be tempted to say: "substantially") real, even though of course psychologically, not physically, real (not a thing of nature, but a mental, intellectual real, a *soul* real, a matter in the psycho-alchemical sense), much like in our metaphor the baby that is born is something real and not a subjective opinion or explanation about the mother (or the embryo). Jung was speaking about the symbol's *own* meaning, the meaning *as which* it exists. How this real, existing meaning should be understood and interpreted by us is an entirely different question which, to be sure is also interesting, but does not enter at all into the question answered by Jung in his "birth of the meaning out of a symbol" theory nor into the argument of my "End of Meaning" paper.

I find it deplorable and shocking that serious Jung-scholars half a century and more after Jung's inauguration of an objective psychology are not capable of getting this crucial point—rendering, as it were, the whole effort of the later, alchemical Jung futile. It is a psychologically fatal mistake to confuse the psychological concept of (the symbol's) "meaning" with "meaning" in the sense of "rational translations and interpretations" of the symbol, a relapse into personalistic or ego-psychology. One can only exclaim with Jung, "You see, it is always the same matter: *the complete misunderstanding of the psychological argument*" (*Letters* 2, p. 572, to Robert C. Smith, 29 June 1960, italics in the original).[3]

Maybe Drob feels that by showing himself willing to "acknowledge that such interpretations represent what might be called a maturing or development ... of human consciousness ..." he obliges my view of things a bit. But not so. I do not at all subscribe to this statement. For me, the "rational, discursive interpretations" are ego-stuff and have no significance for the maturing or development of human consciousness and are uninteresting for an "objective psychology."

---

[3] The context in which he said this and what he referred to were different.

Psychology is not about people and what *they* think or feel. It is about "the soul" (and what it thinks or feels), about the objective psyche, about human consciousness. Of course, like all schooling, academic training, private reading and thinking those interpretations can be important for people's personal development, for the maturing and expansion of the subjective mind. But as to the history of "human consciousness" they are neither here nor there.

We could recall here Jung's oft-mentioned idea, taken over from Leopold Ziegler, of the "metamorphosis of the gods." For example, Jung wrote that (in antiquity) "[m]any of the earlier gods developed from 'persons' into personified ideas, and finally into abstract ideas" (*CW* 13 § 49). When this had happened, i.e., when that which had formerly been gods, or more precisely: when the logical form of "god" for the respective contents had become psychologically obsolete, all of a sudden all sorts of rational interpretations and explanations of the former gods and of myths sprang up, *vide* only those by Euhemeros. But what we have to realize is that those interpretations were precisely not the form in which the birth of the meaning out of the god symbols took place. Rather, they were free-floating, inconsequential ways in which a now disconnected ego-consciousness tried to make sense of the now dead and psychologically alien "symbols" that, true, persisted, but persisted only as erratic, no longer understood elements in historical memory.

All the intellectual speculation and theorizing about the gods is psychologically, in terms of the history of the soul, irrelevant, merely people's opinions, not psychic realities. They are semantic contents of subjective consciousness and as such make use of and thus confirm the prevailing objective constitution of consciousness, much like the furniture and pictures brought into a house have no bearing one way or another on the structure of the house itself. The soul or consciousness is the house, the ego or ego-consciousness is the tenant who furnishes his (private) rooms in the house with his views and interpretations according to his personal likes and needs. The only psychological (in contrast to private, personal, ego) relevance the intellectual speculations and interpretations have is that, as *symptoms* of the (psychological) obsolescence of that which they are about, they display this obsolescence. Whenever the need to explain and interpret

THE EGO-PSYCHOLOGICAL FALLACY

is felt, we know that that which is to be interpreted has lost its significance for the soul and has now become prey to the cut-off ego practicing its external reflection and theorizing upon it as upon the relics of the particular contents of a bygone form of consciousness.

Our result so far is that rational interpretations per se do not represent a maturing or development of human consciousness. But the converse is that it would also be wrong to assume that a real development of consciousness goes along with discursive interpretations and a higher subjective understanding. I already rejected the idea that "with the birth of meaning out of the symbol, the symbol is finally understood" (in the ego sense of understood). The birth of the meaning does not result in interpretations, i.e., in semantic contents. One does not know more or better. One (as individual conscious mind, ego consciousness) is not more conscious, more aware. Rather, the birth of the meaning results in an initiation of consciousness, i.e., in a revolutionizing of the form or logical status of consciousness, so that consciousness becomes an "esoteric" one in Jung's special sense, one that has integrated the meaning of the symbol into its logical form, but *ipso facto* stands ignorant in front of the now empty shells (the now "conventional signs" – Jung) that formerly used to house that meaning and thus used to be living symbols, viewing them from outside, in external reflection. If it does not simply dismiss them, it will probably feel the need to make sense of them on the basis of the newly acquired status of consciousness.

If the kabbalists had the theory of the "infinite interpretability" of the mystic symbols, those symbols must already have been a thing of the past for them, because living symbols need no interpretation: they *are* their meaning. The consciousness of the kabbalists must already have been an esoteric one in Jung's sense, one that from an external, theoretical standpoint reflected *about* the meaning (here = interpretations) of so-called mystic symbols (actually: signs). An exoteric consciousness does not reflect from outside about the meaning of symbols; it is in the *immediate* spell of its presence and truth.

Thus, all that happened when a development of consciousness took place is that consciousness itself has been *objectively* transported to a new level or logical status, a status in which basically the same game as before between unconsciousness and conscious awareness, ignorance

358   *THE SOUL ALWAYS THINKS*

and knowing, repeats and continues, although now in new and different ways and with respect to different aspects.[4] The development of consciousness is a form change, an "alchemical" or logical change, not a rise to a linear increase of subjective consciousness, not a quantitative expansion of personal awareness. In fact, each higher (or deeper) level of consciousness *begins* with a greater unconsciousness and primitivity than had been reached in the final developed phase of the previous status of consciousness.

To explain this by returning to the birth metaphor: with the transition from embryo to baby, the enigma of the former is not lost or diminished. Is the baby—as potential person, mind, and soul— any less enigmatic than the embryo? Of course not. The fact that the baby is now out in the open before everyone's eyes does not resolve the mystery of its nature and being. And the moment we do not confuse the objective meaning of a symbol with our interpretation(s) of the symbol, but comprehend the meaning as a real, the idea of the meaning in the singular that is born out of a symbol does not narrow down the symbol to a single literal "meaning" (in the sense of interpretation), but is open to, more than that: insists on, the inner infinity of this one (real, existing) meaning or mystery as which a baby as well as a symbol exist. The symbol has *its* meaning in the singular, just as a tree has *its* nature in the singular, not in the plural. The choice here seems to be between numeric infinity and inner infinity. But for the psychologist qua psychologist the choice is from the outset determined by his profession.

Birth is not synonymous with rational translation or discursive interpretation; it does not mean that *we* have intellectually *understood* "the baby" or "the symbol's meaning," respectively. It is the objective consciousness that has "understood." Subjectively, the born meaning is normally unconscious, not understood. It simply prevails, rules, as a (in the psychological sense) "natural" fact. As I pointed out, meaning in this psychological sense refers to a reality and not to a subjective "idea about ..." Birth means the meaning's coming to light, its "albedo," if I may say so. And just as the whitening in alchemy only

---

[4] For those who find this statement puzzling I might explain that consciousness is in itself the unity and tension of unconsciousness and conscious awareness. There is not a literal "the unconscious" vis-à-vis consciousness. "The unconscious" is an illegitimate hypostasis and extrajection of one of the internal *moments* of consciousness itself.

means that the matter has turned white, not that the alchemist has provided it with a rational interpretation, so the meaning's coming to light means a *psychological* status change of the meaning itself, instead of an *egoic* intellectual understanding of it. In the "End of Meaning" paper, where I was not concerned, as Jung was in his comments, with the fate of individual symbols, but with that of human consciousness at large, I used in addition to the birth metaphor that of emergence from the waters, an emergence that results in the "Aquarius" stage of consciousness. The "end of meaning" is a logical, syntactical transformation and comes about through the *integration* (and thus also sublation) of the whole former status of consciousness into the structure of consciousness itself.

The inwardization of the whole former constitution of consciousness is dialectically tantamount to the surfacing ("birth") of a new, formerly hidden, unrealized potential of consciousness as such, its rise above its former self.

The notion of integration helps us to be a little more precise than Jung was when he said, very roughly speaking, that "[m]any of the earlier gods developed from 'persons' into personified ideas, and finally into abstract ideas." The birth of the meaning out of the gods, that this sentence expresses, should not be understood such that each individual god changed one-to-one into a particular corresponding abstract idea. Rather, the development of consciousness meant that that stage of consciousness which is characterized by the fact that truth appeared to it in the logical *form* of gods (god images), as personal beings or powers, was *in toto* sublated and integrated into the logical constitution of consciousness, which *ipso facto* had become a post-imaginal, post-mythological consciousness. For this newly constituted consciousness, truth had to present itself in a new form, the form of "abstract ideas" (e.g., Platonic Forms). What in the previous stage were semantic contents of consciousness (images, gods), in the new stage invisibly ruled over consciousness as *its own* inner laws or structure, its syntax, within which this new consciousness now apperceived all its semantic contents. The previous consciousness was, with respect to the gods, comparatively innocent; it had the gods outside, before itself, which means that consciousness in its own constitution was still untouched by and ignorant of them. But the later consciousness did no longer have the same innocence, inasmuch as "the gods" had come

360   *THE SOUL ALWAYS THINKS*

home to it and it now had them, in sublated, distilled form, within itself as its own style or syntax.

Why is it that the born meaning, as I said above, is normally unconscious, not understood, not seen? Because its "birth" means that it is no longer a content of consciousness that we could have before our eyes, but the syntactical form in which we see or think whatever we see or think. And in total contrast to literal, biological birth, which is an empirical, consciously felt event, the birth of meaning happens behind the scenes, unwittingly. Consciousness all of a sudden simply finds itself in a totally new situation without knowing what happened or even being aware *that* something fundamental happened (the only thing to be clearly noticed is something negative: that what used to be of highest meaning to previous generations strangely does not mean anything to oneself any more). This is so because the meaning, by being born, does not appear on the stage of consciousness—on the semantic level—as an insight or interpretation, like the baby indeed appears in the real world as a visible being. Rather, it "reveals" itself by, as it were, directly infecting, undermining, and reconstituting the logical form of consciousness from behind and in an already psychological (subtle, evaporated, distilled), not in a psychic (empirical-factual, experiential, semantic) mode. It is a process in the negativity of the soul, not in the positivity of what the eyes can see.

The consciousness that construes the "birth of meaning" as our providing interpretations to symbols is one that takes its firm footing in what we call "the ego." Maybe because it is, as such, condemned to thinking in *abstractions*, it gets (and possibly feels the need to seek) the non-abstract only outside, before itself, as its semantic contents: for example, as mythic gods and mystic symbols, as the unthinkable and ineffable. This would also explain why it wants to eternalize the gods and symbols into timeless truths, immunizing them from the soul's historical distilling and evaporating work, and why it indulges (by no means in true mysticism, but only) in reminiscences of historical mysticisms, but at any rate in the *form* of *un*consciousness— systematically 'closing its eyes' (*myo*, whence 'mysticism') to the openly displayed psychological truth of the age, an age that knows symbols and the like only as unmistakingly obsolete: as advertised consumer goods on a huge "meaning market," as elements of ideologies and fundamentalisms, as "drugs" for subjective high feelings or for

THE EGO-PSYCHOLOGICAL FALLACY

361

numbing consciousness, as stopgaps to (seemingly) fill one's inner bottomless emptiness, in any case as components of the post-industrial, *medial*[5] phase of modernity.

It is a consciousness that focuses on and clings to mythic images or mystic symbols as stable semantic contents of consciousness in order to be rescued from the danger of having to become aware of the prevailing syntax of consciousness—another example of "the flight into the unconscious." For what is unconsciousness? Not to see the forest for the trees.[6]

---

[5] "Medial": here an adjective to the noun "the media," thus meaning something like 'characterized by the media.'

[6] Thus one can have a multitude of interpretations, explanations, rational translations for all kinds of phenomena, great knowledge, and many insights, and yet be quite unconscious. More interpretations or seeing more trees does not by itself make more conscious.

CHAPTER FOURTEEN

Once More "The Stone Which is Not a Stone"
Further Reflections on "Not"

Many years ago, in *Spring 49* (1989), David Miller presented us with his amazing essay entitled "The Stone Which is Not a Stone," full of insights extending far beyond the immediate theme expressed in this alchemical dictum, insights about "C.G. Jung and the Postmodern Meaning of 'Meaning'" at large. Like myths, fairy tales, symbols, poetry, and works of art, alchemical notions, too, are so rich that it is worthwhile to return to them again and again. In the following paper in honor of David—for whose learned, thoughtful, stimulating contributions to the field, whose long-standing friendship, intellectual support and always prompt, substantial, inspiring responses in our email exchanges I feel and wish to express deep gratitude—I intend to explore the meaning of the pivotal term in the alchemical phrase, the "not."

The word "not" performs a negation. "Negation," "negativity," and "negative" are tied to their opposites, "position," "positivity," and "positive." These important terms are difficult because they give rise to confusions. "Positive" and "negative" have several meanings, and our first task is to keep them apart.

(1) The most common meaning is that of a valuation, the ego and survival sense: the terms mean something like good vs. bad, advantageous (prospective, beneficial, desirable) vs. detrimental,

malignant. So we speak of a positive or negative development, sometimes even of a "positive" or "negative aspect" of archetypes; to get sick or to lose money is negative, to stay healthy or to get a salary raise is positive. This use of the terms positive and negative, which is clearly guided by the perspective of the ego and its survival interests, is not how they are meant here. We must in this context forget this sense. We need to evoke this sense of positive and negative only for the purpose of consciously and explicitly excluding it, keeping it away. There is always the danger that this so very common meaning will unawares creep in. So we have to be on guard.

(2) Positive means, in a strictly *formal sense*, "affirmative," "saying yes," negative then refers to negation, denial, saying "no." E.g., a positive answer, a negative response. In formal logic "positive (or affirmative) judgment." "Negative judgment."

(3) "Positive" is used in the sense of posited, established by human design, in contrast to "given by nature." E.g., positive law in contrast to natural law. Positive law is the actual laws and regulations in a particular state that in our time are put down in writing in the code of law, in statute books. Since the counter-term to this meaning of positive is "natural," "negative" has no place here.

There are also some further meanings that I will not mention here. I will directly go over to that meaning that we need here for our psychological purposes.

(4) Positive here means positively existing, having the status of positive fact, empirically real, demonstrable event, etc. This is the meaning that is prevalent in the philosophical movement of *Positivism*. Positive-factual realities can in this sense also be termed *positivities*. Now what is the meaning of the counter-terms to *this* meaning of "positive", i.e., the meaning of "negative" or "negativity"?

A first approximation might be to think here of the already mentioned term positive law. The written laws made by governments are positivities. The idea of justice, by contrast, is something very different. Many actions and many court decisions may be fully in agreement with positive law, but we may nevertheless feel that justice has not been done. Justice is logically negative, which of course does not mean bad or undesirable, but rather the opposite. Justice can *not* easily be spelled out; it is *not* tangible, visible. And in this sense it is

"THE STONE WHICH IS NOT A STONE"

"negative." While you can point to the individual laws, justice cannot be pointed at. It is *not* positively there.

A similar distinction can be made between positive religion, the official, institutionalized religion of the established churches, which often is felt not to be all that religious, but very worldly, driven by human power interests or commercial interests, a sterile routine, etc. True religion often is felt not to be found in the positively existing churches, in organized religion. You can point at and document the dogmas of the churches, just as you can demonstrate the positive laws of a state. But true religion cannot be demonstrated in the same sense.

Literalism (Hillman) means something similar, but not exactly the same as positivity. And especially the negation of a literalistic understanding of the image is not the same as alchemy's direct negation of the image itself ("not stone").

When we read in Laotse, *Tao te king*: "The WAY that can be expressed in words is not the eternal WAY," we see the role of negation. "Is not!" A rejection of the positive is obviously needed. You cannot say what you actually want to say. You can only negate the positive, that which is not meant. The moment you would spell out what the eternal WAY, the TAO, is, you would have positivized it again. The negation of the positive equivalent is absolutely necessary.

Moving from China to India we find a similar example for negativity, one of many, in the *Kena Upanishad*: "Not what the eyes can see, but what opens the eyes, that is the Brahma." Again: Not!

I give another example from our Western tradition, the New Testament. In the Gospel of John (ch. 4) we learn that Jesus had to leave Judaea and passed through the neighboring region of Samaria. At a fountain he had a conversation with a woman from Samaria. In the course of this exchange, the woman said:

> (20) Our fathers worshipped in this mountain; and ye say, that in Jerusalem is the place where men ought to worship. (21) Jesus saith unto her, Woman, believe me, the hour cometh, when ye shall neither in this mountain, nor yet at Jerusalem, worship the Father. ... (23) But the hour cometh, and now is, when the true worshippers shall worship the Father in spirit and in truth: for the Father seeketh such to worship him. (24) God is a Spirit: and they that worship him must worship him in spirit and in truth.

The question here is what is the right place (the Greek text has *topos*) for worship. And the passage starts out with two *alternatives* as options, "this mountain" versus "Jerusalem." Two features deserve our attention. First, they are obviously both positivities, visible entities in reality. You can point at them. With these two empirical localities as the true places of worship, we are in the sphere of positive religion, not of course exactly in our modern sense of positive religion, but rather as a still ethnic, tribal form of religion, a local cult, a religion tied to national and often political interests. The reference to "our fathers" underlines the dependence on an ethnic tradition. And each ethnic group, tribe, nation with their "fathers" has its own sacred places, literal places in geographic reality. Thus you necessarily get otherness, alternatives, a clash of different local traditions: *our* true place for worship, *their* or *your* true place for worship.

The second feature of interest is that traditional ethnically bound religion singles out from all the places within their own local sphere of empirical or positive reality certain ones as the exclusive (or at least prioritized) places for worship and calls them sacred in contrast to all the other ones, which are *profane* places.

What Jesus does, by contrast, is to push off from and altogether negate both alternatives offered by traditional piety: *neither* on this mountain, *nor* at Jerusalem. And by extension at *no place* at all: *ou topos*. In other words, he negates the whole *level* of positivity as such. Instead, he states that the worship has to take place (!) "in spirit and in truth." Thus he moves the entire question of the "right place" to a fundamentally new level. By rejecting all positive places he does not simply give up the question about the right place. For him, there is indeed a right place. He insists on an exclusive place: "and they that worship him *must* worship him in spirit and in truth" and nowhere else. But spirit and truth as the exclusive place are precisely not a place in empirical reality, nothing positive, nothing literal, fixed. They are really the *sublation* of the very *idea* of "place" or of a "where." *Where* is this supposed to be, "in spirit and in truth"? You cannot say. And yet, it is not either a total utopia (*ou topos*), a literal lacuna, a lack, a nihil or naught. Rather, it is indeed a kind of place, but a *logically negative* "place," a *sublated* place, *topos ou topos*, just as *lithos ou lithos*, the stone which is not a stone. The true worship, we could say, has to take place *in* "absolute negativity" ("absolute," because this negativity is

"THE STONE WHICH IS NOT A STONE" 367

"absolved," freed, from the binary opposition of something versus nothing.) So while you cannot say where this place is in external reality, the expression "in spirit and in truth" nevertheless has a specific (determinate) and concrete meaning. And it receives much of its meaning from the very thing that it negates and sublates. Just like the real TAO is not the literal, spelled-out *tao*, but has a kind of foothold in what is negated, so here too.

We must be wary of not just *acting out* the negation (acting it out in the intellectual realm). Just as in the area of subjective experience and behavior we should not simply live out and let run free any impulses and drives, so that they merely exhaust, spend, waste themselves, but let their dynamic and message come back home to us (*Erinnern*: "remembering," reflection, interiorization into oneself), so the negation should also not just run free. It has to come home to itself, take its own medicine ("self-application"). Then it limits itself, becoming a *determinate* negation. It does not end up in an abstract (empty) nothing, a total uncertainty and not knowing (here I differ from David Miller's 1989 view). It does not become serial, a deferral forever, which would merely show that now the negation itself has become positivized, an end in itself! No, the "not" does land us somewhere. We do arrive. Where? Of course back at the starting point. But at a transformed starting point, because it has absorbed the negation, has become absolute negativity. The "energy" of the negation, rather than horizontally living itself out, came home to, and came to the benefit of, that which was negated and forced *it* (the notion, definition, understanding of it and thus the logical constitution of consciousness at large) vertically to a wholly other level. The negation ceased to be an (endlessly repeatable) subjective *operation* and instead turned into the goal, the *place* of absolute negativity.

The determinate negation is not the negation of the content, the semantics. It is the negation of the logical form of the content. The acted-out negation negates externally. The alchemical negation negates the thing negated from within itself and reveals it as negativity.

Topos ou topos and *lithos ou lithos* have to be seen as abbreviations. Actually, three statements are collapsed into one. 1. The stone is a stone. 2. The stone is not a stone. 3. Despite being not a stone, it is not anything else nor simply nothing at all, but nevertheless a stone. And only as this *in itself* (inwardly) negated stone is it *the philosophers'* stone.

To return to our biblical passage: There is a further point along the same lines. The negation that Jesus expresses does not amount to a wholesale rejection of *worship* as such. He does not say one cannot or should not worship at all any more. No, one should worship, however in a radically new, previously unheard-of way, namely in spirit and in truth.

It is noteworthy that the cultic veneration is here not "psychologized," removed from the external world into the interior of man, as one's inner *mystical* experience or the like. It is not a personal emotion, feeling, attitude. It is something objective, unemotional, sober: *noetic*, something that goes beyond the subjective person: in spirit and in truth. Truth is universal, it is all around us. This is true for scientific truths as much as for the truth that the Gospel of John has in mind. When we speak of the law of gravity or the theorems of geometry, we know that what is meant is not a subjective experience, feeling, or opinion, but something to which everything in the material world is subject. Although in a very different way, the same applies to "in spirit and in truth."

Furthermore, the sublated place "in spirit and in truth" is no longer rooted in an ethnic tradition. It does not belong to any tribe, nation, group. By rejecting this mountain as well as Jerusalem as *the* places to worship God, Jesus (or the writer of this Gospel who puts these words into the mouth of Jesus) of course also negates the ethnic or national rootedness of religion, all local-ness of cult, the tradition of the fathers and thus inherited and in this sense *natural* religion, religion based on kinship, on *blood* relationship. The natural in this sense is what we are born into, like our mother tongue. It precedes our personal existence and as such is, as it were, self-evident, matter of course. "This is how it has always been." So we can say that what Jesus does with such a statement is to perform an *opus contra naturam*. The negation or sublation disrupts one's innocent, naive containment in and unity with tradition, tradition which is "nature" in a *psychological* sense. The same can be said about the negation of the places of worship. What is negated is the natural places, and what is proposed instead is spiritual places, places that are no longer places, much as alchemy is about a stone that is not a stone, *lithos ou lithos*, and as alchemy in general turns against "the physical in the matter."

"THE STONE WHICH IS NOT A STONE"

The negative (or: logical negativity in general) does not refer to a "natural," ontological entity or substance, but is the *result of a negation* of the positive, the result of a pushing off from a specific positivity. "Spirit and truth" *exist* only if, to the extent that, and for as long as, you perform this act of negating and pushing off from. Because spirit and truth never have a positive existence, their existence is fundamentally negative. A mountain or temple, a tree or table exist regardless of whether we see them or do anything with them. Not so "spirit and truth." When we stop being in spirit and truth, *they* stop to be.

What Jesus is saying in this passage amounts to the view that in Christianity there are no sanctuaries, no sacred places at all any more, no temple, no holy mountains, also no holy objects, no holy people; nothing positively real as such is sacred. A church as a building is for this view not a sacred place; it is just an ordinary assembly hall. By contrast, *any* literal place in geographic reality, any building or mountain or valley could become "sacred" in the sense of negativity if there is worship "in spirit and in truth." The sublated place comes out in the other biblical saying (Mat. 18:20), "For where two or three are gathered together in my name, there am I in the midst of them." This "there" is not defined in geographical terms, but by the "name"— a negativity like "spirit and truth"—that brings them together.

It is the *whole difference between sacred and profane* that has (to be sure, not disappeared altogether, but) been sublated, i.e., (a) canceled and (b) preserved on a *new* level. The move that we witness in such a text is that from the *natural* (positive) consciousness to a higher status of consciousness, which is the *result* of a *sublation* of the former. What has been negated by Jesus in what he said is not just two things (this mountain and Jerusalem), but the whole former *form* of religion that distinguishes between the right positive or literal places for worship and those literal places that are not right or at least not as holy. *The whole way of thinking* in terms of sacred versus profane places and objects has been overcome. This difference has been sublated and raised from the *semantic* level of *entities*, things, items, substances, contents that are side by side on the same plane, but have fundamentally different values and dignity (holy vs. profane) to a *syntactical* or *logical* level of truth and spirit, and thereby it has also been interiorized. Now the question is one about where one's soul or heart is, namely whether it is "in spirit and in truth," or not. The question is not whether one is in this building or that one, in this city, holy country, on this holy mountain, or not. It is a movement from positivity to negativity, from nature to spirit.

We can take this thought even a bit more forward. It is not only that this particular difference between sacred and profane is abolished, but also that the "difference as such" or "otherness" is removed. If God is spirit and those who worship him must do so in spirit and in truth—we could also say: they must do so *as* spirit—then we get a uroboric, circular, self-reflective relation. Ultimately it is God himself as spirit who worships himself through man, man having raised himself to the status of spirit and truth. True worship is a self-relation of spirit. All *fundamental* otherness is overcome (in true worship God is no longer "wholly other"). We can think here of Plotinus: like is known through like; one has to oneself become what one wants to see. Or in homeopathy: "Like cures like," *similia similibus curantur.* Or Goethe: "If the eye were not sun-like, it could never see the sun." If Schelling said that in man nature opens her eyes and beholds herself, we can now add that on the level of consciousness reached with the sublation of the literal places of worship it is spirit as sublated nature or as logical negativity that becomes aware of *itself.*

I am here of course not interested in propounding Christian religion or giving a lesson in theology, nor in the question of worship in general. I am discussing this text passage only as a striking example for a move into logical negativity and thus also into the alchemical-psychological "not." At the same time, this Christian example of course *deserves* to be mentioned because Christian thinking, its move *contra naturam*, is one of the historical roots of the articulation and development of this logic in the course of Western history and, as a religious idea, a driving force behind it.

With the wording "in spirit and in truth" logical negativity may be expressed a bit vaguely for us today, because spirit and truth usually do not mean anything to us modern people. They often sound today like empty words, meaningless jingle. Spirit has nothing to do with what "spirituality" means in modernity, in the New Age movement or in esoteric circles. It would perhaps be better to use "mindedness" instead. Similarly, but in different ways, the TAO or the Brahma are

"THE STONE WHICH IS NOT A STONE"

exotic power words for us, but we do not have our own experience with them *rooted* in and authenticated by our own real tradition. So that we also get an example of logical negativity that is much closer to our own experience, I will briefly discuss the notion of life.

Life does not have a positive existence. It is not an entity, a thing-like substance, a life-force comparable to fuel in cars. For example, while you can cut out from the body of a mammal or a human being their lungs or livers and then you really have these organs in front of you as positive objects, you cannot extract the life of a living being. There is no special place where the organism keeps its life-force the way cars keep their fuel in special tanks. Certainly, you can kill a plant, an animal or a human being, you can, as we say, "take" their life. If you take somebody's money, he lost it and you have it. But if you "take" his life, you do not have it. Nobody has it. It is simply gone. By "taking" somebody's life, you do not get it and then have it, you cannot even demonstrate it like you can the lungs or livers that you took out of a body. Life is "nothing," no thing. Life is not either like a vapor, a gas, or like heat or light that in many chemical reactions escapes without our being able to see or touch or sense it with our senses, but nevertheless, with certain instruments, can be demonstrated to positively exist and even be measured. This is not possible with life. It is really "nothing." By contrast, what you do get if you take somebody's life, and *all* you get, is a corpse. The corpse has a positive existence.

And yet, life is a powerful *reality*. There *is* life. But its existence is logically negative existence. Hegel would say that life is a *real* or *concrete Concept* (in contrast to an abstract concept), a Concept that exists, but that, because it is a *Concept* is not a positive thing or entity, cannot be positivized. Life, we might say with our earlier text, exists "in spirit and in truth." However, *as such*, *as* concrete or real Concept, *as* being "in spirit and in truth," it also exists—and *only* exists—in living creatures who have a positive existence. So it is this logically negative reality of life that makes the positive entity alive. And death is the moment when the positive and the negative part company.

But if they part company at death, they must have been joined before. How were they joined? Not like, e.g., husband and wife in marriage. Rather, the living organism is alive because, and as long as, it has the strength to negate its own positivity. When it loses its strength to negate its positivity, e.g., because of old age or illness, then

372   *THE SOUL ALWAYS THINKS*

this positivity (that before had been reduced to a sublated moment within life's negativity) all of a sudden *gains an independence of its own*; it now makes its presence felt *as something in its own right*, and this is what we call a corpse. The corpse is the positivity of the living being that is no longer subdued by, and integrated into, the negativity of life. It has been released from, fallen out of, life's sphere of jurisdiction.[1] Death is the normal, the natural state. Life is, as it were, an *opus contra naturam*. From the point of view of the physical, life is (exists as!) an impertinence, an uprising, arrogation.

The fact that life *as such* exists as the negation and subjugation of the positivity of the living being can be seen, although merely in *acted-out* form, from the fact that animals maintain their life by killing and eating other living organisms and integrating them into their own system. This reality was what was celebrated in the myth and cult of Dionysos, according to Kerényi the primordial image of indestructible life, that is, life that maintains itself precisely despite and even through its own violence against itself. It is "absolved" from the neat *abstract* opposition of destruction and self-preservation. And modern medicine tells us that also we as individual beings stay alive only as long as our body internally keeps winning its permanently ongoing battle against bacteria and viruses, i.e., is successful in negating (killing) them ("immune system"). We exist as living beings only *as* this ongoing "killing."

Like life, soul, too, is logically negative. It is nothing. During earlier times, the ages of mythological thinking, when soul and life were often not really distinguished, one imagined that at death the life or soul of the person left the body through the mouth in the form of breath or a bird, the soul bird. Or later that the devil would lie in wait and try to capture the soul when it leaves the body. This is typical for the mythological imagination: it substantiates and often personifies what in truth is "nothing," namely logically negative or a concrete Concept,

---

[1] By way of analogy I want to mention the fact that when we quickly repeat a word or a mantra a hundred times, we lose its meaning. Then, too, the sounds as acoustic, physical signs slowly push themselves forward and assume an existence in their own right. The sounds are "the corpse" of the word, whereas the word as living one, as meaning, only exists "in spirit and in truth," by virtue of having pushed off from the mere sounds. If a word is to have a meaning the sounds as positivities have to die away. In normal, successful speaking the sounds are only (must only be) a stepping stone. They must not insist on an independent existence on their own.

"THE STONE WHICH IS NOT A STONE" 373

a *real* Concept. The soul is of course not literally a bird or a "subtle" substance like a breath of wind. We know this. However, the images or metaphors of the soul bird or a breath leaving the body have a seductive force. They entice us to unconsciously remain in the mode of substantiating thinking despite our conscious insight that we must not take them literally and must not substantiate them. Therefore: beware of metaphors and images. They suggest that one could simply innocently glide into a nonnaturalistic, nonliteralistic understanding *without* having paid the price: the radical and explicit break with the natural likeness, that break and rejection that is expressed in the hurtful "not" of our alchemical dictum.

In my discussion of the Gospel of John passage about the proper place to worhip, I stated, "When we stop being in spirit and truth, *they* stop to be." The same applies to life. When our organism ceases performing the *act* of living, of breathing, digesting, producing hormones, fighting viruses and bacteria, etc., we are dead. Life is an activity and exists only for the duration that this activity is executed. The point is that life is precisely not a substance that we may possess like property and that may get lost or be taken from us. No, we *keep* alive. It is like a fire that lasts only for as long as it burns...

The abstract concept has its referent outside of itself. For Kant the concept of 100 dollars is different from the 100 dollars that you have in your pocket. For Kant—and for our conventional style of thinking—, the concept is abstract. But life is a *real*, not an abstract Concept. And it is the *Concept* that makes us alive.

What I said here about life referred to biological life. But it is true also for the higher life of "the soul." From what the alchemist Dorneus exclaimed: "Transmute yourselves from dead stones into living philosophical stones!" we can realize that the stone (*lithos ou lithos*), too, is in truth a Concept and not a thing or property.

But when Jung after quoting this dictum bemoans that Dorneus "lacked the concept of an unconscious existence which would have enabled him to express the identity of the subjective, psychic centre and the objective, alchemical centre in a satisfactory formula" (*CW* 9ii § 264, punctuation modif.) he shows that he, Jung, has himself not arrived at the stone which is not a stone. Ultimately, his thought remained stuck in positivity; he thought that there were *two* centers and that one would need the auxiliary concept, i.e., the crutch, of "*the* unconscious" as a third to bring the two together. Jung of course did not speak of "the unconscious" here; he said "unconscious existence." But the latter expression only tells us *what* "the unconscious" is thought to be: positive existence. With "unconscious existence" or "the unconscious" Jung introduces the fantasy of a literal, "empirical" place in the stead of the only place where the stone could really exist: the no-place of "in spirit and in truth." And this despite the fact that the very text by Dorneus that is the starting point for Jung's critical comment already explicitly provides us with the notion of *veritas* (truth), as he himself shows in the same paragraph.

Veritas is the direct opposite of the unconscious. Truth means disclosedness, having appeared and being revealed to consciousness, and thus to knowing. "Unconscious," by contrast, means hidden, split off from consciousness, ultimately inaccessible to human knowing: unknowable. Even if "unconscious contents" are experienced and thus become empirically and semantically conscious, e.g., through dreams, logically or syntactically (as far as their status is concerned) they stay for Jung, as "archetypes of the unconscious," on the other side, dissociated from consciousness, and do not attain to the status of truth, true knowing. "The concept of the unconscious," Jung states, "*posits nothing*, it designates only my *unknowing*" (*Letters 1*, p. 411, to Frischknecht, 8 Feb. 1946). Jung systematically washes his hands in innocence.

"Un-conscious existence" merely negates the *accessibility* for consciousness of what we could call "the essential place," while nevertheless granting it positive existence. It declares an area of consciousness as off limits for knowing. It thus sets up a spatial difference. "In spirit and in truth," by contrast, negates the notion of place itself as well as of anything supposed to be found at this place (such as "the stone"). One's recourse to "the unconscious" tries to get away with a cheap substitute, external negation as the displacement, deportation of the (in themselves untouched!) contents, in order to avoid having to pay the full price: negation as the internal sublation, distillation, evaporation of the contents in question in their *substance* and *positivity*. In this way it manages to be the secret placeholder for logical positivity, while appearing to be its opposite.

In 18th and early 19th century England, convicts were often physically deported to the colonies, above all Australia, and for the

"THE STONE WHICH IS NOT A STONE"

price of this removal from their legitimate home country could escape capital punishment (their own negation), while at the same time being out of sight for the people in England, removed for the latter from the sphere of knowing and conscious awareness. Because of their "metaphysical" content and general character, certain contents of consciousness, namely the so-called archetypal ideas and images, are modern positivism's psychological convicts. Jung understood this. Having armored his positivism with what he believed was his Kantianism, he was keenly aware of the convict character of the archetypal ideas within the world of the modern scientific mind. And responding to their incompatibility he followed, as it were, the British model and (logically) deported them into the psychological Australia invented by him, "the unconscious,"[2] so that they could likewise escape *their* "capital punishment" (their sublation, their *mortificatio* and *evaporatio*).

Another purpose and result of this move of Jung's was that their home country, human consciousness, could feel relieved of its (in this case: intellectual) responsibility for them (of the duty to take a position as to their truth). Because, having once and for all settled in the position of "unknowing" by having deported the incriminated or condemned contents, consciousness was no longer burdened with and bothered by the question of truth.

A third consequence: in both cases this trick of deportation saved the tender-minded "authorities" from themselves having to go through with the tough "execution" of the "not" and from having to shoulder their concomitant loss of innocence.

Finally, the wholesale removal of those contents from the sphere of knowing and the avoidance of the necessary execution also helped Jung to rescue the status of the contents themselves as (simulated) immediacies, as (alleged) facts of nature, objective events (rather than productions of the thinking mind itself[3]), as well as to retain unscathed their imaginal character as natural likenesses, thereby simulating a naivety of consciousness that, having historically become long obsolete, did only become possible through, and always stayed

---

[2] I am of course not suggesting that Jung invented the *term* and *concept* "the unconscious." But Jung invented *his* peculiar concept of it.

[3] The thinking mind of the *homo totus*, the whole man; *not* that of what we call in psychology "the ego," or ego-consciousness.

dependent on, the artificial and not-at-all naive move of logically deporting them.

As far as the "satisfactory formula" for the expression of the identity of the subjective, psychic center and the objective, alchemical center is concerned, "the unconscious" is by definition a vis-à-vis, the object for a subject: for the *experiencing* ego. It is historical England's Australia. The concept of the unconscious posits dissociation, fundamental otherness, the distance of a continent at the other end of the world separated by an ocean; it is for Jung "pure nature" and by definition *not* the mind's, *not* thought's, own depth, inner infinity, and inner transcendency.[4] Its contents remain (and are supposed to remain) logically irrevocably alien to the thinking mind. For otherwise, so the idea goes, they would inevitably produce inflation, madness.[5] Thus contrary to Jung's hope the concept of "unconscious existence" cannot express identity.

Our transmutation into living philosophical stones is even made structurally impossible as long as we hold on to "the unconscious." The philosophical stone as something logically negative, as something that is *not* a stone and *not* a thing subsisting independently, thus also *not* "the objective, alchemical centre" opposite to the "subjective, psychic centre," *is*—from the outset and *in itself* and always-already— the desired identity: because it exists only as thought, in spirit and in truth. It is not in need of the fiction of an "unconscious," having, as it does, everything it needs within itself.

But the stone exists only if, only to the extent that, and for as long as *we* exist as *it*, and only *through* our existing as it. And we exist as it only if we *are*, objectively, the living comprehension of it, only if we *in fact* perform (and are capable of performing) the thinking of it, only

---

[4] In this sentence we see the power of the "not." If it is not executed *as execution*, then it inevitably reappears, but now as being executed in the form of a denial and logical deportation. In the latter case thought's inner transcendency is positivized as its (intra-psychic) external other, its (intra-psychic) Australia. Freud once expressly called the unconscious the *innere Ausland* (inner foreign country). The mind's "not" is thus literally acted *out* instead of being interiorized, instead of self-referentially coming home to the mind itself. And, inasmuch as psychology is the discipline of interiority and self-relation, psychology becomes unpsychological.

[5] Or something bordering on madness. How great the danger is comes out in Jung's emotional tone and wording in the following statement about Schopenhauer: "He had committed the deadly sin of making a metaphysical assertion, and of endowing a mere noumenon, a *Ding an sich*, with special qualities" (*MDR*, p. 70, transl. modified).

"THE STONE WHICH IS NOT A STONE"

if we have, in the logical form of our *consciousness* and our *knowing*, risen to the height of the real, existing Concept and thus explicitly *live as* the real, existing Concept: *are* "in spirit and in truth."

CHAPTER FIFTEEN

"By Its Colorful Tunes the Lark Blissfully Climbs Up Into the Air"
A Few Reflections on Soul-Making as the Making of Psychic Reality[1]

According to a deeply ingrained and almost instinctual assumption, which philosophically is the basis of the school of sensationalism, all knowledge consists of original impressions from without, i.e., from external reality. By contrast, C.G. Jung, more in the vein of the old tradition of idealism, introduced the fundamentally different notion of archetypes, factors that inform the mind directly without coming in via the senses. As incompatible as these two positions are, in a deeper sense they structurally nevertheless follow the same pattern. The mind here is 'pathic.' It is dominated and informed by some other. The sensualist way of thinking clearly operates within the subject–object dichotomy. But, even if in a very different sense, this also holds true for the Jungian conception, inasmuch as Jung teaches us to understand that the subject, i.e., that which initially believed itself to be the subject, is in truth itself subjected to, and thus the object of, archetypal dominants which to

---

[1] I dedicate this text to James Hillman, who introduced the idea of "soul-making" into psychology, in deep gratitude and in friendship—a friendship characterized by *concordia discors*. This paper was written in 2006 as an invited contribution to a *Festschrift* that did not materialize.

some extent are the true subject. The systematic alienation of the mind inherent in the sensualist standpoint somehow continues in Jung's psychology, too, although of course in a much "sublimated" form. It is still a psychology of otherness. The soul is not at home with itself, it is divided from itself. It is not, as the oft-repeated depth-psychological credo goes, master in its own house.

This type of problem was also the reason why Hegel contradicted the long-standing Aristotelian tradition which held that the soul never thinks without image. He insisted that we think in the names, the words, of language. The imaginal representation remains iconic in the sense that it maintains a contiguity with the object referred to. It upholds the natural looks of what it is about. This is even true in the case of fantastic (freely fantasized) objects, like dragons, centaurs, griffons, harpies. Despite its free fantasy activity on the semantic level, syntactically the soul is here ultimately still heteronomous (depending on visual experience). This is very different in the case of words. The names of things in language ("tree," "lion," "star") have no connection whatsoever with the looks of these things, in fact with any visual shape. These names refer to things without preserving any contiguity with the things' natural likeness, which is also why different languages can refer to the same object using words sounding completely different ("tree," "Baum," "arbre," etc.). Names are contingent. The phonemes making up a word have been *produced* by the mind itself, which arbitrarily assigned them to things. By using words the soul may therefore, to be sure, be referring to external reality, but it nevertheless keeps dwelling within itself and deals only with its own property. Because language thus starts out with the *dissolved* alchemical "unio naturalis," with the *severed* "participation mystique," in a true thinking that occurs in the medium of the words of language and has left thinking in images behind, the soul is no longer alienated from itself. It seems that the soul can only come home to itself for the price of the unrelenting logical *separatio* of the *unio naturalis*, which in imaginal thinking is in the last analysis still retained.

In connection with Hegel's thesis we could also think of Genesis 2:19: "And out of the ground the LORD God formed every beast of the field, and every fowl of the air; and brought them unto Adam to see what he would call them: and whatsoever Adam called every living creature, that was the name thereof. {Adam: or, the man}" The naming

"BY ITS COLORFUL TUNES"   381

of things is here described as the free act of man. The name is precisely
not the property of the things, not the necessary result, effect, outflow
of their appearance or inner nature. There is no inherent connection
between name and thing, for if there were, God would not have had
to wait and see *whatsoever* Adam would call the things; the name would
have been rooted in the things themselves. In Adam's naming, the soul
is productive, not receptive.

And yet, this Biblical theory of language is still wanting. Genesis
2:19 makes us think that (1) there is a one to one correspondence of
each word as a name on the one hand and one natural thing so named
on the other and (2) that the names are secondary. First God makes
the things and then he takes them to Adam to have them named. But
we have to reverse this sequence. In language, the soul is truly, fully
productive: itself creative. It does not merely give names to what is
already given to us and found by us. There is a true soul-*making*, a
making by the soul and a making *of* soul, *of* psychic reality. In order
to become able to understand this soul-making, we have to let ourselves
be taught by the lark.

An ihren bunten Liedern klettert / Die Lerche selig in die Luft (Nikolaus
Lenau, "Liebesfeier"): by means of its colorful tunes the lark blissfully
climbs up into the air. There is not a bird here that while rising into
the air also sings. No, its tunes are for the lark, as it were, a ladder by
means of which it can climb up. It is a nonexistent ladder, a ladder in
the status of absolute negativity, both in the sense that it is not a given
object that the lark avails itself of for its climbing, but something it
has to itself produce in and by the very act of climbing, and in the
sense that its production does not produce a persisting product. The
tunes last only for as long as the singing goes on, and only as long as
the tunes last does the climbing continue. The ladder is, we might
say, performative. The singing is itself the climbing and the climbing
can occur only in the mode of singing. (In a more literal, concretistic
sphere this is comparable to how a shaman drums and dances himself
into ecstasy, out of this world into the cosmos, the world of the upper
or lower spirits.) In normal climbing we climb a tree, a mountain, we
lean a ladder against a house wall in order to climb up to the roof.
There is a factual support and a factual goal. But here the climbing is
a climbing into "thin air": concretistically speaking into nothing. But
the fact that this climbing has no concrete, existing object(ive) and

does not get anywhere shows that in truth the singing only "climbs" into *itself*, gets deeper into its tunes, into their inner necessity, their truth. The tunes use themselves as their own means to work themselves up into their own depth or completion.

This is what soul-making is. The only flaw in Lenau's description is that the lark, as the subject of the singing and climbing, remains, as if it were the agent or author of this singing. In reality there is no author, no lark, not a subsisting soul *that* happens to sing and climb. There are only the tunes, and in their singing themselves out "the soul" and that which we call psychic reality is produced. The soul is not ontological (an existing thing). "The soul" makes, produces itself in the singing of the tunes. This means that "the soul" exists only as the *result* of its own self-production (not as the agent of this production), or rather, it does not exist, it always has to come into being, has to make itself. "The soul" is autopoietic. And this is also why soul-making, according to our lines from Lenau's poem, is in itself blissful. 'Blissful' does not refer here to an emotional condition of the lark (or of a person, for example, the poet himself). It is the logical status of the subjectless self-production of "the soul": the bliss of autopoiesis, of absolute autonomy, of singing, making music for no other purpose than that music—soul—be. "The lark" is at most the place where this soul-making happens.

A consequence of this is that psychic reality has to be comprehended as having the nature of tunes, of "thin air." The cosmos of the soul that is productively created through soul-making is airy, vaporous, free-floating—nothing but words, tunes, a *flatus vocis*. The word or tunes are not about something given, some substantial existence. They are only about that which they themselves originarily create; they are, one might say, only about themselves. Nothing solid and permanent. Psychic reality is truly not anything "natural"; it is truly *contra naturam* and absolute-negative. It is *logical life*, where "logical" refers to the *logos* nature of this life. If we nevertheless speak of psychic *reality* we have to know that it means the reality precisely of this *flatus*, of something like colorful soap bubbles, the reality *of* virtuality. *Realitas nostra non est realitas vulgi.* Therefore also no hard-core archetypes, neither archetypes-in-themselves nor time-resistant, eternal archetypal structures. No tree branch to sit on. The only thing

"BY ITS COLORFUL TUNES"

that the lark can rely on is the airy, virtual, ephemeral reality of its own tunes, and it can rely on them only to the extent that it keeps climbing up by means of them, keeps singing them and thereby working itself deeper into their inner infinity.

Climbing here does not refer to the eagle's rise to the heights of spirit or transcendence. The lark climbs up into the *air*, into its nothingness, into the medium of virtuality, not into the heights. And in climbing it establishes this thin air (as which it *is*) in the first place, gives to its virtuality reality. Climbing refers to the persistent, consistent pursual of the tunes' inherent logic and thus to the unfolding, continued elaboration and detailed differentiation of what they entail and demand.

Ordinarily, we think that passionate love, where it occurs, is a mighty instinctual fact. But as Niklas Luhmann showed about 25 years ago, love needs a linguistic code. A supply of tropes and sophisticated phrases is often needed to kindle love. The ritual of wooing was a highly rhetorical activity. Love poems, sonnets played an important role. But rhetorical codes are not only essential for inciting love feelings in the person loved, i.e., for enabling this person to develop the corresponding feelings in herself or himself. Even the original awakening of passionate feelings in the first person alone, who might then woo the other, depends on the words and tropes of language and requires a certain direct or indirect familiarity with the treatment of love in literature. The *human, differentiated, sophisticated* emotion of love needs the rhetoric and tunes of love for "climbing up," working itself up, into the depth of its own airy, virtual reality—even if this use of rhetoric may occur only deep down in the unconscious background of the soul's silent speaking with itself (the *logos psychês pros haytên*) so that the conscious individual may be totally surprised by the result it may spring on him. The real locus of passionate love is in the nonexisting world of language, not the other way around: language is not the expression of a given real emotion. Love feelings are not given to us by nature. They are not, like sexual urges, the simple result of hormones (although, it is true, *without* hormones they might not come about either), nor are they the result of an incursion by "Aphrodite" or "Eros" (or whichever god and goddess of love) into a person's life. The potential to love in a psychological sense is a cultural, linguistic invention, indeed creation. Imagining an incursion by, e.g., Aphrodite is itself part of the *rhetoric* of love. A Caspar Hauser could not have gotten very far in the art of loving.

As a cultural creation, the potential to love is also essentially historical. It is, for example, significant that the plot of the Iliad, despite revolving around two women, Helena and Briseis, revolves around them only as objects of contention, but hardly as objects of love in the deeper sense of involving the personality as a whole. Love in a more personal-feeling sense begins to emerge only much later, to some extent in the Hellenistic period. We know how much the deepening of the feeling of love in our Western tradition owes above all to the courtly love poetry of the Middle Ages and to Petrarca, to mention only these two examples, and this is a poetry of *words, words, words.* These words (and the words of all the other poets that followed) are sunken cultural treasures which created the psychological infrastructure upon which the soul can, even in the modern ordinary individual, form his or her own sophisticated feelings of love. Without these words, without the whole history of language and without our in some way participating in this cultural history through our explicit or implicit education, our loving would probably still be in the status that it had in the Iliad.

Passionate love is only one single example for the virtuality of psychic reality. I chose it precisely because the strong conventional understanding of love has it that it is a natural fact. The naturalistic fallacy prevails not only when one sees in love something basically biological. It also manifests when one views it as a (possibly overpowering) "archetypal *experience*" in Jung's sense. Love, I tried to suggest, is *made*, manufactured, of course not by "the ego," but in and by "the soul." It *makes* itself. If it appears to be an overwhelming experience, then we have to remember, *mutatis mutandis*, the logic expressed in Goethe's "Am Ende hängen wir doch ab / Von Kreaturen, die wir machten" (In the end, we depend on creatures that we ourselves produced). Making and experiencing are not the same, indeed, they are opposites. But love (just as any other psychic reality) is their uroboric, dialectical identity. It can be this self-contradictory identity because rather than being something natural it is absolute-negative. With the conception of the uroboric identity of its own producing what it experiences, the view of "the soul" has lost its alienated form.

The absolute negativity or virtuality of psychic reality is equally as far from "positive empirical fact of nature" as from a Jungian archetypal experience or from a *mundus imaginalis* in the sense of Corbin, both of which lend themselves to some sort of "metaphysical" understanding as preexistent realities. Its absolute negativity character obviously precludes any confusion with natural facts, and the notion of its own making itself destroys the "pathic" conception of the strictly objective nature of psychic reality and the otherworldliness of a separate, preexisting mysterious world of archetypes or images. Soul-making, inasmuch as it proceeds quite concretely via "its own tunes," via the sounds of language of ordinary human origin, is at once down to earth *and* not-natural: a sober "*terrestrial* extraterrestrial."

We live on this earth *in* this *extraterrestriality*. Even this earth and our own bodies and all our experience of and coping with reality have their place in its (this extraterrestriality's) "outer space" and not the other way around. This is what is implied when Jung stated that we are surrounded by psyche on all sides and when he rejected the idea that there could be anything that was not psychic, i.e., not virtual/extraterrestrial, not thin air. Not only love, but all our all-too-real emotions (like rage, joy, sadness, depression), and not only our emotions, but also our perceptions are linguistically fabricated thin air (which is most obvious in the case of color perception, which depends on the color terms that one's language provides).

Even more than that. The lark's climbing up into the air by its own tunes is more than the occasional work of a poet or the occasional experience of some emotion or perception or fantasy. This climbing up into thin air is the differentiation and elaboration process of human civilization as a whole—of languages and especially their vocabulary, of law, morality, religion, philosophy, art, world views. It is the ever deeper exploration, ever more detailed, differentiated unfolding, and real production of the mind's intrinsic potential.

CHAPTER SIXTEEN

"Irrelevantification" or: On the Death of Nature, the Construction of "the Archetype,"and the Birth of Man

As my starting point I take the discussion of the death of nature by Marco Heleno Barreto.[1] His intelligent, well-argued thesis starts out from his observation that the first modern form of the relation between man and nature is one of a drive or will to dominate on the part of man, resulting in a conception of nature as mere raw material and implying a radical alienation between man and nature. He interprets a second observation, that of the increasing diversity of ecological catastrophes in our time, as a sign that this human attitude toward nature contains a fundamental flaw and falsehood, a logical insufficiency. Modern man forgot and even denied, Dr. Barreto states, his dependence on nature. His (modern man's) attitude is, dialectically viewed, only the *negation of the negation* of the original *position*, which in turn can be expressed in the sentence, "man shall be the master of nature." But modern man's attitude is not yet the highest point of the dialectical development, i.e., the *restored position*, which would consist, so he argues, in an *eco-logical* form of

---

[1] Marco Heleno Barreto, "The Death of Nature: A Psychological Reflection," in: *Spring 75* (2006), A Journal of Archetype and Culture, "Psyche & Nature," Part 1 of 2, pp. 257–273.

consciousness that has learned the lesson that the natural disasters entail. By ecological consciousness Dr. Barreto does not merely mean noble ecological concern with the preservation of nature, but rather "a higher level of spiritualization" consisting in "the conscious realization of the full dialectical relation between culture and nature, reached by the interiorization of the domination drive" (its logical interiorization or *Er-innerung* in the sense of a domination of domination). By acknowledging the dialectical interdependence that unites man as "master of nature" and nature itself, this consciousness would have the result that we would find the proper *human place* in nature, our *oikos* (home), inasmuch as it opens up the dimension of interiority that transcends positive nature, and thus comes home to itself. It would correspond to a possible (and legitimate) kind of "resurrection of nature," which dialectically sublates the previous logical moment of "death of nature."

This is only an all-too brief summary of the main line of Dr. Barreto's sophisticated argument, which is in itself consistent and can account for the major aspects of his theme. But I do not think that it does justice to our psychological situation and to the phenomenon of "the death of nature." As much as I appreciate the dialectical interpretation of this topic, I think that it does not address the *real* dialectic that is at stake here and needs to be seen. The dialectic he describes is not the real dialectic because it does not begin with the logical beginning. The logical beginning has to be the primary psychological reality in the area that is the particular topic here.

"Irrevocable Death of Nature" Versus "Irrevocable Kinship to Nature"

There are three problems with taking the statement "man shall be the master of nature" to be the position. The first problem is a formal one. This statement does not express an insight or thesis about reality, i.e., is does not come as a truth claim. A statement about an assumed truth would have the form: "man (or whatever) *is* this or that." By contrast, "man *shall be* ..." expresses a program, a wish, a goal. It is a project, not a truth claim. But the "position" for the unfolding dialectic has to have the form of a truth claim. The second problem is also a formal one. This statement, according to its logical character, is

"IRRELEVANTIFICATION" 389

not really a position as the starting point of formal reflection, but much rather already a (disguised) *negation* of an / of the original position. "Man shall be the master of nature" displays a disrespect for nature. It is the program or project of overcoming nature. And as such it is tantamount to "the death of nature." It is a sentence in which one of the logical *operations* of the dialectical or alchemical process is articulated. But that upon which in this our context this operation is performed, the real starting point of the process, in alchemical terms: the prime matter, in logical terms: the *position*, is something else. It is the highest soul value or soul substance or soul truth, in our case: nature. *It* is what suffers a death on account of that negating operation and is resurrected in totally altered form. The sentence "man shall be the master of nature" clearly points beyond itself to something preceding it, as whose negation it functions, namely to a situation where nature was the master.[2] Because of its own internal (even if masked) *negative* form it in itself contradicts the idea that it could be the *position*. Thus we see that Dr. Barreto does not begin with the real beginning, with the first term of the dialectic. He begins with a second term, with a *negation*.

What "man shall be the master of nature" points to and negates is "nature." Now it is essential to realize that "nature" in the psychological sense does not merely mean literal nature in the narrow sense, the totality of natural things and phenomena over against man. That would be the everyday sense of nature, nature as external fact. Rather, the *psychological* concept of nature means "*Mother* Nature" and thus a specific form of the whole *relation* of man and nature. In other words, nature in this sense is itself the unity of itself and its other, man. And the true beginning of the dialectic, and thus the true initial "position," would be the positive relation between the two, their harmonious unity or man's embeddedness in nature, his awareness and acknowledgement of the human dependence on nature, nature as the *oikos* of man and man as the child of nature.

Now I come to the third problem. "Man shall be the master of nature" amounts to the negation of nature not only according to its logical form. The negation is also visible in the content of this phrase,

---

[2] In terms of the alchemical dictum of Pseudo-Democritos ("Nature rejoices in nature. Nature subdues nature. Nature rules over nature") it would correspond to the first status of nature, that of nature's oneness and perfect harmony with itself.

because it already *presupposes* the severing of the bond between man and nature. The argument in question starts out with the one severed side of the broken unity of man and nature. It begins with alienated man and *ipso facto* with a nature that is totally vis-à-vis man, nature as object. But this means that this nature is already *logically* dead because it is no longer Mother nature whose child man is. Under these circumstances the whole question of whether man wants to and is able to make himself the master of nature or not comes too late. The domination issue is logically insignificant one way or another because the essential issue is already settled: the case of nature is already lost. Nature is reduced to something a priori given (with Heidegger we could say: something in the status of *Vorhandenheit*), an immutable factual entity, that is to say, it has become a positivity. "Mother Nature" was not a positive fact. It was numinous, mythic, imaginal. But if nature is logically a positivity, if it has been reduced to mean the external physical reality, it might as well be empirically-practically viewed as mere raw material.

Nature has been released from its interiority in the soul and become "external reality." If it were still contained in the soul it would be the one side of a relation that as a whole could be subject to a dialectic process. Each stage of such a dialectical development would *redefine* both sides at once. But here, the only dialectical movement left—now being restricted to, and taking place only on, the one, the human side of the whole relation—cannot achieve anything of soul significance anymore; it cannot possibly bring about a real "resurrection of nature," no matter what it will produce, because it is only a cut-off *subjective human* development. Nature itself cannot be reached or touched anymore by the dialectical movement of the thesis "man shall be the master of nature" because the starting point is the split between man and nature and the movement *takes place only on the one side*. We could also express it in the following way: If "man shall be the master of nature" is supposed to be the position, the standpoint of soul has been left and one is now moving in the sphere of ego-psychology. For, as Jung repeatedly stressed, ego means "empirical man," man in the context of ordinary, everyday life.

The paradox of this situation is, however, that precisely because nature is logically cut-off and immunized, consciousness is screened from the insight into the already real psychological death of nature,

"IRRELEVANTIFICATION" 391

an insight that it is, after all, itself witness to, indeed, that is its own precondition. A full-fledged death of nature does not happen here: the death of nature that has long happened and even is the (unwitting) presupposition of this very theory is in this theory nevertheless not released into its being true. In part this is because this death is interpreted as man's fault of merely being oblivious of or denying the reality of nature, but also and above all it is because there has been a surreptitious conceptual substitution: "nature" as a psychological concept (as experienced by the soul, as soul internal) has been replaced by "nature" as a positive fact: external, literal nature. External nature as a whole is of course, from the point of view of human experience, a highly indestructible reality. If you work with *this* concept of nature, the idea of a real death of nature is a priori inconceivable. This is also why ego-consciousness can become enormously impressed by ecological catastrophes and see in them a counter-argument against the idea of the final death of nature; why these catastrophes can be viewed as an invitation to consciously acknowledge our human "irrevocable kinship to nature" and why that "death of nature" that is, to be sure, admitted as a previous moment in the dialectic process, is only seen as a moment that is or will be sublated by a kind of "resurrection of nature." The permanence of nature is guaranteed from the outset—because the term nature is here a physical and not a psychological one.

The paradox or contradiction consists therefore in the fact that precisely because the style of thought that is here critically reviewed has firmly established itself on the *foundation* of the accomplished real death of nature by working with the reduced meaning of nature as positive fact, it manages to escape the necessity of having to suffer the death of nature (in the psychological sense) and can believe in an ultimate continuity of nature. The foundation of this thought is, as we have seen, the radical split between man and nature, so that "nature" is logically reduced to mean literal nature. It is reduced to that nature that is studied in the modern natural sciences and also experienced in modern ecological crises. But this reduction of the concept of nature and this split of the mother-child relation between nature and man *are* in themselves precisely what is meant by "the real and irrevocable death of nature" (in the psychological sense). No further dialectical development of the drive to domination, no learning, induced by ecological catastrophes, to acknowledge our dependence on nature, is capable of undoing this death of nature and this alienation of man vis-à-vis nature, since they are the very basis of this thought. Even if we would find "the proper *human place* in nature" as conceived by Dr. Barreto's vision, it would in truth only be the place in that already dead, literal, alienated nature. This is the one side. The other side is that this truth is *only the factual, but unthematic* foundation of this thinking. It is not made explicit. This theory does not become conscious of it. All that this thinking concentrates on is the logical further-development of the "man shall be the master of nature" thesis. And here the process of the "negation" via the "negation of the negation" to the "restoration of the position" leads to the idea of the possibility of a new *oikos* (home) for man in nature and *ipso facto* of a resurrected nature. In other words, this idea of a possible end of human alienation is itself firmly based on and reconfirms human alienation. The hoped for or demanded sublation of the death of nature to a mere moment rests on the (unseen) irrevocable death of nature.

SOUL VIEW VERSUS EGO VIEW

The problem, so it seems, is that of an equivocation, which is in turn the indication of a shift from a soul (interiority) view of the death of nature to an ego and ego-psychological view. In the spirit of alchemy we can say: *natura nostra non est natura vulgi*. In our context, there are two distinct senses of the one word nature, and not to keep them apart leads to a category mistake. The ecological catastrophes that we experience contradict neither the idea of the death of nature as a psychological notion nor the alleged drive to dominate nature, because those catastrophes refer to literal nature, to the nature "of the people."[3] But this nature has become *psychologically* obsolete and irrelevant; literal nature is what is left of nature in the soul sense of the word after it has "died." Literal nature is the corpse of nature in the psychological

---

[3] Besides, do these catastrophes really negate the alleged drive to dominate nature? Do they not precisely represent a powerful challenge to this drive, to the ongoing dynamic of the human technological conquest of nature? Do they not stimulate a wish, and back up this wish with the sense of absolute necessity so that it turns into a need, the need to deepen and intensify this drive, namely to get a far deeper, better, more comprehensive and sophisticated scientific understanding of nature so as to become better able to control nature? How else, if not through scientific and technological means, can our ecological purposes be reached and we hope to get the better of global warming, the better of the limitation of energy resources, etc.?

"IRRELEVANTIFICATION"

(mythological) sense. There is no soul in this nature anymore. The soul has emigrated from this nature. Nature was only alive as long as it was divine, numinous, Mother Nature, just as on a personal level father and mother were psychologically alive only as long as they were objects of our psychic upward-looking and loaded with "numinous" importance. Ever since the cry "The Great Pan is dead!" resounded in late Antiquity and marked the death of the nature gods, ever since Christianity logically overcame nature as such, nature has been psychologically dead, although it took many centuries for this truth to come home to consciousness. Any "drive to dominate nature" coming one and a half millennia later—at the time of Bacon, Galileo, or Descartes—could not bring about a death of nature, because nature had already been dead for all this time. It is the other way around. Once the death of nature had come home to collective consciousness at the end of the Middle Ages, it, the death of nature, gave rise to modern science and technology.

The ego-psychological view prevailing here shows also in the following detail. Because the dialectical movement is reserved for the human side of the entire psychic phenomenon, the man-nature relation, this movement ceases to be a truly logical development, and instead implicitly and unwittingly takes on the character of a more or less moral task: man is first blamed for his oblivion, denial, and false attitude and then supposed to learn from natural catastrophes and bring about the "domination of domination." This is not *intended* by the author of the article as a moral exhortation to practice a subjective willful self-control, but ultimately boils down to one. It cannot really be thought as the domination drive's own self-domination in the course of its own experience. It can only be thought as man's curbing his own drive. If this intended move were a truly logical change (a change within the domination thesis's own dialectic), it would have to be the "drive to dominate nature" itself that learns from the catastrophes. But a drive cannot learn. It can only be impeded or blocked. Only the human subject can learn from the ecological catastrophes and then perhaps control *his* drive.

Learning is possible only in the sphere of *logos*, of truth claims, not in nature (*physis*). Certain animals can learn because they partake in logos even if only in a limited, "implicit" way. But natural forces like gravity or the forces at work in the movement of the continental plates, in the weather, in volcanos, etc. do not learn from experience. This is and has to be so because they do not exist as truth claims, but as facts. A logical change therefore cannot start out from drives. It can only start out from theses, (alleged) truths, assumptions. An assumption or assertion can be undeceived, taught by experience, refuted by reality, because from the outset it belongs to the mind. A drive, however, is a will, a force. Reality can hinder or check a force, it can block a drive, but not refute or convince it, which would, however, be required for a dialectical process. This is why I think that the mastering of "the will to be the master of nature" (envisioned as a solution in that article) can only be an ego act, the ego's moral behavior, and not a psychological, logical, further-development, not the outcome of a self-movement of the original thesis.

The logical contradiction that prevails here and is the cause for the shift from a psychological to an ego point of view consists in the fact that consciousness on the one hand *has* already experienced and *is informed* by the death of nature, which is why it starts out from alienated man and necessarily restricts the dialectic to a subjective process in him, while on the other hand and nevertheless it insists on holding on to the idea of nature and man's relationship to nature. This does not work. One cannot have it both ways. Once man has experienced himself as no longer a child of nature, nature is— psychologically—dead and *ipso facto*—again psychologically—simply no topic anymore. The idea "man shall be the master of nature" cannot be a starting point for a psychological reflection because this idea is (a) self-contradictory (it expresses a *fixation* on nature and assigns the highest importance to it, while at the same time reducing it to a mere raw material at human disposal) and (b) both man and nature are taken as positivities in external reality and a "power game" determines their relation. In other words, the sphere of the soul has already been left. We are already in the sphere of the ego. It is just like with young adults who in fact have outgrown their status as children of their parents, but nevertheless feel the need to constantly fight with them. With this fighting they resort to an acting out of their status of self-determined beings on the ego level that is supposed to *ostensibly* demonstrate their independence. But by acting it out (psychoanalysis taught us that acting out is a defense mechanism) they avoid to *erinnern*, to interiorize it into itself so that it could prevail as their simple truth.

"IRRELEVANTIFICATION"

What ought—logically—to be their truth, their being (i.e., what they *are*), is reduced to and replaced by an external behavior. By feeling the need to fight against their parents they show that *in reality* (psychologically) they cannot simply live their new truth as independent of their parents, but instead constantly reconfirm their clinging to them. They show themselves not to be independent. Analogously in the sphere of nature, the move to external reality, to positive facts, and to the acting out of a power struggle is a defense against an already prevailing psychological truth.

The Paradigm of "Leaving Father and Mother"

As a paradigm for the psychological understanding of the death of nature, or any such death for that matter, we can use the biblical statement, "For this cause shall a man leave his father and mother, and cleave to his wife" (Mk. 10:7). Growing up means that father and mother have psychologically died. 'Psychologically died' does not mean that they are literally dead, it means: having lost soul importance, having been reduced to *psychological* nonentities. The parents can simply be left behind. The psychic passion, the highest psychic value, the *numinosum tremendum et fascinosum*, has moved out and away from them and now resides somewhere else, somewhere totally new and hitherto unknown, in "his wife," for example. The parents still exist, but now depleted of their former importance. They have become demythologized, demystified and are now ordinary persons, only factually existing *within the ego world* of the *pragmatics* of human life, but no longer in the realm of soul. They have become persons with whom one is, to be sure, connected in a special relationship and with all kinds of feeling simply because of the long prior history of this relationship and also because of what they once used to be for us, but it is nevertheless only an *empirically*, not logically or psychologically, special relationship, just as one has a closer relationship to long-standing colleagues than to complete strangers. For the child the connection to his parents had a quasi ontological dignity. For the adult, by contrast, the relationship to the parents that still exists is merely grounded on the contingent empirical facts of a common past and possibly on personal (egoic) sympathy. But they *are* no longer the man's parents in the psychological sense; he *is* no longer their child. Having grown up, he is now an adult *just as they* are, and thus something like a "colleague" of theirs on an equal psychological footing with them. And sooner or later, the former relation between him and them might even become reversed because, when his parents become old, they may become dependent on being nursed by him like children. "Death" in psychology means irrelevantification. It does precisely not mean that one has to fight, dominate, destroy, kill whatever that reality is that will become obsolete for the soul. To want to fight the parents would on the contrary mean to enhance their superiority, significance, numinosity again.

The man who left his father and mother has ipso facto left his parental *oikos*. But the parental home is not just any house, it is *the* home *kat' exochen*, the only real home, because it is his a priori, and this is what 'home' above all means. It is his a priori inasmuch as it is provided for him by his parents and he has been born into it. Having left this home, he has become fundamentally homeless, alienated. If he now still wants to have a home at all, he has to *establish* his own *oikos* and family with "his wife," an *oikos* which, however, being of his own making, is something totally different from the home of his origin. His self-made home is essentially a posteriori, and despite the fact that he empirically lives *in* it, he is logically above and around it inasmuch as he is its maker and master. So his new home does not undo his fundamental alienation and homelessness. They are irrevocable. They are indeed the basis of his whole future existence and the ground also of the home established by him. Rather, the fact that he established a home for himself means that he fully settled, and made himself at home, *in the condition of his essential homelessness.*

He can of course visit his parents and his former home. The fact that his parents still exist does not contradict their being dead. The first fact is a positivistic truth, the second a psychological or logical one. Also, his former home is still there. But it is his *home* no longer. He can never "return" to it in the full sense of the word; there will never be a revival or resurrection of that *oikos*. Any visit back home will have the character merely of a sentimental journey, and the house in which he grew up will make him wistfully aware of the fact that what he sees there is only the empty dead shell of his former home, a relic of his past, and that there is no way back for him. The parental

"IRRELEVANTIFICATION"

home has inevitably become historical to him, a kind of open air museum, Colonial Williamsburg. The same applies to his parents themselves. As *parents* they have become historical for the adult.

The way I described this change, one could think that it is the act of the son's leaving his parents and his childhood home that brings about the soul's emigration from the primary *oikos* and from out of the persons of his parents into something new. But it is the other way around. Growing up means that the person is, as it were, confronted with and surprised by the irrelevantification of his parents and his home that happened of its own accord. This is by no means the result of his own doing. Unwittingly he finds himself catapulted into a new situation. And only slowly he becomes aware of the fact that the highest soul value, that his "libido," is somewhere else, because the change as an objective reality, as a fact comes generally first and the awareness of it, let alone one's understanding of it, comes only after the fact. Girls are all of a sudden much more important than his parents. So with his leaving father and mother and "cleaving to his wife" he only follows suit to and honors an "autonomous" soul movement that for him had already long ago depleted his parents and his parental home of their soul importance. He makes what is already implicitly a truth for himself explicit for himself and turns it into the foundation on which he stands. It is an act of *psychologically adapting* to his new soul reality.

The word "parents" has now become equivocal. In its now historical, obsolete sense it refers to the parents as all-important personages to whom I as child used to be essentially upward-looking. They were the real, positive presence of the highest soul value. But "parents" also refers to those same-named persons who only once upon a time used to be the persons loaded with numinous meaning, but now are merely ordinary human beings, human, all-too-human, and "colleagues on an equal footing," as I pointed out earlier. The empirical-factual human being has been born out of the former numinously inflated father or mother. We could also say: they have emerged from out of the numinosity in which they had been enveloped; the mythical garment has fallen off of them, so that now they can be seen in their empirical nakedness and positivity. Psychology is wont to express it in still another way: The archetypal projection has been withdrawn from them.

DEMYTHOLOGIZING "MOTHER"

When Jung says, "... but a person with insight can no longer in all fairness load that enormous weight of meaning, responsibility, duty, heaven and hell, onto the shoulders of that frail and fallible human being—so deserving of love, indulgence, understanding, and forgiveness—who was mother for us" (*CW* 9i § 172, transl. modif.), he sort of extracts (not the spirit from the matter in which it had been imprisoned, but conversely) the empirical "matter" from the numinous "spirit." Jung performs the demythologization and reduction and thus also the irrelevantification of the mother; he wants us "to release the human mother from this terrifying burden" (*ibid.*, transl. modified). At any rate, he, too, operates here consciously with the equivocation of the name "mother" and presents us with the notion of "mother" in a merely *historical* sense: she "who *was* mother for us." She is no longer. She *is* only an ordinary human being, frail and fallible, deserving of *our* indulgence, understanding, and forgiveness. Now it is she who needs something from us (and in this sense she is somehow the converse of mother).

The equivocation inherent in the word "mother" expresses the *psychological difference.* The alchemists were perhaps the first to articulate the psychological difference, such as when they, for example, said, *aurum nostrum non est aurum vulgi,* our gold is not the gold of the people (the ordinary gold). Just as I followed this alchemical model when I above coined the formula, *natura nostra non est natura vulgi,* so we could also here say, *mater nostra non est mater vulgi,* our mother— "mother" in the psychological sense, "mother" as loaded with mythic or archetypal meaning—is not the ordinary empirical mother, "mother" in a merely factual (biological, social, or legal) sense. But the interesting point here is that the psychologist Jung, who, after all, is the inventor of the theory of the archetypes of the collective unconscious, pursues the emancipation of the "ordinary mother" from "our, the psychological mother," the "accidental carrier" (*ibid.* § 172) of the title mother from the great mythic burden that comes with the archetypal meaning of it. The mother is *reduced* to human, all-too-human proportions. She is "nothing but" a frail human being and "*only* that!"[4] Because she can be seen through as only being an "accidental

---

[4] With the quote "*only* that!" I refer to *MDR* p. 325, where this phrase, however, occurs in a different context.

"IRRELEVANTIFICATION"

carrier" of the deep psychological mother experience, she is contingent, precisely not archetypal.

For a child, the psychological difference does not exist. The mother is *as* the empirically real person immediately and differencelessly the numinous mother. She as the accidental carrier is totally enwrapped in the mythic garment, where "totally" means that there is no sense whatsoever that something has been *wrapped*. There is a strict identity of both aspects in the same real mother. The child cannot even see that there are two different aspects, "content" and "wrapping." They are completely amalgamated, so that there is only one thing, the real mother, who *at once* carries the enormous weight of meaning that Jung had spoken of. But the process of growing up is the gradual separation (bifurcation) of this primary identity so that the psychological difference that now runs through the word mother and makes it equivocal emerges for the first time. We could even say that growing up is the slow initiation into the psychological difference. Above I stated that with the emergence of this difference the empirical-factual human being in his or her positivity has been born out of the former (now inflated) parent figure. Now I have to add that also the soul as such has been born out of the former amalgamated phenomenon. Only now can there be a psychology proper. Before, there could only be mythology or personal equivalents of it.

But since the difference always emerges only later, it becomes necessary to work with three rather than only with the two forms of "mother" (or whatever the phenomenon in question may be in each case) contained in the formula adopted from alchemy. We get three because the *mater vulgi* of this formula needs to be doubled. *After* the emergence of the psychological difference, after consciousness has begun to negate and push off from the ordinary content "mother" and thus to conceive of, for example, the *mater nostra* and the *aurum nostrum* in contradistinction to the "vulgi" varieties of the same, the *mater vulgi* and the *aurum vulgi* refer to nothing but the depleted content, to the naked empirical-positive factualness of mother or gold, respectively. But there are also the "ordinary mother" and the "ordinary gold" *prior to* the differentiation into this opposition, prior to their depletion, their *kenôsis*. And these primordial ordinary (*vulgi*) forms of "the matter" are the empirical *and* numinous aspects in one: mother and gold *as* positive facts *immediately loaded* with symbolic or soul meaning.

400   *THE SOUL ALWAYS THINKS*

Whereas the *mater nostra* is the mother *idea per se*, the mythic or archetypal meaning, the *mater vulgi* can be either nothing but the literal person or it can be the real person loaded with enormous weight.

THE FUNDAMENTAL DIFFERENCE BETWEEN PERSONAL MOTHER EXPERIENCE AND MYTHOLOGICAL MOTHER AND BETWEEN "MYTHOLOGICAL MOTHER NATURE" AND "MOTHER ARCHETYPE"

With his thoughts about "mother" as described so far, Jung as it were followed the first part of our biblical dictum ("... shall leave father and mother"). But he did not follow its second part, which suggests another ordinary human being as the successor to mother and father, namely the man's "wife." This is a horizontal move. Jung went another way. He stayed with the mother, but went upwards. He said after the statements I quoted, "A mother-complex is not got rid of by one-sidedly reducing the mother to human proportions, so to speak 'correcting' her.[5] By doing this we run the risk of dissolving the experience 'Mother' into atoms, thus destroying something supremely valuable and throwing away the golden key which a good fairy laid in our cradle" (*ibid.*, transl. modif.). It is true, he was all for demythologizing, or "withdrawing of the projection" from, the empirical mother, but then he opted for the preservation of what had been withdrawn as the archetype (or archetypal image) of Mother.

This allows us to see that the *concept* of the archetypal image *in modern psychological theory* is the decal or transfer image peeled off (abstracted) from "Mother" (how the child experienced her). The archetype or archetypal image is, so to speak, a stand-alone "projection," a free-floating, self-serving "projection" per se that no longer needs a real carrier to support it. The notion of "archetypal image" is the product of an abstraction that, however, has secondarily been substantiated so as to achieve independence, indeed, even

---

[5] This formulation is already highly problematic. Jung construes the psychological departure from the mother ego-psychologically and "futuristically" as an act, a manipulation, on the part of man (our reducing or correcting), whereas in truth the only thing necessary is to *become aware of, comprehend*, and integrate into consciousness, what has already long become real, namely the fact that the highest soul value *has* already unexpectedly emigrated from one's mother (perfect tense). Nothing remains to be done in the way of action.

"IRRELEVANTIFICATION" 401

primordiality ("arche-"), and that in addition has secondarily been enhanced by and conflated with a phenomenon belonging to the totally other sphere of the history of *religions* and *mythology*, the phenomenon of mother goddesses.

In medieval paintings we sometimes find the motif of people on their deathbed with the devil nearby, ready to catch their soul that in the form of a little homunculus escapes from their mouth. The corpse then is what is left when the soul has escaped from the body. In a similar way Jung tried to catch the vanishing "souls," i.e., the disembodied numinosity, of the dead parents (of personal biography) and of the dead nature gods (of cultural history), not however in order to put them into hell, but to raise them to heaven as archetypes established as existing on their own account and orbiting like geostationary satellites.

In this way it was possible to dodge the soul's process that we call "history," a process that always follows the logic of the move from, to say it with our paradigmatic example, "parents" to "wife," which amounts to the relentless negation and irrelevantification of that which is left behind. It was obviously possible for Jung to arrest this movement, to avoid really moving all the way to "wife." Jung did of course move, too. But his move was only an upwards move at the same logical or topical place, not a move from 'here' to 'there,' from one *topos* to a new *topos*, where "topos" in each case refers to fundamentally different logical statuses of consciousness, inasmuch as the second is the negation or sublation of the first. Jung's is a move at or within the same old 'here': mother. It is, so to speak, an alchemical sublimating, evaporating, distilling operation. With a terminological distinction introduced by James Hillman, as a theorist Jung left the *literal* mother in order to move to the *imaginal* or *metaphorical* mother. He did not forsake the mother altogether in order to move to wife.[6] We could also speak of an idealization.

---

[6] "For this he would need a faithless Eros, one capable of forgetting the mother and cutting into his own flesh, by deserting the first beloved of his life" (*CW* 9ii § 22, transl. modif.), we could say with Jung, but directed at Jung himself. Of course, this sentence which according to its explicit intention aims for a "leaving (father and) mother," through its wording testifies to the defense against a movement in this direction: the mother is still viewed as the beloved and supreme value and the son's leaving her is branded as faithlessness, whereby the movement "to wife" is thwarted. In reality, however, this is by no means a case of a faithless desertion of the mother by the young man, i.e., of a

402   *THE SOUL ALWAYS THINKS*

We have to be very clear about the fundamental difference between *mythological* Mother Nature or Mother Earth in ancient or primitive cultures and the modern *concept* of the mother archetype. To understand this we first have to comprehend the fundamental difference between the child's experience of "mother" (the human, personal mother) and the cultural experience of "Mother Nature," "Mother Earth," or "the Great Mother" (a mother goddess), which in Jungian psychology and especially by Erich Neumann have been confounded as both being experiences of the mother archetype. The mythical or metaphysical inflation of the notion of the personal mother can be seen when Jung describes her as "Most intimately known and alien like nature, lovingly tender and fatefully cruel—a joyful, untiring giver of life, a *mater dolorosa* and the dark, unanswering gate that closes upon the dead. ... the accidental carrier of that experience which encompasses herself and myself and all mankind, indeed every living

---

doing on his part. Quite conversely, it is a case of the experience that that woman who once upon a time "*was* mother for him" has objectively become irrelevantized. Simple honesty, not faithlessness is what is needed. Because the consciousness prevailing here practices a defense against the simple *insight (cognition)* that the mother as beloved *is passé* and that he *has already been* catapulted beyond her, the quite ordinary condition, appropriate to the son's age, of in fact *having* outgrown the mother is reinterpreted as an *ego achievement* that still needs and ought to be brought about and can be brought about only with great difficulty (capability to cut into his flesh, of forgetting and deserting his first beloved) and moreover as something actually indecent, indeed, prohibited (faithlessness). This is the *neurotic* description of the transition from mother "to wife." In biographical regards, one can under these circumstances probably state that with his anima-beloved (Toni Wolff), whom he kept for himself side by side with his wife (just as analogously he kept for himself his existence in childhood paradise ["Bollingen"] side by side with his existence in the adult world ["Küsnacht"]), he demonstrates that even in his private life he did not truly perform the move "to wife." Rather, psychologically viewed and in the last analysis, in the symbolic guise of his anima-beloved he still unswervingly kept faith with "the first beloved of his life." All anima-only psychology does the same on the theoretical level, even if it does not make use of a literal anima-beloved or a literal Bollingen. The fact that Jung introduces the moral category of "faithlessness" is, however, fully justified. The only problem with it is that the true faithlessness, the real betrayal, does of course not take place where the neurotic interpretation locates it, namely over against the mother, but over against "wife" or against "Küsnacht." (I am here not making a moral statement about the general phenomenon of extra-marital relations or love affairs *as real life behavior* one way or another, because such judgments are altogether outside the psychological sphere of competence. "Faithlessness" and "betrayal" in the present context are exclusively psychological judgments, referring to the keeping faith with "the first beloved" through having an anima-beloved at a time when in psychological reality this first beloved has objectively long been irrelevantized while the move "to wife" is merely "acted out" as literal behavior in external reality, but not allowed to become psychologically true, inasmuch as the actual soul-value is reserved for the anima-beloved.)

"IRRELEVANTIFICATION" 403

creature that comes into being and passes away; the experience of life whose children we are" (*CW* 9i § 172, translation modified).

This identification of the concrete human mother (or the personal experience of one's mother) with the mythological Great Mother is untenable. Just as the child's experience of "mother" is a *particular*, essentially irreducible experience, so also the notion and experience of "Mother Earth" in archaic times was irreducible, something *sui generis*. The latter had not been a transfer image peeled off from the child's mother experience and then transferred upon nature or the earth. Only linguistically was it a "*meta-phorá*" from the human family to the cosmos. In its content or substance, however, it was the authentic cognition and experience of the unadulterated inner truth of human being-in-the-world on the level of an early stage of cultural consciousness and social and economic development. As such it was precisely not a fictional extension of the *child's* psychic experience of mother into the realm of the soul *sensu strictiori*, just as conversely the child's mother experience was not the childish version of the *mythological* mother. Both types of experience are divided and distinguished from each other by the psychological difference and need to be kept apart. They are each phenomena *sui generis*, so to speak autochthonous; the former is *psychic* (anthropological, in the sense of: being based on human *biology*; humans have this experience to some extent in common with certain higher animal species) and has nothing to do with archetypes or mythic images; the latter, however, is *psychological*, having its basis in, and being reflective of, the soul or mind (*Geist*, mindedness) as a reality in its own right.[7]

Both are concepts (thoughts). But whereas the child's concept of "mother" requires its fulfillment in an empirical reality outside itself (in the really existing person of his mother as "positive fact") and is the (psychic) concept of an empirical *interpersonal relation* (a real bond in practical reality), the goddess has no empirical referent.[8] "The earth"

---

[7] What separates 'psychic' and 'psychological' is what I call "the psychological difference."

[8] There is another essential difference or another way to describe this difference. The child's concept of the personal mother is a concept in the sense of an abstract universal that (belonging, as it were, to "The Doctrine of Essence" in Hegel's *Science of Logic*) *ipso facto* has its real referent outside of itself. The Mother Goddess, by contrast, is a concept in the altogether different sense of the third part of Hegel's *Science of Logic*, "The Doctrine of the Concept." As such it is able *within itself* to reach reality (actuality).

or "nature" are not her referent. Rather, the goddess is the divine ground or animating spirit in or behind the earth or nature. Gods and goddesses, as psychological or *soul* concepts (although concepts still in *imaginal form*), are uroboric: they have everything they need, also their fulfillment, a priori in themselves *as* concepts; they are logically negative; they are themselves what they point or refer to; thus they are not in need of empirical fulfillment like the child's concept, which, if it remains unfulfilled in empirical reality (does not find an appropriate "accidental carrier"), leads to terrible pathology, e.g., "hospitalism."

Therefore I have to retract some of my earlier formulations. It is not a "*mythical* garment," the "great *mythic* burden," in which the empirical mother has been enveloped. She is not as empirical mother immediately a "*numinous* mother," although she carries for the child a near-absolute weight. But her significance is not numinous and mythological. Rather, this significance is empirical and practical, concretely real, and she is with this near-absolute significance a different experience from the mythological experience of the Great Mother, simply a different topic.

The fact that the mythic concept is itself its own referent and does not point to anything outside of itself does not at all mean that the mythological "Mother Nature" was an "unconscious" projection of a separately subsisting "transcendent" archetype, the mother archetype, upon nature. No, it was the simple "apperception" (or "awareness") and articulation of one depth aspect of the logic of actually lived life in concrete reality during a particular stage of consciousness, namely the "awareness" of man's real near-absolute dependence on and embeddedness in nature. The same applies, *mutatis mutandis*, to the Christian "our father in heaven" as well as to the God or "the Absolute" of classical metaphysics. They, too, were rooted in the ultimate inner truth of actual lived life rather than in "the unconscious" and rather than being projected fictions or archetypal images. They were, in a psychological sense of the word, "phainomenal," realistic, the "awareness" of course not of the external appearance, but of the inner logic of the prevailing real mode of being-in-the-world. I insist: in both situations (the mythological one and the Christian-metaphysical one), the notion of gods had its source in the respective real experience of the world and of life, not in a separate, isolated unconscious that

"*IRRELEVANTIFICATION*" 405

produced archetypal projections, archetypal dominants of consciousness, archetypal perspectives. Gods were *intellektuelle Anschauungen* (intellectual intuitions), envisioned concepts or truths.

The psychological idea of "archetype," by contrast, is both based on a dissociated conception of consciousness cut off from man's real world experience (which results in the free-floatingness of the "archetypes" as independent primordial images or even archetypes-in-themselves). It is an artificial product. It is the attempt to rescue and immunize the abstracted numinosity or higher meaning of, for example, "Mother" *at a time when* both on a personal (biographical) level the human mother and on a cultural-historical level Mother Nature have become depleted of their numinous meaning, because in both areas man has grown up and "left father and mother." What Jung rescued with his notion of archetypes is, *because he rescued it*, an idle "numinosity" and "upward-looking" that is no longer backed up and authenticated by the actual mode of being-in-the-world, the actual logical status of consciousness. It is not, like the gods of former ages, the simple apperception of the inner truth of human existence at the respective level of cultural development. This is why "the archetype" is not an intellectual intuition, not uroboric, but a theoretical construct, a *hypothesis* of what is supposed to be a *fact*.

And the above quotation about "the experience 'Mother'" with its touching diction and image language for once pulls the usually existing scientistic cover away from the *personal* roots of the theory of archetypes and allows us to sense in a unique way something of the subjective motivation, the deep personal feeling and need that stand behind this construct and fire it. Jung arrived at his archetypal theory because *he* did not *want* the experience "Mother"—and thus his own child status—to be "dissolved into atoms." He felt the absolute need to prevent that thereby "something [in his view] supremely valuable," that is to say allegedly indispensable, would be destroyed or irretrievably lost. By refusing to throw away "the golden key which a good fairy laid in our cradle" and, instead, rescuing it in the form of the theory of archetypes, he reveals for us that—at least on the level of theory—he was ready only for a token growing up, a growing up in an external, literal (psychic or personalistic) sense, while *psychologically* insisting on staying in a child's fairy land. The key to meaning, to the numinous, to myth, to God, is a "golden" one that is to be found regressively in the cradle, in our childhood. It is not, as in our entire tradition, the mature, adult man's *mens humana*, which, as for example St. Augustine thought, is a spark of the divine intellect in man and which needs to be developed through hard work, the labor of the concept.

To sum up these reflections: we have to see that there are three distinct phenomena that need to be kept apart: (1) the child's experience of mother, (2) the archaic experience of Mother Nature, (3) the modern abstract construct of the mother archetype.

JUNG'S REMYTHOLOGIZATION OF MOTHER. THE CONSTRUCTION OF "THE ARCHETYPE"

Jung was quite willing to allow the personal mother to be stripped of her "mythic" burden (as *he* saw it) or of the abstract-universal concept in which she was enveloped (as *I* would put it). He allowed her to become psychically irrelevant. But not psychologically. Rather than submitting to the autonomous process of this divestiture and waiting to see whether the "numinosity" or "meaning" (psychological relevance) that had emigrated from her would show up somewhere else, wherever (in whatever new reality, in whatever equivalent to the biblical "his wife"), or what else the fate of this so-called numinosity might be, he intercepted the psychological process, intellectually taking possession of the now released numinosity, isolating and freezing it, setting it up as substances each in its own right, so that it turned into free-floating "meaning"-entities up in the air: archetypes. Jung robbed the autonomy from the historical process and instead equipped his "the archetypes" and his "the collective unconscious" with it. The notion of a collective *un*conscious was necessary to guarantee the absolute segregatedness of the archetypes from man's real experience in the world, their primordiality over against and independence from experienced reality.

These archetypes were then secondarily retrojected again into the child's experience ("the mother carries for us that inborn image of the *mater natura* and *mater spiritualis*," *ibid.*, which is a psychologically untenable inflation of the child's concept with the very different reality of the mythological concept) and into the past of the ages of myth and ritual (the experience of the gods explained as manifestations of

"IRRELEVANTIFICATION"

the archetypes of the collective unconscious). The late, abstracted decal is interpreted as the true atemporal origin of what it is abstracted from. Satellites set up by the modern theorist from out of *his sorely missing* the meaning and fulfillment that those experiences that have become historical and psychologically irrelevant no longer provide are given out as the primary source of those experiences from which they were actually derived. The psychological root of the archetypal theory is the fear of a lack, a lack that would arise if "father and mother" would be wholeheartedly left. Thus, so we can say with Jung's own words in another context, "... it is simply lack of adaptation, that you are not up to the situation,"[9] namely not up to the move to "wife," to the new locus of the soul value, here to the move into modernity.

If one reviews the mythological ideas, symbols, rituals of all kinds of ancient peoples who lived independently from one another, one will certainly find striking parallels that justify a responsible scholarly mind in introducing the notion of types or *topoi* (in the sense of Ernst Robert Curtius), that is, types as formal, structural categories and practical means of interpretation with a purely functional meaning. But for Jung they have to be much more: ultimate realities ("facts"), causal agents ("dominants"), primordial sources of meaning.

In the same text from which my previous quotes about the mother were taken, Jung makes the following general statement about the concept of archetype as such.

> The archetype is at first far less a scientific problem than an immediately pressing question of psychic hygiene. Even if all proofs of the existence of archetypes were lacking, and all the clever people in the world succeeded in convincing us that such a thing could not possibly exist, we would nevertheless have to invent them in order to keep our highest and most natural values from disappearing into the unconscious. For when these fall into the unconscious the whole elemental force of the original experience is lost. (*CW* 9i § 173, transl. modified)

Here the dogmatist is speaking. Jung *knows* a priori, or decides, what "our" (i.e., the soul's) "highest and most natural values" are. And he can know it because those values are for him themselves absolutely

---

[9] C.G. Jung, *Nietzsche's Zarathustra. Notes of the Seminar Given in 1934–1939*, ed. by James L. Jarrett, Princeton (Princeton Univ. Pr.) 1988, vol. 2, p. 1498.

408   THE SOUL ALWAYS THINKS

a priori: supra-temporal, supra-historical, eternal. He does not have
to allow himself to be taught empirically by the real development of
psychic life what and where the highest soul values in fact are in the
present situation, in each new present. By eternalizing those values,
Jung pursues the ego project of rescuing the meaning and values that
once were. To express it in terms of our biblical saying, he wants to
prevent the highest values from moving away from "father and mother"
to "wife." Even if it is unavoidable, as he admits, that father and mother
as literal empirical persons have become psychically irrelevant, at least
the highest value that they once had must at all cost be preserved.
This, for Jung, is a pressing question of psychic hygiene. The notion
that the highest value could move somewhere totally new and
unexpected is not admitted. Either the value is rescued in the form of
free-floating father and mother archetype or else it is totally lost,
disappearing into the unconscious.[10] In this scheme, there is no place

---

[10] Paradoxically, however, Jung could only rescue the soul values in the form of
archetypes by himself radically expelling them from the conscious life of society and *by
definition* sinking them into the unconscious: "the archetypes *of* the collective
unconscious." In former ages, the highest values and the gods of a people were not in the
unconscious. On the contrary, they were part of "official" public knowledge and they
were likewise publicly, openly, venerated and celebrated in the people's cultic life. Jung
felt he needed to prevent the total disappearance of the highest values into the
unconscious. However, what he feared and tried to prevent could not be *altogether*
avoided. He had to acknowledge it one way or another. He could only dispose of the
values' "disappearance in the unconscious" by absorbing the very thing he feared, this
very "disappearance in the unconscious" and the obsoleteness of those values, into the
very definition of his concept of "archetypes" as "archetypes of the collective unconscious,"
in other words, by incorporating the obsolescence into his theory as its very
presupposition and foundation. The invention of a special segregated "collective
unconscious" was necessary to get the obsolescence of the former soul values *structurally*
(syntactically) once and for all *behind* consciousness (into the [by definition] *un*conscious),
thereby both neutralizing this obsolescence on the semantic level and freeing
consciousness to now being able to concentrate, exclusively "forward," as it were, on
the naked semantic *contents* of the (now obsolete) former soul values. Once the theory
of the archetypes of the collective unconscious existed, consciousness did no longer
have to feel bothered by their obsolescence, because this obsolescence seemed once and
for all, namely logically, syntactically, to have been given satisfaction to and to have
been taken care of: by the hypostasis of "*the un*conscious" as a special sphere or realm
of psychic reality. Stripped of their rootedness in a particular historical time and mode
of being-in-the-world, the former values in their new guise of archetypes of the collective
unconscious would appear to a naïve consciousness as still valid ones. It is a trick, the
trick of splitting the unity of syntax and semantics and making the whole syntactical
aspect disappear "in the unconscious," that is, in psychology's unconsciousness, and at
the same time reducing the syntactical to semantics (the imaginal). For it is clear that
the moment that the obsolescence of the soul's values had to be disposed of on the level
of syntax through the invention of "the unconscious," this unconscious would conversely
dispose of or make disappear the entire topic of the syntactical. And indeed, Jungian

"IRRELEVANTIFICATION" 409

for a real forward movement, a real discontinuity, a historical metamorphosis ("from father and mother to wife"). The only thing allowed, and insisted upon, is a change in the sense of sublimation of the same ("from *literal* and *psychic* father and mother to *archetypal, imaginal,* or *psychological* father and mother," from empirical interpersonal relation to transpersonal relation). The content "father and mother" survives the real change from "literal" to "archetypal," from "psychic" to "psychological" unimpaired, even unaffected. There is no historical transportation from here to there, from one content to a new one (horizontally), but only a (vertical) sublimation and idealization at the same old psychological place or content. Jung is here even willing to sacrifice truth for his ego need to stay with "father and mother." And this ego need to stay put is ennobled as a "pressing question of psychic hygiene."

Jung said: "For when these [our highest and most natural values] fall into the unconscious the whole elemental force of the original experience is lost." Precisely. Such a loss is the whole point of a real change. The whole elemental force of the original experience is gone, has to be gone. How else could there be a real change? Having grown up means that father and mother are—psychologically—*really* dead, the whole logical structure of "father" and "mother" is obsolete, not just the one half of them, their *literal* aspect (the personal parents). It becomes obsolete because this whole structure, rather than remaining in the form of the external fact of an interpersonal relation is psychologized, integrated into consciousness (into its syntax or logical constitution). The linear relation *from* me *to* the parents in positive reality turns back on itself and forms a circle. The former interrelation becomes a uroboric, logically negative self-relation.[11] Only then have

---

theory has been totally oblivious of its own and of the soul's, of the soul phenomena's syntax. It had eyes exclusively for the semantic, for the abstract *contents* of images that come up. But of course, inasmuch as this theory admittedly operates with the notion of a segregated "*un*conscious," thereby instituting a sort-of ontological dissociation from consciousness and from the conscious life of a people, and inasmuch as it thus openly displays its untruth, it is honest.

[11] By moving from personal to transpersonal parents, Jung not only perpetuated the logic of interpersonal relations instead of advancing to the logic of self-relation, he even reverted the very notion of self into the opposite, into an Other, the substantiated "*the* self" *to* which we should develop a relationship or which we should circumambulate. As long as there is for us a self (the Self) *to* which we have to entertain a relationship we hold on to the status of (psychological) unbornness and deprive self from actually being *self.*

the parents *really* been left behind and only then can the son, in "cleaving to his wife," himself become the true father of his children. To be a father, he must totally have ceased being son and child. In him, his father is not eternalized by an *assumptio* into an archetypal heaven. No, he is dead and gone, *buried*, namely buried in the son himself, integrated in the latter's consciousness as part of its syntax. The son integrated his own childhood concept and experience of "father" into himself so that "father" is now reduced to a sublated moment within himself. The father that he now is is the opposite of the experience he had of "father" when he was a child. No continuity! A reversal. To *be* father means to *have* no father anymore. The two statuses are mutually exclusive, inasmuch as the one is the negation of the other. And to *be* father means that "father" is no longer substance, but subject, no longer content, but the logical form of the man's being.

But Jung went precisely the way of the *assumptio*. He adamantly rejected the psychologically *real, wholehearted* death of parents, the unrelenting "one-sided reduction of the mother to human proportions." He allowed only for a (psychological) mock-death,[12] a token demythologization of "Mother." When he demythologized the mother with his one "empirical" hand, he resurrected the mythologization of her with his other "logical" or "syntactical" hand. The mother is dead; long live the mother archetype. *As a theorist*, that is, in "metaphysical" regards, he did not leave father and mother. *Logically* he stayed at home (in the parental home) and preserved his child status, even if empirically—as a private person—he indeed moved out and made himself independent. His exorbitant praise of the new Roman-Catholic dogma of the *Assumptio Mariae* as the only bright spot in our benighted days at long last sort of metaphysically sealed his personal need as a theorist for the preservation of "Mother" and *ipso facto* of the logical status of "child."[13]

When "the whole elemental force of the original experience" is *not* lost, but still active in the adult, we would have to speak of a fixation in the psychoanalytic sense. Jung, however, avoided a *literal* fixation

---

[12] A (psychological) mock-death = a merely psychic death, a death only in the sphere of his personal development..

[13] I discussed this topic of Jung's theories concerning the *Assumptio Mariae* at some length in my paper "The 'Patriarchal Neglect of the Feminine Principle': A Psychological Fallacy in Jungian Theory," in: *Harvest: Journal for Jungian Studies* 1999, vol. 45, no. 1, pp. 7-30.

"IRRELEVANTIFICATION" 411

by substituting for the literal parents, as the "referent" of his concept of parents, the distilled "abstract concept" itself, stripped of its "accidental carriers." This is the archetype: the abstract-universal concept that has nothing else but itself as its (allegedly really existing) referent or carrier. Because it has nothing else that it refers to it is independent of external reality, absolutely self-sufficient, and this is why it seems to be suprahistorical, "primordial": "arche-"type.

Jung feared that "the highest and most natural values" would fall into the unconscious. This shows that he did not realize two things, first, that if he had followed the move from father and mother to wife, these values would by no means have fallen into "the unconscious," but would now have had a new *real* referent in "the wife"; only because he did not follow this movement did he need his anima-beloved side by side with his wife. And secondly, because Jung did not find another *real, empirical* referent or carrier for these values, but nevertheless conceives of those now abstracted highest values as empirical facts and objects of possible experience, it is precisely in his scheme of things that they, that the whole elemental force of the original experiences, had in fact to fall into "the unconscious" (an unconscious, however, that comes into existence only through this very maneuver). The positing of the abstract concept as *its own* (allegedly existing) referent *is* the construction of the Jungian construct of the unconscious. This is also the reason why the archetypes are rightly called "archetypes of the collective *un*conscious" (and inevitably have to be archetypes of the unconscious). They can never be *really* empirical or better concrete concepts, that is, abstract-universal concepts in fact *backed up* by empirical or positively existing referents. They do not have a *real* referent. And therefore they cannot be contents of *consciousness* the same way everything else we think and talk about is; they cannot be part of the world, the same world that all other events are part of. Jung's notion of the unconscious does not really mean "unconscious" in the ordinary sense, namely out of mind, disappeared, gone. It means much rather— quasi-ontologically—a second separate reality, so-called "psychic reality." The duplication of reality and the fundamental segregation of psychic reality from real reality or of the unconscious from consciousness, that is, the exclusion, on principle, of the archetypes or archetypal images from our *one common* world of consciousness, is necessary because the archetypes are not part of the real world with its *real* highest values (their referents are merely mirror images or empty duplications of the abstract concepts underlying the archetypes) and yet are supposed to be utterly real, perhaps even a higher reality than ordinary empirical reality.

The archetypes have the fact that they have no referent in reality in common with the mythic gods. This might seduce one into thinking that even if they are excluded from our one common world of consciousness they at least have the same dignity as the gods of former times and are simply a modern term for the same psychic reality that in mythological ages were called gods. But the reason that those gods did not have an external referent was that they were the "externally" intuited or imaginally apperceived different aspects of the *inner logic* or *soul* of man's real being-in-the-world, the animating spirit of his *really* lived life. As such, as the inner truth of something real they could not possibly have a *referent*. A referent would be a semantic content of or object in the world, but the inner truth of the world is the syntax of the world. The archetypes, by contrast, are abstract concepts or constructs, posited by the modern intellect. They are particular contents, images, or "factors" *in* the world and precisely not syntactical. Their referentlessness is therefore by no means comparable to that of the ancient gods (as the expression of aspects of the inner logic or truth of lived life). Rather, the fact that despite being fundamentally semantic they nevertheless lack a referent makes them free-floating. They are supposed to be the ultimate and self-sufficient "factors," dominants, determinants, causes of our psychic life. We are supposed to be or get into the grip of this or that archetype. The gods were not "factors" or causes behind the real, wire-pullers of what happened. They were, as I pointed out, simply the innermost truth of what actually happened, but this inner truth "externally" *imagined* and *intuited* as a separate shape or personalized figure.

ADAPTATION

What is ultimately at stake with the move from "parent" to "wife" as well as with the move into the eminently modern constitution of consciousness? What is the job of adaptation psychologically about?

For early Jung adaptation is central for explaining neurosis. His view was that neurosis, pathological affects, or all kinds of other

"IRRELEVANTIFICATION" 413

psychological problems arise "when libido is used for the maintenance of fantasies and illusions instead of being adapted to the actual conditions of life" (*CW* 4 § 303). "Affects always occur where there is a failure of adaptation" (*CW* 6 § 808[14]). I agree, adaptation is psychologically vital. However, in the context of a true psychology, a psychology with soul, that is, psychology as the discipline of interiority, we have to depart from that ordinary understanding of adaptation (also prevailing in Jung) that sees it in terms of the subject–object dichotomy, namely as referring to the subject's adaptation to objective or external reality, to social reality. Any thinking in terms of the subject–object dichotomy is *ipso facto* unpsychological because it has deserted the standpoint of soul which is defined by interiority, the hermetic sealing of the vessel. Psychology has no interest in interrelation, but only in the soul's self-relation. Failure to adapt to one's social or natural environment is *psychologically* irrelevant, although it may of course cause serious real problems and great suffering, which, however, are not psychological ones. Neurosis and psychological problems are exclusively due to the soul's mal-adaption to itself, specifically to the discrepancy (dissociation) between its self-understanding, self-interpretation, self-stylization, its mental attitude on the one hand and the logical constitution or status that it in fact happens to be in on the other hand.

This should of course not be confused with early Jung's compensatory idea of a second type of adaptation, "the necessity of adapting to the inner world of the psyche" (*CW* 8 § 66), because this idea remains within the same subject–object opposition and merely replaces an object "out there" by an object "in here." It merely reverses the subject's orientation from extraversion to introversion. The *standpoint* of this type of thinking is ego, not soul.

As a *psychological* concept, adaptation is an adjustment to one's own altered logical constitution, to a new soul situation, one's *new truth*, that one has been thrust into by one's psychic development. It needs to be primarily comprehended in terms of time, time's changes (rather than in terms of the spatial concepts "outer" and "inner"). *Tempora mutantur nos et mutamur in illis.* On a macrolevel, biological

---

[14] Cf. also the comments on "inferior adaptation" already referred to above in C.G. Jung, *Nietzsche's Zarathustra. Notes of the Seminar Given in 1934–1939*, ed. by James L. Jarrett, Princeton (Princeton Univ. Pr.) 1988, vol. 2, p. 1497f.

414   *THE SOUL ALWAYS THINKS*

time transports us, for example, from childhood into puberty and from there into biological adulthood and later into old age, just as historical time transports us into new epochs. There are of course also numerous smaller, more "local" changes. Inasmuch as the changes of time are the result of the soul's self-movement, we are thrust into a new soul truth. The soul does not ask us whether we want this change. We have no say in the matter. The change comes over us *vocatus atque non vocatus* and regardless of whether we are conscious of it and comprehend it in what it is about or not. *Adaptation, now, is the process in which one's new truth—the truth of one's new (biological, social, historical or mental) situation—which is already real, itself becomes explicitly true* (that is to say, in which it is, in addition to its already being factually true, also decidedly released into its truth, acknowledged and honored as being true, subjectively owned as one's reigning truth,[15] the truth as which one lives). "Verification" (in a very different sense from that known from the theory of science). And adaptation is necessary because time's changes are always ahead of us and we, always coming "after the fact," only slowly become aware of them. We are not free to choose the situations we are in. They conversely impose the task on us to psychologically respond to them—one way or another. "The meaning of my existence is that life holds a question addressed to me. ... and I must provide my answer ...," Jung said (*MDR* p. 318). The question always comes first. Man as *responding* being.

This is why the first job of psychology is to attentively listen to "the question" life addresses to us with each new situation, that is, to want to learn to see where the soul is now. Any psychology operating with a *fixed, given* sense of what the "highest and most natural values" are, indeed what "natural" means, what the soul is and needs (e.g., that it is "image" and needs "eros, aesthetics, rhetoric"), or "that the Gods are immortal," is ipso facto ideological. Ideology or *Weltanschauung* instead of psychology! It is ideological because it begins with an answer, with *our* preconceived ideas and presumed knowing, rather than with our listening, and because our fixating a specific sense of "soul" and "our highest values" as a time-immune a priori serves the purpose of gratifying precisely our present

---

[15] The danger of these statements is that they might be misconstrued as being about willful ego actions and conscious decisions. But they have to be actions of "the whole man" (*homo totus*), on the level of the soul's logical life.

"IRRELEVANTIFICATION" 415

(very much time-born) subjective needs or longings. Approaching psychic reality with such fixed notions in the back of one's mind ultimately boils down to our dictating to the soul what nature it has to have and how it ought to appear. It and its "highest and most natural values" are not allowed to appear in a totally unexpected place or in a totally new guise.[16] They have to comply with our cherished expectations, and if they do not, then it surely cannot be soul, it must be something soulless, false values, and our fault, our forgetfulness of soul, our hubris. No readiness and openness to learn from experience. No awareness that we first of all need to allow ourselves to be taught from scratch by the present real situation about the very *definition* of "soul," of "natural" and "highest value" at our time. It is not we who define the soul. It always comes with *its own* definition and imposes it on us. We find ourselves in it. And a particular definition is not static, given once and for all. For this reason, *how* the soul defines itself remains to be seen afresh in each new situation, a posteriori. The soul is alive, a process. It is fundamentally historical.[17] If we prejudge a

---

[16] An example from the Bible for the possibility that the soul's truth can appear in an unexpected, unlikely form is the following experience of Elijah. "And, behold, the LORD passed by, and a great and strong wind rent the mountains, and brake in pieces the rocks before the LORD; but the LORD was not in the wind: and after the wind an earthquake; but the LORD was not in the earthquake: And after the earthquake there was a fire, but the LORD was not in the fire. And after the fire there was the sound of a gentle whisper" (1 Kings 19:11f.). Three times the frustration of one's expectations: "was *not* in..."

[17] The addition of "historical" to "alive" is essential. Taking as a starting point the Goethe quote with which Jung described the soul's life, "Formation, transformation, Eternal Mind's eternal recreation," we immediately see that we can give a harmless and a radical interpretation to the life, i.e., metamorphoses, of the soul. The form change can be understood as a merely semantic one, but it can also be comprehended as a syntactical one. "Semantic" change would mean a transformation on a purely phenomenal level. A demon, for example, may change into a dog, from the dog into a fly, from the fly into human shape and so on, whatever seems opportune. It is always—statically—the same demon, merely in different guise. Kaleidoscopic. – But if, for example, "what natural means" or "what our highest values are" changes its *definition*, we get a syntactical transformation, because this change affects everything, every phenomenon, in the "world," and it changes it not only, or rather precisely *not*, in its external visible shape, but in its inner logical form, in its status, function, and meaning. It is a change of the entire logical constitution of consciousness. And this transformation is *historical* because the change of the entire syntax of the "world" or of consciousness is not random and accidental, but has its own inner coherence and consistency. There is one continuous dynamic, as in the alchemical opus. The process goes through stages, where any later stage only comes about through its having pushed off from its predecessor. – For completeness's sake let me mention an additional form of change that does not fit either of the categories mentioned, but is partly semantic, partly syntactical. We find it in myth, in the metamorphoses as, for example, described by Ovid. These transformations are semantic because they are restricted to one single phenomenon or being in the world, a world whose definition or logical constitution remains intact. But they are logical or syntactical inasmuch as they amount to

416   *THE SOUL ALWAYS THINKS*

situation we cannot respond to the question or challenge as which it exists and which *is* its soul, the inner logic animating it. But then we cannot psychologically adapt to it either.

Animals do not have this need of psychological adaptation or "verification." For them, life does not hold a question and they do not have to provide their own answer. They exist as their by nature always already finished answer. When they, for example, become sexually mature, this their new reality is inevitably and at once also their lived truth. When humans, by contrast, go through puberty so that their now being sexual beings has become their factually real truth, this is, according to what I just said, not enough. Humans, inasmuch as they primarily *are* (exist as) mind or soul and not merely physical beings, have the necessity of, in an additional psychological, mental step, *making* true what factually is already their real truth. There is (needs to be) a duplication. Fact has to be supplemented by a repetition of it on the mental or soul level. Humans have to make what happened to them (and what as fact is still psychically external to them) truly their own. They have to actively interiorize it, embrace it, and take it over as their own responsibility. The blow that was dealt them from outside or the injustice that was done to them they have to perform themselves once more internally upon themselves in order to integrate fact into soul and humanize it, that is, change mere fact into the form or status of truth.[18] And because this their very own necessity can also be avoided or refused, or receive only a fake fulfillment from them, humans have the potential of becoming neurotic, which animals have not.[19] Conversely, the fact that such refusal or avoidance leads to one's psychic illness (rather than to bad external, factual consequences for

---

the absolute-negative interiorization, to the *initiation*, of this one phenomenon or being into its concept, its inner essence, its truth. The nymph Syrinx being changed into a reed is by no means a kaleidoscopic metamorphosis, but her coming home to herself, to what she in truth is and has implicitly been all along, and thus to her fulfillment.

[18] Soul is the organ of truth. The object of the soul, i.e., what soul is concerned with, is truths. Just as the eye reacts exclusively to the visible part of the spectrum, the ear only to acoustic wave lengths, so the soul only (ap)perceives and is interested in truths. It does not have, as the ego-personality does, a stake in fact—things and people and events. Therefore the need for "verification" in the special sense given. The alchemists warned, "Beware of the physical in the matter!" The physical or natural is the "undigested," "unprocessed," "raw," i.e., not "verified" (*wahr* gemacht) fact.

[19] Animals that cannot adapt to dramatic changes in their environment simply die or, as species, become extinct. Likewise, people who do not adapt to their *social environment* simply become outsiders or outcasts, but they do not become neurotic

"IRRELEVANTIFICATION" 417

oneself) shows that, in contrast to social adaptation, *psychological* adaptation—the humanization or "verification" of brute fact—is truly one's own inner necessity as a human being, a being who *is* soul.[20]

With my emphasis on adaptation and "verification" I point out, as Greg Mogenson writes,[21] "that psychological work has to do with what has already psychically come to pass or become real. So much psychotherapy is caught up with trying to promote or foster development or developments, to bring changes about, to make things happen. But the focus can instead be on letting what already *is* come home to consciousness: adaption, verification. A truth emphasis rather than a remediation emphasis." We could also say that I thus radically break with the *utopian* orientation of much of psychotherapy (especially Jungian psychotherapy): "Striving Towards Wholeness" (Barbara Hannah); "The goal is important only as an idea; the essential thing is the *opus* which leads to the goal..." (*CW* 16 § 400). The goal here is a distant, lofty ideal. It lies in the future. We can strive hard to come a bit closer to it, but we will probably never be able to actually reach it. And we *ought to* get there, we feel the moral pressure, but all we can do is to be on the way forever. This conception of psychotherapy sends us on a wild-goose chase. It follows the logic of Moses and the Promised Land. It is like a systematic procrastination. One once and for all *settles* in an unending deferral. A case of shirking.

What I conceive, by contrast, is a "psychotherapy of the perfect tense." No ideal. No wishing and hoping. No *Sollen* and striving. Because there *is* nothing to strive for, no goal set for us. Any developmental goal envisioned by psychology can be seen through as an ego program, *our* own agenda. What is needed instead of all this is

---

(dissociated from themselves). When Jung says (*MDR* p. 140), "I have frequently seen people become neurotic when they content themselves with inadequate or wrong answers to the questions of life," this points to the problem of psychological adaptation in my sense. They become neurotic only if they give the wrong answers to those questions of life that are already *their own* inner truths. Neurosis, as a *psychological* illness, is necessarily a form of self-relation, not of a relation to some literal other, something external to self.

[20] Now it is very interesting that Jung can say that there are people who are *incapable of developing a neurosis* (speaking of psychic troubles that are under certain conditions in store he says, "They will appear either as neurotic symptoms or, in the case of persons who are incapable of neurosis, as collective delusions" *MDR* p. 352). If this be true, does it mean that those people do not fully exist *as* soul? That for them the questions of life are not *questions* really addressed to *them* at all, questions emerging within the context of *self*, but that they have the status of external environmental conditions for them?

[21] Personal communication, email letter of 01 Sep. 2008.

418   THE SOUL ALWAYS THINKS

merely our "catching up with"[22] what has already become real, has
already been reached, is already here. The ground of the real is thus
not left, and the circumference of the present is not transgressed in
favor of one's dreaming of future possibilities and our potentiality. As
the alchemists put it: *Quod natura relinquit imperfectum, ars perficit.*
The imperfect is the real that is only "natural" fact, only "implicitly"
true, but has not yet explicitly (through the adept's *ars*: through a
contribution of human consciousness, *its* acknowledging response)
been *made* true.[23] And verification is perfection, but in the very simple,
down-to-earth sense of completion, of giving to what *is* the finishing
touch—not perfection in the usual utopian idealistic sense.[24] All
development, progress(ion), teleology, if any, is the business of *natura*,
the soul, life itself. *We* don't have to do anything. Our job, a big enough
job, is only to clearly see (in the sense of cognition) the truth that
already *is* and to let ourselves in the form of our consciousness be
consciously and wholeheartedly reached by it.

But the problem is not only the pretentious utopian goals hinted
at. The widespread and time-and-again presented psychotherapeutic

---

[22] On "catching up with" cf. my "The Leap After the Throw: On 'Catching up
With' Projections and on the Origin of Psychology" (1979), now in: W.G., *The Neurosis
of Psychology. Primary Papers towards a Critical Psychology*, New Orleans (Spring Journal
Books) 2005, pp. 69–96. It is essential to understand this phrase dialectically. Our
catching up with what already *is* can be considered to be a forward move on our part (to
bring us up-to-date with the stage reached in the soul's development) only to the extent
that it is much rather, passively, our being reached, penetrated, and permeated by the
inner truth of the real, its soul. We don't have to "get to" any place. "Catching up with
what is already real" thus actually means that it is the already real logic of the situation
that catches up with us, or better: dawns up on us, comes home to our consciousness.

[23] We should not connect any high-flown ideas of an artist as a genius with the
notion of the alchemical *ars*. It is rather to be understood in analogy to the very ordinary,
practical work of an artisan, a handicraftsman. *Ars perficit* simply means that a job has to
be done, although of course in a special Mercurial, speculative-dialectical spirit. Nothing
mysterious or almost superhuman: only owning up to what is.

[24] Jung felt the need to ward off the notion of perfection (*Vollkommenheit*) from his
concept of wholeness (as completeness). This had two reasons. First, he viewed
"perfection" in idealistic terms, and this in turn is, secondly, due to his personalistic,
ego-psychological prejudice: he thought in terms of *our* development, *our* perfection,
our wholeness or completeness. What Jung demanded of the individuals for their personal
psychic process, namely that they learn to distinguish themselves from themselves, he
was obviously not able to do himself on the level of theory with respect to the concept
of the individual, to "us." Psychology's identification with "the human individual"
remained unresolved. For me perfection and wholeness become more or less synonymous
in this context because what for me is at stake is not our (i.e., people's) wholeness, but
the wholeness or completion of the soul's truth. What needs to be perfected, to become
whole (through being made true) is *it*, the soul of the real, the reality that we already live
in and indeed unwittingly already *are*, not we.

view that developmental steps are tasks that the individual has to master and that patients are neurotic because they have not been up to them (for example because they are thought to have too weak an ego and are as yet not ready for the task) is totally misguided. It is the reversal or reinterpretation of what actually is *quite simply* the cognition and acknowledgment of a truth that has already become real, into a task that still lies ahead of the individual and is terribly difficult to master. This is the neurotic interpretation of neurosis. The reinterpretation of an insight (into something that is in the "perfect tense") as a task waiting to be performed or as a threshold yet to be crossed is an excuse. It is the denial that the threshold already lies behind oneself and above all the decision to counterfactually, that is, neurotically, once and for all settle down *in front of* the threshold. Above I already gave an example from Jung himself for this type of interpretation, where he conceives the transition of a son from the mother "to wife" as a terribly difficult task to be performed in the future: "For this he would need a faithless Eros, one capable of forgetting the mother and cutting into his own flesh, by deserting the first beloved of his life" (*CW* 9ii § 22, transl. modif.). The irreal subjunctive is perfectly in place. Because, the way that the situation is construed, the son will never muster the faithless eros and will never have the strength to cut into his own flesh. And the situation is only construed in this way for the purpose that it will never happen. And conversely, precisely if the son, through therapeutic help, were after all able to do it this would be nothing but an egoic acting-out. It would psychologically be irrelevant. It would merely simulate, and lead us to believe in, his having stepped out of his neurosis, while the neurotic *structure* would continue as before, because the level of psychology (the level of cognition) would have been left in favor of the level of action, of moral oughts, and of emotions (one's suffering from one's inability and weakness, one's victim status, and one's fury against those who are guilty of one's own deficiency). Neurotic fuss.

BIOLOGICAL, PSYCHIC, AND PSYCHOLOGICAL BIRTH—AND THE BIRTH OF PSYCHOLOGY/SOUL

The move from a social to a psychological sense that we just made in our understanding of adaptation also needs to be performed with respect to our understanding of marriage. From an external social perspective it looks as if the move into marriage, to focus on it by way of example in the following, was a horizontal move into a "partnership" between two adults as peers and thus a special form of subject-object relation, namely one where the "object" is another subject. But the image of the married couple, which, as the *result* of the movement into marriage, in itself has its own psychological validity ("the syzygy"), nevertheless obscures the psychological direction of this movement itself. Logically, the move into marriage is a downwards movement, a fall, a going under, and has to be seen in the light of the fundamental lifelong psychological task of the birth of man.

For our predominant naturalistic thinking it looks as if birth is a one-time event at the beginning of life and as if with having been born in the literal sense the topic of birth was once and for all finished. We always have our birth, so we think, irrevocably behind ourselves. But this is only the biological birth, our birth as animals. But psychically as well as psychologically a baby is still unborn. Having parents means that it is still contained in an a priori, a primordial origin. The parents are the child's psychological womb, just as the mother's belly is the embryo's biological womb. Through literal birth, the child has become *biologically* independent, biologically a self. Now it also needs to come *psychically* into the world.

A baby, as human being, is from the outset not primarily a biological being, but *is* first of all already psyche. It is the *existing concept*, although only the early form of this concept, *ansichseiend* ('implicit') concept. It is vital to realize that a baby *is* (exists as) the concept. It comes (biologically) into the world enwrapped in the abstract-universal concept that it is, and this concept has at first (in the case of a baby) the form of being the concept of "mother." The baby does not *have* this concept. It *is* the concept of "mother." Long before it can think it *is* the thought "mother."

The content of this concept is more than the mere word "mother" and the notions of nourishment and protection. "Mother" is the initial name of the absolutely fundamental *relation*; it is in itself a relational concept (the concept of the unity of mother and child) and not, as in psychoanalysis, the concept of the "object," not simply no more than the name of a person. The word is pregnant, rich, containing in totally enveloped and latent form all kinds of ideas and values, such as "the

"IRRELEVANTIFICATION" 421

most important thing (for me); (my) highest, indeed absolute, soul value" and "(my) being seen and truly *meant* by and (my) being of absolute importance for (her), [which shows as much in her loving tenderness for me as in her anger at me]." But first of all "mother" means: I am not merely an entity, an object, a (living) thing, contained within myself. Rather, I exist as a subject and thus as a *relation.* Because I *am* this relation,[25] this relation is not a relation to an Other, but my own self-relation. In the course of the child's growing up many or all of the aspects of the concept originally still dormant in it will be born out of it, most notably the notions of "I" and "world," "father," perhaps also "God."

As being the as yet completely abstract and latent, completely ununfolded and undifferentiated concept of mother, the baby is still "in heaven," up in the clouds, in potentiality, not down on earth. In order to come psychically (not yet psychologically!) into the world, it needs to find a real "referent" for this abstract concept. "*Being* this concept" here means precisely not having a clear concept of it. There is no knowledge of it and what it entails. The concept has not yet come out into the open. The baby is *in* this concept as its own being, totally enwrapped in it; the concept is not in its mind (an intellectual idea as an instrument for comprehending reality). The concept exists only as the blind *need* as which the child exists. The baby needs to moor this its concept here on earth, in temporal and material reality, so that the concept does not stay abstract, but can become the concrete concept. In an act of unconditional surrender, for better or worse, it needs to dock onto, and adopt, an external person as his mother in order to *ground* the concept as which it exists. This also explains why, as Jung had said, the mother is an "accidental carrier" of the great experience of "mother." *She* has to carry and embody for the baby the concept as which *it* exists. This is why I would not use the word "dyad" for the baby-mother relation, because *psychologically,* that is to say seen from within and *from the child's side,* it is really a self-relation and not an

---

[25] The things of nature, e.g., stones, are of course also in a or in numerous relations to their environment. Stones are exposed to and affected by the sun, rain, snow, and gravity, etc. All this is external to them. They do not themselves *exist* as relation, they merely have their place within the whole nexus of the universe. In order to be able to have a relation, they would within themselves have to be a self-relation, relate to themselves, which also means that they would have to be within themselves different from themselves.

interpersonal relation or object relation (as which it appears from outside and only from outside).[26]

I already mentioned that where a newborn baby does not have a chance to find its concept of "mother" fulfilled in reality, that is, where it cannot find a real referent for the concept as which it *is*, where there is nobody onto whom it can psychically dock here on the earth, the baby does not really enter the world psychically (keyword "hospitalism") and in extreme cases may even 'undo its literal birth again' by actually dying. The life-long process of being born is stopped or at least impeded at one of its earliest phases. This absolute necessity to find the concept-as-which-it-*is* fulfilled, is the first immediacy of the psychological phenomenon of adaptation, proto-adaptation. It is the attempt to bring its reality (having biologically been born and now being in the real world, being a being in its own right outside the mother's body) in alignment with the concept (the logical constitution of its being-in-the-world as a helpless being) that it already is. I called it proto-adaptation because it is not really a subject's free psychological process, but happens automatically, instinctively, and because it is hardly the baby's achievement, but rather the brutal need to find the real objective correspondent to the concept that it is.

In many archaic societies, who still had an intuitive knowledge about the birth of man as a *human* being and did not confound it with biological birth, it was therefore possible to abandon newly born babies, for example, if they were deformed. In such a cultural context the newborn baby was merely a piece of nature that therefore could also under certain conditions be simply returned to nature. It was not yet a human being. The fact that it was still a piece of nature can also be expressed in the following way: it had psychologically not yet come into the world; it still hovered in extraterrestrial spheres, although biologically it had already been born into the world. It was only brought into the world as a human being, and thus psychically born, through a special cultural act on the part of the parents, namely through their formally accepting the baby as their child (for example by giving it a name or picking it up) and thereby offering themselves to the baby as persons in empirical reality onto which it could dock

---

[26] If one accepts this insight, then the notion of "triangulation" has lost its justification along with that of the "dyad."

"IRRELEVANTIFICATION"

and which it could in its turn adopt as its parents. Humanness is not given by nature. It has its origin in culture. And it is not inherent in the abstract, solitary individual, not the possession of each individual himself, but is a social reality.

But as indicated this amounts only to the child's *psychic* birth or entrance into the world. The psychic birth is not fully and specifically human yet, because the human baby *mutatis mutandis* shares this with certain animal species, the so-called "precocial species." Konrad Lorenz studied this phenomenon called "imprinting." He discovered that, for example, a young duckling learns to follow the first conspicuous, moving object it sees within the first few days after hatching. Normally, this object would be the mother bird; but Lorenz was able to show that he himself could serve as an adequate substitute mother, which, however, forced him to constantly imitate a mother duck's quacking sounds in response to the duckling's questioning sounds. Lorenz found that a newly hatched duckling could even be fooled into adopting an animal of another species as "mother" and model or even a rolling red ball.

The point for us here is that already on the level of animal life in certain species babies come biologically into the world as a (preliminary form of an) abstract-universal concept of "mother" and need to find a real referent for it in order to become also psychically born. It is clear that these logical processes, both in animals and, on a fundamentally higher level, in human babies occur on the level of a still "implicit" logic, a logic still completely immersed in biological instinct and behavior, in the case of the duckling even submerged in a rather mechanical stimulus-response process, but nevertheless on the level of an (implicit) real logic. It is the psyche—the concept—stirring here, a psyche, however, that has not yet come into its own so as to turn into soul.

By having found a referent to his concept and having moored himself to the person who happens to be the "accidental carrier" of this concept, the baby has achieved its *psychic* birth. It has become the concrete concept. *Psychologically*, by contrast, the child remained unborn—if 'birth' means coming out into the open from some protective, enveloping womb, cocoon, or shell. True, the child has been born, but the concept as which it *is* stays enveloped, implicit. Only once the existing concept as concept is also born, can we speak of the psychological birth of man. The baby, although psychically born and having become the concrete concept, is still very far away from psychological birth. Indeed, the *psychic* move into the world occurs precisely (and can only occur) through *psychologically* docking onto some real people as parents, who logically stand between oneself and the world, and through thus embedding oneself without reserve in the cocoon of the psychological protection (and possibly love) provided by them. As paradoxical as it may seem, the act of psychic birth proceeds precisely by the baby's relentlessly committing itself into the state of psychological unbornness.

By contrast, leaving father and mother in order to cleave to one's wife means not only breaking out of the protective cocoon provided by the existence of parents, but also docking with some other, alien person in the outside world.[27] As such it is the first immediacy (no more as yet) of psychological birth. Whereas the parents are one's a priori and whereas one's connection to them, therefore, is logically hallowed by necessity and absoluteness, the connection to "wife" is logically fundamentally a posteriori, contingent, and artificial; it has to be established; and it requires the continuous labor of a rapprochement. Parents cannot be chosen. They are found as always already given to oneself. Although empirically they are "accidental carriers" of the concept of mother and father as which the child exists, logically it is inherent in the concept of parents and in the mooring process that they are adopted as one's absolute a priori, one's true and inevitable parents. The logical act of mooring and adopting is totally unconscious, obliterated. And of course it has to be obliterated, because otherwise the mooring (and thus psychic birth) would not be real. It is real only if it is absolute, without reserve; only if the child has the concept as which it is, its own concept, totally *in* the real parents out there or in the relationship to them.[28]

---

[27] I omit here an important intermediate stage in psychic development between docking onto a parent and leaving one's parents in order to dock unto "wife" or "husband." Often in childhood there appears the fantasy of one's double parents: One's literal parents are only foster parents, false parents, stepparents. In truth one is the child of mysterious other, better, higher, divine parents. These substituted fantasy parents help prepare the ground for "leaving father and mother" and, as one's own fantasy, are a stage in the process of the integration of the parents into oneself.

[28] Rather than in his own mind.

"IRRELEVANTIFICATION" 425

But another person becomes wife or husband through one's (logically[29]) arbitrary choice. It is inherent in the concept of wife that she is *taken* to wife. In marrying, one sets up house by one's own doing and thus becomes, and attests to being, a self. Because the new family is a self-made and in this sense "artificial" (not only "accidental") family it lacks the bliss of being a priori given to us, the gift of absolute primordiality. In cleaving to his wife instead of to his parents, a man therefore not only docks with a contingent person, but also (and this is psychologically the important aspect[30]) *embraces contingency as such*. In this way he has psychologically forsaken the blissful realm of a priori necessity and unconditionality—existence in heaven—and dropped down to earth, *this* earth; he has given himself over to the temporal and empirical, to a-posteriori-ness; he has entered the real world in contrast to the sphere of abstract ideality.

Feelings of love, being contained in a relationship ("I – Thou"), feeling understood and loved is only the ego meaning of marriage. *Psychologically* it is about stepping out of the soul's interiority, innocence, transcendence and instead (psychologically) planting oneself and taking root in the world, investing one's soul-value in some real other out there. The point is to irrevocably entangle oneself with empirical existence. The other person as such is not the essential thing. At bottom, i.e., logically, exchangeable, he or she *is* essential only because one's psychologically planting oneself in empirical reality in its materiality is real only to the extent that he or she is truly *meant* as this specific thou and has in fact *become* unreservedly essential for oneself. One has really *taken* this other person to wife or husband and thereby committed oneself.

There is a curious passage in Jung about the soul. "With her cunning play of illusions the soul lures into life the inertness of matter that does not want to live. She makes us believe incredible things, so

---

[29] Empirically, in social reality, *who* will become one's husband or wife may not be the result of one's own choice. The marriage may be arranged or even dictated by one's parents or, in the case of nobility, by political necessities. But this does not change the logical arbitrariness. However, such conditions do detract from the actual realization of the psychological birth in *the person concerned*, of the emancipation from "primordial givenness," of the true emergence of self.

[30] It is the psychologically important aspect because in practical reality there can of course be factual marriages without *ipso facto* contingency as such having been embraced. It is always possible to literally marry, but psychologically nevertheless stay the child of one's parents for life ("keep cleaving" to one's parents).

that life may be lived. She is full of snares and traps, in order that man should fall, should reach the earth, entangle himself there, and stay caught, so that life should be lived" (*CW* 9i § 56, transl. modif.). What is curious about it is that Jung on the one hand clearly saw and emphasized the need to reach the earth and to get entangled in reality, but that on the other hand he viewed it from the standpoint of resistance to and the fear of life, adopting as his own, as it were, the attitude of the neurotic who wants to stay aloof up in the clouds and does precisely not want to get entangled in earthly existence. You need to be *trapped* into living life. Only because of this stance, what could actually be seen as (one stage of) the birth of man is presented as a Fall, i.e., connected with sin and the loss of paradise (Jung's next sentence explicitly refers to Eve in the Garden Eden), and as requiring snares for the person to be "caught," caught as the fundamental fugitive from life that he or she is presupposed to be. It is this standpoint that gave rise to Jung's particular concept of the soul as ensnaring anima.[31] That to entangle oneself in life could be a person's very own need and wish and that the birth of man could be something quite normal, ordinary, is at least here not provided for.

Because of the necessity, inherent in the psychological meaning of marriage, to embrace contingency per se, it is essential that one always marries so to speak "beneath oneself" (not in a literal social, but in a psychological sense). *Both* persons have to marry down (which is of course only possible in the contradictory world of the soul). Speaking only from the male point of view, the chosen one must not be inflated with anima projections; for the man she must not be the object of his upward-looking: his goddess, his princess, *the* spouse meant for him from eternity, the embodiment of the mysterious immortal "She-who-must-be-obeyed" (Rider Haggard). Rather, to wife and husband applies the same idea that Jung voiced concerning the human mother: they are frail human beings deserving of our love, indulgence, understanding, and forgiveness, and this, the real human being in them, is what needs to be seen and embraced. The human spouse must be "released from the terrifying burden" that in *falling*

---

[31] This (ego-psychologistically viewed) anima must not be confused with that very different, truly *psychological* anima as mediatrix to the unknown, to the underworld and the ancestors, to historical tradition, and the anima as the one side of or within the syzygy!

"IRRELEVANTIFICATION"

in love is inevitably loaded on the shoulders of him or her, a projection and delusion that no doubt is a necessary part of the artful, ingenious motor[32] that initially helps to conduct the libido away from the parents to the other person (just as it had conversely induced the psychologically still preexistent newborn baby to psychically dock onto the real world by means of inflated concepts of the perfection, power, intelligence, and beauty of the real parents as near-divine personages), but a delusional projection that needs to be seen through and left behind once it has done its job.

THE FUNCTION OF JUNG'S *ASSUMPTIO* MOVE

The logic that I illustrated here using the example of personal development from being a child contained in the fold of a parental family to adult husband or wife and self applies analogously to consciousness's cultural-historical development into modernity. By moving from empirical mother to archetypal mother and to his theory of archetypes in general, Jung tried to cement, on the level of psychological theory, what he once referred to as "cloud-cuckoo-land,"[33] man's psychological containment in the realm of the abstract universal, and to prevent at long last the psychological birth of man through his (man's) fall into the contingent and empirical—although this fall had factually and irrevocably already happened in the history of the soul and even been "institutionalized" in how the life of society was organized at his time and even more so in our time. It was in fact the new soul truth. This rescue operation was the *psychological* function[34] of his psychological theory of the archetypes of the collective unconscious. Inasmuch as "the archetype" is expressly stated not to be dependent on scientific proof, but serves the purpose of keeping "our highest and most natural values from disappearing," the theory of archetypes is ideological (in the sense of a theory that rationally underpins and legitimizes irrational *needs*, here by Jung indirectly referred to under the label of the "immediately pressing question of psychic hygiene").

---

[32] This is the small empirical basis for the concept of the ensnaring anima just referred to that Jung erected on it.

[33] In a letter of 9 Apr. 59 quoted in an editor's note to a letter to Freud dated 11 Feb. 1910, *Letters 1*, p. 19.

[34] In contrast to the scientific function as an explanatory principle.

428   *THE SOUL ALWAYS THINKS*

Ultimately, by going the way of the *assumptio*, Jung followed his decidedly anti-Christian impulse of undoing the (for Christianity fundamental and characteristic) logical movement of the *kenôsis*, the divestiture or depletion described in Phil. 2:6ff. ("who, although He existed in the form of God, did not cling to his being equal to God, but emptied Himself, taking the form of a bond-servant, and being made in the likeness of men...") in favor of a (logical, structural, not semantic) repaganisation, which he, however, tried to sell as his "dreaming the *Christian* myth onwards."

When Jung says, "we would nevertheless have to invent [the archetypes] in order to keep our highest and most natural values from disappearing into the unconscious," he not only tells us how indispensable it seemed to him to retain "the parents" for himself and to logically stay at their place,[35] we also realize that the archetypes are *invented as* our *most natural* values. If they *were* in fact natural, they would simply prevail as a matter of course and would not have to be invented. The theory of archetypes is a modern construct devised for the purpose of preventing the conscious awareness that we are already in fact somewhere truly new and different (namely in modernity) and that there has been a real logical negation (sublation), a real cut. But a real negation is presented by Jung as psychologically catastrophic. The suggestion of a catastrophe, however, is needed to erect a bulwark—in the form of terrible fear—against consciously admitting that the expulsion from "childhood" has both biographically and collectively-historically already happened a long time ago and that we find ourselves in the modern situation, irrevocably "alienated" (of course alienated only if "the parental home" *remains* one's standard and measure. If, by contrast, one goes along with the soul's movement and adapts to one's new truth there can be no question of alienation.).

On the other hand, a psychologically real death implies that what hitherto had been our most natural values indeed disappears ("the whole elemental force of the experience is lost"). A psychologically real change amounts precisely to a shift *in what is most natural*. With each

---

[35] Under the section heading of "Token Adulthood" in my "The End of Meaning and the Birth of Man: An Essay about the State Reached in the History of Consciousness and an Analysis of C.G. Jung's Psychology Project" (*IJJTP* vol. 6, no. 1, 2004, pp. 1–65, here pp. 50–53) I discussed in more detail Jung's need to preserve "the parents." See now Chapter Nine in the present volume.

"IRRELEVANTIFICATION" 429

psychological change the "natural" is redefined. And this redefinition is what Jung needed to prevent. Jung wanted to freeze and positivize the notion of what is natural. "The natural" was not allowed to be a *psychological* concept, that is to say, a fantasy of the psyche and ipso facto subject to the development of consciousness, subject to the psychic process, to history. In the archetypes Jung posited, in the spirit of "bad metaphysics," a true primordial origin exempt from time and change. "The archetype is ageless and everpresent" (*Letters 2*, p. 394, to Trinick, 15 October 1957). "The demons have not really disappeared but have merely taken on another form" (*CW* 10 § 431). "Our consciousness only imagines that it has lost its gods; in reality they are still there ..." (*Letters 2*, p. 594, to Serrano, 14 September 1960). That gods, too, and even the very concept of "god" are at the disposal of the soul's process and can thus become historical, i.e., truly die and get lost for good, Jung ultimately did not allow himself to imagine.[36]

OUR NEW *OIKOS*

It has been a long detour via the detailed psychological interpretation of a biblical saying and a discussion of a relevant Jung passage. But with the phrase "our most *natural* values" we have unexpectedly already been redirected to our initial theme, nature and its death. Our paradigm ("... shall a man leave his father and mother, and cleave to his wife") teaches us that psychological change involves a change of subject or locus (*topos*), such as "from parents to wife," a change that at the same time is a fall or going under. The focus of attention and interest changes. Today, we can no longer circle around nature and around the question of the correct relation between man and nature, because nature (which in itself includes the man-nature *relation*) has psychologically been absolutely irrelevantized. Two thousand years ago, the soul emigrated from nature and left it behind as a dead shell. It had lost its numinosity, its soul importance. So if with Descartes the natural world was defined as *res extensa*, and a few hundred years later with the beginning of the Industrial Revolution as mere raw material,

---

[36] This holds true despite his opposite acknowledgment of the "metamorphosis of the gods" (from god into abstract concept) and even of the fact that "the gods die from time to time" (*CW* 9i § 22) and that "When Nietzsche said 'God is dead,' he uttered a truth ..." (*CW* 11 § 145).

a long-standing truth about nature had simply at long last come home to consciousness; consciousness had finally drawn the obvious conclusion from the soul development and taken the new truth into account. It had finally *adapted* to its new truth and later, especially in the course of the 19th century, also become factually equal to it in practical-technical regards. Ever since the nature gods and spirits had left nature, nature had psychologically been fair game.

We have to be very clear about it: For the *soul* it makes no difference whatsoever whether nature is dead or alive, that is, whether it is literally destroyed or whether we develop an ecological consciousness and treat nature well; the soul does not care one way or another whether we survive or not. These two options in each regard are important merely for the ego. *We* want to survive. It is an *ego concern* that we learn to think ecologically. Natural disasters, insofar as they must be understood as results of human interference with nature, have no message for the *soul* in the sense of pointing to a logical insufficiency or even falseness of the hitherto practiced human domination of nature. It is the ego of modern man that they teach to behave differently, more ecologically. It is a very pragmatic issue. Our ego wishes and interests are at stake. Desertification, overpopulation, global warming, an increase of hurricanes and floods, etc., are clearly undesirable. And the answer to these problems is a technical one. We simply have to learn what needs to be done to achieve the desired results. How do we have to behave so that unwanted developments can be avoided? This is the question, and it is about practical learning. It has nothing to do with psychology, in the sense of a psychology of soul. The soul has no stake in nature, no claim on its well-being, no interest in our having an ecological consciousness.

It is much more like the question for the adult person of how to deal with the fact that his or her parents need nursing. Should we take them into our own house and do the nursing ourselves? Or do we find a nursing home for them? These are important practical and moral questions, but as such they are ego concerns and irrelevant for the soul, which we know has emigrated from "father and mother." *It* is somewhere else. When we use the word nature we always have to be aware of the equivocation and the psychological difference running through it. Adapting a bon mot by Lichtenberg we can put it this way: we still say 'nature' just as we say thaler even after the thaler as a currency unit has long disappeared. Just as "Mother" has been "one-sidedly reduced to human proportions" for the adult, so "Mother Nature" has been reduced for modern man to nothing but plain empirical fact. As this fact it needs our respect. We have to be beware of earthquakes, tsunamis, tornados, AIDS and skin cancer, and of such long-range dangers as desertification, the disappearance of tropical rain forests and global warming. Of course. But our practical respect for nature because of physical dangers does not remythologize nature and restore its former soul importance, its numinosity.

We cannot dream of nature as our *oikos*, our home, or of finding the proper *human place* in nature. To entertain such wishes would mean to be barking up the wrong tree. Our alienation from nature is—psychologically—not a mistake to be corrected, just as it is not a mistake to have left the parental home. Alienation from nature is not only irrevocable, but also fundamental, essential for modern existence. There is nothing wrong with it. Just as the man of the biblical saying has a new orientation and establishes his own home with his wife, so an *oikos* can, if at all, only be established somewhere else and definitely not in nature. Nature has become historical for us.

As historical, nature is partly, during workdays, at our free disposal as raw material and puts restraints on our exploitation of it only for our ego interests in our survival and well-being, and partly, during our leisure time, it is a huge literal open-air museum and playground for our indulgence in sentimental-nostalgic longings, which is also egoic.[37]

The soul's real theme and "matter" is god or "highest soul value." Just as growing up brings the painful insight that the highest value of the *personal psyche* is not identical with the initial carriers or representatives of this highest value, one's parents, but that these carriers can all of a sudden be completely stripped naked of psychic importance because this value left them and is now somewhere else, so the history

---

[37] In Christian Churches there is nowadays much talk about the "preservation of the Creation." I ask: which Creation? We know that millions of years ago the Alps did not exist. The Himalayas once were ocean floor. I have read that 95 percent of all the species that ever existed have become extinct, not only the most popular example, the Dinosaurs. Much of what is now Europe was once covered by a huge sea. The presently known continents in early days of earth history together formed one unit called Pangaea. Is the contingent state of the earth at one single moment during its history (in our 20th or 21st century) = "the Creation" which is to be preserved? This project sounds like wanting to freeze a movie at one frame of the film reel.

432   *THE SOUL ALWAYS THINKS*

of consciousness forces the lesson on us that the highest values of *the soul* have an analogous fate. Initially, nature was full of gods and the place of the gods was nature, the natural cosmos. The gods were in themselves natural gods. But then the "gods" moved out of nature. First they turned into the one monotheistic high God and later, with Christianity, this God above nature and above the natural world, the creator of the world, became *spirit* and *self.* This is the cultural-historical equivalent to the personal-biographical "left father and mother and cleaves to his wife." Inasmuch as the highest soul value is truly *spirit* and *self,* there is no external object to which the soul could relate, no positively existing referent. The structure of "self" implies consciousness's self-relation and self-enclosedness. Nature as a vis-à-vis is now truly irrelevant.

To toy with the idea of a "resurrection of nature" means to ignore that it is not the former carrier or representative of the soul value that is reborn in the dialectical process, but the soul value itself. In Christianity, for example, *Christ* was resurrected, not the world of the flesh, not nature and the literal cosmos, not the polytheistic world of the pagans that, on the contrary, were once and for all overcome by Christianity. "Old things are passed away: behold, *all things* are become new" (2 Cor. 5:17). Ultimately the historical move is therefore from nature to technological civilization.[38] The form or logical constitution of reality ("the world") as a whole is radically and irrevocably transformed.

The notion of a human drive to dominate nature operates with an external vis-à-vis and the idea of an interrelation. So does the suggested cure of this drive in its initial pathological form (where it is acted out externally), namely the idea of "the conscious realization of the full dialectical relation between culture and nature." This is still a form of barking up the wrong tree. It is like a wish to reconcile, or compromise between, "father and mother" here and "wife" there. *Psychologically* there cannot be a compromise between the two for the adult man.[39] The one has been left and is once and for all obsolete,

---

[38] Cf. Wolfgang Giegerich, "The Burial of the Soul in Technological Civilization," in: idem, *Technology and the Soul,* Vol. 2 of his Collected English Papers, New Orleans (Spring Journal Books) 2007, pp. 155–211. Originally published as "Das Begräbnis der Seele in die technische Zivilisation," in: *Eranos 52–1983,* pp. 221–276.

[39] But of course on the empirical-practical (or personal) level, a mediation between the two sides is possible and usually desirable. The son may still get along well with his parents while nevertheless "cleaving" to his wife.

"IRRELEVANTIFICATION" 433

and the other is where life now is. There cannot be "a full dialectical relation between culture and nature." Nature is out. It is not a possible real referent for the soul's concepts and values. Consciousness has been on the level of "self" for several hundred years, and the so-called drive for the domination of nature has nothing really to do with *nature*, but with the realization and unfolding of self-consciousness. Once consciousness has recognized *itself* to *be* spirit (just as the mature son integrated "the father" and now must himself *be* "the father"), there is no way back. A status of consciousness once reached cannot be undone. Today there is no choice psychologically but to *be* self—except that with the age of "medial modernity"[40] we begin to realize that the time of "self" and "individual" is once again already over and the highest soul value is somewhere new.[41] Again it is time to "*leave* father and mother" and to move to "wife."

From Content to Form, From Personalism to Absolute Negativity

Having come across the notion of self, another glance at C.G. Jung becomes indispensable. He wanted us to *become* self. He presented the self as a distant goal to strive for or as a mysterious center that could only be circumambulated but never actually reached. He taught that each person has the task of "individuation," of undergoing a life-long individuation process.

There are two problems with this. Firstly, with this theory he projected as a task for the future something that had already been reached and fully accomplished by history. We have all been living within the self as a realized status of consciousness for at least two hundred years. There is no need for a mystification of the self or for a project of "becoming self." The self is old hat. There is nothing that needs to or could still be done about it anymore. It is a completed psychological reality and the ground of modern existence, *now* even,

---

[40] "Medial" refers to "the media." Medial modernity (in contrast to "industrial modernity") is the time from about 1970 on, the time under the aegis of the media and mediality.

[41] Our new *oikos* is language. One unerring sign for this is what has been called the "linguistic turn" in philosophy. – On the obsolescence of "the individual" see my "The Opposition of 'Individual' and 'Collective' – Psychology's Basic Fault. Reflections On Today's Magnum Opus of the Soul", in: *Harvest*. Journal for Jungian Studies, vol. 42, No.2, 1996, pp. 7-27.

as I briefly indicated, the ground from which to push off to something new to "cleave" to.

The second problem explains why Jung did not see that what he felt needed to be sought had already been reached. To understand this, I have to begin with an important insight or demand of Jung's. He insisted that it is psychologically indispensable that we learn to distinguish ourselves from ourselves, to get at a distance from ourselves and learn to see ourselves as if from outside. But he did not do this himself. Or rather, he did it, but only practically, empirically, on the level of behavior, not logically. He did it psychically, in his personal process and therapeutically in work with his patients, but not as a theoretician. As theoretician he confounded the "man" who has to undergo individuation and become self with the empirical individual. The private person was supposed to achieve the task of individuation. In other words, Jung here did not observe the psychological difference, namely that *our "man,"* homo noster, *is not* homo vulgi, *the "man" of the people*, not the literal person, the empirical human being, the private individual. "Our 'man'" is, mythologically speaking, the *purusha*, the *adam kadmon*, the *anthropos*, the *homo maximus*. This, man as such, the *concept* of man, not literal man, is the subject of the soul's processes. What an inflation to think that I personally should have to strive to realize the self, that I should have to individuate (in Jung's sense of these words)!

Contrary to what Jung made of it, "the self" is a general *logical form* of consciousness at large, one constitution of the mode of being-in-the-world that resulted from the history of the soul, not a personal existential experience or substance. And from here I can return to what I said about the first problem. The fact that the self has been fully accomplished by history refers to the "self" as a logical form rather than as a kind of entity in the soul. This is why I said above that we all have been living within the self as a realized status of consciousness. We do not have a self, we have to *be* "self," just as the adult does not have a father, but has to *be* father. To *be* self means to exist as "soul," to be aware of existing as "soul," as "mindedness," as uroboric self-relation (which is not to be confused with an entity or being that in addition to its existence also relates to itself). We are existing soul, existing mindedness, the existing concept.

"IRRELEVANTIFICATION" 435

"Our 'man'" (in the sense of the alchemical diction) did in fact complete the individuation process and fully develop the self, as a concrete historical development in the period extending from, say, the 15th through the 18th century, so that "self" is nothing mysterious, not a numinous goal or content. It is—as a logical form—a cultural reality. But because Jung did not "leave father and mother" he could not move from content to form, from "having" to "having to be." And because of this commitment to the positivity of the semantic level he could not give up immediate identification of the *soul value* "man" with the literal, empirical individual *carrier* of the name "man" and therefore he could not "release the human person from this terrifying burden" of "individuation" and *Selbstwerdung*, but conversely "loaded that enormous weight of meaning, responsibility, duty, heaven and hell, onto the shoulders of the frail and fallible individual human being." The *psychic* process (for example of analysis) was loaded with the enormous weight of *psychological* meaning. As much as Jung strove to ground psychology on the notion of the objective psyche he did not really manage to overcome the logic of personalistic psychology. As much as he warned against, and personally feared, inflation in the life of the literal individual, he practiced it in the constituent structure or logic of his psychological theory.

Avoidance of the psychological adaptation to the new soul situation of modernity *at a time* when it was unmistakingly clear that the old soul situation was definitively obsolete made it necessary to stick to the abstracted, "peeled-off" duplication of the imaginal and numinous essence of an obsolete reality ("the archetype" or, with later Jungians, "the imaginal") and thereby to establish oneself psychologically in a metaphysical *no-man's land* 'above' the real. Namely *neither* with the literal "father and mother" (in the state of 'fixation') *nor* with "the wife," that is to say, *neither* with the traditional and official religious truth *nor* with the modern soul situation, but somewhere in between, with modernized and absolutely privatized replicas of the old, sort of with internal plaster figures as personal devotional objects. "The imaginal" as the *theoretical* equivalent of Jung's extra-marital anima-beloved.

In this way it was also possible to confine psychology's consciousness to the semantic level of substantial contents (positivity)

436   *THE SOUL ALWAYS THINKS*

and to protect it from the modern *necessity* to become aware of the syntactical level of form (logical negativity).

To make this no-man's land psychologically relevant and to simulate some kind of reality, it had to be positivistically sunk into the real individual as his "collective unconscious" (or the other way around: the individual had to be defined as the exclusive access to the "collective unconscious") and fueled by the suggestibility, susceptibility, and emotional excitability of the uprooted modern ego. The empirical individual became for Jung thus "the measure of all things" (*CW* 10 § 523), "the makeweight that tips the scales" (§ 586), the sole place where now the metaphysical "action" was ("the struggle of light against darkness transferred its battleground into the interior [of the psyche]" *CW* 13 § 293, transl. modif.; "For the first time since the dawn of history we have managed to swallow the whole primordial animatedness of nature into ourselves" *CW* 10 § 431, transl. modif.). This, the unity and simultaneity of these two moves up into no-man's land and back down into the existential experience of the private individual,[42] was indispensable for Jung's *psychology* project, but it is also what made it psychologistic (personalistic), where psychologism means the immediate identification of the psychic with the psychological.

Psychology is not about people and what they think and feel and what goes on in them. Psychology is about the absolute-negative soul, the prime matters in the hermetically enclosed alchemical vessel, in fact any matter that is *methodologically*[43] apperceived as having everything within itself and no external base or substrate. The soul has its existence, its ground, and substrate only within itself. This is part of its very definition. It is absolute interiority.

Above I talked about the birth of man, which on the personal level, as we have seen, happened at a first stage as the baby's *psychic* birth through docking the abstract-universal concept, as which one is born, onto some real parent figures and later as the *psychological* birth through the young man's leaving completely behind those parents and his

---

[42] Cf. "The main difficulty here is that the eternal ideas have to be dragged down from their 'supracelestial place' into a biological sphere..." *Letters 2*, p. 559, to Herbrich, 30 May 1960 (transl. modif.).

[43] "The soul" in my parlance has to be always imagined to be enclosed in quotation marks. My statements about it are not ontological assertions, but methodological.

"IRRELEVANTIFICATION" 437

clinging to them in order to unreservedly dock onto "his wife." In the course of life, the concept as which human beings exist goes through changes in form. It develops.

We usually think that it is *we* who grow up. But in reality *what grows up is the concept as which we exist.* This, the concept's further development, is what necessitates our ever new attempts at adaptation: the real adjustment in each case to the new form of the concept as which one already exists. Whereas a child exists as the concept of mother (parents), the concept as which a young man (or woman) exists has changed. He (to speak only of the male case) is now the (still abstract and ununfolded) concept of 'self-reliant being,' which, as abstract, as a mere vague claim, needs the unconditional faith and trust in this alleged self-reliance by a real other. In his wife, he has the realness of his concept of self-reliance, as which he is.

The child had his own concept *in* and *as* the real mother out there. The man already knows *himself* as self-reliance. He has no longer his concept in his wife, but only its realness. The concept has become much more '*for himself,*' more 'explicit.'

Along with the form of the concept, the *form* of adaptation changes too. For the baby, adaptation occurred only in the form of its first immediacy, as a proto-adaptation, namely as the *objective event* of finding the referent or carrier for the concept of mother. For the young man adaptation has already become a subjective task. This is why he can also refuse it or fail at it; he can become neurotic. This freedom did not exist for the baby. It was forced by its own inner necessity (its nature) to find the fulfillment of its concept of mother, and if it failed, it was not the baby's failure, but a fateful mishap.

But with the young man's move from parents to wife, the birth of man is not yet completed. There is an additional stage. This stage of the birth of man comes about by his transcending this "wife" stage. But 'transcending the wife stage' by no means implies (to stay inside this image) leaving, divorcing "the wife," in order to find some new real referent to cleave to, nor in order to free oneself totally of any real referent for the sake of total independence from any ties to something in this world, like certain so-called "free spirits" or existentialists or certain holy men.

438   THE SOUL ALWAYS THINKS

In *The Soul's Logical Life* I referred to the story from an Old Icelandic saga about a young man, a stay-at-home, who finally step by step paved his way into the world by hurling his spear, then running to the place where it had bored itself into the ground, pulling it out and hurling it forward again and so on. If we compare the baby's docking onto mother and father to the first thrust of the spear, the young man's leaving father and mother would then be like pulling the spear from out of the ground and his cleaving to his wife like the second hurling of the spear. If we stay in this fantasy, we might think that in principle this hurling could go on and on with ever new goals to pro-ject the spear onto. But this would be a monotonous, empty repetition, a repetition compulsion, as it were. It would be a constant *différance*, so to speak an unending gliding of signifiers, and as such an eternal deferral of an arrival in psychology.

The pro-jection, absolutely indispensable in the first two instances (parents and wife), in a third attempt would be merely acted out. But in the third instance it needs to be *er-innert*, interiorized into itself. There cannot be a new external referent for the abstract-universal concept. Even the first two instances of docking-onto were not same in kind. The baby's surrender to his parents is total and absolute. But it is also a surrender only of itself as a clean slate, itself only as mere idea and abstract concept. The young man's clinging to his wife, by contrast, is only partial, because he is already somebody real in his own right and retains his identity even in the union with his wife.[44] But the obverse of this is that with the young man it is an already developed, concrete empirical person that consciously and voluntarily enters into the relationship. His docking onto wife is not just a mere natural happening, like the baby's docking onto mother. He actively invests himself. I also already mentioned how there is an increase in subjective freedom with respect to the need to adapt to the (form of the) concept that one is. For the infant this adaptation is still only an objective event (a natural happening, as I said), but the young man has already the option to refuse to go along with this need. From

---

[44] The partialness of his relation to his wife comes also out in the fact that the man may at the same time also "cleave to his king" and "cleave to his God" and that in addition and parallel to his commitment to "wife" and Family he is normally equally committed to his professional life.

"IRRELEVANTIFICATION" 439

instance to instance, there is a logical progress, a gain. A radically different status is conquered each time. And this added value must also be the case with the third stage of the birth of man. It cannot only be a pointless repetition.

Now in this third stage, the hurling of the spear and one's tie to 'referent as such,' that is, *the whole relation* or *logic* itself of abstract-universal concept and empirical referent becomes the new target for the spear. This relation is now turned in on itself, applied to itself and thus becomes self-reflective and self-referential. The very notion of referent is interiorized or reflected into that very concept for whom it previously had to serve as real external referent and thus as its mooring in reality. At this stage, the referent is neither projected out, nor given up altogether. In a "leap after the throw"[45] consciousness logically catches up with its—previously projected—notion of referent and encompasses it. The concept has now its referent and thus its own reality within itself, which also means that the referent becomes absolute and that the concept has ceased being abstract-universal concept and instead has turned into the *concrete* or *really existing* concept. The third stage of the birth of man is not psychological birth, but man's birth as existing psychology. We could also say: the completion of the birth of man is the going under of him as man (as positively existing being, as natural entity, as the concept of self-reliance) into psychology, into the explicit *concept as such*. And the completion of the birth of man—as it is man's logically going under into psychology—in itself is tantamount to the birth of soul. Because soul exists only in and as realized psychology. It does not exist in people, as their property. Logically, psychology comes first. Only then is there soul at all.[46]

---

[45] This phrase is taken from the title of an essay of mine referred to above (note 22): "The Leap After the Throw: On 'Catching up With' Projections and on the Origin of Psychology," in: Wolfgang Giegerich, *The Neurosis of Psychology, Primary Papers towards a Critical Psychology*, Collected English Papers Volume One, New Orleans (Spring Journal Books) 2005, pp. 69–96.

[46] The adaptation to the third stage of the concept as which man exists (= the second metamorphosis of the concept) can of course also be avoided or be experienced as too demanding. The birth of man can be refused, deferred. (The second stage, as we have seen, can also be avoided or refused, which usually results in *neurosis*; the first stage, being a natural happening, as I pointed out, cannot be avoided or refused, but only, due to unfortunate circumstances, it may not take place, with the result, for example, of "hospitalism.")

440   *THE SOUL ALWAYS THINKS*

Summarily reviewing once more what happens in the stages of the birth of man, we can say:

The baby's psychic birth had meant that what had in fact come into the world and become real was the concept in its ideality, its heavenly or up-in-the-clouds nature.[47] The child is essentially wishing, fantasizing, hoping, dreaming, full of illusions about itself, life, and its own future. It lives fundamentally in potentiality. This potentiality-character of the concept, which is reminiscent of its heavenly origin, is here what has become real.

By deserting father and mother, the young man negates this now realized potentiality-character of the concept. And in doing so, he now realizes the concept as an *in itself* truly real one. It becomes empirical, sober, earthly, "realistic," indeed: a positive fact in external reality. In his bond to his wife, the man has the visible symbol of the externality and positive reality-character of the concept now reached by him.

With the birth of man *as existing, living psychology/soul* this externality is negated. And what is now realized as a consequence is the concept-nature of the concept. The concept as such *is* now its own reality. It has come fully down to earth, but *as itself.* Thus it has come home to itself. Before, in the child stage, it had logically been mere wish, hope, or idle assertion, and in the young man stage it had been alienated from itself, because it had not been real *as concrete concept* but as a positive reality. Now it is neither up in the clouds nor external reality. Birth as the coming down to earth has been completed. This is at once the birth of psychology.

Jung, by cleaving to "father and mother" and merely *sublimating* the literal parents into archetypal parents, could never fully shake off the positivity of referent. Despite their deliteralized, evaporated form, the archetypes, being derivative from the precious elemental force of the child's experience of mother and father, are nevertheless burdened by this their emotional origin. (Something similar is true of "the imaginal.") A real cut did not take place. Jung's thinking logically stayed tied to "the (infantile) origin." To be sure, the positivity of the parents has been sublimated, but it has thereby precisely also been preserved. The mother *archetype* is like a balloon freely floating up in the air, but with an almost invisible string

---

[47] Jung had spoken of cloud-cuckoo-land.

"IRRELEVANTIFICATION" 441

attached that is tied to the child's emotional experience of mother. This is the reason why Jung was not free to altogether release the soul into absolute negativity. He willfully decided not to cut the string, not to let completely go. Thus he was logically hampered by the not really renounced (and for him ultimately unrenounceable) empirical base of the archetypes in his childhood emotions.

This had serious consequences: (1) his notion of "archetype" remained an abstract-universal concept and *ipso facto* required some positively real external carrier as positive substrate for archetypal experiences, the individual human being; the soul with all its contents could not be interiorized into itself, not really become uroboric, strictly self-referential, with nothing positive-factual outside itself; psychology could not really overcome its personalistic misconception; (2) "self" was substantiated as *the* Self or as God (God image); (3) the archetypes were likewise positivized and substantiated as a kind of second world and, in their form as archetypal images, as allegedly observable facts; and (4) psychology itself was construed as an empirical science, that is, as a system of externality.

And the other way around, despite his ultimately "religious" and "metaphysical" concern, Jung could not become a philosopher, theologian, or founder of a religion. He *had to* become a psychologist focusing on the empirical person. Only by zooming in on the individual and his segregated (so-called "unconscious") experience was he able to reach what was his (Jung's) historical necessity, namely both to evade the inherited religion (as well as the metaphysical beliefs of the philosophical tradition) *and* to escape the modern form of truth. Psychologistic psychology is the (in itself untrue) stopgap between these two forms of truth, between the past and the present. It is a compromise formation between the positivism of modernity and the religious or metaphysical concern that actually belongs to the mode of being-in-the-world of the pre-modern past.

But because Jung sunk his *deepest, ultimately "religious" and "metaphysical" concern* into the notion of individual existential experience, it is quite consistent that he glorified ordinary psychotherapy, ordinary analysis as immediately having a kind of religious significance. This is a mystification of the human, all-too-human business of be it psychotherapy or analytical self-exploration, a mystification, however, which in turn was later even topped by some Jungians who kitschily pretend—at the end of the 20th and the beginning of the 21st centuries!—that soul work opens up portals to "the Sacred," thereby promoting and celebrating consciousness's becoming unconscious.

CHAPTER SEVENTEEN

"The Unassimilable Remnant": What is at Stake?
A Dispute With Stanton Marlan

In the "Alchemy" issue of *Spring Journal* Stanton Marlan published his remarkable essay, "From the Black Sun to the Philosopher's Stone."[1] It includes a discussion of the differing views that James Hillman and I hold on the alchemical philosopher's stone and related issues central for the basic conception of psychology, most notably the issue of "image" versus dialectic thought. His discussion is remarkable because of the diligence and fairness of his presentation, his learnedness and in-depth perception, his careful weighing of the differences as well as affinities of the standpoints reviewed. In addition one is struck by the sincere commitment that one can sense throughout his article. His presentation is also gracious because it displays a spirit of appreciation rather than derision. Despite reservations and misgivings concerning certain views, I wholeheartedly welcome his essay. I am grateful for it, because it puts very important issues on the table in an intelligent way that provides a sound basis for further discussion.

Meanwhile I have clarified for myself my earlier still vague reservations and present the result of my reflections in this paper. I am only sorry that my article inevitably has to have the character of

---

[1] Stanton Marlan, "From the Black Sun to the Philosopher's Stone," in: *Spring 74 (Alchemy). A Journal of Archetype and Culture*, Spring 2006, pp. 1–30.

dispute and controversy rather than the reconciliatory character that Marlan's paper has. In his own interesting stance he performs a kind of literal at-one-ment of the two compared and contrasted stances, saying that "In Hillman and Giegerich we have two moments of the Stone that not only can live together but also belong together in the same mosaic," a statement to which he, however, feels compelled to add the doubtful question, "or do they?" He also mentions in this connection the alchemists' *solve et coagula*. It is curious to what different interpretations this dictum can lead. Marlan sees the need to complement my formula of "the union of the unity and difference" with the other formula "the difference of the unity and difference," and he insists on an *unassimilable* 'not,' thereby giving even more prominence to fundamental difference. So we see that *in* his theory, that is, on the semantic level, he emphasizes difference and discrepancy, while on the syntactical level he aims for a side-by-side complementary relation of the opposites.

In accordance with my view that the actual place of action for psychology is the level of logical form or syntax, rather than the level of semantic contents, the weights are for me distributed the other way around. The emphasis on difference and negation appears on the syntactical level, between the different standpoints, whereas semantically I stress the union of unity and difference. It seems that in either case you get union as well as difference. They are a pair and as such inescapable. But it makes a great difference where they appear.

Although I would certainly hope that in practical reality, in the sphere of collegiality, "the two moments of the Stone" alluded to by Stanton Marlan (and in addition also Marlan's own standpoint of no mean merit) can live together and maybe even belong together in the same mosaic, I will have the task of showing in the following that and how logically, *on the level of theorizing*, they are in essential regards downright incompatible: two mosaics, indeed two different levels, not one.

I begin with a discussion of Marlan's appreciative assessment of Jung's historical significance, which finds expression in his view that Jung's resuscitation of images amounts to a reversal of the dominant historical process.

"Jung's resuscitation of images: a reversal of the dominant historical process"

To me "a reversal of the dominant historical process" is a strange idea from the outset: is there, can there be such a thing? Is the historical process not essentially irreversible? It seems to me that I have to relentlessly accept the history of personal life as well as of civilization at large and have to acknowledge it as my base and starting point. Rather than letting it be I may wish to push off from this base, but I cannot reverse it. If I have truly accepted my personal history, I can perhaps change the direction of my personal life, but even so I have to build my future life on that base. Any idea that I or somebody else could change the historical process on the cultural level will turn out to be illusionary, because we all are ourselves exponents of our history; the historical impulse is already in us and works through us, even through our illusions, resistance, revolution or revival attempts. Apart from when real disruptions of the cultural process happen through absolute catastrophes, there will only be a continuation of history, either sterile perpetuation of more or less the same or, if "all the bills have been paid," its own further development.

In what Marlan says I hear a contribution to the construction of a popular myth of history: the path of history as pathological and in need of correction or salvation. We hear in this text of "the shadow of Western thought ... since Plato," of the "hatred for image," "the fear of the power of image," the age-old "battle between spirit and soul." Something, so the implication, has gone wrong. And over against all this, Jung and Hillman brought, Marlan thinks, a "reversal" that amounts to "a major advance of consciousness." Ultimately, this assessment of history faintly echoes a Manichean *ressentiment*.

Are we in that magisterial position to decide that the development that *was* is the shadow of the West, that the turn away from image was wrong, and that history should have been different? Quite apart from the question whether the diagnosis of a prevailing "hatred for image" is factually born out or not (what a rich history of art and imaginative literature has there been and how much love for all this!), is it the job of psychology to reverse a given "pathological" development, or not much rather to see it the way it was and to attend to the existing pathology by penetrating to its depth, to the soul in it? Can we allow ourselves, as therapists, to take sides against the way things are?

Be that as it may, I deny this alleged major advance of consciousness brought by Jung's revival of image. No doubt, I am deeply indebted to the work of Jung (and Hillman, but here I am first concerned with Jung), especially to Jung's giving us a concept of "soul" as the basis of true psychological thinking. But I neither think that this amounts to an advance of consciousness nor to a real contribution to the historical process. It is only a contribution to a particular area or field within the present stage of consciousness. It is a semantic, not a structural or syntactical contribution. Jungian psychology does not contribute to the historical process but established a niche, an oasis within it. Precisely when one takes seriously the concept of soul bestowed upon us by Jung, one has to admit that Jungian psychology is a sideline and does not engage the soul of the historical process. The basic motivation behind Jung's psychology, in so far as it *wants* to make a contribution to the historical process (Jung's work has other aspects, too), is a defense against his own time. Jung shares this quasi-Manichean rejection of the dominant historical process as being pathological and in need of a cure. As such his basic stance is, at least in these regards, actually regressive and ideological, notwithstanding all the many marvelous insights that his psychology gave us.

Paradoxically, despite this subjective salvationist intent, Jung's psychology is *objectively* not even meant to engage the historical process or the dominant consciousness: his resuscitation of images is reserved for a logically segregated space, cut off from the historical process. The archetypes are defined as archetypes of the collective unconscious. This is like safer sex. The notion of the unconscious is so to speak the condom around the archetypes and archetypal images. Safer sex means you can have intercourse and the subjective enjoyment and feelings brought by it, but you prevent anything objective from happening, both your own possible infection and the act's becoming in fact productive through the impregnation of the female partner. Inasmuch as Jung's invention of the collective unconscious (or "the unconscious" in general) set up a clearly demarcated second ahistorical compartment

"THE UNASSIMILABLE REMNANT"

over against the collective consciousness and the historical process, and inasmuch as he assigned the archetypal images to this unconscious, he assured that *per definitionem* the images would neither be infected by the dominant consciousness of today's world nor consciousness be logically impregnated by the archetypal images.

Of course, you can have your numinous experiences of archetypal images and perhaps be subjectively shaken by them, but this is much like we can have our feeling experience of lions in a zoo or on television. They cannot possibly bite us. In the same way the subjective archetypal experiences of private individuals cannot possibly reach the soul of the historical process, that is, the prevailing logical constitution of consciousness. The fundamental dissociation between consciousness and the unconscious functions like the bars of the lion's cage. The lion could only make a difference if he were let loose. For the images and the archetypes this letting loose would mean that they would not be logically confined to the unconscious, to a "psychic reality" as a special, separate reality side by side with ordinary reality, but that they would share one and the same space, one and the same consciousness with all our other (for example, modern scientific) knowledge.

But this would of course mean that you could no longer merely imagine and experience them; you would have to think them, that is to say engage them, their contents, on the same level of truth on which we entertain all our other notions about reality.

Since Jung did not want his thinking to become speculative and metaphysical, on the one hand, and insisted, on the other hand, that the images have an immediate present reality (rather than only a historical presence, a presence in Mnemosyne), the price he had to pay was to segregate the images in a special fenced-in space, "the unconscious," and thereby systematically immunize them from consciousness. Now one might say that imaginal psychology is better off, since it does not compartmentalize in the same way. Nevertheless, when it does not compartmentalize anymore it is for the sole reason that it sublimated the fence, integrating it into its very style of thinking. The immunization of the imaginal from the historical process has become inherent in its very form. This notion of form takes me to the next topic.

448   *THE SOUL ALWAYS THINKS*

"THE IMAGE UNDERSTOOD IN ITS MOST RADICAL WAY"

Marlan states that "Giegerich actually misconstrues the way Hillman defines image." He comes to this assessment because he sees a discrepancy between my charge that the imaginal stance is based on "sensory intuition" and a form of "picture thinking," on the one hand, and Hillman's "more radical understanding of 'image'" according to which "we don't see images but see through them," on the other hand. But Marlan here himself misunderstands my critique in the sense of an underdetermination. It is more radical. He thinks that I see "images as pictures" and that this "might be considered to be a remnant of a sensationist psychology that understands images and even the imagination as epiphenomenal to actual things." However, my argument is not on the level of images as contents of consciousness or as "copies" in the mind of the phenomenal at all. Rather than the image in the narrower sense I am critiquing the imaginal style of thought as picture thinking. I take for granted that image is understood by Hillman as "a metaphor without a referent" (p. 6). The notion of a depiction of actual things has never entered my mind in such contexts.

My point is that as to the charge of picture thinking it does not make any difference whether an image is "what you see" or whether it is—"understood in its most radical way"—"the way you see," that is, whether you stay with the image as content of consciousness or see it as a perspective with which we see. In either case the sphere of sensory intuition (*sinnliche Anschauung*) is not left. The image merely recedes from the foreground into the hidden background, from the place in front of consciousness into the very structure of consciousness itself and in this way preserves the visual orientation (but also conceals this its visual character safely from the empirical ego). This imaginal form of the structure of consciousness is the sublimated successor formation to Jung's still concretistic "the unconscious" as a separate container of the images. The new sublimated container is "the imagination," that is, *space as such* (together with the vis-à-vis of one's seeing and what is seen [subject-object], the narrative-temporal succession, and the need to substantiate and personify), whereas "the unconscious" was still imagined as a distinct realm *in space* separate from the other "spatial"

"THE UNASSIMILABLE REMNANT" 449

realm of "consciousness" located "above" the unconscious. To be sure, the image has now, through this quasi transcendental-philosophical move, been deliteralized; it may no longer be visual in the empirical sense, but it stays *logically* visual: "Re-Visioning" (not just a revision), archetypal "perspectives," "seeing through" to the gods or myths.[2] It may have become metaphorical seeing, but it does not advance to *sublated* seeing as thought or conceptual comprehension: "insight," "*intellegere.*"

Marlan quotes Hillman as saying, "We do not literally see images." True, it does not always have to be we as empirical persons that literally see the images, but in all cases it at least has to be "the soul" or the mind in us that actually *sees* the images (which is the indispensable precondition of the possibility of both our empirical seeing through images and of images as "the way we see"). And apart from this, in all our psychological work with images (dreams, myths, fairy tales, etc.) we of course literally focus on images. The move from the literal to the metaphorical is *psychically* a great refinement, to be sure, but *psychologically* does not alter the basic naturalism of this stance. Image qua image inevitably stays tied to pictorial thinking.

It is naive to think that the image in imaginal psychology is not representational simply because it does not have an external referent and is not to be understood in sensationist terms as epiphenomenal to actual things. It is representational just the same—because it represents *itself.* The point here is that it does not make any difference whether there is a literal external referent or whether "referent" has been totally internalized into the structure of image or imaginal seeing itself so that the image is now its own referent: the structure or form of representation has not been overcome merely by overcoming the externally existent referent. The *form* of representation would only be overcome with a transcendence of the form of image as such, that is, with *thought.* Thought does not see or imagine; it thinks. Here one sees how important it is to become aware of the dimension of logical form or "syntax." A merely semantic approach is naturally already satisfied with the difference between "image without external referent" and "epiphenomenal representation of an external referent."

---

[2] Cf. James Hillman, *Re-Visioning Psychology*, New York et al. (Harper & Row) 1975.

450   *THE SOUL ALWAYS THINKS*

"HOW IS GIEGERICH'S IDEA OF THE ALCHEMICAL 'GOLD' TO BE DIFFERENTIATED FROM HILLMAN'S IDEA?"

"Once we have Giegerich's subtle view of 'gold' as totally liquefied Mercurius, can we still distinguish it from lead, silver, or mercury?" This is of course a vital question. If one claims (and I now deliteralize this question) that the imaginal approach is structurally insufficient, that it does not go all the way, then one has to show how an approach based on the idea of the soul's logical life can in fact go further, deeper, or achieve results that on principle grounds cannot be reached by the metaphorical or imaginal approach. Such a demonstration must, however, not be performed in thin air, on the abstract level of talking about the symbol or metaphor of gold. One has to get down to brass tacks, to concrete instances of the work performed on specific matters.

Although I do not claim ever to have actually reached the ultimately desired final result of true gold with my work, I think I have repeatedly shown what my style of work can do. And if you look at any of these examples you will easily see the difference, namely find that with the imaginal approach you could not have gone as far. I refer, by way of a few pertinent examples, to my treatment of Heraclitus' dictum about the depth of the soul, my chapter on the Actaion myth, my discussion of the motif of the slippery or glass mountain, my work on the bottled spirit in alchemy and psychology.[3] Here you can see my dialectical approach in action and what it means to *think* an image all the way through (hopefully) rather than imagining it. It means letting the image decompose, letting it go under into itself, *distilling substance into logical form, semantics into syntax.*

And this is what the imaginal approach cannot and will not do. But this is also why it cannot truly leave behind the physical in the material. The imaginal stance is insensitive, indeed blind, to form-distinctions, and *systematically* blind. It takes semantic similarities of

---

[3] Wolfgang Giegerich, "Is the Soul 'Deep?'—Entering and Following the Logical Movement of Heraclitus' 'Fragment 45'", in: *Spring 64*, Fall and Winter 1998, pp. 1–32. Now Chapter Six above. Idem, *The Soul's Logical Life: Towards a Rigorous Notion of Psychology*, Frankfurt am Main, etc. (Peter Lang) 1998, 3rd revised edition 2001, pp. 203–275. *Idem* (with David L. Miller, Greg Mogenson), *Dialectics and Analytical Psychology: The El Capitan Canyon Seminar*, New Orleans (Spring Journal Books) 2005, pp. 1–24. *Idem*, "Closure and Setting Free or The Bottled Spirit of Alchemy and Psychology," in: *Spring 74 (Alchemy). A Journal of Archetype and Culture*, Spring, 2006, pp. 31–62.

"THE UNASSIMILABLE REMNANT"

different phenomena for imaginal identity and ignores the fact that the logic or syntax (that is, the soul) of the phenomena and the respective status or function they have within the logical constitution of consciousness may make them incomparable. For it Zeus, for example, is still alive today and we still today, in the context of our *modern* mode of being-in-the-world, offer bull sacrifices to him, even if only in a metaphorical way. It can think so simply because it looks for certain external likenesses. It is helpless vis-à-vis the psychology of modern phenomena such as the media, today's most advanced form of capitalism, or nanotechnology, because these are from the outset *in themselves* (in their logical form) syntactical rather than semantic or substantial, so that a thinking guided by images, myths, gods is a priori out of place. The imaginal stance knows of only three alternatives of treating material: taking it literally, making metaphorical use of it, or deserting the matter in the direction of the "poisonous state of splendid solar isolation." There is no place for the fourth possibility, the alchemical decomposition, sublimation, vaporization of the naturalistic form of image into syntactical form ("the Mercurius").

Marlan states, "While Hillman's move takes him beyond the physical, he stays with the material, the concrete, what I have called here the pigment, a certain impurity that for him saves gold from the 'poisonous state of splendid solar isolation.'" Hillman's work is so rich, he has given us so many studies of a multitude of subjects that it would be a serious mistake to lump all his work together. He has said certain things now, and other things at other times; there are instances where his work conveys much more "the negativity of the image" (Greg Mogenson) and comes much closer to a sublation of the image, whereas in other cases the silvery nature of the imaginal approach is much stronger. Any global assessment of his work would go amiss. There are many Hillmans, not only one. So in what I have to say next I will restrict myself to those instances where the approach stays clearly within the confines of the imaginal-metaphorical approach.

But with respect to those instances I deny that his move takes him beyond what is physical in the material. This is precisely what it does not. His move takes him beyond the literal and to the metaphorical, but in this way precisely retains the physical, for which from a *psychological* point of view it is all the same whether it appears in literal or metaphorical form. Whether "simple physicality" (Marlan) or metaphorical physicality—it is physicality; it is naturalistic. And this is what psychologically counts. It is in some ways similar to how Jung believed himself to have left behind the "physical" of his mother fixation by going beyond his literal mother to the mother archetype. True, empirically there is a great difference between the former and the latter form of the mother complex. However, this great difference is only semantic. Psychologically, structurally, syntactically, the mother fixation has not changed.[4] I repeat: the move from the literal to the metaphorical does not take us beyond the "physical" in the material, if "the physical" is itself understood psychologically, that is to say, beyond the basic naturalism that inevitably informs the imaginal style of consciousness.

The phrase "poisonous state of splendid solar isolation" is not mine. For Hillman, it is the certain impurity which he allows his "gold" to have that saves gold from that isolation. Does it really? My critique of imaginal psychology had precisely always been that it cocoons itself in the unreality of a kind of "Platonism," as I once termed it. I had challenged psychology with the thesis that a real cut into the naturalism of the imaginal and metaphoric is indispensable to reach actuality.[5] And I believe that it is precisely by trying to save his "gold" by means of those so-called impurities (that is, through the logically unbroken tie to naturalistic apperception) that this cocooning in unreality takes place.

The fear of the "poison" is, I think, the problem. This is what makes consciousness shrink from going all the way forward and instead makes it turn back again to what it was, after all, itself intent upon leaving through its very move away from the physical in the material. It makes this move, but half-way there (namely after having moved from the literal to the *metaphorical*), it stops. Of course, the danger of splendid solar isolation exists. But the point is that it must be met, not avoided. You have to try to get to the top of the glass mountain. If you avoid the danger, you have psychologically succumbed to it unawares. You

---

[4] Wolfgang Giegerich, "Irrelevantification or: On the Death of Nature, the Construction of 'the Archetype,' and the Birth of Man," Chapter Sixteen above.

[5] Wolfgang Giegerich, "Killings. Psychology's Platonism and the Missing Link to Reality," in: *Spring 54*, 1993, pp. 5–18, which is a brief condensation of "Killings," in: *idem, Soul-Violence. Collected English Papers* vol. III, New Orleans, LA (Spring Journal Books: 2008), pp. 189–265.

"THE UNASSIMILABLE REMNANT"

only truly avoid it by facing it. As Hegel said in a statement quoted by Marlan in another connection: "only by looking the negative in the face, and tarrying with it ..."

"BROKENNESS, INCISION, WOUND, CUT"

The blackness of *sol niger* brought with it for Marlan "the *mortificatio* of brokenness, incision, and wound, castration, cut, negation, with an ultimate 'No' to the ego, with what felt unassimilable." He expands on this theme by first of all amplifying it with a host of experiences and images from different areas of life and culture and by including a section on "Mystical Death" (of the ego). He reminds us that his strategy in his book *The Black Sun*

> ... was to hesitate before this darkness, to pause and then to enter its realm of corpses and coffins, of monsters and monstrous complexity, and to engage its most literal and destructive demons: narcissistic mortification, humiliation, delusion, despair, depression, physiological and psychological decay, cancer, psychosis, suicide, murder and death.[6]

He rightly emphasizes that "the *mortificatio* drives the psyche to an ontological pivot point, to a desubstantiation of the ego, ... leading to a gateway that is both a dying and a new life."[7] And even if only very briefly, he connects this with a shamanic-like initiation and describes by way of analogy the absolutely gruesome Tantric rites of Kali.

All these are experiences and images of negation. But the problem I have with them is that the negation remains decidedly naturalistic: experiential, sensible image, ritual behavior, *mystical* death of the ego. The negation does not come home to itself and cut itself loose from its tie to and immersion in immediate experience and natural(istic) image. So there is a cut, but it does not cut all the way through. The desubstantiation of the ego is not enough. Where is the desubstantiation of substantiation itself (of the form of substantiation and personification)?

---

[6] Marlan, *The Black Sun*, p. 14.
[7] *Ibid.*

Our thinking is here tied to ancient modes of experience, shamanic initiation, Tantric ritual. But it is clear that we cannot go back to them (which is of course not suggested by Marlan). My question is: is it enough to use these references as *metaphoric* ones? Does it psychologically make a difference if we literally go back to ancient modes or only imagine our experiences metaphorically along the lines of archaic psychic realities? The soul remains in the spell of those images which, however, do not provide a concrete way for the modern soul to go. The soul is lured imaginally back into the modes of the past and down into the experiential field. It is held captive there because the metaphor, which after all does not have a referent, does not open up to anything that could have a real meaning for a modern person. And this is also why the death of the ego has to be seen as a *mystical* death and why Marlan's paper, the more it draws to a close, moves into the mysterious. The problem with the "mystical" is that you cannot say what it really is. You cannot account for it. You talk about it, but you cannot take responsibility for what you say—because in the last analysis it reveals itself for Marlan as being "the unthinkable" and "unspeakable." With "the unthinkable" we each have carte blanche. It is anything and nothing, a void. In the notion of the unthinkable, the imaginal style of thought imagines, and betrays, its own innermost nature, its total freedom from any real restraints, its free-floatingness.

We also hear, for example, of a move toward "a Zen-like perception of the ordinary, the 'sheer mereness of things.'" Things? Things today, in the age of television, advertising, throw-away society, advanced capitalism? Of course, we still have the word "thing" in our language and use this word, but things in the strict sense (in the sense of their "sheer mereness") and along with it the ontology of things have been extinct for two hundred years, at least as far as the reality of the psyche is concerned. The *mortificatio* may have driven the psyche to the ontological pivot point, but it obviously did not drive it to the other side. The imaginal approach is the hidden recess into which the old ontology of "things" informed by "perception and imagination" has withdrawn and made itself less discernible. The cut did not really cut.

Marlan feels the need "to raise a number of concerns about any move that relegates images to a status secondary to thought." I connect this his concern with a desire not to have the cut cut the cut itself.

"THE UNASSIMILABLE REMNANT"   455

The most terrible perturbations of the ego are permitted, but not the perturbation of the logic (or, if you wish, ontology) of the naturalistic orientation, of the image and of things.

Actually it is not meaningful to say that image is secondary to thought. This is the wrong pairing. It is the imaginal *approach* that is secondary to thought. Image itself, by contrast, is itself thought, garbed in sensible form, much like animals are thoughts or concepts garbed in a physical body.

The mystical turns easily into mystification. When I once wrote in connection with the theme of the death of the ego that "The art of psychological discourse is to speak as someone who is already deceased," this should not be construed as referring to the result of a mysterious existential death experience, as a kind of personal rebirth into a higher state of existence like that of a shaman, a sage, someone illumined or "individuated," one who has been in contact with the unthinkable and unspeakable or has had a satori experience. All these mystifying ideas have to be kept away. What I said has a very concrete practical, namely strictly *methodological* meaning. It is very much down to earth. Very sober. Nothing unspeakable. It can be described. It is not a statement about the state reached by a person, not about a human being, but about the logical subject that wants to do psychology or the logical constitution of consciousness necessary for psychology, a methodological stance to be taken by the psychologist *if* and *when* he wants to do psychology. That's all. The empirical person remains in his or her private life the same ordinary person.

Owing to its naturalism, to its unbroken connection to the *form* of the visible (in the sense indicated above), the imaginal approach is ultimately a resistance to "the death of the ego." It is the resistance to "let *intellectually, logically* go" without reserve, to "go under" into thought (thinking). Thought proper is the result of the full-fledged cut. As I pointed out elsewhere[8] following Hegel's insight, we think, *if* we think, in names, in the words of language, not in images, and words are contingent sound clusters with no relation to the looks of the things that they "mean," sound clusters freely *produced* by the

---

[8] Wolfgang Giegerich, "Psychology—the study of the soul's logical life," in: *Who Owns Jung?*, edited by Ann Casement, London (Karnac) 2007, pp. 247–263, here p. 256. Now Chapter Twelve in the present volume.

456   *THE SOUL ALWAYS THINKS*

thinking mind itself.[9] In thought, therefore, the cut with the natural and sensible has really and fully happened.

"The Unassimilable"

Time and again Marlan insists on there being something unassimilable. The blackness of *sol niger* is his proof and paradigm. Here he says he encountered a darkness that refuses conscious assimilation. But is this really true? No doubt, this blackness was initially "*felt* unassimilable" (my italics). But did it not in fact become "assimilated"? First of all, by his tarrying with it, it revealed itself to be in itself the opposite of itself, light, "the light of darkness itself," "the *lumen naturae*." The eyes of consciousness must have become adjusted to the darkness to be able to see the light of this darkness, which in itself is already an assimilation of this darkness into consciousness. But above all, Marlan wrote a whole book on the black sun and the darkness of *sol niger*, with rich amplifications and deep insights. He himself proved the assimilability of the black sun through his own achievement. What more could be expected, what better conscious assimilation could we get? What else could assimilation possibly mean?

This question points precisely to the problem. Marlan elucidates the meaning of conscious assimilation that he has in mind with the following formulations: a black sun "that would not yield or be incorporated by an ego stance. It would not dissolve, go away, or be lifted up..." It "did not allow itself to be possessed by ego..." What is

---

[9] Although fully aware of the decidedly arbitrary connection between sound and meaning, Paul Kugler advanced the very different thesis that "on a synchronic level" the sound patterns are "nonarbitrarily tied through phonetic parity to a cluster of archetypally related meanings." (Paul Kugler, *The Alchemy of Discourse. An Archetypal Approach to Language*, Lewisburg, PA [Bucknell University Press] *et al.* 1982, p. 103). – It may well be true that this is valid for reduced or pathological states of the psyche, where it functions merely mindlessly like an automat. But I don't think psychology should *base* its own theory on such observations. Chickens whose heads have just been cut off are said to sometimes still run around for a while. Should this be one's basis for a theory of chicken behavior? "In geometry, if I may use a remote comparison, it is possible to arrive at Euclidean parallels by reducing the curvature of a non-Euclidean space to zero, but it is impossible to arrive at a non-Euclidean space by starting out with Euclidean parallels. In the same way, it seems to be a lesson of history that the commonplace may be understood as a reduction of the exceptional, but that the exceptional cannot be understood by amplifying the commonplace. Both logically and causally the exceptional is crucial, because it introduces ... the more comprehensive category." Edgar Wind, *Pagan Mysteries in the Renaissance*, New York (Norton) 1968, p. 238.

special about that? If this is the sense of "conscious assimilation" there cannot be any conscious assimilation of whatever at all. Because this applies to all psychic reality, all symbols and archetypal images. Does the image of a lion or of the philosophical tree dissolve, the motif of dismemberment go away, the symbol of virgin birth become possessed by ego, the glass mountain yield, the image of the Crucified become incorporated by an ego stance? Can Apollo or Zeus be assimilated in an ego sense of assimilation? They all are and remain what they are, even if the darkness reveals its inner nature to be light, if the crucifixion leads to resurrection, if dismemberment leads to restitution of wholeness. And of course in all these cases the ego could, conversely, possibly be possessed by them or, another possibility, claim to have possessed them by *replacing* the phenomena by some concocted interpretation of its own making.

But the fact that the psychic images have their own internal solidity, integrity, and intactness and don't go away even when assimilated in no way means that there is an "unassimilable remainder" in the emphatic sense. If "unassimilable remainder" is supposed to mean more and something else than the basic Jungian insight that psychic reality is really real, Marlan has not proven his point. The reality of the darkness of *sol niger* is the same ordinary reality of all psychic images and different only with respect to its specific content.

Even the very image of consciousness, the sun, the *light* of the sun, cannot be possessed by ego, inasmuch as it is "*Sol et eius umbra*: light without and darkness within. In the source of light there is darkness enough..." (*CW* 14 § 129). The clear consciousness of something does not see this *consciousness's* own unconsciousness. What I am driving at is that the notion of "conscious assimilation" *in the sense of* incorporation by an ego stance, of going away or dissolving does not apply in any case. It is utopian, fictitious, has no base in reality. Conscious assimilation means something else, much more sober, concrete, and simple, for example, writing an insightful book about the black sun (with all the psychic and mental labor that goes along with this). But that fiction is the ground for the dogma of the "unassimilable remainder." The "remainder" exists only for that position that expects assimilation to mean that everything should be incorporated by an ego stance. Marlan, it seems to me, confuses the "ultimate 'No' to the ego" (which logically is inherent in anything truly psychological) with a remainder. But psychological work is not defined as attempted incorporation by ego from the outset. It is the attempt to allow the psychic phenomena to self-unfold their inner complexity, to reveal their (soul) meaning, their "truth." And such an attempt is what I call *thinking* the phenomenon or image.

This is why I have trouble with statements like the ones quoted from Hillman that the Stone "does not allow itself to be held in meaning," "[i]t does not yield to understanding," or when he says of a particular alchemical process that it is "designed to obliterate a psychological *episteme* ..." Transferring this from the Stone to the black sun, I can agree that it does not allow itself to be held *in* meaning. But what is implied or suggested betrays much more, namely a general anti-meaning, anti-understanding, anti-knowledge stance. My thesis, by contrast, is that each psychic phenomenon, each symbol or archetypal image *is* its own meaning, *is episteme*, *is* its own concept, *is* a thought. The blackness of *sol niger* thus does not have a meaning, it is meaning and it is only the meaning or thought *as which* it *exists*. This fact, namely that psychic phenomena *are* meaning or concept, is the reason why we have to *think* them. Thinking means to think (to step-by-step repeat in our mind) "the *soul's*" thoughts that "it" thinks in the phenomena in which it manifests itself for us.[10]

It is not really we who assimilate the Stone or any other psychic phenomenon. Rather, it is the phenomena's own work. When their time has come they integrate and absolute-negatively inwardize themselves into consciousness. They cease being a content of consciousness or object before consciousness and enter the logical constitution of consciousness itself. Assimilation in the strict sense means the transition from semantics to syntactical form. We can only

---

[10] *Historically* as well as *biographically* speaking there can indeed be something that is (as yet) unassimilable. As long as a psychic phenomenon is in the status of a true symbol with its mystery and its power to fascinate consciousness, it is still only *pregnant* with meaning. The meaning is only implicit, it can only be vaguely (but nevertheless possibly intensively) felt and divined. The thought as which the phenomenon *is* is deeply sunk into and enveloped in its imaginal form or, even more hidden, in the form of a symptom (be it behavioral or physical) or of a "fact." A phenomenon can only be assimilated once its meaning *has been born out of it* and it has died as a "symbol" (cf. *CW* 6 § 816). Assimilation has to wait until the phenomena are ready to give birth to their meaning. There cannot be a psychological Caesarean. Another wholly different type of unassimilability may be given through our personal shortcomings—lack of depth, of psychological refinement and intelligence. I will briefly touch on this *phenomenal* unassimilable further down in this chapter.

"THE UNASSIMILABLE REMNANT"

think or comprehend those phenomena whose semantics have already been absorbed into consciousness's syntax so that consciousness is logically up to the thoughts as which they exist(ed), in other words, only those phenomena that are psychologically already dead. Psychology always comes after the fact.

All the problems here with darkness, unassimilability, the remainder, and meaning seem to arise because "the ego" is the hidden standard and measure, the secret ruler inside the intellectual stance, or, to use an earlier formulation, because the cut has not really happened and one's thinking does not begin on the other side of the "ontological pivot." If you define "conscious assimilation" as assimilation to an ego stance, I agree there is something unassimilable. But why define it so?

To be sure, despite this ego stance the defeat is supposed to happen for the ego; this defeat is, as it were, "preached" and celebrated. Perhaps I could also say it is merely circumambulated. But it has not already happened. The death of the ego is here, on the one hand, a threshold before which one's theoretical stance tarries and thus it is constantly deferred to a (possibly imminent, but never gotten-over-with) future; on the other hand, it is *imagined* and *ipso facto* pushed down into and held down in the sphere of the merely psychic (the subjective, emotional *experience* of *mortificatio*, the *mystical* idea of death, etc.). It is never the accomplished starting-point, the ground and background from which psychology proceeds.[11]

The point of the death of the ego and its strange nature is that it can never happen. It is not such that it could happen. It is such that it can only be if it always already has happened; it comes into being as its own perfect tense. This one cannot imagine. It can only be thought. And this is why it is never an "experience." Any experience of the death of the ego inevitably confirms the very ego whose death it is supposed to bring. Emotional states solidify the personalistic prejudice; they tie back the notions of the death of the ego, of individuation, or of transformation in general to "me" as person. As long as one thinks in terms of a personal process, one cannot get beyond the mystical, beyond an ought, beyond hoping, and vague

---

[11] I discussed this important point (for example under the label "*hysteron proteron*") in my *The Soul's Logical Life*, Frankfurt/Main et al. (Peter Lang) 1998, pp. 20f. See also p. 62.

divinations. One does not get beyond the stage of merely "dreaming" about the goal. Psychology does not become *real.* Real psychology has the goal behind itself as its pre-sup-position, as the condition of its own possibility. And real psychology is only possible if the purpose of *soul life* is understood to be *psychology-making* and not *our* "process," the realization of psychology and not our self-realization. "The soul" wants to become real, and psychology is its realization.

When Jung stated that "The goal is important only as an idea; the essential thing is the *opus* which leads to the goal: *that* is the goal of a lifetime" (*CW* 16 § 400) he showed two things. First that at least here he opted for merely "dreaming" about and striving for the goal throughout one's life, that is, for never reaching it and for a linear, vector-like conception, although the soul is by definition uroboric, having its *telos* always behind itself as its *arche.* Secondly, he stays stuck in a personalistic conception of the work, the idea of the goal of *our* life. The two aspects require each other. It is clear that the moment that you are identified with the soul process, thinking that it is about you and that the goal is the goal for you, the moment that you are incapable of distinguishing yourself from "the soul," it would be a case of inflation and hubris to claim that you either had already reached the goal or could possibly reach it. Jung simply had to go "linear" and defer the goal into a never-reached future, once he confused the soul process with our development as people. And the other way around, with his linear thinking he precluded that psychology as psychology could begin, because it could only begin if it had already its goal behind itself as its beginning.

I know that for most people it is very disappointing, but the death of the ego is *logical* death, a *mortificatio* on the cold, "objective" level of soul and its logical life. It is the birth of psychology as a *methodologically* based enterprise. Nothing spectacular, emotional, mysterious, numinous. Only if the death of the ego is comprehended as a logical death, can it become real. Nay, this comprehension, if it is real, *is* the reality of this death. It is the breakthrough through the imaginal stance into thought, through the ego's personalism, emotionalism, enthralment by sensible intuition, through its need to substantiate.

Different archetypal images have different "meanings," are the manifestation of different concepts or truths. It is clear that, e.g., an

"THE UNASSIMILABLE REMNANT"

idea like *sol et eius umbra* has a totally different telos from *sol niger*. Now it might well be that the particular telos of the appearance of the latter idea is precisely that of initiating the mind to whom it appears into thought and dialectics. The blackness is the objective negation of all imaginal seeing. But it is not negation in the sense of point-blank elimination. Rather, the blackness forces on consciousness the realization that it, the blackness, negates *itself* and reveals itself to be light. Marlan thus rightly wonders, "Could this darkness be called sublated?" The thought that only sets in once the blackness has radically cut off any way back to the imagination shows itself to be the *sol niger's* own thought (or the thought of "the soul" AS *sol niger*). It is not a human concoction, an ego activity. It is the self-thinking, self-movement of the matter at hand. The appearance of the *sol niger* is also an attempt to initiate into the notion of soul as uroboric self-reflection. No otherness. The blackness is not in need of an external light source. No lack. It has everything it needs within itself.

But the telos of the initiatory appearance of the black sun is only reached, the initiation has only taken place, if the black sun does not merely stay an experience affecting subjective consciousness (the ego), but becomes logical, theoretical, that is, radically changes the intellectual stance, its logical constitution, one's "ontology," I could also say, if it becomes an objective method of psychology. The appearance of the black sun has to come home to itself. It has to negate itself *as emotional or imaginal experience*.

From here it is possible to understand what the function is of such ideas in Marlan's paper as the unassimilable, the remnant, the unthinkable. We have to be very clear about this: all these ideas are not phenomena, not observed facts, impressing themselves on the mind of their own accord. The blackness of the black sun is by no means unassimilable, although of course not in the sense of assimilation as being incorporated by an ego stance. The point of psychological thinking is anyway to let each phenomenon think itself. The phenomenon is not supposed to be assimilated to the ego in the first place, but to "the soul" whose own thought, for example, this blackness is.

The latter is also by no means unthinkable. We can think it as the soul's need to negate the ego stance, the imaginal approach, the perception-governed mind. It does by no means "drive the soul toward the unthinkable." On the contrary, it drives, if one dwells with it and follows its lead, "the soul" to the *lumen naturae*, that is, to its, "the soul's," own light (because "the soul" always talks about itself, thinks, displays its own truths and wants to bring *itself* as human consciousness to comprehend these its own truths). The blackness does not resist consciousness, but illumines it with its own (rather than with an ego) light. And why should we call the *sol niger* a remnant? A remnant of what? Is it not just one soul phenomenon, one prime matter, like all the myriad of other phenomena that may come up? The fact that its particular quality or property is blackness is on exactly the same level as that the ordinary *sol's* character is light, or that the character of dismemberment is dismemberment.

In the ideas of the unassimilable and the unthinkable, unspeakable, the blackness of *sol niger* is literalized. The initial experience and appearance of it is singled out of the entire process and frozen. The unthinkable, unspeakable is pure blackness. But *sol niger* is precisely not purely black. It is blacker than black, namely light. The self-movement of the black sun beyond its blackness is noted in Marlan's paper, but does not enter and transform the style of thinking about it. Semantically we are informed about the shining light of nature, but the syntax of consciousness or the theoretical standpoint holds fast and solidifies the initial absolute blackness.

The ideas of the unsurmountable "not," the unassimilable remnant and the unthinkable are *posited*. They are theoretical constructs and dogmatic prejudices. They are not the result of experience, but the outcome of a decision, a will or interest in having them: postulates. And their function is, I think, to give to psychology an a priori *reservatio mentalis*. Not a mental reservation as a personal behavior, but one built into the structure of one's theoretical stance itself. And a mental reservation not about particular contents or ideas, but the empty general (logical, methodological) *form* of a reservation. In the ideas of the unassimilable "not" and the unthinkable, the theoretical standpoint that entertains these ideas beholds the semantic reflection of its own logical refractoriness, its syntactical decision not to allow this standpoint without reserve to go under into the dynamics and fluidity of the theoretical process. In the apodictic idea that there is *necessarily* and *on principle* something that "resists conscious assimilation" and does not "dissolve" and "yield," we can see the projection, objectification, hypostatizing of a fundamental resistance to yielding.

The blackness of *sol niger* amounts to a *mortificatio* of the ego. But there are many ways the ego can be mortified (other examples are Dionysian dismemberment, Christian crucifixion, even passionate love). What is the specific type of ego death brought by the black sun? Here I have to come back to what I already hinted at above: absolute blackness, by cutting off all avenues back to any seeing and envisioning, to images and perspectives, and by furthermore *dialectically* revealing itself as its own opposite, light, could be interpreted as that particular "death of the ego" experience through which "the soul" wants to initiate a consciousness under the sway of the imaginal mode into veritable thought and dialectical thinking. And if this experience is said to "drive the soul toward the un*think*able," we see that consciousness has indeed somehow already got the message. It understands and admits that now it would actually be a matter of thinking rather than seeing or imagining. But we also see that it refuses to go on, to move across the threshold separating the imaginal from thought and into the sphere of thought proper. "The *un*thinkable" means that a real entrance into the realm of *thought* is declared to be off limits. The limits have been reached, but must not be crossed. The mental reservation, rather than being a reservation with respect to a particular content, is indeed a *mental* reservation in the strict sense, a reservation with respect to nothing but mind or thought itself: the *form* of thought.

Again it must be stressed that this resistance to yielding or to going all the way must not be misunderstood as belonging to personal psychology. It is not on the level of personal development, experience, or subjective attitude. It is inherent in the objective *logical form* of the theoretical stance. The alchemists had a saying that one should not begin with the work before everything has turned into water. In our context we could also add: or into flame or vapor, at any rate in all cases into a non-solid, not positive state, a state of negativity. I mention this alchemical dictum because of the "everything" in it. They did not say: do not start before *you* have reached such and such a state. They talked about the state of the objective contents, the matter, which according to this statement must have been transformed in its totality, with no remainder. But in our text, it is decreed in advance that there has to be a resisting remainder. This stance wants something absolutely

464   *THE SOUL ALWAYS THINKS*

hard, firm, impenetrable, unreachable and untouchable, something that is by definition exempt from the "alchemical" process.

"The unassimilable" is thus a kind of *fundamentum inconcussum*, but other than that of Descartes it is not a real content or a substantial truth, but rather merely the empty, hollow form (of an indestructible substance or fundament): a "not," an "un-"—or rather *resistance per se*. And it is of course not really a *fundamentum*, something known to be the ground of all that follows, but what once was ground has here been pushed to the edges, the border: as mere remainder. We would probably not go wrong if we stated that this standpoint is the hollowed-out and inverted Cartesian one: the Cartesian "doubt" absolutized and precisely as such turned into a (not ontological, but psychological) "foundation."

We could also describe the dogma of "the unassimilable" as a reified categorical imperative, "Don't yield all the way," where, however, this imperative is again not directed at the human subject, but at the logical form of the contents. It means: resist total liquefication or transmutation into the state of absolute negativity. More concretely, it means that the contents are only allowed to move from the literal to metaphor or image, but not beyond. Psychology's (subtle, sublimated) naturalism, the imaginal (thing-like, personified) form of the content of images must be protected. In other words, the ego. The assimilation that Marlan himself has already performed is not owned up to; what is already a fact is not allowed to also be released into its being *true* and thus to become the very standpoint and starting point of consciousness. Marlan does not theoretically catch up with the position factually already reached by him. He holds onto an alleged "unsurmountable 'not'" that he himself has already surmounted, having long arrived at the *lumen naturae*. The death of the ego remains "mystical," although consciousness has long gone through the concrete experience of it.

The idea of "the unthinkable" is the point where any theory that entertains this idea becomes a metaphysical one in the pejorative sense of the word. How could we possibly know that there is an unthinkable? We would have to have transcended our own mind. But in this its concept of the unthinkable, because of the categorical prohibition built into this concept, such a theory has brought its own metaphysicizing under its own control. It has completely surrounded and neutralized it, much like viruses in our body are sometimes encircled and rendered harmless by our immune system. In this way such a theory can indulge in its metaphysicizing as its *general* logical outlook while seemingly not making itself guilty of it in a practical sense, since it, after all, precisely abstains from thinking "the unthinkable" and from making a metaphysical system of it. It celebrates this its metaphysical orientation merely by reverently circumambulating "the unthinkable" like a tabooed invisible fetish and maybe once in a while, like Paul Kugler, by making "Raids on the Unthinkable" (whatever that is supposed to mean): the *zero stage* of metaphysics.

Jung, at *his* historical locus, saw himself confronted with a "barrier across the mental world which made it impossible for even the boldest flight of speculation to" get beyond. It was for him a "wall at which human inquisitiveness turns back" (*CW* 18 § 1734, translation modified). The result of this turning back was the duality or dissociation of the non-speculative, not-thinking empiricist observer here and "the unconscious" to be carefully observed over there. At the historical loci at which Hillman and Marlan have their place, this duality, that is, the whole Jungian *relation* between empiricist observer and the unconscious, has been sublated into "the imaginal stance." The imaginal no longer operates with an observing mind vis-à-vis its object, "the unconscious." It is logically much more refined, more subtle, because it is both at once, having collapsed and integrated them both into itself: it is both the seeing *and* what is seen at same time.

What for Jung was still imagined as an external obstacle, a wall that forces human inquisitiveness from its striving forward toward knowledge back into itself, into "the *un*conscious" as the result of inquisitiveness's (*consciousness's*) logical about-turn, is for the imaginal stance no longer an external barrier. This stance has the brake that prevents it from moving into thought built into its own style of operation. It *is* the tarrying at the threshold, the "ontological pivot." And the idea of the unassimilable and unthinkable is the explicit objectification of this internalized, integrated brake, an objectification, in which the imaginal approach provides itself with the logical justification for not going under. It now *cannot* go under because there *is* something unassimilable and unthinkable.

But the imaginal approach has a *semantic* equivalent to Jung's logical barrier, something to be avoided at all cost. It is the "poisonous state of splendid solar isolation," the peaks of spirit, at one end, and literalism at the other.

Inasmuch as the Jungian observer and the numinous archetypal symbols that he observed have in imaginal psychology become collapsed and *interiorized* into the very logic of image as such, and, as perspectives, have become more or less indistinguishable (cf. "We do not literally see images." "An image is not what you see but the way you see"), the cocooning effect of the imaginal approach is obviously much greater than in the case of Jung's set-up. It is due to the high degree of interiority and comes out in the emphasis that is put on the aesthetic and "sense-certainty" quality. The image in imaginal thinking bestows much more anima-like innocence, unwoundedness by the animus, even immunization against any such wounding, than the "symbol" did for Jung, which was, after all, beheld (as well as intellectually "understood" and "put into ethical practice") by an "external" observer, the ego. The logical fusion of symbol and observer into one has a suction effect and tends to prevent "alienation" (the intrusion of the animus) on principle.

Just as "the image" is the (much more subtle) successor of (the far cruder *combination* of) symbol+observer, so the enthralling aesthetics of the imaginal is the successor of the Jungian "numinous experience." The numinous experience is a special massively emotional event. It happens at certain times to certain people. The "beauty" of the images is no longer a particular event and not literal beauty. It is, again much more subtly, the general objective *mystique* of image as such. And in the postulates of the unassimilable and unspeakable, this mystique so to speak exudes from the imaginal and crystallizes into the theoretical construct of a (quasi ontological) absolute mystery existing in its own right, as an unknown and unknowable object to be reverently "gazed" at, or to be more precise: merely divined, in silent wonder. Rather than forcing an about-turn and a logical shrink-wrapping of psychic contents in "the unconscious," as was the case with Jung's barrier, the "unassimilable unthinkable" invites and attracts consciousness, but attracts into nothing, into its void or darkness. It is the *hypostatized* mysticism (abstract mystical quality) of the imaginal.

Jung's constitutive move to, and bouncing back off, the barrier across the mental world and Marlan's move to an "unsurmountable 'not'" invite a comparison with the kind of move suggested in

"THE UNASSIMILABLE REMNANT"

Heraclitus's fragment 45 (Diels): "You would not find out the boundaries of soul, even by traveling along every path: so deep a logos does it have."[12] Heraclitus sends us forward all the way; we have to keep moving without reserve. And instead of then letting us bounce against a solid barrier or an unsurmountable 'not,' *his* 'not' negates the very idea of our ever coming to a limit. Heraclitus precisely frustrates our expectation of a stop sign. You can go as far as you want, you will *never* end up at an "unthinkable." Instead of presenting us with a reified negation, *his* negation interiorizes the forward move *itself* into itself and only in this self-contradictory way causes this decided forward move to be a recursive move into soul and its depth. Or should we say: for the first time creates the space of soul at all? Because soul is nothing ontological. It exists only if and when and for as long as it is *made*, and it is made through the *opus* of absolute-negative inwardization. The forward move began as a move in spatial imagination. Through his 'not' Heraclitus forces this move out of spatial imagination and its naturalism altogether into thought, into the logos of soul. The forward move becomes self-contradictory: *recursive* progression, an active move forward into its own going under.

If, as Heraclitus claimed, you can never come to a boundary of soul, no matter which road you take and how far you travel, how then did Jung get to his barrier and Marlan, with all the philosophers he cites behind him, to the unsurmountable 'not'? Did they disprove Heraclitus and show that there *is* a limit, after all—or is what they found perhaps something very different from a boundary of soul and its deep logos? Or is it their own putting a stop to the movement suggested by Heraclitus, that is, to the unreserved movement into this movement's own self-negation, into its further and further going under into itself? The barrier and the remainder are ultimately the *reified* 'not.' And whereas this reified 'not' allowed Jung to turn his back on it, when it has the form of the unassimilable remainder it allows one to always keep it at the same safe distance in front of oneself while one is moving, instead of oneself moving deeper and deeper into, and exposing oneself to the work of, the *living* negation (where "oneself" does of course not refer to the person, but to the logic of consciousness). Could it be that both Jung's empiricist observer and his "the

---

[12] For a detailed discussion of this fragment see Chapter Six in the present volume.

unconscious" are located outside the sphere of soul, in the land of positivity? The soul all right, but displaced from its native state and translated into the foreign language of positivity and naturalism?

Freud once said, "It is a most remarkable thing that the whole undertaking [of analysis] becomes lost labour if a single concession is made to secrecy. If at any spot in a town the right of sanctuary existed, one can well imagine that it would not be long before all the riff-raff of the town would gather there."[13] The notion of "the remainder" is the theoretical equivalent of that concession to secrecy in the practice of psychoanalysis and that right of sanctuary in a town. The negation is safely shelved. Consciousness can wash its hands of it.

"The unassimilable," "unthinkable," and the "remainder" that we are here talking about must be distinguished from the common (*vulgi* version of the) experience of something unassimilable. The former unassimilable is a building block of psychological theory and a postulate, a principle apart from concrete practical experience or work. The latter unassimilable, by contrast, is phenomenal. It is the not unfrequent experience that one cannot make sense of this particular dream image today, this pathology, this symbol or this detail in a myth or fairytale. Here the remainder that resists understanding is not a general principle anymore. It is due to a personal limitation, a lack of intelligence or knowledge. Also, it may not stay ununderstood forever, because at a later time it may dawn on one what it means, or somebody else can make sense of it. In my work, both in the consulting room and in my study, I go to work and try my best. My best may, however, not be good enough so that there will be a resisting remainder. I have no difficulty accepting the idea of this (practical, phenomenal) type of "remainder," but this is not what has been our topic here.

"A critical stance toward the Hegelian dialectic"

Hegel per se is of course not a topic for us. We cannot be Hegelians in the 21st century, just as we cannot be Thomists or Cartesians or neo-Platonists in good conscience today. It would be ideological. Hegel was the philosopher of his time. There is no way back. We have to make our own bed. When I nonetheless stress the importance of Hegel,

---

[13] "Further Recommendations in the Technique of Psycho-analysis," in: S. Freud, *Collected Papers*, vol. II, London 1953, p. 356n.

it is mainly for two reasons. It is to my mind an obligatory part of cultural education and a general training of the mind to have gone through a process of studying Hegel. It is part of one's homework and indispensable for being able to understand at least part of the modern world. And secondly, psychology in particular needs the capability to think dialectically in order to do justice to "the soul." Hegel is a great help in acquiring and strengthening a sense of absolute-negative inwardness. But in both regards we do not "buy" his philosophy as a whole.

Marlan does not turn to Hegel directly, but reviews the critiques of a number of thinkers of the 20th century of Hegelian dialectic. We have to be very clear about it that in this way we do not really approach Hegel. We have lectures by Hegel himself about the history of philosophy. But nobody in his right mind would read those lectures in order to learn something, for example, about Plato. You have to read Plato (and perhaps Plato scholars) for that purpose. Similarly, it would be an error to think that in reading what Heidegger or Derrida said about Hegel you would really address the topic of Hegel. Heidegger and Derrida are philosophers in their own right, not ordinary scholars. And true philosophers always talk about their own philosophy even when discussing other philosophers.

Besides, Heidegger and most of the major French philosophers of the 20th century were divided from Hegel and classical metaphysics by a gulf. They are *modern* thinkers, and all in one way or another started out and pushed off from Husserl's phenomenology, which from the outset obstructed any avenue to a real understanding of Hegel. When they criticized Western metaphysics they projected (retrojected) fundamental problems of the modern situation into it, problems that metaphysics did not have. The label "metaphysics" in their discussions has the character of a kind of screen-memory.

It is furthermore clear that a thinking committed to deconstruction, deferral, a sliding of signifiers is diametrically opposed to and precludes an understanding of dialectics, of absolute-negative interiorization, or of alchemical decomposition and distillation. Deconstruction is a style of (intellectual-theoretical) acting out and going away, on and on; a method of how the form of consciousness reserves *itself* over against the process of the deconstruction of 'the text.' Dialectics and alchemy, by contrast, stay with the one (hermetically enclosed) matter at hand and in both it is always so that the form of

470 THE SOUL ALWAYS THINKS

the dialectically or alchemically thinking consciousness *itself is subjected to the same process of the matter that is dialectically decomposed.* The distillation of the one is at the same time the distillation of the other.

"At first one goes into the water believing one wants to wade through it, until it gets deeper and deeper and one is forced to swim" (Goethe).[14] But the point of both the modern philosophical and the imaginal approach is not to go into the water in the first place. They maintain the fundamental (logical) difference, their own distance to the water. They walk along the river bank letting the water move on, the signifiers slide, or following the "polytheistic" impulse.

The notion that emerges most prominently from Marlan's review of the philosophers who faulted Hegel for his dialectic is that of engulfment, of an all-embracing tendency, a restricted, 'speculative' philosophical economy, and of an incorporation of all contradiction. The spirit and fantasy underlying this conception comes out best in those views of Derrida according to which "trying to undo Hegel is like trying to decapitate the hydra" and "that every attempt to refuse such engulfment is seen as error…" "How do we escape the perpetual reversal entailed in any oppositional system of thought?" Hegel, it emerges, is a terrible, nearly invincible monster. One can only hope to escape from or, if one is a Hercules, undo this monster. Hegel's philosophy is a dynamically growing prison. Any move you make will just enlarge this prison. To my mind this is a rather paranoid fantasy.

The will to escape and undo "Hegel" is the root and motivation, and I claim that it is this will that itself creates the engulfment that it wants to escape from.

This type of reaction could perhaps be compared to an imaginary reaction to paintings like those of Mantegna, Leonardo da Vinci, Dürer, Claude Lorrain, a reaction that would consists in the will to undo them because everything in them is subject to and restrained by central perspective. Even if one is a modern abstract painter, can one not truly appreciate those old masters, too?

But this interpretation of *Hegel's* dialectic as being an instrument for incorporating, engulfing, and assimilating everything is very odd indeed. The dialectic is not aiming for a totalitarian system. It starts with a concrete particular notion or reality and unfolds the logical life

---

[14] In a letter of 21 December 1804 to Schiller, my translation.

contained in it. It is not a trick or technique to capture or engulf more and more other *views*. Hegel's thought is not operating on the level of views in the first place. Views are the views of people; they belong to human discourse. But Hegel works with or on *concepts* as quasi alchemical objective matters (cf. "the matter's cold march of necessity").

But even if *Hegel's* intent were indeed such an engulfment, it would be obvious that *in psychology* dialectics could not possibly have this effect inasmuch as the psychological *opus* is only concerned with a particular matter in its "eachness" and has no interest in an all-embracing system. The methodological maxim of the psychological approach is, as I stated numerous times, that the image or psychic phenomenon at hand has everything it needs within itself. The goal is interiority, the inward depth of the same, not extension, accumulation, or hoarding.

About Heidegger's Hegel critique Marlan states, "The 'not' is more than a dialectical alienation on the way to a sublation." But such a "not" is not a dialectical one in the first place. It is a hypostatized or *positivized* "not," one extracted from the real process. It is now something in its own right and has therefore, allegedly, become subject to an illegitimate attempt on the part of Hegel to "assimilate" it. But for dialectics there is no "not" that could be, or would have to be, *assimilated*. Let's take a simple practical example, constructed by me. An orchestra in which many musicians play their particular instruments is in turn the instrument upon which the conductor plays. The musicians have become sublated moments in the new instrument, the orchestra. There is no "not" here that would be a separate reality which could either be assimilated or "resist assimilation." The negation is inherent in the musicians as real members of the orchestra. Dialectical thought reveals to us the negation or "not" that already exists in the real phenomenon, namely the orchestra musicians' self-negation as former soloists playing on their instruments.

I suspect that the charge of an *assimilation* of the allegedly self-sufficient 'not' and the setting up of the 'not' as self-sufficient is actually and unwittingly a reflection of the fact that both the modern philosophical and the imaginal-psychological stances keep their own logical form of consciousness out of *what* they discuss. The fact that Hegelian dialectics does not maintain this neat difference, but exposes

472   *THE SOUL ALWAYS THINKS*

its own form of consciousness to examination at each stage is sensed by those critics of Hegel, but this *coniunctio* is misconstrued as an illegitimate assimilation of the 'not.' The alleged independent reality of the 'not' that Hegel is supposed to have ignored is actually the 'not' of the modern stance's (logically) *not* going into the water.

Especially with what Marlan cites from Derrida's Hegel critique, the impression is created that dialectics is an almost imperialistic endeavor, an attempt to conquer more and more ground and to subdue every objection, every other view. The result of this view is that "Absolute Knowing" becomes almost comparable to an all-comprehensive world government.[15] The perspective guiding this interpretation is power, domination (and its obverse, the fight against domination), that is, an ego interest. But we already know that dialectics is nearly the opposite, the self-exposure to and self-immersion in the process of the conscious standpoint's going under, its self-distillation. Inwardization and *recursive* progression instead of engulfment. In the case of Hegel's *Phenomenology of Spirit* and *Science of Logic* it is the self-distillation, self-liquefication of all semantics of the metaphysical tradition into syntactical or logical *form*. In the terms of our earlier discussion we could say: it is the *assimilation* or *integration* or *inwardization* of the content of metaphysics into the form of consciousness.

Sublation is not a *goal* towards which one could be on the way. The "not" is neither a remainder nor "a momentary hiatus in the dialectic." It is not something separate or in between two statuses or phenomena, not what happens to, is done to, or is inflicted upon a given stance. It's the realization that the matter has all along *not* been what it had seemed to be. And this is at once the (first immediacy of the) recognition of the new form of the matter.

The inclusion in Marlan's discussion of the critique of dialectics by modern thinkers and their idea of a positivized "not" serves to prepare the ground for and to underpin the psychological ideas of the unassimilable remnant and the unthinkable, which, as we already found out, safeguard the imaginal stance (the form of consciousness

---

[15] Compare with this despotic fantasy the implications of Hegel's own statement that "The True is thus the Bacchanalian revel in which no member is not drunk" (*Phenomenology of Spirit*, tr. by A.V. Miller, Oxford [Oxford University Press] 1977, p. 27).

"THE UNASSIMILABLE REMNANT"

of this stance) from itself having to go under into the "alchemical" process and to be itself exposed to the transformations of the matter.

CONCLUSION: THE NEEDS AND DEMANDS OF PSYCHOLOGY

Quite apart from what the merits of a general philosophy may be that insists on a "'general' economy," fights logocentrism, and celebrates otherness and difference, the needs of psychology are precisely to cultivate "a restricted economy," for which the closed, hermetically sealed vessel is our alchemical symbol. Psychology, despite being committed to the soul of whatever is, is nevertheless, or precisely because of this, aware of having only modest aspirations and modest relevance and of on principle belonging only in an out-of-the-way corner of modern life as a whole. Psychology does not compete with philosophy. It is not, as philosophy is, so to speak a global player; it does not have a grand mission to better the world. This empirical or semantic modesty concerning the sense of its own importance is, on the logical or syntactical level, reflected in the fact that its general stance and particular theses do not come with the claim to be ontologically relevant, but to be merely methodological: *if* one wants to do psychology one has to approach, treat, and interpret things in the way specified. But nobody needs to want to do psychology.

The closed vessel demands a commitment to absolute interiority. Because the vessel systematically *excludes* the whole ego-world (*mundus vulgi*)—all external 'positive' reality and thus externality as such—what is in the vessel is not only inside it, but in itself (in its own logical form) "inner, inward" that is to say, a self; it has self nature, is uroborically self-reflective, self-contained, without a real (external) Other and without absolute difference. As a self it has its other within itself. And this its own other is in principle transparent for it. It can— in principle—be known and thought. Because it has been generated by itself.

Psychology boldly *privileges* unity by preferring *coniunctio* over dissociation and therefore also by preferring "the unity of unity and difference" over "the difference of the unity and difference."

And because it is committed to the alchemical warnings against the physical in the material, psychology *professes* its decided (but methodological) logocentrism and essentialism (*anima naturaliter essentialistica*).[16] Its business is to deal with (existing) meanings, that is, only with "matters" that *are* in themselves meaning, nothing but meaning ("thoughts," "the soul's" thoughts); in other words, that are in the status of absolute-negativity (rather than positivities). Its business is to deal with the *logos eôn* (the subsisting logos, Heraclitus) or rather the particular subsisting *logoi* of all the diverse prime matters in their eachness as the soul that lives in them.

In its work psychology therefore strives toward an inwardization of the matter at hand into itself, which, if it succeeds, amounts to the matter's deepening, liquefying, and distillation: the freeing of its mercurial soul from its imprisonment in the positive-factual, the thinking the thought or existing concept as which the particular soul phenomenon *is*.

How else could it be psychology? How could there be psychology if one faddishly insisted on fundamental difference and otherness, anti-essentialism, and the unthinkable? "No man can serve two masters." Or rather, a *man* can perfectly well serve several masters, because he can be a psychologist, politically active, scientifically interested, a lover, a believer, a sportsman, a philosopher, all in personal union. But psychology cannot serve two masters. If it does not want to become a mongrel, a chimera, it has to abide by its principle, its definition.

---

[16] We must not take exception to the fact that logocentrism and essentialism are historically obsolete. "The soul" is the *historical* presence of what is no longer a present reality. Psychology is to some extent comparable to the modern institution of museums, which, too, house archeological finds and cultural treasures of the past in the middle of our modern technological civilization. Like museums, psychology provides a kind of oasis in modern life. Objective symbols of this oasis are the consulting room in physical or rather social reality and "the interior of man" as an idea or fantasy. Psychology is thoroughly modern because it is conscious of the decidedly pre-modern ("archeological") nature of what it is dealing with as well as of the pre-modern logic with which it approaches its subject-matter. It is modern because in it the pre-modern has been sublated so as to have merely methodological validity. It is, after all, nothing but psychology, not metaphysics, religion, physics, not poetry or art.—Jung of course saw the archeological nature of "psychic reality" quite clearly, but nevertheless, forgetting all modesty, claimed present reality and immediate meaning significance for the archeological. "The archetypes are timeless and ever-present." That's not only a fiddle; it also does not do justice to psychology, for which obsolescence, deceasedness, disdain (cf. the *lapis in via ejectus*) are constitutive (they are psychology's *home*) and by no means corrigible or to be overcome. Where the obsolescence is obliterated or obscured instead of respected as belonging, and where psychology claims to be immediately relevant for today, psychology becomes inevitably nostalgic and/or ideological, which in psychology's present-day reality is already the case to a large extent.

CHAPTER EIGHTEEN

Imaginal Psychology Gone Overboard:
Michael Vannoy Adams' 'Imaginology'.
A Defense of the Image Against the
Detraction by its Devotees

In his paper "Imaginology: The Jungian Study of the Imagination,"[1] Michael Vannoy Adams advocates that "Jungians adopt a new terminology, which I believe would be advantageous." On the basis of Hillman's statement about the ego that "it too is an image" and of Jung's dictum that "the psyche consists essentially of images," he uses, and wants us to use from now on, the terms "ego-image" and "non-ego images." Why and how this new terminology would be advantageous is not explained. It remains for us to look at what happens when these terms are employed in his article in order to form an opinion as to whether they indeed bring an advantage.

THE PERSONIFIED IMAGE

The first thing to be noticed is that the term ego-image is used in sentences of the following type. "The ego-image, however, regards non-

---

[1] Michael Vannoy Adams, "Imaginology: The Jungian Study of the Imagination," in: Stanton Marlan (ed.), *Archetypal Psychologies: Reflections in Honor of James Hillman*, New Orleans (Spring Journal Books) 2008, pp. 227–242.

ego images as ..." "The ego-image employs the familiar, famous defenses of ..." "... the ego-image rarely exhibits any initiative in regard to ..."

I wonder how in heaven's name an *image* is supposed to take an initiative? An image is just an image. It does not do anything. It does not pay any attention to other images, let alone regard them as ... or employ defenses against them. While we can certainly have images *of* curiosity or defensiveness, it is not the image that is "curious" or "anxious" or "suspicious." Even diametrically opposed and thoroughly incompatible images, to the extent that they are images, coexist peacefully, just as you can, in the world of things, put the Bible and Mao's *Little Red Book* (or an anti-Christian invective or a hard-core pornographic book) next to each other on your bookshelf—and nothing happens. The Bible does not get defensive or start a crusade against the other book. It does not get embarrassed by the pornography. Nor does the other book "take the initiative in regard to" the Bible. Unless *we* do something with or to those books they will, still years later, calmly sit next to each other at the same place on the same shelf. Similarly, the myth of Hercules, that of Aphrodite, of Dionysos, *qua* myths, do not react to each other. Mythic gods, inasmuch as they are myth-*internal* figures, may be at war with each other, but not their myths. Only people who adopt the one and reject the other myth can become enemies. Likewise, the words "love" and "hate" can be written next to each other on a sheet of paper without the one word feeling troubled by the other.

The image of water does not extinguish the image of fire. However, *within* a dream image, water may extinguish a fire, or fire may make water go up in steam. The distinction between what is within an image and the images themselves is crucial.

It is true, we can speak of an angry book. But that is a metonymy. The book is not angry. Only the content of the book is. However not *really* the content either, because ultimately the anger resides in the author who wrote the book or in the reader who senses the anger through the mediating text of this book. Be that as it may, at any rate the book as such has no emotion at all. But Adam's new terminology is not meant metonymically or figuratively. It is precisely meant literally. The ego-*image* and all the non-ego *images* are straightforwardly said to feel anxious or to be curious, to defend themselves or to make conversely an effort to transform the ego-*image*.

IMAGINAL PSYCHOLOGY GONE OVERBOARD

The image is treated here as if it were an agent, a person, a subject. It is of course true that we are used to saying things like: this image shocked me, this book moved me to tears, this text made me angry. In such phrases, too, the image, the book, the text are linguistically presented as acting agents, efficient causes. But is it really the image as such that shocked me? Is it not much rather the sense *I made of it*, in other words, what it means to me? It is not the book itself that moved me to tears. Because the book is just a book and has no effect of its own. It is *my* reading the book, my understanding of and feeling the drama described in it, which had this effect. If I am not sensitive enough or misunderstand the same book, it may possibly appear completely boring to me. Also, if I were somebody else, the book might have left me cold.

We see: the seeming effect of the book as a seeming agent depends entirely on the human subject. For it to have an effect, a *thinking* and *feeling* mind or soul is required in whom alone the (by itself dead) text or content can come alive. By the same token, only in and for a thinking and feeling soul, not for the image itself and by itself, can an image be shocking, anxiety-causing, or delightful. My seeing and interpreting what I see in this or that way, i.e., in *my* way, first creates that which affects me emotionally. And most importantly, an image *is* image only if it is perceived imaginally, poetically, and that means, perceived poetically *by a real I*. Without an imaginally thinking mind there is no image. Image is not simply given as an objective fact.

An image can portray or represent acting subjects, but an image cannot itself be considered an acting subject. It can be an image of a defensive attitude, but the image itself cannot be defensive. Any purpose, intentionality, teleology that one may wish to ascribe to an image is not of the image, but of what it is the image of. It could perhaps make sense to say that "the ego" is defensive or curious, that "the ego" exhibits an initiative or regards the manifestation of the non-ego as dangerous. It does not make sense to say this of the ego-image.

PHANTOMIZATION: THE SUBSTANTIATION OF A PREDICATE

Hillman's statement that the ego too is an image has the word image in the position of the predicate. This is important. The predication of an image character of the ego entails a challenge to us, the invitation, if not exhortation, to actually think the ego imaginally. It also holds "ego" and "image" apart, preserving the difference, while at the same time of course establishing a connection between them. The copula syntactically separates "the ego" as sentence subject from "image" as predicate and in one and the same act semantically declares them united. When Hillman made this statement it was a startling move. He had spoken into a situation in Jungian psychology in which "the ego" was thoroughly reified, considered to be an entity, an existing, more or less thing-like component in the makeup of the personality or psyche ("ego-complex"). His new view broke through this dry, stalemate convention. It pushed open a gate. The ego was no longer a given and as such fixed entity. Being an image, a product of the imagination, it, that is, the *theoretical concept* of "the ego" and thus OUR *theoretical thinking* about it, had come alive and become flexible. *We* had to become flexible. *We* had to stop taking it for granted and instead start imagining it. Hillman's insight revolutionized our style of thinking about the ego. It made our "definition" of ego fluid. But Adams' move wants to face-lift *the ego* itself.

Adams, probably wanting to draw the conclusion from the result of Hillman's new insight and turn it once and for all into the presupposition or base of all psychological work, made "image" the new subject to which "ego" (or "non-ego") was added as a specifying attribute. His overzealous attempt to be absolutely serious about the imaginal approach introduced by Hillman into psychology made Adams paradoxically and unwittingly go back full circle to a pre-imaginal psychology and, more than that, convert the very notion of image into its opposite. It is the undoing of imaginal psychology by overdoing it. I want to point out a few aspects of this undoing.

Generally, to draw the conclusion from the result of a thought process or experience is what ought to be done. A result in its first immediacy is not enough. It needs to come home to itself. It also needs to become the starting point for a new process, for new insights. Why then does Adams' drawing the conclusion from Hillman's result end in failure? I think it is because he does not take the whole result, but only the letter without the spirit: merely the naked *word* "image." A real result has the whole thought process that led to it within itself as its animating spirit. But much like hedge funds want to milk

IMAGINAL PSYCHOLOGY GONE OVERBOARD

companies for quick profit, sort of for naked cash, without the least interest in the milk-giving companies in their own right or the products produced by them, so Adams takes from Hillman the abstract word "image" as an item or jetton that one can operate with. We could also express it in a more psychological way. Whereas normally a new result "infects," maybe even revolutionizes, the style of consciousness as a whole, the way of our thinking, propelling consciousness onto a new level or into a new status, Adams treats Hillman's result as a mere content that he simply inserts into the same old consciousness. A new piece of furniture in the old apartment.

For Adams, "Jungian psychology is what I call imaginology," where imaginology means that "Jungian psychologists study images." Sometimes it is unfair to attribute too much weight to a casual comment. But the cited statements are not casual comments but deliberate theoretical assertions and completely representative of Adams' stance. They are born out by what he in fact does in this his entire text. *What* they show is that the higher logical complexity of the subject-subject-object relation reached by Hillman's imaginal stance is reduced to the simple subject-object relation between Jungians as subject(s) here and images as object(s) over there. Except for the names there is no difference between the idea of an ego-complex and an ego-image. In Adams' usage, "image" has become an entity, an objective fact. It has become reified. He takes "image" absolutely literally. Image ceases to be a predicate of the actual subject or "substance," here the ego, or to be (in the form of the word "imaginal") an adjective ("the imaginal ego"), but is substantiated, ontologized. The result is that the *image becomes a phantom.*

Using a Kantian term[2] we can say that by turning, in his theorizing, a quality or style of seeing into an existing entity Adams commits the fallacy of subreption (*vitium subreptionis*)—the positing of an (objective) substance or subject where in truth there is a (subjective) function, act, or performance. Here it is the freezing of imaginal fluidity into "images" as personified things. The image is now a positivity (but, since it is nevertheless image, the positivity of a phantom). Conversely, the terms "the ego-image" and "non-ego

---

[2] I say "Kantian" term (although the term dates back to Jungius and was also used before Kant by Leibniz, for example) because I use it in the special Kantian sense.

images" shrinkwrap in the plastic foil named "image" the ego (or rather the real imaginal I) and the real figures occurring *in* an image (in a dream, myth, fantasy).

According to Adams, the ego-image itself is defensive against non-ego images, and the latter images "attempt to contact and impact the ego-image in an effort to transform it." He who says this is, just as in 19th century science, the outside observer of the strictly "objective" interplay that happens *out there* in front of consciousness, on the level of alleged objects, between two quasi-physical things, forces, or natural "beings" (the ego-image and the non-ego images) that are usually in some tension, if not opposition, to each other. Structurally his imaginology therefore takes us right back to the long-overcome standpoint of the psychic apparatus, with the only change that the latter's components are now no longer termed "agencies" or "complexes" but "images." Instead of psychology we get a new artificial mythology of the modern psychologist's own making, a mythology peopled by diverse "ego-" and "non-ego images." We know this fallacious mythologizing—Kant's "subreption"—from other popular misuses of Jungian terms. Especially Jung's orientation functions, the shadow, and the anima are likewise often turned into phantoms, as if they were acting persons, subjects.[3] But it is not my thinking function that thinks in me. It is I who think. It is not my shadow that did something evil. It is I who did this evil. And so it is also not my ego or "the ego-image" that defends against the psychic other. It is I who feel threatened by it. But this real me *is* of course imaginal in nature; it is (part of) the *psychology* (the imagination or theory) that I have, that I live, or as which I exist, not a natural part of the human organism.

The Truncation of the Subject-Subject-Object Relation

Is the *term* image enough? Does the mere use of the name image guarantee that one's approach, that so-called imaginology is still imaginal? I already pointed out that the image in the sense of imaginal psychology is absolutely dependent on *our* imaginal thinking, *our* capacity to think poetically. The image is imaginal only if *it*, as our

---

[3] Certain present-day neuroscientists commit the same fallacy, thinking that the brain thinks, which would be like saying that a car drives. A car may roll somewhere, but it never drives. The driving is done by a driver.

IMAGINAL PSYCHOLOGY GONE OVERBOARD

object, contains from the outset our imaginal thinking within itself, or to be more precise, if it is apperceived or construed as a priori containing it. It is, *when* it is, in itself a priori subjective-objective, that is to say, as image it has the subject indispensably in its objectivity. Whereas facts of nature can be comprehended within the simple subject-object relation, an image needs to be understood in terms of a subject-subject-object relation. It is a reality of a higher logical complexity. The moment that this duality of "subject," namely first the subject as the mind of the psychologist studying images, and second the subject as the psychologist's poetic apperception already inherent in the "object" (in the image studied), disappears so that the psychological theoretical stance relapses into the subject-object relation, the image has lost its imaginality. Images are not simply given. Jung's sentence, "the psyche consists essentially of images," must not be understood as analogous to a statement like "this house is built of bricks." The psyche, according to Jung's statement, is not made up of image-phantoms as its building-blocks. Rather, what Jung is trying to say is that what the psyche is made up of has image quality and not fact or entity quality. Not substances, positivities, but fantasies, ideas; not "hardware," but "software": *mental* realities instead of natural facts. Jung's attribution of an image quality to the "components" of the psyche shows that he too operates within the subject-subject-object relation at least in this instance: the human mind is already inherent in the object of psychology; prior to our studying the psyche, that which it contains is already imagined, fantasized, thought, interpreted from the outset; what psychology studies is already the *psychologies* that we have.

But in the theory presented in this essay of his Adams has once and for all left the subject-subject-object relation. He clearly tries to get away from the subjectivity inherent in the psychological object. There is one instance where this move away from subjectivity is clearly documented in his paper. After having quoted Freud's dictum that "The ego is the actual seat of anxiety," he cites Jung's reference to Freud's dictum, "In this way, as Freud rightly says, we turn the ego into a 'seat of anxiety,' which it would never be if we did not defend ourselves against ourselves so neurotically." Apart from the fact that Adams mistakes this statement as Jung's agreement with Freud's view,

482 THE SOUL ALWAYS THINKS

whereas it is a subtly-worded polemic against it,[4] he feels the need to reword Jung's diction: "What Jung means when he says that 'we defend ourselves against ourselves' is that the anxious ego neurotically defends itself against the unconscious."

A fundamental change. Jung spoke about "*us*," i.e., himself and me and you. He expressed himself in terms of the First Person pronoun, appealing to our subjectivity. Adams, by contrast, cleanses Jung's statement of all subjectivity. He eliminates the First Person and replaces it by the Third Person: instead of "we against ourselves" he prefers "it (the ego) against it (the unconscious)." And then, before introducing his suggestion that Jungians adopt his new terminology of "ego-image" and non-ego image," he explicitly points out that "'Ego' means 'I.' The ego-image is the 'I'-image." So it is clear that the attack aims at the "I." It is really the sense of "I," of "me" that is supposed to be overcome. "I" am supposed to be replaced by "the ego-image," and this means, to be dissolved into a phantom. It is by no means only the dream-I (the "I" occurring in a dream or other fiction).

Do Jung's and Adams' statements really express the same idea? Does Adams really elucidate Jung's meaning? Or is in this reformulation Jung's sentence not much rather deprived of its very point, namely Jung's rejection of "the ego" (Third Person, a thinking in terms of objects) in favor of "we" (First Person, subjectivity)? Only because *we* defend ourselves against *ourselves*, this is Jung's thesis, can

---

[4] Jung's charge in this paper against Freud's theory of the ego as the seat of anxiety is that it misses the real issue behind neurosis and *ipso facto* falls "into the same trap as the neurotic" (*CW* 10 § 365). "The loss of the great relationship is the prime evil of neurosis, and that is why the neurotic loses his way among ever more tortuous back-streets of dubious repute, because he who denies the great must blame the petty" (§ 367, transl. modif.). Of course, one does not have to agree with Jung's view of this problem. But regardless of one's own preference in this matter, one is obligated to avoid creating the impression that Jung accepted Freud's view on this point. Jung's radical critique of Freud's "The ego is the seat of anxiety" comes out much more clearly than in the quoted paper (published 1934) in his private letter to Arnold Künzli written about nine years later. "Question: is it an object worthy of anxiety, or a poltroonery of the ego, shitting its pants? (Compare Freud, 'The ego is the seat of anxiety,' with Job 28:28, 'The fear of the Lord, that is wisdom.') What is the 'anxiety of the ego,' this 'modestly modest' overweeningness and presumption of a little tin god, compared with the almighty shadow of the Lord, which is the fear that fills heaven and earth? The first leads to apotropaic defensive philosophy, the second to γνῶσις θεοῦ." *Letters 2*, p. 333 (16 March 1943). For Jung, the theory of the ego as the seat of anxiety is an apotropaic theory. It must not be taken for granted.

IMAGINAL PSYCHOLOGY GONE OVERBOARD

"the ego" be turned into the "seat of anxiety." The theory of the anxious ego is, Jung suggests, the result and expression of an existing neurosis, which in turn means that this theory is itself a manifestation of neurotic thinking; the doctor, by explaining neurosis in this fashion, rides the same hobby-horse as his neurotic patient (cf. *CW* 10, § 362. Also: "The topsy-turvy view of the human soul is turned into a theory of psychic suffering." *Ibid.* § 368).

In addition to the elimination of the First Person by the objective Third Person, Adams' reformulation also gets rid of the identity, in Jung's sentence, of the subject that defends itself and whom the subject defends itself against. We against ourselves. A self-relation. Adams turns this self-relation into the opposition between two fundamental others, two strangers, "the ego" and "the unconscious," which, I mention this only as an aside, on top of everything also gets rid of the *neurotic* character of the relation that Jung talked about. For as problematic as the defense of one thing against another thing may be, it is not neurotic. Otherwise it would also have to be considered neurotic that our immune system defends against bacteria and viruses. It is nonsense to say that "In a very real sense, every neurosis is an anxiety neurosis." Whatever it may be, it is certainly not *neurotic* if the ego or if I regard(s) non-ego images as dangerous and if the ego is anxious or suspicious instead of being curious and receptive. Anxiety can mean a realistic fear on the basis of a realistic self-estimation; in other cases it can mean cowardice; it can of course, in still other cases, also mean a terrible rigidity. But the point is that none of this is neurotic. The designation neurotic can only be used for cases of a self-contradiction, for the defense against or denial of or dissociation from one's own truth.[5] (Therefore, to go back to my earlier reference to the immune system: on the body level, *autoimmune* diseases would be an analogy to neurosis.)

It is Adams' move away from all subjectivity, clearly exemplified in how he rephrases Jung's statement, that prepares the ground for the strictly objective (thing-like) interpretation of "the image" in

---

[5] It should be mentioned that there are other places where Jung, too, considers the defense of the I against the unconscious (i.e., of "it" against another "it") as neurotic. So he does not always, as in the present quotation, and consistently make it clear that neurosis is to be understood in terms of our self-relation—that particular type of self-relation that is a self-contradiction. Jung at times even said that neurosis consists in mere one-sidedness. But one-sidedness obviously does not per se make neurotic.

484   *THE SOUL ALWAYS THINKS*

Adams' conception. After "we" or "I" and "ourselves" and "myself" have been once and for all eliminated, the path is free for the additional step of moving from "the ego" as sentence subject to "the ego-image," a concept which has totally left behind all traces of our subjectivity. "The (ego-)*image*" is irrevocably an "it," whereas "the ego" at least *semantically* still retained the First Person, despite the fact that syntactically it came as a Third Person noun (a pronoun substantiated into a self-sufficient noun). In "the ego-image," the last trace of the First Person still semantically retained in "the ego" is completely subsumed under the Third Person concept "image."

As Bruno Bettelheim pointed out a long time ago, Freud in his own idiom did not, as in the official English translations, speak of "the ego" (as in general he did not use scientific-sounding technical terms taken from Latin), but used the ordinary-language term "I" ("das Ich"). So also when he spoke of the seat of anxiety. The same is generally true of C.G. Jung. But in our passage Jung even leaves the substantiated form "das Ich" behind and speaks the way we really speak in ordinary language: "if *we* did not defend ourselves..." Is this a slip on Jung's part, a psychologically inadequate form of expression? Perhaps a concession to the average lay reader? Should he, to be psychologically correct, have stuck to "*das* Ich" or even used "the ego" instead? The question of *what* is psychologically at stake in choosing "the ego defends itself" (let alone "the ego-image defends itself") over against "we defend ourselves" is crucial. The two wordings involve more than a stylistic or rhetorical difference.

With the move away from "we" or "I," that is, from actual human beings, to "the ego" or, worse, to "the ego-image," psychology goes up into the air, up into the sphere of free-floating, self-sufficient concepts. It loses touch with the real world, or rather, with the sense of reality as such, cocooning itself in a self-contained ideal sphere as if in outer space. Speaking of active imagination, Adams says, "The ego-image actively engages the non-ego image in a dialogue." This description makes a shadow play out of active imagination, the playing of a player piano, scarecrows engaging scarecrows, but it is not active imagination. The real subject has been filtered out and replaced by a phantom. But active imagination is a real event, here and now, and it depends on its being *my* imagination, on *my* committed presence in the act of actively imagining. A string must connect the balloon of

IMAGINAL PSYCHOLOGY GONE OVERBOARD 485

fantasy with a real person on earth. In active imagination I—*really* me (neither *the* I, nor the ego, nor the ego-image)—enter an image, which ipso facto is a *real* image. The standpoint of "psychic reality" depends entirely on *our* presence, our presence as real. *I* actively engage (*not* the non-ego image, but) the other *figure*, the imaginally *real* figure, depicted *in* this image. It is a direct encounter in earnest, not an encounter up in the air between two space-suits called "images."

In Psychoanalysis there is a defense mechanism called *Dazwischenschieben* (to interpose, interject, namely between oneself and a real experience). In Adams' discourse the artificial construct of "the ego" (and even more so "the ego-image") is interposed between me and what I am confronted with. As ego-image and non-ego image, both sides are derealized and, as I said, shrinkwrapped. I can stay out of it, but at the same time the soul has been deprived of its reality, too: phantomized.

The Necessity of Forgetting "Image"

The fact that my real active engagement of the real non-ego figure in a dialogue only happens *within the image* (because I, really I, have committedly *entered* the image) and that it thus *is* an imaginal dialogue ("imaginal" as attribute or predicate!) is misconstrued by Adams as one image talking with another image. This shows that, to be sure, he takes note of the imaginal quality of the interaction, but reifies it and thus inevitably views it completely from without, turning things inside out. He assigns the realness to the image quality (the ego-*image* as a real agent that poses questions or listens), whereas for the soul it is precisely the events and figures themselves *in* active imagination, *in* dreams and visions, *in* mythic images that are brutally real and are not images. If one merely *imagines* active imagination from without and so stays an external observer, then *they*, the ego-image and the other image, talk and listen to each other. If one enters the concept of active imagination, one forgets—or always already has forgotten—about the image character and so things become (precisely *in* the image, which one has forgotten) absolutely real: me in my psychological nakedness really confronted with my other in its reality. To think imaginally, you have to forget that you are dealing with images. Having taken your standpoint inside the image, you have to be exclusively devoted to *what* the image contains, to the events and figures shown in it. As psychologists, we should not operate with or study images ("imaginology"), but think *imaginally*, that is, engage the contents of dreams, myths, life situations, etc. *as* real. Psychology is not *about* images.

In addition to "subreption" and to the false substantiating (or mythologizing) of predicates in the sense of the latter's phantomization, the fundamental fallacy of Adams' approach can therefore also be described as the reversal of inside and outside. What was inside the image and ipso facto imaginal, is now construed, according to its logical status, as an external, positive reality called "the ego-image" and "the non-ego images." And the absolute realness that originated from my real entering the image gave way, in his scheme, to a merely externally observed or imagined shadow play between automated parts of the "psychic apparatus"-like psyche.

Still another way of describing it would be to say that his scheme amounts to the confusion of the standpoint of *reflection* and *theory* with the standpoint of *experience* and/or *practical approach*. The statement, "The ego too is image" is spoken from, and true only for, the standpoint of reflection. For our work with image-material to be imaginal we must with methodical awareness "forget" this truth that the reflection arrives at in order to return to a (by no means naïve, but rather methodically produced) naïvety vis-à-vis the contents of the image. Conversely, to make the image-aspect supraordinate, as Adams recommends, turns the standpoint of reflection into the ego's standard stance and thereby kills the reflection, because instead of having something *whose* reflection it could be, it is now itself the primary material that might or might not become subject to a possible reflection. The reflection is literalized.

The insight about this methodical forgetting is true despite the essential fact that psychology, as an enterprise following the uroboric logic of the soul, is the simultaneous unity of reflection *and* practice, alchemically expressed: of laboratory *and* oratory. No switching back and forth, now this, thereafter that. Reflection is not a subsequent pastime, the way the theory of science is a separate additional discipline supplementing the practice of science. But the unity of reflection and practice in psychology is neither an initially given *unio naturalis*, nor the result of a merger, but the methodically

IMAGINAL PSYCHOLOGY GONE OVERBOARD

produced unity of what before has systematically been separated. In the contradictory logic of the *mysterium coniunctionis*, the separation is always logically prior to the union of the opposites, and the psychological unity has and retains irrevocably within itself the difference between the opposites.

By the same token, psychology is the unity of Lesmosyne and Mnemosyne, forgetting and remembering, but in such a way that the forgetting (here of the fact that image is image) also possesses logical priority and is *not* canceled by the remembering. In their unity they nevertheless remain separated.

We can summarize our insights about the nature of the image in imaginal psychology in four statements:

1. It all begins with the insight of reflection that the image is *image*. As a part of the decidedly modern world, psychology has left the naïve stance of mythological consciousness for which images were immediate realities, apparitions. It is no longer innocent. It takes place in the domain of reflection and alienation. For psychology, myth is dead. It has seen through to the image nature of myth and dream, so that for it a difference is opened up between "image" (myth, dream, etc.), on the one hand, and "what the image shows," on the other—a division that would be absolutely deadly for the standpoint of immediacy and for the innocent reception of images.

2. Our thinking is only imaginal if and when with methodical awareness it "forgets" or "brackets" the insight gained by reflection so that we can devote ourselves with a secondary (methodically produced) naïvety to the contents *in* the images (to what is shown in them) and view their contents directly *as real figures and events* and *not* as images themselves (because this would turn them into phantoms)—precisely because images (dreams, myths, etc.) present their contents (not once more as images, but) as absolutely real. By means of a relentless (although methodical) immersion in the image, we have to go along with what the image itself does with its contents, with how *it*, the given image, perceives and presents *them*.

3. Those figures in images have their reality as "personalities" only *in* the images (dreams, fictions, myths, novels, ...). Only within them can they have emotions, interests, intentions, a purpose, and "regard something as..."

488   THE SOUL ALWAYS THINKS

4. The images (in which such figures appear) are images in the first place only if there is a real I (not the phantom of an ego-image) as an in fact imaginally perceiving and feeling mind.

THE LOSS OF IMAGINALITY

Adams' not forgetting, his bringing the "image" into and keeping it in the limelight of the sentence-subject position, has the grave consequence—and herewith we at long last come to the answer to our question above, whether the use of the name image guarantees the imaginality of the approach—that all the imaginal or poetic quality of his "the ego-image" is lost. Its problem is not only the Third Person, or thing-like entity, aspect. Much more serious is that the very term "image" has now also become decidedly unimaginal. "Image" here is an abstract concept.[6] In his text it functions as a given building-block of the psyche that can occur in two possible states, defensive or receptive, anxious or curious. The word image in Adams' usage paradoxically became unimaginal because of his very attempt to draw the conclusion from Hillman's move to imaginality (imaginality even with respect to "the ego") by raising "image" from the predicate or attribute position to that of the sentence subject. Through this move, the distance between "I" and "image" was lost. Subject and predicate were collapsed into one. And because of the loss of distance—the loss of the difference between a real referent on the one hand and the image-nature predicated of it, i.e., the poetic quality, on the other hand—"image" itself in its new sentence-subject or substance sense turned into a self-identical, flat, hard-core reality to be taken as a given. In Hillman's imaginal psychology, by contrast, it signified a *quality of how* phenomena could be or were supposed to be understood. The very notion of "image"—once introduced to push off from the literal—was thus itself totally literalized, positivized. Its imaginal quality has been extrajected from it: *pre*-supposed, and thus reduced to a slogan or catchword that one can freely use. It has degenerated into a mere label: a word-fetish.

---

[6] The concept of the concept underlying the use in this my entire paper of the term concept is the abstract (formal-logical) concept that has its referent outside of itself. It must be distinguished from the *psychologically relevant* concept of the concept or notion that figures in some other publications of mine.

IMAGINAL PSYCHOLOGY GONE OVERBOARD

Using a distinction introduced by Abraham into libido theory, Freud, in his afterword to the question of lay analysis, remarked that concerning the embrace of psychoanalysis by the medical profession he was suspicious about whether it amounted to an appropriation for the purpose of the destruction or the preservation of the object. Other than Freud, in the case of Adams' move we do not have to think in terms of a purpose or sinister intention. And on the other hand, again other than Freud, we do not have to be merely suspicious but can be certain that in its result, in what it in fact achieves, Adams' advancement of imaginal psychology beyond Hillman's "it too is an image" amounts to the undoing of the imaginal approach as performative, as a style of perceiving and thinking.

His advancement beyond Hillman has the problem of word-fetishism in common with a recent powerful trend, the societal insistence on "political correctness." Although the latter is indeed sinister[7] and thus different from Adams' proposal, it nevertheless likewise works with (often euphemistic) renamings and thus with the complete withdrawal of meaning from the mind's living (i.e., always *practiced* afresh) thought into external linguistic labels that one merely operates with in a technical (mindless) fashion. Linguistic operationalism. Spirit retreats into, and disappears in, words (words as mere sounds). One only has to go through the motions. The mechanical replacement "out there" of one "incorrect" word by another, "correct" one, in other words, the manipulation of language,[8] has the function of relieving us from our constant obligation to try "in here" to transform our attitudes, our actual ways of thinking and feeling, that is, to practice a more adequate way of apperception in each concrete real-life instance with a renewed effort. A sham. It is simply taken for granted that the use of the correct word just like that guarantees that the correct spirit is at work. The "correct" words are ready-mades—*vorhanden* once and for all.

---

[7] Its actual home is in dictatorships. It is a fundamental suppression of the freedom of speech and thought.

[8] The manipulation of language is a violence performed upon *language*. By the suppression of free speech we usually mean that *people* are hindered from freely expressing their opinions. But there is a much more fundamental suppression of free speech, namely the hindrance of *ideas* or *experiences* or *matters* to spontaneously find their own words and styles of expression according to *their* own inner necessities. "For out of the abundance of the heart the mouth speaketh" (Matth. 12:34).

490   *THE SOUL ALWAYS THINKS*

But, to return to the field of psychology, a soulful, imaginal way of perceiving has to be produced or conquered for oneself each time anew from scratch. The subject, our subjectivity, and its thinking effort are psychologically indispensable. Psychology is performative. You have to do it. There is no "imaginal world" to do it for you. And in doing it you have to prove each time that what you are doing and how you are doing it is in fact truly psychology. Psychology is not a science, a doctrine or theory *about...*

What we have discussed so far can be further developed in its ramifications. The fact that Adams' paper has left the ground of imaginal psychology shows also in several other ways. His theory of neurosis based on the anxiety of the ego and following one of Freud's views clearly has regressed to an ego-psychological standpoint. It stays on the surface, trying to explain neurosis from without, rather than from within (from the standpoint of soul). All depends in Adams' scheme on the ego (or "the ego-image"), whether it is anxious or curious. The ego-image tips the scales. The truly *psychological* view that neurosis might be produced by the soul rather than by the ego and could be an (albeit thoroughly pathological) way of soul-making has no chance under these circumstances.

THE ABSTRACT FORMAL-LOGICAL CONCEPT AS THE HORIZON OF "IMAGINOLOGY"

My insight that "the ego-image" is an *abstract concept*, a construct, and not itself an image, not an example of imaginal thinking, is also supported by Adams' recourse to formal logic in his attempt to expose Jung's archetypal stance as "conceptual essentialism," in contrast to his own alleged "imaginal essentialism." He states, "Gregory Bateson notes that in formal logic a class is 'on a *different level of abstraction'* from the members of the class. As a result, the class cannot be a member of the class, and a member cannot be the class." This is certainly correct. But it is of course correct and meaningful only in formal logic, only in the logic of the sciences and of everyday life, which as exponents of the world of "the ego" are both governed by the laws of formal logic. The horizon of Adams' psychological thinking is this abstract formal logic.

IMAGINAL PSYCHOLOGY GONE OVERBOARD

But what about the world of soul? Is Bateson's point really applicable to it, too? Is the alchemical Mercurius not both a sort of "class" (the world of alchemy at large, the hermetic spirit of the whole work) *and* a particular embodiment, figure, and image possibly occurring in that "class"? Are the mythic gods not each the whole world (experienced from a particular perspective) *and* a figure at times manifesting in that world? Is psychology not the unity of the comprehensive theory of all psychic phenomena *and* nevertheless the particular psychology "that I have"? Is "the soul" not the all-encompassing "class" of all psychic reality *and* a specific psychic phenomenon within psychic reality, e.g., as an anima-figure, or as the event of a soulful (in contrast to a soulless) interpretation of a given phenomenon? If, as Jung insists, we are surrounded by soul on *all* sides, then the soul is the unity of itself *and* of what it is not, the soulless. It has nothing outside of itself.

Even in philosophy itself we find Hegel's thesis that a universal genus may be one of its own species, that, for example in the case of the Concept and its moments, the Universal is both a genus *and* a particular species of this genus parallel to its other two "species," the Particular and the Individual, and, conversely, that "Each moment of the Concept is itself the whole Concept" (*Enz. I*, § 163), i.e., that each species, here the Universal, the Particular, and the Individual, is itself the genus of which it is one specification.

Be that as it may, at any rate the soul's logic is not abstract-formal logic, not ego logic, but uroboric logic. Which is why formal logic must not be the horizon within which our psychological thinking takes place (if it is supposed to be the thinking of a psychology with soul).

However, with his Bateson quote Adams does not have the purpose of establishing formal logic as the horizon for psychology. His referring to it merely incidentally underlines for us once more that it in fact is the horizon of his "imaginology." But his purpose, the real reason why he introduces the abstract formal-logical dissociation between class and member of the class, is that he needs it to accuse Jung of working with "concept[s], which [are] abstract forms" and of "replac[ing] the image with a concept." Now it is quite clear that Jung was not an imagist in Hillman's sense. But he was nevertheless truly devoted to images, even if he did not clearly distinguish between images and symbols. It is absolutely unfair to classify Jung as anti-image in the sense that he "reduces it [image] to a concept" or "privileges the concept over the image." Repeatedly Jung stressed explicitly that "[...] all the dream images are important in themselves, each one having a special significance of its own [...]" (*CW* 8 § 471). "Concepts are coined and negotiable values; images are life" (*CW* 14 § 226). Nor is it tenable to suggest that Hillman's statement that we must "stick to the image" is in contrast to Jung's allegedly strictly conceptual stance, since this very statement, which before Hillman had already been expressed by Lopez-Pedraza, ultimately goes back to Jung himself: "To understand the dream's meaning I must stick as close as possible to the dream images" (*CW* 16 § 320).

Nonetheless, there are also those statements by Jung on which Adams bases his interpretation. Jung does say that it does not matter if the treasure is a ring, a crown, a pearl, or a hoard. He does say that "It matters little if the mythological hero conquers now a dragon, now a fish or some other monster." Adams fails to see, however, that the statements according to which it does not matter which precise image is chosen in a myth and the other statement about the special significance of each particular image are compatible because they belong to different discourses. It is perfectly reasonable of Jung to insist, in the context of an elucidation of his theory of archetypes, that the dragon in one myth and the fish (or whatever monster) to be conquered by the mythological hero in another myth are *structurally* or *functionally analogous*. With respect to this analogy, it does indeed not matter if the one or the other image is chosen. In this kind of context Jung is speaking as a theorist. He observes such analogies or *typical* motifs and explains them (the equivalent functions that diverse images have in corresponding myths of different cultures and times) by positing his arche*types*. At times Jung sets these archetypes up as "archetypes-in-themselves" in contrast to the specific "archetypal images." We do not have to agree with this move of his (or with his theory of archetypes, for that matter). But it does not in itself prove any privileging of the concept over the image. It only shows that Jung *in addition to* working with particular phenomena also felt the need to provide a conceptual ("scientific") explanation for those phenomena that he observed.

When, by contrast, Jung insists on sticking to the image, he is speaking (not as a theorist, but) as a practitioner in the sense of one

IMAGINAL PSYCHOLOGY GONE OVERBOARD

who practices the art of dream or myth interpretation. When he is concerned with individual texts, Jung wants to be true to the specifics of each image. He then is devoted to the particular phenomenon at hand. It is clear that both concerns do not exclude each other, because they come to bear at different moments or in different situations of the work and on different levels.

THE DIFFERENCE BETWEEN IMAGE AND CONCEPT

But Adams' unfair treatment of Jung in this point is not my main concern here. My interest is in Adam's abstract conception of "image." He works with the (formal-logical) distinction between "class" and "member of the class" and correlates "class" with concept and "member of the class" with image. "Monster" and "treasure" he thinks are classes and *ipso facto* concepts, whereas "dragon" and "fish" in the one case and "ring," "crown," "pearl" in the other case are members of their respective class and *ipso facto* concrete images. The criterion that distinguishes image from concept is the former's greater specificity. "The concept," he says, "is nondescript: it possesses no distinctive qualities. In contrast, the image possesses quite distinctive qualities ..." "Although it is extremely difficult—I would say, impossible—to define the essence of a concept, ... I argue that it is possible ... to ... accurately define the essence of an image, because an image is a concrete content with distinctive qualities."[9] Concepts "are intrinsically vague," whereas images have "distinctive qualities." "Concepts are generalizations; images are particularizations."

This is a terrible confusion. Whether monster and treasure on the one hand or dragon, fish and crown, ring, pearl on the other hand— they all are equally concepts. Subclasses are just as much concepts as the class itself. By going, in the hierarchy of classification (the *arbor Porphyriana*), down to the *infima species*, you do not leave the range of

---

[9] A very odd, unusual view. It is generally thought that it is much easier to define an abstract concept, precisely because it is a priori limited, than a concrete image which is characterized by its inner infinity. Obviously when Adams says image he does not have that *imaginal* image in mind that is in itself essentially infinite, but a well-circumscribed abstract concept, and when he thinks that it is nearly impossible to define the essence of a concept, his notion of concept is different from the concept that he calls image solely through its enormous generality or comprehensiveness (like philosophy's term Being) and his notion of defining the essence of *this* concept boils down to enumerating everything that falls under it (which indeed is probably impossible).

concepts and suddenly arrive at "image." The difference between concept and (imaginal) image has thereby not yet been sighted. It is not the greater or lesser generality, the higher or lower degree of abstraction. Even when he explicitly speaks of "image," Adams nevertheless operates solely within the sphere of abstract concepts.

A large amount of literature has been produced in the history of thought both about the concept and about image. They are complex topics, and much could be said about them. In the present context, however, it suffices to introduce only the traditional distinction between *repraesentatio generalis* and *repraesentatio singularis* to get a very basic handle on the difference between concept and image. The concept is a general representation of what is *common to* several objects; it is concerned with the qualities or properties that things, events, phenomena have *in common*. As such it abstracts from singular individual things (this tree over there, the Eiffel Tower in Paris, my father, Einstein) and is the property of thought in the strict sense, of the Understanding. An image, by contrast, belongs to Intuition (*Anschauung*) or imagination, not to thought, and as such it has precisely singular individual things or ideas as its content. In tales, poetry, and (most important for the psychologist) in dreams we are generally dealing with images: this swan, this monster, this moon, this dark unknown man who follows me, this toilet, this endless maize of hallways, etc.

The central distinction between image and concept—in this context—is thus what we might call the thisness of any image, a thisness which identifiably *locates* the content in question in a particular context (in the world or landscape created by *this* poem, dream, story, vision, fantasy) or in time and space (*this* experience in the empirical world). Concepts are by contrast the abstraction from this thisness, an abstraction on account of which the (abstract) concept is a *Gedankending*, a noumenon, something which has its locus only in the mind (in the absolutely open, timeless and spaceless sphere of the mind) and not as a singular entity in empirical or imagined reality. (But, this is the other side of it, for this very reason the concept is what alone enables us to truly *comprehend*, intellectually *grasp*, and *speak about*, the real.)

The degree of abstraction from *distinctive qualities* is irrelevant for the distinction between image and concept. What alone counts is the

IMAGINAL PSYCHOLOGY GONE OVERBOARD 495

abstraction or not from *thisness*. It is the achievement of images (dreams, myths, etc.) to present the figures and events in them in each case as a "this," and this is precisely what provides the imaginal characters with their *realness*. The image itself presents its contents as real and not as images.

Jung reports having had a dream in which he was at night in a fog making his headway against a mighty wind while carrying only a tiny light in his hands. "Suddenly," he says, "I had the feeling that something was coming up behind me." (*MDR*, p. 108)

This "something" has hardly any distinctive qualities. It is completely vague, nondescript. But it is a full-fledged image. For it is a this. The apparition of a ghost may be very foggy, but as an apparition here and now it is an image. By the same token, the general words "monster" and "treasure" can be just as much dream images as dragon, fish, or ring, just as, conversely, "something," "monster," and "dragon" can also be concepts. It all depends on whether they are *envisioned* by us as singular individuals—or *thought* as generic. When young boys, having read *Treasure Island*, go out with a pickax and shovel to search for a treasure they do not have a concept but an image of treasure, although they may not have any clear idea about the treasure, whether it might turn out to be rings, crowns, pearls, gold coins. Nor do they care; all they are fascinated by is the general mystique of "treasure," not the particularities of what it may consist of. "Man" in "Socrates was a man" is a concept because it could also be predicated of Cicero, Napoleon, Freud, and numerous other people. But in "A man tried to break into my house" in a dream text, "a man" is an image despite his having no face or any other distinctive characteristics. Adams' binary opposition of image and concept, where everything depends on the *type of objects* (certain ones, like "monster" and "treasure," belonging to the one and certain others, like "dragon" and "ring," to the other category), is untenable.

I said that the image of "something" in Jung's dream—"something was coming up behind me"—is completely vague. But I hasten to add that this particular vagueness *is* the distinctive quality of this particular image, as already Hillman had pointed out many years ago. The vagueness is precisely part of the precision and exactitude of this image. When Adams, by contrast, speaks of the distinctive qualities of images, he does so in terms of the abstract formal logical distinction between

496   *THE SOUL ALWAYS THINKS*

genus and *species* or class and member of the class; the higher a concept is in the pyramid of concepts the fewer distinctive qualities it has and the lower the more. Adams, committed to formal logic, *counts*, as it were, *the number* of qualities in order to distinguish image from concept. His is a quantitative, positivistic concept of distinctive qualities.[10] Imaginal or poetic thinking, committed to the thisness or eachness of the image at hand and deprived of the possibility to compare (because *this* image is all it has and all it is concerned with), uses a qualitative concept of distinctive qualities. It is simply a question of the actual how and what of the image, so the lack of details is an equally good qualification for being image as would be a richness of details.

It is a most curious, puzzling fact that after pages of insisting on the described view of the difference between image (e.g., dragon or fish) and concept (e.g., monster) Adams all of a sudden admits that "a dragon and a fish are also concepts and not images. 'Dragon' and 'fish' are classes with members…" This is correct, but contradicts the whole thesis of his paper. And it is curious because it remains absolutely without consequences. The earlier views are not retracted or revised. The whole paragraph in which he makes this comment strikes one as a late addition (perhaps to accommodate objections raised by others to a previous version of his paper?). At any rate it sticks out like a sore thumb because its message is really out of place in his argument.

In addition, this new insight is also incomplete. While he realizes that "dragon" and "fish" are also abstract concepts, he does not realize that conversely "monster" and "treasure" can also be images. Nor does he provide any idea why and when such terms are images and why and when concepts.

Ideological Partisanship: "Good" Images versus "Bad" Images

"Replacing images with concepts—for example, interpreting a snake as 'fear,' 'sexuality,' or the 'mother-complex'—is, Hillman says, 'killing the snake.'" This is true. But this does not at all mean that "any concept is the very death of any image." Adams here establishes an absolute opposition or mutual exclusiveness between concept and

---

[10] Just as he thinks that the essence of a concept can possibly not be defined because he seems to understand defining as *enumerating* all the objects that fall under the general concept.

IMAGINAL PSYCHOLOGY GONE OVERBOARD

497

image. But since we are thinking beings, anything we think or say about images in the way of interpretation must needs make use of concepts. It would be an illusion to think that we can do without concepts, could utter meaningful statements or think in terms of images and work with images without any concepts. Concepts are unavoidable. The images themselves contain numerous concepts, albeit implicitly. Therefore, as far as our work with images is concerned, it all depends on (only depends on) whether our concepts fit or not: whether they are intrinsic, the images's own concepts. In the above example, what kills the snake is not *that* concepts are used, but (1) that these particular concepts are far-fetched, absolutely external associations (labels stuck onto the image) and (2) that they are meant as substitutions for "snake," translations of "snake," that is, that they are tacitly prefixed by an equals sign, rather than being introduced by way of elucidation and exploration of what a snake is, what all is inherent in the image "snake." But if in my interpretation I make use, in a circumambulating fashion, of terms such as poison, earth, healing, to sneak, which are also concepts, the snake is by no means *ipso facto* killed (although the question of course remains whether these concepts are truly relevant to this particular snake in this dream).

Given the interest that Adams has in not killing the image it is ironic that he gives the reader the following advice concerning the image of the dragon-killer: "Actively imagine a dialogue between St. George and the dragon or between Captain Ahab and the fish: not St. George lancing the dragon or Captain Ahab harpooning the fish— not a concept killing the image—but St. George and the dragon and Captain Ahab and the fish conducting a reciprocal conversation and experiencing a mutual transformation." What is this other than an instance of killing the image? Other than wanting to replace it by another, allegedly "better" image?

Adams does not show any respect for the dignity and integrity of the images of St. George and of Ahab, and, by extension, of the dragon-killing hero at large, who also figures in his paper. Underlying his suggestion to manipulate their content is the fact that he has obviously replaced the image of the dragon-killing hero by his own modern-ideological concept of it, for which he relies on a statement by Hillman, one which I find deplorable: "Killing the dragon in the hero myth is

498

nothing less than killing the imagination."[11] There is here no attempt to understand what this time-honored image of the dragon-killer psychologically means in its own terms. It is instead a modern moralistic[12] condemnation (here of "killing"[13]), a condemnation that in another context Adams himself disparages in the same paper of his: "The neurotic reaction of the ego-image to the non-ego image is a function of what I call moralistic, scientific, and aesthetic oppositions— good versus evil, true versus false, and beautiful versus ugly. These oppositions provide the ego-image with a convenient excuse to repress— or 'kill'—non-ego images that it considers evil, false, or ugly—and, as a result, dangerous." These two sentences are his inadvertent self-interpretation of his response to the stories of St. George and Ahab, and to the hero-myth (that he in one instance even calls "insane").[14]

---

[11] James Hillman, "The Great Mother, Her Son, Her Hero, and the Puer," in: *Fathers and Mothers*, ed. Patricia Berry (Dallas, TX: Spring Publications, 1991) p. 191.

[12] Adams cites Hillman's incensed reaction to Esther Harding's speech "in favor of killing the dragon": "so moralistic!" But the denunciation of dragon-killing is the same moralism, only in the opposite direction. The contra is in no way better than the pro. Both are unpsychological: ideological.

[13] The very notion of "killing" seems to be a banal, literal, completely unpsychological one, one that might be appropriate when discussing Westerns or newspaper reports, but not ancient myths, rituals or dreams. The question what "to kill" means for and in the soul, and here particularly in the hero myth, has not been raised by Adams, nor by Hillman for that matter. Just as "death" means something else for the soul than for the ego, so also "killing." "Our 'killing' is not 'the people's' sense of 'killing.'"

[14] It should be noted that it is a psychological mistake to simply lump together such fundamentally different stories of monster-slaying as that of archaic Siegfried and Hercules on the one hand and the much later Christian St. George on the other hand, merely on account of the external, superficial similarity of their plots, their semantics. The "monster" in the archaic situation is psychologically something *toto coelo* different from the one after the rise of Christianity (with its notions of "evil" and the devil), and again something *toto coelo* different in modernity (Melville's *Moby Dick*). Terentius: *Duo cum faciunt idem, non est idem* (when two people do the same, it is not the same). Discern the *spirits*—the different logic or syntax—in each case! Don't be deceived by "the same" semantics. Discriminate!

In addition to our need to discern the spirits, there is another indispensable discrimination, as particularly Jung taught us: *the psychological difference between the great and the petty*. It is an abuse of psychological tact for Adams to mention such dignified imaginal figures as Captain Ahab and St. George in the same breath as presidential candidate Barack Obama and former Deputy Chief of Staff Karl Rove. What a debasement, a leveling down! In general, what in heaven's name have the shallownesses and petitesses of daily politics and election campaigns—sort of the "psychopathology of everyday life," the trivia of the ego-world—to do in a psychological essay, what do they have to do with soul and myths and what do soul and myths have to do with them?! The cobbler should stick to his last, the Jungian psychologist to the life of the soul. "*Our*" great is not the "great" that hits the media (be it the top politicians, Lady Diana, and other celebrities, or be it "September 11th." They are of no psychological interest, as long as psychology is a "psychology with soul" and not a psychology of ego emotions). Do Jungian psychologists completely lack the feeling function?

IMAGINAL PSYCHOLOGY GONE OVERBOARD

Is the myth of the dragon-killing hero not a "non-ego image" for Adams' own "ego-image"? Why is his "ego-image" not receptive and curious? And apart from this, is the motif of the killing of the dragon not in general a ("non-ego") product of the *soul*? Adams practices censorship. He wants to bring out these old stories in new expurgated, improved, politically correct versions. Harmless versions. This is plain ego-psychology. He approaches these stories, that over centuries have been so precious for the soul, with a moralistic agenda of his own.

Psychology's job is not to be for or against, not to advocate or condemn, not to condone or criticize the images produced by the soul, but to elaborate and comprehend their psychology: to discover what through them the soul achieves for the soul.

Hillman's statement, "Killing the dragon in the hero myth is nothing less than killing the imagination" is mimicked by Adams: "When the ego-image regards a non-ego image as a monster, however, it tends to commit what I call *imagicide*." Both statements perform a *salto mortale*. They do not stay in and dwell with the image, but leap out of it, out of the imagination and out of "the soul," into "the ego's" abstract conceptualism and moralistic judgmentalism. The hero's killing the dragon happens *precisely in the imagination* and *as an image* and thus, rather than killing the imagination, confirms it and enriches it with one of its possible moments.[15] The same is true for the so-called ego-image. "Its" regarding a non-ego image as a monster is not imagicide, but an instance of ongoing imagination, imagination as a real event.[16] Both authors tear apart the unity (the alchemical *ligamentum, vinculum*, the logical *copula, desmos,* or *syllogismos*) of the

---

[15] By the way, if the dragon were indeed a representation of "the imagination," as it is viewed by Hillman and Adams, then Adams himself would *malgré lui* have given an example of the soul's uroboric logic that he explicitly rejected in favor of abstract formal logic, because then "the imagination" would here, as it were, appear as a "member" of its own "class."

But if the dragon were a representation of "the imagination," a *psychological* view would still not see in the hero's dragon-killing the literal killing of the imagination, but view it in terms of its own insight into psychology's notion of "nature," namely that *its* "nature" is "the nature that conquers nature" (*CW* 12 § 472, transl. modif.) and that analogously *its* notion of "imagination" is "the imagination that conquers the imagination." The overcoming of the imagination would happen within the soul's own imagination and as its own *opus* for its own purposes. And the result, one's being *beyond* a merely imagining mind, would not altogether have dropped out from the soul's imagination, just as "the soulless" stays within the soul.

[16] It could of course be pathological. But even so, did Hillman not teach us that pathologizing is one of the modes of soul-making?

uroboric soul, whose serene sovereignty shows in its ability to affirm, maintain, and even enhance itself precisely in and through its negating itself. Instead they imagine a linear and absolute opposition between hero and dragon, *coniunctio* being replaced by *disiunctio*. They confuse the soul-internal, image-internal, and thus thoroughly imaginal, thoroughly psychological killing of an element *in the image*—killing as one of the soul's deepest modes of *coniunctio*—with a literal killing (in the sense of annihilation) of the literal imagination itself, i.e., the imagination outside the image. It is the logic of Baron Münchhausen who was able to pull himself out of a bog by his own hair.[17]

---

[17] Interestingly enough, Münchhausen's remarkable feat (which, although formal-logically an impossibility, nevertheless and *ipso facto* confirms a thinking in terms of formal logic) is the reverse of that logic by which the soul moves. The soul progresses precisely by its absolute-negatively interiorizing itself deeper into itself, for example, by its "killing itself into being" (as in the case of sacrificial slaughter) or by "nature's conquering nature," "imagination's killing the imagination" (as in the case of "alchemical" progress in the direction of higher degrees of distillation). Not superseding itself by getting out of the initial *massa confusa* status ("the bog") and leaving it behind and below, but self-sublation, self-overcoming by getting deeper, and going under, into the *massa confusa*: *deepening* itself into *higher* levels or statuses of differentiation and sublimation—through self-negation and self-application.

CHAPTER NINETEEN

Psychologie Larmoyante:
Glen Slater, For Example.
On Psychology's Failure to Face the Modern World

In his interesting paper "Numb,"[1] Glen Slater compiles an impressive number of significant observations about fundamental changes in society that recently have taken place in Western culture at large and that can all be subsumed under the single idea of a "general numbing of the psyche." "The sense of psyche *as psyche* is becoming unconscious." Some of the phenomena he discusses include the following features that I will merely hint at by citing a few key-notions:

- Symptoms are often no longer felt as symptoms; they "have not been conquered, they have been assimilated—blended into normality." "[T]he capacity to actually feel what is wrong is fast eroding."
- "Hollywood-style outing of psychopathologies, the ubiquitous psychobabble, and the acculturation of defense mechanisms…"
- "Epidemic levels of depression and anxiety are read neither as calls for inner exploration, nor as indications of wayward

---

[1] Glen Slater, "Numb," in: Stanton Marlan (ed.), *Archetypal Psychologies: Reflections in Honor of James Hillman*, New Orleans (Spring Journal Books) 2008, pp. 351–367.

lifestyles, nor as comment on the soulless contours of the world at large."
- "[D]issociation is present today as a more pervasive means of managing incompatible emotions and perceptions."
- The fast growing online diversion of "Second Life" shows that "When actual life is unpalatable, an alternate one is a mouse-click away."
- A general loss of body, emotion, eros.
- Psychotropic drugs are widely used to create states of artificial happiness.
- "The 'googled' information that appears alongside a vast array of links and *associated* material is mostly *dissociated* from author, lineage, place, and genre."

Slater's description of these phenomena and the overall picture that emerges from his compilation and discussion, the picture of a major development in stark opposition to the situation that early 20th century psychologists were confronted with, are accurate. His conclusion concerning the effect of these phenomena is: "[P]sychology proper ceases to exist." What he means becomes clear when we consider that earlier in his paper he had given very clear expression to the contrast between the direction that this new development is taking, on the one hand, and what the role of psychopathology and neurosis used to be during what we might call the good old days of depth psychology, on the other hand, by saying about neurosis: "Having once appeared to lead us into a new realm of psychic understanding, that harbinger of complex and creative lives we call 'neurosis' now appears to have headed back underground." The new processes Slater describes do not only seem to undo the whole work of 20th century psychology and psychologists, but also the work of the psyche itself which during that century, as Slater sees it, created neuroses precisely as our psychopomp, our leader into a new realm of psychic understanding and possibly even into creative lives.

I have no difficulty with "the case" Slater presents nor with his view that it is pathological. But I nevertheless do have difficulties with his stance as a whole.

PSYCHOLOGIE LARMOYANTE

THE PSYCHOTHERAPEUTIC STANCE TOWARDS PRESENTING COMPLAINTS

If the material that he spreads out before us is the general cultural pathology of the beginning 21st century (or one aspect of it), then what Slater provides is like the "presenting complaint" of society as a transpersonal patient. For a psychologist or psychotherapist, to be confronted with a patient's presenting complaint is nothing unusual, and the fact that this complaint is about things that are thoroughly pathological and wrong, sad and possibly destructive, sometimes horrid, is nothing shocking for him, but rather his daily bread. In fact, what else could he expect when meeting a new patient? What enables him to be a therapist in the first place is precisely that all this pathological material does not give him the jitters. Rather, he is able to take it in his stride, to face it squarely, to hold his place vis-à-vis, and—most important—to view it, alchemically speaking, as the prime matter to be worked with. The first task of the therapist is to become the unshaken, unperturbed holding vessel for the patient's pathology.

Jung once wrote in a letter, "As a medical psychologist I do not merely assume, but I am thoroughly convinced, that *nil humanum a me alienum esse* is even my duty."[2] A crucial insight. It seems to me, however, to be demanding a bit much that "*nothing* human is alien to me." It is, I think, always possible to become confronted with totally unexpected turns of events, with unplumbed depths of the human psyche, and with human atrocities that one has not been prepared for and did not imagine to be possible. So I would want to reformulate Jung's statement a bit: It is, yes, my duty as psychologist even in those cases where I at first was deeply disturbed by the content of the "presenting complaint" to at least try as soon as possible to *acquire* for myself that frame of mind towards the disturbing pathology that Jung expressed with his Latin quotation. It is my duty because it is the *sine qua non* for any therapeutic work with this patient. My patient is entitled to expect from me a genuine firm composure vis-à-vis the horrid aspects of his story. *Gelassenheit.* I must be able to honestly *allow* his story *to be* the way it is, without wishing it away or to be otherwise. We might even say that I must, in some way, embrace it, to harbor it within myself. Despite its possibly horrid and inhuman appearance,

---

[2] Letters 2, p. 589, to Read, 2. Sep. 1960.

504   *THE SOUL ALWAYS THINKS*

and this means despite the fact that for me as the empirical I (the
human-all-too-human person and ordinary citizen) that I am, it may
indeed be deeply upsetting or even frightening—nevertheless as
therapist, as "the *vicarius animae* on earth" (the representative of
the soul standpoint in real life) I must accept it as *not*-alien and
thus, with methodical awareness, give it its own place within the
sphere of what is *humanum* and soulful. Each new pathology is a
challenge and invitation to me to conquer for myself the soul
standpoint once again by overcoming in myself the "ego," the
habitual everyday or man-on-the-street point of view, and so also my
fear of or disgust for the abnormal.

CONDEMNATION INSTEAD OF PSYCHOLOGICAL EXPLANATION

For Slater, however, the presenting complaint is only cause for
lamentation. His whole paper boils down to a sob-story about how
bad the development is that he sees. The world is getting worse! How
terrible! We are moved to tears. The story of his "patient" scares the
hell out of Slater. The content of his observations ("a general numbing
of the psyche") leaves *him* numb with aversion. Like an innocent young
nurse-in-training who has to witness her first surgery, Slater faints at
the sight of the presenting complaint. He does not hold his place vis-
à-vis the phenomena, but allows himself to be driven into downright
apocalyptic fears: what is happening in his eyes amounts to the end
of the world of psychology ("psychology proper ceases to exist") and
thus probably also to the end of soul as such. A psychological Ragnarök,
the twilight of the soul.

But his assessment "psychology proper ceases to exist" is in reality
only a self-fulfilling prophecy. It merely describes what is happening
in his own paper. He nicely reports the facts, but what one is entitled
to expect from a *psychological* paper after this report, namely an in-
depth psychological analysis of the facts, is missing. He simply does
not get started on the psychology of the matter. What would turn his
paper into a psychological one is omitted. It is as if a student of
literature felt it completely sufficient to retell the story of a novel
without discussing it, or as if an art historian described a painting
without making any attempt at interpreting it, or as if a
psychotherapist sent his patient home after hearing his story. Yes,

PSYCHOLOGIE LARMOYANTE

psychology proper ceases to exist—but only because no effort has been made to begin with it. Psychology is not the dishing out of food, but the digestion of it, the digestion of this particular dish in front of me. Putrefactio, fermentatio, distillatio, sublimatio...

Psychology is not an abstractly existing reality that could on account of adverse circumstances cease to exist. No, just as music needs to be played to exist, i.e., *to come into existence*, and just as it lasts for as long as it is played, you need to *do* psychology if it is supposed to exist. Psychology has to be made. And its making is always a just-in-time, on-the-spot production, each time afresh and from scratch, each time a movement all the way from conventional everyday perception to the soul perspective (continually higher degrees of depth of this perspective). And it must be made in such a way that this production is not so much our doing; it is much rather the work of the material at hand to be psychologically comprehended. It is not we who make the presenting complaint psychological, it makes us psychological, provided, of course, that we truly devote ourselves to it.[3] It (or *this* dream or whatever else is our prime matter here and now) is the true agent, our psychopomp, our teacher. And it is the element or the catalyst through which and the circumference within which alone we can work ourselves up from the level of conventional thinking to that of psychological awareness. Psychology does not come about *in abstracto* and once and for all. It is not, in the way the sciences imagine themselves, the slow construction through many hands of an edifice, nor a ready-made tool that would merely need to be applied each time anew. Psychology is always the unity of tool-making and working with the tool, in such a self-contradictory way that the working with the tool is itself the first-time making of it. *L'appétit vient en mangeant.*

Instead of a psychological digestion of what is presented to us, all that we get in Slater's piece is something in the order of "cultural criticism," a rejection or condemnation of what he sees, in other words, something that could just as well have been written by a journalist or a sociologist. Jung once cited the joke about a person who comes home from church service and, when asked what the minister preached about,

---

[3] The process is dialectical, uroboric. Our devotion to it gives the material the chance to make us psychological so that we in turn can see the soul in it. Our strictly passive receptivity requires our concentrated involvement. And our involvement has to be nothing else but the intensive willingness *to be* (become) informed by the matter at hand. It must not be *our* wish to accomplish the understanding of it.

said, "about sin." And when the first question was followed up by "well, what did he say about it?," his answer was, "he was against it." This is exactly the spirit in which Slater approaches his "patient's" presenting complaint: he is against it. To the extent that he thinks that his paper is a contribution to psychology, he has succumbed to the fallacy of the (as I call it) *damnatio explanandi*, the condemnation of that which actually would have to be "explained"—alchemically cooked, psychologically interpreted, made sense of, mined for insight. Condemnation takes the place of psychological discussion, a negative affect takes the place of comprehension. All thinking and effort go in the direction of defensive measures.

THE FIGHT AGAINST THE NEW PROPHETS IN THE NAME OF THE OLD PROPHETS

Before I comment on those defensive measures, let me return to a sentence I already quoted above. "Having once appeared to lead us into a new realm of psychic understanding, that harbinger of complex and creative lives we call 'neurosis' now appears to have headed back underground." Yes, once upon a time, during the late 19th and at the beginning of the 20th centuries, it was classical neurosis that was a harbinger of the newly arising depth psychology. But why was classical neurosis able in the first place to "lead us into a new realm of psychic understanding"? Only because the early psychologists-to-be refused to approach it with the everyday, man-of-the-street condemnation of neurosis as pathological, abnormal, disgusting and to supply common-sensical rationalistic admonitions of the "pull yourself together" type. Instead, they accepted it as a harbinger, as their guide to a new understanding. For them, neurotic pathology was interesting, even fascinating. They were driven by a compelling intellectual curiosity to dwell with and devote themselves to it instead of wanting to immediately return to normality. They wanted to solve the puzzle it presented to them, to penetrate into the pathology's own depth. They did by no means deny or conceal that it was pathological, sick, wrong. And of course they did not condone it. But they wanted to mine the "symptom," this sick phenomenon, for insight, much as the alchemists turned to dung to try to make gold of it and turned to what was *in via ejectum* in order to learn to see precisely in it the *lapis philosophorum*.

PSYCHOLOGIE LARMOYANTE

The move on the object side from dung to gold, or from what has been cast away as *vilis* and perverse to the *lapis*, is on the side of the subject parallel to the move I mentioned above, the move from the conventional everyday perspective ("the ego") to the standpoint of soul. In fact, maybe they are not two moves at all, but only one and the same move seen from two different sides.

We know from the Old Testament stories how time and again a new prophet was condemned by his contemporaries precisely in the name of the prophets of previous times, ironically prophets who during their own lifetime had also been condemned by their own contemporaries. A prevention of something (allegedly) in the name of that very something. Allegedly, because a prophecy that happened way back in the past is no longer a prophecy for us. A prophecy is only what it is supposed to be if it is the soothsaying about the yet unborn future, or unknown inner truth, of this our own present. By the same token, a former harbinger of something that meanwhile has become old hat is no longer a harbinger.

The same logic I illustrated by this brief reference to the fate of prophets we see repeated in an altogether different context in Slater. The good old neuroses of former times that had been condemned by the mainstream thinking of the day are for him the hallowed leaders into new realms of understanding, the true, time-honored prophets of the past. But present-day pathology is a false prophet to be cast out, or rather no prophet, no harbinger at all, just a mistake, a fundamental aberration from what the old prophets brought us; not a guide into new realms of insight, but a killer of all possible insight, indeed of psychology as such.

THE PARADIGM OF THE COMING GUEST

In stark contrast to this disparagement and rejection of a new doubtlessly "pathological" development we still find in old man Jung the same intellectual curiosity that distinguished the early pioneers of true psychological research, a curiosity about what another truly "pathological" new development that he described may bring and contain.

> "We have no dominants any more, they are in the future. Our values are shifting, everything loses its certainty, even *sanctissima*

508   *THE SOUL ALWAYS THINKS*

> *causalitas* has descended from the throne of the axioma and has become a mere field of probability. Who is the awe-inspiring guest who knocks at our door portentously? Fear precedes him, showing that ultimate values already flow towards him. Our hitherto believed values decay accordingly and our only certainty is that the new world will be something different from what we were used to."[4]

No "Looking Backwards." Yes, there are very sad losses, there is decay, and this amounts to a truly fearful situation for Jung, too. Nonetheless, he does not want to cling to "what we were used to." He does not side with the old prophets. Judging from the tone of this quotation as well as from what we know about his general attitude from other texts, we may assume that as far as his personal feelings were concerned the traditional forms of a "symbolic life" would have been much more to his own liking. But Jung knew that what he liked, and whether he liked or not what he sensed was coming, was psychologically irrelevant.[5] He knew he had to distinguish himself from his subjective feelings and needs in order to be open to the objective psyche. And so we see him here relentlessly oriented towards the unknown future,

---

[4] *Letters 2*, p. 590, to Read, 2. Sep. 1960.

[5] An important aspect of the reason for Jung's reaction is his general view of the relation between the empirical ego-personality and the objective soul. This view comes out succinctly in the inscription he placed over the entrance to his Küsnacht house: *vocatus atque non vocatus deus aderit*. In matters of the soul process it does not matter very much whether we agree or not. It will happen anyway. In the Füssen *Dance of Death* depiction (Jacob Hiebeler, 1602, Anna Chapel, St. Mang, Füssen, Germany) we read, "*Sagt Ja, sagt Nein, getanzt muß sein*" (Say yes, say no, but dance you must). However, depending on whether the guest comes *vocatus* or whether he comes *non vocatus* there is a great difference in *how* his arrival will happen, that is to say, what it will mean for us and how it will affect us. Seneca wrote, and Jung would certainly have agreed: *Ducunt volentem fata, nolentem trahunt*, "If you are willing, fate will guide you, if you are not, it will drag you" (*Epistulae morales*, 107,11). Similarly, Thomas Mann said (in *Joseph and his Brothers*), "If you can do it, you will do it. If you can not, it will be done to you." That's the difference. And it makes all the difference *for us*, the difference between "suffering blind victim" and "comprehending and feeling human being." But it makes also an essential difference for the arriving new reality. If we resist, this reality will be mechanical and soulless. If we see the guest in it, *our* guest, indeed our deepest self, it can appear in redeemed form. Jung in our passage speaks of the knocking of a guest at our door. This sounds as if this guest politely asked whether we want to permit him to enter or not. This should, however, not be misunderstood as implying that if we don't invite the guest in he will turn around and go away again. No. The guest is not just anybody on the same level with us, just another human being, and he is not totally other. He is the objective soul, the soul of the real, and as such *our own* deepest *truth*. In *him* we find our truth (Jung might have said: our self). This is what makes this guest on principle inescapable. "*Sagt Ja, sagt Nein, getanzt muß sein.*"

PSYCHOLOGIE LARMOYANTE

just as in his early days he had approached neurosis from a final-prospective point of view instead of from a causal-reductive one. He views the visible "pathology" as the already audible knocking of an unknown guest at our door and as the already present harbinger of an as yet unimaginable "new world." The "ego" only sees the surface, the almost unbearable loss and "pathological" decay, but the *vicarius animae* in Jung already senses the guest who announces his future arrival through this very pathology as its harbinger.

In other words, despite the sacrifice it meant for him concerning his subjective emotional-ideological needs and cherished values, Jung showed *respect* for what was coming. He respected the soul dignity of the upheaval envisioned by him. More than that. By speaking of the "guest" he shows that there is in him a hospitable attitude towards him. In fact, by saying "guest" Jung has *logically* already let him in, although literally he is still in front of our door. What is coming is not viewed as enemy, senseless, and utterly alien, totally unrelated. Although as yet unknown, it is nevertheless a priori connected to us. There is an intrinsic bond between what is coming and us. It belongs. It has a right to come. It is well possible that when he chose the word guest Jung had, as a foil and warning, dimly in the back of his mind the Biblical "He came unto his own, and his own received him not" (John 1:11). The coming of the guest means the advent of our (new) Truth.[6]

(The term "guest" is of course not a metaphoric way to refer to the new world itself with all its individual positive-factual features.[7] Rather, this image refers to the soul *of* and *in* the new reality,

---

[6] One could think that the advent of the guest implies fun and joy and that the arrival of our Truth would be harmless. After all, it is our own Truth. But on the contrary, the advent of our own Truth is always a terribly upsetting event, the guest is "awe-inspiring," the signs of his coming are "portentous," and "fear precedes him." The encounter with our Truth is nothing for sissies.

[7] The word *vocatus* in the *vocatus atque non vocatus* adage therefore does not mean that we would have to *wish for* and try our best to *promote* the new world of technology and the anaesthetized mind or any other positive-factual features of this development. All it means is to see "the guest" *in* the technological development and respect him as such. For this reason, *vocatus* may in our context be too strong and misleading. Seneca's *volens* is better, but still does not hit the mark. It is not really a question of willingness either, which refers too much to an ego volition. Rather, the point is seeing through to and comprehending in what is coming the coming new form of the *soul* or our Truth, and to be reached and touched by it in one's mind and heart. All the soul, the coming guest, our deepest truth, needs is to have a real echo, a resonance in ourselves, to be seen, acknowledged, and appreciated for what it is.

510 THE SOUL ALWAYS THINKS

alchemically speaking to the spirit Mercurius in it, in other words, to its inner logic or syntax.)

FEELING AS BRIDGE TO THE SOUL

The notion of a coming guest is not an abstract scientific concept, but expresses a felt relationship reverberating with deep and very old ethical, indeed religious values (just think of Zeus Xenios as the god of hospitality, but also of the cited statement from John 1:11). His use of this term shows that Jung was able to *feel* in a psychological, objective sense (to feel the real that he saw, or feel into the real), and that he made use of his potential to feel. Feeling in the psychological sense is a *rational* function (Jung), a *"judgment* of taste" (Kant), and thus must not be confused with our *having* feelings, with our emotions, with sentimentality, with our subjective likings or antipathies, all of which are merely *psychic events* and not psychological. Without feeling, the soul cannot be apperceived. Feeling in this sense is what has the power to connect modern consciousness with the soul-in-the-real across the gap of our fundamental alienation from it. The capacity to feel is the bridge across the psychological difference, the bridge also across and beyond our subjective positive or negative feelings, so that we may become open to the heart of what *is*.[8] It is not the dream that is the *via regia* to the soul, because dream material is only a psychic fact or event and per se not yet psychological. Dream texts can be viewed very soullessly. Psychologically, dreams as such do not deserve any privileging. No, the *via regia* to soul and the sine qua non of a psychological perception of things (of *making* soul when faced with a

---

[8] In his typology, Jung distinguished the thinking function and the feeling function as rational functions from sensation and intuition as irrational because the latter supply consciousness with new data, whereas the former functions only *formally* process or evaluate already available data, each in their own different ways. My term feeling is different. I call it "rational" mainly to ward off any sense of emotion or sentiment, and for me it is not a merely processing or evaluating function (e.g. according to the "good-bad, pleasant-unpleasant, etc." categories which are always measured from the ego point of view), but it also makes something new accessible and, as in this way providing us with new "input," has thus a kind of "irrational" aspect, too. However, this new material is not, horizontally, new empirical data as in the case of the sensation and intuition functions, not "what the eyes can see," but vertically a new *dimension* ("what opens the eyes"), the depth dimension of what has already been made available by sensation or intuition. The philistine and the art lover may see the same painting. But his capability to feel makes accessible to the art lover something in that painting seen by both that for the philistine simply does not exist.

PSYCHOLOGIE LARMOYANTE

given dream text, pathology, symbol, or situation) is feeling as a "judgment of taste." In the case of the present passage about "the coming guest," it was his power to feel that enabled Jung to sense the soul and *our own* Other in the developments in question even *despite* his personal aversion to them.

Why does feeling have the capability of performing the miracle of allowing one to sense or intuit the *lapis* in what, after all, appears in *exilis* (uncomely) and utterly *vilis* (cheap), if not disgusting and pathological shape? The miracle of on this, our side, the psychic side, opening our eyes to the psychological, to the soul's life, to the inner truth contained in what is yonder, out there, e.g., to what is in a particular development of our civilization, or in a given dream text, and hidden under its external, abstract, positive-factual, maybe even nonsensical form? Why is feeling able to open a first access for empirical consciousness to what *ipso facto*, and only *ipso facto*, turns into a prime matter, that is, into the stuff that psychological *thought* can then begin to work with, begin to absolute-negatively interiorize into itself?

The reason for feeling having the power to be the door-opener to soul is that feeling, the type of feeling I have been talking about, is that mode *in* the empirical I in which the I with its initial egoic survival[9] interests has gone under, has learned to be silent—has *died* as "the ego." Feeling is the soul's ambassador, ally, advocate, "fifth column" in the empirical person, or, as I put it above, the *vicarius animae*. And as such it is the *copula*, the *ligamentum* or *vinculum* in the sense of alchemy, between empirical man ("I") and the soul (in our context especially the *opus magnum*) as well as between positive-factual reality and the Mercurial spirit "imprisoned" in that reality.

Among the coexisting phenomena in the world there are many that externally, as far as their phenomenal appearance or their "semantics" are concerned, may look pretty much alike. In such a case we need a cultivated capability to feel, feel deeply, in order to separate the wheat from the chaff, that is to say, to differentiate what is, in a psychological sense, "great" from what is "petty,"[10] what is an authentic expression of soul (what really has soul depth, soul dignity; what really is our Truth) from what, despite a possible content-wise similarity, is

---

[9] Survival in the widest sense, including the interest in heightening and beautifying life.

[10] The distinction between the great and the petty occurs in *CW* 10 § 367.

512   *THE SOUL ALWAYS THINKS*

only a human, all-too-human production. A description of what one sees does not help. It is like in literary or art criticism. A truly great work on the one hand and some other maybe popular, but nevertheless cheap or shallow work on the other hand may have a very similar content and message, but the fundamentally different *ranks* of the two works cannot be discerned on that basis. You need (objective) feeling—the power of aesthetic judgment, a well-differentiated judgment of taste.

Feeling is what connects us to the soul, it is what bridges the gap across the psychological difference, but as a *judgment*, the judgment of taste, it only bridges this gap by being an act of sundering, *separatio*, holding apart, namely *by first establishing* this psychological difference that it bridges, the difference between "petty" and "great" phenomena or (within one and the same phenomenon) between "the petty" and "the great" in it, that is, between the phenomenon's empirical, positive-factual foreground and its soul-depth (the "hinterland of the soul," as Jung put it metaphorically). In feeling, bridging and sundering are equiprimordial, two sides of one and the same. Conversely, this lets us see that the psychological difference has its origin in an act of feeling.

Jung's appreciation of the coming guest (who is seen by him as being inherent in a development that he personally certainly did not welcome) is not utopian thinking. Utopias present us with pictures of a better world. They want to anticipate the future. Jung has no picture to offer. Nor does he come with a program. He comes empty-handed. He insists precisely on the future's being fundamentally unforeseeable. It cannot be anticipated. We will have to wait and see. And the question whether it will be good or bad for us is neither here nor there. We can only try to get—perhaps—a little more ready to receive it.

THE COUNTER-PARADIGM: ABERRATION, NOT GUEST

In contrast to what we learned from Jung's reaction to the new developments, and here I come to the defensive direction of his piece, Slater is, in the psychological field, still completely in the spell of the Rousseauan impulse that in different ways so powerfully determined so much of the thinking and feeling of the last two centuries. Without using these exact terms, he views the new reality described by him as an aberration, alienation from our true nature, as a corruption, a kind

PSYCHOLOGIE LARMOYANTE

of Fall. Slater's thinking is motivated by an unspoken wish to hold on to or rather, since he realizes that it's already too late for that, to *return* to "what we were used to" and to prevent the emergence of a new world. He is a psychological reactionary. His psychological stance amounts to an acting out of his *Unbehagen in der Kultur* (his "Discomfort with Civilization,"[11] officially translated as *Civilization and Its Discontents*). He speaks of today's "wayward lifestyles," of "the soulless contours of the world at large," and laments that people do no longer feel "what is wrong." His reaction to the developments observed stays on the level of the subjective psyche ("the ego") and as such takes the form of point-blank rejection. He does not give the pathology of numbing that he detects any chance. He refuses to listen to it and to be taught by it about ourselves, our own truth, our soul.

No guest. Totally unconnected. No *ligamentum*. Absolutely dissociated. Not our own. Only something utterly alien and wrong. Slater describes the underlying process of numbing as dissociation, a dissociation that "seems to grow out of the contemporary scene." "This style of dissociation has become cultural, normative..." This is well observed. But he does not see the dissociation already at work in his own seeing, his own approach to the pathology that he sees himself faced with.

The "guest" is the paradox of newcomer, truly other, unknown on the one hand *and* "our own" on the other hand. His arrival implies an encounter, a meeting. As the opposition between truly other and "our own," "the guest" is in itself the psychological difference. The counter-idea of an aberration or corruption is also paradoxical, but on both counts the reverse of the first-mentioned paradox.

- Whereas the "coming guest" implies an enrichment, the encounter with something truly new, the pathology described by Slater is, as aberration, only the corruption of, or our own deviation from, the old healthy state. This is why I said that his reaction stays on the level of the subjective psyche. He thinks in terms of an "internal" change (a decline) of one and the same. The ego remains self-contained,

---

[11] This is the translation originally suggested by Freud himself. It comes closer to what is meant.

514   *THE SOUL ALWAYS THINKS*

undisturbed. No advent. No otherness. No encounter. No unknown future (*Zukunft*, "that which comes to us").

- However, whereas the "guest" is always already (at least implicitly) viewed as "our own," that which is seen as our aberration must precisely be *disowned*, rejected, cast out. It is *not* our Truth, but our untruth, a fundamentally false state.

Since Slater does not relate to what he becomes aware of through *feeling* it, feeling does not connect him to the soul in the real. This in turn makes it impossible for him to show any respect to what is happening as to an expression of the movement of the objective soul. Other than for Jung who said about neurosis "We do not cure it—it cures us,"[12] it is for him the pathology that needs to be cured: he wants to "undo numbing" (that is to say, the very harbinger of a fundamental change), he wants to "counter the anaesthetized mind," thereby paradoxically showing how anaesthetized his own feeling is: merely egoic. He wants to "put people squarely back in their neurosis." In other words he says, as it were: Gimme that old-time neurosis, it's good enough for me. After having cited a passage from Hillman about the significance of "re-entering Dionysian consciousness" (re-entering? A Dionysian consciousness in the year 2008?) he states, "In turning the tide of dissociation we could do no better than go back to these reflections..." Yes, to "go back" is what he wants.

Unless, as we can say with Jung, we "hit upon the saving delusion that *this* wisdom is good and *that* is bad," i.e., "the artificial sundering of true and false wisdom,"[13] we are stuck with and have to learn to live with the pathology as well as with the consciousness that *is*. We have no choice, that is, no choice between a nice classical neurosis or the new pathology of an "anaesthetized mind" as described in Slater's paper; no choice between a Dionysian consciousness or modern consciousness. In the context of the problematic presented in this paper, it would be an irresponsible manipulation to try "to put people [those people who are beyond that stage] squarely back in their neurosis, to help them suffer honestly..."[14] Obviously the soul's point

---

[12] *CW* 10 § 361 (in the German original, the whole sentence is in italics).
[13] *CW* 9i § 31, transl. modified. Unlike the "sundering" through the judgment of taste, this sundering is "artificial" because it is based on "the ego's" arbitrary preferences.
[14] By this I do not wish to imply that in the consulting room, when faced with a patient, a real human being, it might not be appropriate to "put him back in his neurosis."

PSYCHOLOGIE LARMOYANTE

is no longer this honest suffering on the part of the individual. The soul is somewhere else and has other needs. By the same token, it does not want today's "[e]pidemic levels of depression and anxiety" any more to be read "as calls for inner exploration." The soul is, so it seems, beyond that interest in "the inner" ("the ego's" or *our* inner). Could it not be possible that we are witnessing the beginning of its finally trying to go through with the notion of an *objective* psyche?

Maybe it is possible today to *simulate* a Dionysian consciousness, I don't know, but this would be phoney, worse than today building houses in the neo-Gothic style. It is an ego illusion that we could exchange our styles of consciousness like we change our garments. Our only real choice is between a superficial perception from outside of what happens to *be* and a perception of the same from the soul standpoint. And the question is totally useless whether a Dionysian consciousness would perhaps be better than, for example, a monotheistic or a technological one—because in any case we have to work with what we've got.

THE EGO'S CLAIM TO SOVEREIGNTY AS DEFINER OF SOUL

The *point* of a reactionary response to what one sees is happening is to deny and prevent change, change as such. In psychology it is an attack on the movement of the soul, or rather on the soul *as movement*, as logical *life*. Change in a psychological sense does not simply mean that this or that changes, that there are new events, that day turns into night and night into day, that a child is born, somebody dies, that a war arises, that old enemy nations make peace, that horse-drawn carriages are replaced by automobiles, or that an earthquake destroys a city. These are semantic changes within the same old definition or syntax of the world. Psychological change applies to the change

---

In the consulting room we are concerned with people, persons, who may have to learn to distinguish and emancipate themselves from the great cultural development, that is, from the soul, which may have absorbed them into itself so that they became its will-less exponents. *They* may indeed have to learn again that they are "*only* that!," merely human beings with their own personal human needs and that they are merely surrounded by and exposed to the great changes in the soul's life. But here we are not in the consulting room. We are in psychology. As such we are not concerned with people, with those members of society who were weak enough to become swept by the tides of the soul's logical life. In Slater's paper our concern is with the astounding soul phenomena of numbing themselves.

of the *definitions* of the same old things that continue to exist, but that on account of that new definition are really something totally new. A real change in a more concretistic sense happened, for example, during the French Revolution: the redefinition of the State from monarchy to republic.

But as indicated, psychological change refers in particular to the definition of the world, indeed, the definition of the very notion of soul. This is what Jung was referring to in the quoted passage about the awe-inspiring guest. The guest is the new definition of the soul and of the world. Our old values, our old ideas, conceptions, expectations about what soul is and how the world is have had their day. The "ultimate values already flow towards him [the guest]," i.e., towards the new still unknown definition of the world and of the soul.

Similarly when 2,000 years ago another fundamental redefinition of what soul and world are announced itself, for example, in the words, "Therefore if any man be in Christ, he is a new creature: old things are passed away; behold, all things are become new" (2 Cor. 5:17), this epochal psychological change did not refer to the things *in* the world. The Roman Empire, the social structure with its slaves, the trees, rivers, mountains and the people empirically all remained what they had been before. What the "new heaven" and "new earth" (Rev. 21:1) imply is a completely altered *logical constitution* of the same old world, a fundamentally new determination of the soul of the real.[15]

The psychological reactionary finds the idea intolerable that the soul is alive, that from time to time it redefines itself, re-invents itself and confronts us at such times with new definitions of itself that require the adaptation of our consciousness to them. The reactionary wants to freeze the sense of soul in a single definition, the one definition that he cherishes and has become accustomed to and that is (1) developed in reaction to, or better: as counterpoint to, the spirit of the present age and (2) uses ready-made props from the property room of former times (such as a "Dionysian consciousness," or soul as "anima," as "image," as "polytheistic"). This definition has to be eternal. It must have been, so this view thinks, the one and only definition of soul

---

[15] And of course, when the logical constitution of the soul or the world changed, it is very likely that, as a consequence, in the course of time concrete empirical aspects of the real will also change, such as the societal institutions, the laws, people's views and behavior...

PSYCHOLOGIE LARMOYANTE

already prevailing in prehistoric ages and it must still be valid in all the millennia to come.

This means nothing less than that "the ego" demands to have the peculiar right to provide the definition of soul (the *Deutungshoheit*). The soul in its definition is fixed, static. We are by no means the recipients and experiencing "victims" of this definition. We do not time and again have to see and to allow ourselves to be taught by the actual ongoing development and the actually emerging pathologies about how the soul wants to define itself in each new age. We do not have to—probably painfully—adapt to this new definition in the logical form of our consciousness. Rather, it is we who know, we who dictate what soul means. And if the actual soul process possesses the impertinence not to comply with our definition of it, if it, for example, dares to move into cyberspace and produces all the symptoms of numbing described by Slater, we simply call what it produced soulless, *not*-soul. It is not the emergence of a totally unexpected new world. Rather, we prefer to think that the real problem is that "the world is getting *worse*." "The painfully obvious difference," Jung tells us as if already commenting on and ironizing such moves, "seems like a contravention of the natural order, like a shocking mistake that must be remedied as speedily as possible, or a misdemeanor that calls for condign punishment."[16] How could it be soul? The soul would never do what is contrary to our ideas of it!

Here another passage comes to mind from the letter of Jung's that I already quoted twice. "*We* decide, as if we knew. We only know what we know, but there is plenty more of which we might know if only we could give up insisting upon what we do know."[17]

THE FEAR OF HISTORY

Why must the possibility at all cost be prevented that soul escapes our *Deutungshoheit*, that it can be seen as having a life of its own, its own history? The static, fundamentally ahistorical definition of the soul has to fulfill the function of stabilizing the habitual logical *form* of consciousness. *Within* this habitual form of consciousness, that is, on the semantic level, the level of *contents* of consciousness, new ideas

---

[16] *CW* 10 § 277.
[17] *Letters 2*, p. 591, to Read, 2. Sep. 1960.

are allowed, even all sorts of (by mainstream standards) deviant, revolutionary positions may be entertained, such as the position of a polytheistic, Dionysian, underworldly imagining—as long as the form of consciousness is not called into question. This is the problem not only of Slater's paper, but of archetypal, imaginal psychology at large. The reactionary fight, which in the last analysis is a fight against the intrusion of the idea of change and process into the very *notion* of soul, serves the purpose of protecting consciousness from itself having to undergo adaptation, and that always also means self-negation, self-overcoming, redefinition, rather than merely exchanging some of its accustomed ideas for other ones. The freezing of the single definition of soul is at the same time the freezing of consciousness—and thus also of psychology itself—in the definition that one prefers. But adaptation is not only a task for the individual with respect to the changes in the soul's life during his personal life span, but also the task of psychology itself with respect to the great epochal changes. As Slater rightly says, without realizing that this applies to his own position, "The mind closes when it can no longer imagine past its own self-absorption and engage the ideas that make an epoch."

Despite all the talk in psychology about "the objective soul" and "the autonomous psyche"—as long as "the ego" secretly insists on the right to define soul and in this way to screen psychology itself from the changes in the soul's life, the soul is in reality still *subjective soul.* It has not been released into its objectivity and autonomy. Logically, "the ego" has not let go of it. The soul is only truly objective and autonomous when the subject (be it the individual person or psychology itself) has to empirically (i.e., always *a posteriori*), slowly and perhaps painfully, find out how the soul defines itself now, this time. Learning from experience. From "the guest." Psychology, if it wants to be one of the objective soul, must not feel to be in possession of the definition of soul and approach phenomena with a given definition in the back of its mind. It always has to start out from the position of *not* knowing what soul is.

Now we know why Slater's paper gave us his compilation of the symptoms without in any way beginning to go into their psychology. To look at them *psychologically* would have been like opening (imaginal or "anima-only") psychology's Pandora's box. What would have

PSYCHOLOGIE LARMOYANTE

emerged from letting oneself in for them would have been the fundamental threat to the ego's sovereignty as definer of soul, thus also the threat to one's own view that there is only one single and eternally valid definition of soul, the threat to *psychology as an ideology*. And it would inevitably have forced psychology to open itself to the idea of a *history* of the soul and of soul *as* history, which would include the insight into the historical relativity and limitedness of present psychology's own definition of soul. God forbid! (Or should I say here, politically correct: Dionysus forbid?) Anathema be any *history* of the soul!

The price for this avoidance, however, is high. It is that the whole paper remains on the level of lamentations in the style of cultural criticism. Instead, through what it does it proves its own point that "psychology proper ceases to exist." The psychology of what is discussed is omitted. Such an exploration of the psychology would require the questions: "What does the soul want with this new pathology, with this numbing, with the production of the anaesthetized mind, with the dissociation from an 'honest suffering' of one's discomfort?[18] What is the telos of all this? What are these terrible pathological phenomena the first immediate, literalized, acted-out form of? What do these phenomena want to tell us, teach us?"

BACKWATER PSYCHOLOGY

But the paper stays throughout under the dominion of "the ego" and its interests. This has two aspects. First, all the details described about the new situation are only introduced for the purpose of creating

---

[18] Here we see again the *damnatio explanandi* at work. The word dissociation becomes a reproach in his text. And he thinks by calling what he sees "dissociation" his psychological work is finished, as if this were the answer to the problem. But this new phenomenon of dissociation, rightly observed by him, is in reality the question, not the answer. At the time when it was a matter of trying to understand hysterical neuroses, the notion of dissociation could be considered an answer. In his context, however, "dissociation" is by no means, as he suggests, the *unconscious "underlying process" behind* numbing, in which case it could qualify as explanation. "The anaesthetized mind," "numbing," and "dissociation" are simply synonyms. The dissociation he points to has now precisely taken the position of the symptom in need of being psychologically explained. This dissociation is the obvious behavior, has become phenomenal (that which shows itself). Slater himself describes it, in contrast to hysteria, as having "become cultural, normative." It is therefore the topic or problem that psychology is confronted with, not its analysis or interpretation.

a menacing wall from which consciousness can rebound into the pleasant fields of old-time psychology and psychopathology with their hollow promise of their being "rooted in emotions and the living life as destiny," of their making "the connection between mind and body," of their providing us with a pantheon of actual gods "within the connective tissue of the *mundus imaginalis*," and, of course, of their being a harbinger of "creative lives." At the point where psychology should begin, consciousness turns around and moves into backwaters. In other words, it avoids becoming psychology and turns into ideology. Psychology would begin on the other side of this wall, a wall, of course, that for it precisely does not exist at all because it does not, by refusing to proceed to the actual psychological work, build it up in the first place.

For this wall to be created, it was essential that the phenomena not be allowed to be presented as if they were like a book that needed to be opened and read. We could also say: they were not allowed to be seen as harbingers of the coming guest. The way they had to be presented, they were constricted to the status of flat facts, one-dimensional positivities, literal behavior. They were only allowed to be seen from outside, from the ego perspective that focuses on people and their observable behavior: on, as I say with *Kena Upanishad*, "what the eyes can see, not what opens the eyes." Because only then could they be simply rejected (provided they were pathological or horrid enough). But the topic of psychology is not the real *as* literal facts, the surface appearance of things, but the *soul* of the real.

Its conception of the symptoms as a wall (through rejecting them) shows this theoretical stance's wish to return to itself, to stay self-contained within itself. As such it is the logical exclusion of the possibility of any coming, the coming of a guest, of any psychological other (that as psychological is nevertheless "one's own" other). It is the prevention of the psychological difference. By contrast, true psychology's move "beyond the wall" (which for it, as pointed out, does not come into existence in the first place) is dialectical. Its own going forward is in itself the experience of some other coming towards it. Seen in the light of this insight, backwater psychology's return to itself can be understood as its wish to itself take over control of the

PSYCHOLOGIE LARMOYANTE

(unavoidable) "coming movement," to do the "coming" all by itself and to itself take the place of the other or guest. This is why it is pure ego-psychology (cf. Jung's "*We* know...").

The second aspect does not concern the material presented but the presenter. Construing the material as an insuperably horrid wall for consciousness to shrink back from relieves him from having to perform the indispensable task of anybody who wants to be a psychologist: the task vis-à-vis the presenting complaint or prime matter of overcoming himself as empirical I (overcoming "the ego" standpoint within himself), in order to slowly work himself up into the standpoint of soul using the very material at hand as his guide as well as ladder. He can stay identical with himself, continue to remain committed to the everyday point of view, which is and remains for all of us our inevitable starting-point in each new situation, but should for the psychologist be no more than a starting-point. The psychological difference does not have to come alive in him and as himself.

Since for Slater the psychological difference is not opened up, neither in himself nor on the objective side of the real, since for him the literal facts of the developments are all there is, he is of course right to be afraid of devoting himself to them. Devoting himself to them would in the case of a positivized view of reality be condoning, advancing these developments, becoming totally absorbed into them. This fear becomes clearer in an earlier paper of his on "Cyborgian Drift: Resistance is not Futile,"[19] in which he among other things reacts at the very end to my attempts at elaborating the psychology of the technological world, when he says that my move "beyond the imaginal" into thought "ultimately props open the door to a robotic existence." But to *think* technology does of course not mean to promote the trend "to unconsciously drift along and passively adapt to its [technology's] innovations." *Psychological* adaptation is not passive and not unconscious anyway, and it is precisely not *our* adaptation, in our behavior, to technology's *innovations*, not absorption into or inflation by the powerful trends of literal technology, but consciousness's adaptation, in its logical form, to the *soul* or logic or syntax of technology. Adaptation presupposes my clear distinction of myself

---

[19] Glen Slater, "Cyborgian Drift: Resistance is not Futile," in: *Spring 75, Psyche & Nature Part 1*, Fall 2006, pp. 171–195, here p. 190.

from the soul process. I do not act the soul out, but merely "get the message" it contains, the message that "the guest" brings. Adaptation is my *response* to it, not my being swallowed by it. I must hold my place vis-à-vis it. But since the psychological difference does not exist in Slater's scheme, he can probably not imagine what is meant by these differentiations. And perhaps they cannot be imagined at all. Because they have to be thought. For him the only alternative available seems to be: rejection or succumbing, defense or acting out. *Tertium non datur.*

But neither is psychological.

The cited title of this earlier paper makes it explicitly clear that his response to the "new world" is resistance—which sounds strange, indeed amazing, to a psychoanalytically trained ear. To be sure, he is right to warn in this paper against "obfuscating the difference between relating to an archetypal impulse and being swept by it." But what we see in his work is that, as much as he certainly does justice to the negative task of avoiding the mistake he warns of (the mistake of becoming swept by technology), he does not in any way realize the positive half of the job. He altogether refuses to *relate* to technology—to *feel* it, feel into it. By ignoring one half of the task, he, to be sure, does not obfuscate but rather totally eliminates the difference. He simply stays plain common-sensical, on this, the ego side of the psychological difference. Where Jung was able to see the approaching "guest," he only sees "viruses" that need to be combated by "antibodies." As we all know, antibodies do not exactly do what we mean by "relating." They neutralize or kill viruses. Slater does not want to *imagine* and see through technology, but wants to "derive from the imagination" insights that "function as [those] antibodies." He wants us to be on the lookout for "compensating images" and "the psyche's own counteracting response[s]"—an abuse of the imagination for alien, indeed, adverse purposes. He wants to force the imagination to serve his ego resistance, his immune system. It is supposed to provide him with weapons against the objective psyche, the *opus magnum*.

The childlike, "humanistic" conception of soul

I leave it to the reader to judge whether the particular resistance Slater has in mind is indeed "not futile," as he claims, or whether it is not perhaps much rather hopelessly helpless—innocent and childlike,

PSYCHOLOGIE LARMOYANTE

hardly scratching the surface of this overwhelmingly powerful phenomenon of technology, whose direction he wants to change.[20] I cite only one example from his "Cyborgian Drift": "Sometimes, when you live with technology for a time, you discover this kind of relationship—naming cars, coaxing computers into cooperation, caring for equipment in a hands-on way... Sensitivity to such things would keep technology within the bounds of human concern, and perhaps even open a soul space for engaging our gadgets." Maybe he should have added to his list spray-painting trains with our favorite colors or with our favorite slogans.

How touching, how very dear: to name our apparatuses, to coax them, to care for them—maybe even stroke them? A very loving, kind approach to technology. But wait a minute, not to technology. All that Slater is aware of and relates to in such a charming childlike way, is technical objects, things, the foreground of positively existing entities. *Technology*, by contrast, let alone the *soul* of technology, has not been sighted by him at all. He perceives the trees, but cannot apperceive the woods. The woods, of course, cannot be perceived and handled, because woods is a *concept* and therefore woods exist only for him who rises to the level of concepts, thoughts. But Slater stays, as we could say with Heidegger, on the level of the ontic and scotomizes the ontological, and, as we could say with Hillman, on the level of the literal while being blind to the imaginal. He operates on the level of the psychic, but ignores that of the psychological.

And this is also why when *he* speaks of "soul," all that he has in mind is *ego sentimentalism*,[21] not really soul at all, at best a child's idea

---

[20] That resistance is always *possible* is beyond doubt, especially for analysts. What is neurosis other than a person's resistance against his truth? But there are good reasons to doubt that it is meaningful, reasonable, and *not futile*. Jung at least felt that "To protest is ridiculous—how protest against an avalanche? It is better to look out." *CW* 10 § 1020.

[21] "Numbing is the absence of feeling response in the face of suffering, trauma, or general discontent." His word feeling is completely different from what I discussed in this paper under the same heading. One has to be aware of this equivocation of two fundamentally different things. He means what the ego feels (or should feel): human sentiments, "honest suffering," *affective* responses to what causes oneself "discomfort and cognitive dissonance," sympathy, compassion. He fraternizes with *our* discomfort, *our* pain! *They* get his "feeling," and this reveals how limited and enclosed his term feeling is within the precincts of the human, all-too-human. Humanly it is of course nice enough to show sympathy for our human pain and discontent. It only has nothing whatsoever to do with doing psychology.

of soul. "Soulful" in his way of thinking means simply the inverse of his *Unbehagen in der Kultur*. This is of course not exclusively his problem. It is widespread in Jungian psychology (and beyond).

Is it not very sad that psychology so often is devoid of feeling, of the "judgment of taste"? That it prefers fundamentally *abstract* sentimentality? The appearance of sentimentality is, as already Jung pointed out, the tell-tale sign that feeling is missing or at least poor. Sentimentality presupposes the lack of ("objective") feeling, because it is the ersatz for the latter. It naturally fills the vacuum that is left when feeling does not take place.

Slater's conception of soul comes from a very harmless, "nice" thinking, a thinking still contained, as we might say, in the anima's *hortus conclusus*. He projects his personal emotional and ideological needs and his cherished "humane" values, his preferences and wishful thinking onto the soul and confuses the former with the latter. The authorial I that conceived his papers has not distinguished itself from itself. It has not stepped out of the walled garden of the humane into the open, not out of the horizon of the human, all-too-human.[22] What *he*, Slater, calls "a soul space for engaging our gadgets" is in reality only an ego playroom.[23]

In this sense, his is a thoroughly *humanistic* notion of soul (in Hillman's derogatory sense of humanistic), inasmuch as all the approaches he suggests are merely intended to humor "the ego." They are the ego's self-gratification, a game it plays with *itself, only* with itself, high above the reality of the technical apparatuses. And therefore they do not really, as I was willing to concede above, relate to or engage the technical *objects* (our "gadgets") at all, let alone technology. This would, of course, be innocent enough (why should he not play games if he is so inclined?)—if it did not have the terrible function of pulling the wool over our eyes, of first diverting, in a paper *devoted* to technology (!), his and our attention away from technology to technical items and of then cocooning those technical items in our sweet talk and fussing about them, and of finally pretending that *this* merely cosmetic

---

[22] As I pointed out earlier, it is *feeling* that makes the connection to the soul in the real possible even when the real evokes fear or aversion in us.

[23] The *soul* does not provide any space for "entertaining our gadgets" anyway. A category mistake. Soul and gadgets are on fundamentally different levels.

PSYCHOLOGIE LARMOYANTE

retouching was "keep[ing] technology within the bounds of human concern."[24] Camouflage.[25]

And is it really the job of psychology to *change* the direction of developments in the first place? Would this not be like wanting in psychotherapy to change the patient's *behavior*? But all psychology is called to do is to focus on and attend to the *psychological background* of behavior, not on the behavior itself. Instead of wanting to *change* or *better* anything, to *prevent* or *undo* what seems to be bad, all psychotherapy wants is to liberate the matter at hand from its imprisonment in the initial positivistic, literalistic understanding of it. Psychology is not in the business of correcting or improving people nor of saving the world. It wants to free the spirit Mercurius captured in it, to release the phenomena into their truth, their soul.

THE AVOIDED PSYCHOLOGICAL DIFFERENCE RETURNS AS THE ONTIC DIFFERENCE BETWEEN "GOOD" AND "BAD" PHENOMENA

Slater, however, obviously does not think in terms of the difference between the "hinterland of the soul" (Jung) and the empirical foreground. For him there is only the one (and one-dimensional) level of the positive-factual. The horizon of his thinking is people, what *they* do and what technology does to *them*, in other words, the human, all-too-human. This is why, when confronted with the unpleasant, pathological aspects of the technological world or the information society (the new "'medial' reality"), all that he can envision is the wish to change the actual course of events for the better (and why, conversely, he fears that without these changing efforts we would eventually all turn into something like literal robots).

Where the psychological difference is missing, you have to replace it by literal (ontic or positivistic) differences (empirical splittings on

---

[24] As this his phrase betrays, Slater seems to hold (or be enthralled by) the naïve ego-centered, "humanistic" view that technology is for *our* benefit, for man's sake. He has not understood that, so to speak, "man was made for the Sabbath, and not the Sabbath for man." The soul does not exist for our well-being, comfort, wish-fulfillment. It exists for its own sake and produces what it produces (here: technology) to realize *itself.* The soul is soul precisely because (and one could add: to the extent that) it does *not* have "human concern." It is what begins *outside* "the bounds of human concern" and frequently directly violates human interests and feelings.

[25] It is fascinating to see how easily an egoic humanism can surreptitiously reappear in, and thrive under the cover of, archetypal psychology, a psychology that after all once upon a time expressly started out under the motto of "Dehumanizing or Soul-making."

the semantic level); it is then that, as Jung put it, you "hit upon the saving delusion that *this* wisdom is good and *that* is bad," that this development is positive and that terrible, that certain pathologies (e.g., neuroses) are healthy and others (e.g., "numbing") sick, or that so-called "psychology proper" is "soulful" and the coming world "soulless,"[26] so that our only choice vis-à-vis the "bad" phenomenon in each case is: rejection or being swept-up, defense or acting out. The inescapable psychological difference (a vertical and as such logical or syntactical difference), when avoided, reappears projected onto the semantic plane of positivity,[27] much like in geometry a three-dimensional figure can be projected onto a two-dimensional plane. It

---

[26] These splittings could but should not be confused with those distinctions referred to above between empirical phenomena that are "great" and others that are "petty". In both cases it is a matter of separating the wheat from the chaff. Both separate on the semantic level. But whereas the good-bad type distinctions are horizontal, have the ego as arbiter and belong entirely to the semantic or empirical level, the criterion for the other distinction is the presence or absence of verticality. This differentiation is based on *feeling* as arbiter, which points away from the ego. Those phenomena that are said to be "great" have the vertical difference between surface and soul depth within themselves, whereas what is "petty" is comparatively flat, *only* semantic. "The great," too, appears on the phenomenal level as a semantic content, like all the other semantic contents, which is why without "feeling" it can be mistaken as being merely one of them. But it sticks up out of their ranks because it does not mean a semantic content that it seems to represent. In truth, *as semantic* content it nevertheless expresses precisely the logical form of the whole, the syntax of man's being-in-the-world or of consciousness. The guest whose knock on the door Jung had become aware of is thus not just a new person or new empirical phenomenon that wants to enter. It is the announcement of some new definition of the whole, a new logical status of consciousness.

[27] The traditional privileging of dreams as the *via regia* to soul is also based on an "artificial sundering" on the horizontal semantic level of positivity: "*this* phenomenon (dream) is particularly expressive of soul, all *those* other phenomena are not, or not to the same degree." In this way, the idea of a special access or bridge to soul is literalized and positivized: you don't need psychological sophistication to know what a dream is; already an uneducated small child and even the most soulless person are competent to tell, and they both can even *have* dreams. But in psychology there is no bridge to soul as an externally existing fact, as an instrument *given* by nature (let alone given to us in our sleep) that one merely would have to avail oneself of. Rather, what we call bridge in psychology only comes into being for the first time *through* and *in* one's going across it, *through* and *in* one's soul-*making*, and it "exists" only for the duration of this crossing-over movement. It is, as I pointed out, the act of feeling as a "*judgment* of taste." This act is needed if a dream is supposed to be *turned into* a possible topic for psychology (into a "prime matter") in the first place, which the dream as a natural, merely *psychic* fact is by no means per se. Of course, the positivistic "dream as *via regia*" idea dates back to the early days of psychoanalysis, when it was not a question of getting to soul at all, but still one of getting to "the unconscious." As we now are better able to see in retrospect, the distinction between "the unconscious" and consciousness was/is itself logically thoroughly positivistic (despite its factually *fictitious* character!).

is reductive. To be sure, the "facts" remain, but a whole *dimension* is lost. The soul dimension.

And where *feeling* does not establish for us a connection to the soul and heart of the real out there, beneath its positive-factual surface, where our commitment is not to the inner *Truth* that prevails at a given time, where we are not capable of seeing in it *our own* other, there the question whether a real development that we observe is good or bad will quite naturally preoccupy us and, depending on the answer, make us be *for* or *against* it. The "survival" interest takes over. By making us be for or against, "good" and "bad" make *us*, make "the ego," be the center of things. "The ego" then tips the scales. "*We* decide," as Jung had said; it is *we* who are for or against. *Our* fervor is what counts. However, *what* we are for or against is not really all that important. It is reduced to a mere means for rousing our fervor for or against, which shows that ultimately the whole purpose of all this is nothing else than the constellation and further consolidation of "the ego" in us or of ourselves *as* "ego," so that the soul or inner truth of that reality for or against which we are may totally disappear from our field of vision and be simply forgotten.

Apart from the misconception about what psychology's job is (the reformatory idea), it hardly needs mentioning that the wish to change the direction of such a more-than-human, daimonic reality as modern technology is megalomaniac, as illusionary as would be the project of a worm to divert an express train.

Summarizing the complex movement in Slater's thinking we can say that his own omission of or refusal to see through the material that presented itself to him is objectified and appears in front of his consciousness as the material's, the phenomena's fault, *their* threat to psychology. The anaesthetized *psychological* feeling in him forces him to take the *corresponding* cultural phenomenon of *psychic* numbing out there at face-value and blow it up into an apocalyptic threat. The phenomena are to be blamed for his refusal, so that this their fault (that he sees in or rather into the phenomena) in turn seems to retroactively justify his omission as well as his defensive move into backwaters.

But what is at stake with his omission and refusal and what necessitates this whole resistance? It is the feeling of an indispensable need to hold on to the dogma of the ego's sovereignty as definer of "soul," in order to thereby absolutize the habitual logical *form* of consciousness as the only possible one and immunize it against change, against history, which is also what turns it into an ideology. This need is only felt and arises precisely because there is already a clear, although repressed knowledge that both this dogma and this form of consciousness have long been rendered untenable by the actual course of events and that the still defended definition of soul has long been obsolete. This need comes too late and is secretly *known* to come too late. It is, after all, reactionary—the need to settle in backwaters when the stream of the soul's life is far ahead. Just as a neurosis, so, too, the reactionary move is always the spite against one's own (secret) knowledge that the familiar organization of life and logical form of consciousness are irredeemably over.

WHO IS AFRAID OF THE POSSIBLE END OF "PSYCHOLOGY PROPER"?

The moment one would truly want to take seriously the phenomena discussed by Slater, irrespective of their clearly pathological form and their first-immediacy status, that is, take them seriously as the harbingers of "a new way of psychic understanding" and as the heralds of a new world, *then* it might perhaps not be completely wrong after all to say that with them "psychology proper ceases to exist"— provided that we understand that what is here euphemistically called "psychology proper" is merely the conventional 20th century form of psychology that we have grown fond of, and not *really* psychology proper, true psychology. This so-called "psychology proper" can in retrospect, precisely through those new phenomena, be seen through as being only the first immediacy of true psychology. Could it not be that the phenomenon of numbing might possibly contribute to opening our minds to the insight that, on the one hand, personalistic psychology (the psychology that focused on the individual and what is going on inside people, with its emphasis on "honest suffering," on relating, development, growth, on body, emotion, eros, introspection, dreams, and meaning) was itself one of the great delusional ideas of the 20th century and that, on the other hand, an "anima-only" psychology with "gods," with "aesthetics," and of a *mundus imaginalis* is also merely a kind of (subtle-bodied) drug that promises to *numb us* into "states of artificial happiness" and dissociates us from real life,

PSYCHOLOGIE LARMOYANTE

from the soul of the real? Are, for instance, Slater's questions—"if the symptoms of these diseases are no longer felt, what becomes of the gods? What becomes of us without the gods?"—not themselves a perfect example of the "ubiquitous psychobabble" that he rightly bemoans, although admittedly "psychobabble" of a more "ennobled" variety and "ubiquitous" only in certain Jungian and New-Age quarters? Heidegger reports a joke of a man who comes enervated into the local pub moaning that his wife talks and talks and talks. When asked what she talked about, his answer was, "*That* she does not say." Did Slater *say* anything with his "what becomes of the gods? What becomes of us without the gods?"?

Why could it not be that psychology's *adaptation* to those epochal self-redefinitions in the soul's life that become manifest both in the phenomena described by Slater and in the other ones pointed to by Jung in the letter quoted might include the possibility of its, psychology's, having in full consciousness to move into its own end, into its being superseded by something else, something new? In individual psychology, Jung thought, the beginning of what he called the second half of life was "the birth of death." Can a psychology that expects patients to learn to face their own death afford to be afraid of its own possible death? Should it not, just like a person is supposed to, have a critical distance to itself, distinguish itself from itself?

Psychology the way we have known it arose very late in history, during the latter half of the 19th century. If it is something that came into being, it might just as well have to pass away when its time has come, just as the world of myth and ritual, just as later in history religion and still later metaphysics had to yield to their respective successors and as during our time the latest bearer of the baton of the soul's truth, science, seems to be losing it, to be having to pass it on to "the media."

But then, has psychology ever been a full-fledged bearer of the baton of truth like the aforementioned institutions, really their peer, and not much rather only a sidetrack? Be that as it may, psychology is itself a product of the soul's life and exposed to its further development. It is *in* the retort. Not the external observer and immune interpreter or artifex of the processes in the retort.

And in the last analysis, is "that psychology's time has come" not the very experience which all the phenomena of numbing would have had in store for Slater if he had been willing to go into them? And is this their threat to psychology not what all his defensive efforts try to ward off?

CHAPTER TWENTY

C. G. Jung's Idea of a "Metamorphosis of the Gods" and the History of the Soul

C.G. Jung took the phrase "*Gestaltwandel der Götter*" ("metamorphosis of the gods") from the title of a 2-volume book by Leopold Ziegler. Ziegler (1881–1958) was one of the most famous and popular philosophers during the first half of the 20th century in the German-speaking world and, much like for example Oswald Spengler, widely influential especially in nonacademic circles. His cited book appeared in 1920 and as early as 1922 it already had its third printing. In 1920, the same year as this book appeared, Ziegler received the Nietzsche prize and in 1929, as the third prizewinner and one year before Freud, the Goethe prize of the city of Frankfurt. From his youth on interested in Eduard von Hartmann, the 19th century "philosopher of the unconscious," as he has been named, Ziegler felt the need during the early 1930s to deepen his view of the unconscious and to familiarize himself more thoroughly with mythic symbols. In connection with those studies he also carefully studied Jung, especially Jung's early main work, *Wandlungen und Symbole der Libido*. Jung on his part was certainly familiar with Ziegler's book and not only with its title. But here I do not want to go into the interesting question whether Jung may have been influenced in his own thinking by Ziegler's ideas in the sense that, along with this catchy phrase, he also took over the author's theory that came with it, or whether Jung more or less simply took over the phrase alone, but made use of it for his own different purposes, inserting it into the context of his own thinking. May it suffice here to have given a few hints about the provenance of the phrase "metamorphosis of the gods" that plays a not unimportant role in Jung's own thinking.

In a certain way one can see the idea of a metamorphosis of the gods (or at least the basic logic informing it) already prefigured, eight years prior to Ziegler's work, in the title of Jung's already cited early main work, *Wandlungen und Symbole der Libido*, "Transformations and Symbols of the Libido." "Transformation" is synonymous with "metamorphosis," both meaning a change of form (*morphê, forma*). The first word of Jung's title suggests such a form change, and the next noun in it tells us that the forms which change are called "symbols." "Wandlungen und Symbole" is clearly a hendiadys, a title wherein one is expressed as two. *What* changes its form from one symbol to another symbol is here, during these early days of psychoanalytical thinking and under the influence of Freud, called "libido." Per se the latter is irrepresentable and can only become visible in different "symbols." The libido, which Jung did not comprehend as a qualitative force (e.g., a sex drive), but as totally abstract, contentless energy (mere degrees of quantity), is, as it were, the underlying absolutely invisible, inaccessible soul substance that, without itself appearing, makes itself felt and known through processes of symbolization. The logic informing Jung's title thus follows that of a metaphysics of substance. There are two levels. On the one, the level of the symbolic forms, there is change, development, history. The libido does not manifest itself once and for all in one single form. There is movement, and as the subtitle of Jung's work, *Beiträge zur Entwicklungsgeschichte des Denkens* (Contributions to a Developmental History of Thought), suggests, "transformation" does not mean just any serendipitous change, but rather a progression, some kind of consistent development. However underneath this changing phenomenal level, there is something that persists, something permanent that does not enter the developmental process and is not affected by it, something which, as I pointed out, is in this early phase of Jung's thinking called "the libido," but ultimately would be best simply considered an "X," a formulation which would probably have

"METAMORPHOSIS OF THE GODS"

found Jung's consent. (From our present-day point of view it should of course be seen through as a stand-in for the soul in its absolute negativity.) While the form develops, the content or substance maintains itself as always the same.

I give below a number of passages in which Jung explicitly refers to the *Gestaltwandel der Götter* from diverse texts and from very different contexts.

> We are living in the *kairos* for a "metamorphosis of the gods," that is, of the fundamental principles and symbols. This concern of our time, which is certainly not of our choosing, expresses the changes that are going on in the inner and unconscious man. Coming generations will have to account for this momentous change ... (*CW* 10 § 585, transl. modified)

> But the "metamorphosis of the gods" rolls rumbling on and the State becomes lord of this world: more than half Europe is already swallowed up. (This is a comment in reference to the contemporary [1934] political situation. *CW* 10 § 1020.)

> With the loss of the past, which ipso facto has now turned into something "unreputable," devalued and incapable of revaluation, the saviour has been lost too, for the saviour is either the unreputable thing itself or else arises out of it. He originates in the "metamorphosis of the gods" (Ziegler), as it were ever anew, as the harbinger or first-born of a new generation and emerges unexpectedly in a most unlikely place (sprung from a stone, tree, furrow, water, etc.) and in dubious form (Tom Thumb, dwarf, child, animal, and so on). (*CW* 9i § 267)

> The biographical "metamorphosis of the gods" is decidedly more popular than their static immutability. (*Letters 2*, p. 250, 2 May 1955, to Cortis. See also *CW* 11 §§ 193, 206, and 145).

These occurrences of a reference to the "metamorphosis of the gods" are very brief and do not reveal much of the theory behind this formulation. To get a better insight into what Jung has in mind when he speaks of the "metamorphosis of the gods" let us look at a passage from a text that dates from 1929, Jung's "Commentary on 'The Secret of the Golden Flower.'" It succinctly explains the "metamorphosis of the gods," although without literally citing this phrase. It reads,

> For this reason many of the earlier gods turned from persons into personified ideas and finally into abstract ideas, because animated unconscious contents always appear at first projected outward and in the course of mental development they are gradually assimilated by consciousness via spatial projection [*via Raumprojektion*] and transformed into conscious ideas, a process through which the latter lose their originally autonomous and personal character. As is well known, some of the old gods have, via astrology, become mere descriptive attributes (martial, jovial, saturnine, erotic, logical, lunatic, etc.). (*CW* 13 § 49, transl. modified)

This brief passage contains in a nutshell an entire theory about the life of the soul on the collective level. I will try to unfold it in a number of theses or points.

1. What Jung envisions is an actual historical process. He is talking about an empirically real development. He is here not concerned with archetypal processes, with movements within the *mundus imaginalis*, but rather with soul history as concrete earthly events and social changes that are in principle datable (even if only roughly), that is to say, that belong to the temporal, not the archetypal sphere. Another quote may clarify this rootedness of Jung's thinking about this topic in literal history. Speaking of the collision and encounter of the Mediterranean culture of late antiquity at the end of the Roman Empire and the early Middle Ages with "the Teutonic man of the North," Jung said of the latter, "His polydaemonism had not yet reached the level and clarity of Mediterranean polytheism, and in this state he was suddenly confronted with a religion and view of the world that had sprung from the decay of Olympus and the transformation of the gods into philosophical and theological ideas" (*Letters 2*, p. 337, 20 Nov. 1956, to Père Bruno de Jésus-Marie). What Jung has here in the back of his mind is, on the one hand, the Greek historical development from early polytheistic religion to late Hellenistic and neo-Platonic philosophy (including philosophical modes of mythologizing) and, on the other hand, the historical Age of the Germanic Migrations (*Völkerwanderung*) and their consequences.

2. This historical development is *geistige Entwicklung* (mental development), however not a mental development of the individual, but rather of the human mind at large (or at least a development of

"METAMORPHOSIS OF THE GODS"

the human mind in the Western cultural sphere, which is probably Jung's tacit main focus here). We will not go wrong in interpreting this mental development as history of consciousness.

3. This history of consciousness is described in terms of a history of the gods. Why the gods? Why single them out? Our passage does not contain any answer to this question. But the reason that we can give is that the development of consciousness is best analyzed through its central and supreme content, that exceptional content that expresses the *principle* of consciousness itself and thus also of all possible contents. On the archaic level this content is the gods (in the plural). Consciousness defines itself—on this level—through its gods. In the gods, and only in them, it becomes (implicitly, indirectly!) aware of its own constitutive logic or syntax. We could also say, the latter, which governs it "from behind" as it were, becomes a visible or imaginable shape for it, indeed a person (or rather persons). In the gods, consciousness relates to its own innermost (but otherwise irrepresentable, inaccessible) truth, to the cornerstone of itself.

4. We are also told *what* the specific stages of this (macro-level) historical development are. The process is not nondescript, indeterminate, open for all kinds of possibilities, but instead has a definite and linear, indeed irreversible direction. We can describe it best in alchemical terms as sublimation, distillation, evaporation. It begins with gods as concrete persons who change into personified ideas, which in turn become abstract ideas (and finally these ideas may possibly even be diluted and desubstantiated into mere qualities; linguistically speaking, adjectives instead of nouns).

5. This is a *form* change. The content or "soul matter" stays the same. But form change not in the sense of a change in *visible shape*, as we know it from many myths where, for example, Zeus at one time appears as a swan, at other times as a bull, an eagle, or a flash of lightning, and Daphne changes into a laurel or the nymph Echo into a reed. These transmutations and all the numerous other ones described for example by Ovid in his *Metamorphoses* are transformations of one thing into *another thing*, in other words, "horizontal" and semantic changes on one and the same plane of natural objects. The change from god to abstract idea, from person to notion, from nearly-physical substance to abstraction or from noun to descriptive attribute or

adjective is a form change in an altogether different sense. It is a "vertical" change of the logical status or level, a refining and distilling process, a transformation from the level of substantiated entities into "spirit," "vapor," indeed, from matter or substance into *form as such* (logical or syntactical form). We could also say that the first type of metamorphosis is a "physical" change, whereas the latter is a "chemical" one. The "physical" change works by means of replacement of one form by alternative forms. There is from the beginning a plurality of possible guises like ready-made costumes to choose from. The change therefore remains external to that which changes. "Chemical" change, by contrast, comes about through the *internal processing* of one and the same given "raw" *form* of manifestation *itself*, so that *it*, this initial form, within itself turns into another, more refined one.

Alchemy is about internal form changes in this latter sense. It works on the *form* of the matter. And the alchemical process is absolutely dependent on the hermetical sealing of the vessel in which the matter is kept, because what needs to be prevented at all cost for the alchemical process to become possible is that the—always fugitive—Mercurial matter escapes and pops up somewhere else in an alternate form (i.e., visible shape) and thus as something else. Alchemy holds the matter in its original raw form absolutely tight and subjects it (its "physical" or substantiated or personified form) to processes of decomposition and putrefaction and later subjects the result of this procedure to higher processes of distillation. This kind of process can therefore serve as a model for us when we try to understand the type of metamorphosis that is meant in our Jung quote by the change from "gods as persons" into "personified ideas" and finally into "abstract ideas." It is a transformation of the *inward logical form* of the content in question.

Of course, gods are not literally physical, not positive facts. They are from the outset soul property, imaginal beings. Nevertheless, *as* those psychological or imaginal realities they contain a strong physical element. They are imagined in the likeness of real people or animals (or as composed of parts of different beings, partly human, partly animal) and thus have a strongly substantial character. The imagination is naturally naturalistic. In addition they are first nature gods; although not identical in a positivistic sense with natural phenomena (sun, moon, life and death, storm, lightning, earthquakes, etc.), they are nevertheless still closely attached to them. These real natural

"METAMORPHOSIS OF THE GODS" 537

phenomena are not only their respective areas of competence, the gods also have their epiphany in them. The gods also live in nature, in the real natural world, and at particular places existing in geographical reality (Mount Olympus, Cyprus, Delphi, etc.). So on both counts (their substantiated character as persons and their near-identity with nature or particular aspects of nature), "the physical in [their imaginal] matter" is predominant. And in a truly alchemical sense, it is the cinders of this "physicalness" that in several steps get gradually worked off during the history of consciousness. The history of consciousness— if viewed not in terms of *intellectual history* as a history of contents (ideas, etc.) but *psychologically* as a history of form changes, logical or "syntactical" changes—is a distillation process, a truly alchemical opus.

6. I mentioned the irreversibility of the process. It is clear that in alchemy it is impossible to go back to the original form once it has been pulverized, decomposed, putrefied, dissolved, or burned up. By the same token, no way leads back from "abstract ideas" to the initial "gods as persons," just as there is in people's personal development no possibility to go back behind puberty and behind an awareness of one's "shadow" to childhood innocence or in cultural history back behind Enlightenment skepticism to a naive medieval faith. Here we may remember something Jung said in his seminar talk about "The Symbolic Life." "... we cannot go back to the symbolism that is gone. ... Doubt has killed it, has devoured it." And Jung also made it very clear that the problem is not the content, but the form. "I know it is the truth, but it is the truth in a form in which I cannot accept it any more." (*CW* 18 § 632). Elsewhere we read that "the gods die from time to time ..." (*CW* 9i § 22). In this context we must also include Jung's idea about the death of symbols (*CW* 6 § 816) that I discussed elsewhere.[1]

Once the process of metamorphosis has entered the phase of "personified ideas," the symbolism of "gods as persons" is gone; it has been "killed," decomposed, distilled. In other words, the irreversible process of the metamorphosis of the gods involves real discontinuity. The change of discreet forms implies a succession of distinct stages or statuses of consciousness. When early Jung spoke of the transformations

---

[1] Wolfgang Giegerich, "The End of Meaning and the Birth of Man," in: Journal of Jungian Theory and Practice vol. 6, no. 1, 2004, pp. 1–65, here pp. 11 ff. Now Chapter Nine in the present volume.

538   *THE SOUL ALWAYS THINKS*

(C) and symbols (B) of the libido (A) we can speak in this new context of the transformations (C) of the supreme contents (B) in which consciousness (A) reflects and symbolizes itself, that is, in which it displays the respective logical form corresponding to that status that it has achieved in the course of its development.

7. The "transformation of the gods into philosophical and theological ideas," even "abstract ideas," is a development away from the mythic imagination to thought. As "fantastic" as it may be, the imagination still thinks according to the model of visible shapes and entertains its contents in close correspondence to natural entities and events. Thought, by contrast, has left the sensory behind and operates with forms that are solely its own property, generated by itself. In thought consciousness has come home to itself. It is no longer alienated from itself, as it is in the mode of imagination which requires images of natural things or shapes as a vehicle for doing its thinking (much like small children need their fingers, or apples and other images, as a visual aid for counting and performing simple mathematical operations).

8. At the beginning of our quotation, Jung merely lists the three different major stages of mental development by naming the specific forms in which the different statuses of consciousness he focuses on crystallize: gods as full-fledged persons—personified ideas—abstract ideas. He mentions the predominant form of products produced by each stage. But in the clause beginning with "because" he also tells us something about how the transition from one form or status to the next one comes about. The question how such a progression from gods as persons to abstract ideas is possible indeed demands explanation. In order to provide a few hints for comprehending the logic of this transformation, Jung begins by going back behind the content "gods as persons," explaining how the gods arise. He speaks of "animated unconscious contents" and says of them that they "always appear at first" in projected form. The term content at the beginning is of course inaccurate. To begin with there are no contents. "Contents" are only the *result* produced by this projection. It is a naive and wrong idea that consciousness is a kind of sack full of unconscious contents, some of which can become animated (or constellated) and because of this animation get projected outward. No, the act of projection is the first

"METAMORPHOSIS OF THE GODS"

production of specific contents. Consciousness as such is only logical life, performative, a way of processing.

And therefore, *what* is projected cannot initially be anything else but consciousness's own logical form, the logic of the mind's (mindedness's) own way of operation, of the human world-relation (interchange with the world). Inasmuch as the contents of consciousness are always *in front of* and *vis-à-vis of* consciousness, projection is indispensable for contents to come into existence, unless it is a matter of contents that, being given to consciousness by perception, are external realities from the outset. Although gods in early ages have their predominant place in nature and are experienced there, it is clear that they are not external realities, but internal properties of the mind, of consciousness itself. But by being projected outward and thus becoming a "content" in front of consciousness in the first place, this consciousness's own inner constitution or syntax in its complexity becomes substantiated, concrete image, personified—gods as persons. In itself the inner constitution of consciousness is not only "unconscious" but per se above all "irrepresentable" and "unimaginable." The gods are the first immediacy of consciousness's becoming conscious of *itself*—first immediacy because although in the gods consciousness has become conscious of itself, it does not in any way know that what it is conscious of is its own inner logical functioning. Rather, it takes the gods as external realities, substantial entities, beings, although beings of a special kind, different from merely-empirical facts.

9. After having briefly hinted at how gods come about, Jung proceeds to the further "course of mental development." Its purpose and achievement, he says, is to bring about the gradual assimilation of the gods by consciousness, so that they are no longer gods imagined as externally existing beings, but have become "conscious ideas." That they now have become "conscious ideas" means that through this advancement consciousness has inwardized, or integrated into itself, what before it used to imagine "out there" but now has and knows as its own property, as mental realities, contents of the human mind. In other words, through this transformation the gods, at first the product of projection away and out of consciousness, have now in a literal sense come home to consciousness.

540   THE SOUL ALWAYS THINKS

And as a matter of course, this form change from gods to abstract conscious ideas means that the "originally autonomous and personal character" of the contents is lost. The moment the content is no longer external (and as such outside the "jurisdiction" of consciousness itself), the moment it instead has been integrated into itself, it is no longer wholly other and irrational, unpredictable, but falls within the range of consciousness's own competence. And when the autonomous character of the contents is gone because they have meanwhile (objectively) been seen through as contents of consciousness, it is once more clear that there can be no way back to gods imagined as fundamentally independent external forces, as persons with a decisive will of their own.

10. Now it is interesting to see that here Jung does not explain the movement from the projected content to the assimilated or integrated content in the standard way, namely by having recourse to the idea of a "withdrawal" of the projection. On the contrary, he attributes this inwardization of what had been projected outward to a *second projection*, which he calls spatial projection. The bringing home into consciousness of what has been cast out according to this text obviously does not proceed by a literal fetching back, the way an escaped convict is recaptured and returned to jail. Surprisingly, indeed completely paradoxically, it happens through another forward move on the part of consciousness. The projection, rather than being undone, is overtopped.

Jung does not explain what he means by *Raumprojektion*, and since, as far as I can see, he does not discuss this term and concept anywhere else in his work, we are called upon to infer what is meant from the immediate context.

We have two clues. The first clue is that the spatial projection has to be seen in contrast to the original projection. The second clue is that it must be comprehended as a soul move that achieves the inwardization postulated. As to the first point, it is clear that the original projection that produced the gods is concerned with specific contents or entities that exist in, or are imagined as existing in, the world, in space. Consciousness sort of takes, entirely unconsciously, empirical space for granted and simply projects the god images into it. This is of course the general nature of the imagination and imaginal thinking. It is only aware of the things, shapes, persons, events, but oblivious of

"METAMORPHOSIS OF THE GODS"

the natural space that it makes use of as the stage for its imaginings. The second projection, on the other hand, projects out the very notion of space, which means that it first of all has now become conscious of such a thing as "space," a totally new category, and secondly *ipso facto* has occupied the whole sphere or *dimension* in which the gods used to exist. And its having conquered this sphere for itself is tantamount to having taken possession of it as its own property, as the space or realm of consciousness. It is thus an expansion of consciousness, a fundamental widening of its horizon. And this also at once explains why the asserted inwardization or integration of the gods into consciousness through such a second projection is plausible.

The conquering and claiming of this whole sphere for itself is comprehended by Jung in another passage as a *swallowing*. He states,

> "Well, after all we managed—for first time since the dawn of history—to swallow the whole primordial animatedness of nature into ourselves; not only did the gods descend (or rather were they dragged down) from their planetary spheres and transformed into chthonic demons, but, under the influence of scientific enlightenment, even this host of demons, which at the time of Paracelsus still frolicked happily in mountains and woods, in rivers and human dwelling-places, was reduced to a miserable remnant and finally vanished altogether."[2]

We see that by this step nothing is done to the gods themselves. *They* are not recaptured and integrated. Rather, all that happens only happens to consciousness itself. It widens its sphere of competence. It advances to a fundamentally new category or dimension. Having hitherto only been aware of its contents, the gods, as the expression of its highest values, its truth, it now all of a sudden becomes conscious of itself, namely of itself as "space" *for* whatever contents: conscious of itself as consciousness. And the moment this happens, it has moved beyond the level of contents; it no longer imagines itself in terms and by means of its highest contents, the gods, but has risen to the level of the realm that is the stage for all the contents. With this move from the What to the awareness of the Wherein, consciousness has *ipso facto* once and for all *left the mythic imagination as such behind*, the imagination as the organ of its truth, and opened the door to the *form*

---

[2] *CW* 10 § 431 (transl. modified).

of thinking as its new access to its truth. With its advance to the dimension of the "space" for contents, the imagination is obsolete, of course not in the sense that it would now no longer be possible to imagine and that consciousness did not retain the imagination as one of its psychic faculties, but rather in the sense that imagining has been reduced to a sublated moment within it, either an instrument that consciousness can now avail itself of at will or incidental happenings (e.g., dreams, visions) of merely subjective importance or an ingredient in, or mere mode of expression of, thought (e.g., poetry, poetic images). At any rate, in contrast to the mythic situation, the imagination is now no longer the medium in which consciousness or the soul is in contact with itself, its logical life, its innermost truth.

This also shows why the gods have ceased being gods. They are now fundamentally sublated, they are *only* contents of consciousness, "ideas" that consciousness entertains, no longer gods (consciousness's *supreme* principles), because consciousness itself is already far ahead of all contents on its new level of self-consciousness. It is logically already too refined to be able to reflect itself meaningfully in any content and to content itself with such images as its valid self-manifestation. Consciousness, having transcended beyond the sphere of contents or entities, as a matter of course can no longer find satisfaction in the highest contents of the previous stage, gods, as its true self-reflection. They are incapable of accounting for and giving adequate expression to consciousness's precious new acquisition, its awareness of "space" as such, i.e., of itself. The gods "cannot do anything any more for" consciousness. They have done their job. They have lost their *raison d'être*. Consciousness now is on the way to comprehending itself as mindedness, as logical form and logical life.

As long as the gods were, if I may express myself disrespectfully, "state of the art," that is, the absolutely highest form of consciousness's self-knowing, they were precisely not yet contents of consciousness, not yet its ideas, despite the fact that for us, *in retrospect*, they were, as ontic beings, projected contents of consciousness. Above (see # 8) I stated that the term content at the beginning, prior to the initial projection, is of course inaccurate and that such a thing as "contents" are the result of this projection. But now we see that even the use of the *term* content for this result is wrong, premature. As long as there is no consciousness that is aware of itself as consciousness, as the

"METAMORPHOSIS OF THE GODS" 543

dimension and space for all contents, there are properly speaking no contents either. The gods *as concrete visible or imaginal shapes* were in themselves the contradictory indissoluble unity of "entity" (being) in front of consciousness and all-encompassing space (a whole world) all around consciousness, and being both at once they were neither object/content nor space. This undifferentiated unity of being and space is what their compelling numinosity consisted in. Only once object and space have parted and consciousness has advanced to an awareness of itself as "space" does it make sense to speak of contents. It is the "container" that generates the possibility of contents. But the moment the gods have become "animated unconscious contents" they are of course gods no more. They have dropped out of the race. As ideas, one can now think *about* them, *believe* in them (or not believe in them), but they are *ipso facto* gods no longer. They have lost, as Jung put it, their autonomous character, and this simply means their reality as gods. We could also say they have lost their absolutely convincing numinosity.

The coming home to consciousness of projected contents can only occur as the advancement of consciousness as such to a fundamentally new logical status of itself, "a leap after the throw," as I once put it.[3] Assimilation or integration amounts to a lesser or larger revolution of the very constitution of consciousness. A simple addition of another, hitherto unconscious content to all the contents it already contains will not suffice. We could say the same thing in the following way. The integration into consciousness is a syntactical change of consciousness, not merely a semantic one.

One particular form of the former gods' having become obsolete because consciousness has advanced to a new structural or better logical level of itself is the "survival" (of sorts) of pagan gods after the Christianization of Europe. About the Grimm fairytale "The Spirit in the Bottle," Jung states, "It is worth noting that the German fairytale calls the spirit confined in the bottle by the name of the pagan god, Mercurius, who was considered identical with the German national god, Wotan. ... Our fairytale thus interprets the evil spirit as a pagan

---

[3] Wolfgang Giegerich, "The Leap After the Throw: On 'Catching up With' Projections and the Origin of Psychology," now in: *idem, The Neurosis of Psychology. Primary Papers towards a Critical Psychology*, Collected English Papers vol. 1, New Orleans (Spring Journal Books), 2005, pp. 69–96.

god, forced under the influence of Christianity to descend into the dark underworld and be morally disqualified. ... In fact the spirit behaves just as the devil does in many other fairytales: he bestows wealth by changing base metal into gold; and like the devil, he also gets tricked." (*CW* 13 § 246). The same idea is expressed in another passage, where Jung, speaking of the vision of a "Radiant Boy" found in English ghost stories, tells us that, "This apparition was supposed to be of evil omen. It almost looks as though we were dealing with the figure of a *puer aeternus* who had become inauspicious through 'metamorphosis,' or in other words had shared the fate of the classical and the Germanic gods, who have all become evil spirits" (*CW* 9i § 268, transl. modified).

Charles Baudelaire had already in 1861 voiced a similar view concerning the one classical goddess of love. "Radiant classical Venus, foam-borne Aphrodite has not gone unpunished through the dreadful darkness of the Middle Ages. No longer does she inhabit Olympus nor the shore of the fragrant Archipelagus. She withdrew deep down into a cave ... By having taken her place in the underworld, Venus came close to hell, and at certain ghastly festivities she probably never fails to pay her respect to the arch-demon, the prince of flesh and the lord of sin."[4]

But is it psychologically appropriate to say, as Jung did, that the pagan gods were forced under the influence of Christianity to descend into the dark underworld and be morally disqualified? I do not think so. As Jung himself had shown us, the "gods as persons" had simply died. They had turned into and been superseded by "abstract ideas." Consciousness had advanced to a fundamentally higher level. There was no need to force the pagan gods to descend. Christianity did not need *to do* anything to the pagan gods, to repress them. Consciousness was simply beyond them, on a completely different level where those gods simply did not matter any more. And the pagan gods did not really descend either. They were simply dead and the soul was far above them. What we have to understand is that the *appearance* of their having been forced to descend and their moral disqualification are nothing but the reflex or *symptom* of the soul's own knowledge that it is regressive when it not only artificially keeps,

---

[4] In: *Revue européenne*, 1 April 1861.

"METAMORPHOSIS OF THE GODS"

against its better knowledge, the old gods alive, but thereby even affords the luxury of clinging to *the old but now obsolete, namely the mythic, imaginal level of consciousness!*

The defense of the whole outdated level of consciousness is something much more serious than merely holding on to or reviving obsolete contents. The soul knows that it does something wrong; that it fails to in fact rise to and hold itself on that level to which it actually has already advanced. That the classical and the Germanic gods have all become evil spirits is the innocent self-representation on the part of these contents that the form of consciousness which they represent is no longer up to date. It is simply out of place. The new evilness of the pagan gods is the soul's projection of something *it* does unto its *contents* as *their* character. It projects its own act, as subject, of violating its own moral law, namely the law not to regress behind the status that has already been achieved. We could also say that in the evilness of the gods is symptomatically reflected the objective prohibitedness for the soul of the old mythic stage of consciousness. Nobody morally disqualified the pagan gods. No, in the gods' now evil nature the objective soul *objectively* morally disqualifies merely its own regressiveness, but displaces this disqualification so that it appears as the demonic character of *what* it is devoted to, the pagan gods. There is no moralism here, no preaching from on top. All there is is the objective logic of regression, the objective self-reflection of its distance to consciousness's now valid norm, a self-reflection in the form of the very thing to which it regressed. A soul that is in fact beyond the gods can still experience those gods in spontaneous apparitions as authentic psychic phenomena, attested in innumerable local legends, but only as monstrous demons or evil spirits. The regression has its price.

But, by interpreting this situation as a violent act on the part of Christianity of forcing the gods to descend into the underworld, Jung fraternizes with the regressive tendencies of the soul and views and evaluates things from the worm's eye view of the regressive position, resenting and blaming the higher stage of consciousness as suppressor. From here it is only a small step to the view contained in another passage from the same work of Jung's from which the text was taken that I discussed in the foregoing pages at some length, his "Commentary on 'The Secret of the Golden Flower.'"

The former passage came from § 49, the new one, only a few paragraphs down, from § 54.

> It must stir a sympathetic chord in the enlightened European when it is said in the *Hui Ming Ching* that the "shapes formed by the spirit-fire are only empty colours and forms." That sounds thoroughly European and seems to suit our reason to a T. We think we can congratulate ourselves on having already reached such a pinnacle of clarity, imagining that we have left all these phantasmal gods far behind. But what we have left behind are only verbal spectres, *not the psychic facts that were responsible for the birth of the gods.* We are still as much possessed by autonomous psychic contents as if they were Olympians. Today they are called phobias, obsessions, and so forth; in a word, neurotic symptoms. The gods have become diseases, and Zeus no longer rules Olympus but rather the solar plexus, and produces curious specimens for the doctor's consulting room, or disorders the brains of politicians and journalists who unwittingly set off psychic epidemics. (*CW* 13 § 54, transl. modified)

Absolutely astounding. Only five paragraphs earlier we had heard that through the metamorphosis of the gods into conscious ideas "the latter lose their originally autonomous and personal character." This happened more than two thousand years ago. Now the autonomous character of the contents is all of a sudden back in full force, "we are still as much possessed by autonomous psychic contents as if they were Olympians." Jung had also specifically told us that the Germanic tribes of the North at the end of antiquity were confronted with a "religion and view of the world that had sprung from the decay of Olympus and the transformation of the gods into philosophical and theological ideas." Now, two thousand years after his decay, Zeus is all of a sudden presented as if alive and kicking again. We could of course put this reference to Zeus down to mere rhetoric— if Jung did not expressly and in full earnest state that "The gods have become diseases," which corresponds to other statements of his: "Our fearsome gods have only changed their names: they now rhyme with *-ism*" (*CW* 7 § 326); "The demons have not really disappeared but have merely changed their form. They are now unconscious psychic potencies" (*CW* 10 § 431, transl. modified).

"METAMORPHOSIS OF THE GODS"

This is a totally different theory of the "metamorphosis of the gods" from the first one. And it is incompatible with the latter. Whereas the first-discussed theory could be interpreted in analogy to the alchemical processes of decomposition, distillation, sublimation, evaporation, this new one is unmistakably anti-alchemical, namely materialistic, psychologistic, and personalistic. Rather than thinking in terms of overcoming the initial "physicalness" of the gods as psychological matter, he views them here as having become *more* physical; they are buried in the materiality of the solar plexus, or the brain, or in human neurotic diseases. Diseases are positive facts, fundamentally *individual* events (enclosed in the bodies of people), whereas both the Olympic gods and the later "abstract ideas" into which they developed were Universals. Jung's commitment here to an anti-alchemical downward direction into a deepened physicalness of "the matter" comes also out in another text, e.g., when he writes, that "spirit too, as Heraclitus says, has descended from its fiery heights. But when spirit becomes heavy it turns to water..." (*CW* 9i § 32), a statement followed up in § 50 of the same essay by the following sentences: "Symbols are spirit from above, and under those conditions [i.e., in an age or culture that possesses symbols] the spirit is above too. ... Our unconscious, on the other hand, holds living water, spirit that has become nature [*naturhaft*, physical]..." (transl. modif.). Not more refinement, evaporation, but more coagulation, more physicalness.

The first theory of a metamorphosis of the gods had an obvious phenomenological basis. The process described can easily be seen in the course of Greek history from ancient to Hellenistic times and beyond to neo-Platonism. But the new theory has no leg to stand on. It is just an assertion without any empirical or phenomenological backing. This phenomenologically completely implausible identity of our neurotic diseases with gods would need to be demonstrated in detail, but it cannot be demonstrated. Why is it really *Zeus* that rules the solar plexus? Zeus is a god with specific features. What is divine in or behind our phobias and compulsions? What justifies the use of the terms god and demon? Jung does not say. He does not even give a hint.

Interestingly enough, "Zeus," "gods," "demons" have in his parlance here become completely abstract terms devoid of concrete content. However they are abstract precisely not in the same sense that the gods according to the first metamorphosis thesis had turned into "abstract ideas." No, they have *only* become abstract, depleted, *without* having turned into ideas in the high philosophical sense, but as such abstract terms they have nevertheless retained their original names, status, and alleged autonomy. In other words, the terms "Zeus," "gods," and "demons" now have merely a musical function; they are supposed to be *suggestive* of a vague religious mood and feeling. Jung's introduction of the "god"-topic is due to his own emotional-ideological wish to still today have some kind of gods or meaning. It is not due to and necessitated by observed psychic phenomenology. Jung's interpretation amounts to a mystification, an inflation of petty, indeed downright sick realities with a higher, even divine aura.

The only argument Jung seems to have hinges on the idea that through our neurotic symptoms we show ourselves "still as much possessed by autonomous psychic contents as if they were Olympians." But this argument does not work. First of all, if A is autonomous and B is autonomous it does not follow that A = B, just as their being both sovereign does not make two sovereign States identical. In addition, the autonomy of neurotic complexes is something very different from the autonomy of gods, especially since the gods are cosmic forces (if not even creators of the world), whereas neuroses are strictly personal illnesses. What kind of a god would that be whose sole field of activity is an individual's private psyche?

Secondly, are the psychic contents that stir within neurotic symptoms truly autonomous in the first place? They are certainly "non-ego," but "non-ego" precisely because neurosis is a condition of dissociation. If, as Jung himself holds, neurotic symptoms are compensations for a false or one-sided attitude of consciousness, there is not much left of their autonomy. They are much rather dependent on the conscious attitude. That personality that denies its full truth denies its own other side; it may *ipso facto* drive the split-off contents into "autonomy" and become possessed by them. But this is then a *produced* autonomy of those contents, not an originary one. Neuroses are man-made.[5] Jung wrote, "A neurosis is truly 'finished off' when it has gotten rid of the falsely minded

---

[5] This does not mean that my view is that neuroses are made by the conscious I.

"METAMORPHOSIS OF THE GODS"

I [*falsch eingestellte Ich*, the I that has a false attitude]" (*CW* 10 §
361, transl. modif.). If the gods have become diseases, have turned
into our neurotic symptoms, into our phobias, obsessions, etc., then
a cure of the neurosis (the false attitude of consciousness) would "finish
off" the gods too. But what gods would that be?

Jung's thesis is that the "gods have only changed their names,"
that they "have not really disappeared but have merely changed their
form." What his second thesis amounts to is a mock metamorphosis.
According to his first theory, the gods truly disappeared and lost their
autonomous and person character because they had become integrated
into consciousness (as "conscious ideas"). The conscious ideas were the
successor form of the original form of divine persons. Now nothing
disappeared, nothing has been "killed" by doubt. There is no real and
fundamental form change, at most only a superficial costume change.
In this new theory, unbroken continuity wins out over against the
discontinuity that was the essential characteristic of the first theory of
a metamorphosis of the gods. Any discontinuity one might still
diagnose on the surface is now only a seeming one, more or less only
due to our illusions: "what we have left behind are only verbal spectres."
True, Zeus no longer rules Olympus, but he is still just as active and
autonomously powerful. The reality is the same. Only our words
changed and, because we believe in and are deluded by our words,
our ideas about the facts also changed.

In the title of *Transformations and Symbols of the Libido* it was the
irrepresentable "libido" that stayed the same throughout the processes
of transformation, while the symbols, the forms, in which the "libido"
manifested itself underwent a radical change. Similarly, the soul or
consciousness was what maintained itself in the "metamorphosis of
the gods" while the primary forms of the "contents" in which
consciousness reflected itself were rendered fundamentally obsolete and
were succeeded by radically new ones. Now, however, Jung works with
a literal *reductio in primam figuram*: it is still Zeus who rules. It is still
the demons of old that are the true determining factors. This is like
saying that a butterfly is still a caterpillar—a denial of the radical
discontinuity prevailing between these two discreet, irreducible forms
that succeed each other while there is nevertheless also a continuous
identity, but precisely not on the level of the metamorphosing
phenomenal forms, but only on the level of irrepresentable substance.

Jung now, as we could put it in terms of the notions contained in his early book title, takes one of the "symbolizations" of the "libido," one of the forms that come up in the transformation process of the libido and treats it as if it were itself the irrepresentable substance behind the transformation process and remains identical with itself through all its changes. This prioritizing of one form reduces all the other forms to irrelevancy. They are either deformations (e.g., neurotic symptoms) of the only true form—the gods—or illusions, delusions, deceptions that disguise and hide the truth.

Jung here cancels the psychological difference that was operative both in the title formulation of his early work and in the "metamorphosis of the gods" idea. The difference between the two levels (the irreducible distinctness of the level of "the libido" or "the soul" or "consciousness" on the one hand, and the level of the metamorphosing "symbols" or "psychic phenomena," "psychic contents" in which the soul articulates itself on the other hand) is collapsed into one. Here the phenomena, the neurotic symptoms, are both at once. This new theory is reductive. The form change and the continuity of the substance occur on one and the same level. It is still the same Zeus, although he no longer rules Olympus but our solar plexus.

This reductive abolition of the psychological difference manifests also in Jung's interpretation of the insight he quotes from the *Hui Ming Ging*, that the "shapes formed by the spirit-fire are only empty colours and forms." Jung commentary on this is, "That sounds thoroughly European and seems to suit our reason to a T. We think we can congratulate ourselves on having already reached such a pinnacle of clarity, imagining that we have left all these phantasmal gods far behind," and later he states "Instead of taking [this Eastern insight] as additional confirmation of his view that the daemon is an illusion, Western man ought to experience once more the realness of this illusion. He should learn to acknowledge these psychic forces anew..." (§ 55). Here we see very clearly how spellbound Jung is by the surface appearance of the phenomenal level (the compulsive power of symptoms) and that here he does not have eyes for the level of soul. When speaking of Western man he personalistically looks at *people* and their behavior, their symptoms, their subjective ideas and feelings, etc. His horizon is the consulting room and the personal psychology of

"METAMORPHOSIS OF THE GODS"

the individual. And on that level it is of course doubtlessly clear that no pinnacle of clarity has been reached. People are always only people, a little more or a little less conscious, wise, crazy, morally good, courageous and cowardly—no matter on what level of cultural development and at what stage of consciousness. What else could one expect of people?

But when doing psychology, when it is a question of whether such a high degree of distillation of the form of consciousness has been reached or not, one must not stare at people (empirical man) and at the empirical psychic foreground. One has to look at the soul, at the logical constitution of modern consciousness, at the objective inner *form* of Western culture. Of course it is not *we* who have reached the highest distillation of consciousness. However, *the soul* has reached it. We live in a culture and at a level of consciousness that have in fact undergone a long historical transformation process in that direction. The element *in* which we live—the soul—has been distilled. And in that element in which we as modern Western man live, the daemon *is* an illusion, objectively so, in other words, *quite independently of whether an individual consciousness is up to this level or not*. People's consciousness usually lags behind the soul's development. Therefore the *soul* of Western man does not need any additional confirmation that the daemon is an illusion, because that this is so is old hat; a wish to confirm it would be carrying coals to Newcastle. Daemons, ghosts, gods *are* superstitions *at the stage* of consciousness reached in Western civilization, and any real consciousness that seriously (not only intellectually) believes in them is ready for the madhouse.

So we don't need to *pretend* "that we have left all these phantasmal gods far behind" in order to have something to pat ourselves on the back about. That we no longer live in the Stone Age nor in polytheistic or in medieval times cannot even be used to flatter our vanity because it is not our doing at all. It is the work of the history of the soul that transported us to where we now are. It is a form change of consciousness, a metamorphosis of the soul's truth *into which* we people happen to be placed. Although the particular soul truth in which we live naturally also informs us in certain ways, nevertheless, it does not make us any better or higher or wiser. We as people stay human, all-too-human.

When Jung says, "So it is better for Western man if he does not know too much about the secret insights of the Oriental sages to begin with, for, as I have said, it would be a case of the 'right means in the hands of the wrong man'" (§ 55), my response is that it would be a case of "preaching to the converted." It is like offering a primer book to a university graduate. The content of the Oriental insight in question has long been integrated into the real syntax of Western consciousness. But Jung feels that Western man should be protected from it because it would come to him prematurely. By saying "it is better if he does not know ... *to begin with*," Jung holds out the prospect of a future time when we will perhaps have become ready for those Oriental insights. In other words, what is a long accomplished past he presents to us as a future promise. He is driven to do this because he focuses on the consciousness of people instead of on the soul, the logical form of modern consciousness.

Only because it is a fact that the obsolescence of the gods and spirits is psychologically the already prevailing self-evident truth for us can Jung feel the need in the first place to *tell* Western man that they are by no means obsolete. If the gods and demons were still alive it would not need Jung's preaching. And conversely, only because Oriental man (who still today consults fortune tellers, for example, about auspicious days for marrying, or uses rhinoceros horn powder as an impotency cure) still *needed* this message was he in this Chinese text told that the "shapes formed by the spirit-fire are only empty colours and forms." Obviously, this message is addressed to a consciousness that takes these shapes at face value. For this consciousness being freed from its persisting naive belief in those shapes formed by the spirit-fire is in this text a distant goal to be striven for, because as a matter of course it still takes them to be substantial, self-sufficient realities. As Jung himself realized, this message contains a "secret insight of the Oriental sages"—a *secret* of the subjective *conscious* (*intellectual*) awareness of *a few sages* precisely because it is by no means the lived, prevailing truth of the objective soul at large. What for the Chinese text is an explicit message, so to speak a news item, is in the West a living social reality.

We modern people of the West are certainly not in the situation of that consciousness for which the "urgent instructions" of *The Tibetan Book of the Dead* were intended, namely for the "simpler, polytheistically-minded mentality of Eastern man"; *it*, not modern Western consciousness, needed to "be instructed not to take these

"METAMORPHOSIS OF THE GODS"

figures for truth" (§ 50, transl. modified). And conversely, this instruction was not at all necessary because the danger is great "that consciousness will be disintegrated by these figures" (*ibid.*). This danger did not exist for that consciousness since those figures were firmly established, and generally familiar, constituents of that type of collective consciousness that has such a "simpler, polytheistically-minded mentality." They are elements of the self-articulation of this consciousness and as such rather support and confirm it rather than threaten it. No, those instructions are necessary for a purpose in the opposite direction: to set before this naive polytheistically-minded consciousness the distant goal (*terminus ad quem*) of an enlightened consciousness, which is *mutatis mutandis* the "same" goal that for Western civilization has long objectively become the real basis on which it stands and from which it already moved on to yet further forms of consciousness.

The gods and demons have become dead to such an extent and are so far removed from us that modern man can safely use them again as abstract clichés and merely rhetorical devices in a "polytheistic psychology." For we have to keep apart two entirely different topics. The one is the survival of the old pagan gods in the shape of evil spirits, especially during the Middle Ages; Jung gave an example by referring to the Mercurius in the fairytale of "The Spirit in the Bottle." We can speak of a survival of sorts because these gods or spirits were rooted in authentic soul phenomena, the events of actual (although regressive) *spontaneous apparitions.* The other topic is the artificial revival of "gods" in polytheistic psychology. They have no phenomenal basis. They are *intellectual* contents of consciousness, ideas that solely stem from modern man's higher education and serve as mere labels. Like very old sun-bleached bones that are so far beyond all disturbing traces of a decaying body that one can touch them without revulsion, so one can use these "gods" without having to fear any consequences. One can now freely speak of "personal myths" and of "portals to the sacred" without having to incur any cost (obligation), indeed without having to mean anything concrete by those phrases. Just nice-sounding jingle. And because vampires and ghosts *are* in fact unreal for modern consciousness we can lightly enjoy their appearance in horror movies as thrilling.

It is a psychological mistake that Jung psychologistically levels the psychological difference down by identifying the empirical subjective symptomatology of the individual person with something of soul importance and by exclusively concentrating on "semantic" contents while ignoring the dimension of the form or "syntax" of consciousness. Jung actually knew better. He had already discussed the "metamorphosis of the gods" in that same text, and in 1935 he wrote explicitly in a letter to Friedrich Seifert that the historical development of the functions "is a very complicated affair, since it would have to be treated not in terms of the contents that have remained more or less the same in the history of civilization but in terms of form" (*Letters 1*, p. 194, 31 July 1935). What applies to the history of the functions (if there is such a thing) applies to a much higher degree to the essential history of the soul at large. Soul history is a history of logical forms. The logical or syntactical constitution of consciousness is what counts in psychology, not so much the positive contents that appear in consciousness. But in his commentary on the Chinese text Jung is oblivious to the problem of form and shows himself exclusively impressed by the neurotic contents, the symptoms of people. Why? Probably because he wants to hold on to the *prima figura*, the *form* of gods, demons, symbols, etc. who all still have the substantiated *form* of semantic contents, beings, autonomous persons. Semantically he speaks of a form change, but syntactically he tries to rescue and eternalize the *prima figura* ("rescue" it long after it has dissolved!). That is, he wants on the intellectual, theoretical level[6] to regress behind that form of consciousness that after a long historical development has assimilated or integrated those contents into itself. I already pointed out that Jung took the worms' eye view basing himself in the regressive tendency. And the moment one form is prioritized and singled out as the exclusive form, consciousness becomes unconscious of the problem of form as such and thus also of the difference between form and what it is the form of, between the level of syntax and the level of semantics. From now on it is inevitably only interested in the *What*, the contents, the images. It now moves solely on the level of semantics.

---

[6] In contrast to the regressive *spontaneous apparition* in medieval times of demons in whom pagan gods survived.

"METAMORPHOSIS OF THE GODS"

Criticizing Freudian psychoanalysis Jung wrote, "The loss of the great relationship is the root problem of neurosis, and that is why the neurotic loses his way among ever more tortuous back-streets of dubious repute, because he who denies the great must blame the petty" (*CW* 10 § 367, transl. modif.). Is it not sad to see that Jung here, with his "The gods have become diseases," unwittingly himself denies the great, only on a much more subtle level than Freud and in a disguised way, namely by systematically distracting from this reductive move by *upgrading* petty neurotic realities to manifestations of gods? How he himself thus loses himself among the tortuous back-streets of dubious repute, even while thinking that he is precisely doing the opposite, namely paying respect to the great? The second Commandment reads, "You must not misuse your God's name." I think we should expand it to read, "You must not carelessly misuse the word 'god.'" Is it not irresponsible to claim that *the gods* have become diseases?

This is a *metabasis eis allo genos* (jumping into another domain), or actually a *katabasis eis allo genos*, inasmuch as it is a descent to a categorially lower level. Jung inflated the petty to give it the significance of the great. In order to get an idea of the soul in ancient times, we turn to the real "great," to the highest, most advanced cultural phenomena of early cultures, namely to their myths, rituals, gods, symbols. We do not look at the private psychology of individuals of those times, what they thought and felt, what symptoms they had (and this not only because we have no way of knowing anything about those personal phenomena). Rather it is because what we are interested in in Jungian psychology is the objective psyche, the "collective unconscious," as Jung termed it (despite the fact that it was in reality precisely not unconscious but socially celebrated public knowledge). But in our context Jung treats "the petty," what he finds in the consulting room of the psychotherapist, i.e., in the personal psychology of modern individuals, as if it were on the same level with those myths and rituals. These are two incomparably different dimensions. One cannot compare personal neuroses with archaic gods. But Jung precisely looks at the great from the worms' eye view (the diseases are gods since the gods have become diseases). The real functional equivalent to what the myths, rituals, and symbols were to ancient peoples would nowadays be what is "the great" today, that is to say, what informs our modern culture in the depth, the philosophies, scientific knowledge, our determining political ideas, the great literary and artistic creations, the existence of the *institutions* of newspapers and television,[7] etc., in short, the logic of modern life. This is the modern equivalent to ancient myth. With all that, one would move on a comparable level, and the moment one would stay faithful to this level throughout, the psychological problem would naturally reveal itself as a problem of logical form and the soul's history as a metamorphosis.

"But what we have left behind are only verbal spectres, *not the psychic facts that were responsible for the birth of the gods*" (§ 54; the italics are in the German original). "If tendencies towards dissociation were not inherent in the human psyche, psychic partial systems would never have been split off; in other words, neither spirits nor gods would ever have come into existence" (§ 51, transl. modif.). If the psychic facts that were responsible for the birth of the gods still existed, it would simply be impossible for gods not to exist still today. Our age is of course only "so utterly deprived of gods and desacralized" (§ 51, transl. modif.) because "the psychic facts" have changed. Jung mentions (*ibid.*) the modern view that "God is a hypothesis that can be subjected to intellectual treatment, to be affirmed or denied" and feels the need to *criticize* this view instead of recognizing in it a psychological *phenomenon*, a tell-tale sign, that reveals the state of the soul and needs explanation or interpretation. It speaks for itself. It is of course true that this view is based on a misunderstanding of what "God" actually means. But the fact that there is this misunderstanding is exactly what is of *psychological* relevance, whereas a critique or refutation of this misunderstanding is merely of *abstract intellectual* interest. Whether a view is correct or not is psychologically neither here nor there. What counts is that it exists and prevails. The psychological question is how this modern view (that God could be disputed) could come about in the first place and what that is that it reveals. It clearly demonstrates that "God" had psychologically become a relic of the past in modern consciousness. The word, the idea still existed; consciousness found it in the inventory of its language, but it simply could not connect any *real* soul meaning and feeling with it any more. Consciousness had

---

[7] Not what is written in newspapers and shown on television.

"METAMORPHOSIS OF THE GODS"

outgrown it, much like we have outgrown stone axes. "God" was no longer backed up as a matter of course by any "psychic fact." This is why it had to be a puzzling question, an intellectual, debatable hypothesis. What else could it be after the soul had no stake in it any longer? In earlier ages, the hypothetical nature of God or gods would have been totally out of the question, because the gods in those ages came as unquestionable realities with absolute convincing power. Gods were the soul's own truth, the (projected) self-reflection of consciousness as such on that cultural level.

Jung's attempt here is to argue away a real "psychic fact" of the modern soul and to supplant it by the idea of *alleged timeless psychic facts*. No, there is not today, in this regard, a "fanatical denial of the existence of autonomous partial systems" (*ibid.*, transl. modif.). It's the other way around. Jung needs to claim such a fanatical denial in order to use the power inherent in this invented but rejected *fanaticism* to lend power to his idea of those split-off autonomous partial systems as the timeless psychic facts responsible for the birth of gods.

The timelessness of "psychic facts" in Jung's thinking does not betray a kind of Platonism (eternal ideas). On the contrary, it is due to the opposite, his naturalistic, positivistic bias.[8] The psyche is seen by Jung in analogy to the biological body. Just as the human body and its organs were pretty much the same from the Stone Age to today, so Jung perceives of the psyche and its partial systems personalistically as constant "psychic facts" that modern man shares with mankind of all previous ages. Since the gods and demons are split-off psychic partial systems for Jung, and since these partial systems are the same "psychic facts" as in archaic so in modern man, this is the logic of Jung's thesis, Zeus and the demons cannot have disappeared.

This positivistic conception of the soul is not tenable. The body and its organs as well as its historical continuity can indeed be shown to be positive facts. Not so the soul. There is no such thing as the soul. It is logically negative. The soul has to be comprehended as the self-display, self-articulation, self-representation of the inner logic and truth of man's world-relation, his interchange with the world. The soul is from the outset *product, result, display* and not naturalistically a set of

---

[8] This is Jung's basis for insisting on "gods." The basis for the same insistence in "polytheistic psychology" is very different: *rhetoric*.

558   THE SOUL ALWAYS THINKS

"psychic facts" *behind* this result. It exists *only* in how it shows itself. The idea of immutable "psychic facts" that are "responsible for the birth of gods" is positivistic. In long-bygone days the truth of man's world-relation articulated itself in the gods, and later in the one God. Because the human world-relation drastically changed from man as hunter via man as agriculturalist and man as craftsman to man as industrialist and so on, the self-articulation of the inner truth of his interchange with the world was also bound to change. And so here at the end of our exploration we see that we have to return again to Jung's first theory of a "metamorphosis of the gods" in the sense of "transformations of the self-articulation of the soul's truth."

* * *

By way of an appendix I have to briefly mention another theory of Jung's about the metamorphosis of the gods that is radically different from the one above, which had operated with the idea of the integration of "the gods" into consciousness by means of what Jung had called "spatial projection," that is to say, consciousness's having become conscious of *itself*. The other theory explains the death of the gods in a very different way, by means of the idea of "awakening reason" and "reflection." Speaking of the "iconoclasm of the Reformation" and the crumbling away of nearly all sacred images, Jung wrote about those images,

> They became awkward, for they collided with awakening reason. Besides, it had long been forgotten what they meant. Had it really been forgotten? Or could it perhaps be that men had never known at all what they mean, and that only in more recent times did it occur to the Protestant part of mankind that actually we do not have a real knowledge of what is meant by the Virgin Birth, the divinity of Christ, and the complexities of the Trinity? It almost seems as if these images had just lived, and as if their living existence had simply been taken for granted, without doubt and without reflection, much as everyone decorates Christmas trees or hides Easter eggs without ever knowing what these customs mean. The fact is that archetypal images a priori carry their meaning within themselves so that people never think of asking what they might mean. The reason why gods die from time to time is that man suddenly discovers that they do not

> mean anything, that they are made by human hands, useless
> things formed of wood and stone. In reality, however, he has
> merely discovered that up till then he has not had any thoughts
> whatever about his images. And when he starts thinking about
> them, he does so with the help of what he calls "reason"—which,
> however, in truth is nothing more than the sum-total of his
> prejudices and myopic views. (*CW* 9i § 22, transl. modified)

This thesis about the death of the gods and sacred images is not restricted to the particular case of the Reformation. A few paragraphs down Jung works again with this explanation, now applied to the death of the classical gods, thereby showing that this is a general theory for him, at least in this essay.

> The gods of Greece and Rome perished from the same disease
> as did our Christian symbols: people discovered then, as today,
> that they had no thoughts on the subject. The gods of the
> strangers, by contrast, still had unexhausted mana. Their names
> were weird and incomprehensible and their deeds mysteriously
> dark—quite in contrast to the hackneyed *chronique scandaleuse*
> of Olympus. ... (§ 26, transl. modified).

For at least two reasons this is a poor theory. First of all, it is a theory from the standpoint of external reflection, of "the ego." Jung thinks in terms of a clash between two given facts, the existing gods or images here and the demands of the intellect there. He simply takes for granted the emergence of "reason," of a necessity to have rational thoughts about the meaning of the divine or sacred images, without in any way developing where this intellectual necessity "suddenly" came from and why and how it originated, what the soul need or purpose behind it was. And this takes us already to the second point. His thesis begs the question. The fact that people discovered that they did not have any real knowledge about their gods and symbols is not the explanation but that which needs to be explained. The gods of Greece and Rome did of course not perish *from* this discovery. Rather, this discovery presupposes that the gods have already become obsolete (had no "unexhausted mana" any more) and consciousness has risen to a higher level. Only then can the need to understand what they mean arise in the first place, because only then have the gods dwindled to mere *objects* of, or semantic contents *within*, a (now superior, encompassing, *self*-conscious and as such *reflecting, thinking*) consciousness as "space for all contents." As long as they are alive, such a necessity could not possibly be felt, because then the gods would be the expression, in imaginal form, of the *ground* as well as *outside borders* of consciousness as such, of its truth, its logical life. As "objects" whose semantic claim is precisely to be nonpositive and supra-objectual they are as a matter of course puzzling for consciousness and demand *reflection*, whereas as consciousness's own ground and outside borders they are *worshiped*; their experienced overwhelming numinosity ("mana") speaks for itself; the soul's deepest feelings naturally and spontaneously flow towards them. But now their numinosity and divinity have been reduced to no more than part of their dictionary definitions, the list of their attributes in mythology books. And conversely, the moment they have become objects of reflection and reasoning, it has simply become impossible to worship them, sincerely worship them without having had to make some contorted efforts at silencing one's intellect.[9]

It is also interesting, in the light of his other statement that "The gods have *become* diseases," to note that here Jung lets the gods die *from* a disease. And that what in the first-mentioned theory of the metamorphosis of the gods was a progression of consciousness, in the second one is denigrated as a disease.

I called Jung's theory about the death of the gods through people's discovery that "they had no thoughts on the subject" a poor theory. But it is nevertheless helpful because it makes us aware of an aspect of the metamorphosis of the gods that we have not explicitly noted so far. When Jung spoke of the gods' turning from persons into personified

---

[9] But here we have to be cautious. "Worship" does not only refer to naive religious practice on an archaic or popular level of cultural development. In classical metaphysics up to the time of Hegel we have the phenomenon that God was sincerely worshiped— however, on the wholly other level of philosophical thought (*metaphysical* thought); and accordingly, the God that was worshiped was no longer image and no longer polytheistic nature gods in the plural, but also in himself thought. Jung's opposition of only two states, one of a naive religion and another one of a situation of "awakening reason" where man discovered that he "has not had any thoughts whatever about" the gods and images does not cover all of our real history, nor does it in any way apply to our situation today. A more differentiated view is needed. Our modern situation of not being able to make sense of the old religious motifs, of the gods, and of God precisely follows upon a period of more than two millennia during which there had been very deep and very thorough *thought* "about" God, without his having been a mere object or content of consciousness. Metaphysical thought *as* a form of worship.

"METAMORPHOSIS OF THE GODS"

ideas and finally into abstract ideas he had addressed himself to a different phenomenon from the present one of the discovery that one cannot make sense of the gods. The difference comes about because a psychological metamorphosis such as that of the gods leads to a bifurcation.

When the nymph Daphne changed into a laurel tree, she as nymph had disappeared (at least on the narrative level; logically what is narratively portrayed as two distinct states has of course to be seen through as simultaneous aspects of one and the same being). But when historically the gods have become abstract ideas, the gods as persons have not totally disappeared. They remain as historical relics. We now have a true duality: (a) the new "abstract ideas" as the authentic successors of the now obsolete gods and (b) the now obsolete gods as persons themselves who, although obsolete, may nevertheless survive in public religious institutions and ritual practices, in acquired personal deep-rooted feelings, as components in our historical knowledge about the "religious ideas" of former ages or peoples, as metaphors, allegories, or as popular superstitions and modern artificial revivals. What I called Jung's first theory of a metamorphosis of the gods focused on (a), the internal form change of the *life* or *truth* of what originally used to have the form of gods as numinous persons. The life and truth that originally were in the gods remained, but the "personal god" form of this life and truth was left behind in favor of a new form. On the other hand, with his theory of the death of the gods on account of people's noticing that the gods do not mean anything Jung focused on (b), the abstract form of the *literal* images (pictorial representations) of gods as historical relics. Here there is precisely not a succession, not a progression of life, but a retention, a conservation of the *prima figura* (the gods as persons), almost reminiscent of a mummification.

This also means that the notion of a metamorphosis of the gods becomes equivocal. It can mean (a) the transformation of the inward logical form of the gods from persons to philosophical ideas, as discussed above, but it can also mean (b) that change through which what had once been the expression of the soul's highest life and truth was precisely depleted of its life and prevailing truth and reduced to the lifeless shell of accurately preserved historical relics. This change from living god to lifeless pictorial representation is a metamorphosis too. But rather than being an internal form change of those conserved gods themselves, it is a change external to them: the floor has been pulled out from under them, as it were, and this caused their demise. The logical constitution of consciousness or the mode of being-in-the-world in and for which the gods had been the authentic imaginal portrayal of the soul's truth no longer exists. Underneath the literal gods (as persons), consciousness imperceptibly glided over centuries to a new logical status or syntax. At a certain point in time, consciousness objectively all of a sudden finds itself in this new status without subjectively being fully aware of it or having embraced it. It is a status in which and for which those gods as persons all of a sudden have no vital function any more and do not make sense any more. They are now foreign bodies, relics from the past. And this is why all of a sudden the need discussed by Jung arises for people to come up with theoretical ideas about the gods and what they mean, especially when the former religious practices and the corresponding claims that one ought to respect the gods are still retained and the sense of their former deep significance still has a strong emotional hold over consciousness.

CHAPTER TWENTY-ONE

There is Psychological Progress.
Can There Be Progress of Psychology?

The belief in progress is an inheritance of the Age of Enlightenment. It developed into a most powerful and popular ideological force during the 19th century. In its form as Cultural Darwinism it could easily be allied with other historical forces such as imperialism, colonialism, and racism as their ideological justification. In the amazing and indubitable progress of the sciences, technology and industry during the 19th century it had its obvious factual underpinning. The constant and seemingly unending advances on the scientific and technical fronts with their numerous innovations in material culture and the ensuing changes in social life were an enormously impressive experience in real, practical life to be felt by everyone on a day-to-day basis. *Psychologically* this experience necessarily had a powerful impact. It produced a particular existential feeling, a particular sense of and attitude towards life. This feeling in turn led to and gave, as a matter of course, a vigorous boost to a more generalized idea that life at large, life also in the area of human culture, insight, and ethical development, follows a similar pattern of progress.

"Progress" in this later context always involves a value judgment. It means better, greater, higher: improvement, perfection. When I speak, by contrast, of psychological progress I do not have this notion of progress in mind. I merely mean progression in analogy to how we imagine biological evolution, as a development from very simple unicellular forms of life to ever more degrees of complexity and differentiation. True, we also speak of the "higher" mammals, but in biology this is not a value judgment. It does not at the same time mean better. All it means is higher degrees of complexity. The term progression or progress is appropriate because there is really *pro*-gress (not merely diversification), inasmuch as the more complex types of organisms presuppose the simpler types. They build on the solutions realized on the stages of evolution reached so far and push off from there to again a little more differentiated forms. In other words, I use "progress" as a merely descriptive term.

Progress in the history of the soul proceeds likewise by the soul's again and again pushing off from a prevailing constitution of itself to logically more complex ones. Since the theme of *psychological* progress is not my topic here, but only a backdrop for my actual question, I will just mention three major phenomena representative of different stages of psychological evolution as examples of psychological progress on a macro-level: crudely speaking, polytheism – monotheism – the end of God or religion (in the sense of "the birth of man"). Monotheism is *sublated* polytheism, the birth of man is *sublated* monotheism. In each case the later form would not have been possible without the prior one, and despite the negation by each later form of its predecessor there is nevertheless a certain *continuity*, precisely because any later form is the negated or sublated earlier one. The changes occur within one undisrupted cultural memory, rather than each one's being a random and context-free realization of any one of all abstractly possible forms of consciousness. This is what allows us to speak of progress.

At first glance, one might of course object to the idea that the move from polytheism to monotheism, let alone the step from monotheism to the birth of man, is progress in the sense of higher differentiation. Is not polytheism, the system of many gods and cults parallel to each other in one society, quite obviously more complex than monotheism with its one single God? This objection is correct, but only as long as one looks at things from a psychic or semantic level. Many is more complex than one. But it is not tenable when it is a question of the psychology, the logic, or the syntactical aspect of the matter. From such a point of view, monotheism is logically or psychologically much more complex. It presupposes a much higher degree of differentiation

PROGRESS OF PSYCHOLOGY? 565

of consciousness. In polytheism, the differentiation or complexity is, as it were, acted out; it is "literal," all "out there." It is the complexity of the contents of consciousness. But *ipso facto* it is not yet consciousness's own differentiation. In order to have come into existence, monotheism, by contrast, must have interiorized this external differentiation on the content level into the very constitution or logical form of consciousness itself. It has, as we can also put it, integrated it. It can no longer deal with the complexity on the level of contents that it has in front of itself and thus itself stays clear of it. It has to *exist as* this complexity. *Mutatis mutandis* the same can be said about the psychological situation in which there is no God at all any more. At this stage, "God" has been sublated, that is to say, inwardized into the form of consciousness (which for this very reason has become incapable of having a God vis-à-vis or above itself, as a content of consciousness).

I mentioned this only by way of an example, so that one can have a better idea of what I mean when I say that "there is psychological progress." But in order to begin with the question that in this paper is my real interest, namely whether there can be progress of psychology, progress in psychological knowledge or insight, I will use a famous quotation from Max Planck from his *Wissenschaftliche Selbstbiographie* (1948) as my starting point.

> The usual way a new scientific truth becomes generally accepted is not that its opponents are persuaded and stand corrected, but that its opponents gradually die out and the next generation grows up with that truth from the start.[1]

As true as this statement is, and as much as it is borne out by experience, it is nevertheless shocking. It deals a death blow to the idea that science is governed by rationality. All scientists, so one should think, would immediately become convinced by a new truth, simply because it is a truth. "It is a scientific truth" is not to be understood here in terms of a metaphysical truth. It means no more than that it is a thesis supported by the best arguments and empirical support available at the time. The mere word "opponent" (of the new scientific truth) introduces something irrational into the progress of scientific

---

[1] My translation.

566 THE SOUL ALWAYS THINKS

insight. It sounds as if science were a matter of a power struggle between parties or interest groups, or a matter of preferences and personal likings, and not a matter of solid reasoning and empirical proof. How can a scientist, committed to rational argumentation, be an opponent of a new truth? Incredible, but obviously true. If its opponents have to die out for a new truth to have a chance, if, in other words, the victory of the new truth depends on the defenders' of the obsolete views being removed from the scene through the *natural, contingent* event of their death and on their being replaced by *other*, young, not yet committed persons freshly entering the arena of science, then scientific progress is dependent on external serendipitous factors.

But when I said Planck's statement deals a death blow to the idea that science is governed by rationality, I was not accurate. I confused the difference between science itself and the scientific community, that is, the multitude of human individuals in and through whom science realizes itself. These are really two distinct realities. What Planck described refers only to the second reality, to the people who are scientists and *their* human psychology, not to science itself, which is an abstract reality belonging to the ideal or noetic sphere. The moment people are involved, an irrational element comes in. Science itself, by contrast, is not touched by Planck's description. In science itself as the abstract realm of ideas and knowledge, a new truth, if it is really a truth, is as a matter of course simply the truth with respect to the particular issue. There cannot be any doubt or resistance to it. Science per se develops strictly on the basis of the best argument. But the moment human beings come into play, we have left the ideal sphere and entered a totally different scene. A scientist, although a worker in the field of science, is not identical with science. Rather, he is within himself the unity of and difference between science itself and the human, all-too-human. As a human being, a scientist is limited. And by saying this I am not referring to the possibility of *bad* scientists, those who, for example, for ulterior motives (fame, career, jealousy of others, more research funding) forge or invent the results of experiments. I leave this possibility completely aside and concentrate only on the ideal case of conscientious scientists *without* ulterior motives. Even so we will have to consider the human factor.

Considering the point made by Planck, the main human factor that creates "opponents" to a new scientific truth can probably be

PROGRESS OF PSYCHOLOGY?

identified as the force of habit. It is, however, not a habit in the usual sense of an attachment to old traditional views. It is a habit in a special, very personal, biographical sense. The members of the scientific community are scientists, that is, they do research, they themselves attempt to advance science. The scientists of a given generation have themselves covered a distance, having moved from a starting point (the point representing "state-of-the-art" knowledge when they began) to the state to which their own investigations led them. The life of a scientist is thus essentially the movement from a *terminus a quo* to a *terminus ad quem*.

In order to arrive at the latter, throughout their lifetime the scientists had to invest into their work lots of time, zeal, and sweat, and in addition many deep emotions: disappointments to be combated, satisfaction with successful advances, joy at arriving at new discoveries. So the *terminus ad quem*, i.e., the convictions slowly gained, hard-earned, time and again tested and confirmed during their lifelong study as scientists, is for them their crowning achievement, something like the "treasure hard to obtain." Through their long slow labor at arriving at their results they have become attached to them, indeed we might even say they have become one with them, grown together with them. This unity is an *embodied reality* with some stability. These scientists are like an old tree that cannot freely be bent this way or that way any more. They are set.

In addition, we have to realize that in order to get to where they are they exhausted themselves. The convictions gained through a lifetime's research and teaching have for them psychologically the character of having *arrived* at a goal, a finish. And if in this situation there is all of a sudden a radically new scientific truth, it is for them as if a runner were to be told at the end of a race that he should immediately begin a new and possibly longer race.

On both counts, we can understand that and why a new scientific truth has little chance with the old generation. Its representatives simply have to die out. Instead it requires new, young persons if it is to be accepted—and turned into a new *terminus a quo*. However, these new, young persons will in turn, when their time has come, have to disappear to make way for a new generation for the same reason. The people who produce science, one after the other must be discarded so that science itself may triumph. "*It* must increase, but they must decrease." They are ruthlessly thrown out into and buried in the cemetery called "history of science," which, instead of a cemetery, could alternately also be seen as a huge wastebasket. Thus the relation between the human workforce in science on the one hand and science itself on the other hand can in some ways be compared to the building of a mediaeval cathedral that extended over several centuries and consumed many generations of construction workers.

This human "recycling" does not hamper scientific progress itself. It is rather required for the progress of science. The constant consumption and disposal of human scientists does not impair science. Science stays untouched, unaffected in its eternal peace and splendor, just as a cathedral or an Egyptian pyramid in no way shows any sign of the suffering, wounds, deaths of all the workers used up for its construction. In science itself, or on the level of science as a noetic reality, scientific truths, once discovered, irrevocably replace previous ideas, now proven wrong, about the same subject. The old, now falsified ideas suffer their *real*[2] death precisely *in* the literal deaths of the old generation scientists who advocated them. For the symbolic experience of the soul, their adherents take the obsolete ideas with them into their graves. And for the new and future generations of scientists it will *ipso facto* be impossible to return to the superseded ideas.

The ongoing substitution of one generation by another in science is necessary for overcoming what one might call the "stickiness" of insights, their tendency to solidify, become fixated, "materialized," by growing together with and getting stuck in a really existing person (the scientist) as his unshakeable conviction. A ruthless cut is necessary to sever the bond that connects scientific truths to, and tends to amalgamate them with, their naturally existing carriers, the consciousness of people who are the discoverers of those truths. It is (literal) death, the death of the scientists, that finally and ultimately liberates the truths from their initial contamination with nature and releases them into an existence in the purely ideal sphere of knowing. It is a fundamental shortcoming of the natural sciences that they cannot by themselves and within themselves perform this releasement of their own truths, but instead are dependent on an external force, namely nature, to bring this cutting loose about, in the form of a

---

[2] Real in the sense of not only logical, noetic. In material reality.

PROGRESS OF PSYCHOLOGY?

positive fact, a fundamentally contingent event—death. The natural sciences do not work with truths[3] that would either come as a priori released from nature or that would within themselves have the strength to perform this severing of their own accord as their own inherent logic.

One could assume that something similar could be the case in psychology (and when saying "psychology" I restrict myself here mainly to Jungian psychology). Inasmuch as psychology has a very strong empirical aspect through the psychologists' daily experience in the consulting room, one could expect that there would be a process of learning from experience so that here, too, certain old psychological ideas would become falsified in the work with patients and at the same time new insights into psychic reality would be gained. And why should the generations problem pointed out by Planck not take effect here, too, his observation that the opponents of a new truth simply have to die out for it to become accepted?

But this is obviously not the case. And that it is not the case in psychology shows that psychology is not a science. The question is what makes it so different from a science.

A superficial glance suffices to make us realize that the process of psychology cannot, like that of the sciences, be compared to the work by numerous workers on the construction of one cathedral. Rather, psychology inevitably falls apart into a multitude of parallel universes, not only the Jungian school beside all the other schools of psychology, but also within the Jungian field itself. Under these circumstances there cannot be any progress of the field, because different views about the same thing can peacefully coexist in those multiple universes. Only if there is a fundamental unity of the field can a deviant hypothesis be

---

[3] In this paper I retain Planck's traditional term "truth" for the sciences despite the fact that strictly speaking this term is inappropriate. Science is not after truth, not even after "correct" statements, but after *reliable* ones. As Heidegger for one pointed out, science is at bottom and from the outset technological (rather than, as is popularly believed, that technology is applied science). And as Niels Bohr realized as early as 1963, "It is a mistake to think that physics has the task of finding out what nature is. Physics is concerned with what we can say about nature." Here, however, because I am concerned with the question of scientific progress, I work with the understanding of science in the traditional sense, where it was the voice of truth, and because progress comes about through the simple separation of what is true from what is false ("verification" and "falsification"). This "truth" is pragmatic, not metaphysical: it is our best confirmed knowledge at the present time. No higher claims ("eternal truths") are connected with it. – This naïve, pragmatic sense of truth must also be distinguished from my term truth in strictly psychological contexts.

either true *or* false and a true elimination process of the false take place. Without this unity nothing can be discarded, once and for all be rendered obsolete, so that only the victorious idea, the new truth, remains. Even the death of the old generation of psychologists does not help, because here the new generation does not grow up with "the new truth" as a matter of course inasmuch as there is now a whole array of "truths," new and old, side by side competing with each other. The "old truths" do not get buried together with their adherents. They stay alive as one possible option.

In fact, the very idea of a truth as in science does not makes sense here any more. There are only *different* ideas, views, conceptions, not true and untrue ones. This is why there cannot be any learning from experiences in psychology. Experience at best provides new ideas. It does not mercilessly negate any old one, at least not in a way that would be binding for the generality. Why this is so is again something that needs to be explained.

Why is there not one single edifice for all psychologists to work on? And why do the insights of psychology not have the character of truths (the way that scientific results come as truths in the sense described above)? The reason for this fundamental difference between science and psychology is that psychology (depth psychology, in particular Jungian psychology) is a discipline that is not constituted through a structural difference between subject and object, mind and nature. As Jung saw very clearly, in psychology the soul explores the soul, the subject studies the subject. There is for it no "Archimedean point" outside of itself. This means that psychology is logically so constituted that it operates within a fundamental identity. It is structurally not different from itself. Symbolically expressed: it is uroboric; it bites its own tail. It is self-contained, cocooned within itself, with no chance of getting out, of arriving at an "objective" other. This is very different in science. Here the discipline comes as structurally a priori distinguished from itself. Underlying it as its constitutive act there is a fundamental cut. Science is set up as having its object of study *logically* (not only empirically and factually) outside of itself, and thus irrevocably outside.

The irreversible logical division between subject and object which is given with the structure of science has consequences for the subject as well as for the object. The structural division inherent in the field

PROGRESS OF PSYCHOLOGY?

of science as such necessarily imparts itself to both. The moment a person enters science (truly enters it, which means that he or she has tuned into and is informed by the logic constituting it), a severing has always already taken place in him or her as subject, a division between the subject's merely personal, private subjectivity and a (through this entrance newly instituted) intersubjective subjectivity. To the extent that a scientist is truly a scientist he does not think as his private self, but has *logically* taken the standpoint of consciousness-as-such, the consciousness of any and all scientists (regardless of whether he or she is empirically, subjectively fully able to hold himself/herself at the height of this standpoint). The point here is that the objective field comes with this distinction and *ipso facto* constellates the universalized subject the moment the field of science has truly been entered. It is precisely not the personal task of the individual to achieve, through its own struggle, this abstraction from his or her personal subjectivity. The logic of the institution of science has always already taken care of that for the scientist. All the individual has to do is to fully enter science. And it is here, in the degree to which this entrance succeeds or not, where the human, all-too-human shortcomings of the individual may come in after all and interfere with the purely scientific standpoint.

Only because a scientist has on principle left his private subjectivity behind simply by becoming a scientist and thinks as consciousness-as-such do we get in science that situation that I compared to the construction over centuries of a cathedral through many builders. In the case of each scientific question there can only be one single truth valid for all scientists. Scientific consciousness-as-such is common to all scientists, and so is truth. It is one and the same shared consciousness that decides what is true or false, regardless of how many individual scientists may empirically be participating in it and who in particular may be speaking at a given time. Each individual is only this general consciousness's temporary human stand-in.

Now I want to look at what the structural division that constitutes science does to the *object* of science. The division that sets subject and object apart shows in the object itself in its having been stripped of any subjectivity. It is purely "objective," that is to say, it has a firm nature or essence as its own inalienable property independent of who the subject may be who is studying it. As such it is resistive, unyielding.

572   *THE SOUL ALWAYS THINKS*

It can say "No!" to the subject's questions and hypotheses about it. And it reliably gives the same response to the same question no matter how often it is questioned and by how many different people. Reality is here a priori construed as positive fact.[4] Because the object is resistive and can give its *independent* answer to our human questions there is in science the possibility of learning from experience.

The independent being-so and hardness of the object has to be understood (seen through) as the result or product of the logic of science which puts its own object radically and irredeemably vis-à-vis itself. The solidity is not itself a fact, something naturally given. The relentlessness of the logical act of severing that underlies the institution of science is what in science gives the object its hardness. This becomes all the clearer the more we confront the resistive nature of the object in science with the object of psychology. Being constituted by a uroboric logic of identity, the object in psychology does not show an unambiguous being-so of its own, independent of the subject. It does not offer the same kind of resistance. It is more to be compared to water. When I try to grasp water, it simply yields. And it indiscriminately adjusts perfectly to the shape of whatever vessel or obstacle. Water, rather than having a shape of its own, receives its shape from whatever surrounds it. In a similar way the object of psychology is characterized by a great plasticity. The object simply does the subject's bidding.

This comes out in the fact that all the diverse psychological theorists found their theories confirmed by their empirical observation, e.g., in their therapies. Jung, being keenly aware of this problem,[5] tried to show that one and the same case can quite as well be interpreted

---

[4] The new, 20th century insight, for example, by Niels Bohr quoted in a previous footnote that "It is a mistake to think that physics has the task of finding out what nature is. Physics is concerned with what we can say about nature," while turning aside from the earlier naïve idea of the possibility of a direct access to objective nature nevertheless retains, even confirms the notion of a positive-factually given essence of nature ("what nature is"). Science still today operates within the pattern of human question/hypothesis and a Yes or No from nature.

[5] But we also have to see that there is another side to Jung, too. He pointed out that an analyst's wrong interpretations simply will not work so that there is, through the patients' real being-so, a corrective factor in therapy after all. Again another (and problematic) aspect of his thinking is that when he was attacked for his general views, e.g., his theory of archetypes, by non-analysts, he worked with the argument that if only these critics had practical therapeutic experience they would naturally be forced to accept his theories.

PROGRESS OF PSYCHOLOGY?

from a Freudian as from an Adlerian or from a Jungian point of view. Obviously, the case material does not of its own accord say "No!" to another interpretative hypothesis. It willingly accepts any one and all of them. But if there is no falsification, there cannot be any learning from experience either. Patricia Berry demonstrated something similar.[6] She presented the same dream to so many different Jungian analysts and received equally many different interpretations. In psychology, psychic reality does not correct the psychologist's ideas about it. Without resistance it lets itself be molded this way or that way, depending on the perspectives and convictions with which it is approached. Psychology, therefore, has nothing external to push off from. If it does push off after all, then it necessarily only does so *within itself* and *from itself* (or from what is already its own internal property or what it has made its property), as we shall discuss below.

Along the same lines Shamdasani points out that,

> If there is one thing that psychology and psychotherapy have demonstrated in the twentieth century, it is the malleability of individuals, who have been willing to adopt psychological concepts to view their lives (and that of others), in terms of a play of conditional reflexes, a desire to kill one's father and sleep with one's mother, a psychomachia between the good and the bad breast, a parade of dissociated alters, a quest for self-actualization through peak experiences or contorted twists through the hoola hoops of the symbolic, imaginary, and the real."

And he insists, "'Psychic reality' is, par excellence, the fabricated real" and states that "its most remarkable 'property' was its capacity to present itself according to whatever theory one held about it.[7]

The phrase "The fabricated real" contains, one would think, a devastating verdict. On the one hand this verdict is justified, inasmuch as in psychology the object is not an independent reality that resists false understandings of it and disproves them, but allows itself to be molded according to the needs or perspectives of the subject viewing

---

[6] Patricia Berry, "An Approach to the Dream," in: P. Berry, *Echo's Subtle Body. Contributions to an Archetypal Psychology*, Dallas, TX (Spring Publications) 1982, pp. 53–79.

[7] Sonu Shamdasani, *Jung and the Making of Modern Psychology*, Cambridge (Cambridge University Press) 2003, p. 11.

it. Interpretations in psychology "fabricate" that which they interpret, and the act of interpretation is in itself this fabrication. This shows once more the uroboric character of psychology. On the other hand, the phrase "the fabricated real" does not go far enough. It is meant to be critical, if not devastating. In some way it still uses as its standard, and thus confirms, the idea of an "objective" real that is *not* fabricated, as we find it in the "nature" that science is about. But to understand psychology and do justice to its uroboric nature we have to leave the idea of an "objective" reality *completely* aside as totally misleading. That psychology "fabricates" the "real" that it studies is not its shortcoming, but its special character, from a certain position we might even say its virtue and distinction. Since in psychology there is not that structural vis-à-vis, that fundamental severing of subject and object which characterizes the underlying logic of science, there cannot be a clear-cut division between subjective view here and objective reality over there. Rather the two aspects, interpretation and reality, are here two *integral moments* of and within one and the same act of doing psychology. They are uroborically intertwined.

Again, Jung saw this very clearly. He knew that in psychology ultimately *Bekenntnis* and *Erkenntnis*[8] (confession / subjective self-expression / self-display, we could also say "projection," on the one hand, *and* recognition / scientific discovery / objective knowledge, on the other hand) go together; the one *is* only as the other and vice versa. By the same token he realized that, for example, Freud developed his particular psychology because he *had* a "Freudian psychology." Freud's psychological theory was the self-portrayal of the psychology that he, Freud, lived or as which he existed. The same principle applies to any psychologist who designs a psychological theory and thus of course also to Jung himself. In psychology, other than in science, the logic of the field does not a priori strip the consciousness of the researcher of its individuality so that what would be present in all psychological researchers would be the same single universal consciousness-as-such shared by all. Rather, each person working in psychology has his or her private consciousness. This also means that each has—potentially—his or her own truth. There is no external touchstone of

---

[8] Cf. *GW* 10 § 367; also "Über Psychologie," in: *Neue Schweizer Rundschau* 1933, 1, pp. 21–27 and 2, pp. 98–106, here p. 22.

truth. What is true, needs here to be determined from *within* the particular psychological theory alone. Each psychology has its touchstone within itself.

As Jung pointed out, psychological work inevitably proceeds under the rule of "the personal equation." This is the equivalent on the side of the subject to the plasticity that we discovered on the side of the object. And both aspects are of course inseparable; they naturally mirror each other, because subject and object are not definitively separated by the logic informing psychology. But if it is *logically* not one single universal consciousness that studies psychological reality, no matter how many individual *empirical* researchers there may be, there cannot either be a universally valid truth in psychology.

We have seen that, on the one hand, the object of psychology is not unambiguously *so* and not otherwise; it is not resistive and does not unforgivingly correct our mistaken assumptions. And we have seen that, on the other hand, the subject of psychology inevitably falls apart into as many individual consciousnesses (and therefore so many personal truths) as there are researchers. Under these circumstances it is clear that progress in psychology is unthinkable. Instead of progress you get multiplication.

Jung once stated that he was the only one of Freud's followers who developed further two particular ideas that were most important to Freud. In other words, in his own estimation he *progressed* beyond Freud's position. David L. Miller also diagnosed an instance of a kind of progress in psychology. "If James Hillman's work on 'archetypal psychology' represents after Jung himself second wave Jungianism, the work of Wolfgang Giegerich may well indicate third wave Jungian thinking."[9] If these two views were correct (which is not an issue in our context), would they contradict my thesis in this paper that there cannot be any progress in psychology? By no means. Because in all cases mentioned, the psychological position that has been overcome by the later move nevertheless continues to flourish undisturbed side by side with the further developments. Its having been overcome does not outclass it. Thinking of Planck's statement that the opponents of a new truth have to die out for it to become accepted, we could point

---

[9] Edward S. Casey and David L. Miller, "Introduction to the Philosophy and Psychology Issue," in: *Spring 77. A Journal of Archetype and Culture*, Spring 2007, p. 6.

out that, in the case of Jung's real or imagined progress beyond Freud, the latter indeed died during Jung's lifetime—the best precondition, according to Planck's dictum, for Jung's view to become accepted. But nothing of the sort happened in reality. The progress has no effect outside of itself, no effect on the theory that has been overcome by it.

What we have to realize is that even if there is progress, as certainly there is, for example, in the case of Hillman's "re-visioning psychology," this progress is nevertheless something completely different from the one that Planck had in mind when he was speaking of a new scientific truth becoming generally accepted. Quantum physics transcended Newtonian physics *within science at large* and *for science as such*. But Jung further-developed Freud's views (in those two areas he had in mind) only within *his own* psychology and *for* his own thinking. As one can show, there is really a move beyond Freud in Jung's theory. But it has no consequences for Freud's theory. By the same token Hillman re-visioned psychology only within his own psychology and for it, just as I pushed off from imaginal psychology only within my own psychological position and for it. What is overcome in each case is only overcome within and for the new scheme, but does in neither case overcome its predecessor *outside* this scheme. So there can indeed be *logical* progress *in* a psychology, but not *factual* progress *of* psychology as such.

Now it is important not to view this *coniunctio* of *Erkennen* and *Bekennen* set out by Jung as a handicap that should not be, and ought to be overcome. But here one can find fault with Jung for not really having drunk his own medicine to the dregs. He does not go all the way to the end with his own marvelous insight into the logic of psychology. For example, he said,

> Our psychological experience is still too young and too little extended to permit of general theories. Further research is needed to assemble many more facts before we could dare to make a first attempt at putting forward universal propositions (*CW* 16 § 236, transl. modified).

Although Jung has clearly understood and affirmed the uroboric logic of psychology, he still firmly holds on to the fantasy of and wish for psychology as a future possible science. Psychology is merely *not yet* there. For the time being it is still too early. Psychology is still too

PROGRESS OF PSYCHOLOGY?

young. Much more preparatory work is needed. But when all this necessary work will have been done, then, one day in the distant future, psychology will be able to advance to universal propositions after all.

What Jung says in this quote is untenable, given his seminal insight into the identity of recognition and self-expression, because then there are (1) no facts in the first place and (2) a general theory in the sense of universal propositions is completely out of the question. All so-called facts are in themselves interpretation and only produced by this interpretation in the first place, its articulation. And each epoch, each interpreter will re-interpret them according to its / his needs and *ipso facto* create "the same" "facts" as different, new ones. No, the idea of a universal theory has to be given up altogether along with the idea of "facts," of an external "real." The lesson of the uroboric intertwinement of "fabrication" and "reality" in psychology is precisely that psychology is the discipline of interiority, which here means that the very notion of the real and the very notion of truth are logically absolute-negatively inwardized into the production process, into the act of doing psychology. The production or interpretation process has the real as its product within itself. Psychology is productive. Much like art, it produces itself as that real that it is about; it *produces* truths and does not find or discover them. Psychology is soul-*making*, not explanation of soul. And this real that it "fabricates" is in itself interpretation. It is not a positive fact, or it is the fact of there being this interpretation, this view.

There is for psychology not any given metaphysical "essence" or substance that would need to be expressed or interpreted, neither as an external real nor in the sense of one's own true inner nature. But psychology is not totally "essence"-less either. No, it *produces* essences as the *result* of its doings. It is inventive.

There are for psychology two possible main problems, two things that can go wrong. A first problem arises if the scientific or pseudo-scientific stance with its logic of externality ("facts," an absolutely independent and "objective" real) and a single universal consciousness-as-such is retained and as one's indispensable standard and measure informs one's thinking even about psychology, while what is done in psychology itself is in fact governed by a totally different logic. We found an example of this problem in the Jung passage quoted above in which his hope, even if only for some distant future, comes out for

578   *THE SOUL ALWAYS THINKS*

universally valid propositions and thus for psychology as a science, despite his clear insight into the uroboric intertwinement of recognition and confession.

The second problem comes about when what is inherent in the logic of psychology, namely its "subjective" confession character, is taken literally as a *licence* for the ego to indulge in its subjectivity with all its idiosyncracies, shortcomings, and personal needs or wishes. This second problem is, I would say, the normal state of affairs in Jungian psychology. For those who become or are Jungians, psychology usually serves the purpose of self-gratification, self-indulgence. It is an ego-trip. People who go into Jungian or into archetypal psychology are for the most part drawn to it because they hope it can provide *solace* for their deep discontent with the modern world, for the enormous intellectual demands it makes on everyone who participates in it, the abstraction of modern life, its metaphysical and religious emptiness; and that secondly it can provide *meaning*, a kind of belief system, an ideology, and thus serve as a substitute religion; and that thirdly it can provide all this *immediately*, without further ado, because each person is thought to already carry all the desired treasures within himself. Concerning this belief-system you do not even have to subject yourself to fixed articles of faith that you would have to study in order to understand them adequately. And you do not *really* have to believe in anything, in the sense of a binding belief with practical consequence. All it takes, by contrast, is (a) to *experience* yourself and to experience *yourself* or (b) to *indulge* in images, myths, symbols. Ultimately *anything* you experience *goes*, just as does any image, any myth. It does not matter *what* it is. There are no criteria of truth. No hard work is needed, no discipline, no intelligence. Beautiful images and certain mantras take the place of thought. An intellectual land of Cockaigne that makes meaning readily available *while* one is asleep (dreams!) and that, for the waking mind, has in store plenty of intellectual fast food and sentimental baby food. This kind of psychology caters to the emotional and ideological needs of *people*.

Because of their being motivated by such needs and hopes, Jungians each have *vested interests* in their own version of Jungianism that satisfies their particular emotional-ideological need. Since their particular interpretation of Jungian psychology matches their needs, those needs in turn confirm this interpretation. It is a self-sustaining

PROGRESS OF PSYCHOLOGY?

system. And since there are enough people with the same kind of needs among their patients and in the general public, this interpretation even gets support from outside.

Both problems need an answer. The answer to the first problem is that rather than to keep toying with the hope of finally maybe after all arriving at a science of psychology, what is necessary for psychology is to systematically adopt the position of the contradictory unity of recognition and confession. There is no external truth for it, neither the historically primordial form of truth (the truth of the fathers, the ancestors, the dead, the gods, the prophets, the ancients, tradition, any authorities) nor the later form of truth (the scientific truth of positive facts and rational argument). Psychology has to relentlessly let go of any external support that it could hold on to and of any hope or wish for such a support and instead with full determination dive into the process of soul-making as the *production* (yes, fabrication!) of its own truth. What Jung merely described as a deplorable fact

> [P]sychology inevitably merges with the psychic process itself. ... no explanation of the psychic can be anything other than the living process of the psyche itself" (*CW* 10 § 429). "With regard to scientific status, we thereby [i.e., by describing or interpreting the psychic process] have not in any way removed ourselves to a level superordinate to or alongside the psychic process ... (*ibid.*, § 421, transl. modified),

we have to consciously embrace as our methodological principle. But this means that although there is no progress of psychology, our doing psychology (our soul-*making*) nevertheless at least partakes of the *psychological* progress mentioned at the beginning, the historical progress of the psychic process, inasmuch as it is one of the latter's moments.

The answer to the second problem is that it is a misunderstanding (and abuse for egoic purposes) of psychology's uroboric logic that it grants to the psychologist licence to go on his own ego-trip while nevertheless giving this out as "psychology." There is nothing to be said against going on your own ego-trip. But this is not psychology. If we want to do psychology then its uroboric logic does not dispense us from the necessity of obtaining a distance to our private, merely-personal subjectivity. Any field or discipline depends on that distance,

580   *THE SOUL ALWAYS THINKS*

although depending on the type of field this distance will have different characteristics. The fact that, other than science, psychology does not a priori provide the distinction of the subject from itself simply through the fundamental subject-object division inherent in its internal logical constitution much rather means that in psychology the subject itself has to systematically *produce* the equivalent of this division as its own methodological work *within* psychology. Science has this division outside itself, as its a priori and presupposition, which is why the individual scientist is relieved of such a task. The field has always already done it for him. But psychology as the discipline of interiority has everything within itself, and so also the need for the subject to actively perform the task of the subject's self-distinction by ruthlessly cutting into its own flesh. In psychology we always begin as empirical I, as "the ego," the ordinary everyday personality that we are. But for psychology to become truly able to come into existence, within psychology we have to logically abstract from ourselves as merely-private individuals, indeed, with full methodological determination to go under as "the ego," in order to be able to do psychology as "already deceased ones."[10] Whereas in science, according to Planck, progress depended largely on the generational difference and the contingent event of the literal death of the opponents of a new truth, in psychology the "death" indispensable for its coming into being is methodologically produced and intrinsic.

We always have to remember that psychology, as the soul's speaking to itself about itself, is not about "us," about people, not about external objects, but about *itself.* Jung had already warned us that "We should never forget that in any psychological discussion we are not making statements *about* the psyche, but that the psyche is inevitably expressing *itself*" (*CW* 9i § 483, transl. modified). In other words, even if we are not aware of it, even if in our doing psychology we believe that we (as "ego") are the ones who are speaking, in truth it is nevertheless the psyche that is speaking. However, Jung's insight takes us only to an inevitable fact, so to speak a fact of nature. But the fact is not enough. True psychology begins only when this factual, implicit truth has become explicit for psychology itself, that is, when it has

---

[10] Cf. Wolfgang Giegerich, *The Soul's Logical Life. Towards a Rigorous Notion of Psychology,* Frankfurt/Main et al. (Peter Lang), 1998, ⁴2007, pp. 24 (fn.) and 80.

PROGRESS OF PSYCHOLOGY?

actively and with methodological awareness been adopted as psychology's own standpoint and, as a consequence, in fact *shows* in the perspectives and style of our speaking. Psychology has only begun once we with our self-interest have become silent so that in and through our psychologizing it can be the soul that is speaking to itself. Paul said, "I live; yet not I, but Christ liveth in me" (Gal. 2:20). Analogously the psychologist should come to a point where he is able to say because it has become explicitly true in his work, "I do psychology; yet it is not I, but it is (objective, impersonal) psychology itself that *makes* itself in me."

As long as psychology is in fact acted out as one's private self-indulgence, it is truthless. Just fun, entertainment, or self-stabilization. To be sure, here too it is the psyche which is inevitably expressing itself, but precisely only the psyche as the subjective psyche, the psyche reductively narrowed down to "the ego" ("the empirical man") with all that it involves—even if explicitly one declares oneself to be devoted to the collective unconscious or the *anima mundi*. But when the subject has acquired for itself its own distinction from itself then it becomes open to the objective soul, which, cold and alien, may in no way correspond to our own emotions and emotional-ideological needs, but follows its own necessities. What it ultimately means to have become freed from one's being identified with oneself and one's own feelings, needs, and ideas is that one has been let in to the sphere of thought, has become open to the real, objective thought as which the soul exists and unfolds itself. When truly confronted with the objective soul—the soul of and in what *is*, as it manifests in those conditions of our modern reality into which the history of the soul has transported us—then the question of whether the psychological insights to which we are led are pleasing or not no longer matters. And although truth in the sense of the scientific true-false distinction is on principle out of the question for psychology, it can find—produce—its own truth within itself, through the *opus* of absolute-negatively interiorizing into itself whatever is given to it as its "prime matter," regardless of what this may be in each case. This inwardization of the matter is the process of releasing it into its truth, through the "matter's cold march of necessity"—a march where to? Of course, into nothing else but the matter's going under into itself, into its inner logic or syntax—its truth, its soul.

582   *THE SOUL ALWAYS THINKS*

* * *

I cannot leave the question of "progress of psychology" without turning to a powerful tale—the *classical* tale in our tradition—about the problem of progression from one status of consciousness to another. We all know it. It speaks of people in a cave, so tightly bound that they cannot move and are forced to look exclusively straight ahead at the back wall of the cave. On it, they see the shadows of objects carried past them behind their backs, shadows thrown by a fire burning even farther back. Their entire "world experience" is thus restricted to the play of the shadows. Now, if one of these persons were freed and turned around, he would suddenly be confronted with the real objects whose mere shadows he had seen before, but only in the artificial light of the fire. If he got out of the cave altogether he would see the world in daylight and even become aware of the sun itself. His world experience would have become immensely enriched by completely new dimensions. If he would go back into the cave to his former comrades in order to share his experience of the new dimensions of reality with them, they, firmly convinced that their experience was the only reasonable and true one, would laugh at him and, if he tried to lead them out of the cave, probably try to kill him.

Although the particular metaphor chosen in this story of cave people absolutely fixated on and enthralled by the images (shadows) appearing on the wall might for us Jungian psychologists immediately suggest the position of a dogmatic imaginal psychology indulging in ancient mythic images as the ultimate horizon of its thinking, we should rather understand this tale as a general parable about any historical situation of a discrepancy between a cherished, established position and a new position that transcends it. Each new revolutionary position gained will in the course of time inevitably itself turn into the new cave-dweller position and will sooner or later find itself superceded by a newer revolutionary position. We can understand our tale as being about the situation of what in the history of science we nowadays call a paradigm shift (in the sense of a shift from a poorer, simpler model to a deeper, more complex and comprehensive one: shadows of objects are two-dimensional, real objects three-dimensional; and the experience of shadows is a black-and-white experience, the world outside the cave in the daylight is colorful).

PROGRESS OF PSYCHOLOGY?

The people who stayed in the cave cannot possibly make sense of the report by someone who had been outside. He cannot, as it were, explain to the color-blind what color is. The two-dimensional experience has within itself no room for a third dimension. The cave-people are thus bound to interpret reductively, in terms of their own two-dimensional categories, all that is said about a three-dimensional colorful reality and inevitably see in the homecomer's report about the latter nothing but nonsense, claims absolutely incompatible with all reason and with their experience of the world, if not a sacrilegious attack on their own belief-system, which, after all, is for them *the* truth.

In general, two possible reactions of the people who stayed behind are feasible. The first reaction is the one exemplified in our story. The cave people become, as it were, apologists who probably keep merely reiterating the traditional views, insisting on the verity and reasonableness of their own experience (a verity and reasonableness that now, however, is no longer an innocent one, but one that has already become *challenged* because of its confrontation with the message of their returning colleague). More than that, in our tale they turn into fanatic Defenders of the Faith of Orthodoxy who, in the last analysis, are even willing to kill the disturber of peace.

It is well known to what degree Freud felt that his "revolutionary" theory of psychoanalysis was rejected by the established academic world of his time[11] (but how he also seems to have cherished and cultivated the idea of being disdained). Early Jung confronted with the same situation consoled himself with an idea that comes close to Planck's "sequence of generations" theory. He said about psychoanalysis that we could conjecture "that something extremely significant is going on here, which the learned public will (as usual) first combat by displays of liveliest affect. But [and now comes the consolation]: *magna est vis veritatis et praevalebit* [Great is the power of truth and it will prevail]" (*CW* 7 § 441).[12] In his old age, this optimism had left him.

---

[11] For example: "... the general revolt against our science, the disregard of all considerations of academic civility and the releasing of the opposition from every restraint of impartial logic," 18th of his *Introductory Lectures*, Standard Edition vol. 15, p. 285.

[12] Jung significantly added to this quote from *Vulgate* 1 Esdras 4:41 (*magna veritas et praevalet*) or from Tertullian, *Adversus Praxean* 26, the word *vis* and changed the tense of the verb to the future. Jung had already used this quote in the form *Magna est vis veritatis tuae et praevalebit* ("Great is the power of *your* truth and it will prevail") in his letter to Freud of 11 Nov. 1908.

584   *THE SOUL ALWAYS THINKS*

He was overcome by resignation, if not despair, concerning the impact of the psychology he had bestowed upon the world. In his late letters his lamentations abound about not being understood, even by his very disciples, and being combated or disdained.

The other reaction of the "cave people" (to stay within our metaphor) can be exemplified by young man Luther's well-meaning spiritual guide, Staupitz, who, when he, as still medieval man, was confronted with Luther's decidedly post-medieval inner experiences could only state: "I do not understand it." An honorable reaction! Still having his place firmly within the horizon of medieval conceptions, he *of course* did not understand, could not possibly understand, the experiences of someone who had been catapulted beyond it. Nevertheless, he simply acknowledged it without a priori condemning it as absurd or heretical, the way the people in our cave story would have done. Such a reaction is of course rare, since it requires some self-awareness and courage (inasmuch as it does not automatically locate the problem in the other person who has the unheard-of views, but in how he judges the for him alien experience Staupitz stays with himself, with his own limitation to understand. Thereby he leaves it open whether the new position may have any merit or not. *Ultra posse nemo obligatur*.). The non-appearance of an *understanding* did not cause Staupitz to switch levels by reacting to the unununderstood with the usual "displays of liveliest *affect*" (as Jung had put it). He remained on the intellectual level, and precisely by acknowledging its having been disappointed or negated confirmed his continued desire for insight.

Theoretically, there is of course also a third possibility, namely that a person might be willing to follow the promptings of the one who returned into the cave and to find out for himself what the homecomer's claims might be worth. But in practical reality this is forgettable.

In addition, I should also mention the possibility of non-reaction, which is probably the most frequent one in reality: that people do not show any interest at all in what the returning person has to say and simply ignore it, be it that it goes over their heads or that they are absorbed by their own things.

Now let us look at the position of the person who originally left the cave and gained his more-dimensional world experience. In our

PROGRESS OF PSYCHOLOGY?

tale he returned to his fellows in the cave driven by an ethical impulse and a pedagogic eros. But I wonder whether this impulse is truly ethical. Should we not instead of a pedagogic eros much rather speak of a desire to missionize?

This reminds me of a passage of Jung's in a letter to Herbert Read of 2 September 1960. "I asked myself time and again why there are no men in our epoch who could see at least what I was wrestling with. I think it is not mere vanity and desire for recognition on my part, but a genuine concern for my fellow-beings. It is presumably the ancient functional relationship of the medicine-man to his tribe, the *participation mystique* and the essence of the physician's ethos. I see the suffering of mankind in the individual's predicament and vice versa" (*Letters 2*, pp. 586, 589). This is pretty much the same stance that the hero of the cave parable presents. A genuine concern for his fellow-beings (who are only a *suffering* mankind because they are still in the cave and have not yet advanced to the level of what Jung is wrestling with). The physician's ethos. The relationship of the medicine-man to his tribe.

It sounds great.

But is it really? Is it not really an inflated position? An identification with the healer archetype, the mana-personality? And an identification precisely on the part of that analyst who taught the necessity of the "dissolution of the mana-personality" (*CW* 7 § 398), of one's distinction from any archetype (as well as from oneself), and who preached *individuation*, that is, becoming what one is (in the sense of "I am *only* that!"). 20th-century Jung adopts the stance of an archaic medicine-man or shaman toward his tribe. The psychologist who demanded of us to dissolve the *unio naturalis* here justifies his suffering from lack of recognition with a *participation mystique*! I cannot help but detect a kind of missionary zeal behind the stance taken here by Jung. Is it not a presumption to feel that he, C.G. Jung, as human being and ego-personality ought to be the one who should shoulder a responsibility for "his tribe"? Why could he not leave people to their own devices and leave it to the soul how mankind will develop? Who appointed him medicine-man, who authorized him?

The medicine-man or shaman of old is precisely medicine-man for his tribe because the people of his tribe in fact come to him for help and advice and thus acknowledge him as their wise man. Likewise, the psychotherapist of today becomes active only when people come to consult him and thus authorize him. He does not, like a missionary or prophet, all on his own initiative, go to the people to save them regardless of whether they want to be saved or not. If no men in our epoch see what Jung was wrestling with, this speaks for itself. Why did he ask himself "time and again" this question? Is it not obvious? And: is it not fair enough? It is the simple self-display of the objective relation that exists between him and the others. Furthermore, does what Jung once said about neurosis not also apply to the misunderstanding or rejection that he who advanced to a new level may find himself confronted with? Jung had said (*CW* 10 § 361, transl. modif., Jung's italics): "We should even learn to be thankful to it.... *Not it is cured, rather it cures us*"! Why? Because the misunderstanding and rejection, *if* thankfully received, could help to put him in his place. It is a cauterizing therapeutic agent. It works at "dissolving the mana-personality," the inflation.

Surprising for a psychotherapist is also Jung's reaction to the suffering of mankind and of individuals. It sounds here as if he saw (psychological) suffering as the noxa to be cured away, whereas psychologically it is after all people's "own best enemy or friend," their psychopomp. It is the way to go, their only *real* path to psychological progress (in the spirit of the statute of Zeus reported by Aeschylus, *pathei mathos*). Suffering is simply the *form* in which psychic change takes place as a real change below the ego level, one that inscribes itself into the flesh. Not Jung and his insights ought to be their teacher. They have their *only* authentic teacher in their very own "spiritual" plight, which has everything it needs within itself. "In reality this suffering contains the soul of the sufferer; to lose it would mean to become pointless," we could say adapting certain of earlier Jung's own formulations (*GW* 10 § 355). Jung seems to think that if people were at least able to see what he was wrestling with and if they maybe even followed his answers to the collective problem, this would help them. But it would probably merely amount to "a substitute for legitimate suffering," just as in fact today many Jungians want to cheat people (and ideally even society at large, if only it were possible) out of their own authentic suffering from a lack of meaning by offering them a "Jungian worldview," a compensatory alternative to the "one-sidedness" of modern life, and

PROGRESS OF PSYCHOLOGY?

so-called "numinous experiences"—as gratification of and consolation for the ego. Plugging the crevice to "the underworld."

How different is all this from a position Jung had taken twenty-five years earlier in his Tavistock Lectures.

> I say what I see, and if somebody agrees with me it pleases me and if nobody agrees it is indifferent to me. I can join neither the Adlerian nor the Freudian confession. I can agree only with the Jungian confession because I see things that way even if there is not a single person on earth who shares my views. The only thing I hope for is to give you some interesting ideas and let you see how I tackle things. (*CW* 18 § 276)

Certainly, everyone is pleased if he finds that somebody agrees with him. But the opposite, that "if nobody agrees it is indifferent to" oneself sounds a bit dubious, a show of a greater indifference than is likely to exist. It is never pleasant to meet with disagreement or rejection. However, so much is clear, one should at least be able to accept it without misgivings and comprehend that it is simply the price for having gone one's own way, a price that has to be *paid*. It is the same price that in our cave story is shown in its ultimate consequence: being killed (the paradigmatic example in history is of course Socrates, who, by the way, went into his death without grudge). *Psychologically*, there is nothing wrong with this possibility. It is, if it happens as a literal fact, merely the literal acting out of the *truth* of the objective discrepancy that has come about. He who goes his own way and advances beyond the level of consciousness of his fellow-beings has himself created this discrepancy by having advanced to this new level.[13] And he has to be willing to pay for it. No bitterness. One cannot have it both ways: go ahead, and yet insist on approval from those left behind. Maybe if one says "if nobody agrees it is indifferent to me," thereby playing down the fact that it is annoying or maybe even hurts, the paying of the price is circumvented.

But the other point Jung makes in this passage is admirable. "I say what I see" and I "let you see how I tackle things." No keeping of his ideas exclusively to himself (the way the mathematician Carl Friedrich Gauß, simply because he feared the "clamor of the

---

[13] Less subjectively worded we would have to say: "the soul" created this discrepancy by advancing *in* and *through* him to this new level...

588   *THE SOUL ALWAYS THINKS*

Boeotians," held back during his lifetime his revolutionary work on non-Euclidean geometry). But also no educational mission, no healer or educator attitude. Just an offer, a presenting of his case to the public for what it may be worth and, of course, *arguing* his case as best he can. Goethe, adapting lines of the Persian poet Hafis, once wrote in a poem something like: "Throw your cakes into the water [river], who knows who may enjoy them."

And "I can agree only with the Jungian confession because I see things that way even if there is not a single person on earth who shares my views," because I, C.G. Jung, am the way I am; I am *only* what I am. It is my necessity to see things this way.[14]

Both this latter position of Jung's and the cave parable remind me of something Kant wrote. "I freely admit that it was the critical points David Hume had made which, many years ago, first interrupted my dogmatic slumber and gave my investigations in the field of speculative philosophy a completely different direction."[15] And in a later passage in the same work he said of a certain remarkable product or result of pure reason (in its transcendental use) that it is "what is also the most forceful agent among all to rouse philosophy from its dogmatic slumber and to induce it to undertake the difficult business of the critique of reason itself" (A 142). The metaphor used by Kant actually amounts to a compression of the cave story into a nutshell. Kant's dogmatic slumber was the equivalent of the cave people's being completely enthralled by the shadows on the cave wall. Then his slumber was interrupted, he was turned around into "a completely different direction," and this led him later on to his critical insights.

But there is also a decisive difference. As the one who has awakened from this dogmatic slumber, he does not want to turn around again and go back "into the cave," in order to awaken *others* (philosophers, human beings). Rather than focusing on people, on the philosophers, and "what *they* say," but also rather than focusing like Jung on his (likewise merely personal) "confession," he is only concerned with philosophy itself, the objective mind. It is *philosophy* as objective structure—and by the same token in our case *psychology* (as the objective

---

[14] If it is merely *my necessity* to see things this way (just as it is the necessity of others to see things differently), my seeing things this way is nothing to be proud of, nothing to let go to my head. My having advanced to a new level does not put *me* above the *others*.

[15] Immanuel Kant, *Prolegomena* A 13.

PROGRESS OF PSYCHOLOGY?

soul having become explicit)—that needs to be roused from *its* dogmatic slumber, *not* philosophers and psychologists from theirs. And only on this level, on the inconspicuous background level of the logic of psychology, *its* standpoint and form of reflection, might it even possibly be true that *veritas praevalebit*. Although during our age, the age of mass culture, mass media, "spiritual" consumerism, and the unabashed marketing of "myths," "images," "the sacred," and ecological salvation schemes—in short, during an age of the explicit and deliberate *institutionalization* of the soul's dogmatic slumber in the cave—this seems admittedly rather unlikely. Be that as it may, one thing is sure, the clamor of the Boeotians will not fail to make itself heard.

Index

aberration, new reality as 512–15

absolute interiority 137–39, 148, 150, 151, 156

"Absolute Knowing" 472

absolute knowledge 59

absolute swallowing 278–82 *see also* Saturnian swallowing

abstract, as equivocal term 9

abstract art 96

abstract formal logic 490–93

abstract ideas 359

abstract thought 19, 119–25, 120

abstraction 38–39, 85 of archetypal perspectives 86 Platonic Forms 86–87

abstractness, senses of 333

acting out 43, 394

active imagination 484–85

activism 102–3

Adams, Michael Vannoy 475ff

adaptation 412–19, 437, 518, 521–22, 529

Adler, Alfred 346

adulthood, token 268–72

adult-parent relationship 395–96

advertising 68

aesthetic response 68–69

aisthesis 68–69

albedo 358–59

alchemical gold 450–53

alchemical opus 317–19 first phase 319 second phase 319–20 third phase 320

alchemy 469–70 as form change 536 as model for psychology 332

alienation 43

all-importance 286–87

ambiguity, usefulness of 95

Analytical Psychology 243

Ananke 95, 117

ancient Greeks, world view 195

anima 328–29

anima mundi 64, 66–67, 87, 304

animalized cosmology 87

animalizing 74

animals 210–11, 215 adaptation not needed 416 consciousness 216 ideas of 75

animus 328–29

animus possession 2

"Anstrengung des Begriffs" 55, 60

anthropological fallacy   337
"appearance"   54
Aquarius consciousness
   264–66, 276–77, 359
archetypal depth   20
archetypal experiences   24, 38
archetypal perspectives,
   abstraction of   86
archetypal psychology   278–82
archetypal realm   319
archetypal theory   427–28
   as prejudice   48
   psychological root   407–12
archetypes   90, 100, 272–73,
   407
   as artificial products   405
   of unconscious   374
Aristotle   334–35
artifex   16
artists, great   253
assimilation   456, 458–59, 464,
   471, 472, 543
assumptio   427–29
Átányi   294–96
Atlas   293
atom bomb   35, 47
authenticity, of ritual   28
autism, of the soul   311
"autistic" reality   311
autonomy   518, 548
awareness, psychological   90
axis of the world   318–19
   centers of the earth   294–96

changing views of   285
dangers of viewing soul as
   286–88
dual function   294
interiority   296–300
modern axis   300–303
money and media   301–3,
   305
mythological axis   298–99
soul as   303–6
temporary centers   296–97
verticality   289–94
view of soul   307

baby   358
   as piece of nature   422
baby-mother relation   420–22
backwater psychology   519–22
balloon analogy   89
Bandera, Cesáreo   27
Barreto, Marco Heleno
   387–88, 392
Bateson, Gregory   490–91
bathýs   144–45
Baudelaire, Charles   544
beauty   466
"Begriff"   54, 61, 102
behavior, mechanical   27
Berkeley, George   1–3, 334
Berry, Patricia   573
Bettelheim, Bruno   484
Bible   231–32
big words, thinking in   102

biotechnology 201

birth 211–14, 436–37
 of humankind 218–24
 of meaning 354–55,
  357–58, 360
 soul and consciousness 217
 stages of 440

black sun 453, 456–57, 458,
 461–62

blindness 70

Bollingen 263–64, 266–67,
 272, 277, 278, 282

borders 136

boundaries
 reaching 141
 of soul 134–36, 465–67

brokenness, incision, wound,
 cut, 453–56

Camillo, Giulio 93

cargo cults 70

Cartesian split 142–44

cave story 582–9

center, as discarded idea
 300–301

centers of the earth 294–96
 temporary 296–99

change
 psychological 515–16
 psychologically real 428–29
 reactionary response 513,
  515, 518

child, concept of mother 403

Christ, as mediator between
 heaven and earth 300

Christian mythological images
 24–25

Christian symbolism 30

Christianity
 loss of validity 231
 preaching 80
 realized 45
 as superseded 46–47
 world view 197

Christmas customs, as living
 myth 29

Christmas tree
 as allegory 35
 change of symbolic meaning
  34
 earliest use 30–31
 loss of symbolism and
  allegory 36
 obsolete symbol 44
 roots of meaning 29–30
 as symbol 24, 31–32

classification 493

cloud-cuckoo-land 427

collective unconscious 42,
 244, 262, 272, 555

coming guest
 counter-paradigm 512–15
 paradigm of 507–10

commercialization 24, 36

Concept 333
 concrete 371, 372–3

concepts, and images   493–96

concreteness   124

condemnation, in place of explanation   503–6

confusion, within psychology   173

conscious assimilation   456–57

consciousness   11–12
  birth of higher   276
  change through history   39–41
  of consciousness   140–41, 216
  cultural-historical development   427
  development of   349, 357–58
  differentiation   565
  ecological   387–88
  general logical form   21
  history of   535
  inescapability of   148–49
  initiation of   357
  lunar   37
  modern   42, 551–53
  nature of   292–93
  outdated   544–45
  as performative   292–93
  pre-modern   282–83
  self-recognition   222
  solar   37
  and unconscious   42
content

to form   433–42
  use of term   542–43

contentedness   234–35

context   19–20
  of phenomena   50–51
  temporal   39–40

conventional signs, of religion   224

copula   197

2 Corinthians 5:17   516

corpse, as positivity   371–72

cosmological views   194

cosmology, animalized   87

"Cosmology for the Soul"   73

cosmos   6, 74
  animalized and as perspective   81–83
  form of discourse defeats message   79–81
  metaphysical position   77–79
  out of touch with actual world   74–77

costumes   82–83

counter-paradigm   512–15

creative illness   180

creativity   253

credibility, of depth psychology   173

Crow Indians, legend   165–66

Cultural Darwinism   563

cultural pathology   503

cultural phenomena   18

curiosity   506, 507–9
"Cyborgian Drift"   523

Daphne   561
David   106
Dazwischenschieben   485
death   59, 229
   of ego   454, 459, 463
   of God   274
   as natural state   372
   psychological   395
death of nature   *see*
  irrelevantification; nature
decadence   79
deconstruction   469–70
defamation, of thought and
  character   120–21
deportation analogy   374–76
depth   93
   archetypal   20
   metaphorical   145
   real   146
depth of soul
   meanings   132–34
   as misleading   148
   new consciousness   149–50
   questions to pose   131–32
Derrida, Jacques   469, 470, 472
Descartes, Réné   142, 464
desubstantialization   89
"determinate nought"   147
dialectical approach   450
dialectics   468–73

difference   525–28
differentiation, of consciousness
  565
Dionysian consciousness
  514–15
dissociation   261–64, 513, 519,
  556
   consciousness and the
    unconscious   42
dogmatism   109
Dorneus   373
downsizing   250–57
dragon killing   497–500
dream images   161
dreams   259–60
   exaggerated significance
   254
   Jung's   276–78
   not way to soul   510–11, 526
Drob, Sanford   351–53, 354,
  355
dualism   111, 113
dullness   75
Durer, Albrecht, woodcut   92

eachness   75–76, 93
earth, forsaking   87–89
ebonics   124–25
Eckman, Barbara   53–61, 64
ecological catastrophes
  387–88, 391, 392
ecological consciousness
  387–88

ecological thinking, as
  ego-concern   430
ego
   death of   454, 459, 463
   as distinct from soul   3
   experiencing   375
   imaginal approach   478
   in philosophical thinking
      125–26
   reached by symbols   38
   right to define soul   517, 518
   standpoint of   38
   theoretical construct of   91
   transformation   59–60
"ego concoctions"   124
ego personality   160–61, 162
ego sentimentalism   523–24
ego-consciousness   92
ego-identity   126
ego-image, use of term
   475–77
ego-psychological fallacy
   351–61
El Capitan Canyon Seminar
   165
Elgonyi people   25–27, 216
Eliade, Mircea   197
emancipation   108
   psychological   200–201
   of soul from soul   349
empirical approach   341
empirical splittings   525–26
empiricism   58

empty vessel   8–9
end of meaning   351–61
energy, technical appropriation
   202
epistemology   65
Erleben   254–55
eros, philosophical   121–22,
   127
erotic relation   119–21
Erscheinung   96
esoteric spirituality   172
esoteric standpoint   206
essentialism   473–74
ether   6
evasion   100
evasiveness   88–89
evilness, pagan gods   545
"Excursion on Perspective in
   Painting."   91
existence, dialectical nature
   162
"exoteric"   25
exoteric standpoint   206
experiences   121
experiencing ego   375
explanation, replaced by
   condemnation   503–6
external reality   300
extraterrestriality   385

fabricated reality   573–74
Fall   85, 111
fallen stars   245

fatherhood   410

Faust   238

feelings   527
   as bridge to soul   510–12, 514
   privacy of expression   128–29

felt experience   254–55

Fichte, Gottlieb   335

"flip flop"   168–69

forgetting   486

form, exclusion of problem   245–49

form change   535–36, 540, 550, 554

formal logic   4–5, 333

fragment 45 (Diels)   144, 467
   interpretation   132–34
   and Psalm 139   140–41

Freud, Sigmund   175, 326, 468, 484, 489, 583
   idea of unconscious   184
   on sexuality   339
   split with   183

Freudian psychoanalysis   555

"From the Black Sun to the Philosopher's Stone"   443

function   337

functionalization, of image   44

fundamentalism   224

fur coat analogy   86

future, control by unconscious   275–76

Future of an Illusion   175

future task, of psychology   175–76

gamos   291–92

Gauß, Carl Friedrich 587

general representations   494

Genesis 2:19   380–81

genetic engineering   201

geographical views   194

Gerhardt, Paul   30, 32–33, 45

Gestalt perception   168

Gestaltwandel der Götter   531

Giegerich, Wolfgang, identity with Jung's ideas   48

glass mountain fairy tale   165

goal, of life   460

God   56–57
   death of   226, 274
   as disputable   556–57
   end of   564–65

gods   49–50
   in archetypal psychology   279–80
   death of   560
   fate of   224–30
   as imaginal beings   536–37
   intellectual intuitions   404–5
   lack of   221–22
   as memories   224
   move out of nature   432
   pagan   543–44, 545

sublation   542
going back   454
going under   176, 177
  importance of   188
  Jung's experience   178–80,
    181–83, 186, 188
  nature of   180–81
"great dream"   252–53
Guthrie, W.K.C.   144

habit   566–67
Hardy, Thomas   26, 128
harmonia   6
heaven   194–95
Hegel, Georg   53–55, 58–59,
  64–66, 111, 122, 335–36, 371,
  380, 491
Hegelian dialectic, critical stance
  468–73
Heidegger, Martin   68–69, 469,
  471
Heraclitus   6–7, 8, 10, 131, 145,
  146–47, 155, 156, 244, 331, 467
  as father of psychology   163
  and Jung's psychology
    152–55
  new insight   151
  view of psyche   141–42
    see also fragment 45 (Diels)
heroes   100
higher consciousness, birth of
  276
Hillman, James   63–66, 73–74,

91ff, 278–82, 309, 334–35,
342–44, 345, 365, 443, 448,
451, 458, 477–79, 488–89, 496,
576
  allopathic stance   88
  dimension of soul   132
    see also self-contradictions
historical process, irreversibility
  445
history
  bond of   90
  of consciousness   535
  fear of   517–19
  of soul   534
home   396–97
homosexuality   281
horizontality   289
house for the soul   107, 110–11
Hui Ming Ging   546, 550
human inquisitiveness, turning
  back   465
humanism, conception of soul
  522–25
humankind
  as afterthought   28–29
  alienation from nature
    390–92, 431
  birth   218–24
  burden of lack of gods   228
  child status   211–12
  continuity   209
  interpretation of self   208
  as modern subject   91

position in world   193

relation with nature   387–88

the unborn   210–17

as unborn   213–14

variation   217

humanness, as cultural   423

humility   236

Husserl, Edmund   219, 252, 469

I   9–10, 337, 482, 484

ice-age analogy   103–4

Ideas, Platonic   86–87, 97

identity, personal   126

ideological partisanship   496–500

ideology   414, 520

avoiding   108–9

Iliad   384

illness, creative   180

image

functionalization of   44

interiorization of   341

imageless thinking   334–35, 336–37

images

and concepts   493–96

good vs. bad   496–500

mythic   13

nature of   475–77, 487–88

necessity of forgetting   485–88

radical understanding

448–49

reification   479

as representational   449

resuscitation of   445–47

sticking to   106

as thoughts   334, 455

imaginal approach   14, 146, 341, 342, 344, 348, 450–51, 454, 455, 465–66, 470, 478

imaginal dialogue   485

imaginal mode   12–13

imaginal psychology   449, 452

nature of the image   487–88

imaginal thinking   333–34

imaginality, loss of   488–90

imagination   14

moving away from   538

structural deficiency   146

imaginology   479, 480

"Imaginology: The Jungian Study of the Imagination"   475ff

immediacy   108, 258–59

animal   84

loss of   75–77

return to   83–84

impartiality   109

impression   13–14

imprinting   423

imprisoned thoughts   18

individuals

atomization   199–200

reality and substance   198

individuation 60, 108, 433–34, 435

inescapability, of consciousness 148–49

infinite interpretability 357

infinity 135–36, 139
internal 148

initiation 315–16, 349
of consciousness 357

"inner" 177–78

in-ness 141
in archetypal psychology 281
containment in language 218–19
end of 199–203
interiorization 261
metaphysical 194
new 208–9
reactions to end of 203–5
as reality of pre-modern ages 193–98

innocence 66–67, 83
atemporal 70–71
impossibility of return 141
loss of 359–60

insight 419

institutionalization 280

integration into consciousness 348–49, 359, 472, 543

intellect, sacrifice of 245–49

intellectual curiosity 507–9

intension 139

interdisciplinarity 176

interiority 147, 165–72, 177, 297–98, 314, 413
absolute 137–39, 148, 150, 151, 156
axis of the world 296–300

interiorization
of image 341
self-interiorization 315–16

internal infinity 148

internal logic form 265

internality 187

introspection 172

Inverted World 147

inwardization 315–16, 359, 467, 472, 474, 581

irrelevantification 387
adaptation 412–19
assumptio 427–29
birth 419–27
conceptions of mother 400–406
content to form 433–42
death of nature vs. kinship to nature 388–92
demythologizing mother 398–400
leaving father and mother 395–97
"man shall be the master of nature" 388–90
new *oikos* 429–33
remythologization of mother

406–12
soul view vs. ego view
392–95
stages of birth 440
irreversibility, metamorphosis
of the gods 536–37

James, William 192
Jeweiligkeit 93, 95
John 1:11 509, 510
John ch. 4 365–66, 368, 373
Joseph and His Brothers 132
Jung, C.G.
acting out 155–56
Adams' treatment of
481–84
adaptation and neurosis
412–13
autonomous psyche 56
boundary of human
inquisitiveness 465–67
Christmas tree 24
consciousness and the
unconscious 42
construction of ego 91
death of symbols 205–9
demythologizing mother
398, 400
dismissal of culture and
technology 273–74
on dreams 16
Elgonyi people 26–27
fog dream 495

foundation 156
goal of life 460
going under 178–79,
181–83, 186, 188
as heir to Freud 326
and Heraclitus 152–55
historical necessity 440
historical significance
445–47
humans as twice-born 126
idea of unconscious 184–85
image as soul 14–15
as imagist and theorist
491–93
individuation 108
intellectual curiosity 507–9
letter to Herbert Read 584
logic and genesis of
psychology 239–83
loss of in-ness 204
meaning as therapy 233–34
motivation 446
mythic images 25
nature of psyche 481
on neglect of later work 325
neutrality 162
on piety and will of God
106
power of unconscious ideas
109
present-day demands
39–40
problem and solution

239–45
problem of Christianity 47
psyche as all around 111
on Pueblo Indians 195–96, 211–12
as reactionary 158
reality of theories 56–57
recording dreams 14
rejection of Hegel 54–55, 59
remythologization of mother 406–12
on sexuality 339–41
split tongue 153
split with Freud 183
status of Gods 94
stuck in positivity 373–74
Tavistock Lectures 587
temporality of gods 49
theory of synchronicity 157–58
understanding of Kant 55–58
Jungian psychology, attraction of 578–79
Jung's razor 163
justice 364–65

kabbalists 357
Kant, Immanuel 55–58, 96, 331, 335, 373, 588
Kena Upanishad 365
Kerényi, Károly 372

Kierkegaard, Soren 190
killing 372
kitsch 12
kitschification 24
knowing 55–56
knowing too much 223
knowledge, absolute 59
Kronos *see* Saturnian swallowing
Kugler, Paul 465
Küsnacht 263–64, 266–67, 278

language 218–20, 336
generation of meaning 344–45
images in 346
thinking in 380
Laotse 365
lark analogy 381–83, 385
legends 165–72
Lenau, Nikolas 381–82
liberation 108
libido 532, 549–50
Liebrucks, Bruno 86
life
as activity 373
goal of 460
meaning and worth of 192
notion of 371
opus contra naturam 372
light 32
like-ness 370
linguistic turn 218

literalism   365

locus   19–20

logic
  modern   300–301
  need for   69
  of soul   491
  two-stage   108
  understandings of   65–66,
    330–31

logical approach   341, 342, 344

logical drama   340–41

logical negativity   370–71, 372

logocentrism   473–74

logos   6–7, 8
  bipolarity   9–10

logos eôn   331, 333

loneliness   221, 231, 269

Lorenz, Konrad   423

loss, critique of feeling   230–38

Love   322–23

love
  as cultural and linguistic
    383–84
  of the world   71

Luhmann, Niklas   383

lunar conscientiousness   37

man   *see* humankind

"man shall be the master of
  nature"   388–90, 394

mana-personality   585f.

Mann, Thomas   132

Mark 10:7   392

marketing analogy   66–67

Marlan, Stanton   443ff

marriage   420
  meaning of   424–27

Marx, Karl   102, 190–91

mass media   76

Matthew 18:20   369

Meaning   207

meaning
  birth of   354–55, 357–58,
    360
  end of   351–61
  living without   230–33
  loss of   202–3, 228–29, 239
  self-contradictions in search
    for   191–93

meanings, of utterances   218

mechanical behavior   27

media
  as axis of the world   301–3,
    305–6
  modern form   305–6
  as vampire   320

meditating yogin dream
  276–78

memories, creation of   14

Memories, Dreams, Reflections
  178, 236, 237

memory, reproductive   335–36

Memory Theater   93, 112

Menschheitsproblematik   255,
  256

mental development   534–35,

538–39

mental experiments 134–35

mental reservation 463

metamorphosis 111

  mythological 317

metamorphosis of the gods
316–17, 356, 531ff

  emergence of reason
558–60

  second theory 546–49

  theories of 561–2

metaphors 343

  pregnancy-birth metaphor
353–54, 358

  of soul 373

metaphysics 297–98

  Western 222–23

Midgard 194

Miller, David 363, 575

mind, as performative 292–93

mindedness 370

miracles, as truths 40–41

modern axis 300–303

modern humanity, complexity
of psychic situation 39

modern logic 300–301

modern subjectivism 125–29

modernism 199

modernity 218, 348

  avoidance of 282–83

  religion under 225–26

  spirituality in 370

Mogenson, Greg 417

money

  as axis of the world 301–2,
305

  modern form 305–6, 348

  as vampire 320

monosemy 344

monotheism 564, 565

  and perspective 91

  pluralism 93

Mörike, Eduard 37

Moses 88

mother

  baby's relation to 420–21

  child's concept of 403

  demythologizing 398–400

  differences between
conceptions of 400–406

  remythologization 406–12

mother archetype 400–402

mother goddesses 401, 403–4

Mother Nature 389–90, 404

motifs 109

movement of the soul

  active involvement of people
314–15

  alchemical opus 317–19

  fifth type 316–23

  fourth type 314–15

  initiation 314–15

  Okeanos 308–11

  projection 312–14

  second type 311–14

  third type 314–15

movements, aims of 348–49

museum analogy 242, 243

mysterium coniunctionis 487

Mysterium Coniunctionis: An Inquiry Into the Separation and Synthesis of Psychic Opposites in Alchemy 326–28

mystical, unthinkable and unspeakable 454

mystification 455
  of therapy 251–52

myth 7–8, 10, 12, 20, 189–90
  absolute interiority 150
  birth into 212
  self-estrangement of soul 319

"myth of consciousness" 274

mythic images 13

mythic imagination, moving away from 538

Mythic Meaning 208

mythological axis 298–99

mythological man 293–94

myths
  as definitions of the soul 307
  historical presence 43–44
  loss of 218
  as paradoxical 151

nakedness 231, 270–71

names 336, 380–81

Nathan 106–8

natura naturata, and *natura naturans* 346

natural world
  ensoulment 319
  redefinition 429–30

naturalism 96–98

nature
  alienation of humankind 390–92, 431
  changed role 202–3
  dependence on 198
  external 391
  humankind's relation with 387–88
  literal 392–93
  no longer natural 45
  psychological concept 389
  reduction of concept 391
  resurrection 432
    see also irrelevantification

"nature alive" 74

necessity 116

Necker cube 168

need, critique of feeling 230–38

negation 367
  experiences and images 453

negative 364
  as negation of positive 369

negative interiorization 322

negativity, absolute 365–67

neuroses 160–61, 190, 233, 346–47, 419

cause 413
as human 416
recovery 268–69
and understanding 506
neurosis, Adams' theory 490
"neurotic" dissociation 257
neurotic split 159–60
"new form" 264–68, 275
Nietzsche, Friedrich 126, 190,
191, 208–9, 210, 221, 240
night 32–33, 37
nihilism 190
"not" 363–77, 471–72
"Numb" 501ff
numbing 513–14, 528–30
numen 255–56

object
effect of science 571–72
of psychology 572
objective psychology 355–56
objective soul 581
Odysseus 9–10
oikos 429–33
Okeanos 150–51, 156, 307–9,
311–13, 322–23
movement of the soul
308–11
one, and the many 93
onesidedness 176–77
"ontological pivot" 465
opinions, as distinct from
thinking 1–2, 4

opposites, union of 159
oppositional structure 328
opus contra naturam 321–22,
332, 368
orientation functions, typology
of 3–4
otherness 141–42, 380
overanimal 210, 220–21
overman 208–9, 210

pagan gods 543–44, 545
pagan symbolism 29–30
paganism 96–98
painting
non-perspective 92–93
perspective in 93
paradigm of the coming guest
507–10
paradigm shift 329–30
parenting 201–2
parents, as psychological womb
420
partisanship, ideological
496–500
Pascal, Blaise 331
passion 122
pathologizing 77–79
patience 19
perception 345–46
performativeness 490
personal equation 575
personal mother 402–3
personalism, to absolute

negativity   433–42

personalistic psychology   299, 303, 338

personality   155, 160
  containing psychic   184

perspectives   81–82
  awareness of   101
  choosing   103
  discovery of   90
  polytheism   112
  polytheistic multiplicity as logical monotheism   89–95
  seeing through   85–87
  spatial   91–92, 93–94
  temporality   111–12

phainomenon   46
  splitting   85–86

phantomization   477–80

phenomena, good and bad   525–28

phenomenon   46

Philippians 2:6ff   428

Philippians 2:9ff   302

philosophical eros   121–22, 127

philosophizing   99–100

philosophy
  argument against   99
  drained of life   88
  emancipation of psychology from   98–99
  fear of   87–89

phonemes   344–45

physicalness   547

physiognomonic perception   70

piety, and will of God   106

Planck, Max   565, 575

Plato   97–98, 144, 210, 309, 469

Platonic Forms   86–87

playhouse   155

pluralism, of monotheism   93

plurality, of views   569–70, 573

political correctness   489

polysemy   343–44

polytheism   112, 564–65

Popper, Karl R.   331

popularization, of psychology   174

positive   364

positive law   364–65

positive religion   365–66

positivism   364, 557–58

post-modernism   282

poverty   231

practice   103

pregnancy-birth metaphor   353–54, 358

pre-logical mentality   296

presenting complaints, of society   503–4

prime mover   335

privacy   128–29

privatization   250–57

problem, of form   245–49

problem and solution, Jung's
  view of   239–45
productivity   201
professional mourners   27
progress
  belief in   563
  psychological effect   563
  in psychology   563–64,
    569–70
progress, in history of soul
  564
progression   46
projection   312–14, 348–49,
  538–39
  spatial   540–41
projections   154
promised land   88
prophets, old and new   506–7
Psalm 139   137–41, 148,
  151–52
Pseudo-Democritus, axiom
  349
psyche
  atemporal innocence   70–71
  creative nature   347
  Heraclitus, view of   141
  numbing   501–2
  objective   115–16, 126
psychic, contained in
  personality   184
psychic birth   422–23
psychic facts   557–58
psychic phenomena, as meaning

  458
psychic reality   379–85
  as fabricated   573–74
psychic transformation,
  objective   46
psychoid archetypes   54, 60
psychological awareness   90
psychological birth   11, 423–24
psychological change   428–29,
  515–16
psychological death   392, 395
psychological difference   398,
  525–28
psychological reactionary
  516–17, 518
psychological reality   162–63
Psychological Types   205, 352
psychologizing   99–100
psychology
  avoiding ideology   108–9
  backwater   519–22
  conceptions of   328–29
  as delimited   153
  deplorable state of   173–75
  as future science   576–77
  ground   4
  insufficiency of pure
    98–105
  nature of   491, 504–5
  needs and demands   473–74
  negligibility of   286
  object of   572
  objective   355–56

opening to philosophy 101–2

place of   338

possibility of   298

problems of   577–79

real   460

as self-portrayal   574

terms of   48–49

psychology of the unconscious 186–87

psychology proper, possible end 528–30

psychosis   59

psychotherapy   417–18

psychotic reaction   184

Pueblo Indians   211–12

message of   235

world view   195–96

pure psychology, insufficiency of   98–105

Pythagoras   223

Rabbi anecdote   236

"Radiant Boy"   316–17, 544

rational psychology   56

Raumprojektion   540–41

rawness   258–59

reactionary response, to change 513, 515, 516, 518

Real   110, 333

real psychology   460

reality

external   300

fabricated   573–74

meaning as   355

new, as aberration   512–15

psychic   379–85

psychic and real   410

as soul   111

reconstruction   347

reenactment, dialectic of   299

reflection   43–44, 85, 89–90, 110, 220, 486, 487

inescapability of   149

Reformation   558–59

regulation, effect on psychology 174

relicts, of mythic experience 23

religion

end of   564–65

fulfilment of task   222–24

and modernity   225–26

positive   365–66

as present reality   225

remembering   346–47

remythologization of mother 406–12

Renaissance art   91

Christian character of 96–98

representations, general and singular   494

reproduction   201–2

reproductive memory   335–36

res cogitans   142–43

res extensa 142–43
resignation 229–30
resuscitation of images 445–47
return, Hillman's concept of 77
Revelation 21:1 516
re-visioning 576
Revisioning Psychology 74, 91
Rilke, Rainer Maria 19
ritual 6–7, 8, 10, 12, 315
  accurate performance 27–28
  creation of center 297–99
  crisis as 183–84
  and initiation 315–16
  non-ego 27
  performance of 128
  performed without thinking 24–26, 246
  self-sufficiency 299
  in temporal context 23–24
ritualistic mind 298
rock analogy 165–72
Rosegger, Peter 31

sacramental deeds 7
sacred, and profane 369–70
sacred places 365–68, 369
sacrifice, of intellect 245–49
sacrificial slaughter 314–15
Sandplay 212–13
Saturnian swallowing 243–45,
259–60, 261, 272–78, 279
  see also absolute swallowing
Schelling, Friedrich 16, 335
Schiller, Friedrich 311
Schulbegriff 331
science
  development of 566–69
  effect on object 571–72
  entering 571
  psychological meaning 46
  structural division 570–71, 580
sciences, orientation 177
scientific knowledge, as embodied reality 567–68
scientific progress 567–68
scientific truth 565–66
scientism 58
scientists 567–68
seeing through 100
self
  being 434
  as cultural reality 435
  as enough 235
  as goal 433–34
self-articulation, of soul 312–14
self-centeredness 127
self-constitution 332
self-contradictions
  animalized cosmos and cosmos as perspective

81–83

to "cosmos" as move into "universe" 83–85

cosmos out of touch with natural world 74–77

form of discourse defeats message 79–81

of legends 167, 169

metaphysical base 77–79

polytheistic multiplicity of perspectives as logical monotheism 89–95

in search for meaning 191–93

self-destructiveness 113

self-division 85

self-estrangement 319

self-growth 172

self-indulgence 580–81

self-inwardization 315–16

self-negation 10

self-sufficiency, of ritual 28

semantics 444

sensation 68

sensationalism 379

sensualism 380

sentimentality 524

sentimentalization 29

separation 328

sexual liberation 200

sexuality 339–41

logical drama 340–41

Shamdasani, Sonu 573

side-slipping 88–89, 101, 105

as therapeutic tool 90

singular representations 494

skin 105–6

Slater, Glen 4, 501ff

society, presenting complaints 503–4

sol niger 453, 456–57, 458, 461–62

solar consciousness 37

Sophocles 111

sophon 6

soul

as autogenetic 5

as axis of the world 303–6

boundaries 134–36

changed sense of 303–4

character of 322

depth *see* depth of soul

depth of logos 163

dimension of 132–34

as distinct from ego 3

house 107, 110–11

humanistic conception 522–25

inescapable 111

logic 491

logical life 330–31, 332–33

mythical depictions 307–8

nature of 491

objective 581

oppositional fantasy of 84–85

as performative 292–93
place of 338
redefinition 516–17
as self-defining 415
self-estrangement of 319
self-reflection 5–6
as thought 15
Western theoretical neglect
73–74
see also movement of the
soul
soul history 534, 554
soullessness, of universe 111
soul-making 379–85
sounds, in language 344–45
sovereignty, as definer of soul
515–17
space-suit image 214–15, 220
spatial perspective 91–92,
93–94
spatial projection 540–41
spear analogy 438–39
speculative knowledge 188
"speculative sentence" 60
"spirit and truth" 368–69
spiritual poverty 270–71
spirituality
esoteric 172
in modernity 370–71
splittings 525–26
St. Augustine 230
St. Lucy's Day 30
St. Paul 302

State, effect on psychology
174
Staupitz, Johann von 584
subjectivism, modern 125–29
subjectivity 482–84
Hegelian sense 61
of thought 126
subject-object dichotomy 379,
413
subject-subject-object relation
480–85
sublation 43, 44, 45, 46, 97,
262, 472
of gods 542
of sacred 369–70
submission, of humankind
198
subreption 479, 480
substantiation 440
suffering 43, 586–87
superficiality 120
superscience 286
swallowing 541
symbolic life 198–99, 208
symbolism
Christian 30
pagan 29–30
symbols
authentic 36
death of 205–9, 351–52
failure to reach soul 38
replacement 206–7
synchronicity 158–59

syntax 444

synthesis 328

syzygy 6, 328–29, 420

Tao 365

technology 113, 523

   psychological meaning 46

   purpose 45–46

Temple, building of 106–8

temporal context 39–40

The Black Sun 453

"The First Christmas Tree in the Forest Home [*Waldheimat*]" 31

"the great" 555–56

the imaginal 435

"the petty" 555

The Relations Between the Ego and the Unconscious 326–27

the secondary 272–73

"The Stone Which is Not a Stone" 363–77

the unassimilable 456–68

the unthinkable 454, 464–65

theorizing, as abstract 123

theory 103

theory of decadence 79

theory of synchronicity 157–58

therapy 21

   futility of 59–60

   mystification of 251

   soul's wish for 114

things 454

thinkers, great 253

thinking

   as bound 16

   ideas of 3

   imageless 334–35

   imaginal 333–34

   in language 380

   nature of 341–42

"thinking again" 16

thisness 494–95

thought

   abstract conception of 119–25

   as autogenetic 8

   dynamism 10–11

   quality of 17–18

   self-sufficiency 121

thoughts, nature of 334

three monsters 88, 104

time 20

   awareness of 115–17

   bond of 90

topoi 407

totalitarianism 286–87

Tougas, Cecile T. 119–29

transcendence 172

transformation 532

   personal 60

transformation processes, contemporary 337–38

"Transformations and Symbols of the Libido" 532

transition, childhood to
  adulthood   268–69
transpersonality   256
traveling, in thought   146–47
true thought   18
truth   38
  as opposite of unconscious
    374
  in psychology   570, 575, 581
  scientific   565–66
  universality   368
turning back, human
  inquisitiveness   465–67
two-dimensionality   290, 293
two-stage logic   108
types   407
typology of functions   3–4

UFO dream   276–77
"unassimilable remainder"
  457, 459, 461–62, 464, 468
unborn-born   354
unbornness
  in archetypal psychology
    281
  rescue of   261–64, 268
unconscious   42
  control of future   275–76
  as discovered fact or means to
    end   249–50
  as empirical force   184–85
  Jung's notion   410
  as label   247

nature of   187
  as performative   260
unconscious existence   374
understanding, need for
  246–47
underworld, as locus of
  psychology   298
unio mentalis   320
unio naturalis   321–22, 332,
  486
unity   473
  being and space   543
  forgetting and remembering
    487
  scientific   569–70
universal genus   491
universe   74
  curing   114
  as fact   103
  perspective   82–83
  shift to   81
  soullessness of   111
"unthinkable"   468
uroboros   6, 309
utopianism   240, 286
utterances, meanings of   218

vanishing lines   93–94
verification   416, 417, 418
verticality   132, 289–94
  loss of sense of   300
vested interests   578–81
view, as unchangeable   82–83

*Wandlungen und Symbole der
Libido* 183
"We shall overcome" 71
Weltbegriff 331
Western metaphysics 222–23
white psychology 99, 101
whitening 358–59
"wholly other" 81
wife, as successor to parents
397, 400, 410
Wilde, Oscar 119–20
will 314–15
women philosophers 119–20
mission of 122–23
words, as images 342–43
World Parents 194, 290–92,
293
world pictures 304
World Spirit 60
World Tree 194, 285, 288,
290, 291, 293
world view, metaphysical
297–98
worship 560
nature of 370
place for 365–68, 369
"in spirit and in truth" 368

xynon 7

young adults, relationship with
parents 394

youth, idolization 201

Zeus 546–48
Ziegler, Leopold 531